There has long been a need for an up-to-date textbook on administrative aspects of government, designed to meet the needs of the Australian student. The purpose of this book is to outline the workings of Australian government administration at Commonwealth, State and local levels, and to discuss some of the problems of organization and management that arise in these fields. Its eighteen chapters have been written by an expert group of senior public servants and university teachers, at the invitation of the Public Service Board of New South Wales, whose Chairman introduces the book. It is specially aimed at the working administrator, but contains much that will also be of great interest to the university student and to the general reader. Its editor is the Professor of Government and Public Administration in the University of Sydney.

G 78713—1   K 5673

PUBLIC ADMINISTRATION IN AUSTRALIA

Edited by

R. N. SPANN

With an Introduction by
WALLACE C. WURTH, C.M.G.

**V. C. N. BLIGHT, GOVERNMENT PRINTER,
SYDNEY
1967**

First Edition, 1959

Second Edition (Revised), 1960

PREFACE

This symposium was originally planned some years ago. A series of mischances prevented its completion at that time, although a number of chapters had been written and its original editor had done a good deal of work on it. When he found that he could not continue, I was invited to edit the book by its sponsors, the Public Service Board of New South Wales, and to arrange for the writing of the additional material needed. The original contributors kindly agreed to revise their chapters to bring them up to date.

The book as completed has a more modest aim than the one first planned. It makes no claim to great originality or to be the fruit of prolonged research, though some of its chapters include much previously unpublished material. The primary object of its editor and contributors has been to produce a serviceable textbook for young public servants. The New South Wales Public Service Board, in initiating the enterprise, has had in mind particularly the candidates for its Higher Grades examination in Government Administration, who have lacked an up-to-date text. We hope that it may also be of interest to public authorities generally, to universities and colleges teaching in this field, and to overseas readers.

Some of the sections on State government may be found to draw rather heavily for their examples on New South Wales. We apologise for this, and would not wish it to be thought that we regard the affairs of other States as less important. It is often more generally enlightening to deal with one or two systems in some detail, than to try to keep six balls in the air at once.

The contributors represent no particular doctrine or outlook, and have been left free to express their own opinions. A number of them have given generous help in reading and commenting on the drafts of other contributors. I shall not thank them here individually, except Mr. R. S. Parker and Mr. S. C. Derwent, whose help and guidance have been of particular value. Special thanks are also due to the Chairman of the New South Wales Public Service Board, Mr. Wallace C. Wurth for his great interest and assistance at every stage; to Professor P. H. Partridge, the original editor; and to Mr. W. J. Campbell, Mr. S. Encel, Mr. J. Frape, Mr. F. A. Larcombe, Mr. J. C. Conway, Professor G. Sawer, and Mr. D. Swanson. Mrs. M. Daniel and Miss J. Benson who gave valuable help in the final preparation of the manuscript. The index was prepared by Mrs. P. J. Williams.

R. N. SPANN.

CONTENTS

6

INTRODUCTION

For as long as I can remember, those responsible for the training and development of public servants in New South Wales have deplored the absence of a good text book dealing adequately with government administration in Australia. The many excellent texts on some aspects of the subject did not provide a sufficiently wide treatment for training purposes.

The explanation of this state of affairs was very simple. There was not one man anywhere with the knowledge and experience required to cover the breadth of topics involved. The solution has been a joint effort by various well-qualified authors drawn from the Universities and the Commonwealth and State Public Services.

In a career service, the ambitious and able public servant must not be allowed to be satisfied with merely acquiring skills which are essential for the job to which he is immediately assigned. He must take a broader view. His own experience is not enough: he must profit wherever he can by the experience of others, from the lessons already learned.

"Public Administration in Australia" is designed primarily to meet the needs of the younger administrator, who should make himself familiar with problems ranging over the broad field of public administration before he actually has to meet them. The authors are to be congratulated not only on the thoroughness and competency with which they have covered their various subjects, but also for the way in which they have been able to avoid the use of technical language. This is particularly important when it is realised that they are catering, at least in part, for readers without a substantial background knowledge of government.

I feel that the book will be of considerable interest to students of public administration at all levels. I hope, too, that it will be read by many who are interested in the workings of government, even although they are not themselves part of it. The public services play an important role in the economic and social life of the community. Just as the public servant must keep himself as well informed as possible about community affairs, if he is to do his job properly, so there are very many people who can gain practical benefit, as well as increasing their tolerance and understanding of the work of government institutions, through the study of the practice of public administration.

The functions of government in the modern state are complex indeed. Many of the greatest problems arise through the necessity for defining, dividing and co-ordinating the work of the authorities in the different governmental fields. Two chapters have been devoted to Federal-State relations.

In a federation there are special problems not met within countries such as Great Britain which enjoy a unitary system of government. Australia has seven governments, each sovereign, each not only exercising the regal functions of government but providing also a wide range of community services.

It is small wonder that instances of overlapping of functions and duplication of services have arisen. The only surprising thing is that there have not been more of them and this, I think, is due generally to the quite elaborate machinery of consultation at all levels that has been developed between Commonwealth and State organisations.

Over the years I have been most outspoken about this problem. As a result of the joint efforts of the Public Service Commissioners of all States and the Commonwealth, supported by the various Governments, much has been done to eliminate it.

Duplication and overlapping, however, still exist and will always exist and tend to increase if not watched consistently. It is a matter of the very greatest importance for every public servant to inform himself fully of the work being done by other authorities in his field, whether Commonwealth, State, semi-government or Local Government, and to take steps to ensure that public money is not wasted by unnecessary duplication of effort and services.

The avoidance of overlapping and duplication calls for the utmost goodwill on all sides and a readiness to concede that another party may be in the best position to carry out functions on behalf of all interested authorities.

This work discusses this problem in some detail and gives an indication of the way in which it has been tackled in recent years.

Two other chapters refer respectively to the functions of local government bodies and statutory corporations. The work of public service boards and commissions is constantly referred to throughout the book; for instance, the chapters on management and control, organisation and method, personnel problems, training and executive development, deal with matters with which the boards and commissions are concerned. However, one of the most important considerations—the relationship between governmental bodies and the public—has not been dealt with separately, although it is of fundamental importance in public administration.

One of the things which should concern all public servants vitally is the quality of their public relations.

Individually, public servants are respected in the community. The teacher at the local school, the court officer, the postmaster, the agricultural adviser —each is accepted as performing an essential function and as being a good and worthy citizen. Collectively they are described by the press as "bureaucrats" and are pilloried unmercifully.

The press, unfortunately, is prepared to misrepresent the role of the public servant. All are loosely classified as "non-producers". In other words, a compositor in the Government Printing Office engaged in setting up in print a valuable scientific work is a "non-producer". His counterpart in industry who is engaged on the printing of a race book is regarded, oddly enough, as a "producer".

Much of the criticism of the public service stems from a work "The New Despotism", published about thirty years ago by Lord Hewart, The Lord Chief Justice of England.

On the subject of law, Lord Hewart will be accepted as a leading authority. Concerning the public services he was obviously not so well informed. He set out to expose what he regarded as a growing tendency towards improper delegation of authority by parliament to ministers and public servants. Some of the issues he raised there are dealt with in the chapter on Administrative Law in this book. In the process he made a number of sweeping statements about the United Kingdom Public Service, all unsupported by authority, which, in the intervening years, have come to be used as catch-cries by other critics.

His Lordship condemned public servants generally because he considered that they dealt with the rights of members of the public without hearing both sides of a matter. Yet he was quite prepared to deal likewise with the Civil Service and reach very serious conclusions without hearing the "other party"; in this case, the Service itself.

Within the space of a few pages, he was prepared to complain that public servants have too much authority, that the parliamentary organisation is not appropriate for detailed consideration of legislation, that members of parliament take no interest in bills passing through the House and do not know what is in them, that cabinet and not parliament is running the country anyhow, and that public servants are usurping the functions of parliament.

All this is very confusing even to the moderately well informed.

I have no doubt His Lordship would have been the first to complain of an attack on the judiciary by one who did not have a complete knowledge of the subject of law and of the functioning of the courts.

Publications such as the present one serve a most valuable purpose in that they tell the true story of the public services. In their way they help to correct the false impressions created by such works as that just referred to.

Government departments are no longer confined to regulatory and inspectorial functions: they provide social, educational and research services which have become essential to the life of the community. Most of the problems (of policy at the ministerial level, or practice at the departmental level) encountered by a government can be regarded as variants of the simple question—what is the most satisfactory and efficient way of serving the public in this matter?

In introducing this book to you, I must place on record my appreciation of the very real contribution made by its Editor, Professor R. N. Spann, Professor of Government, University of Sydney. He is deserving of special commendation.

WALLACE C. WURTH.

PART 1

ADMINISTRATIVE STRUCTURE
AND FUNCTIONS

Chapter One

PUBLIC ADMINISTRATION, SCOPE AND PROBLEMS

R. N. Spann

The literature of public administration belongs mainly to this century. In the nineteenth century the activities of government were more restricted than they are today. The emphasis was on preserving law and order, defending the national territory, and a few other basic tasks. In favoured countries like Australia, even defence was not of much importance; though conversely the development of a new country made certain demands on government—regulating land purchase, building railways—not met with to the same extent in the United Kingdom, where the land was already settled and railways were built by private enterprise. Writings on government reflected this; they were mainly concerned with the work of Parliament, Ministers and the Courts. When people spoke of "the Administration" they still meant the Ministers of the Crown, that is, what we now tend to call "the Government", though the old use also survives. One of the first English books on government to recognise the existence of the permanent official was Walter Bagehot's *The English Constitution* (1867)[1], and what he says on the subject is still worth reading.

Nowadays the position has greatly altered. Governments intervene in many different fields. Chapter 3 gives a good picture of their present activities in Australia. The growth in the functions of government is well illustrated by employment figures. In 1900 public authorities in Australia, Great Britain and the United States each employed only five or six per cent. of the working population. (The post office and, in Australia, the railways were the only large public enterprises.) There have been great changes since then. By 1950, in Australia about one in five of the working population was a government employee; in Great Britain one in four; in America about one in eight.

In Australia the total number of occupied persons is around three and three-quarter millions (it was 3,650,000 at the 1954 census). Of these, in June 1956, 734,788 were government employees; we should add another 52,900 if we wish to include the permanent defence forces. Most of them were not "public servants" in the popular, and too often abusive, sense. They included workers in railways, banks, air transport, teaching, broadcasting, power stations, government factories and munitions works and so on. Railways alone employed about 145,000; the post office about 90,000. There were 13,000 policemen, and about 50,000 teachers in government schools.

Commonwealth government agencies employed 208,000, under 10,000 in Canberra itself. State and local governments employed 190,000 in New South Wales, 135,000 in Victoria; at the other end of the scale, 20,000 in

---

[1] The best modern edition is in the *World's Classics*. See especially Chapter VI.

Tasmania. Many were not under the Public Service Acts, but worked for statutory agencies not subject to Public Service Boards or Commissions. This was true of about one-quarter in the Commonwealth, nearly three-quarters of New South Wales State employees, and an even larger fraction in most other States.

Government expenditure tells a similar story. In many countries, including Australia, public agencies are spending 20 per cent. or more of the national income. (A detailed breakdown for Australia is given in Mr. Gates' chapter.) Most of it is raised and spent by the central government. In the United Kingdom, the central government spends about 80 per cent., local government the rest. In the United States, the federal government spends about two-thirds, State and local governments one-third. In Australia the equivalent figures are about 60 per cent. and 40 per cent.; but the Commonwealth government raises over 80 per cent. of public revenue. (American States can still levy income and sales taxes, and by these and other means raise most of their own revenue.) Australian public authorities have an even larger slice of total investment, around one-third in recent years.

It is not surprising that students of government have become more interested in public servants, in what they do, and why, and how they might do it better. There are now many books dealing with this administrative side of government, especially in the United States and the United Kingdom. Australia has not been so well off, though Professor F. A. Bland in his many writings has done important pioneer work. There is also much good material to be found in annual reports of departments([2]), reports of Royal Commissions, and so on. Bodies have been formed to further the study of administrative problems, such as the Royal Institute of Public Administration in the United Kingdom, which has nine Regional Groups in Australia and the Territories([3]). Many universities and colleges, including such institutions as the newly-founded Australian Administrative Staff College, offer courses of training and study in this field([4]); and a good deal of training and some research also take place nowadays in the public services themselves.

It is beyond the scope of this book to examine in detail the reasons for the great growth of state activities. Some of it has arisen from the demand for "social justice", and the growing view that private action needed regulating and supplementing to bring this about. Sometimes leaving certain decisions in private hands seemed to make everyone, or nearly everyone, worse off—think of public health or traffic control, once there were big cities and large numbers of motor cars. Some services seemed best provided on a large scale, say, electricity generation; and to lead to monopolies or concentrations of power that were felt to require close public control; or to need more capital than could be raised privately, as was true of Australian railways. Sometimes minorities have pressed for

([2]) Some are uninformative; and it is a pity that there are departments (especially in the Commonwealth) not required to report annually.
([3]) The British and Australian sections each publish a quarterly journal called *Public Administration*; the two journals are distinguished below as *Pub. Admin.* (*London*) and *Pub. Admin.* (*Sydney*).
([4]) See S. Encel, 'The Study of Public Administration in Australia', *Pub. Admin.* (*Sydney*), XV, Dec., 1956, and Sir Douglas Copland, 'The Australian Administrative Staff College', *Pub. Admin.* (*Sydney*), XVI, June, 1957.

special consideration, such as farmers. Partly it is just that some of the previous limitations on state power have been removed. Improved communications make central control easier. Greater wealth means that countries can spend more on older functions of the state, such as defence ; or on large-scale development, which may only yield returns in the remote future. Other limitations have been removed by greater knowledge of the possibilities ; we now know, for instance, that certain types of government control can mitigate or control booms and slumps ; we know that certain types of government propaganda will persuade people to adopt healthier habits (or to believe that some groups of persons should be exterminated).

This growth of control has been accompanied by important developments in methods of control. There are many different techniques that a government can use to control social life. Some of them are very simple, though possibly far-reaching—it is a great error to confuse complex controls with effective controls. The old "rule of the road", whether left-handed or right-handed, is a regulation that prevents countless collisions, and yet it is simple to understand and easy to enforce. A change of central bank policy may alter the whole economic climate and influence millions of other economic decisions by consumers and businessmen ; yet it may be effected by a few men sitting round a table, and the desired consequences produced largely by letting other people react spontaneously to the new situation. Methods of control run the whole gamut from fairly simple rules or decisions which can be put into effect without fuss, to highly detailed types of control which may require many complex regulations and large numbers of subordinate employees to be effective. It is activities of the latter kind that raise the most difficult problems of administration.

Many of these problems are not confined to the operations of the state, but are met with in other fields, for instance, private business. Both government and industry are now often organized on a large scale, and are carrying on many complicated activities involving great numbers of employees. The latter have each a specialised task inside the organization they serve ; they have to be recruited, and their work so arranged, that the policies they carry out are carried out effectively. This is the basic administrative problem and it is a difficult one to solve in a big organization, especially one the demands on which are changing all the time.

The chapters in this book will be concerned with the problems of administration as they affect the activities of government, that is, with Public Administration. This has some special features. All the same, there is no sharp line between the administrative problems of government agencies and those of other organizations. This is especially true nowadays, when governments administer business undertakings ; and when business firms are sometimes so big that they can become as "bureaucratic" as the most-abused public department ; "There are far more bureaucrats outside the government service than inside it"[5]. Many of the issues discussed in this book are applicable to all types of organized human activity. The study of administration is, in fact, the study of some general problems of human organization ; and public administration is one part of this study.

---

[5] K. C. Wheare, 'The Machinery of Government', *Pub. Admin. (London)*, XXIV, Summer 1946, p. 77. A recent estimate is that, during the last half-century, the ratio of "administrative" to "production" employees in British and American industry has increased from about 1:12 to 1:5. See R. Bendix, *Work and Authority in Industry*, 1956, p. 214.

THE PROBLEM OF ORGANIZATION

"The moment I find Organization creeping into this Ministry I shall stamp it out ruthlessly." (Attributed to Lord Beaverbrook.)

What is the central problem of administration? It is not easy to state it in a simple way. But a useful start would be to say that it is the problem of how to organize a group of people for a purpose. There is an objective. This objective requires for its realization the co-operation of a number of people. Getting them to co-operate constitutes a problem for those responsible for fixing the objective.

This account already raises a number of difficulties. For example, it is usual to distinguish "administration" from "politics". Does the above definition enable us to do so? In part it does. We could say, politics is concerned with fixing objectives, administration with carrying them out. The politicians decide to provide education for all, to cut imports, to develop hydro-electric power, and so on; the administrators tackle the problem of how to do it. We shall see later that this distinction is not clear-cut; administrators often play an important part in policy. Still, it is roughly true that administrators are working within a framework of set aims, which they have not chosen themselves.

However, it may be asked, is not an important part of politics concerned with "organizing" groups of people in support of certain policies as opposed to others? What then is the difference between the political problem of organization and the administrative problem? A first approach to this would be to consider the following example. Suppose you had to persuade a million people that it was a good thing to fight a war—that would be a politician's job. Suppose you had a million people all convinced that it was a good thing to fight a war—then putting them in a position to do so effectively would be an administrator's job. "Getting people to co-operate" has, in fact, two meanings—getting them to want to, and making it possible for them to do so.

But even this account leaves some difficulties. A politician, you may say, does not primarily want to persuade people to accept his (or his party's) objectives, he wants them to behave in ways consistent with them, e.g., vote for him. If they do that, it may not much matter to him why they do so, or what is passing through their minds at the time. This makes him like the administrator running an organization, who is also trying to get people to behave consistently with his agency's aims—which, incidentally, may include encouraging their loyalty to those aims. In this sense as well as others, a good administrator is also something of a politician.

Perhaps the best way of drawing the distinction is this. There are some kinds of purpose, or objective, which cannot be achieved by voting, or bargaining (or by leaving it to individuals to work out their own destinies). The only, or the best, way of doing the job appears to be deliberately to organize people in fairly complex ways, involving a good deal of *specialization* of function (division of labour) and a good deal of conscious and planned *co-ordination* and *control* (adjustment of relations between the units by superiors). Achieving this result in ways best suited to the aims of the organization becomes a problem requiring special skills. These are the skills of the administrator.

So the administrative problem starts from an objective—a job to be done ; and certain requirements imposed by the job. There may have been a time when it was left to uncontrolled individual initiative, or initiative controlled only in a few simple ways, say, by a statute which imposed a certain penalty for non-performance, enforced by a handful of inspectors and the ordinary courts of law. But a time comes when an enlarged notion of the objective makes more complex arrangements necessary.

An example would be education. The first schools in Australia were established by the Reverend Richard Johnson in 1793, and financed by the Society for the Propagation of the Gospel. The number of church schools increased, and the government began to provide money. By 1820 there were thirty schools, some of them wholly government-supported. A system of public elementary schools gradually developed alongside the church and private schools. The Australian colonies decided that the job of education could not be done merely by handing out money, and this involved them in all kinds of new problems,(*) teacher-training and salaries, school buildings and equipment, curricula. The Board of National Education established in New South Wales in 1848 was soon involved in administering an elaborate code of regulations ; and by 1865 it had over 250 schools under its direct control.

The next stage was to establish parliamentary control, under a Minister and Department of Public Instruction. In the same period public aid to church schools ceased ; it had stopped as early as the 1850's in South Australia. A changed and enlarged notion of the educational task, "free, compulsory, and secular", gradually involved the colonial governments in a mass of new administrative problems. We begin the story with a few private schools. We end it a century and a half later with Departments of Education employing up to 18,000 people, and with an elaborate headquarters organization of administrative directors, inspectors, accountants, research officers, with divisions or branches for buildings, teachers' appointments and training, education programmes in the schools, transport, physical education, guidance and counselling, and so forth.

It is important to stress, then, that the problems of administration arise, often inescapably, out of the objectives which are set for (or sometimes by) administrators. Such an emphasis will help us to avoid certain fallacies.

As Mr. Bourke says in his chapter, many writings on administration give the impression that there are a large number of golden rules of good administration-in-general. If we keep in mind that administration is concerned with getting things done, and that the things to be done differ, it will teach us some healthy scepticism about this. Of course, it is just as silly to deny that there *are* some common problems and some general skills to be learned. There is such a thing as the "good administrator" who will do as good a job in a defence department as in a social service department. But not mainly because he deludes himself into thinking that it is the same job, rather that he is a skilled adapter to a different job, of familiar means to new ends.

Stress on the objective may also remind us of the advantages of organizing work so that the objective is clearly seen, and that the people concerned have the command over men and materials needed to achieve it. This

---

(*) cf. Francis Anderson, cit. C. M. H. Clark (ed.), *Select Documents in Australian History* (1851-1900), p. 690.

home-truth is often neglected; it helps to avoid one danger which has been well christened "the displacement of goals", that is, we begin to think of our procedures as ends in themselves. This point is touched on further below. It also reminds us that one way of solving the administrative headaches caused by a particular task, is to ask oneself whether, if it causes so much trouble, it is worth doing at all. An important function of the working administrator is to recall to his superiors, who may be other administrators or politicians, the unworkability of some of the tasks he is set.

Of course, it is an over-simplification to talk of "the objective" in this way. The task is always changing; there is always room for argument about what it is at any moment of time; or, as most departments are multi-purpose, about the weight to be given to the different tasks, about which different members of the department may have different views. Many quarrels about methods are really disguised quarrels about ends.

Why does the pursuit of certain objectives create a problem of organization? Some tasks involve the co-operation of fairly large groups of people. There are decisions to be made too complex for one or a small number of persons, and great advantages (in the shape of improved skill and efficiency) from the division of labour, from each of a largish group having a more or less specialized job. A *problem* of co-operation arises when, to get the specialized units to work fruitfully towards the objectives, there is need for a small number of leaders to co-ordinate their activities in fairly detailed ways; both by deliberately designing their tasks so as to get the best out of them, and so arranging the total structure that what one does fits in with what others are doing.

Some kinds of objectives raise this problem of co-ordination in an especially acute way. In ancient Egypt the complications of building and regulating a network of waterways produced an early example of large-scale administration; similarly in China (it has been argued) the problem of irrigation and flood-control was the root-cause of the growth of the old Chinese bureaucracy, with its elaborate rules and authoritarian controls. Other early examples are the large armies that some countries wished to maintain, and which needed to be elaborately organized to be effective. We may remember that the modern term "civil service" was first used by the East India Company, a combination of army, large-scale business firm and government which once ruled India on behalf of the British Crown.

Bureaucracy

The attempt to solve these problems has produced the kind of administrative organization we call bureaucracy, using the word in a neutral sense. The sociologist Max Weber, who was the first to give a clear account of this kind of structure, included among its characteristics([*]):

> (1) *Specialization of function.* The members of a bureaucracy are "officials", that is, they fill offices or positions with fairly fixed duties attached to them. The discretion of each unit is prescribed and

---

([*]) I have somewhat re-worded his account and omitted one or two points, e.g., that members of a bureaucracy do not own any of the assets of the organization, and have no property-rights in the job.

limited so as to produce a high degree of specialization of skill and function.

(2) *Hierarchy.* Offices form a structure, with different levels, so that each lower office is under the control and supervision of a higher one. This means that there is a high degree of "control from the top", with a few persons exercising a great deal of power, through a series of intermediaries.

(3) *Rules and regulations,* defining the responsibility of each member and the relations between them.

(4) *Objectivity,* or elimination of personal bias or attachments from work.

(5) *Qualifications for office,* e.g., a career service recruited on a merit basis, with promotion by seniority or merit, or both.

Weber is, of course, setting up a model, and no actual bureaucracy completely fulfils all his criteria. Still we can recognize that many modern government departments and business firms have these characteristics. We shall say something of the differences between governmental and private bureaucracies later.

The growth of bureaucracy has not been solely due to considerations of administrative efficiency. The leadership of organizations is an important source of status and power Some people in charge of them, or sections of them, like them to grow in size or to become more dependent on decisions made at the top. They are "empire-builders". It has also been argued that some societies and individuals attach a high value to bringing things about deliberately, as opposed to letting them happen; they would tend to be predisposed towards bureaucracy. Some people, both officials and clients, feel safer when bounded by rules and regulations; or prefer the apparent "fairness" of a rigidly consistent rule to the greater efficiency that might result from more discretionary behaviour. This partly explains why many organizations develop bureaucratic characteristics which have no real need to do so.

It is also important to remember that bureaucracy is only one of a number of ways in which people can act together. There are relatively non-hierarchical methods of co-operation, where decisions are made on a basis of formal equality, by voting or bargaining or informal kinds of co-operation. There are fruitful relations between people that depend very little on anyone setting out to plan the total result. There are also non-bureaucratic kinds of leadership, for example, where the leader influences and controls mainly through some form of personal or traditional attachment, because he has a commanding personality or charm or his father led before him. Most actual bureaucracies incorporate some of these non-bureaucratic elements; and it is doubtful whether they would be workable if they did not.

The bureaucratic method has enabled all kinds of things to be done which would have been difficult or impossible without it. But it also carries various costs, which have to be measured against the advantages in deciding to use it; and which need minimising if it *is* used. What are these costs?[*]   (1) It uses men and resources not to give people what they want

---

[*] Some of the following analysis is based on R. A. Dahl and C. E. Lindblom, *Politics, Economics and Welfare,* 1953.

or need but to see that other people do this.   The best educational administrator is not teaching anybody, though he may be helping teachers to teach better.   (2) It raises control and enforcement problems.   Bureaucracies are hard to control from outside.   Outsiders (think of shareholders or back-benchers) are generally ill-informed, relatively ill-organized, and run up against the very loyalties which are necessary to a good department or firm.   They are also hard to control from inside.   Decisions have to be communicated through many persons, rules and regulations have to be made, and someone has to see that they are carried out.   The procedures can also easily become an excuse for "passing the buck".   (3) It tends to be inflexible.   To make a large organization work, jobs and procedures have to be more or less prescribed, or no-one knows where they are.   But this may mean that they are poorly-adapted to individual cases, and may produce an attitude of mind obsessed with procedures, regardless of how badly they work.   Changing needs may make the prescriptions out of date. The people who see this may find it hard to make those members of the hierarchy who are protected from the direct impact of the world outside see the need for change.   (4) It tends to become over-centralized—the top men may be too confident of their own superiority, or alternatively (having worked their way up slowly) still have the concern for minor detail appropriate to men lower down.   (5) The fact that it involves so much fairly strict defining of duties and subordination of one man to another is sometimes held to be destructive of human freedom, equality, spontaneity.   Many people view with distaste the extension of centralized control and break-up of autonomous social groups that resort to bureaucracy often encourages, as a threat to human values.   (6) It may concentrate power in too few hands.

Finally, bureaucracies are often said to be wasteful.   Too many decisions have to be taken in them without proper knowledge of the preferences of their clients, or knowledge of alternatives that might have been better.   It is hard to give each unit in them a measurable standard of success, and reward it accordingly (in pay, status, social approval, or some other way). Some people argue that business bureaucracies are better at this than government departments, partly because of the nature of their activities. We shall have more to say about this later.

From this, we may draw two conclusions:—

(a) A careful weighing of the advantages and disadvantages is needed in each particular case before the bureaucratic method is used.

(b) Administrators must do everything they can to improve their organizations, which sometimes means incorporating some of the advantages of non-bureaucratic methods into the bureaucracy itself.

The latter conclusion is worth particular stress in this chapter.   Public servants cannot do too much about the former.   Many of their functions are thrust on them by politicians or public opinion, and it is often most unjust to say that they seek more and more control.   They would sometimes be content to manage less, if they were allowed to.   But they can do a good deal under our second head, and already do a certain amount.

There are broadly two ways of improving a bureaucratic organization which may appear, and sometimes are, contradictory.   The first is to make it a more perfect bureaucracy—for example, establish clear lines of control, improve the design of forms or the classification of jobs, and so on. The second is to make more use of non-bureaucratic ways of doing things—such as encouraging individuals or small groups to act on their own initiative even at some expense to orderly routine and strict control of expenditure, being friendly with one's employees even at some expense to discipline, resorting to frequent committees and conferences, and so on. A. W. Gouldner(°) has published an interesting case-study which bears on this point. It describes how the new manager of a plant, unfamiliar with its customary ways of working, and with poor informal relations with the workers, who were still loyal to his predecessor, could only establish his control by making the structure more "bureaucratic", insisting on regular returns, closer supervision, etc. He succeeded in asserting his control, but at some cost in other directions. Some paragons claim to be able always to mix both in ideal proportions.

Finally, it is clear that bureaucracy has come to stay. In many fields of activity it is the most efficient way of doing things. When we criticise its failings, we need to remember that many of them are the inevitable result of the objectives we set ourselves. It is, of course, also true that (for reasons given above) we are often more bureaucratic than we need be.

Building an Administrative Structure

Some writers on administration distinguish "organization" from "management". The organization of an agency is its structure, the regular pattern of relationships inside it ; and the task of organization is the job of building the structure. Management is concerned with working the organization so as to achieve its objectives. The distinction is far from watertight, but useful for some purposes.

The task of management might be defined as "getting co-operation". This is sometimes taken to mean beating the big drum, exhorting, inspiring, appealing for loyalty, and so on. All this has its place. But generally speaking in administration, "getting co-operation" is not primarily a question of causing a group of people to accept, in some psychological sense, a common set of objectives, but of getting them each to perform effectively an appropriate set of duties, to fill an "office", to play a "role". A condition of doing this is that someone has devised a set of "offices", or "roles" for them to fill. Spontaneity and initiative are needed, as a job can rarely be specified so completely as not to leave considerable room for flexible adjustments between individuals. But in most cases the individual officer needs to be told the core of his duties in some detail, and its broad limits. This may be done in some cases by mutual discussion and agreement. But, generally speaking, the "offices" and "roles" are determined from above. This is the task of organization.

So we get the *formal structure* of the agency—a prescribed set of offices (positions), each of which consists of a cluster of duties and responsibilities, carrying with them a certain command over the resources needed to carry out the duties. It may be embodied in part in written documents—an organization chart, a set of job specifications, departmental regulations. But there will be many features of the organization that cannot easily be written

(°) *Patterns of Industrial Bureaucracy*, 1954.

down, or at any rate have not been written down.   Some writers on administration have called these features the *informal structure* or organization, the part that is not prescribed in laws and regulations.   The term is somewhat misleading, as many unwritten rules and procedures are in practice very stable and set, and may be rigidly enforced.   Perhaps "formal" and "informal" are better used (as by some writers) to distinguish those relationships which are consciously and deliberately controlled from those which are not.

Of course, most administrative structures have not been planned as a whole at some one time.   They have grown up historically, either by the subdivision of existing units or by adding new units to old ones. The history of administrative agencies is an interesting study.   It may explain some apparent illogicalities in the present set-up.([10])   It may throw some light on what will be relatively easy and what relatively hard to change in the future.   Builders of administrative structures in practice depend very much on past example.   They add a bit here and there, or copy from another country or department.   It is very hard to design a successful organization "from scratch" as the history of some war-time departments illustrates.

Anyone designing an administrative structure has also to take account of the people available to fill the jobs. The problem of structure cannot be divided from that of *personnel*.   Even if the organization is new, the people in it are not "new".   Their past experience and training will be important, positively or negatively.   It will partly determine their success in filling the offices prescribed for them.   You may be able to use it, or have to take measures to counteract it, or to develop it in certain ways.   It is no good devising a lot of positions of great responsibility if there is nobody capable of filling them.   In that case you may have, for example, to shape it so that most of the work is reducible to fairly simple routines ; though it is true that something can be done to fit the individual to the work by good recruitment and training programmes.   Some writers on administration talk as though one could create ideal administrative structures *in vacuo,* by simply considering the objectives to be attained and then juggling with the "logic" of various ways of dividing up the work.   This is not so.

The Division of Work

However, there are some general points to be made about the division of work, which may help to clarify our ideas on the subject.

Let us start by considering a fairly small group of persons who find that some conscious thought has to be given to the best way of doing a job.   We may think of them as meeting to discuss the matter.   Even this may involve some organization.   If the question is at all complex, they may form a committee.   A small committee has a fairly simple formal organization—the only designated offices are chairman, secretary, member

---

([10])   Compare Montesquieu's proverb: "Good laws which have helped a small country to grow, become a burden to it when it has grown".

—though its informal organization may be very complicated.([11]) This may take various major decisions. But a committee is not an efficient instrument for most tasks, which have to be carried out by individuals. The task has, in short, to be divided up.

This division of the task, at whatever level of administration we are thinking of, raises two main problems: (a) the number of units, (b) the grouping of functions. In each case a balance of considerations is involved.

In general the greater the number of units at any level, the harder they are to co-ordinate.([12]) This is true whether we are thinking of the number of Ministers in the Cabinet, or the number of divisions in a department, or lower down. On the other hand, if the number of units at any one level is reduced, this may lead to an increase in the number of levels. If the Cabinet were to consist of only six Ministers, their departments might become bigger than they could manage. This might lead to their handing some powers to a new layer of junior Ministers; or to their leaving more to the permanent head, who in any case would be finding his burden intolerable, and might set about appointing a new layer of deputy heads. In the effort to simplify the Cabinet's problems, we have complicated the works further down by increasing the number of levels in the organization. It is clear that some balance between the number of units at any level, and the number of levels, is involved. This is, needless to add, a much over-simplified way of stating the problem.

The other problem is that of grouping of functions and here again a few general comments may be made.

If we look at the functions of government described in Chapter 3 of this book, it will be noted that they can be classified in several different ways. We can, for instance, classify them according to major *Purpose*, the main social objective for which the task is carried on. An elementary classification in these terms would be: Protection (Law and Order, External Peace), Economic Control and Development, Social Services; or we can have a more detailed breakdown in which, for example, Social Services are subdivided into Education, Public Health, Social Security, and so on. This is a common way of subdividing the tasks of government in practice. So a State will have a Department of Education and a Department of Health; and within the Education Department, there may be sub-units dealing with Primary Education, Secondary Education, and so on.

But this is only one form of classifying government activities. Another would be in terms of *Process*, the method or means used to achieve the objective. Take, for example, Finance—the process of getting, spending,

---

([11]) The committee is, in fact, quite a sophisticated organizational form, and one which (as most readers will have experienced) is hard to work really well; in particular, committee chairmanship is a highly complex business, about which books have been written, e.g., Lord Citrine, *The A.B.C. of Chairmanship*, 1952. Lord Citrine learned how to handle committees in the British Trade Union Movement. Unfortunately, most of the rules of good chairmanship are not easy to specify in a book.

([12]) That is, if their functions interlock, i.e., need co-ordinating. This is the origin of the famous principle of the "span of control", which was first systematically discussed by V. A. Graicunas in L. Gulick and L. Urwick (ed.), *Papers on the Science of Administration*, 1937. For a criticism of it, see H. A. Simon, *Administrative Behavior*, 1947, pp. 26-28.

and accounting for the money used in forwarding the education, health, etc., of the community. It is convenient to group together a large number of the tasks associated with Finance in a Treasury Department, and perhaps also in a Finance Division in the other departments. The "means" may involve a recognised type of skill—engineering, medical, statistical, accounting. It may be just a set of procedures, drafting legislation, issuing licenses, checking income tax returns, which it is convenient to have done in the same office.

These are two of the most important ways in which the work of government is subdivided. Two others are Person and Place. An example of the former would be an agency which dealt with a given set of individuals for a whole variety of Purposes and by all manner of Processes. Examples are not easy to find, as this is not usually a happy way of dividing up the business of government. A historical example is the English Poor Law, which once tried to treat "paupers" as a distinct class of persons, whose economic support, health, work, and so on, were catered for by a single agency. Some approach to this form would be found in the Repatriation Commission, whose functions are listed as: *"In respect of members of the Forces* (i.e., of a category of Person) . . . determination of applications for the treatment of disabilities, provision of in-patient and out-patient medical treatment, determination of claims for . . . service pensions, etc., etc.".* The defence departments similarly provide a wide variety of services for present members of the Forces. Of course, even in these cases, the whole needs of servicemen and ex-servicemen are very far from being met by one government agency. Subdivision according to Place may be illustrated by the division of functions between States, which is based on the principle that each State Government serves a defined territory ; or by regional offices, or local government.

Most government agencies embody a mixture of these different ways of dividing up the work. Each method has its own conveniences and inconveniences.([18]) A department which has a single social aim, e.g., educating children, building good roads, and which can marshal many different kinds of means to this end, can develop considerable driving force. It is organised around a clear task, the value of which is apparent both to its officers and to the general public. On the other hand, there often seem to be advantages in grouping all the experts in a particular process together—a single department for finance, or purchasing, or personnel work, or research, can make good use of specialist skills, or take advantage of the economies of large scale. A central printing agency can be more mechanised than a series of departmental printers could ; and a central publishing agency (like Her Majesty's Stationery Office in the U.K.) might improve the quality and appearance of government reports. One of the disadvantages is sometimes said to be that specialists in means are liable to lose sight of the end. Similar arguments can be used in favour of or against the other ways of dividing up work, e.g., one can argue that it is advantageous to a certain group of persons to have to deal with only one office for their varying

---

([18]) Luther Gulick discusses some of the pros and cons of different ways of dividing up work in *Papers in the Science of Administration,* 1937, Ch. I. See also H. A. Simon, *Administrative Behavior,* 1947, Ch. 2; and D. N. Chester and F. M. G. Willson, *The Organisation of Central Government, 1914-56,* 1957, "The Grouping of Functions", pp. 349 ff.

needs. Which combination of them is used in practice is a matter of good judgment.

The important thing to realize is that these different classifications conflict, not merely with one another but also internally. The education or foreign affairs department may argue that it should control its own personnel, as one means of achieving its overriding objective. The personnel agency may reply that *it* should control all personnel matters, as it is valuable to consider personnel problems in relation to one another irrespective of department. There may be good arguments for both sides and some compromise may be reached, e.g., for certain purposes the one controls its staff, for others they are controlled by a central staff agency. This is a case of a very common kind of conflict that arises between Purpose and Process.

Another conflict is between Purpose and Person. A central objective of an Education Department is "educating children". But it may feel that it cannot educate children without also doing other things for them. It may, for example, want to interest itself in the health of school children, guidance in their future careers, and so on. This may bring it into conflict with other departments concerned with health or with child welfare outside the school, including children's employment. Some people will always be found to object to the subdivision of concern for children (or other groups of citizens) between various agencies. A new function is sometimes given to a department simply because it already has the closest contacts with the persons concerned.

The conflicts may be internal, since most of the social objectives of government are ambiguous. Take education again—are we to include in it all forms of training? Clearly not; other agencies will not be willing to agree that all their training branches are to be absorbed by a single department of education. What about technical education? Is this best controlled by the department concerned with other forms of education, or not? Or is it a distinguishable objective, which needs treatment on its own merits? What about university education? Does the same apply there?([14]) Plenty of examples will come to mind from other fields. The courts and the police are both concerned with "law and order." However, catching offenders and giving them a fair trial are activities that involve very different habits of kind. So it tends to be thought desirable that this ambiguity in the notion of "law and order"—is it primarily a matter of keeping order or of seeing that justice is done?—should be recognized by confiding the care of the courts and those of the police-force to different hands. Most public agencies are multi-purpose, and this may lead to conflict about which objective should receive the most stress. Police catch criminals, control traffic, preserve public order, and so on. Mental hospitals segregate their patients from the public, but also try to make them well again. Education departments provide a high-grade "academic" training for some, but a more elementary type of education for many more.

This problem of classifying and dividing up work occurs at all levels of

---

([14]) Universities are generally anxious to keep clear of Education Departments, partly because they feel that their problems are different from those of schools, and that Education Departments are "school-minded". If they must be supervised by a government department, they tend to prefer one which will not be tempted to feel that it has a close professional interest and expertness in their educational policy.

government. At a lower level, it might take the form of having to decide whether it is better to give an official concerned with a particular subject-matter his own typist (organize her into a small "purpose" unit) or to make him draw on a typing-pool (organize her into a "process" unit). It is in one sense just part of the problem of *specialization*. In government, as in other collective enterprises, individuals and groups of individuals have to specialize. We want them to do so to the greatest advantage. What are the criteria we use? In their most general form they are, first, grouping tasks together so that doing one of them facilitates the doing of another. A ludicrous example of failure to do this would be to assign to each typist the job of typing one letter of the alphabet in every piece of correspondence. The inconvenience of this largely results from the nature of typewriters, but also from the nature of typists, who can develop very great skill at performing a certain set of inter-locking operations; but in other situations will find the group of tasks they have to do recalcitrant to their efforts to improve performance.

The same applies at higher levels of government, though the profit and loss are more difficult to calculate, and complicated by other issues. The question still is partly: is the grouping of tasks such that doing any one in a given group helps towards the doing of another in that group, and helps more than any other conceivable arrangement? There will be much more controversy here as the variables are more numerous and harder to assess. The techniques devised by "Organisation and Methods" specialists (described in Mr. Grainger's chapter) are often less easily applicable at high levels than lower ones. The very word "helps" conceals a host of problems—helps how? by facilitating the acquisition of skills? by raising morale and improving incentives? It may "help" to put two different jobs under the same Minister simply because he wants them, and will make trouble if he doesn't get them; or because the power and prestige he derives from the one, may facilitate his task in getting things started in the second field.

In practice, of course, the division of work we find in government is the result as much of history and political pressures as of logic. For example, it causes an upset to rearrange functions and if an existing arrangement does not work too badly, there will be a strong incentive to leave things as they are. A sub-division of tasks represents a balance of power as well as a balance of efficiency. Many departments or units will tend in practice to sponsor an interest. It may be an outside interest; Departments of Agriculture in some countries have had a way of becoming Departments for the Defence of Farmers, ex-servicemen prefer to be looked after by their "own" department rather than have its functions transferred to other departments performing similar functions for other citizens. It may be simply its own interest, the empire-building of its Minister and/or top civil servants, or its "point of view". It is a matter of common observation that an interest or viewpoint does not get full consideration if it has no reasonably powerful department to defend it.

The second main criterion is that the sub-division of tasks should simplify the work of co-ordinating the units concerned. Some ways of sub-dividing work need a minimum of co-ordination. A simple way of cultivating a large piece of land is to divide it up into small plots, and give a plot to each man. This might involve very little machinery of central control. But some people would say that it was a poor way of getting maximum production out of the land, that there were much better ways of specializing the human talent available. This might be true ; but any other way of dividing up the work might involve more administrative effort to see they did not get in one another's way. This is the case with the activities of government. Indeed, the problem of keeping the various tasks of government in line with one another is a difficult one ; and in deciding on the way to sub-divide tasks, we always have to take into account which method will make it easiest to relate them one to another.

Some of the Process departments that we mentioned above grew up as a means of co-ordinating already existing agencies. The Treasury and the Public Service Board are examples of units linking the work of different departments through control of the "financial" and the "personnel process", in ways discussed below in Chapters 3, 7, and 10. But it is an over-simple idea to think that you master the problem of co-ordination by setting up a new department. Indeed in a sense the opposite is true. There are two ways of thinking of the Treasury. It may be set up, or its activities expanded, with the aim of linking the other departments more closely on the financial side (as a co-ordinator and "controller" of finance). But, once it is in existence, it is in part just another department, with its own policies and points of view. *It* itself may need, almost certainly will need, co-ordinating with the so-called spending departments, to see that the two do not get unnecessarily in one another's way. You can imagine a sort of nightmare situation in which the government set up agency after agency to co-ordinate the existing ones, and each new agency had itself to be co-ordinated with all the others. So there is often a case for a sub-division of duties that makes the task of co-ordination as simple as possible, the kind that can be done by informal contacts, a few inter-departmental committees, and an occasional Cabinet decision. This may involve some sacrifice of the advantages of specialization, but the sacrifices may be worth making.([15]) An elementary requirement of good administration is being able to "fix the responsibility" for a set of tasks. There is a great deal to be said for an administrative structure that minimises the possibility of buck-passing.

An allied point is the one made by Simon that "specialization must be sacrificed [sometimes] in order to retain the use of the individual brain as a co-ordinating mechanism. It is not very easy to thread a needle if one person holds the thread and another the needle".([16]) This is, among other things, part of the case for the jack-of-all-trades as administrator. A few people with a good general knowledge of developments and ideas in a wide range of subjects can work wonders in a complex administrative machine. You can say if you like that they are not specialists ; or you can say that they specialize in co-ordination.

Levels of Responsibility

We have spoken up to now of the division of work horizontally ; at a given level of responsibility. We must now take account of the fact that

---

([15]) A similar point can be made about specialized Planning or Policy units. They are set up to overcome the limitations of a department in adjusting to change. But they may also complicate the works.

([16]) *Administrative Behavior,* p. 238.

levels of responsibility differ, that in the administrative machine the individuals and units form part of a *hierarchy*. Each subordinate is responsible to a superior at the next level. So we get what is sometimes called a scalar chain of formal authority running from the top to the bottom of the organization.

In many organizations, public and private, you will find the following levels.([17])

   (i) Criticism, review, final control—Parliament, shareholders.

   (ii) Governing authority—Cabinet, Board of Directors.

   (iii) Link between policy-making and operations—Departmental Minister, active director.

   (iv) Operating authority—Permanent Head, Director-General, Managing Director/General Manager.

   (v) A variety of supervisory grades down to those who have no authority over anyone else.

It is quite common in large organizations to find nine or ten levels from operating head to the bottom of the pile.

As you move down the grades, it is often (not always) true that supervision of higher over lower officers increases, and responsibility([18]) decreases ; tasks become more particular and concrete. The actual scope of decisions made at different levels, the degree of delegation of power, varies from department to department. An attempt is usually made to define as precisely as possible what the scope of decisions is at each level—so that an officer knows who are his subordinates, what equipment is at his disposal, what are his objectives and which directives he is supposed to carry out. Tests by which his achievement can be measured have to be devised (if his superior cannot keep a direct and continuous eye on him, it may be necessary to have periodical inspections, or to insist on written returns or reports). Rewards and penalties have also to be provided.

The fixing of levels of responsibility in an organization has much in common with the horizontal division of work which we dealt with above. They are, in fact, both ways of dividing up the work. They look different because of the element of so-called *command* in the division of work between different levels. Two individuals or groups doing different work at the same level have, it is said, no authority over one another ; whereas this relationship does exist between levels. This is important, but too much should not be made of this distinction. Writers on administrative theory a few years ago were laying great emphasis on the importance of a clear line of command, and of precise definitions of authority. But there has been some reac-

---

([17]) See L. Urwick, *Elements of Administration*, 2nd. ed., 1950, pp. 63-64.

([18]) "Responsibility" is hard to define. Some would want to do so in terms of the "importance" of decisions taken (measured in some way or other) or of numbers of subordinates. An interesting recent account is in E. Jaques, *Measurement of Responsibility*, 1956. Dr. Jaques argues that, in an industrial firm, two important existing criteria, influencing pay and status, are (*a*) the "time-span" of discretion—the period in which each worker exercises his discretion without outside review (*b*) (in the case of manual workers) "wastage"— the worker's power to damage the firm's resources. See also Chapter 18 below.

tion from their views (some would say we have over-reacted). We have become aware of the fact that many successful organizations operate very little on the basis of commands or orders. The problem is rather seen as one of arranging the division of tasks between different levels, and training individuals to perform them, so that everyone understands what is required of him and "does the right thing without being told."([19]) Waldo has christened this "built-in rationality."

Once we start looking at administrative hierarchies in this way, the problem of dividing work between levels begins to look more akin to that of dividing it between formal equals. It becomes the problem of "vertical specialization," and the same general criteria apply:

   (i) to create sub-units in which tasks are grouped so that one facilitates the doing of another.

   (ii) to minimise the problem of co-ordination between levels, *i.e.*, to minimise order-giving, buck-passing, and fruitless conflict, and to enable most of the necessary adjustments to take place by informal discussion, a few staff conferences, and so on.

Just as in the case of the division of work between departments or sub-units of departments, there were the two questions: (*a*) how many sub-units? (*b*) on what principle is sub-division to take place? ; so in the case of levels, we have the questions (*a*) how many levels? (*b*) what shall each do?

Delegation and decentralization

"What shall each level do?"—is the same question as, how much delegation and decentralization shall there be? We are periodically told that Australian government has become too centralized. Sometimes what is being talked of is a tendency to concentrate more power in federal hands, sometimes the failure of the States to give more power to local government, or to regional offices ; or it may be argued that Public Service Boards, Treasuries and Prime Minister's or Premier's Departments have increased their power in relation to other departments ; or that too much in a particular department has to be referred up to the top for approval. In all these cases the same kinds of argument recur ; that centralized control is administratively inefficient, and that by concentrating decision-making in too few hands, it endangers freedom and democracy.

It is hard to deal sensibly with such a controversy while it is stated in blacks and whites. If we confine attention here to the first point, it is clear that a balance of advantages and disadvantages is involved. It is at ground level that the shoe pinches, and any decision made there is liable to be quicker and better adapted to local conditions. It may also produce a greater sense of responsibility among the officials concerned. Pride in a job partly depends on being able to recognize one's own work. But it may be cheaper, or cause less conflict, or make better use of talent, to concentrate certain

---

([19]) An important early influence in this direction was Mary Parker Follett. See her essay, "The Giving of Orders", reprinted in *Dynamic Administration*, 1941, with its stress on the need to depersonalise orders, and make the subordinate feel that the so-called order is itself given in obedience to the "law of the situation". The perfect product of such methods, with co-operativeness "built-in", is currently under fire in America; see W. H. Whyte, *The Organization Man*, 1957.

kinds of decision-making. There is no general rule about this; and the balance of advantage will vary with the service concerned.

It should be added that decentralization and delegation in all their various forms can be made easier by good training—both in the sense of widely-spread skill, and that of a widely-shared habit of co-operation; by exploiting to the maximum the possibilities of control through fairly simple devices, so that a few central decisions provide an adequate framework within which other decisions may be made by large numbers of persons without producing major disharmonies; and by trying to avoid getting into situations where such things are difficult to arrange.

Leadership and Control

The most obvious fact about a hierarchy is that its constituent units are unequal. There are leaders and followers, superiors and subordinates, controllers and controlled, however you care to name them. Notions like "leadership" and "control" are far from simple. How do you for instance measure the amount of control, or influence, A has over B? It certainly cannot be done in terms of the number of decisions taken by A—it is likely that the leader of an organization will make only a few decisions (but the important ones), and the people lower down more, but less important, ones. Nor does a leader necessarily initiate much business. He may spend most of his time endorsing, modifying, or vetoing other people's proposals, though it is important that he can always initiate activities if he wants to. Nor is it even always helpful to think of leaders as deciding broad policy but not "interfering in details"; an effective leader may have little time for details, but he reserves the right to interfere, and if he is wise he sometimes will.

Recent work on leadership has tendered to discredit the notion that there is any one set of leadership qualities applicable to all groups of people in all situations. It is easier to point to examples of good and bad leaders, than to say why. So a good way of studying leadership is to read biographies, and a good way of training leaders is to let people work with leaders. Different types of leader suit different situations—this should in fact be fairly obvious. Some units may be highly dependent on the personal decisiveness and creative intelligence of the men at the top; in others, which are highly institutionalized and have set routines, it may be hard to find a leader at all. All you can say is that everybody knows his job and is doing it. In the latter case, unless it is felt that the agency needs a shakeup, the best people to have in senior positions may include a good many who simply have the most experience; or whose creative function is to make people feel that their routines are useful and important, not that they need changing.[20] There are leaders who carry their followers along new paths, those who hold them together on old ones; a recent writer has christened them "dux" and "rex".

"Control" is another difficult concept. We may first think of organized control machinery, with a definite set of directives and means of enforcing them. This is what we are partly thinking of when we talk about Treasury control or say that the Public Service Board controls many personnel mat-

---

[20] On this subject, Chester Barnard, *The Functions of the Executive*, 1938, A. W. Gouldner (ed.) *Studies in Leadership*, 1950, and P. Selznick, *Leadership in Administration*, 1957, will be found enlightening.

ters. But "control" exists at all levels of an organization, whether we use the word to mean simply "influence", or (more narrowly) "deliberate influence", or (still more narrowly) to mean "watching results and taking the necessary corrective action". In all these senses everyone plays some part in "controlling" finance, personnel, materials, and so on.

There are a number of formal ways by which management at any given level may control the performance of subordinate units. They include (i) prior approval of specific projects, (ii) fixing budgetary limits, (iii) setting standards of performance, (iv) reporting and inspection, (v) approval of key appointments. Each has its own advantages and disadvantages. Specific approval may be appropriate where control through more general directives is hard to establish, or would involve so much detailed spelling-out of rules as seriously to hamper initiative and flexibility. But it may also be time-wasting or be felt as a mark of lack of confidence. It may, of course, be delegated to some point to lower levels, e.g., power to approve projects up to a certain limit. Allotting a maximum sum of money to be spent in some particular field can be a flexible instrument of control, and is the basic one of modern governments; but it has an element of arbitrariness and may unduly restrict one activity while encouraging other departments to spend up to the limit. Setting standards of performance is valuable where they can be made reasonably precise and where "living up to them" is a true measure of efficiency; and where compliance with them can be determined by some fairly simple reporting or inspection system. Periodical reports may be required to check compliance with any or all of the above, or simply to get a general impression of the performance of an administrative unit. It is important not to demand unnecessary information; reporting can easily get out of hand.[21]

Inspection is often a valuable way of informing the "top" about what is happening lower down, and at the same time of establishing relations of mutual confidence. But it may crucially depend on the high individual quality of the inspectors; in the wrong hands it can become a tiresome kind of fault-finding. There are many other problems in creating good reporting and inspection systems. For example, if they are over-formalized they may miss many points or become unduly burdensome.

Often the most effective type of control is simply to take great pains in appointing good people to the key positions, so that most things can safely be left in their hands. "In the whole organization . . . . there are about 200 people who take on themselves the decisions which make or mar the success of the business as a whole . . . The biggest job of top management is to ensure the quality of this 200".[22] This applies at all levels, even where there may be many other controls—forms for standardized procedures, bulky regulations or instruction books, and so on—and in most areas of activity. To appoint, say, in charge of local taxation offices, or schools, or consulates, individuals who can safely be left to plan the programme of work and make final decisions in most of the problems coming to

---

[21] A useful exercise would be to look at the annual report of a government department and ask oneself (a) what it puts in that would be better left out, or presented more intelligibly, (b) what it leaves out that ought to be in.

[22] Sir Geoffrey (now Lord) Heyworth, Chairman of Lever Bros., in G. E. Milward (ed.) Large-scale Organisation, 1950, p. 177.

them, is often the most valuable instrument of control a headquarters department has.

This may serve to remind us of the important general point that the problem of control is much wider than the problem of "command", that is, of who gives the orders and sees that they are carried out. People are often controlled by influencing their expectation of rewards and penalties; and direct orders usually play a small part in this. The basic limitation of commands is that they offer no reward; on the contrary they may simply frustrate the receiver, be troublesome to enforce, and invite evasive action.

Many of the most effective methods of control do not try directly to influence particular acts, but to influence personality or environment—for example, by teaching the response appropriate to a task, or by adapting the task to the characteristics of the person concerned. If you like, they are often problems of training and organization. It saves a lot of trouble if rewards and penalties can be, as psychologists say, "internalised", in conscientious behaviour or feelings of loyalty to the organization, so that the controls exercised are felt to be "right" (of course, this can be done to good or evil ends—no doubt there are many conscientious members of the Soviet secret police). If there are rules, it helps if their purpose is understood and approved, and they are clearly seen to serve that purpose.

This is all part of the problem of *incentives*. Many of the latter are of a more concrete character, e.g., pay, promotion prospects. They have to be properly graded to satisfy justice and to encourage effort in the right direction. Campaigns to boost morale are not of much value if these basic conditions of efficient work do not exist. A public servant in a Department of Public Health may conceivably be unconcerned about the health of the public. That may not matter if he can be interested in doing his own job (say, compiling figures) with reasonable efficiency. He will still be a useful person to have in the office. Some very zealous departmental heads like to think that every employee feels personally concerned in the agency's policies. But it would be a sad thing if the fate of a department depended on this, though it is helpful up to a point if they do.

Communication

Good control depends on good communications, which are needed to prevent "involuntarily inconsistent" behaviour. It is quite possible even for a group of people with aims in common, to behave in ways quite inconsistent with their achievement. Anyone who doubts this should watch a body of amateur removal men trying to get a large piece of furniture through a small door. The most loyal and belligerent armies have often lost wars. This does not happen only because the individuals concerned lack skill, but also because of poor communications between them. A lacks knowledge of B's proposed activities, B does not know what is expected of him by C, and so on. There are often situations in which we can only take advantage of all the potentialities of the division of labour by also building up an elaborate net-work of communications.

The requirement is that each official has the data relevant to the performance of his particular task. The relevant information has to be passed from one person to another, and has to be as clear and complete as is necessary for him to do his job properly. It would be misleading to say "as clear and complete as possible," and as accurate to say "no clearer and completer than necessary". We very often have to act on unclear and incomplete information. The conveying of information carries with it a cost—for example, it takes time ; we do not want to incur a greater cost than is necessary. Where the extra cost of a bit of information exceeds the extra advantage of having it, it is not worthwhile to pass it on (a fact frequently ignored by officials who insist on detailed returns without asking what trouble it takes to prepare them, and how much use will be made of them when prepared). On the other hand, where the costs of misunderstanding are high, it will be necessary to reduce the possibility of it to a minimum. The armed forces have developed a complex set of communications and a rigidly defined language of communication partly for this reason—it is, for example, not possible to rely on correcting ambiguities later when quick decisions have to be taken. Such a language may also develop out of a great emphasis on the need to fix responsibility for mistakes, or on the need for fairly precise statements of rights and obligations, as in the case of the law.

So all kinds of questions are raised. What information do people at various levels need? How can it be conveyed most economically in words and figures? How can people be trained to get the most out of it?

The information needed may become available at many different points in the administrative structure—it may, for example, be a policy formulated at the top and passed down, or data collected at the level of contact with the outside world, over the counter, in the class-room, on the census form. It may also arise at various intermediate levels, as every employee is expert at something, and knows something which is useful to others. It may arise in the ordinary course of duty, or have to be specially obtained, at additional cost, by an investigating branch or an accounting unit.

It has then to be transmitted from those who have it to those who need it. An established structure will develop regular "channels" or "lines of communication" to this end. They must be as direct and short as possible.([28]) If information has to pass through many persons or levels, this increases the time taken to act on it and also sometimes multiplies the possibilities of misunderstanding it. It is tempting to the persons at the top to want to know everything, as well as to decide everything ; and this is the impulse that makes for centralization. But the cost of their knowing more than a certain amount may be greater than the advantage. The problem of communication is simplest where much of the information required by a person to act arises at the point of action, and does not need to be passed on. The decision can be taken by the man who knows. Consider the case where a simple and unambiguous rule can be given to all counter-clerks: sell a stamp to anyone who offers you 4d. for it. All the information needed is that X, Y, Z have the money and no one needs to know it but the clerk. A somewhat less simple case is where the rule is: pay a pension to anyone fulfilling a, b, c conditions—more complex because a line of communication to another level may be needed for interpreting doubtful cases. The need for more and more complex communications systems increases

([28]) See on this Chester Barnard, *Functions of the Executive*, pp. 175 ff. On communication generally see: A. J. Ayer, etc., *Studies in Communication*, 1955.

steadily as the policy to be applied becomes less easily translated into clear and unambiguous rules for those at the point of action.

Communications will be partly reduced to rule—certain papers have to be sent to certain people, certain formal reports required, there may be "rules of access" (e.g., you don't normally "go above" your immediate superior or write letters save through certain channels). It is important to decide how far to formalize communications (e.g., a standard form of application saves time, but may be inflexible). In any event many communications will be "informal"—the telephone has become an important medium of informal administrative contact. Informal contacts may supplement or even cut across the formal pattern. There are also informal devices for limiting contact—you may have the right to see the boss but be unable to get past his secretary.

Various different kinds of thing have to be communicated in administrative systems. First there are "the facts" in the popular sense—what is happening inside and outside the system, including the sorts of facts contained in statistical returns, pensions, applications, balance-sheets and so forth ; second there are policies, decisions, rules, interpretations, orders, advice, feelings, wishes—in language which is often necessarily imprecise and whose meaning may vary with the person who uses it. X may say, "I would like you to do this as soon as you can", and in fact expect it to be done as quickly as Y who habitually says, "I want this now". This is an elementary lesson in interpretation.

At the other extreme may be a top-level directive such as that "only essential peace-time production is to be provided for".([24]) How is this to be interpreted? It would be quite meaningless except to someone in touch with the whole context of the directive—what has gone before, what other clues there are to present intentions, and so on. Knowing what is expected of one has become a problem of the greatest complexity, involving a wide knowledge of many matters, including the people concerned. One reason why it is often hard to work new organizations properly is that there has developed no regular structure of mutual expectations and no store of accumulated knowledge, with reference to which particular communications can be interpreted.([25]) Even quite a small group, such as a committee, works better when its members know one another reasonably well and even better when they have acquired some experience of discussing the same subject together, because they have built up such a structure. This is also an important reason why physical propinquity is important for officials or departments that have

---

([24]) This (which is part of a war-time directive) continued: "Military items are to be given a lower priority where they cater only for the European theatre and new items of equipment are not to be manufactured unless a serious loss of efficiency would be involved by not providing them"—none of which could have made it much easier to interpret.

([25]) cf. Sir Geoffrey Vickers, in A. J. Ayer, *op. cit.*, p. 79: ". . . the (British) National Coal Board was required to come into full activity at a time when its three upper levels of authority had only just been recruited. When opinions, orders and information began to fly up and down these newly improvised channels, everyone concerned found at first a curious difficulty in making himself understood. We became aware how much we are normally accustomed to rely, for the understanding of all we say, on the understanding accumulated during past intercourse with the same minds on the same subject."

much to do with one another. The chance of frequent discussion is not simply a way of exchanging "facts", but of learning about attitudes, as well as of persuading and being persuaded.

The above remarks may also help us to understand the importance of training and experience. Two of the objects of training are to see that a man knows what to do without being told and to see that he is more receptive when he is told; and experience teaches the same lessons. They both reduce the need for communication; and are specially important when communication is difficult. "Training . . . . has its greatest value in those situations where the exercise of formal authority through commands proves difficult," owing to "the need for prompt action, . . . spatial dispersion of the organization, ... the complexity of the subject matter of decisions which defies summarization in rules and regulations. Training permits a higher degree of decentralization".([20]) Compare the following, by a British civil servant, "In many government departments the nature of the work is such that it is possible to lay down rules as to who decides what . . . . Practically none of the Colonial Office work is of that kind. Every officer has to exercise judgment in dealing with any question, whether to settle it or 'send it on'. This is where tradition, training and experience count".([27])

It may be added that the greatest deficiency in communication is often that which runs from the top down, especially where changing policies are involved. It may be hard to communicate the needed understanding even of existing plans and programmes; it is still more difficult to convey the rationale of change. New policies that may have been, in some vague way, long-mooted in the select circle near the top, that senior officers may have contributed to and in some sense "got used to" even before they are implemented, can arrive as bolts from the blue on those mainly involved in or affected by the agency's routines (which the change may affect in the sharpest and most concrete way). It is hard for the most benevolently disposed leader to realize how little he really passes on in time of the way in which his own mind is moving or of what he sees approaching over the distant horizon.

"Human factors"

There has been a good deal of discussion lately of what are called "human factors" in administration. It is true, of course, that the whole of administration is concerned with human factors, since it is an affair of human beings. But the term has been invented to call attention to the fact that the behaviour of human groups can never be completely rationalized, because they are composed of individuals who react as "wholes" and not simply in terms of their formal place in the organization, and who are subject to the pressures of a social environment, both inside and outside the department they serve. Some administrative reformers, of whom Jeremy Bentham is the first and most famous, have assumed that you can dispose of all problems by water-right systems of recruitment, inspection, accountability, rewards and penalties. But this is not the case. Almost everyone

---

([20]) H. A. Simon, *Administrative Behavior*, pp. 170-171.
([27]) Sir Charles Jeffries, *The Colonial Office*, 1956, p. 124.

in an administrative unit has some discretion that cannot be precisely checked. There are forms of apathy, defensiveness, resentment, red-tape-mindedness, and minor persecution of subordinates, which the most perfect system of administrative control cannot deal with, but which may seriously affect the morale of an agency, "the degree of willingness to participate in the organization's tasks."

There are many different influences acting on individuals in an organization, home environment and early training, social attitudes to the public service and various group-influences (trade union, church, etc.). Some social attitudes may be of great importance. Consider the influence of a society that looks lightly on corruption in the public service ; or that puts a high value on efficiency or fairness ; or where deference and hierarchy play a large part in social relations ; or in which the public service has low prestige. All these attitudes may have marked effects on the way public servants carry out their duties. Then there are influences received from the formal structure—job, orders, training, rewards and punishments—and those acting more informally through friendships, loyalties, rivalries that develop in the course of work. Any one of these influences may reinforce or weaken others. For example, informal loyalties may support or undermine the administrative structure.

A good deal of emphasis has been placed in recent administrative theory on the importance of the "primary group", the small working unit or "face-to-face" group in which most people do their daily work. Most people's happiness depends on being able to develop strong attachments to such a unit—a labourers' gang, a typing pool, a group of clerical workers who share an office. Its attitudes will tend to become those of any individual who joins it, unless he or she is highly ambitious, unsociable, or otherwise strongly enough motivated to tolerate deviating from the group's standards. Its influence may be stronger than that of the larger unit of which it forms part, if the two should happen to be in conflict. In such a group the leader (for present purposes, the member with the most influence on activities relevant to work) may play a decisive role. If he happens to correspond to the formal supervisor of the unit, on behalf of the larger unit of which it forms part, he can do something to reconcile the group's attitudes with the requirements of the agency ; or to alienate the one from the other.[28]

The social and educational background of public servants is another important influence on their behaviour. (Some might, for example, argue that the fact that most modern public servants derive most of their social prestige from their status in the administrative hierarchy has various consequences). A number of interesting studies have been made of the social background of public servants. It can be dangerous, of course, to draw over ready conclusions from such studies. A good example of this is the famous prediction of Professor Laski, repeated by many others, that a Labour government in Britain would run into serious trouble because of the predominantly upper-middle class character of the senior civil servants who would administer its policies. Most people are agreed that this did not happen. We cannot, in fact, assume a close link between background and

---

[28] Hence some of the present emphasis on the "training of supervisors." See Chapter 18.

official behaviour. One important reason for this has already been indicated, that a well-established public service closely moulds its own members.

Efficiency

People have been saying for at least a century that government should be made "efficient".([20]) "Economy and efficiency" was for a long time a catch phrase of administrative reformers; though it was associated with a minimising view of State functions that finally helped to discredit it. But it is right that the words should be closely linked; efficient action is economical action, whether one is thinking in terms of large expenditure or small, or simply of economy of effort, of "maximising output for a given input".

A great deal of talk about efficiency is confused by failure to realise that any measure of it must be concerned with relating an output of something to an input of something. In other words, we have (1) to know what the aim is (2) to be able to measure (at least roughly) the degree to which it is being achieved and (3) what resources are being used to achieve this, and ideally, (4) what alternative uses of these resources are being foregone. Business firms often use money as a measure of over-all efficiency—the surplus of income over costs. This has some defects as a test even in business; and is not much help even there in determining the efficiency of, say, a personnel department, the contribution of which to income cannot be directly measured. Public bodies can often measure their input in money terms, but rarely their output.

Stating the objectives of government in such a way that progress towards them can be measured is a difficult task. It is no good simply listing adequate defence, good health, housing, education, and so on. What are the measures of progress towards these? We may be able to list certain measurable criteria—mortality rates, housing space, size of classes in schools—and relate progress to costs and it is important that we should do this whenever we can.   But it is hard to find units in which many objectives can be measured (how far is our educational system turning out "good citizens"?). It is hard to measure the contribution of particular sections of departments to objectives (is the headquarters staff of the Department of . . . . . doing an efficient job?). It is also very hard to weigh the merits of different objectives that may conflict. Is it a better use of given resources to improve school buildings, or to pay teachers more? To reduce the T.B. rate or to improve mental health services? Should we spend more on housing and less on defence? There is no common unit to which these choices can be reduced, and they often tend to be made in more or less irrational ways, depending on the pressures of the moment and the prejudices of individuals.

Assuming that we know a particular job needs to be done, and that we can measure the degree of success in doing it, and the resources needed to do it, we can be fairly clear about what it means to do it more or less

---

([20]) "Efficiency" seems to have started its popular career about a century ago. "It was not until September, 1855, that Sebastapol fell: by that time public opinion had passed from wholehearted enthusiasm for the (Crimean) war to scathing criticism of its maladministration. 'Efficiency' became a Radical slogan." (A. Briggs, *Victorian People*, p. 69.) The First World War launched Planning, the Second popularized it and added Organisation and Methods.

efficiently. Many of the most successful applications of Organisation and Methods techniques have been to tasks that satisfy these conditions. In general, it is easier to do this at the lower levels of administration than higher up, and easier in repetitive jobs than others. It is simpler to measure a typist's efficiency than a department head's; and, as has been said, quick replies to letters are a safer test of efficiency in the Department of Social Services than in the Department of External Affairs.

So it is worth remembering: (*a*) that "efficiency" has no meaning save in relation to some objective. Hence people who say, for example, that talk about efficiency neglects "the human side" are confusing the issue—*if* you want to be humane, there are still more and less efficient ways of doing it; (*b*) that the more measures we can devise of efficiency (by better accounting, clearer thinking, intelligent comparisons) the better; (*c*) that this is subject to the proviso that we must rely a great deal on common sense judgments, and on putting people we trust in a position to make them; and that it may be positively dangerous to look for measurable indices of progress, if it leads us to suppose that the things we cannot measure accurately are less important than the things we can. Mr. Bourke discusses some of these problems at greater length in his chapter.

SPECIAL CHARACTER OF PUBLIC ADMINISTRATION

Up to now, although we have drawn most of our examples from the field of public administration, the points we have discussed have largely been applicable to many types of administrative agency. Here we must consider some problems more particularly relevant to the field of government.

"Public" is in some ways a misleading adjective to apply to government bodies and their work. Mr. Kewley in his chapter prefers "governmental". As he points out, many hospitals are rightly called public; but most of them would not be classed as State agencies, though they receive government subsidies. However, in this book we have retained the term public administration, which is well-understood, to refer to the administrative activities of governments.

What is the special character of public administration, as contrasted, say, with the administration of private business? It is by no means all contrast; the two share many problems, and many of the management techniques and skills of the one are applicable to the other. There is everything to be said for each keeping in close touch with developments in the other. As is pointed out in Chapters 15 and 18, Organisation and Methods work in the public service was an outgrowth of "scientific management" in industry, and the same is true of some recent developments in public personnel management. The administrative problems of large-scale operation, how to delegate authority, how to keep good communications, how to preserve incentive, and so on, exist in a large business often in much the same form as in a large government department. There are lively public agencies as well as lively firms; and bureaucratic business empires as well as bureaucratic departments. Big businesses may be more like government departments than they are like small businesses. This does not stop businessmen and public servants from commenting scathingly on each others' activities.

Yet there are some important differences between the two, and the State is not simply a large business concern. First, the public administrator is the servant of political decisions. He has a Minister, sometimes one who changes quite frequently and who is often not primarily chosen because he is a good administrator. (The latter is sometimes true of business heads.)

Policy may change for reasons quite unaffected by considerations of administrative efficiency. A department may get functions it does not want, and knows that it cannot administer well. Parliaments, unlike shareholders, meet regularly, maintain a correspondence with the firm, and include an Opposition with a vested interest in criticism. Many of the decisions that a department makes may involve matters of political controversy. The natural fear of letting more than a very small number of very experienced public servants deal with them may mean that these are over-worked, while their subordinates' discretion has been severely limited by strict rules.

Second, the customer of the public services is not usually in the same position as a firm's customer. Except for State trading enterprises, most public services are given free or below cost as far as individual customers are concerned. There is no simple test of whether they are getting the things they most want, or would prefer to buy something different. An individual section of a public department may have some notion whether its customers are on the whole pleased or displeased; but that may be simply because it has managed to do relatively well in the allocation of funds.

It cannot, however, be left to decide this, which may simply lead to other more urgent needs being left unmet. Who is to decide? The Treasury? It is certainly less biased than the spending departments, and has information available to it from all of them. Its views will certainly be important. But by and large it knows even less than the departments about the various particular demands that have to be evaluated. It can often only judge on the basis of last year's figures. The Treasury's views are subjected in turn to the political process, where the politicians keep their ears to the ground, try to decide the relative strength and significance of public complaints, and have their hunches periodically tested in a broad though decisive fashion by elections. The customer can for once speak his mind—though it will still be unclear just *why* he failed to return the Government? Was it because age pensions were not raised enough? Or because taxes were raised too much or for some other reason?

In the absence of other criteria complainants may get too much attention; and too much energy may be spent, or mis-spent, on the hunt for mistakes, with outsiders hot on the trail for some glaring example of mis-spending; the exposure of which will in turn leave a comforting feeling that the budgetary process is after all potentially a rational one, that is, if we keep a vigilant eye on the misuse of ministerial cars. Psychologists tell us that one consequence of a feeling of failure rationally to control a situation is an excessive attention to detail.

A related point is that the financial fruits of special efforts do not accrue to the person or department making them. In these respects public and large business agencies differ only in degree, though the latter are perhaps more successful at relating earnings to output, mainly because more measures of output are available to them.

The State is, over a large part of its activities, a monopolist with compulsory powers, including the power to tax. It is the one firm the public has to go to; and it seems to them therefore specially important that it should act in a controlled and "fair" way. This demand is reinforced by a common belief that the State should have higher ideals than business, and in particular be concerned more with justice as between man and man.

These demands express themselves in various ways. There is a special concern for consistency of treatment, that apparently similar cases must be treated similarly. The concern to avoid charges of inconsistency, which may carry with them the charge of favouritism or bureaucratic muddle, affects a great deal of public administrative activity, and is an important factor in the reliance on rules and precedents. It extends into the organization of the public service itself, where recruitment and promotion tend to become encased in a similar framework designed as much to avoid suspicions of injustice as with a direct eye on efficiency. A higher standard of honesty and integrity is also demanded of, and often supplied by, the public servant. The greater fear of being imposed upon by the State may also lead to well-meant public relations activities being less readily approved than equivalent activities by private business.

All this explains a good many of the special characteristics of public departments, including some that are much criticized, for example, so-called "red tape" (once defined as "the application of a rule to the exception"). Government files expand partly because every expenditure has to be "justified", partly to provide materials for answering questions, assuming that every decision may be challenged sooner or later. There is less room for acting on hunches, partly because the basis of a hunch cannot be explained on paper. Another consequence is that control in government agencies is more often divided. An operating unit may have little say in many activities very important to it—for example, who it employs and what it pays them. Its top management, as has been said, often "looks up to a bureaucracy as well as down to one". One authority may have fixed its functions, a second its staff, a third the funds it gets. Such a phenomenon is not, of course, unknown in large businesses; but they can escape from it more easily if they want to.

Nothing said in this section should be taken as implying any judgment about the relative merits of public servants and businessmen, or of public and private enterprise. The only conclusion we may validly draw is that government is to some degree different from business, though many of the problems overlap; and that, to the extent that it is different, different talents are needed to operate it successfully. Most of the points we have made would suggest that government is the harder sphere in which to achieve assured successes. However, there are some things which tell in the other direction. At its best government can call upon a high degree of loyalty and devotion to duty; the finest sort of public servant has a largeness of view and capacity for disinterested service that can achieve results open to few private firms. We might remember, too, how much of the research and developmental work that brings long-term advantages depends (especially in Australia) on the initiative of government; and not simply because it commands the resources, but also because it is often less blinkered in their use. Some of the disadvantages that confront the public administrator can be reduced by public attitudes that encourage enterprise and experiment among public authorities, and do not judge them mainly by their mistakes; as well as by doing everything possible to introduce measures of efficiency into the public service, and incentives to economical working.

Policy and Administration

Who defines the objectives of the government administrator? Many people would say that Parliament does. Parliament passes a law, and this is "executed" by the administration, by applying it to particular cases. There is certainly some truth in this, provided we remember that most of the laws modern Parliaments pass are not initiated by them, but by Governments ; and that, when we say the Government or a Minister has introduced a bill, we remember that many of the ideas embodied in it came from a variety of sources, including public servants.

It may be argued that public servants advise on legislation, but the decision whether to introduce it lies with the Government, and Parliament has the final word in deciding whether it becomes an official directive or not. But is it true, even so, that the statutes passed by Parliament define all the objectives, leaving to the administrative departments only the job of devising ways and means? The inspection of a few Acts of Parliament will show us that this is not the case. A law will to some point define the task, outline machinery, provide funds, lay down some main procedures. It is the authority for the actions of the administration ; the courts will refer to it if a question arises whether the administration is justified in acting in a certain way. The departments must act according to law. But this does not take one very far (as courts often find out). The statute will only define the objective in broad terms. The powers of the agency will not usually be stated with any precision, and sometimes in a way that makes them especially hard to control, e.g., when the Minister may act if "satisfied" that it is "requisite", "necessary" or "expedient". Quite frequently the law does not say that such-and-such is to be done, but that it "may" be done. The Minister, or whoever heads the agency concerned, may even be given an express power to fill the gaps in the statute by making regulations, i.e., legislating for his own department.

The law also normally says very little about machinery and procedures. Having established that the job is to be done by a Minister, or perhaps by a Board or Commission appointed in a stated way, it generally works on the theory that the Minister and the Board are best able to order the doings of their own agency, under some supervision from the Treasury and the public service authority, and within the limits of the money voted for this particular activity. In practice most Ministers accept the structure as they find it, and even new departments are usually formed round an existing nucleus and ordered according to existing rules. In short administration works within a framework of law, but the law allows a good deal of *discretion*.

Statutory enactment is not, of course, the only means the elected representatives of the people have of controlling administrative activities. We have spoken as though laws are given to officials to carry out. But this is not the case. The powers are usually granted to Ministers, or if not, as in the case of some Boards and Commissions, at any rate to a small number of persons over whom some Minister is usually given certain legal powers of supervision and control. These Ministers are themselves drawn from Parliament, and directly responsible to it. They are in one aspect members of the administrative machine, carrying out the laws with their official subordinates. In another, however, they are those members of Parliament invested with a special responsibility for "policy-making". It is through them that the generalities of law become translated into more concrete policy-objectives, and that many projects with which the law has little or no concern, e.g., in the field of economic and foreign policy, take form and shape. Parliament itself can act in this area mainly through critical comment in debate, and by the well-timed question.

So we can widen our statement above and say that administration works within a framework of law and policy. But when Ministers make policy (as when they initiate bills) they derive some of their advice from officials. In some important areas they can hardly be said to have views on policy at all; they "leave it to" officials. Thirdly, their policy-directives usually leave a good deal to be filled in, and may be susceptible of more than one interpretation. Occasionally the policy may even contain internal contradictions, which the administrator has to resolve as best he can.

This means that the public service is inevitably concerned to some point with policy-making. It does not mean that Parliament and the Cabinet are not very important determinants of the objectives of administration. On crucial matters their decision is clearly the one that counts. What particular areas politicians interest themselves in, and decide are "crucial" for the moment, will depend on many factors, including their personal preferences and "the dissatisfaction of citizens, multiplied by their number and strength, modified by their geographical-jurisdictional location and by their persistence and techniques of agitation".([30])

One result of this is that we must expect to find political pressures operating directly at the official as well as the parliamentary and ministerial levels. Outside interests will seek access to those who they consider can influence decisions which affect them. This is discussed below. Second, a public servant's efficiency will depend partly on his capacity to adjust his department's policy to give satisfaction to interested parties, to make its programmes acceptable—at its crudest, to "keep the department (or his Minister) out of trouble"; in the longer run, to see that it adapts itself to changing needs and pressures, as far as is possible within the existing law and within its budget. This is particularly true of the top officials. In countries such as the United States, where the pressures on administration are great, this has resulted in some of the top administrative posts being treated as frankly political appointments. The English tradition, which Australia has largely inherited, lays great stress on the neutrality of all officials below the Minister; though it is not wholly unknown for a little administrative reshuffling to follow a change of government.

The Role of the Public Servant

This emphasis on the neutrality of officials has many virtues. It assists the development of a career service in which the highest posts are open to permanent officers; which in turn gives the public servant a professional status and encourages him to adopt a professional attitude to his work. He can develop pride in his technical skill, and learn to distinguish his

---

([30]) Paul Appleby, *Policy and Administration*, p. 61. As Appleby says, "Any particular problem is capable of being pushed upward for resolution by political processes"; and even the "normal" level at which decisions of a certain kind are taken is fixed partly by political considerations.

personal view of a matter from the demands put on him by his office. The career public servant is encouraged to think of himself as mainly a "practitioner of means", working out of the limelight and anonymously to put into effect policies decided by others, on which he may have offered advice, and which may leave him scope for considerable discretion, but which he should not consciously distort in response to other viewpoints and pressures. Such an attitude of mind is a vital element in an effective public service.

It is partly a product of service tradition.([31]) The public service, like any profession, closely moulds its own members. New entrants find themselves occupying positions in a well-defined structure and with fairly well-defined criteria of proper behaviour and efficient performance of duty. If this structure is well-established (as it is, on the whole, in Australia) it acts as a very powerful influence on all individuals within it; it also, of course, only attracts the sort of person who thinks he would like that kind of thing.

But the role of public servants is also safeguarded by formal provisions. They are recruited on a merit basis and have in practice great job-security. There are rules prohibiting the passing-on of information obtained in the course of duty, and the use of outside influence to get promotions or other privileges. They are officially debarred from public comment on the working of government departments.

A case of special interest is that of political activity. The old view was that they should be very stringently controlled in this respect. In eighteenth century England, many public servants were debarred from voting; as recently as 1903 in Victoria they were segregated into special constituencies (though this was a short-lived experiment). Their claim to form staff associations used to be looked on with some suspicion, and in Britain these were for a time debarred from outside affiliations. Australian public service unions have mostly been content to preserve their own freedom from obviously political links, though there are important exceptions.

In general, Australian opinion has accepted reasonably free trade union and political activity on the part of public servants.([32]) Staff associations have often had good parliamentary contacts, and there have been periods of intense political activity, as over depression salary cuts. Views about the political rights of public servants as individuals have mellowed. The original Commonwealth rule prohibited any public political activity. However, in 1909 it was replaced by the present regulation which merely prohibits public comment on departments and disclosure of information; it was also ruled

---

([31]) cf. W. C. Wurth. 'The Public Servant and Responsible Government', *Pub. Admin.* (*Sydney*), XV, June, 1956, p. 83. "It is a sense of trustworthiness that is communicated by older to younger officers; it ensures that honest advice is given to Ministers and others who make final decisions. It is present in the teacher before the class, the clerk at the enquiry counter, the architect or the engineer at his drawing board, the government doctor and the government solicitor. It is peculiarly the creation of the service itself."

([32]) In 1955, there were 62 public service unions with 203,437 members. But this does not include the many outside unions that have government employees among their members. See also: J. D. B. Miller, "Public Service Associations and Politics", *Pub. Admin.* (*Sydney*), VI, Sept., 1947; V. Subramaniam, "Political Rights of Commonwealth Public Servants," *ibid.*, XVII, March, 1958; "The Public Servant and Politics", F. A. Bland (ed.), *Government in Australia*, 1944 ed.. Ch. XX; and A. Wildavsky and D. Carboch, *Studies in Australian Politics*, 1958, pp. 202-209.

that Commonwealth public servants might contest State elections without resigning if State laws did not forbid this. New South Wales allowed public servants to contest State elections without resigning in 1916, Victoria in 1935. Public servants still have to resign to contest Federal elections, but are normally reinstated without loss of privileges in case of defeat.

The relative freedom of Australian public servants is no doubt partly due to the existence of strong barriers (in the shape of independent public service authorities) to widespread political patronage; but also to the looser hold than in Britain of the notion that a Crown servant is a "person apart", and should not have at least the rights of all other workers. This is also reflected in another field—that of the State's rights as an employer. Its right to fix salaries has been eroded by arbitration; its right to promote by appeals tribunals. Its discretion in the matter of recruitment and dismissal has also been sharply curtailed.

The traditional common law view is that all servants of the Crown are employed, and can be dismissed, at the pleasure of the Crown. In practice, in both the United Kingdom and Australia, most public servants have permanent tenure, and can only be dismissed for misconduct or gross inefficiency; and there are other safeguards for their protection from arbitrary treatment. However, in the United Kingdom these and other rules governing public service matters are rarely embodied in legislation, but take the form of Orders in Council, Treasury minutes and departmental regulations. They are, so to speak, rules made by the Crown for itself in its dealings with its servants and are not enforceable in the courts; so an aggrieved civil servant has no legal remedy for wrongful dismissal.

In the absence of the statutory provisions about to be mentioned, the position in Australia would be the same; indeed, it can happen that owing to gaps in the statutory provisions, there are occasionally "common law" Crown servants even today. Some Australian Court decisions suggest that even in such cases, the Crown servant has a contract of sorts, and should be able at least to recover salary for services actually rendered, and recent English decisions support this view. But the question is in practice of little importance, because the six States and the Commonwealth have enacted Public Service Acts which lay down methods of recruitment, promotion, demotion and dismissal, and vest disciplinary powers in special tribunals. The Courts have interpreted these statutes as creating enforceable rights. Of course, the statutes in their own terms often leave wide discretionary powers to the executive government in its dealings with Crown servants, but nevertheless the body of legal decisions in which the courts have intervened to declare or protect civil rights is very considerable.([38])

It is not a complete description of the good public servant to say that he must do a fair day's work, be personally honest, loyal, discreet and observe the standards of "neutrality" indicated above. The fact that he may have a significant influence on an agency's policies carries with it inescapable obligations. He may be called upon to help to formulate some of the major schemes of his department—say, trade relations with Japan,

---

([38]) See Gould v. Stewart (1896) A.C. 575; and references in W. Friedmann, *Principles of Australian Administrative Law*, pp. 57-59. On the position in the United Kingdom. see J. A. G. Griffith and H. Street, *Principles of Administrative Law*, 1952, pp. 258-261.

a new approach to mental health services, or a new plan for secondary education. He may have considerable discretion in carrying out policies once decided—say, the control of imports to correct a balance of payments deficiency,([34]) or the control of building in a town-planning scheme. All this imposes on him the task of thinking and creating, within the framework of his loyalty to the law and to the elected government he serves. It also brings him into contact with the outside world, and it is to problems raised by this contact that we now turn.

Public Administration and the Public

Once we recognize that carrying out Government policy is a more complicated affair than forming fours on command of the sergeant, the way is open to considering the relations of public administration and the public.

"The trained official hates the rude, untrained public," wrote Bagehot.([35]) This is no doubt an exaggeration, just as it would be to say that the public in general hates officials. Public servants are bound to earn some unpopularity, if only that, in this unsatisfactory world, we need someone to blame for the fact that we don't all get what we would like ; and a large, anonymous, allegedly tea-sodden, bureaucracy is a good candidate.

The problem of Public Relations, broadly interpreted, has many aspects. From the administrator's point of view, he wants to tell the people things they need to know to make use of the services offered (a simple case would be a railway time-table) ; to get the information from them needed in the department (from their incomes to their possible attitudes to proposed changes) ; and to persuade them, i.e., to change their views and attitudes, including trying to convince them that the department is efficient, and individuals that they are being fairly treated. All these raise problems of communication. Even in the case of plain informing, there may be difficulties in attracting attention and conveying the facts intelligibly and memorably. It is harder still to persuade, particularly if you are trying to change people's convictions.

Three things are perhaps specially worth emphasising. The first is that public relations are not something that can be left to a Public Relations or Information Officer. Every public servant plays a part in the maintaining of good communications. The second (which partly follows from this) is that it greatly simplifies the problem of communication if what is to be communicated can itself be kept simple ; as the Public Service Commissioner for Queensland wrote some years ago, "an avoidance of complexity of departmental procedures and regulations will relieve citizens of unnecessary embarrassment in their relations with the Departments".([36]) The third is that simply exhorting people to do things very differently from the way they do them at present is a great waste of time. It will be seen that the problem of relations with the general public does not differ basically from the problem of an agency's relation with its own employees.

([34]) An interesting insight into the role of the public service in this field may be gained from J. G. Crawford, "The Organization of the Department of Trade", *Pub. Admin. (Sydney)*, XVI, Dec., 1957; cf. P. B. Marshall, "The Professional Ethics of Administrative Discretion", in R. S. Milne, etc., *Bureaucracy in New Zealand*, N.Z. Inst. of Pub. Admin., 1957.

([35]) *The English Constitution*, World's Classics ed., p. 172.

([36]) *Report*, 1949, p. 41.

We have been talking up to now from the "manipulative" point of view —how the public servant gets the public to do what *he* wants. But there is a wider problem. The administrative machine is an important part of government, and government nowadays an important part of society. It is arguable that a democratic society requires certain attitudes of mind among its administrators—to be responsive to outside opinion, to respect individuals, to encourage knowledge, interest and participation in government by citizens. The public must also be free to criticize the administration, and has some right to know what is going on. It all takes time, of course, and there is a duty to get through the day's work ; and there are also things to be said on the other side. One could argue, for example, that an expert class of professional administrators is a valuable counterpoise to the elected member and the outside pressures on him. In politically unstable countries, we are often told that it is the public servants who keep the ship of state on a reasonably even keel. In all countries administrators have some duty to protect the integrity of the service from outside invasion.

A large part of public relations is concerned not with an undifferentiated "public", but with many different "publics" or groups of persons, sometimes highly organized to promote particular aims. Freedom to organize is one of the basic freedoms of a democratic society, and a growing number of organizations are interested in the kinds of decision made by modern governments, and will seek to influence them, both at the political and the administrative levels. There is nothing wrong in itself about this. In fact, a good deal of modern government would not be possible without such organized groups, which among other things greatly simplify the administration's task of getting the information it needs to make decisions.

Public servants are rightly suspicious of letting outside groups far inside their offices. They fear it may cause their agency to lose sight of its basic task as an organ of public policy. The orthodox view is that Parliament is the appropriate point at which interests express themselves, and even there we think of the lobbying as best done by the political parties themselves, and are suspicious of outside organizations that are too obviously trying to influence members. However, once we see that all "policy" cannot be settled in a statute or by a single Cabinet decision we must expect to find these forces operating at every level, and that the administrator would have to take account of them.([87])

The most obvious kind of pressure that the State has to deal with nowadays is that coming from organized economic groups, e.g., trade associations, trade unions, farm-groups. But there are also professional organizations (such as the British Medical Association), reforming bodies (such as a Prison Reform Council), bodies representing ex-servicemen, pensioners, and so on ; as well as powerful groups inside the public service itself.

The activities of outside groups affect the State in many different ways. They may act in ways that conflict with public policy, e.g., monopolies, and which call for some public control. The State may, on the other hand, actually be called upon to help them extend their control over their members

---

([87]) The discussion of this problem has mainly been in American books such as P. Appleby, *Policy and Administration* (1949), and D. B. Truman, *The Governmental Process* (1951), esp. Ch. XIV.

or over "non-joiners", e.g., producer-controlled marketing boards, compulsory unionism, bodies that are given powers to protect professional standards and discipline their members ; or to help them protect themselves against "outsiders", e.g., by tariffs. It may impose obligations in exchange for privileges, on unions to abide by established negotiating machinery, to register and accept some rules regarding their internal organization and procedures. The State may give subsidies in return for co-operation with its objectives, as to voluntary bodies working in the social service field ; or just give subsidies (or levy taxes) ; or give other special privileges, say preference in employment to ex-servicemen or disabled persons, or special medical benefits to pensioners. It may be called in to mediate in group conflicts.

All such activities, and many others, bring the administrator in touch with organized groups outside. How far should he bring them inside? There are various ways of occasional consultation, ranging from personal contacts and discussions in private to some quite formal hearing such as a public inquiry, during which interested parties may give evidence. Assuming that it is desired to consult interested groups or individuals, it may be a nice question when it is better to insist on formalized procedures and when to encourage informality and privacy. The latter may encourage co-operation([38]) (including co-operation between interests, for example, employers and trades unions), it also creates a suspicion that the way is open to settlements against the public interest.

There will be different things the administrator is trying to do in consulting outside parties. He may simply be using them as "experts" on the facts ; Mr. Else-Mitchell in his chapter suggests that this is the main point of consultation. But it is undeniable that he may also want to know their "interest" in the matter, with an eye on adjusting policy to give them greater satisfaction ; or simply on convincing them that a decision already made is fair.

There are two main methods by which outside groups can be formally incorporated into the administrative process (i) through *advisory bodies,* (ii) by creating *statutory boards* or commissions with outside representation, or by giving some executive powers of a "public" character to an outside body.

(i) Advisory Bodies

Two main types of advisory body are used by governments. There are "standing" committees, that is, groups including outside persons which have a semi-permanent character, and which are expected to give some continuing advice on a range of problems. Examples would be the network of advisory committees working with the C.S.I.R.O. and the A.B.C., the Ministry of Labour Advisory Council, and (at the State level) the Child Welfare Advisory Council. The other kind are "ad hoc" committees, such as Royal Commissions and Committees of Inquiry, which will normally report on a particular problem, and then cease to exist. Recent examples at the Commonwealth level are the Royal Commission on Espionage, and the Committee on Australian Universities.

([38]) In private the administrator may employ elementary group-therapy, express sympathy or threaten, soothe wounded feelings, suggest face-saving devices, make tentative promises—in a word, practise diplomacy.

A full study of the use of these devices in Australia has never been made. Australian governments seem to use them less, for some purposes at least, than the United Kingdom. For example, two quite common types of publicly-appointed standing committee in the latter country are joint bodies representing the two sides of industry and councils set up to represent consumer-interests in connection with government enterprises. (On the other hand the federal system has produced a crop of interesting and sometimes powerful bodies representing Federal and State governments described in Chapter 8). Royal Commissions used to be a popular device—the Bruce-Page Government appointed twenty-one in six years. But they are nowadays not much used in Australia to advise on government policy in some broad field, but more to investigate some alleged scandal or charge of maladministration; the quite common British practice of making them fairly large bodies, sometimes including representatives of interested parties, is rarely followed. They have commonly been three-man or one-man bodies, with the legal profession well represented among their members;([39]) and enquiries have often tended to be judicial inquisitions, with witnesses protecting their interests by employing counsel.

There have been a few important policy-forming commissions and committees including in the past some influential individuals and groups reporting on the public service itself, referred to in Mr. Bourke's chapter. But on the whole, modern Australian governments seem confident of their own capacity for fact-finding and policy-formulation, doubtful of the possibility of getting a meeting of minds from a representative group of outsiders in any published report; and prefer to get outside advice either by informal consultation or from committees whose views can be obtained in private.

It may be added that the appointment of an advisory body including outside persons is not necessarily evidence that a government or a Minister has not already largely decided what to do on the matter involved. They may simply want some outside support, and know in advance broadly how the committee will report, if it is asked to report. (After all, they choose the members and frame the terms of reference.) The advisory body may, of course, still be an important aid in working out details; and some of the most successful examples are those where the commission or committee has the task of clarifying and detailing plans already favoured in a more or less vague way by the appointing authority.

(ii) Statutory Boards

The device of the board or commission set up by Act of Parliament and endowed with executive powers has been widely used in Australia, as is indicated in Chapters 3 and 4. The general principle has been not to put many statutory limitations on the choice of members, but also that they should not (at least openly) represent interests.

([39]) Of a sample of 72 New South Wales Royal Commissions, 48 were "sole commissioners", and only nine had more than three members; over half had a judge, magistrate or barrister as president or sole member. See J. R. Thomas, "Royal Commissions of Inquiry in New South Wales", unpublished thesis, Department of Government, Sydney University. Of 84 Commonwealth Royal Commissions appointed 1901-50, 54 had 3 members or fewer. Many of the others had a large representation of M.Ps., and were sometimes mere extensions of Parliamentary Select Committee inquiries.

Occasionally, as Mr. Kewley shows in his chapter, the statute provides for the appointment of members with "experience" of certain fields of activity; the use of this word lays stress on the fact that they are being appointed as experts, not as interested parties. There are some exceptions to the exclusion of interests. The various commodity marketing boards normally have a large representation of producers and other interested parties. Mr. Kewley in his chapter also mentions public boards established to maintain professional standards, in fields such as medicine, dentistry, nursing, pharmacy, etc., which are representative of the professions concerned. The attempt has rarely been made to include potentially conflicting interests in public boards with executive powers. A conspicuous failure of this kind was the short-lived Stevedoring Industry Commission (1947-49), which included representatives of shipowners and unions in this industry.([40])

Administration and Social Change

Modern government cannot be (if government ever could) a static thing. It has to be highly adaptable to changing needs. More than that, it is nowadays an important factor in bringing about social change. To take only one example, governments now play a leading role in scientific research. The Commonwealth Scientific and Industrial Research Organization (C.S.I.R.O.), the parent body of which was established in 1920, is now spending about £6,500,000 a year, and is by far the largest research organization in Australia. The Australian Atomic Energy Commission, the Bureau of Mineral Resources, the State Departments of Agriculture are among other public bodies in the field; and much of the money spent on research in the universities comes from government grants. Private industry, in comparison, makes a poor showing.

In the social and economic field, there have developed planning agencies and "policy" departments or branches of departments, such as the General Financial and Economic Policy Branch of the Commonwealth Treasury, first created during the Second World War. The recent emergence of the Department of Trade is a good example of an agency designed mainly to handle changing trade policies, with the more routine functions of trade regulation left to departments such as Customs.

All this is having important reactions on the structure and personnel of higher administration. The expert has arrived; so, as we must expect when change is rapid, have the smart operator and the empire-builder; sometimes to the disgust of the older type of administrator, who has still many great qualities but is also in danger of being a little out-of-date. The public service, of course, needs more than advisers. It also needs first class "managers", able to keep large organizations alive and adaptable; and it does not always get them.

The reader should bear in mind, in reading the chapters that follow, this central issue of how public administration can best be organized to deal with change. Some of the kinds of problems that arise are:—

([40]) The present Australian Stevedoring Industry Authority, established in 1956, includes one member from the employers' side of industry and one from the trade union movement, but neither is connected with the stevedoring industry.

(1) What are the effects of the changing role of government on federal institutions? Australia has been a Federation of States since 1900, when a new written constitution handed over certain activities to a Commonwealth Parliament, leaving others to the States or shared between the two. Several of the chapters in this book are variations on the theme that governmental functions now interlock too closely for Commonwealth and States to live in anything like water-tight compartments. Mr. Davies and Mr. Gardner both point to the emergence of close working relations between the two in many fields, some of them distinctly by-passing Parliaments. Dr. Mendelsohn considers that federalism "is still operated too much as a system of rival governments . . . instead of as a working partnership". What are the problems of establishing such a partnership, or a "co-operative federalism" as some American writers have called it? And how far do the same problems arise in the relations of State and local government, discussed by Miss Atkins? Another pertinent question would be: Is "co-operative federalism" really federalism at all?

(2) What are the other administrative demands of the newer economic and social activities of government? Modern States have been administratively fairly inventive in these fields. A large range of possibilities has developed between the direct administration of a service by a government department and unregulated private activity. Mr. Kewley in his chapter discusses some of the varied uses to which the device of the statutory corporation has been put, and the great variations in these bodies themselves. He also mentions the "mixed undertaking", in which the State shares ownership and control with private interests, though Australia has not made much use of this method up to now. The State may also contract with private interests to carry out a service on its behalf. It may subsidise private activities ; it may control prices or credit terms ; and so on. We badly need a full study of the place of governments in the modern Australian economy.

(3) What bearing do new functions of government have on the public service itself, and the way it is recruited, trained, promoted, controlled? The general pattern of the departmental service was settled in many parts of Australia over half a century ago, and Mr. Bourke and the other contributors to Part II of this book consider that in many ways it was a good pattern. But much has happened since then. The departmental service has multiplied many times over. Public servants have become involved in policy-decisions of an importance not dreamt of in 1900 in relation to national development, immigration, relations with the outside world, especially with Asia, and so on. A great body of public employees has grown up outside the old "public service". Inside it, many new professional and semi-professional skills are called for. The old picture of the official working to a well-set pattern, honest, sober, but unenterprising, was never quite fair, now it certainly needs drastic modification. It is by no means clear that we are awake to all the changes called for in our thinking about public employment.

Another question of great importance concerns the bearing of modern administrative developments on the maintenance of a free society. One of its aspects is discussed by Mr. Else-Mitchell. Efficient government often involves the giving to administrators of a large "discretionary" power, and this raises the issue of how they can best be controlled in the exercise of this discretion, especially where it seems to involve activities that liberal-democratic theory assigns to Parliament or to an independent judiciary. But this is only one side of the general problem of securing democratic control and individual liberty in the modern State, which involves not only protecting individuals from arbitrary acts of government but giving them some genuine participation in its activities. There are people who believe the latter to be a hopeless task; others think it could only be achieved by decentralising our societies and trying to work them through smaller and more manageable units; a third group think there is still considerable scope for "democratizing" our present instruments of rule.

It is a defect in this book that it only touches on this last question incidentally. We might have spent more time than we have in discussing the limitations of centralized authority and hierarchical control, or the important problems connected with the administrator's relations with the public and with what Jeremy Bentham called "publicity" (neither to be confused with what usually passes for Public Relations).([41]) We might have turned a more detached and critical eye on the qualities we are breeding up in our great bureaucracies, private as well as public, and compared them with some "abridgment of all that is pleasant in man". We might have done for Australia what Mr. Frank Dunnill has in some measure done for the British Civil Service in his valuable book.([42]) I mention these matters here mainly to give me a chance of saying that they are problems we should all be thinking about, and especially any young public servant who may read this book. He will learn from it a number of things that will make him more knowledgeable, but not much that will make him more creative and more humane. Perhaps it is something that cannot be learned from books, or at any rate, not from books on Public Administration. One might learn more from characters in novels, such as Hawthorne's Mr. Smooth-it-away, "who, though he had never visited the Celestial City, yet seemed as well acquainted with its laws, customs, policy, and statistics, as with those of the City of Destruction, of which he was a native townsman".

([41]) The opposite of publicity is secrecy. The opposite of good Public Relations is giving a bad impression. Bentham thought that bad administration *should* be made to give a bad impression; then it might improve.

([42]) Frank Dunnill, *The Civil Service, Some Human Aspects*, 1956.

Chapter Two

FEDERAL RELATIONS

A. J. DAVIES

Before federation the six separate territorial governments were called colonies. Responsible government has existed in New South Wales, Victoria, South Australia and Tasmania since 1856. In Queensland responsible government was granted in 1859 and in Western Australia in 1890. There were marked differences between the colonies, notwithstanding the largely British origin of the colonists and the common inheritance of the spirit and form of British parliamentary government. Some, such as New South Wales and Tasmania, had a history as original penal settlements with friction between convicts, emancipists and free settlers. South Australia and Western Australia had their origins in deliberate and optimistic colonisation ventures by enterprising Englishmen like Wakefield and Peel. Each had its own problems, which occupied most of its attention—whether it was the sale and control of Crown lands, the establishment of free, compulsory and secular education, the restriction of Kanaka labour, the encouragement of secondary industry, or the overcoming of periodical financial and economic crises. Each differed in economic character and outlook. In 1893 secondary industry represented 30 per cent. of total production in Victoria, but much less in most of the other colonies. They differed in rate of growth; at the extremes, Victoria (worst hit by the depression of the 1890's) hardly increased its population at all between 1890 and 1900; while Western Australia, with a population of only 48,500 in 1890, almost quadrupled it in the next ten years.

Yet the colonies were also becoming increasingly aware of certain issues that required uniform action. One was the establishment of inter-colonial free trade. Another was the desire for a common, and tighter immigration policy. A third was the need for uniform legislation on certain social and economic matters. A fourth was defence.

There were other features of colonial life which had an Australia-wide character: the spread of trade unionism and the development of a political Labour party; concentration of high percentages of population in colonial capitals which were themselves in growing touch with one another; the feelings of mateship and nationalistic chauvinism (expressed vociferously in the Sydney "Bulletin") and an awareness of social problems epitomised in the words of Henry Lawson:—

"They lie, the men who tell us in a loud dicisive tone
That want is here a stranger and that misery's unknown"[1].

It is difficult to indicate the degree of importance to attach to each of these various differences and similarities. Nor does it seem possible to state

---

[1] Henry Lawson, *In the Days when the World was wide* and other verses, **Angus & Robertson**, 1913.

when the balance of interests among the various colonies was tipped to favour some uniform action over a range of governmental activity. One can say that federation was a gradual process wrought of man (or men with particular interests and objects in view).

As the events leading to federation have been treated adequately in a number of books([2]), it is not proposed to discuss them in detail here. Although the cause had ardent advocates such as Parkes, Deakin, Barton, and Griffith, there were others like Reid (of "Yes-No" fame) and Want of New South Wales who were lukewarm or opposed. Yet despite intercolonial jealousies, personal antipathies, and party divisions between colonial delegations to the 1891 and 1897-8 Constitutional Conventions, a federal solution was finally accepted by a substantial majority of the 61 per cent. of qualified voters who took part in the last referendum.

The Commonwealth of Australia Constitution Act took effect on 1st January, 1901. It is said that one of the Founding Fathers reckoned the per capita administrative costs of federation at "less than the price of a dog licence" and Professor Portus has remarked, "In the event it proved to be an extremely expensive dog and nothing seemed able to stop its growth"([3]).

The Commonwealth Constitution was a federal constitution on the American model. It provided for distribution of legislative powers between the new Commonwealth and the existing colonies, in future to be called States. However, it retained the British institution, familiar in the former colonies, of cabinet government—an executive chosen from and responsible to Parliament, and not (as in the United States) led by a separately elected President. Federalism, according to A. V. Dicey, is characterised by weak government, legalism and conservatism. In practice, cabinet government and the development of nation-wide political parties have helped to offset some of the federal "checks and balances" and to permit an increasing unity of legislative and executive action. To-day, for example, it is acknowledged that the Senate has been a lamentable failure in achieving the object assigned to it by the Founding Fathers, to act as a "States' Rights" house and to man the barricades for those less equipped in population and material resources. The reason for this failure is commonly ascribed to the working of the party system.

COMMONWEALTH POWERS

The Constitution enumerated, mainly in section 51, certain Commonwealth legislative powers such as those concerned with overseas and interstate trade, taxation, postal services, defence, banking, marriage and divorce, immigration and emigration, external affairs, invalid and old age pensions. A few of these, e.g., customs and excise([4]), were *exclusive* to the Commonwealth. But most of the powers listed in section 51 were to be shared with the States and are termed *concurrent* powers. Both had, for example, the

---

([2]) Students may refer to: L. F. Crisp, *The Parliamentary Government of the Commonwealth of Australia*, 2nd ed., 1954, Ch. 1.: G. Greenwood (ed.), *Australia: A Social and Political History*, 1955, Ch. IV; and Alfred Deakin, *The Federal Story*, 1944.

([3]) G. V. Portus, *Britain and Australia*, 1946, p. 38.

([4]) The "defence power" is sometimes said to be an exclusive power; but, strictly speaking, it appears that this is not the case, though only the Commonwealth may have armed forces, declare war and make treaties.

right to levy income tax, to legislate with regard to banking, divorce and so on. Provision is made in section 109 for the supremacy of Commonwealth laws in case of conflict. All other governmental powers, termed *residual* powers, remained with the States. These include the control of most agricultural and industrial activities, trade and transport inside each State, and many social services, including education.

To watch over this Constitution and to interpret it in case of dispute there was created a new judicial body, "a Federal Supreme Court, to be called the High Court of Australia". Thus, in the classic pattern, the federal system provided for the supremacy not of Parliament but of the law. Section 71 vested the judicial power of the Commonwealth not only in the High Court but "in such other federal courts as the Parliament creates, and in such other courts as it invests with federal jurisdiction". Consequently the State judicial systems could be authorized to act as Commonwealth tribunals for certain purposes and duplication and additional cost could be avoided. In contrast, in the administrative sphere, the Commonwealth government made little use of State agencies but built up its own centralised administrative organisation.

Shortly after federation the 1904 Annual Report of the N.S.W. Public Service Board summarised the activities of that State in these words:—

> "The State constructs and manages railways, tramways, bridges, roads, harbour works, docks, printing offices, abattoirs; it provides for and controls popular education; it takes measures to preserve the health of the people; it establishes hospitals and asylums; it has vast machinery for dispensing justice, for restraining and punishing crime; it regulates all matters relating to the purchase, leasing or transfer of lands; it regulates forestry, mining, agriculture ......; in a word it touches the life and enterprise of the people at a thousand points".([5])

These activities and others are still carried on by State governments, as Mr. Parker shows in his chapter. Why then does one read and hear that "since 1939, the issues of federal politics have seemed large and familiar, while the contents of the State field have seemed rather miscellaneous and mysterious"?([6]) How widespread is the belief that in the Australian house the States are disgruntled tenants pre-occupied with the preservation of antiques in the attic? Is such a belief at odds with reality; an Australian myth to be placed beside that of the "tall bronzed men" who are said to inhabit our land?

MAIN TRENDS SINCE 1901

"It is not always the residuary legatee who comes off best under a will", sagely observed Mr. Justice Higgins. Some of the major changes which have occurred in Federal-State relations since 1901 may be considered under the following headings:—

Constitutional Amendment

Section 128 of the Constitution states, in effect, that the Constitution shall not be altered unless at a referendum the proposed alteration is accepted

---

([5]) N.S.W. Public Service Board, *Report*, 1904, para. 60.
([6]) Alan Davies, "Victorian Government and Politics", in *Introducing Victoria*, 1955, p. 286.

by a majority of the voters as a whole, and by a majority in at least four States. Quick and Garran's comment on this provision was: "If the Federal Legislature could change the Constitution it might transfer itself from a subordinate law-making body into an organ of sovereignty; it might destroy the federal system altogether, and substitute a consolidated form of government".([7])

The formal amendment process has proved very rigid and the Australian electorate, which some of our Fathers feared might be over-prone to radical change, has borne out Dicey's view of the conservatism of federal constitutions. Between 1905 and 1951, twelve referenda were held at which 25 proposals were put forward, covering more than 40 specific amendments. Only four proposals were accepted, and only two of these amendments have been important in increasing Commonwealth power. Section 105A provided for the taking over of State debts and paved the way for legislation giving the Loan Council statutory authority in 1928. Section 51 (xxiiia), added in 1946, gave the Commonwealth the "social services" power expressed as—

> "The provision of maternity allowances, widows' pensions, child endowment, unemployment, pharmaceutical, sickness and hospital benefits, medical and dental services (but not so as to authorise any form of civil conscription), benefits to students and family endowment".

Section 51, xxxiii, xxxiv, xxxvii and xxxviii, provided that the State parliaments could refer legislative powers to the Commonwealth for specific matters, e.g., for the acquisition of State railways and State railway construction and extension, or generally with respect to any subject. But this has been almost a dead letter. In 1942 a convention, representing both Labour and Non-Labour politicians, was held at Canberra to consider proposals for the reference by the States of certain powers claimed to be necessary to permit the Commonwealth government to deal with the problems of post-war reconstruction.([8]) The States' representatives agreed to request their respective parliaments to refer "adequate" powers to the Commonwealth for a period of five years from the cessation of hostilities. At the end of the period, or at an earlier date, a referendum was to be held to secure the approval of the electors to the alterations of the Constitution on a permanent basis.

However, only New South Wales and Queensland passed the Powers Bill as agreed by the convention. South Australia and Western Australia amended it. Victoria's Act was made dependent on all States passing uniform laws. It was left to the Tasmanian Upper House to refuse assent to the transfer of power requested; and "its obdurate stand on State rights, or on what others would call narrow parochial interests, forced the Commonwealth Government to take a referendum on the matter of transference of powers, and this referendum the people of Australia rejected".([9]) Ironically enough

---

([7]) J. Quick and R. R. Garran, *The Annotated Constitution of the Australian Commonwealth*, 1901, p. 988.

([8]) *Convention of Representatives of the Commonwealth and State Parliaments on Proposed Alteration of the Commonwealth Constitution* (held at Canberra, 24th November to 2nd December, 1942), Commonwealth Government Printer. A good account of the convention is given in G. Greenwood, *The Future of Australian Federalism*, 1946, Ch. VI.

([9]) W. A. Townsley in F. C. Green (ed.), *A Century of Responsible Government in Tasmania*, p. 38.

the Tasmanian Premier had moved the motion on the transfer of powers at the 1942 Convention.

Referenda have been initiated by both Labour and Non-Labour governments. In most instances they have failed at least partly because the opposing political party contested the proposals and fought the issue on the basis of "you cannot trust *that* government with these powers". It is especially likely that voting on constitutional changes will bear small relation to the merits of the particular proposals. It has been said that "the people, as such, have no fixed or even long-term views about the federal constitution or about the distribution of legislative powers under it, because federalism and its legal implications are a mystery to the bulk of them".[10] That the prevailing social climate may affect the views of the people on great issues is demonstrated by the following Gallup poll findings on one vital question at two separate periods[11]:—

Question: "Should State Governments be abolished or continued?"

	November 1942	September 1948
	%	%
ALL STATES, MEN AND WOMEN VOTERS		
Abolish State Governments	60	30
Don't abolish them	22	56
Undecided	11	14
No answer	7	..
	100	100

There was no very striking degree of popular interest even in the making of the federal Constitution itself.

High Court Decisions

Decisions of the High Court have had an important effect on the character of Commonwealth-State relations. Cases known popularly as the *Engineers' Case*, the *Uniform Tax Case*, the *State Banking Case*, the *Bank Nationalisation Case* and the *Communist Party Dissolution Case*, to name a few, have greatly influenced Commonwealth-State relationships. Nationalisation schemes, civil rights, marketing, banking, commerce, external affairs, taxation, industrial regulation and other matters of political content have been examined by the Court in its role as interpreter of the Constitution.

The members of the first High Court said in *The King v. Barger*[12] "Our duty is to declare the law as we find it, not to make new law".[13] But the Court cannot avoid making new law. Many of the sections of a constitution are always vague ; more than one interpretation can be given to them. The decision may depend on the Court's general notions of the nature of a constitutional document. Take. for instance, the case just mentioned, which involved defining the word "taxation". A majority of the Court stated that:

---

[10] R. S. Parker, "The People and the Constitution", in G. Sawer, etc., *Federalism in Australia*, 1949, pp. 169-70.

[11] Table from Parker, *op. cit.*, p. 189.

[12] (1908) 6 Commonwealth Law Reports, 41.

[13] *Ibid.*, p. 64.

"The primary meaning of taxation is raising money for the purposes of government by means of contributions from individual persons". One of their conclusions was that "even if the term taxation, uncontrolled by any context, were capable of including the indirect regulation of the internal affairs of a State by means of taxation, its meaning in the Constitution is limited by the implied prohibition against direct interference with matters reserved exclusively to the States".[14]

This doctrine of "implied prohibitions" became a recurring theme in the judicial interpretation of the Constitution. It was thought to have succumbed in 1920, but reappeared periodically and swelled forth again in 1947 in the State Banking Case.[15] William, J. then expressed the doctrine in these words:—"Neither the Commonwealth nor the States may exercise their respective constitutional powers for the purpose of affecting the capacity of the other to perform its essential governmental functions". How far such a view of the nature of the constitution is held, will clearly make a considerable difference to the interpretation of its particular provisions.

Broadly speaking, the history of High Court decisions on the Constitution may be divided into three periods:—

(a) 1901-1920. In this period the High Court mostly interpreted the Constitution as a "federal compact", a sort of contract between the States, and regarded the exercise of powers by either State or Commonwealth as being limited by what were considered to be the logical implications of such an agreement. The personnel of the first High Court may have influenced the general trend of judicial reasoning. Griffith, Barton and O'Connor were former politicians who had themselves helped to shape the Constitution.

In *Deakin v. Webb*[16] the Court applied the "implied prohibitions" reasoning to exempt from Victorian State income taxation the salaries of Federal officers. This rule of inter-governmental immunity, extending to the officers and instrumentalities of the government concerned, was known as the doctrine of "immunity of instrumentalities". It appears to be, as Professor Sawer has said, "a particular application of the doctrine of 'implied prohibitions' " . . . .[17] The Court borrowed this doctrine from the United States Supreme Court, where it was formulated by Chief Justice Marshall in 1819 in the famous case of *M'Culloch v. Maryland*.[18]

The Court treated the doctrine as mutual between Commonwealth and States. For example, in the *Railways Servants' Case*[19] the Court held, in effect, that the Commonwealth Arbitration Court could not enforce a settlement of a dispute between a State and its own employees. The general effect of these and later decisions was "(1) An implication that States and Commonwealth must not interfere with each other's governmental activities.

---

[14] (1908) 6 Commonwealth Law Reports, pp. 68, 78. See also G. Sawer (ed.), *Cases on the Constitution of the Commonwealth of Australia*, 2nd ed., 1957, pp. 27-30.

[15] (1947) 74 C.L.R. 31, p. 99.

[16] (1904) 1 C.L.R. 585.

[17] *Cases on the Constitution of the Commonwealth of Australia*, 1st ed., 1948, p. 16.

[18] Cf. D'Emden v. Pedder (1904) 1 C.L.R. 91.

[19] (1906) 4 C.L.R. 488.

(2) A presumption that Commonwealth powers should be given a narrow construction in order to avoid trenching on State powers".([20]) Some emphasis was laid on section 107 reserving residual powers to the States, as adding weight to this contention.

(b) 1920-1947. This period begins with the *Engineers' Case*([21]) when the Court virtually threw overboard the previously dominant doctrine. *The Engineers' Case* reversed the decision of the *Railway Servants' Case.* The majority decision held that the Commonwealth Arbitration Court could make awards binding on State employees and therefore on State governments. Full weight was now given to section 109 of the Constitution, which provides that "When a law of a State is inconsistent with a law of the Commonwealth, the latter shall prevail, and the former shall, to the extent of the inconsistency, be invalid". The general effect of the decision was the establishment of a rule that the constitutional powers of the Commonwealth are to be broadly interpreted, and not restricted by presumptions about the powers of the States. In particular, Commonwealth laws could bind the States and their instruments of government. (A State could also bind the Commonwealth, but the latter could escape by passing a law inconsistent with the State law.)

This interpretation was re-emphasised in the *Uniform Tax Case,*([22]) where legislation which made it so difficult for the States to levy income tax that they were driven out of this field, was deemed valid despite the argument that it was directed towards destroying or weakening the constitutional functions or capacities of the States.

The essence of the *Engineers' Case* was deemed to be that henceforth the Constitution was to be interpreted without implications, as with other British statutes, and the words of the Constitution were to be given their full, ordinary, natural and grammatical meaning. The former High Court minority (Higgins and Isaacs, JJ.) had become a majority. Higgins had declared his view before he joined the Court:—"Judges, in interpreting and applying the law, have no right to assume the functions of legislators. The justification for judges introducing words that have not been expressed must rest on logical necessity, not upon political expediency".([23])

Isaacs, J., in the *Engineers' Case,* stated, inter alia, that "possible abuse of powers is no reason in British law for limiting the natural force of the language creating them".([24]) Later, in the *Uniform Tax Case,* Latham, C.J., said, "It is not for this or any other court to prescribe policy or to seek to

---

([20]) G. Sawer, etc., *Federalism in Australia,* 1949, p. 17.

([21]) (1920) 28 C.L.R. 129.

([22]) (1924) 65 C.L.R. 373. The States of Victoria and New South Wales challenged the uniform tax legislation in 1957, and the High Court judgment held invalid one part of it, Commonwealth priority in tax payments. But otherwise it upheld the legislation and substantially confirmed the view that there is no constitutional hindrance to Commonwealth domination of State activities through conditional grants. See (1957) Argus L.R. 761.

([23]) Nettie Palmer, *Henry Bournes Higgins,* p. 247, *cit.* L. F. Crisp, *Parliamentary Government of the Commonwealth of Australia,* 2nd ed., 1954, p. 268.

([24]) 28 C.L.R., p. 151. However, some have suggested that what appears to the Court as the "natural force" of language is not wholly unconnected with the broad picture of a good society and a good constitution in the minds of the various Justices (e.g., Sawer, in *Federalism in Australia,* p. 19).

give effect to any views or opinions upon policy. We have nothing to do with the wisdom or expediency of legislation. Such questions are for Parliaments and the people . . . . the Court is not authorised to consider whether the Acts are fair and just as between States—whether some States are being forced, by a political combination against them, to pay an undue share of Commonwealth expenditure or to provide money which other States ought fairly to provide. These are arguments to be used in Parliament and before the people . . . . the validity of legislation is not to be determined by the motives or ultimate end of a statute".([25])

(c) 1947 *to present*: From the "broad" interpretation of the Constitution which operated mainly in a pro-Commonwealth direction the Court swung some way back to a "narrow" view in the *State Banking Case*.([26]) Section 48 of the Banking Act, 1945, provided that a bank should not conduct any banking business for a State or for any authority of a State, including a local governing authority, without the consent in writing of the Commonwealth Treasurer. The majority of the Court held that, by reason of the federal character of the Constitution, a State and its instrumentalities are immune from Commonwealth laws that discriminate against them, or single them out for the imposition of special burdens or are aimed at controlling or interfering with them in the exercise of their governmental functions. In the words of Dixon, J., the proposed law was construed as "directly operating to deny to the States banking facilities open to others, and so to discriminate against the States or to impose a disability upon them".([27]) Perhaps there is a parallel between the trend of public opinion over this period and that of judicial interpretation. However, the case has not had such marked effects as was expected.

On the whole it can be said that the High Court has helped the Commonwealth Constitution to move with the times. An example would be the *Radio Broadcasting Case*([28]), in which the Court adopted an interpretation of "telephone, telegraph and other like services", so as to include radio broadcasting and wireless telegraphy. One might also instance the defence power, which has been given a wide construction. It has, for example, permitted price and manpower control in war-time and some continuance of rationing and other controls when hostilities were over.([29])

So the Court's decisions have provided some flexibility in a document which legally appears rigid. Certainly the Constitution has not proved as flexible as some groups in Australia would desire. It has been said to be a disadvantage that the Commonwealth government, unlike the government of a unitary State such as the United Kingdom, cannot in peacetime "peg" wages even as one step in a co-ordinated anti-inflation plan; and cannot nationalize industries. On the other hand the Court has also been able to limit Commonwealth activities in the sphere of civil liberties, e.g., in the *Communist Party Dissolution Case*([30]).

([25]) 65 C.L.R., p. 409.

([26]) (1947) 74 C.L.R. 31.

([27]) 74 C.L.R., p. 84.

([28]) (1935) 54 C.L.R. 262.

([29]) See D. I. Menzies, "The Defence Power", in R. Else-Mitchell (ed.), *Essays on the Australian Constitution,* 1952, pp. 132-155B.

([30]) (1951) 83 C.L.R. 1.

Changing Needs

That the needs of the people do not stop at arbitary State boundaries was one of the reasons for the establishment of federalism in Australia. Functions of government overlap. This is not necessarily to be condemned as long as policy and administration between different levels can be dove-tailed so that the people are given service with reasonable efficiency and with minimum friction. This is not easy to achieve in a federal system. The very continuance of the federal pattern implies that there are differences sufficiently significant between the States and between State and Federal political parties and pressure groups to prevent unification being achieved. The virtues of experimentation, political and administrative; of the greater satisfaction of local needs; of the encouragement of local communities of interest, are said to be better nurtured in a federal climate. It may be that federalism is but a stage on the road to unification or it may be that it will really provide the best of both worlds. One cannot always make a fetish of efficiency or uniformity. For example, some types of democracy are not as efficient as some types of totalitarian state, and yet both the British and American peoples have preferred democracy; and the Americans have also preferred federalism.

There are many differences between the Australia of 1901 and the Australia of the present. In 1901 Australia was regarded as a primary producing country with a few local factories and scattered secondary industry. 32.9 per cent. of the working population was employed in primary industries and mining, and only 18.4 per cent. in manufacturing. In 1947, 18.7 per cent. of the work force was employed in primary industries including mining; 27.9 per cent. in manufacturing and 53.4 per cent. in tertiary service.[31] Since then the post-war immigration programme has given a further impetus to industrial development[32]—though in terms of exports Australia still rides on the sheep's back. The population of Australia in 1901 was 3,774,000; in 1956 it was estimated to be 9,428,000. The growth of population and of the work force, of the "welfare State", changes in location and type of industry and commerce, have given rise to new demands, require new regulation and control and are mirrored in the changing functions of government. Industry now increasingly operates on an inter-state basis. We have also to take account of the growth in importance of the "defence power". Total defence expenditure in 1901-2 was under one million pounds. It was one hundred and ninety million pounds in 1956-7.

These changing needs have been an important direct cause of the growth of Commonwealth power. This has been phenomenal whether one measures by the size of its purse or by the expansion of its public service. For example, at federation there were 11,181 permanent officers in the Commonwealth Public Service, and 13,179 New South Wales public servants (i.e., under the Public Service Board's jurisdiction) as at 30th June, 1902. By 1939 the Commonwealth service was about twice the size of the New South Wales service (but three-quarters were still accounted for by the Post Office). By 1952 the Commonwealth service was four times the size of the New South

---

[31] See J. Andrews, *Australia's Resources and their Utilisation*, Part 2, 1949.

[32] By June, 1955, over a million Australians were employed in manufacturing.

Wales service. The table on this page gives some indication of the respective growth in the numbers of Australian public servants for the period 1939 to 1952.

We get an even more striking picture of the change if we look at expenditure. In 1901 the Commonwealth spent £4m., the States £29m. In 1938-39 Commonwealth expenditure from consolidated revenue was £79m.,[33] and State expenditure £128m. In 1953-54 the equivalent figures were £772m. and £465m. The difference is still more impressive if we consider that most State expenditure in 1938-9 was still from their own revenues (Commonwealth payments to or for States amounted only to £15.7m.). By 1953-54 Commonwealth payments to or for States amounted to £194,000,000.

The breakdown of Commonwealth expenditure tells us a good deal about what has happened. The £772 million of 1953-54 is made up as follows: defence services £190m.; war and repatriation services (war debt, pensions, etc.), £147m.; National Welfare Fund (social services) £177m.; Post Office £98m.; Territories £16m.; subsidies and bounties £21m.; other (including cost of departments) £122m.

PUBLIC SERVICES—VARIOUS STATES AND COMMONWEALTH[34]

		1939	1952	Percentage Increase
Commonwealth	(a)	47,043	150,543	220
New South Wales	(b)	24,914	38,307	54
Victoria	(d)	7,350	11,574	57
Queensland	(c)	43,014	58,124	35
South Australia	(d)	2,563	4,507	76
Western Australia	(d)	1,856	3,895 (1953)	110
Tasmania	(d)	1,264	2,821	123

Notes: (a) Includes permanent, temporary and exempt employees.
(b) Includes the teaching staff in schools.
(c) Total Crown employees.
(d) Public Service Act staff only.

Finance: a major factor in Federal-State relationships

Federal financial relationships are being treated in another chapter but as this topic is so fundamental, some broad comments appear essential. The theory of divided sovereignty and the practice of dual government are weakened if there is a vast difference in the resources, particularly the financial resources, available to the various governing bodies. Federalism under present-day circumstances could lead to "unification by default". To-day the fear expressed by the States is that they will be so starved for finance by the drying up of their sources of revenue that they will be unable to carry out the governmental functions reserved to them by the Constitution.

The basic problem is not new and is not peculiar to Australian federalism. How are financial resources to be distributed so that they will enable both central and regional governments to retain, each in its own sphere, independence and the power to carry out the functions granted them in the basic division of governmental powers? Over the years there has been

[33] Excluding payments to or for States. The figures are from the Commonwealth Year Book.

[34] From: South Australian Public Service Commissioner, *Report on the Efficiency of the South Australian Public Service*, 1954.

impatient criticism of section 87 (the "Braddon Blot"), the Surplus Revenue Act of 1908, the "per capita" payments operating from 1910 to 1927, of the Commonwealth Bank set up by King O'Malley and Federal Labour in 1910, and especially of the Uniform Tax legislation of 1942. The Loan Council, functioning on a statutory basis since 1928, and the Grants Commission established in 1933, have not escaped criticism, particularly the former, where it is alleged that the Commonwealth, with its two votes and a casting vote to the single vote possessed by each of the States, and coupled with the financial primacy which it has possessed since 1942, assumes the role of a feudal overlord meeting vassals. Not only are South Australia, Western Australia and Tasmania "claimant" States, runs the theme, but the other States have also become mendicants instead of partners. The Commonwealth on the other hand is able to finance the great bulk of its loan programme from revenue.

This perpetuation of financial imbalance, it is alleged, fosters political irresponsibility and promotes discord where there should be harmony. It encourages "buck-passing"—the Commonwealth can say it lacks the power, the States with equal truth that they lack the money, to take effective action in many fields. At the same time it is true that the Commonwealth Government, whether Labour or Non-Labour, is enabled to provide uniform treatment to the people, whether of richer or poorer States, in such matters as old age and invalid pensions, child endowment, maternity allowances, hospital and medical benefits. Again it is now able, through its control of finance, not only to use budgets to raise revenue through taxation, direct and indirect, to provide services but also to employ them as an instrument of economic policy. In these Keynesian days budgets are deliberately "deflationary" or "inflationary". Economists remind us that the Commonwealth Government is expected to provide flexible economic policies to suit changing economic circumstances. In addition the Commonwealth Government is able to use progressive income taxation to redistribute incomes between individuals, as well as between States.

Unity, diversity and interdependence

One does not solve current problems and satisfy modern requirements by returning to a rigid 1901-type federal division of powers. Sometimes this latter course is advocated by interested individuals and groups whose attitude is motivated by opposition to increased governmental powers as such. Invoking the sacred symbols of "sovereignty" and "states' rights" lends strength to these pleas by marshalling traditional loyalties. To others it seems more important to consider how Commonwealth and States can best co-operate for the benefit of Australians.

The preamble to the Commonwealth Constitution refers to "one indissoluble Federal Commonwealth". One could cite any number of instances of the "essential oneness of the Commonwealth and States" to use the phrase of the then Victorian Premier, Mr. J. G. B. McDonald, at the 1950 Premiers' Conference. For example, if Commonwealth immigration policy is to bring thousands of migrants each year to these shores, then in Mr. McDonald's words, "State Governments must provide schools, hospital accommodation and other services". Most of the functions of State Government involve the investment of men, money and materials in developmental projects and in services from which no immediate returns can be expected but which in the long-term will promote the economic and social well-being of the whole nation. Health, education, agriculture, conservation and public works are notable examples.

Federal government must promote both unity and diversity. Unity may be promoted by central direction and control by one government or by co-operative action. Diversity implies opportunity for unilateral action, for the evolution and implementation of experimental methods, as in the case of the Tasmanian area schools, or experimental political and social ideas, such as family endowment was in New South Wales. Diversity enabled Queensland under a Labour government to abolish the Legislative Council in 1922 and thus to become the only unicameral State. Each State tends to have special characteristics of its own. Some claim the leadership that comes from established wealth and development; others are more in the pioneering stage. "Western Australia, like Queensland, is essentially a pioneering State still; its energies are concentrated upon economic development, and the conventional slogans of the political parties are subordinated to discussions of how that development, both rural and industrial, can be hastened".([35])

It seems that there are both beneficial and harmful effects flowing from the existence of separate State and Commonwealth governments. Beneficial effects would flow from healthy rivalry and State pride in the quality of primary and secondary production, competition to attract inter-State and overseas investors, the encouragement of local verve, initiative and innovation and in stimulating what the Americans refer to as "grass-roots democracy". On the debit side of the ledger would appear items such as unilateral action in one State having unforeseen adverse effects on the others lack of co-ordination in matters where common continent-wide action is deemed necessary (some would instance here inter-State marketing, arbitration, wage and price-fixation).

Governmental functions and co-operative action

Instead of viewing Federalism as a political Janus in which the loyalty of the people is divided, as are the governmental powers, between State and Federal authorities, there is much to be said for the view that "the National Government and the States should be regarded not as competitors for authority, but as two levels of government co-operating with or complementing each other in meeting the growing demands on both".([36]) An example of a governmental function involving co-operation in Federal-State-local relations would be the Salk polio vaccination campaign in Australia. In this instance the Commonwealth procures and pays for the serum; the State organises distribution, provides doctors, arranges distribution points; the local authorities provide premises, publicity and so on.

To meet the felt necessities of the times there is an active need for governments and people to re-think the problems of federation in a functional context. A good example of inter-governmental co-operation on

---

([35]) J. B. D. Miller, *Australian Government and Politics*, 1954, p. 31.
([36]) J. M. Gaus, in *Pub. Admin. Review* (U.S.A.), XVI, Spring, 1956, p. 106.

functional lines is the Australian Agricultural Council established in 1934.([37])
Another is the conferences of Public Service Commissioners, the first of
which was held in Canberra in September, 1937. There have been common
inquiries and consultation on such problems as the national need for, and
training of, apprentices, and on the codification of building regulations.

To a much greater degree than is realised the task of government at
State and Commonwealth levels is carried on by co-operative methods
arrived at through Premiers' Conferences, conferences of Commonwealth
and State Public Service Commissioners, and by political agreements between Commonwealth and State governments. Some major projects arising
from political agreement are discussed in Mr. Gardner's chapter. From
the earliest days of federation there was a necessary inter-relationship
between State and Federal politics, e.g., Alfred Deakin's "New Protection"([38]) where a Commonwealth policy providing for a protectionist
tariff encouraged the growth of secondary industry in the States as well as
the idea of the "basic wage". Scores of examples could be quoted of how
governmental activities at the different levels spill over and intermingle.

Principally through the medium of grants made under section 96 the
Commonwealth and the States have been able to co-operate on the construction and maintenance of the nation's roads, on the education of New Australians, and the provision of Commonwealth Scholarships for tertiary
education, on free milk for school children, on public health and preventive
medicine, and on soldier settlement on the land. Under the Commonwealth and State Housing Agreement, Commonwealth and State governments
co-operate in the field of housing.

Duplication of functions

There can be little quarrel with Commonwealth and State agencies working toward the same ends so long as waste of resources is not involved.
Sometimes this happens. For example, when the Commonwealth introduced
a Child Endowment Scheme in 1941 and the N.S.W. Family Endowment
Office ceased to function, despite the fact that trained staff was available
in the State organisation, the Commonwealth asked for the services of only
six State officers.

At times duplication of function may arise through lack of knowledge
of other existing facilities rather than through deliberate political or administrative design, but at other times the desire to build an independent empire
may also be present. Is there warrant for a Department of Primary Industry
or of Health at the Commonwealth level? And if so, is there not room for
further rationalisation of function and joint agreement on spheres of activity?
Similar problems exist inside the States, where there has been varying
emphasis on decentralisation, e.g., in education, health, housing, forestry, soil
conservation, child welfare, lands and the administration of justice.

([37]) On the work of this and on inter-governmental co-operation generally, see
below, pp. 234-257, and R. Anderson, "The States and Relations with the Commonwealth" in R. Else Mitchell (ed.), *Essays on the Australian Constitution*, 1952, pp. 94-131.

([38]) See G. Greenwood (ed.), *Australia: A Social and Political History*, 1955, pp.
216 ff.

CONCLUSION

The Constitution provides for some separation of Commonwealth and State legislative powers, but in many matters the line of demarcation is not clear. The history of concurrent powers may be likened to that of the royal prerogative in the British constitution. By a process of attrition, supplemented by firm frontal attack when absolutely necessary, the prerogative powers of the Crown have been reduced to the point where they are largely a formality. By much the same process, particularly in gaining control of the purse-strings, Commonwealth governments have left the States progressively fewer effective concurrent powers. Even in the sphere of residual powers, Commonwealth influence through such bodies as the Grants Commission, Loan Council, Commonwealth Bank and Commonwealth Treasury has resulted in many of these powers becoming conditional rather than absolute.

Federation began as a bundle of compromises and to-day it bears the marks of its imperfections. Yet it remains a powerful element in the Australian way of life. For many a year to come it will have to be taken account of, shaping and being shaped by personalities as a democratic people continues to doubt and question, to seek after certainty, for the benefit of Australia.

Chapter Three

STRUCTURE AND FUNCTIONS OF GOVERNMENT

R. S. PARKER

In this chapter we are concerned firstly with the structure of Australian governments and their growth since 1900, secondly with the distribution of functions between the Commonwealth and State governments, and between the various departments and agencies of each government. The relations between Commonwealth and States—the division of constitutional powers, financial relations, and administrative co-operation—are treated in Chapters 2, 7 and 8.

STRUCTURE OF GOVERNMENT

In both the Commonwealth and the States, there are three broad categories of governmental institutions. They are, firstly, the institutions connected with the parliaments—including the Cabinets which in every case except the Commonwealth (since 1956) contain all Ministers of the Crown; secondly, the departments for whose operations, in all respects, individual Ministers are responsible to their parliaments; and thirdly, a miscellaneous category, including statutory corporations and boards, law courts, and elected local government bodies, whose operations are either wholly or partly free from detailed control by Ministers and their departments. In all State governments, though not in the Commonwealth, the administrative agencies in this third group have become at least as numerous and important as those in the second, departmental, group. Some of them are discussed in Chapters 4 and 6.

Parliamentary Institutions

These are very clearly and simply described in Geoffrey Sawer, *Australian Government Today* (fifth edition—revised, Melbourne 1957). Here we need only indicate briefly their relation to administrative departments and other agencies.

Since 1948 the Commonwealth Parliament has been easily the largest in Australia (182 members compared with 154 in New South Wales); and its Ministry is also the largest, with twenty-one Ministers (there are sixteen in New South Wales), though since 1956 only twelve of these have been included in the Cabinet. For administrative purposes the main difference between the parliaments is probably that members of the Commonwealth Parliament, living throughout the continent, find it more difficult than State parliamentarians to press their constituents' claims and grievances upon the appropriate administrative agencies, most of which have their head offices in Canberra or Melbourne. Indeed, some Commonwealth members maintain that this is not part of their duty as national legislators. This view has become harder to defend since the Second World War, when the Commonwealth has undertaken more and more functions closely affecting the private interests of citizens, notably in the field of social services. Even before that, the Commonwealth had long been administering repatriation benefits and pensions. Services like these create many small demands for members to intercede with officials, and it must be easier for the State parliamentarian to familiarise himself with the working of departments that are concentrated mostly in his own State capital city.

For similar reasons the detailed Ministerial control of departmental day-to-day administration is probably more effective in the States generally than in the Commonwealth, and more effective in a small State like Tasmania than in a large and populous one like Victoria or New South Wales. Adequate knowledge and control of the working machinery of their departments is made more difficult for Commonwealth Ministers not only by the dispersal of their staff throughout Australia and the Territories, and the division of their main offices between Melbourne and Canberra, but also by the fact that Ministers' own offices are concentrated in Parliament House in Canberra, and in separate buildings in Sydney and Melbourne, so that they never work inside their own departmental offices as is generally the practice in the States (and also in the parent government in Great Britain).

What is meant by the statement that "a Minister is responsible for all the operations of an ordinary department"? Primarily, it means that in this realm powers and duties are conferred by statute, or by virtue of the Royal prerogative, upon Ministers, and not upon "departments" or public servants. In performing their departmental duties the latter are merely exercising the powers of a Minister. For this reason it is Ministers and Ministers alone who can report, explain and defend in parliament (whether in answer to questions or in ordinary debate) what is done in the exercise of their powers and duties. (Of course, public servants as well as Ministers may be answerable in the Courts for illegal acts under certain circumstances). And since this is one of parliament's main ways of exercising control over administration, it *expects* Ministers to answer politically for departmental acts in this manner.

It has long and often been said that responsibility also involves the liability of a Minister to resign if parliament disapproves of some act or omission of his department, whether or not the Minister knew or approved of what the public servant in question had done. However, this view has recently been called in question, not only because parliaments have excused Ministers when officials acted without their approval or knowledge, but also because enforced resignations, even when the Minister's personal "responsibility" was clear, have in fact been very rare.[1]

In the case of agencies other than Ministerial departments, parliament's methods of control are as varied as the agencies themselves, and are often very indirect and tenuous. Many acts of parliament (statutes) allocate powers and duties to administrative boards, ranging from those in charge of massive public enterprises like Trans-Australia Airlines or the State Electricity Commissions, through regulatory bodies like the Commonwealth

---

[1] See S. E. Finer, "The Individual Responsibility of Ministers", in *Pub. Admin.* (*London*), Winter 1956.

Broadcasting Control Board or the South Australian and Western Australian Betting Control Boards, to primary products marketing boards and Registration Boards set up to maintain standards in the trades and professions. Parliaments have also conferred statutory powers on individual non-Ministerial officials such as the Auditor-General, the Solicitor-General and the Public Trustee.

Boards and officials like these have no right to appear in parliament to explain or defend their acts and policies, and it is hardly practicable (and so extremely unusual) for any parliament to exercise its power to call individuals to the "bar of the House" for this purpose. In some cases, such as the judiciary or the Councils of Universities, it is public policy that they should be as independent as possible in carrying out their functions, provided they do not exceed the powers conferred on them by statute. Only parliament itself can dismiss judges, Auditors-General, and in the Commonwealth and New South Wales at least, members of the Public Service Board, and their salaries are, as it were, guaranteed by "permanent appropriations". These are regarded as two means of assuring their independence—from influence by the government of the day.

A large part of the revenue of local authorities is levied by the councils from rates, and that of many government business undertakings comes from charges to their customers, so that to this extent they are not dependent on parliament's annual appropriations. The power of granting money to carry on constitutes, however, at least an indirect form of parliamentary, indeed of governmental, control over most of the non-departmental agencies, even those with a large degree of formal independence like universities. So does the government's power to appoint all or some of their members.

Parliaments have powers of varying effectiveness to review or even "disallow" regulations made by many of these agencies (see Chapter 9). Ministerial approval is required for local authorities to make by-laws, raise loans, and in New South Wales even to alter street names! Public corporations are often subject to rather ill-defined controls by Ministers, either over specific matters such as capital expenditure and rates and charges, or in general terms over policy decisions. In this respect Commonwealth and Victorian corporations are in general more autonomous than those of New South Wales, most of which, "in the exercise of their powers, authorities, duties and functions", are "subject in all respects to the control and direction of the Minister". One would expect the Minister's willingness to answer questions in parliament about the activities of corporations to correspond to the nature and degree of these policy-controlling powers. However, in Australia, as distinct from the United Kingdom, even Commonwealth Ministers generally try to answer as many questions as they can. This topic is more fully discussed in Chapter 4.

One other form of control being increasingly practised in the Commonwealth is the requirement that either the numbers or the salaries and working conditions of staff, or both, shall be determined by the corporation "subject to the approval of the Public Service Board". The fact that most of these agencies are required to make annual reports to a Minister or to parliament is a potential form of control, but it is scarcely effective in practice since these reports are hardly ever discussed in parliament.

Departments

From what has been said of departments as being merely the instruments of Ministerial action, it can be seen that a special legal enactment is not generally required to establish, abolish, sub-divide or reorganise a department. In general, Commonwealth departments have been established by order of the Governor-General in Council, and this is often done in the States. However, departments have sometimes been established by act of parliament, or on the other hand simply by a Cabinet Minute or Ministerial decision. If any official definition of a "department" existed, it would probably refer to a group of public servants organised under a single permanent head responsible directly to a Minister. However, in many cases the head of a smaller organisation, regarded in public service lists and budgets as a "branch" or sub-department, also has direct access to a Minister, and is virtually independent in running his own unit. For example, departments such as the Prime Minister's or Premier's, the Department of Interior or Colonial Secretary's, and the Treasuries, consist of a "core" head office or administrative section, together with a group of semi-autonomous agencies, with unrelated functions in some cases. Under the aegis of the New South Wales Colonial Secretary's Department we find such diverse units as the State Fisheries Branch and the State Electoral Office. Under the Treasury are grouped the State Lotteries Office, the Stamp Duties Office, the Bureau of Statistics and Economics, and the Government Printing Office, among others.

Under the Minister, the permanent official head of a department is usually called the Secretary, in Commonwealth departments, or the Under-Secretary in the States. However in both cases the title is sometimes Director-General, Director, Registrar, etc., while the permanent head of the Commonwealth Attorney-General's Department is also the Solicitor-General. With some exceptions in the "portmanteau" type of department just mentioned, the permanent head combines the role of chief official adviser to the Minister with that of a kind of general manager to the department.[2] There may be a Deputy Secretary, and there are usually a number of other senior officials heading broad divisions or branches of the department, often known as Assistant Secretaries. It is becoming commoner for one of these to be in direct charge of the organization and staffing matters throughout the department, and for the others to manage different functional aspects of its work. Although the Assistant Secretary (Administrative) or his equivalent may have close contacts with the Public Service Board and the Treasury, he is wholly responsible to the permanent head, and Australian governments do not follow the British practice of designating certain senior officers as Accounting or Establishments Officer (usually in the former case the permanent head himself) with certain cross-responsibilities to the Treasury.

The rest of the departmental organization varies according to the character of the department. For instance, there are comparatively small "policy" departments like the Commonwealth Department of Trade or the N.S.W. Ministry of Transport, whose staffs are almost entirely in a single office in a capital city. Apart from the Trade Commissioner Service over-

---

[2] See the article on "The Role of the Permanent Head", by Mr. J. G. Crawford, then Secretary of the Commonwealth Department of Commerce and Agriculture, in *Pub. Admin.* (*Sydney*), XIII, September, 1954.

seas, the Department of Trade consists of three main Divisions in the Canberra office, the Import Division, Industries Division, and Trade Policy Division, each headed by what is virtually a First Assistant Secretary. Above these there is a Deputy Secretary assisting the Secretary in managing the work of the department as a whole, and there is also a Policy Secretariat of half a dozen people who help the Secretary on problems affecting more than one Division. There is also an Administrative Division, which by an unusual arrangement shares library, accounting staff and records system with the Department of Primary Industry. Even the Department of Trade has small regional offices in State capitals. These are not nearly so elaborate, however, as the regional organizations of large administrative departments, such as the Postmaster-General's or Customs, or a State department of Agriculture, Lands or Public Works. Such big Commonwealth departments have generally retained the States as units of territorial decentralisation, and each State division would be headed by a State Director or equivalent senior officer, with a large office controlling operations within the State. Similarly, among New South Wales State departments, for example, there is considerable decentralisation to regional Directors' offices in the cases of Agriculture, Education, Housing and Public Works.

Table I on page 72 shows the growth in size and number of Commonwealth departments up to the beginning of World War II and then up to 1955. The first group of seven were the original departments formed at Federation, the first three absorbing the corresponding departments transferred from the States. In addition to the 11,661 permanent officers of these seven departments in 1904, there was a sizeable staff of manual workers "exempt" from the Public Service Act. The dates opposite the other departments indicate when they were established substantially in the form in which they appear in the table. In many cases there were previous departments under similar names, which had been abolished, subdivided or absorbed elsewhere. Not all of the departments had a continuous existence between the dates for which figures are given: for example, External Affairs, which in 1904 was really concerned with territories, was absorbed partly into Prime Minister's and partly into a department of Home and Territories in 1916, emerged as a separate unit again in 1921, then disappeared in 1924 into Prime Minister's and re-appeared as an independent foreign relations department in 1935. An indication of the way in which departments are brought to birth by fission or combination, as well as by fresh creation, is given in the following notes on the additional departments which supplemented the original group in June, 1939 (based on a not wholly accurate summary of changes up to 1952 in the 29th annual report of the Public Service Board):

Prime Minister's—established 1911.

Health—established 1921.

Commerce—Department of Markets and Migration established 1925 ; re-named Markets, and then Markets and Transport, 1928 ; separated into Markets and Transport departments 1930 ; Markets absorbed into new department of Commerce 1932. This was re-named Commerce and Agriculture 1942 ; and divided into two departments of Trade (absorbing part of Trade and Customs) and Primary Industry 1956.

Interior—Department of Works and Railways established 1916, absorbed the original Home Affairs; Home and Territories established 1916 (absorbing External Affairs, which was re-established 1921) was renamed Home Affairs 1928; Home Affairs, Transport and Works and Railways absorbed into new department of Interior, established 1932; shed part of functions to new department of Works, 1938; re-absorbed Works, 1939 (latter re-established as Works and Housing, 1945; renamed Works, 1952).

Civil Aviation—established 1938.

Supply and Development—established 1939 (became Supply and Shipping during the war; shed Shipping and resumed original name 1948; separated into Supply and National Development departments, 1950).

The table shows a Commonwealth departmental service of 47,043 in June, 1939 (including 14,614 temporary and "exempt" employees), working in twelve departments. It also illustrates an important point—that up to that time the Postmaster-General's department had always accounted for at least three-quarters of all departmental employees, and well over four-fifths of the permanent staff.

It is a striking symptom of the transformation of the Commonwealth service since 1939 that this ratio of permanent postal staff to total staff fell to less than half and remained so even after the disbanding of many wartime departments. The transformation has been both quantitative and qualitative. It can be seen from the table that while the Postmaster-General's staff had doubled by June 1955, total departmental staff had more than tripled. There were twelve more departments (rising to thirteen with the splitting of the Commerce department in 1956). At least half of these had existed in embryo within the 1939 group, and Repatriation had been exempt from the Public Service Act from 1920 to 1947. Nevertheless, some of the latter such as Territories, Social Services and Defence Production had opened up fresh fields of Commonwealth activity just as much as the entirely new departments like Labour and National Service, Immigration and National Development. Even long-standing departments had acquired new functions, as in the case of the Treasury which had taken over State income taxation.

Thus the Commonwealth Public Service as a whole has twice as many Ministerial departments (twenty-five in 1956) with more than three times as many employees as it did before the last war. How does this compare with changes in the States?

Broadly speaking, the States have shown a far less spectacular development in this departmental field. For example, A. F. Davies remarks of Victoria that "there are very few major activities at present in train that are not to be found in a state of fairly mature development before federation", and again: "There are at present fourteen departments, and this pattern was consolidated well before federation. Few changes have occurred since. The new departments are Forests (until 1908 a branch of the Lands Department), Labour (a factory inspectorate within the Chief Secretary's Department until 1915), Premier's (until 1936 also within Chief Secretary's), and Transport (a small co-ordinating unit, created in 1951)".[3]

---

[3] See forthcoming publication, edited by S. R. Davis, on *The Government of the Australian States* (Longmans, Green, Melbourne).

TABLE I
GROWTH OF COMMONWEALTH DEPARTMENTS

Department			1904	1939		1955	
			Per-manent	Per-manent	Total	Per-manent	Total
Postmaster-General	..	..	10,323	25,314	35,066	48,779	77,680
Trade and Customs	..	..	1,099	1,671	1,886	2,678	3,157
Defence	.. .. ..	..	124	1,029	1,291	287	585
External Affairs	.. ..	..	16	29	30	314	740
Home Affairs	.. ..	..	48	..	..	..	..
Attorney-General	.. ..	..	10	375	437	681	922
Treasury	.. .. ..	..	41	1,746	2,109	6,152	8,389
Prime Minister's*	..	.. 1911	..	360	398	1,013	1,345
Health	.. ..	.. 1921	..	313	576	971	2,298
Commerce	.. ..	.. 1932	..	589	953	715	1,128
Interior	.. ..	.. 1932	..	907	4,051	1,461	3,991
Civil Aviation	..	.. 1938	..	90	240	2,609	4,875
Supply	.. ..	.. 1939	..	6	6	1,706	4,096
Air	.. .. ..	.. 1939	..	..	..	783	2,351
Army..	.. ..	.. 1939	..	..	..	1,600	4,732
Navy	.. ..	.. 1939	..	..	..	1,293	2,335
Labour and National Service		1940	..	..	..	1,117	1,689
Territories	.. ..	.. 1941	..	..	..	276	761
Works	.. ..	.. 1945	..	..	..	1,598	12,021
Immigration	.. ..	.. 1945	..	..	..	641	2,286
Social Services	..	.. 1946	..	..	..	2,095	3,122
Repatriation..	..	.. 1947	..	..	..	3,643	8,240
National Development		.. 1950	..	..	..	303	581
Shipping and Transport		.. 1951	..	..	..	1,102	686
Defence Production		.. 1951	..	..	..	1,283	3,888
Totals	.. ..	..	11,661	32,429	47,043	82,330	151,898

* Figures include staff of Auditor-General's Department and Public Service Board.

The situation in New South Wales is a little different in form but similar in principle. The table shows a service of seven Ministerial departments in 1904, with a permanent and temporary staff of 13,275. The number of departments had risen to thirteen by 1939, and the staff also had doubled—but it should be noted that nearly half the people listed as New South Wales departmental staff are school teachers. Of the additional departments, three had been operating modestly within the departments of 1904—Public Health in the Colonial Secretary's Department, Labour and Industry as part of Public Instruction, and Forestry in Agriculture. Only Transport and Social Services were new departures: other expansions of State activity had been accommodated in the traditional departments.

The changes in New South Wales between 1939 and 1955 were of much the same order. Substantial functions and blocks of staff had been transferred to the Commonwealth. Although the number of departments had risen to nineteen, this was largely a result of separating pre-existing sub-departments, some of them quite small. Child Welfare had been withdrawn from Public Instruction and combined with Social Services in a single new

TABLE II

GROWTH OF NEW SOUTH WALES DEPARTMENTS
(Employees under Public Service Act)

Department	1904		Permanent + Temporary	
	Permanent	Total	1939	1955
Chief Secretary's*	1,887	2,047†	405	272
Treasury	1,181	1,459	2,497	4,229
Attorney-General and Justice	1,359	1,375	1,762	2,554
Lands	732	813	717	1,061
Public Works	853	960‡	1,351‡	2,761
Public Instruction	6,096	6,132	12,626	17,785
Mines (and)	} 305	489	{ 176	248
Agriculture			756	1,643
Premier's .. 1909	..	..	222	658
Labour and Industry .. 1910	..	..	585	503
Ministry of Transport .. 1932	..	..	21	28
Public Health .. 1938	..	..	3,205	4,487
Social Services .. 1939	..	..	339	¶
Local Government .. 1941	..	..	..	369
Ministry of Housing .. 1941	..	..	..	21
Conservation .. 1944	..	..	..	1,028
Tourist Activities and Immigration .. 1946	..	..	..	92
Child Welfare and Social Welfare .. 1946	..	..	..	616
Technical Education .. 1949	..	..	..	2,090
Ministry of Co-operative Societies .. 1953	..	..	..	48
Employees under Public Service Act in non-Departmental Agencies—				
Public Service Board	..	..	34	84
Hospitals Commission	..	..	..	49
Electricity Authority	..	..	..	39
Housing Commission	..	..	..	924
Forestry Commission .. 1915	..	..	218	§
	12,413	13,275	24,914	41,589

* Includes Auditor-General's Department.
† Includes Public Health section.
‡ Includes Local Government section.
§ To Conservation.
¶ To Child Welfare and Social Welfare.

NOTE.—These are only a few examples of transfers of sections and departments.

department; the insignificant registry of Co-operative Societies had been separated from the Chief Secretary's Department (whose name had altered though the Minister is still strictly speaking the Colonial Secretary), as had the departments of Technical Education from Education, and Local Government from Works. The only substantially new department was that of Tourist Activities and Immigration. The small Ministries of Housing and Conservation were superimposed on existing agencies. The increase in total staff of three-quarters over the 1939 figure is modest compared with the tripling of Commonwealth departmental employment. However, comparison with the State's population increase of one-quarter during the same period shows that State departments also are still increasing their participation in community life, whether by economic regulation or by services to industry and to individuals.

Developments in New South Wales and Victoria are reasonably indicative of the role of State departmental administration generally; but it would be wrong to attempt quantitative summaries for the States as a whole— detailed differences in structure and in the kinds of functions and employees included in Ministerial departments make it impossible to present comparable statistics.

Non-departmental Agencies

Among agencies of this kind, developments since 1900 have been spectacular in both the Commonwealth and States. The significant change is not so much in the number of these bodies, since they have always been so numerous that it is impossible to count them precisely. There are about fifty Commonwealth statutory authorities. Victorian researchers found 100 such agencies in that State in 1954. New South Wales had at least 400 before the last war, and more than 500 in 1955.

What is important is the growth in large public utilities and business undertakings under the corporate form, and the way in which they have come to dominate the politics and public finance of some, if not all, of the States. The increased use of corporations for these purposes may be due in part to some vague long-term theories about their political and administrative appropriateness. But there are such inconsistencies in the choice between corporate and departmental form for particular functions, and so many unaccountable variations in the degree of "independence" of corporations, to say nothing of minor discrepancies, that much of the corporation-making can only be attributed to the influence of habit or to political expediency. This last may well be a partial explanation of the spawning of corporations, especially in New South Wales and Victoria, during the period when State development, insofar as it depends on the central governments' loan programmes, has been closely controlled by decisions of the Loan Council under the Financial Agreement of 1927. "Local authority and semi-governmental" borrowing is not legally subject to Loan Council control and so the entrusting of more functions to these bodies has left greater freedom for manoeuvre, even since 1936, when the Premiers made a "gentlemen's agreement" to regulate the borrowing of these bodies in accordance with accepted Loan Council principles.

The Commonwealth, with its limited responsibilities in the fields of development, economic regulation and community services, has always been under less pressure than the States to extend its activities in these directions. Nevertheless, when it has done so, it has invariably resorted to the corporation device, with the major exception of the Post Office, the largest enterprise of all. Before the last war the Commonwealth had established, in addition to a number of commodity marketing boards, many regulatory and quasi-judicial agencies, such as Taxation Boards of Review, the Tariff Board, the Commonwealth Grants Commission, the Court of Conciliation and Arbitration, and the Public Service Arbitrator. However, its only large public utility or service corporations in 1939 were the Commonwealth Bank (1912), the Commonwealth Railways (1917), the Australian Shipping Board

(1923), the Council for Scientific and Industrial Research (1926) and the Australian Broadcasting Commission (1932). The total direct government employment in non-departmental agencies in June, 1939, was 20,820, compared with 47,043 in the Ministerial departments.

By June, 1955, Commonwealth non-departmental employment had risen to 53,233, thus increasing one and a half times compared with the three-fold increase in departmental staffs. Although this meant a decline, since 1939, in the proportion of non-departmental to total Commonwealth employment from about 1 in 3 to 1 in 4, the number of major non-departmental agencies had increased more than three-fold, the principal new ones being the Australian Shipbuilding Board (1941), the Aluminium Production Commission (1944), National Airlines Commission (1945), the Overseas Telecommunications Commission (1946), the Joint Coal Board (1946), the Stevedoring Industry Authority (1949), the Australian Shipping Board and the Australian Whaling Commission (1949) (the latter since abolished on sale of the undertakings in 1957), the Snowy Mountains Hydro-Electric Authority (1949), Commonwealth Hostels Ltd. (1952) (operating migrant camps), and the Atomic Energy Commission (1953).

As already shown, non-departmental agencies of all kinds are far more numerous in the States than under the Commonwealth government. These vary enormously as to their functions, area of jurisdiction, membership, financing, staffing, relations with Ministers and departments, and whether they operate administratively or quasi-judicially. A logical classification of them, based on any one of these elements, would produce a highly artificial result, since the elements are combined in so many different ways. The following is not a classification, but merely a list showing the kinds of bodies operating in New South Wales in 1956, grouped according to certain major characteristics, in some cases functional and in some cases formal.

TABLE III

N.S.W. STATUTORY BOARDS AND COMMISSIONS, 1956

1. *Major Public Utility and Business Undertakings*

   Transport
   Railways Commissioner.
   Main Roads Commissioner.
   Commissioner of Government Transport.
   Sydney Harbour Transport Board.
   Maritime Services Board.

   Power and Fuel
   Electricity Commission.
   Sydney County Council.
   State Mines Control Authority.*

   Other Commercial Undertakings
   Rural Bank.
   State Dockyard.*
   Government Insurance Office.*

---

* Statutory authorities with staff under Public Service Act.

Metropolitan Meat Industry Board.
State Brickworks.*
State Tileworks.*

Water Supply and Conservation
Water Conservation and Irrigation Commission.
Forestry Commission.*
Metropolitan Water, Sewerage and Drainage Board.
Hunter District Water Board.
Broken Hill Water Board.

Other Services
Housing Commission.*
Pre-cut Homes Undertaking.*

2. *Regulatory and Co-ordinating Authorities*
Hunter Valley Conservation Trust.
Electricity Authority of N.S.W.*
Conservation Authority of N.S.W.*
Hospitals Commission.*
Commissioner of Motor Transport.
Library Board of N.S.W.*
Joint Coal Board.
Public Service Board.*
Auditor-General.*
National Fitness Council.*
State Cancer Council.
State Nutrition Committee.

3. *Quasi-departmental Administrative Agencies*
State Bush Fire Committee.*
Aborigines Welfare Board.*
Board of Fire Commissioners.
Board of Health.*
Pastures Protection Boards.
Commissioner of Police.
Hospital Boards.
Grain Elevators Board.
State Superannuation Board.*
Lord Howe Island Board.*
Consultative Council for the Physically Handicapped.
Ambulance Transport Service Board.
Prickly-pear Destruction Board.*
Western Lands Commissioner.*
N.S.W. Film Council.*
Bursary Endowment Board.*

4. *Quasi-judicial Tribunals*
Coal Industry Tribunal.
N.S.W. Industrial Commission.*

---

* Statutory authorities with staff under Public Service Act.

Workers' Compensation Commission.*
Crown Employees' Appeal Board.*
Fair Rents Board.*
Licenses Reduction Board.*
Local Land Boards.*
Land and Valuation Court.*

5. *Commodity Marketing Boards*

Egg Marketing Board.
Milk Board.
Marketing Boards for Rice, Wine Grapes, Navy Beans, French Bean
    Seeds, Potatoes.
Dried Fruits Board.
Dairy Products Board.

6. *Educational, Cultural and Recreation Trusts*

Public Library Trustees.*
Art Gallery Trustees.*
Australian Museum Trustees.*
Botanic Gardens and Government Domain Trust.*
Royal National Park Trust.
Public Park Trusts.
Museum of Applied Arts and Sciences.*
Universities (3).

7. *Professional Registration and Examining Boards*

Veterinary Surgeons' Board.*
Medical Board.*
Dental Board.*
Architects' Board.
Surveyors' Board.*
Public Accountants' Registration Board.*
Optometrical Registration Board.*
Pharmacy Board.*
Nurses' Registration Board.*
Physiotherapists' Board.*

Employees of non-departmental agencies in New South Wales numbered
about 117,000 in 1955, of whom over 100,000 were included in category
1 above. The largest single employers were the Railways, with a staff of
more than 50,000 ; the Department of Government Transport (trams and
buses) with 10,000 ; the Electricity Commission and the Metropolitan Water
Board with about 7,000 each ; the Department of Main Roads and the
Water Conservation and Irrigation Commission with about 4,000 each.
Thus the non-departmental agencies account for nearly three-quarters of
all State government employment in New South Wales, compared with
one quarter under the Commonwealth Government. The proportion of
State employees outside Ministerial departments in other States except
Queensland and Tasmania rises very much higher than in New South Wales.

---

* Statutory authorities with staff under Public Service Act.

In all States the pattern of non-departmental agencies is broadly similar to that given above.

The Governmental Machine

No simple summary, whether in words, figures or diagrams, can faithfully represent the complexity of relations between the institutions of government.

For example, for purposes of budgeting and of Ministerial responsibility. (e.g., introducing legislation and answering questions in parliament) as well as in the usual statistics of government employment, the Public Service Boards and Auditors-General are treated as though they are part of the Prime Minister's Department (Commonwealth) or Premier's Department (N.S.W.), although their heads are "independent authorities". Again, "non-departmental employment" is generally equated in the statistics with "employment not subject to the Public Service Act". But there are some Ministerial departments which have large staffs outside the Public Service Act, and many public corporations whose staff in whole or in part is employed under that Act. (See footnote to Table III).

Some "non-departmental agencies" are required to make annual reports direct to Parliament (e.g., Auditor-General), some to the Governor (e.g., N.S.W. Public Service Board), some to a Minister "for presentation to Parliament" (e.g., Commonwealth Public Service Board to Prime Minister), some to a Minister *and* "to be laid before Parliament" (e.g., Electricity Commission of N.S.W. to Minister for Local Government), some to a Minister "for the information of Parliament" (e.g., N.S.W. Forestry Commission to Minister for Conservation), and some simply to a Minister.

Again, the chapter on Statutory Corporations shows the remarkable degree of Ministerial, Treasury, Public Service Board, and Auditor-General's control over general policy, specific acts, staffing and finance of many non-departmental agencies. Since these different forms of control are not associated in consistent patterns with particular kinds of agencies, the relationships cannot be summarised in any simple form.

All that can be said about "structure" in this sense is that not only departmental units, but nearly all non-departmental agencies are "associated", in one or other of the ways mentioned, with some particular Minister or department, and so it is possible to present a broad picture of the scope of governmental institutions by simply listing departments and their sub-divisions, together with the "associated" non-departmental agencies.

The following are such lists of Commonwealth and New South Wales departments, sub-departments and agencies. They cannot pretend to be exhaustive.

TABLE IV

MACHINERY OF COMMONWEALTH GOVERNMENT, 1957

Parliament consists of:

    Governor-General.
    Senate, 60 members.
    House of Representatives, 122 members.

Parliamentary "Deparments" (i.e., officials):

Senate, headed by Clerk of the Senate.
House of Representatives—Clerk of the House.
Joint House Department—Secretary.
Parliamentary Reporting Staff—Principal Parliamentary Reporter.
Commonwealth National Library—Librarian.

Courts

High Court of Australia—Chief Justice and six other Justices.
Commonwealth Industrial Court—Chief Judge and two others. The Court has most of the judicial powers formerly exercised by the Commonwealth Court of Conciliation and Arbitration.
Commonwealth Conciliation and Arbitration Commission—President, Deputy President, Senior Commissioner, eight Commissioners and three Conciliators. The Commission exercises the industrial arbitral powers formerly exercised by the Arbitration Court.
Federal Court of Bankruptcy—One Judge.
Supreme Court of the A.C.T.—One Judge.
Supreme Court of the Northern Territory—One Judge.
Central Court of Norfolk Island—One Judge.
Supreme Court of the Territory of Papua and New Guinea—Chief Justice and three Judges.
Central Court of Nauru—One Judge and ten Magistrates.
Supreme Court of the Territory of Cocos (Keeling) Islands—One Judge.

Executive Government

Executive Council:

Governor-General and Ministers of the day, and all surviving ex-Ministers. But the latter are not "under summons" for current meetings.

Ministry, 1957:

Cabinet Ministers:

Prime Minister.
Treasurer.
Minister for Labour and National Service.
Minister for Trade.
Minister for External Affairs and in charge of C.S.I.R.O.
Minister for Defence.
Vice-President of the Executive Council and Attorney-General.
Minister for National Development.
Minister for Immigration.
Minister for Territories.
Minister for Supply for Defence Production.
Minister for Primary Industry.

Other Ministers:

Minister for Repatriation.
Minister for Shipping and Transport and for Civil Aviation.

Minister for Health.
Minister for the Army.
Postmaster-General and Minister for the Navy.
Minister for Air.
Minister for the Interior and for Works.
Minister for Social Services.
Minister for Customs and Excise.
Parliamentary Secretaries (three).

Departments and Agencies:

Departments and Sub-departments	Associated Non-departmental Agencies
Prime Minister's Department:	
Head Office (Canberra). High Commissioner's Office (London). Office of Education (Sydney).	Historic Memorials Committee. Art Advisory Board. Commonwealth Literary Fund Committee. Commonwealth Archives Committee. Public Service Board. Auditor-General's Office. Commonwealth Grants Commission. Universities Commission.
Treasury:	
Head Office (Canberra). Defence Division (Melbourne). Sub-Treasuries (States and Territories). Commonwealth Loans Organisation (States). Commonwealth Advertising Division (Sydney and Melbourne). Government Printing Office. Bureau of Census and Statistics. Taxation Branch.	Superannuation Board. Defence Forces Retirement Benefits Fund. Australian Loan Council. National Debt Commission. Commonwealth Bank. Taxation Boards of Review. Valuation Boards. *Interdepartmental Committees*: Treasury Financial Committee. Commonwealth Local Stores Board.
Attorney-General's Department:	
Head Office (Canberra). State Crown Solicitors' Offices. Legal Service Bureaux. Courts and Titles Office (Canberra). Reporting Branch. Bankruptcy Branch (States). Commonwealth Investigation Service (all capitals). Patent Office.	Commonwealth Practitioners' Board. Board of Examiners of Patent Attorneys.

Departments and Sub-departments	Associated Non-departmental Agencies
Department of External Affairs: Head Office (Canberra). State Offices (Sydney and Melbourne).	

Department of Defence:
Head Office (Melbourne).
Canberra Secretariat.
	Interdepartmental Committees:
	Council of Defence (Ministerial and Chiefs of Staff).
	Defence Committee.
	Chief of Staff Committee.
	Joint War Production Committee.
	Commonwealth War Co-ordination Committee.
	Principal Administrative Officers' Committees:
	    Maintenance and Material.
	    Personnel.
	
	Advisory Committees:
	Defence Research and Development Policy Committee.
	Joint Planning Committee.
	Joint Intelligence Committee.
	Joint Administrative Planning Committee.
	Board of Business Administration.

Department of the Navy: Navy Office (Melbourne). Naval Establishments—All States and some Territories.	Naval Board. Naval Staff.
Department of the Army: Head Office (Melbourne). Commands (All States and N.T.). Army Canteens Service Board. Royal Military College, Duntroon.	Military Board.
Department of Air: Head Office (Melbourne). Commands, Areas, etc.	Air Board.

Departments and Sub-departments	Associated Non-departmental Agencies
Department of Supply:	
Central Administration (Melbourne).	Australian Aluminium Production Commission (Minister for Supply is "Minister in Charge").
Research and Development Branch—R. & D. Establishments.	Atomic Weapons Tests Safety Committee.
Board of Management for Atomic Weapons Tests:	
Design and Inspection Branch.	
Planning Branch.	
Stores and Transport Branch.	
Directorate of Contracts:	Contract Board.
State Representatives.	
Department of Defence Production:	
Central Administration (Melbourne).	*Interdepartmental Committee*:
Munitions Factories.	Defence Production Planning Committee.
Aircraft Factories.	
State Representatives.	
Department of Customs and Excise:	
Head Office (Canberra).	Literature Censorship Board.
Collectors of Customs (all States).	
Commonwealth Laboratory (Melbourne).	
Commonwealth Film Censorship Board.	
Department of Trade:	
Head Office (Canberra).	Tariff Board.
Administrative Division.	
Policy Secretariat.	
Trade Policy Branch.	
Imports Division.	
Tariff Division.	
Industries Division (Melbourne).	
State Branch Offices.	
Trade Commissioner Service.	

Departments and Sub-departments	Associated Non-departmental Agencies

Department of Primary Industry:

Head Office (Canberra):
  Inspection and Administration Division.
  Division of Agricultural Economics.
  Division of Agricultural Production.
  Fisheries Division.
  Marketing Division.
  Stabilisation Division.
  War Service Land Settlement Division.
State Branch Offices.

Australian Agricultural Council.
Standing Committee on Agriculture.
Apple and Pear Board.
Canned Fruits Board.
Dairy Produce Board.
Dried Fruits Control Board.
Egg Board.
Export Sugar Committee.
Fruit Industry Sugar Concession Committee.
Meat Board.
Potato Advisory Committee.
Wheat Board.
Wine Board.
Wine Research Institute.
Wool Bureau.
Wool Realization Commission.
Flax Production Commission.

Postmaster-General's Department:

Central Administration (Melbourne).
State Administrations.

Overseas Telecommunications Commission.
Australian Broadcasting Control Board.
Australian Broadcasting Commission.

Department of the Interior:

Head Office (Canberra):
  Administration Branch.
  A.C.T. Policy Co-ordination and Establishment Branch.
  A.C.T. Services Branch.
  Housing and Accommodation Branch.
  News and Information Bureau.
Directorate of Civil Defence (Melbourne).
State Branches.
A.C.T. Police Force.
Official War History.
Australian War Memorial.
Commonwealth Electoral Office.
Ionospheric Prediction Service.
Forestry and Timber Bureau.
Commonwealth Bureau of Meteorology.

National Capital Planning and Development Commission.
Australian National Film Board.
National Memorials Committee.
A.C.T. Advisory Council.

Departments and Sub-departments	Associated Non-departmental Agencies
Department of Labour and National Service: Head Office (Melbourne). Regional Administration (all States and A.C.T.).	Public Service Arbitrator. Coal Industry Tribunal. Australian Stevedoring Industry Authority. Commonwealth Hostels Ltd. Ministry of Labour Advisory Council. Standing Committee on Productivity.
Department of Shipping and Transport: Head Office (Melbourne). Commonwealth Handling Equipment Pool. Marine Branch. State Offices. Transport Branch.	Australian Coastal Shipping Commission. Australian Shipbuilding Board. Australian Shipping Board. Commonwealth Explosives Transport and Port Facilities Committees. Commonwealth Railways. Australian Transport Advisory Council.
Department of Works: Head Office (Melbourne). State Branches. Commonwealth Experimental Building Station.	
Department of Civil Aviation: Central Administration (Melbourne). Regional Directorates.	Australian National Airlines Commission.
Department of Social Services: Central Administration (Melbourne). State Headquarters (all States).	
Repatriation Department: Head Office (Melbourne).	Repatriation Commission. Repatriation Boards (all States). War Pensions Entitlement Appeal Tribunals. Assessment Appeal Tribunals.

Departments and Sub-departments	Associated Non-departmental Agencies
Department of Immigration: Central Office (Canberra). Branch Offices (all States and N.T.). Overseas Representatives.	**Advisory Bodies:** Commonwealth Immigration Planning Council. Immigration Advisory Council.
Department of Health: Head Office (Canberra). Divisional Offices (all States, N.T. and London).	National Health and Medical Research Council. Medical Board of the A.C.T. Dental Board of the A.C.T. Pharmacy Board of the A.C.T. Nurses' Board of the A.C.T. Optometrists' Board of the A.C.T.
Department of Territories: Head Office (Canberra). Sydney Office. Australian School of Pacific Administration. Northern Territory. Norfolk Island. Territory of Papua and New Guinea. Nauru. Cocos Islands. Ashmore and Cartier Islands. Custodian of Expropriated Property (New Guinea).	British Phosphate Commissioners. Christmas Islands Phosphate Commission. Papua and New Guinea Copra Marketing Board.
Department of National Development: Central Administration (Canberra). Melbourne and Sydney Offices. Division of Fuel. Commonwealth Mica Pool. Bureau of Mineral Resources. Division of National Mapping. War Service Homes Division.	Snowy Mountains Hydro-Electric Authority. Joint Coal Board. River Murray Commission.

Agencies Not Associated with Particular Departments (each "in charge" of a Minister):

Commonwealth Scientific and Industrial Research Organization.

Australian Atomic Energy Commission:

Advisory Committees: Uranium Mining, Scientific, Business Advisory Group.

TABLE V

NEW SOUTH WALES MACHINERY OF GOVERNMENT

Parliament consists of:

Governor.
Legislative Council, 60 members.
Legislative Assembly, 94 members.

Parliamentary Departments— Officials

Clerk of the Parliaments.
Clerk of the Legislative Assembly.
Librarian.
Editor of Debates.
House Secretary and Accountant.

Courts

Supreme Court of N.S.W.—Chief Justice and Justices.
District Courts—Judges.
Courts of Quarter Sessions—District Court Judges (Chairmen).
Courts of Petty Sessions—Stipendiary Magistrates or Honorary Justices of Peace.
Licensing Courts—Stipendiary Magistrates.
Warden's Courts (Mining)—Stipendiary Magistrates.
Land and Valuation Court—A Supreme Court Judge.
Industrial Commission—Members (status of Supreme Court Judge).
Crown Employees' Appeal Board—Chairman (status of Supreme Court Judge).
Workers' Compensation Commission—Members (status of District Court Judge).
Transport Appeal Court.
Coroners' Courts.
Children's Courts.

Executive Government

Executive Council: Governor and Ministers of the day.

Ministry, 1956—(All Ministers are members of Cabinet, as in other States).

Premier and Colonial Treasurer.
Deputy Premier and Minister for Education.
Attorney-General, Minister of Justice and Vice-President of the Executive Council.
Colonial Secretary, Minister for Immigration and Minister for Co-operative Societies.
Minister for Agriculture and Minister for Food Production.
Minister for Health.
Minister for Child Welfare and Minister for Social Welfare.
Minister for Local Government and Minister for Highways.
Minister for Transport.

Minister for Housing.
Secretary for Public Works.
Minister for Conservation.
Minister without Portfolio.
Secretary for Lands and Secretary for Mines.
Minister for Labour and Industry.
Minister without Portfolio.

Departments and Agencies

Departments and Sub-departments	Associated Non-departmental Agencies
Premier's Department:	
Head Office.	Auditor-General's Department.
London Office.	Police.
Division of Industrial Development.	Public Service Board.
Ministerial Motor Services.	
State Governor's Establishments.	
Chief Secretary's Department:	
Head Office.	Aborigines Welfare Board.
State Fisheries Branch.	Bush Fire Committee.
Weights and Measures Office.	Lord Howe Island Board.
State Electoral Office.	State Electoral Commissioner.
	Board of Fire Commissioners.
Department of Public Health:	
Central Administration.	Board of Health.
Division of Industrial Hygiene.	Hospitals Commission — Hospital Boards.
Pure Food Branch.	Consultative Council for the Physically Handicapped.
Tuberculosis Division.	
Maternal and Baby Welfare Division.	State Cancer Council.
School Medical Service.	State Nutrition Committee.
Division of Epidemiology.	Ambulance Transport Service Board.
Division of Dental Services.	
Nurses' Registration Branch.	Dental, Medical, Nurses', Optometrical, Pharmacy and Physiotherapists' Boards.
Health Inspection Branch.	
Analytical Laboratory.	
Microbiological Laboratory.	
Dietetics Branch.	
Government Medical Officers.	
Chemical Laboratory.	
Health Education.	
Master in Lunacy.	
Mental Hospitals.	
State Hospitals and Homes.	

Departments and Sub-departments	*Associated Non-departmental Agencies*
The Treasury:	
Head Office.	State Superannuation Board.
Stamp Duties Office.	Government Insurance Office.
State Lotteries Office.	Maritime Services Board.
Bureau of Statistics and Economics.	Rural Bank of N.S.W.
Government Printing Office.	Public Accountants' Registration Board.
Government Stores Department.	Pre-cut Homes Undertaking.
Government Real Estate Office.	
Government Cleaning Service.	
State Clothing Factory.	
Commissioner of Taxation.	
Ministry of Transport:	
Head Office.	Commissioner for Main Roads.
	Commissioner for Railways.
	Commissioner for Government Transport.
	Commissioner for Motor Transport.
	Sydney Harbour Transport Board.
Department of Attorney-General and Justice:	
Head Office.	Fair Rents Board.
Rent Control Office.	Council of the Auctioneers, Real Estate and Stock and Station Agents.
Court Officers.	
Sheriff.	
Clerks of Petty Sessions.	
Crown Solicitor.	
Public Trustee.	
Prisons Department.	
Registrar-General's Department.	
Adult Probation Service.	
Department of Lands:	
Head Office.	Land and Valuation Court.
War Service Land Settlement Branch.	Western Lands Commissioner.
Central Mapping Organisation.	Closer Settlement Advisory Boards.
Survey Co-ordination.	Land Boards.
Letter Delivery Bureau.	Prickly-Pear Destruction Board.
	Surveyors' Board.

Departments and Sub-departments	Associated Non-departmental Agencies
Department of Public Works:	
Central Administration.	State Brickworks.
Survey Branch.	State Tileworks.
District Offices.	State Dockyard.
Water Supply and Sewerage Branch.	Architects' Board.
Government Architect's Branch.	
Harbours and Rivers Branch.	
Government Motor Garage.	
Plant Branch.	
Stores Branch.	
Building Construction and Maintenance Branch.	
Testing Branch.	
Local Government Engineer's Branch.	
Engineering Design Branch.	
Department of Local Government:	
Head Office.	Local Government Superannuation Board.
Department of Valuer-General.	City, Municipal, Shire and County Councils.
Town and Country Planning.	Water Boards.
Gas Engineering Branch.	Electricity Commission of N.S.W.
	Electricity Authority of N.S.W.
Ministry of Housing:	
Head Office.	Housing Commission.
Department of Co-operative Societies:	
Registry of Co-operative Societies.	
Registry of Friendly Societies.	
Department of Education:	
Head Office.	Bursary Endowment Board.
Area Administration.	Library Board.
School Library Service.	Public Library of N.S.W.
Visual Education Branch.	Australian Museum.
Teacher Training.	National Art Gallery.
Furniture Workshops.	N.S.W. Film Council.
Furniture Service Branch.	National Fitness Council.
Research Office.	
Guidance Office.	
Physical Education.	
Conservatorium of Music.	
Sydney Observatory.	
State Emergency Service—Civil Defence Organisation.	

Departments and Sub-departments	Associated Non-departmental Agencies
Department of Technical Education:	
Head Office.	Museum of Applied Arts and Sciences.
Correspondence Teaching Division.	
Audio-visual Education Section.	
Research and Information Section.	
Guidance Office.	
Technical Colleges.	
Department of Child Welfare and Social Welfare:	
Administrative Division.	
Field Division.	
Establishments Division.	
Social Welfare Division.	
Department of Labour and Industry:	
Ministerial Office.	Arbitration Tribunals.
Youth Welfare Section.	Factory Welfare Board.
Inspectors of Factories, Scaffolding and Lifts.	Apprenticeship Commissioner and Councils.
Prices Branch.	
Department of Mines:	
Mines Inspection Branch.	Coal Industry Tribunal.
Miners' Pensions and Long Service Leave Branch.	State Mines Control Authority.
Accounts Branch.	Joint Coal Board.
Geological Survey.	Coal Conservation Committee.
Mining Museum.	Mines Subsidence Board.
Registrar's Branch.	Prospecting Board.
Explosives Branch.	
Chemical Laboratory.	
Department of Conservation:	
Head Office.	Conservation Authority of N.S.W.
Soil Conservation Service.	Water Conservation and Irrigation Commission.
	Forestry Commission.
	Hunter Valley Conservation Trust.

Departments and Sub-departments	Associated Non-departmental Agencies

Department of Agriculture and Food Production:

Central Administration.
Division of Information.
Division of Plant Industry.
Division of Horticulture.
Division of Dairying.
Division of Animal Industry.
Division of Regional Extension Services.
Division of Science Services.
Division of Marketing and Agricultural Economics.
Hawkesbury Agricultural College.
Wagga Wagga Agricultural College.
Experimental Farms and Nurseries.

Botanic Gardens and Sydney Domain Trust.
Grain Elevators Board.
Board of Tick Control.
Pastures Protection Boards.
Marketing Boards.
Metropolitan Meat Industry Board.
Milk Board.
Veterinary Surgeons' Board, etc.

Department of Tourist Activities and Immigration:

Government Tourist Bureau.
Immigration Section.

State Park Trusts for individual parks.

FUNCTIONS OF GOVERNMENT

Commonwealth versus State Administration

It has become fashionable to say that Commonwealth administration has grown in scope and stature. in power and prestige, while State administration has been reduced to the level of a local County Council in Great Britain.   On the other hand, it is also suggested that Commonwealth administration is remote from the people, relatively abstract, and centralised in Canberra, while State administration more closely concerns the daily lives of citizens and is more directly in touch with the economic and social activities of the community.   Other related contrasts are sometimes made. It is said that Federal administrators tend to be more concerned with broad policy issues, requiring constant and rapid adjustment to changing circumstances, while those of the States are mainly engaged in routine management of long-standing, stable regulatory functions, public utilities and social services. Finally, it has been observed that Federal programmes are generally better financed than those of State level.

Only the last of these contrasts can safely be applied as a generalisation about Australian government today. By the introduction of uniform income tax in 1942 the Commonwealth claimed the lion's share of all government revenues. The metaphor itself suggests the inevitable corollary—that the States must subsist, like jackals, on the financial scraps they can glean from the Commonwealth's leavings.   But it is precisely this relative impoverishment of the States that has helped to bring the Commonwealth increasingly into certain fields of "domestic" legislation and administration. With the State governments lagging for want of funds, the Commonwealth has had to provide the incentive, the financial means and, sometimes, the administrative machinery, for an anti-tuberculosis campaign, for University scholarships, for extended social services, better roads, the development of industries, even the encouragement of literature. Thus Commonwealth predominance in finance has helped to blur any broad distinction between Commonwealth and State functions. How far can such a distinction be made?

An important basis for the distinction is the distribution of the fundamental "constituent" functions of government—those which are bound up with the nature of political government itself. At Federation the national parliament was inevitably made exclusively responsible for defence, for external relations, the government of territories, the control of migration into and out of the country, and the control of external trade and of trade between the States. It also, of course, had to be given the power needed by every government to raise its own revenue, and this included a general power of taxation as well as a monopoly, after the first ten years, of the proceeds of customs and excise duties. On the other hand, the States retained almost complete control of one of the basic "constituent" functions of government —the preservation of internal law and order, including the administration of common law and statute law, both civil and criminal, with all their varied influences on the personal, economic and moral relations between citizens. This responsibility alone is sufficient to raise State government above the level of local authorities.

Thus there is a fairly clear-cut division of the constituent functions between the Commonwealth and the States, and it is broadly true that in this field the States' share more intimately touches the private affairs of individuals. Even here, however, the Commonwealth's control of overseas and interstate trade brings many of its officials into direct relations with those citizens who are exporters, importers or engaged in interstate commerce.

Beyond this field we must recognise that, especially since the last war, the Commonwealth has become involved in every one of the broad categories of regulatory and service functions that have been undertaken by State governments in Australia and unitary governments abroad. As a result, Commonwealth public employees are not concentrated in remote Canberra nor detached from the direct impact of government policies. They are widely dispersed through the continent in the conduct of grass-roots administration. Of the 152,000 departmental employees in 1955, only 7,289, or less than 5 per cent., were working in Canberra. The rest were distributed throughout the States roughly in proportion to their population.

As to the distinction between flexible policy functions and routine service functions, we have already seen that more than half the Commonwealth's departmental employees are post office workers. Others engaged in similar "bread and butter" functions include about 6,000 in routine services to air, land and sea transport, from lighthouses to weather stations ; about 13,500 paying out social service and health benefits and administering repatriation benefits ; about 10,000 collecting taxes and customs duties ; and about 3,000 doing regular chores for parliament and other departments. To these should be added the 20,000-odd employees of non-departmental agencies running Commonwealth railways, airlines, shipping lines, banks, migrant hostels, telecommunications, power generation and broadcasting services.

In fact, only slightly more than a quarter of departmental employees, or a fifth of all Commonwealth employees, are serving in departments concerned with external affairs, immigration, defence, economic and trade policy, and the development of resources, and this includes much routine work in supply and munitions factories and the day-to-day administration of Commonwealth territories.   A substantial proportion of these activities is devoted to the promotion of economic development, marketing of primary products and building of public works—functions which are also carried out in their own spheres by State governments.

Thus, apart from the constituent functions, it is difficult to make any clear distinction between the nature of Commonwealth functions and that of State functions.   But some rough lines can be drawn.

In the field of long-term economic development and conservation of natural resources, the Commonwealth's role is relatively restricted and indirect. For example, its Co-ordinator-General of Works collates the States' public works programmes for annual consideration by the Loan Council, in which the Commonwealth government has great power.   The Commonwealth can thus influence the total scope of development programmes (so far as they are dependent on loan expenditure) and to some extent the priorities among them. Its own works are mostly for its own enterprises and for defence purposes. The States must initiate, plan and carry out the detailed programmes for extending railways and highways, building dams and controlling floods, providing power and light and wheat silos, conserving soil and forests and training scientists and technicians. The Commonwealth helps some of these projects by making grants of money; but again the example of South Australia in recent years shows that the States can do much to determine the distribution of industry. Two other examples may illustrate this relationship. The Commonwealth Scientific and Industrial Research Organisation aids development mostly by carrying on basic research and publishing the results. The State Departments of Agriculture and of Industry do some similar work, but primarily they must ensure, through their extension services, that new knowledge and techniques are understood and applied in practice by farmers and industrialists. Again, the Snowy Mountains Hydro-Electric Authority is a Commonwealth agency to generate bulk power and a by-product will be the diversion of water into the Murrumbidgee and Murray Rivers. It will be up to the States of Victoria and New South Wales to plan the distribution of their shares of power and build the irrigation works for using the additional water. This direct responsibility for long-term economic development is the second major State function (the first being the making of criminal, commercial, industrial and social law) that quite clearly distinguishes the States from mere local governing bodies.

In the field of short-term economic policy for maintaining full employment and controlling fluctuations, the Commonwealth necessarily has a major role to play through the central bank's regulation of credit, the Treasury's taxation powers and the control of imports by the departments of Customs and Trade. The State parliaments have more specific powers which can contribute to the regulation of the economy: for example, they can impose price controls and alter wage levels and working conditions. However, this is an area in which the federal constitutional distribution of powers militates against coherent and co-ordinated action. Monetary and fiscal measures need to be dovetailed with import and price regulation and with wages and taxation policy. Some of these functions can only be exercised by the Commonwealth government, some only by the States, some are shared between them, and a good half of all wages are fixed by Commonwealth arbitration tribunals judicially independent of any government's direction. And economic policy is so closely bound up with the political convictions of governments that even in the depth of the Great Depression it was not possible to secure unanimous concerted action.

In the field of social services the Commonwealth now administers the major benefits (medical benefits; invalid, old age, widows', and other pensions; maternity allowances and child endowment, etc.) that involve, for the most part, purely monetary payments on a large scale. It also pays large sums to help the States to carry on certain services, e.g., provision of housing, university scholarships, hospital and pharmaceutical benefits, milk to school children, and the anti-tuberculosis campaign. The States are responsible for social services requiring not merely money payments but detailed administration and personal attention, the major ones being education and public health, the others ranging from child, youth and aborigine welfare to the building of State houses and the provision of community centres.

Finally, in the field of public enterprise and public utility services, while both Commonwealth and States conduct some services of the same kind, these activities are, relatively speaking, peripheral to the Commonwealth, involving less than a quarter of its employees and a smaller proportion of its finance; in the States, on the other hand, they tend to dominate the budgets, the employment picture, and political life itself. Together with education, conservation and economic development, the work of the great corporations providing transport, power, and water supplies constitutes what a Victorian survey has called "the fast-running current" of State politics and administration.

Commonwealth Functions

Table VI is the Public Service Board's summary of Commonwealth departmental functions showing the numbers employed on each at 30th June, 1955, and 1956. This can be supplemented for Commonwealth agencies as a whole by reviewing the list of agencies already given, and by consulting *The Federal Guide,* June, 1957, on which the list is based. There is no specific legal provision for dividing the executive functions of government among Ministers or departments. This is generally done in the first place by simple Cabinet decisions. However, the Commonwealth, carrying somewhat further the provisions of s. 64 of the Constitution, has adopted the practice of publishing from time to time in the Commonwealth Gazette an Administrative Arrangements Order, made by the Governor-General on the advice of the Prime Minister, setting out which functions and which statutes have been allocated to the several Ministers and departments. This statement, of course, is never up to date for long, and is not an authority for carrying out any function. That must be sought in specific legislation, in Government decisions supported by Appropriation Acts, or in the Treasurer's approvals of specific expenditure([3]).

TABLE VI
COMMONWEALTH FUNCTIONS

	Employees 1955	1956
Communication Services—Conduct of postal, telephonic and telegraphic communications, and services to air, land, and sea transport	83,814	85,281
Service and Supply—Defence policy and organization and control of the Armed Forces; civilians in the Forces; Defence Scientific Service; production and supply of stores and equipment for the Forces	18,003	18,836
Social Services and Rehabilitation—Provision of social and health benefits to ex-servicemen and the community as a whole; training and rehabilitation of handicapped ex-servicemen and others; provision of homes for ex-servicemen	13,461	13,485
Development and Conservation—Construction and maintenance of aerodromes, public buildings, etc.; development of productive and mineral resources	12,752	11,762
Revenue and Regulatory—Collection of income and other taxes; collection of customs and excise revenue; maintenance of standards of imports and exports	10,539	10,610
Territorial and Local Government Activities—Administration and development of Australian Capital Territory, Northern Territory, and the Territory of Papua-New Guinea	3,358	3,455
Economic and Trade Policy and Services—Agencies providing advisory and information services to the Government on economic policy; services to primary and secondary industry and overseas trade	3,595	3,865
External Relations and Immigration—Diplomatic representation abroad; general international policy matters; Antarctic research and exploration; selection, transport and assimilation of migrants	3,410	3,256
Agency Services—Services to Parliament and ancillary services to the Commonwealth Service generally; general, legal and education services	2,966	3,050
	151,898	153,600

([3]) See Commonwealth Joint Parliamentary Committee of Public Accounts, *Third Report*, 1952-53.

State Functions

A broad view of the main kinds of State functions has been given in the discussion of the division of functions with the Commonwealth. Somewhat similar headings have been used in listing Victorian functions of government in G. W. Leeper *ed., Introducing Victoria,* Melbourne, 1955, and in *The Government of Victoria* (Melbourne University Press, 1958). These can be read for comparison with the following summary of the distribution of functions among departments and agencies in New South Wales. A more detailed account of the nature, financing and parliamentary control of New South Wales functions is given in W. J. Campbell, *Australian State Public Finance,* Sydney, 1954.

A. "CONSTITUENT FUNCTIONS"—LAW, ORDER AND REGULATORY

1. *Protective, legal and registry services* include the work of the courts, police and prisons, the Master in Lunacy, and child welfare and reformatory institutions ; of the Registrar-General, Industrial Registrar, and Registrars of Co-operative and Friendly Societies ; the statistical services of the Bureau of Statistics and Economics ; the Civil Defence Organisation ; some protective functions of the Public Trustee ; and the management of the electoral system by the State Electoral Office.

2. *Regulation of quality standards* is maintained mostly by the devices of inspection and supervision, licensing and publicity. The purity of food supplies, drugs and medicines, and other chemical preparations, is the responsibility of the departments of Public Health and (in the case of meat) of Agriculture and the Metropolitan Meat Industry Board. Safety and quality in building and engineering are policed by the departments of Public Works (building materials and steelwork), Labour and Industry (factories, scaffolding and lifts), and Mines (explosives). Electrical work and appliances are supervised by committees under the Electricity Authority of N.S.W., and ground vehicles and road traffic are licensed and controlled by the Commissioner for Motor Transport, who also issues Co-ordination Licenses for air and water passenger carrying vehicles. The consideration of safety and traffic of water vessels generally is the concern of the Maritime Services Board.

3. *Regulation of professional and occupational standards* is the care of licensing or examining committees and boards for electrical contractors and electricians, architects, doctors, dentists, nurses, optometrists, veterinary surgeons, pharmacists, surveyors, public accountants, auctioneers and estate agents, mine managers, boiler inspectors, etc.

4. *Regulation of primary production* involves such matters as the supervision of working conditions, control of pests and diseases, protection of pastures, enforcement of safety rules in mines, and sometimes control of output, and falls to agencies associated mainly with the departments of Agriculture, Mines and Lands.

5. *Regulation of industry and commerce* applies some of these controls to secondary industry, as in the inspection of factories and shops, or the control of poisons by the Pharmacy Board, and also the regulation of prices (by Labour and Industry Department), rents (by the Rent Control Office and Fair Rents Board under the Attorney-General's Department), and

wages by various tribunals already listed; it also includes control of competition with the railways (by the Commissioner for Motor Transport); the supervision of co-operative societies, trade unions, auctioneers and estate agents, the liquor trade (the last by the Licenses Reduction Board); and prevention of harbour pollution (by the Maritime Services Board).

6. *Internal administrative services* include the raising of governmental revenue and the control of expenditure by the Treasury and the Auditor-General, the supply and control of staffing and organisation (in Ministerial departments mainly) by the Public Service Board, and various centralised services to government agencies generally, as by the Letter Delivery Bureau, Motor Garages, Government Architect, Bureau of Statistics, Government Printer, Government Stores, Real Estate Office, Cleaning Service, Valuer-General, Superannuation Boards, Public Library and Government Insurance Office.

7. *Local Government services* are provided by wholly or partly elected statutory authorities. The wholly elected authorities are city and municipal councils for urban areas and shire councils for the non-urban incorporated areas which cover 60 per cent. of the State (i.e., excluding the Western Land Division in which there are still very few local authorities). These authorities provide roads and bridges and street lighting and drainage, sanitary and garbage services, local electricity or gas supply, parks and, in some cases, swimming pools, libraries, baby clinics, abattoirs and aerodromes. Sydney's electricity is reticulated by the Sydney County Council, indirectly elected by local authorities in the metropolitan area, and there are over forty other such county councils in various parts of the State, providing local public utility services such as noxious weeds control, electricity or water supply. Three similarly constituted authorities administer town planning schemes, the Cumberland County Council for the Sydney area, the Northumberland County Council for Newcastle, and the Illawarra Planning Authority for the Wollongong-Port Kembla district. Water, sewerage and drainage services are controlled by boards partly elected by local authorities, partly appointed by Cabinet, for Sydney, Newcastle and Broken Hill.

B. CONSERVATION AND ECONOMIC DEVELOPMENT

8. *Conservation of natural resources* involves complex co-operation among many agencies concerned with flood control, water, soil and forest conservation, bush fire control, land use and pest control.

9. *Promotion of industry* by the State government is confined almost wholly to primary industry and includes closer settlement administration by the Department of Lands, agricultural research and extension services by the Department of Agriculture, Rural Bank and other financial assistance to farmers and prospectors, development of mining, marketing schemes, provision of grain elevators, subsidies to transport, etc. On the secondary industry side, a beginning has been made by the Division of Industrial Development in the Premier's Department.

10. *Developmental works* include the construction and maintenance of harbours, dams, water and sewerage systems and public buildings (mainly by the Public Works Department), promotion and co-ordination of urban

and rural electrification (by the Electricity Authority and the Electricity Commission), town and country planning under the Local Government Department and the planning county councils, building of water and irrigation works by the Water Conservation and Irrigation Commission, the building and maintenance of harbour and wharfage facilities by the Maritime Services Board and local authorities, railway extensions and highway construction by the Main Roads Department and by local authorities with the department's supervision and financial aid.

C. SOCIAL SERVICES

11. *Education, culture and recreation* are provided for mainly by the two departments of Education and by the various cultural and recreational trusts previously listed.

12. *Public health services* can be gauged from the functional divisions of the Department of Public Health listed above. There are also the minor health services of local authorities, the hospital and ambulance services and research and publicity activities carried on by bodies like the State Cancer Council, State Nutrition Committee and the State branch of the National Fitness Council.

13. *Social Welfare activities* include the provision of Children's Homes and other services of the Department of Child Welfare and Social Welfare, promotion of soldier settlement by the Department of Lands, youth welfare schemes under the Labour and Industry and Social Welfare Departments, pensions, long service leave and workmen's compensation schemes, care of deceased estates by the Public Trustee, assistance to indigent accused in the courts by the Public Defender, the work of the Factory and Aborigines Welfare Boards and the low rental provision of State housing.

D. PUBLIC UTILITY SERVICES

14. Some of these have been mentioned under previous headings. There are also the twenty-one great State corporations listed in section 1 of Table III.

The range of functions in other States is very similar to this and, on the whole, they are organised in a similar way, though naturally there are numerous minor differences. Every State has either a Premier's or a Chief Secretary's Department, or both, and the other departments common to all States are those of the Treasury, Attorney-General or Justice, Lands, Public Works, Public Health, Education, Labour and Industry, Mines and Agriculture. (The titles vary in some cases.) The scope of the departments under these names is not always the same, one reason being that some States have established as separate departments sections of the public service which, in others, have been grouped in one of the major departments under the control of a permanent under-secretary. For example, in South Australia the Agricultural College, Produce Department, Woods and Forests and Chemistry Departments are independent of the Department of Agriculture, though controlled by the same Minister; while in both South Australia and Western Australia public health departments are still nominally sub-branches of the Chief Secretary's Department.

A second reason for differences in the scope of departments with similar names is, of course, the different grouping of functions and therefore of sub-departments, particularly those which, as we have seen in the case of New South Wales, have no organic relationship with each other and so tend to be grouped haphazardly under "portmanteau" departments like Treasury, Chief Secretary's or Attorney-General and Justice. Taking, for example, the Chief Secretary's Department, compare the list of sub-departments already given for New South Wales with that for the corresponding Western Australian department, which comprises Medical and Public Health, Harbour and Lights, Registrar and Statistical, Prisons and the Observatory. In any one State this grouping is changed from time to time, as when in New South Wales Child Welfare, formerly in the Department of Education, and Social Welfare, formerly in Labour and Industry, were removed from these departments and linked in a new and independent department.

A third source of differences in the organisation of State functions is that a function which is entrusted to a ministerial department in one State may be administered by a non-departmental board or commission in another. Forests are controlled by Ministerial departments in Victoria, Queensland and Western Australia, but by statutory Commissioners in the other three States—though even in these States most of their staff are subject to the Public Service Acts. Water conservation and irrigation are departmentally administered in Victoria and Queensland, but entrusted to an independent Commission in New South Wales. In general, however, there has been a trend in all States to organise the same major public utility and developmental services under non-departmental, statutory agencies.

The Co-ordination of Functions

Problems of co-ordination naturally arise from the piecemeal growth of administration (whether Commonwealth or State), from the constant reorganisation of departments involving the transfer of functions from one to another, and from the increasing scope of government regulation and services which results in different agencies working in the same field. Sometimes the problem is to co-ordinate different agencies of a State government, sometimes to promote joint action between State and Commonwealth agencies. For example, the development of the irrigation areas in the Murray-Murrumbidgee basin involves co-operation and co-ordination between a multitude of Commonwealth and State agencies. To regulate the Murray's total flow into South Australia there is the River Murray Commission, a joint agency of the governments of the Commonwealth and three States. Water conservation, drainage and flood protection are generally entrusted to the Department of Water Supply in Victoria, to the Water Conservation and Irrigation Commission in New South Wales. The W.C. and I. Commission's work involves co-operation with the New South Wales Department of Lands in developing holdings for War Service Land Settlement; with the Commonwealth Snowy Mountains Hydro-Electric Authority on problems of the diversion of Snowy waters into the Murray and Murrumbidgee systems and its effect on irrigation; with elected local authorities and land boards in the irrigation areas; with the Commonwealth Scientific and Industrial Research Organisation and the State Department of Agriculture on soil surveys, irrigation research and extension services; and with many private citizens' associations concerned with the development of these areas.

Co-ordination problems generally are of three broad types—concerning administration, finance, and policy—and they are met by various techniques.

In administration, advisory committees help to link government agencies with two kinds of private knowledge and experience: technical expertise, and the views of the people being regulated or receiving service. Inter-departmental committees avoid overlapping and help to work out practical methods of co-operation. Special agencies like the Public Service Boards, in consultation with departments and corporations, can strive for a more rational organisation of the various parts of the governmental machine as a whole, and a proper allocation of staff among them. No comparable agency in other States or the Commonwealth has the powers or the influence of the N.S.W. Public Service Board in this respect. (See Chapter 10.)

Financial co-ordination is necessary to allocate money in due proportion among the many activities of government, and to keep their total expenditure within available resources. The Treasuries, and, ultimately, the Cabinets, are responsible for making this allocation; and since much of the money spent by the States is raised by the Commonwealth, there are inter-governmental agencies both at the official and the Ministerial level for deciding how this money shall be shared out. The most important of these are the Premiers' Conference and the Loan Council. (On financial co-ordination see Chapter 7.)

Financial allocations are closely dependent on policy co-ordination, since they depend on decisions about the relative value and urgency of different programmes. In New South Wales and the Commonwealth the collation of data on which these decisions are based is greatly helped by regular systems of co-operation and joint review as between the Public Service Boards and the Treasury; in New South Wales in particular the Board has become a knowledgeable and respected adviser of governments on policy co-ordination. In other States such top-level official co-ordination is not so highly developed. But it is not so necessary in the smaller States where personal contact between Ministers and the higher officials is easy and it is possible for Cabinets to acquire a direct acquaintance with all important aspects of administration. In all governments the Cabinets are helped in policy formation by small secretarial staffs in the Prime Minister's, Premiers' or Chief Secretaries' Departments.

Thus in the Commonwealth and at least in New South Wales, the three main co-ordinating agencies are the Prime Minister's or Premier's Department, the Treasury and the Public Service Board. The first-named departments are responsible for the secretarial work relating to the Cabinet and its committees and prepare the Cabinet agenda and minutes. The Treasury advises on general economic and financial policy, and relates the expenditure plans of the departments to one another through the Estimates. The Commonwealth Treasury, for example, has a General Financial and Economic Policy Branch, a Budget and Accounting Branch, a Banking Trade and Industry Branch, Social Services Branch, a Defence Division, and so on.

For policy co-ordination between governments there are, in addition to the Premiers' Conference, very many joint councils and committees such as the Australian Agricultural Council or the Australian Transport Advisory Council (see Chapter 8) and innumerable consultative bodies perform similar functions within each government. There have also developed in some governments in recent years, special co-ordinating devices for particular areas of policy. For example, in New South Wales the Conservation Authority includes a Commissioner of the Water Conservation and Irrigation Commission, the Commissioner for Forests, the Commissioner of the Soil Conservation Service and the Under-Secretary, Department of Conservation. Similar joint boards exist for the co-ordination of transport policy at the State level. A final example of systematic attempts at policy and financial co-ordination is the Commonwealth practice of appointing a Treasury official as a member of many of the statutory corporations.

However, it must always be remembered that day-to-day co-ordination, whether in administration, policy or finance, would be impossible without the constant informal contacts not only between Ministers, senior officials and influential private citizens, but also between officials of different departments and agencies at all levels.

Chapter Four

THE STATUTORY CORPORATION

T. H. KEWLEY

There are three main types of governmental administrative agencies in Australia—ministerial departments, local authorities and statutory corporations. Local authorities, which are the creation of State Governments, are discussed in Chapter 6. Statutory corporations are used at both State and Commonwealth levels. They are the main concern of this chapter.

If asked to define a statutory corporation (or "public corporation" as this agency is sometimes called overseas) most people would probably reply by giving an example—the New South Wales Government Railways or the Australian Broadcasting Commission. Such caution is warranted for, whilst this agency is usually recognisable, it is less easy to define. There is no single pattern or model and the functions of corporations are diverse. What mainly distinguishes a statutory corporation from a ministerial department is that in exercising its statutory powers and duties it does not have full and direct responsibility to Parliament. In other words, some measure of independence is granted to the corporation in carrying out its functions. The degree of independence differs greatly as between the several corporations: the essential point, for the purpose of definition, is that an attempt has been made to grant some measure of independence.

The statutory corporation has for long been a familiar agency of government in Australia. Some resort to it was had during the first half of last century. Two reasons which then favoured the adoption of the corporate structure remain important. "Firstly, the 'Crown' as a legal personality was a most unsatisfactory basis for the organization of any enterprise which might be involved in daily dealings with property and in litigation, owing to the cumbrous procedures connected with Crown property and the strict limitations on Crown liability to legal action. Secondly, an activity identified with the Crown almost inevitably became a political activity, and this might be either bad for the activity or embarrassing for the politicians."[1]

Towards the end of last century a more conscious awareness developed of the political and administrative advantages that the statutory corporation might possess over the ministerial department for operating government enterprises (and also for recruiting and controlling public services). That awareness arose chiefly in relation to railways. Railways had been government owned and operated in both Victoria and New South Wales since the eighteen-fifties. Once established they provided considerable opportunities for patronage and for corruption of various kinds. Victoria in 1883 took the first deliberate step to provide a suitable instrument for government in business. Railways legislation of that year established a distinction between the construction of new lines, and the operation of the existing system. The former function was recognised as inescapably political and was left in the

---

[1] G. Sawer, "The Public Corporation in Australia" in W. Friedmann (ed.) *The Public Corporation,* 1954, p. 10.

hands of a ministerial department. The latter function was considered technical and commercial, and suitable for administration without political interference. It was consequently transferred to a statutory corporation, consisting of a Chairman and two Commissioners, appointed by the Governor for seven-year terms and with security of tenure for that period. The Commission was given complete authority over the appointment and control of the railway staff. In two years, the railways, which had shown repeated deficits, were showing a profit. This system was then adopted with variations by the other States, beginning with New South Wales in 1888.

During the present century the statutory corporation has become widely accepted in Australia as an instrument for operating government enterprises. The fields in which it was early used include ports (for example, the Sydney Harbour Trust, 1901) ; savings banks (e.g., the N.S.W. Government Savings Bank, 1906) ; and developmental activities such as irrigation (e.g., the Victorian State Rivers and Water Supply Commission, 1905). Gradually its use was extended to cover a number of public utility services ordinarily associated with local authorities. For a number of such corporations some connection with local government is maintained by the election of some members of the governing boards, but in most instances the Boards are appointed by the State governments to which they owe varying degrees of responsibility.

The statutory corporation, although widely accepted as an instrument for operating government enterprises, has not been invariably chosen for that purpose. Some enterprises are run as adjuncts to ministerial departments. The Commonwealth Department of Defence Production, for example, runs several munitions and ordnance factories. In the States, too, are to be found examples of departmental administration of business enterprises. That has been specially true of Queensland, though it has often happened in that State that the Head of the Department of Industry has been incorporated as a corporation sole for the purpose of running a particular activity. Other examples are to be found in Western Australia.[2] When, during the second decade of this century, New South Wales embarked upon a number of business ventures, including fish trawling, brickworks, tile works, saw-mills, timber yards and ship-building, it enacted in 1912 an Industrial Undertakings Act which laid down an administrative and financial code to be followed by all undertakings brought by proclamation within its provisions. Several undertakings functioned under this legislation for a number of years, but they have since passed from the scene, and the blanket enactment has been repealed.[3] Two business undertakings at present in existence are the State Brickworks and the Government Engineering and Shipbuilding Undertaking (the State Dockyards). Although established by special statute, these have not been incorporated. They are run by a manager under the control of the Minister.

---

[2] E.g., State brickworks, saw-mills, engineering works, shipping service, even a State hotels department.

[3] Some were part of a conscious policy of State enterprise espoused by W. A. Holman, as Attorney-General and Premier, and the Minister for Public Works, Arthur Griffith. See R. S. Parker, "Public Enterprise in New South Wales", *Aust. Journal of Politics and History*, Nov., 1958, and H. V. Evatt, *Australian Labour Leader*, 1942, ch. XLII.

Another device, of which some limited use has been made, is the "mixed undertaking", in which there is a partnership between government and private enterprise. Two notable examples at the Commonwealth level were Commonwealth Oil Refineries and Amalgamated Wireless (Australasia) Ltd., but the Government has now sold its shares in these. They were registered as companies under State law. Little use has been made in Australia of the ordinary company laws for governmental purposes. Two governmental agencies incorporated under such laws are Commonwealth Hostels Ltd., the migrant hostels authority; and Qantas Empire Airways Ltd., all the shares in which were bought by the Commonwealth in 1947. The extent to which the company form has been adopted for operating public enterprises is, however, very limited. The agency most usually chosen has been the statutory corporation.

The advantages over the ministerial department generally claimed for the statutory corporation by those who were its enthusiastic advocates about the turn of the century have been summarised by Professor Sawer broadly([⁴]) as follows:

(1) The technical legal advantages of an entity with perpetual succession, capable of suing and being sued by ordinary process of law and of obtaining, owning and giving title to property, free from the cumbrous restrictions and immunities of Crown law. (This consideration has become less important with the reform of Crown law in general.)

(2) The political advantage of administration free from the irrelevant issues of partisan politics at any time, with consequent ability to concentrate on short and long-term policies appropriate to the activity, and on technical and managerial efficiency.

(3) The administrative advantages of building up a personnel structure appropriate to the activity and free from the rigidities of ordinary public service rules.

(4) The possibility of representing on the governing boards various functional interests or outlooks appropriate to the activity—the technical expert, the producer and so on.

(5) The advantage of removing the undertaking from the immediate political pressures that bear upon the party in power.

(6) The possibility of careful accounting practice designed to run the activity as economically as possible and, where it is a revenue earning activity, to run it on "business" lines, that is making its income pay for interest on capital, depreciation, reserves for development and running costs.

The advantages claimed for the statutory corporation would, of course, differ somewhat from activity to activity. Underlying these general claims, however, is the assumption that the corporation would enjoy a large measure of independence. That broadly was the situation until the 'thirties. Since the 'thirties, and especially since World War II, there has been a tendency to restrict the independence of corporations. Whereas the emphasis was earlier placed upon their independence, the more recent trend has been to

---

([⁴]) op. cit, pp. 12-13. See also F. W. Eggleston, *State Socialism in Victoria,* 1932, pp. 41-48.

emphasise their public accountability. This is true of the Commonwealth as well as of the States, as will be seen later.

A more immediate point that needs to be made is that, implied in the above list of advantages is the assumption that corporations invariably have a number of features in common. That, however, is not the situation even with corporations operating business enterprises. And not all of them are operating enterprises: some have only regulatory functions. Whilst it is most usual, for example, for the staff of corporations to be outside the jurisdiction of the relevant Public Service Board or Commission, that is not always the case. Likewise there are important differences in the composition of the governing boards of corporations. Some boards, for example, include serving public servants as members, others do not. Part of the reason for these and other differences between corporations is that they have been created at different times in answer to the needs of the moment rather than in response to long-range plans (as for example were the corporations operating the nationalized industries in Britain) or to considerations of organizational symmetry. It could be broadly said that almost the only significant features they invariably have in common are that they are created by special statute and have the legal status of a corporate body with independent legal personality.

The statutory corporations operating in Australia are thus so diverse in character as to defy any simple classification. Certainly they do not permit of classification on a functional basis in the manner attempted by Professor Friedmann for Great Britain, where he distinguishes between commercial, social service, and supervisory (or regulatory) corporations.[5] Even if such an exercise were attempted for Australia, little of the constitutional characteristics of the corporations would be revealed, for constitutional characteristics do not correspond with functional. The constitutional characteristics of the corporations are examined later in this chapter.[6]

THE STATES

New South Wales

In the Australian environment, the pursuit of an energetic developmental programme has always been a vital matter to governments, and from the earliest days a large proportion of public expenditure has been directed to this purpose. Internal development has remained fundamentally a State, rather than a Commonwealth function. The main group of statutory corporations in New South Wales are those operating undertakings such as railways and water conservation, which have occupied an outstanding place in the development of the State. The fact that these undertakings are, for the most part, of a business character, should not be allowed to obscure their developmental character. Government subsidy has been held to be justified by the enhancement given to the general revenues as a result of their operations. On strictly business lines they might be expected to return direct revenues equal to their annual costs, including debt charges, thus freeing the Government from the need to share in their operating expenditures. However, they often fail to do so.

---

[5] See his chapter in W. Friedmann (ed.), *The Public Corporation*, pp. 166-67.
[6] For a more detailed account of New South Wales statutory corporations see W. J. Campbell, *Australian State Public Finance*, 1954.

The corporations which may be grouped together because they carry out activities that are, to a greater or less degree, of a developmental character are the Government Railways; the Maritime Services Board, established in 1936 to operate the port of Sydney (formerly the responsibility of the Sydney Harbour Trust) and also to operate the other main ports in New South Wales; the Water Conservation and Irrigation Commission,[7] created in 1912, which is concerned with the conservation of water resources and the utilisation of those resources by means of irrigation projects; the Forestry Commission (1916) which is responsible for the preservation, development and use of the State's forests; and the "Department" of Main Roads [8] (1925), which has the duty of constructing and maintaining a system of highways. Another corporation in this group is the Rural Bank, which began operations in 1933.[9] This Bank has evolved in a series of stages from a savings to a rural and homes lending institution. In 1947 its charter was extended to include all classes of general banking business. It also conducts a Government Agency Department, the function of which is to administer several forms of rural lending on behalf of the State. Two corporations of more recent creation are the Electricity Authority (1946) and the Electricity Commission (1950). The former is largely a planning and regulatory agency.[10] It also administers a subsidisation scheme for the extension of electricity supply to rural areas and thus influences rural development. Partly for that reason, and partly because of its relationship with the Electricity Commission, it is included here. The prime function of the Electricity Commission, which also has some planning functions, is to generate and supply electricity in bulk to the distribution authorities, mostly local authorities, throughout the State.[11]

The above corporations operate over the whole area of the State. Partly for that reason, the Metropolitan Water, Sewerage and Drainage Board,[12] which operates in the Sydney metropolitan area and environs, has not been included with this group, although it has a long record of developmental activities. It seemed more appropriate to group this with other corporations which likewise provide, over a limited area, a public utility service of a kind usually associated with local authorities. These are the Sydney County Council,[13] which was established in 1935 and whose function was reduced in 1950, by the acquisition of its generating system by the Electricity Commission, to the distribution and sale, within the City of Sydney and environs, of electricity purchased in bulk from the Commission; the Metropolitan Meat Industry Board, which conducts the Homebush Abattoirs; and the

---

[7] See C. K. Jacka, "Conservation and Increased Food Production", *Pub. Admin. (Sydney)*, XI, Dec., 1952.

[8] See H. M. Sherrard, "Main Roads Administration in New South Wales", *Pub. Admin. (Sydney)*, XV, Sept., 1956.

[9] See C. R. McKerihan, "The Rural Bank of New South Wales", *Pub. Admin. (Sydney)*, XVI, March, 1957.

[10] For further discussion of this authority, see chapter by Ruth Atkins below.

[11] See H. C. Conde, "The Electricity Commission of New South Wales", *Pub. Admin. (Sydney)*, XVI, March, 1957.

[12] See J. W. Goodsell, "The Metropolitan Water, Sewerage and Drainage Board", *Pub. Admin. (Sydney)*, XIV, March, 1957.

[13] See D. J. Nolan, "The Sydney County Council", *Pub. Admin. (Sydney)*, I, Dec., 1939.

"Department" of Government Transport, established in 1932, which operates the tramways and omnibus services in the metropolitan area of Sydney and Newcastle. For good measure, and also to illustrate one kind of factor that has sometimes led Australian governments into the field of public enterprise, it is appropriate to include here the Sydney Harbour Transport Board. Following upon the financial failure in 1951 of a ferry company operating over the waters of Sydney Harbour, this Board was established to purchase the assets of the company and to carry on the services. The Act empowered the Board to delegate the work of operation and management. This it has done to a privately owned company on an agency basis in terms of an agreement with the Board—an arrangement which is unusual in this State. The losses on this service (and, for that matter, on other government transport services) have continued with monotonous regularity.

Two of the corporations, the Sydney Water Board and the Sydney County Council, differ from the other corporations with which they are grouped in that they retain a link with local government.[14] The members of the Sydney County Council are elected by the aldermen and councillors of the relevant municipalities: the Chairman being elected by and from the members.[15] The members of the Water Board are similarly elected, except for the President (a full-time member) and the Vice-President, who are appointed by the Government. Another authority that has retained a link with local government is the Board of Fire Commissioners.[16] Of the five members of this Board, one is elected by the local authorities (which contribute one-eighth of the expenditure); one by the fire insurance companies (which contribute three-quarters); one by the volunteer firemen; and one by the permanent firemen. The President is appointed by the Government, which also contributes one-eighth. The Board of Fire Commissioners resembles the "mixed undertaking", referred to above. In fact, it seems desirable to break with custom, and to regard this authority as a mixed undertaking rather than as a statutory corporation.

With two exceptions, the statutory corporations mentioned above may be said to be operating monopoly undertakings or services, though some of them are, of course, subject to indirect competition such as that between the railways and the road hauliers. The exceptions are the Rural Bank, in respect of its general banking activities; and the Metropolitan Meat Industry Board. The latter, however, operates under sheltered conditions. There is a third group of statutory corporations which operate enterprises that are in competition, to a greater or lesser degree, with private undertakings. The oldest of these is the Public Trustee who, in 1913, was constituted as a corporation sole with power to carry on the business of executor and trustee. Another is the Government Insurance Office. This was estab-

---

[14] Another such corporation is the Hunter District Water Board. It is similar in most respects to the Sydney Water Board.

[15] Unlike other county councils in N.S.W., the Sydney County Council does not derive its constitution solely from the Local Government Act. It operates under a special charter conferred by the Gas and Electricity Act. An interesting feature of that Act is the provision it makes for the division of administrative responsibility between the Council and the General Manager.

[16] See T. J. Smith, "Fire Administration", Pub. Admin. (Sydney), II, March, 1940. The constitution of the Board was changed to the above in 1956.

lished in 1926 as a sub-branch of the Treasury, primarily to provide employers with a means of insuring their liability under the Workers' Compensation Act of that year. A wider charter was granted by legislation in 1941 when the Office was constituted as a body corporate, under a general manager, and empowered to carry on any class of insurance in the manner of a private insurance corporation. A third corporation in this group is the State Mines Control Authority, which controls certain State-owned coal mines.

There remain several other major corporations that need to be mentioned. These include the Hospitals Commission, a principal function of which is to distribute government subsidies to the hospitals which form the "public" hospital system of the State; the Housing Commission; and the Public Service Board, all of which are discussed elsewhere in this book. There is the Grain Elevators Board, which is responsible for the storage of wheat and the operation of the State's grain elevator system.

The statutory corporations mentioned above do not exhaust the list of governmental administrative bodies in New South Wales that have been given a corporate structure. The Comptroller-General of Prisons, for example, has been incorporated as a corporation sole. There are also a large number and variety of trusts, such as the Royal National Park Trust, which have been established for the management and protection of public amenities. Some of these trusts, for example the Taronga Zoological Park Trust, engage in activities which are substantially of a commercial character. The commercial activities of most others are minimal. The members of these trusts are appointed by the Governor and serve in a voluntary capacity. In some cases, however, certain privileges are enjoyed by the trustees.

These trusts have been incorporated under one or other of three general statutes—the Public Trusts Act, 1897, the Crown Lands Consolidation Act, 1913, and the Public Parks Act, 1912.([17]) There consequently seems little case for regarding them as "statutory" corporations. If the term "statutory corporation" is to have a manageable connotation, it would seem necessary to limit it to those corporations established by special statute which defines the powers and functions of the particular corporation, and not to apply it also to bodies that have been incorporated under some general statute. Such a limitation would not suffice, however, to exclude all of another group of trusts, namely those concerned with certain cultural and educational activities. Some of these trusts, for example, the Public Library and the Australian Museum, have been incorporated by special statute. They will not, however, be further discussed here, for they throw little light on the more general questions relating to the statutory corporation.

In New South Wales, as in other States, numbers of Boards have been established for the purpose of registering and disciplining members of learned professions, or of trades in which only registered persons are permitted to practice after proof of competence, and subject to de-registration for loss of competence, conviction of crime and such matters. Some of these boards, for example the Pharmacy Board, have been incorporated: others, for example the Medical Board, have not. Whether the lack of con-

---

([17]) The only trust concerned with the management and protection of public amenities which has been established by special statute is the Kosciusko State Park Trust. That body, however, has not been incorporated.

sistency in this matter results from accident or design is not clear. What is clear, however, is that presence or absence of the corporate form in such cases is a question of very minor importance.([18])

It should perhaps be stressed that this essay is concerned only with *governmental* administrative bodies that have been incorporated. Apart from legal judgments, which, in any case, seem to have produced merely a "wilderness of single instances", there appears to have been no general discussion of what constitutes a governmental body. The writer understands that the Government Statisticians of the several States have discussed this question at their conferences held in recent years, but that no agreement upon a suitable definition, or definitions, has been reached. The terms "public" and "governmental" are sometimes used as synonyms. It is preferable, however, to speak of governmental and non-governmental bodies rather than public and private (or non-public) bodies. The words "public" and "private" have an emotive content for many people and their use is likely to cause some confusion. It might be argued by some, for example, that the Australian Red Cross Society was a public body in a way that Broken Hill Proprietary Company Limited could not be said to be. It would be less easy to argue that it was a governmental body.([19])

The term "governmental" necessarily excludes a wide range of corporate bodies such as the public hospitals throughout the State; the University of Sydney; and the marketing boards established under the Marketing of Primary Products Act. Some may contend that these bodies should be included on the grounds that they were established by Act of Parliament and/or that they receive annual grants from the Government. Neither of these tests can be usefully applied, however, to determine whether a body is governmental. The first test is much too general. It would bring in, for example, the Australian Gaslight Company, which is not usually considered to be a governmental body. The second test likewise presents difficulties. To suggest that all bodies receiving annual government grants are governmental would mean including, for example, the New South Wales Geographical Society and the New South Wales Council of Social Service. And nobody would reasonably make such a claim for these. The test applied by the writer in deciding whether a corporate body was governmental, was to enquire whether all, or a majority, of the governing board were either appointed by the Minister (or Governor) or elected by local authorities.

Upon examination it will be found that the corporate bodies excluded by this test are, in fact, not usually regarded as governmental bodies. The public hospitals, for example, are usually described as voluntary organisations. Some may consider that the marketing boards established under the New South Wales Marketing of Primary Products Act (and similar Acts in other States) should be regarded as governmental. There is little reason, however, for so regarding them. The initiative in creating a marketing board lies with the producers of the relevant commodity, and all, or the majority, of board members are derived from election among the producers. More-

([18]) Sawer, *op. cit.,* p. 32.
([19]) See D. N. Chester, "Public Corporations and the Classification of Administrative Bodies", *Political Studies,* Feb., 1953, pp. 40-41.

over, on the vote of a sufficient number of producers the board may be disbanded, as happened with the Potato Marketing Board.([20])

An exception should be made of the Milk Board, which is constituted by special statute and whose Chairman and members are appointed by the Governor. That Board should perhaps be grouped with the other statutory corporations mentioned above, such as the Sydney Water Board, which operate over a limited area of the State. Another exception is the Fish Marketing Board, constituted under the Fish and Oyster Farms Act. Under that legislation the Chief Secretary (a Cabinet Minister) is incorporated for the purpose of carrying out fish marketing and distribution. That agency had best remain in a category of its own. A note on marketing boards will be found in Appendix I.

Other States

The general character of public corporations in other States does not show any marked differences from New South Wales, and in some cases there is a close parallelism. For example, Queensland and South Australia appointed Railway Commissioners about the same time as New South Wales, and the other States followed with some time-lag. Some of them have alternated between one and multi-membered commissions as has New South Wales. Victoria created a Board to deal with main roads (the Country Roads Board) in 1912, and three other States set up Main Roads Boards or Commissioners in the 'twenties, as New South Wales did. Most of the States have Electricity Commissions or Trusts, which control the bulk of generation and have extended in varying degrees into the field of sale to the final consumer. Victoria's State Electricity Commission (1919) and Tasmania's Hydro-Electric Commission (1930), itself preceded by a State Department, were earliest in the field, and have the widest functions. In Western Australia, the State Electricity Commission (1946) replaced the Railways and Tramways Department (for generation) and local authorities (for distribution). The Electricity Trust of South Australia took over a private undertaking in 1946. Queensland's Commissioner for Electricity Supply has powers to own and operate electricity supply undertakings, but so far has only exercised these through membership of Regional Electricity Boards which also include local authority representation, and the Southern Electric Authority, a public corporation operating in South Eastern Queensland. The State Electricity Commission as such exercises regulatory, co-ordinating and consultative functions.

Harbours are mostly controlled by harbour boards and trusts, most public housing by State Housing Commissions or Trusts. Many of the States operate banking and insurance institutions, which have sometimes existed for a long period, e.g., Victoria's Savings Bank (1841) and Rural Finance Corporation (1950), South Australia's Savings Bank (1875) and State Bank, Queensland's Agricultural Bank (1901) and Government Insurance Office (1916), Tasmania's Agricultural Bank (1907) and Government Insurance Office (1919), Western Australia's Rural and Industries Bank (1944) and

---

([20]) The Commonwealth marketing boards differ from the State boards in a number of important respects, and there may be a case for regarding them as governmental agencies. For an account of them see G. Sawer, op. cit., pp. 21-24, and Appendix I.

State Government Insurance Office (1926). The Queensland Coal Board has regulatory functions similar to those of the Joint Coal Board in New South Wales. Most States now have State-wide Fire Brigades Boards or Commissions with operating or co-ordinating functions (Victoria has separate boards for Melbourne and the rest of the State). Victoria's State Rivers and Water Supply Commission (1905) pioneered the idea of a State-wide corporation for water supply and irrigation.([21]) State boards or trusts operate public transport services in Adelaide, Hobart (where the trust represents both State and city), Melbourne, Perth, Sydney. Only in one State capital, Brisbane, is passenger transport in the hands of a local authority— the Brisbane City Council.

There are some differences. Victoria's Gas and Fuel Corporation (1950) is the only public body in Australia created specially to re-organise gas supply.([22]) Tasmania's Railway Commissioner has been superseded by a Transport Commission (1938) which has wider functions and also operates many bus and other services. The Melbourne and Metropolitan Board of Works (1890) has the functions of Water Boards in other capitals, but now also has other important tasks, e.g., town planning. In some States forestry is controlled by a State-wide commission, in others by a Ministerial department or sub-department. (Victoria's Forests Commission is called the Department of State Forests for public service purposes and its staff are under the Public Service Act.) Some States have several harbour trusts, others a more powerful State authority covering all or a number of harbours. Some have bodies special to themselves, e.g., Tasmania's Aluminium Production Commission (jointly with the Commonwealth) and Salmon and Fresh Water Fisheries Commission. Queensland's Public Service Act appears to cover a somewhat wider scope than that of other States, where corporations are not usually subject to the Public Service Board or Commission, though there are important exceptions. Management by a single Commissioner is also most popular in Queensland.

Commonwealth

Because of its comparatively limited activities during the earlier years of Federation, the Commonwealth Government made little use of the statutory corporation. An early Commonwealth experiment with this type of agency was the Commonwealth Bank, created in 1911 by a Labour Government. In its original form there was no Board: the powers were given to a Governor appointed for seven years. In 1917 the Commonwealth-owned railways were unified under a single Commissioner. The same model was used the next year when the ill-fated War Service Homes Commission was created. The principle of the one-man commission was thus established in the early days.

The corporations established in the 'twenties by the Bruce-Page Govern-

---

([21]) The Act creating it, the Swinburne Water Act, 1905, was a very advanced measure for its day (cf. F. W. Eggleston, *State Socialism in Victoria*, p. 75). A separate Board supplies Melbourne's water. The Commission is now known as the Department of Water Supply for Public Service Act purposes.

([22]) In Western Australia the State Electricity Commission has power to regulate gas supply; and it shares the manufacture and distribution of gas with a private concern. In most other States gas is supplied by private enterprise or local government.

ment were usually of the multi-member kind, and clearly intended to resemble boards of company directors as closely as possible. This was true of the Shipping Board, which operated a shipping line from 1923 to 1928 ; the reconstituted Commonwealth Bank (1924) ; and the Council for Scientific and Industrial Research (1926). The new model that thus emerged was the board of part-time members, with a full-time chief executive ; though there were some minor exceptions. The Australian Broadcasting Commission, established in 1932, was also a part-time body, with a full-time General Manager. Here the model of the B.B.C. in the United Kingdom was expressly followed.

The Australian Broadcasting Commission was the only statutory corporation established during the 'thirties. With the great increase in its activities during and since the Second World War, the Commonwealth has made extensive use of this type of agency. The post-war period really begins with the 1942 Report of the Joint Parliamentary Committee on Broadcasting. It made the first notable study in Australia of the principles that should be adopted in creating a statutory corporation. Most of its recommendations were embodied in the re-organization of the Australian Broadcasting Commission which followed, and they also influenced the character of some of the post-war corporations. The first of these was the Australian National Airlines Commission, established in 1945. During the following year the Overseas Telecommunications Commission and the Joint Coal Board were established. (Earlier legislation, in 1944, had created the Australian Aluminium Production Commission.) Later legislation created the Broadcasting Control Board (1948), the now defunct Australian Whaling Commission (1949) ; the Snowy Mountains Hydro-Electric Authority (1949) ; the Atomic Energy Commission (1953) ; the Australian Coastal Shipping Commission (1956) and the Export Payments Insurance Corporation (1956).

Of special interest are the corporations established by the Commonwealth Government in co-operation with a State Government. These "joint authorities" are the Aluminium Production Commission, created by the Commonwealth and Tasmania to develop the aluminium industry in that State ; and the Joint Coal Board, established by the Commonwealth and New South Wales to regulate and rehabilitate the coal industry in New South Wales (in which State about 90 per cent. of Australia's black coal is produced). These authorities have been given legal structure and powers by both Commonwealth and State legislation. This has been done because the Commonwealth has lacked constitutional power, or was uncertain of its constitutional power, to embark upon the activity solely on its own authority. It has consequently supplied financial support and such constitutional power as it possesses, whilst the State, being glad to have the activity fostered within its boundaries by financial support from the Commonwealth, has supplied the necessary legal basis. They are discussed in Chapter 8.

The extensive use of the statutory corporation by the Commonwealth during the post-war years, and especially before 1950 when a Labour Government was in office, should not be taken to mean that it has been employed as an "instrument of nationalisation", as in the United Kingdom. There are constitutional limitations upon the Commonwealth in this respect, as witness the fortunes of the banking legislation in 1947. Of the corporations which are conducting commercial enterprises, few control the whole field in which they operate. In neither broadcasting nor television has the Australian Broadcasting Commission been granted a monopoly. It does not, however, have to compete with commercial broadcasting stations for advertising revenue; it receives its revenue from the Government. Of the Commonwealth corporations conducting commercial enterprises, only two monopolise their field, the Commonwealth Railways Commission (which operates rail services between South Australia, Western Australia and the Northern Territory and within that Territory) and the Overseas Telecommunications Commission. The latter derives its monopoly from an international agreement.

CONSTITUTIONAL CHARACTERISTICS

The constitutional characteristics of statutory corporations are of special concern, for it is these which throw light on the main common feature of statutory corporations—their "independence" or "autonomy". It has been stated above that what mainly distinguishes statutory corporations from ministerial departments is that, in exercising their statutory powers and duties, they do not have full and direct responsibility to Parliament. In other words, to a greater or less extent, they have been placed outside the normal system of control and accountability that has been developed in relation to the departments. An examination of the main points at which political controls may be exercised over corporations is therefore necessary.

Key points at which control may be exercised are: the constitutions of the governing boards, finance, staff, and those matters where the Minister is granted statutory powers. In the following discussion, the constitutions of some statutory corporations are examined in relation to these. The discussion mainly deals with corporations engaged in trading and commercial activities.

Boards: Appointment and Tenure

Apart from the elective boards, such as the Sydney Water Board, it is usual for the statutes to provide that the boards shall be appointed by the Governor-in-Council. This means in practice that appointments are made on the recommendation of the Cabinet. Statutory provisions relating to the tenure of Board members are far from uniform. Sometimes the period for which the appointment is to be made (subject in most instances to renewal) is specifically stated. In other cases the legislation merely states the *maximum* period, i.e., "not exceeding" three, five or seven years, for which the appointment might be made. There are usually certain statutory disqualifications for continuance in office. The provisions differ slightly as between the various Acts, but generally they state that a member is deemed to have vacated office if he becomes bankrupt; or of an unsound mind; has, except under certain specified circumstances, an interest in any contract or agreement with the corporation; or is absent without leave from Board meetings for a specified period. The appointment may usually be terminated for inability, inefficiency, or misbehaviour.

Some of the statutes make no provision for security of tenure. The Grain Elevators legislation in Victoria, for example, empowers the Governor-in-Council to remove any member of the Board from office at will. Mostly, however, the statutes provide for a comparatively secure tenure during the specified period of the appointment, which tends to be three to five years, though often a longer period, for example, seven years, for the Chairman, or where the appointment is full-time. In a few cases, for example the Rural Bank of New South Wales, tenure is until retiring age.

The provisions regarding tenure are of importance in that they can influence the independence of the Board. Where appointments may be terminated at the will of the Minister, the influence of the Minister upon Board members can be considerable. The independence of the Board may also be influenced when the legislation specifies merely the maximum period for which the appointment is to be made. This allows the Minister to make appointments for a shorter period than the maximum. In Victoria, for example, there have been occasions when re-appointments have been made for as short a period as six months. And during the earlier years of the Australian Broadcasting Commission members were sometimes re-appointed for even shorter periods than this.[23] This power to make short-term re-appointments may place the Minister in a position where he can exercise a very strong influence over Board members, particularly over a full-time member who, as often happens, regards his service as a career in which he would normally continue until retirement.

Composition

The size of the boards varies. In most instances provision is made for a small compact membership, varying from three to seven. This is also true nowadays of the corporations constituted on an elective basis, with the exception of the Melbourne and Metropolitan Board of Works. The deficiencies of a large board are well-illustrated by the history of the Sydney Water Board between 1925 and 1935.[24] Sometimes the authority is con-stituted as a "corporation sole", that is, a one-man corporation, as are the New South Wales Forestry Commission, the Snowy Mountains Authority, the Commonwealth Railways and the Export Payments Insurance Corpora-tion. In the first two cases, however, the Commissioners are assisted by two Assistant Commissioners who, like themselves, are full-time.

The Australian statutes do not usually specify any qualifications for mem-bers. In this they differ from the statutes creating the boards for the nationalised industries in the United Kingdom, where members are usually required to have had wide experience in specified fields of activity. The Commonwealth banking legislation requires that members of the Bank Board shall have engaged in one or other of several specified fields of activity, and the broadcasting legislation requires that one member of the Australian Broadcasting Commission shall be a woman. But these are exceptional. Usually the statutes include little more than some vague pro-vision about the appointee being a "fit and proper person".

It is sometimes contended that the absence of specified qualifications for board members makes it easier for party political appointments to be made. That some such appointments have been made is beyond question. There

[23] Joan Rydon, "The Australian Broadcasting Commission", *Pub. Admin.* (*Sydney*), XI, Dec., 1952, p. 191. The broadcasting legislation has since been amended to provide for terms of three years.

[24] See Goodsell, *op. cit.*, p. 61.

is little reason to believe, however, that the specifying of qualifications for board members would necessarily present any serious obstacle to the making of party political appointments. The quality of persons appointed to the Boards of corporations depends rather upon the rectitude and ability of the political leadership. With some corporations political experience could well be a desirable qualification.

As well as the fear that political appointments will deprive the boards of independence, there is also the fear that such appointments may give them too much independence. Labour members have often complained about the independence of boards which they consider to be composed of anti-Labour men. These complaints arise in part from the belief, not without foundation, that non-Labour governments have sometimes viewed the independent statutory corporation as a means of preserving continuity of policy for an undertaking and safeguarding it from the "wrecking" activities of Labour governments. This partly explains why Labour governments, at least in the States, have tended to favour ministerial control of corporations.[25]

Some of the statutes provide for the representation of various interests on the board. The State Electricity Commission in Western Australia, for example, is composed of seven members, two of whom represent consumer interests in town and country respectively, and one of whom represents employees.[26] A second example is the New South Wales legislation which requires that two of the members of the Maritime Services Board of New South Wales "shall be identified with such interests as . . . [the Minister] may think desirable". In introducing this legislation the Minister stated that these members "will represent shipping and commercial interests outside the department". The members of some harbour trusts are elected by interested parties. Of the two members of the Sydney Metropolitan Meat Industry Board, other than the Chairman, one is appointed as a representative of the producers of cattle, the other as a representative of the employees.

There are to be found a few examples of legislation providing for trade union or employee representation on the Board. Such provision has usually been made with a view to meeting the somewhat vague demand for this within the Labour movement. It should not be taken to mean that there has been any substantial discussion of the question of trade union representation amongst the Australian trade unions, such as took place in Britain for many years prior to the enactment of the nationalisation measures. Few specific demands for trade union representation have been made. Two exceptions are the Miners' Federation which has quite vigorously demanded representation on the Joint Coal Board, and the New South Wales Branch

---

(25) It also partly explains an earlier hostility to the statutory commission as such. "At the last election, like knights in shining armour, the members of the Labour Party went out to kill the dragons of boards and commissions. . . . Anything that began with a 'B' was doubtful, but . . . if it were a 'committee' that might be passed, a 'council', possibly, but a 'commission', never" (according to an Opposition critic, J. G. Latham, *Com. Part. Debs.*, v. 123, 21st March, 1930, pp. 386-7).

(26) Bruce Graham, "Administrative Structures and Problems of State-owned Utilities in Western Australia", *Pub. Admin.* (*Sydney*), VIII, June-Sept., 1949, p. 119.

of the Australian Railways Union which has, at various times, sought representation on a reconstituted Railways Board.

The legislation of the Chifley Labour Government establishing the earlier post-war Commonwealth corporations makes no provision for trade union or employee representation on the Boards. That legislation, in fact, makes no provision for the representation of sectional interests of any kind. This could well have resulted from a recognition that, for the efficient running of commercial undertakings, the conception of the Board as a meeting place for the representation of interests is wholly mistaken. The knowledge that the official view of the trade union movement (and also of the Labour Party) in Britain was opposed to the direct representation of employees, or their trade unions, on the boards operating the nationalised industries might also have been of some influence.

In Britain, rejection of the notion of direct representation of interests on the boards of the nationalised industries has been partly offset by the establishment of advisory committees; machinery for joint consultation between employer and employees; and consumers' councils. In Australia, there are no consumers' councils, little attempt has been made to establish machinery for joint consultation and, with the notable exception of the Australian Broadcasting Commission, little use has been made of advisory committees.

A feature of many Australian corporations, which is absent from the British corporations, is the appointment of serving public servants (and especially Treasury officials) as part-time members of the Boards. The New South Wales Electricity Commission, for example, has the Under-Secretary of the State Treasury as its Vice Chairman. In the Commonwealth sphere, the broadcasting legislation of 1948 is singular in specifically providing for such appointments. That provision, which was repealed during 1956, increased the membership of the Australian Broadcasting Commission from five to seven in order to include an officer of the Treasury and an officer of the Postmaster-General's Department. During the regime of the Chifley Labour Government public servants were appointed as part-time members of a number of other boards. This practice has not, however, met with favour by the Liberal Government which succeeded the Chifley Government in 1949.

Little attention has been given to the question of the effects that this practice may have upon the independence of the boards.([27]) Some aspects of this practice were, however, considered by the Commonwealth Parliament Joint Committee on Public Accounts during 1954 in the course of its inquiry into the affairs of the Australian Aluminium Production Commission. The Committee found that the presence of a Treasury official on that Commission had created some confusion and misunderstanding. There was naturally a tendency for the other members of the Commission not so skilled in matters of finance as the Treasury representative could be expected to be, to rely upon him for guidance in this field. The Treasury maintained,

---

([27]) In the context of Australian politics it is, of course, possible to envisage situations in which a board's independence may be strengthened by the inclusion of a serving public servant as one of its members, for the public servant may be more skilled than other board members in handling the Minister.

with the support of the Solicitor-General, that the status, functions and responsibilities of the Treasury representative were no different from those of other members of the Commission. The Committee was of opinion that, if this view be accepted, there was little purpose in making such an appointment. It concluded that in most cases it was not necessary, and might even be inexpedient, to appoint a Treasury official to the governing board of a statutory corporation. The Committee also questioned the wisdom of appointing other departmental representatives to such positions, and especially a representative from the "responsible department". One factor leading the Committee to this view was its recognition of the conflict of loyalties to which the official may become subject. On the one hand he is responsible to a Minister; on the other hand he has duties as a board member and would be less than human if he did not develop loyalties towards his fellow members.[28]

The statutes do not usually state whether members of the boards are to be appointed on a full-time or a part-time basis, although where the amount of salary or other remuneration happens to be stated the nature of the appointment is, of course, clear. The practice has mostly been to appoint the Chairman on a full-time basis, and the members on a part-time. The majority of the boards are thus what have been called "policy" boards, as distinct from "functional" boards; meeting perhaps monthly, as do the Australian National Airlines Commissioners.

An interesting exception is the Snowy Mountains Authority. Although constituted as a corporation sole, in practice the Commissioner and the two associate commissioners are collectively a policy-making body, but in addition each assumes responsibility for a particular group of functions within the organisation.[29]

Staff

Control over the appointment and conditions of employment of staff has generally been regarded as an important element contributing to the independence of statutory corporations. The granting of this power results largely from the notion that corporations operating commercial enterprises should, so far as possible, approximate to the ideas of business management and be free from the more rigid rules which apply to the public service proper. It might therefore be expected that the staff of purely regulatory corporations would form part of the ordinary public service. That, however, is not invariably the situation. Nor have all commercial corporations been granted freedom in controlling their staffs. The staff of the New South Wales Government Insurance Office, for example, are subject to the control of the Public Service Board. Mostly, however, with the notable exception of Queensland,[30] the staff of commercial corporations are excluded from the provisions of the relevant Public Service Act.

---

[28] *Twenty-first Report*, pp. 13-14, and *Twenty-second Report*, pp. 71-72.

[29] For a general discussion of this issue, see W. A. Robson, "The Governing Board of the Public Corporation," in W. A. Robson (ed.), *Problems of Nationalised Industry*, 1952, pp. 97-98.

[30] C. J. Hayes, "The Administration of State Public Services", *Pub. Admin.* (*Sydney*), XV, June, 1956, p. 121.

The multiplicity of corporations outside the jurisdiction of the public service controlling authorities does not necessarily imply a great diversity in methods of recruitment, salaries and other conditions of employment. In New South Wales, for example, where well over two-thirds of all public employees (a large proportion of these being transport workers) are outside the jurisdiction of the Public Service Board, many of the corporations have adopted similar methods of recruiting to those of the Public Service Board. Moreover, in that State, at the request of the Premier, regular conferences have been held since 1950 between the Heads of the Corporations and the Chairman of the Public Service Board with a view to securing a measure of uniformity in salaries and other conditions of employment. In addition, regular meetings have been held between the industrial officers of the several authorities.([31]) In other States, too, attempts of various kinds have been made to secure some measure of uniformity in conditions of employment for all public employees. It cannot be said how successful these attempts have been, for no comprehensive study has been made either of the conditions of employment, or of personnel practices in the statutory corporations. There does, however, seem to have been a general tendency to bring methods of recruitment and conditions of employment more into line with those applying in the regular public service.

The post-war Commonwealth legislation imposes a number of restrictions upon the corporations in staff matters.([32]) Most of the statutes require the corporations to recruit on the basis of open competitive examinations, except for specified classes of positions. They also require that Ministerial approval be sought for the appointment, transfer, or promotion of an officer where the salary exceeds a specified amount, usually £2,500. Sometimes, as with the Overseas Telecommunications Commission, the statute contains lengthy provisions about staff which deal with such matters as the grounds on which an officer may be promoted, dismissed, or retired. In some other cases, as with the Snowy Mountains Authority, they require that the terms and conditions of employment shall be approved by the Public Service Board. Because they operate competitive enterprises, the National Airlines Commission and the Coastal Shipping Commission have been allowed greater freedom in staff matters. The staffs of these corporations have also been excluded from the jurisdiction of the Public Service Arbitrator.

FINANCE

Financial control is the most vital of all forms of control. The degree of autonomy enjoyed by corporations tends to be related to the extent to which they are financially self-sufficient. Clearly, other things being equal, a corporation that has its own, independent source of revenue from sales of services (the National Airlines Commission) or from assigned revenues (the N.S.W. Department of Main Roads) is likely to be subject to much less parliamentary (and therefore ministerial) control than is a body financed wholly out of annual parliamentary appropriations of the usual departmental kind. There are considerable variations in the degree of financial autonomy

---

([31]) New South Wales Public Service Board, *Report*, 1956, p. 32.

([32]) See T. H. Kewley, "Some General Features of the Statutory Corporation in Australia", *Pub. Admin. (Sydney)*, XVI, Mar., 1957, pp. 13-17.

enjoyed by the Australian statutory corporations. The following outline of the situation in New South Wales is, however, broadly indicative of the situation in the other States.[33]

New South Wales

With the exception of the Rural Bank and the Sydney County Council, which are financially self-sufficient, most of the New South Wales corporations fall into one of two categories: those whose capital is wholly provided by the government, and those whose capital is partly provided by the government and partly raised through loan issues.   Important in the first category are the Railways Commission and the Maritime Services Board. For historical reasons and because of the importance of their operating results for State financial management, they are taken into the annual budget. Their expenditures are subject to annual appropriation. The appropriation process when applied to a business enterprise such as the railways, however, tends to lack the force it has in relation to purely governmental expenditures, for the outcome of operational needs rather than vote allocations will determine the volume of expenditure. The expenditures of the Department of Government Transport are also subject to annual appropriation, although the relevant statute does not direct the adoption of that practice. That authority, unlike the above instrumentalities, is empowered to raise public loans, but this power has not been invoked.

Other authorities wholly capital financed by the Government, for example the Government Insurance Office, are excluded from the budget and the attendant fund appropriating processes. Their operating funds are, nevertheless, kept in the Treasury, on the self-liquidating principle, as also are the funds of the Railways Commission, the Maritime Services Board and the Department of Government Transport. Unlike the latter, though, their funds are available for the purpose of expenditures simply upon requisition by their managerial authority.

Of the corporations in the second category—those possessing some independent borrowing powers—the more important are the Electricity Commission and the Sydney Water Board. These authorities directly control their own funds outside the Treasury system. Their operations are not included in the budget, nor are they subject to the processes of parliamentary appropriation. The Metropolitan Meat Industry Board also enjoys autonomy in the control of funds. Its capital is wholly Government financed, however, and the Board does not possess any outside borrowing powers other than by bank advances.

Control of the loan raising practice of a corporation possessed of independent borrowing powers is laid down by statute.[34] The provisions applying to the New South Wales State Electricity Commission may be regarded as broadly typical of the requirements. The Act sets out, amongst other things, the purposes for which capital may be borrowed, requires that the Governor's approval first be obtained, that a reserve for loan repayment be

---

[33] For a fuller account see Campbell, *op. cit.,* Chapters XIII and XIV.

[34] Corporations possessed of independent borrowing powers are not subject to Loan Council restraint. Exercise of their borrowing powers is regulated, however, by a "gentleman's agreement". See p. 231.

created, and stipulates the measures for the custody, investment and use of the reserve for loan repayments. Securities are to be in the form of debentures, bonds or inscribed stock. The loans are declared to be secured on the income of the enterprise, and are guaranteed by the Government.

Power over the disposal of profits is one element in the financial freedom of a corporation. Mostly the New South Wales statutes are silent as to the contingency of profit or loss. In only one or two cases of minor importance is provision made for the payment of surpluses into the general revenues. An unusual provision in the legislation relating to the Government Insurance Office, however, requires that any funds in excess of those determined from year to year as necessary for the purpose of the office should be set aside in the Treasury for capital expenditure upon hospitals. Whilst there has thus been some statutory provision concerning the disposal of surpluses and deficiencies, practice has mostly been influenced by the course of events. Most corporations have retained their profits, but on occasions when the Government has been seeking budget assistance, legislation has been enacted for the transfer of portion of the surplus funds of the more affluent authorities to the general revenues. In many cases losses fall automatically upon the general revenues

The corporations are required to submit annual reports, accompanied by statements of account. Their accounts are audited by the Auditor-General, who may report to Parliament upon them. In carrying out his audit responsibility, the Auditor-General is possessed of powers of enquiry similar to those conferred upon him in connection with the State's general finances.

Commonwealth

The Commonwealth corporations, unlike some of the State corporations, lack independent borrowing powers.([85]) The permanent capital required by them is appropriated by the Parliament and advanced to the corporation on terms and conditions decided by the Treasurer. Where a Commonwealth corporation has a temporary need for capital to supplement funds provided by parliamentary appropriation, its recourse is to bank overdraft, almost invariably with the Commonwealth Trading Bank and mostly under Government guarantee.

The expenditures of the Commonwealth Railways Commission and the Australian Broadcasting Commission form part of the budget and are appropriated annually, like those of an ordinary government department. The finances of the other Commonwealth corporations have, however, been separated from the budget, and are not subject to annual appropriation. Each corporation is authorised to maintain its own bank account, into which are paid capital moneys and revenue, and from which it has a very substantial measure of freedom to make drawings to meet capital and operating expenditure. This is a rather broad statement of the position. Important differences in financial methods exist between one corporation and another. These mainly relate to the provision of capital funds, the return required on such funds, and the question of repayment of capital. These differences

([85]) This could well be due to the fact that the Commonwealth has for some years financed its capital works from revenue.

depend upon the nature of each individual enterprise, the existence or other-wise of competition, and a number of other factors.

The Australian National Airlines Commission may be taken as an example of the kind of provisions which apply where a corporation is in competition with a private enterprise. The funds required by the Commission to carry out its functions are provided (*a*) by capital advances from parliamentary appropriations, nominally repayable but not subject to any sinking fund conditions ; (*b*) by overdraft accommodation as required with the Common-wealth Bank, subject to a statutory limit of £1m. at any time. Operating profits or losses are carried in the Commission's account and, in lieu of a **fixed interest charge on its capital indebtedness to the Treasury, there is** provision for distribution to be decided by the Treasurer. This payment is in the nature of a dividend. For 1955-56 it was £174,800, equivalent to **4 per cent. on capital.([36])**

The Commission is required to submit to the responsible Minister annual estimates of receipts and expenditure ; to keep its accounts in such form as the Treasurer approves ; and to submit to Parliament an annual report and statement of accounts, the latter certified by the Auditor-General. In prac-tice, the Commission's accounts are kept on a "commercial" basis. The Commission is subject to income and other taxation, and in most respects its finances parallel those of its private enterprise competitors.

A somewhat different approach to the financing of corporations has been adopted with monopoly undertakings. A monopoly undertaking is charged interest on moneys advanced to it from the Treasury, and enjoys immunity from income taxation but not other Commonwealth taxes, the basic idea being that its charges for service provided should be related to the real cost of providing the service (including interest on capital employed). During the developmental stages of such an undertaking, the decision might be that interest will be charged but payment deferred until it is producing revenue. As with the Snowy Mountains Authority, interest indebtedness accumulated during development is capitalised and written into operating cost over a period of years.

The different financial methods that have been adopted with the corpora-tions in regard to capital funds have resulted less from statutory prescription than from decisions made by the Treasurer under discretionary powers in relation to these matters conferred upon him in the relevant statutes. The statutes do, however, contain a number of detailed provisions regarding financial methods. They usually specify, for example, what may be done with any profits and also the conditions under which money may be invested. Most of the corporations are empowered, subject to the approval of the Treasurer, to set aside such sums as they think proper for reserves and depreciation of assets. Some are required to keep their accounts in a form approved by the Treasurer ; others have the form of their accounts prescribed by regulation. The statutes also require that the accounts of the corporation shall be inspected and audited at least once yearly by the Auditor-General of the Commonwealth.

A restriction on the autonomy of the corporations in financial manage-ment that deserves special notice is the statutory requirement that certain

---

([36]) See *Eleventh Annual Report*, 1955-56, p. 4.

transactions be reserved for the approval of the Minister. The Australian Coastal Shipping Commission, for example, shall not, except with the approval of the Minister, purchase or dispose of assets for a consideration exceeding £50,000. With most of the other corporations the amount is less— usually £5,000.

While the nature of the statutory restrictions upon the financial autonomy of the corporations can readily be ascertained, the extent to which their financial autonomy is otherwise restricted in practice cannot so readily be discovered. A few of the corporations work in accord with financial directives, presumably issued to them by the Minister, with the Treasurer's approval. These apparently define in some detail the procedures that are to be followed by the authority in fulfilling the financial provisions of the legislation.[37]

CONTROL BY MINISTERS AND PARLIAMENT

The statutes establishing statutory corporations, as well as prescribing the constitution, powers and duties of the corporation, also empower a Minister to exercise some control over the operations of the corporation. Some of the kinds of powers granted to the Minister have already been noticed. Often, for example, the statute requires that the Minister's approval be sought before the corporation does certain things, such as purchase or dispose of assets above a specified value, or pay a salary above a specified amount. Sometimes also the statutes empower the Minister to give directions on particular matters. The Minister may, for example, direct the National Airlines Commission to establish, alter, or continue to maintain, any specified airline service if he considers it in the interest of Australia so to do.[38]

The matters over which the Minister may exercise control vary from corporation to corporation, and need not be further enumerated. The essential point to be noticed is that there has been a marked tendency to increase the Minister's powers of control over the governing boards of the corporations. In some states, especially those with a long record of Labour Party rule, many of the corporations have been placed under all-embracing ministerial direction and control. In New South Wales the relevant statute usually contains a provision which reads: "In the exercise and discharge of its powers, authorities, duties and functions, the Commission shall be subject in all respects to the control and direction of the Minister."

Ministers are responsible to Parliament for the exercise (or the non-exercise) of all their statutory powers and duties. Thus the more statutory powers of control possessed by a Minister in respect of a particular board, the more the affairs of the board are directly the concern of Parliament. The extent to which Parliament does, and should, exercise control over the

---

[37] For a copy of the financial directive issued to the Snowy Mountains Authority, see Commonwealth Parliament Joint Committee on Public Accounts, *Twenty Second Report*, p. 104.

[38] The relevant legislation provides, however, that if in any year any such service operated at the direction of the Minister shows a loss, and the whole of the corporation's operations show a loss, then the corporation is entitled to be reimbursed by the Government to the extent of the lesser of the two losses.

boards of corporations is a difficult question which will not be discussed here. Reference will be made merely to particular forms of parliamentary control.

Neither at Commonwealth nor State levels have there been established special Parliamentary committees, such as the Select Committee on Nationalised Industries in Great Britain, to acquire knowledge of the operations of statutory corporations necessary to make parliamentary control more effective. Following upon the report of the Parliamentary Joint Committee on Wireless Broadcasting in 1942, the Commonwealth Parliament established a Standing Committee on Broadcasting with a view to reconciling "the Australian Broadcasting Commission's independence with the political conception that all activities of government or quasi-government authorities should be subject, in the final analysis, to parliamentary control". That committee was in existence for a number of years, but was not successful in securing the objects for which it was appointed and was abandoned.[39]

The statutes require the corporations to render annual reports and financial statements to the Minister who is usually, but not always, required to transmit these to Parliament. Usually neither these reports, nor the Auditor-General's report on the financial statements, provide an occasion for debate in Parliament upon the affairs of the corporation concerned.

Parliamentary questions about the activities of corporations tend to be treated in much the same way as questions about the activities of ministerial departments, partly, no doubt, because there are so many points at which the Minister has been granted powers in relation to the corporation's activities. Sometimes the Minister will give information supplied to him by the Board on matters for which he will not accept responsibility.[40] There has been little discussion about the principles which should relate to Parliamentary questions on the affairs of the corporations; nor has the Speaker given any specific ruling upon this subject as has happened in the House of Commons.

While that is the general position, the role of the Joint Committee of Public Accounts in the Commonwealth Parliament requires special mention. That Committee, first appointed in September, 1952, has been re-appointed by subsequent parliaments, and from the outset has had as its Chairman Professor F. A. Bland, who formerly occupied the Chair of Public Administration in the University of Sydney. The duties of the Committee include examining the accounts of the receipts and expenditure of the Commonwealth and also each report and statement of the Auditor-General, and directing the attention of Parliament to any matter in these, or any circumstances connected with them, which it deems fit. The Committee thus has some responsibility for inquiring into the accounts of the statutory corporations. An inquiry of special importance was that made by the Com-

---

[39] See Joan Rydon, "The Australian Broadcasting Commission, 1942-1948", *Pub. Admin.* (*Sydney*), XI, Dec., 1952, pp. 194 ff.

[40] For example, when questioned about the cost of the new Commonwealth Bank at Hobart, Senator Spooner replied for the Treasurer: "The question concerns the internal administration of the bank, which is a matter for the bank to determine. However, the Governor of the bank has informed me that the total cost of the bank's new Hobart premises . . . was about £1,000,000." *Com. Parl. Debs.* (*Senate*), V. S. 4, p. 905, 21 Oct., 1954.

mittee during 1955 into the Australian Aluminium Production Commission. The Committee was led by this inquiry into a general examination of the nature and status of the statutory corporation. Its reports represent something of a landmark in the development of thought about the statutory corporation in Australia if only because they reveal some of the consequences of the failure to profit from Australia's long and varied experience with the statutory corporation.

CONCLUSION

Examination of the constitutions of selected statutory corporations in Australia has revealed great diversity among them, both in form and in degree of independence. In only a few cases, for example, the Rural Bank of New South Wales, do they possess the degree of independence envisaged by those, who at the turn of the century, favoured the adoption of this instrument of government. The general tendency, which has become more marked since the thirties, has been to restrict the independence of the corporations.

This tendency has been lamented by some writers, who have suggested that it has resulted from the inherent inability of politicians and public servants to leave well alone. However that may be, there appear to be other and more important reasons for this trend, which is also to be observed in many other countries, including the United Kingdom, Canada and the United States. The trend has occurred during a period in which the economic activities of governments have greatly increased and in which new kinds of responsibility for the economic health of the nation have been assumed by governments. These developments have required that an attempt be made to co-ordinate and control the policies of corporations so that the policy of the government as a whole might be free from contradiction.

Because of the importance to the Australian economy of the many enterprises operated by statutory corporations, there would be fairly general agreement that the question of the public accountability of these corporations could not have been ignored. Not all would agree, however, that the forms of control to which the corporations have been subjected, provide the most satisfactory solution to this question. In particular, it would appear that the increase in Ministerial powers, and especially the granting of all embracing powers to the Minister, as in New South Wales, has tended to blur the distinction between a statutory corporation and a ministerial department. This could create a situation in which the corporation becomes an instrument for combining the worst, rather than the best, features of the two worlds of business and government.

These developments do not necessarily mean that the statutory corporation has lost its usefulness as an administrative agency. They do, however, suggest that it is important to examine more closely than hitherto the reasons for establishing statutory corporations and the circumstances in which this agency is to be preferred to a ministerial department. It is customary to claim that a statutory corporation has superior flexibility and business efficiency. Such a claim has reference only to a particular class of corporation, that engaged in commercial activities. It ignores the wide range of other governmental activities apart from commercial enterprise where the statutory corporation has proved its usefulness. It also ignores the fact that, as a result of the controls that have come to be exercised over its operations, the qualities usually claimed for the statutory corporation have largely disappeared. One consequence of an examination of the kind suggested could be a recognition that, for the administration of some activities, a ministerial department is to be preferred to a statutory corporation. Another consequence could be a clearer recognition of the fields in which the statutory corporation is a particularly suitable agency because it can overcome certain limitations of the ministerial department. The upshot could well be that, where the statutory corporation is the agency chosen, more satisfactory methods than hitherto will be devised for blending autonomy and public accountability.([44])

([44]) For a general discussion of this question see Leicester Webb, "Freedom and the Public Corporation", Pub. Admin., (Sydney), XIII, June, 1954, pp. 101 ff.

Chapter Five

SOCIAL SERVICES

RONALD MENDELSOHN

By social services we mean those services of government designed to maintain or improve the personal welfare of individuals, as distinct from protecting their physical security or helping economic activities. Because the social services cover many needs, and because they have grown up one by one in response to particular requirements, they now form a large and rather ill-assorted group. As a result, they can be classified in various ways, two of which may help in understanding what follows.

On the one hand we may distinguish *individual* or *direct services* from *environmental services*. The former directly help the individual to cope with the vicissitudes and hazards of life, sometimes by economic aid, as with unemployment allowances, and sometimes by personal advice or supervision, as with vocational guidance or probation services. Child endowment would come under this heading, even though that implies that a family is one of the vicissitudes of life! The environmental services, such as public health, factory inspection or the provision of public parks, are intended to create and maintain favourable conditions for the personal development of whole classes of people or of the community as a whole.

This classification helps us, by the way, to see that social services do not consist entirely of hand-outs or benefits to everyone. They may involve supervision of the individual's behaviour in his own interest, as in the cases of child welfare and probation. They may impose standards of behaviour on individuals in the general interest, as in the cases of factory inspection, sanitary regulations or public health requirements. These and other examples also show that none of the classifications is watertight when applied to particular activities of government. Education is a direct service to the individual, and so not an "environmental" service. But it is provided, and compulsorily, for everyone in a given age-group, not just to meet the specific emergencies of particular individuals. Again, some government functions have both an economic and a social service element inextricably combined in them, as for example industrial arbitration which may be used to maintain economic stability as well as to protect the employee.

The second way of classifying the social services is to distinguish the *social security services,* which maintain or raise people's income by providing money to the individual or family to meet some actual or assumed need, and include the various types of pensions and also child endowment ; and second, the *social welfare services,* including benefits in kind, skilled services and treatment, which cannot conveniently be obtained by an individual through his own efforts. Examples of the latter are public health services, education, and child welfare services. In Australia, with certain exceptions, the social security services have tended to pass into the hands of the Commonwealth

Government, while the welfare services have become a major function of the States.

This division of functions is the result rather of accident than design. The social services are mostly a product of the twentieth century, and their wide development was not visualized by the fathers of Federation. But the division is quite a good working arrangement, because as a rule the more a function requires to take into account the individual needs of the citizen, the closer it should be to the "grass roots", and the further away from the central government. Conversely, the more a function can be reduced to routine, especially if it involves payment of money, the greater are the advantages of centralized administration. And the social security services in Australia have been administered essentially as a fairly impersonal business, in which equality and uniformity of treatment between individuals and regions have been the keynotes; while the social welfare services have laid stress on the needs of the individual, and the separate treatment of each person.

The present division can best be seen by listing the functions of Commonwealth and State Governments:

COMMONWEALTH

Age Pensions.
Invalid Pensions.
Widows' Pensions.
Unemployment Benefits.
Sickness Benefits.
Special Benefits.
Child Endowment.
Tuberculosis Allowances.
Maternity Allowances.
Public Health (certain aspects).
Milk in Schools Scheme.
National Health Service.
Rehabilitation of the Physically Handicapped.
Commonwealth Employment Service.
Home Nursing Subsidy.
University Benefits—
    Commonwealth Scholarships
    Grants to Universities.
Repatriation Benefits—
    Including war pensions for ex-servicemen and their dependants, physical and other rehabilitation and treatment of ex-servicemen (Commonwealth Reconstruction Training Scheme, hospital treatment, etc.).

STATE

Education.
Public Health.
Child Welfare.
Hospitals.
Mental Hygiene.
Maternal and Child Hygiene.
Health of Schoolchildren.
Housing and Slum Clearance.
Relief (residual).
Workers' Compensation.
Home Helps.
Protection of aboriginals.
Corrections (prisons, probation, remedial training, etc.).
Legal assistance.
Protection of Workers (factory legislation, minimum wage legislation, etc.).
Physical Education.

G 78713—5   K 5673

The principal items in the Commonwealth list are thus monetary benefits, and the principal State activities are devoted to humane service. There are certain overlaps, for example public health in some of its aspects is a concern of both Commonwealth and State. The Federal Government is necessarily concerned with external aspects of health, particularly quarantine, and the Constitution visualized that the Commonwealth would be restricted to this field. But for various reasons the Commonwealth has tended to expand its activities, as described later in this chapter. An item in the list above that may appear anomalous is the rehabilitation of the physically handicapped. The justification for Commonwealth intervention in this field has been the urgency of starting a nation-wide programme; it grew out of an initial concern with the rehabilitation of ex-service personnel.

The division between "social security" and "social welfare" can only be partial as the two main divisions of social service rarely function in isolation from each other. The Commonwealth has found it necessary, for instance, to employ constantly expanding staffs of professional social workers within such Departments as Social Services and Immigration to extend personal casework services to individuals, supplementary to the main statutory services such Departments were initially established to provide. Conversely, State agencies, primarily organised around individual counselling and supervision, nevertheless pay initial regard to the client's financial or material need, where such exists, either by contribution from the agency's own resources (e.g., N.S.W. Child Welfare) or by such organisation of community resources as the situation requires.

The retention by the States of the function of material relief to certain persons is an historical survival from the formerly complete responsibility of the States for monetary assistance to individuals. Step by step the States have surrendered the function, but there remain a few people whose needs are not covered by Commonwealth benefits, and some also for whom the Commonwealth benefits are inadequate; and the States have continued to provide for them. The residue are largely people with special problems, who require case work treatment; and this is in most instances an obvious State function.

HOW THE SOCIAL SERVICES AROSE

Every Western country during the last hundred years, and particularly during the last half-century, has developed a fairly full programme of social services, and it would have been surprising if Australia had not participated in the movement. But each country has its own history and its own conditions, and in some directions the development of Australia's social service system has been unusual. Australia was settled in the nineteenth century, largely by migrants from the British Isles. There, in the field of community provision for the needs of the unfortunate, two factors were paramount. One was the prevailing dislike of State intervention, and the other was the special form taken by relief to the destitute.

At the beginning of the nineteenth century Britain had a chaotic and demoralizing system of relief, which was felt by influential people to have caused the poor to lean too heavily on charity. The Poor Law of 1834, which was enacted to correct this state of affairs, was a unique administrative device. First, it laid it down as the duty of the State to support all those in distress, a social obligation which, for example, has never been expressly accepted in Australia. But because of the belief in the dangers of pauperism, people were to be discouraged by every means possible from asking for that relief which, if demanded, had to be accorded to them. The Poor Law administration was therefore made as harsh as possible.

The early Australian immigrants carried with them an abiding horror of the Poor Law. Of course, they also brought a social system which in its essentials closely resembled the one they had left behind. The same social problems were encountered; unemployment and the trade cycle, unequal distribution of wealth and income, poor working conditions. Australia never duplicated the deep poverty and distress of the mother country. But the workers were just as insecure as their counterparts in Britain against the hazards of sickness, poverty in old age, unemployment, and widowhood, and the burdens of bringing up a young family on a small income. Medical science and the practice of public health were in the same state of backwardness, and even the knowledge available was not being applied. Moreover, the characteristic clustering in the capital cities began early, bringing with it slums and disease.

Since the need for communal help arose very early, and the dislike of Government charity prevented the development of a regular system of relief, other means had to be found. In part private charity came to the rescue. The New South Wales Government, for example, chose as its agent the Sydney Benevolent Society, which it subsidized, and the Victorian Government did the same with the Victorian Ladies' Benevolent Society. But the independent nature of the settlers caused development to be slow. There was a striking lack of care for the under-dog, largely on the ground that the country ought not to be producing under-dogs. Since it was felt that the new society ought to be a more perfect one, it was at first denied that bad social conditions were reproducing themselves in the colonies. On the other hand, the radical outlook of many of the new settlers made them advocates of legislation to improve the lot of the worker. The influence and numbers of this group increased after the depression of the 1890's, when the vision of unlimited plenty for all disappeared. There began a period of social experiment which for a time placed Australians in the forefront of social advance.

A distinction should be made here between the first State regulatory activities, which were largely concerned with improving working conditions, and the later legislation by which the State itself took steps to improve individual welfare. The early reforms did not involve much government expenditure. The period of the 1890's, which earned the country its reputation for advanced social reform, was devoted mainly to attempts to protect the workers—minimum wage legislation, shop and factory legislation, protection for women and children at work. This legislation was concerned with regulating the relations between citizens. Only at the end of the century was there some old age pensions legislation in New South Wales and Victoria. So in 1900 the social services were still not visualized as likely to be the source of much governmental activity, especially at the federal level, and the Australian constitution contains little more reference to social service matters than the United States Constitution of 1787, or Canada's Constitution of 1867. The only specific references were the powers given to the Commonwealth by section 51 to legislate on quarantine and on invalid and old age pensions.

Four distinct periods can be traced in Australian social service development. In the first period, up to the foundation of the Commonwealth, action was largely confined to the environmental services of health and education, though, almost coincidentally with Federation, State old age pensions were introduced. In the second period, between 1901 and 1914, the Commonwealth introduced invalid and old age pensions and maternity allowances, and the States began to pass workmen's compensation laws.

The third period begins with the outbreak of the 1914 war, when fresh social legislation largely ceased, and ends with the outbreak of the second war in 1939. The first war was responsible for legislation to protect and rehabilitate ex-servicemen and their dependants, and this legislation was extended in the second war. But inter-war social legislation was meagre, though N.S.W. pioneered widows' pensions and child endowment, Victoria made some provision for widows, and Queensland introduced unemployment insurance. The Commonwealth made two attempts to introduce social insurance legislation, both of which failed because of opposition from interested groups. And all States were forced during the depression of the 1930's to set up emergency relief schemes; but these left no permanent trace. More progress was made on the social welfare side, with the slow building up of the State educational, health, maternal and child welfare and similar projects; and towards the end of the period three States enacted slum clearance legislation, and Victoria actually started slum clearance operations.

The fourth period, still unfinished, began with the introduction by the first Menzies Government (1939-1941) of Australia-wide child endowment. Then the Labour Governments of Curtin (1941-45) and Chifley (1945-49) brought in laws giving widows' pensions, sickness and unemployment benefits, funeral benefit, hospital and pharmaceutical benefits, and making provision for a national health service. The latter they were unable to implement, but it is being progressively brought into force by the later Menzies administrations (1949 onwards).

The Chifley Government codified the newly enlarged social security structure into the 1947 Social Services Consolidation Act. This Act followed the referendum of 1946, which gave to the Commonwealth power to legislate on "the provision of maternity allowances, widows' pensions, child endowment, unemployment, pharmaceutical, sickness and hospital benefits, medical and dental services (but not so as to authorize any form of civil conscription), benefits to students and family allowances". These were all subjects upon which the Commonwealth had previously legislated (relying upon its general powers to raise and spend money for its own purposes) but which had been thrown into doubt by a judgment of the High Court. The Commonwealth still possesses no widely drawn powers in the social service field, and presumably it is unable to legislate in any new area not specifically listed in the Constitution. For example, it probably could not introduce a social security type plan to replace workers' compensation, as Great Britain has done.

Four interesting developments round out the story of the growth of the social welfare State. The first is the establishment during the war years of the Commonwealth Employment Service, a general placement body linked with the Department of Social Services for unemployment benefit purposes. The second is the establishment of the Commonwealth Office of Education and the Universities Commission, which are mainly concerned with the support of students and subsidy of University expenses. Third is the emergence of the States as major construction authorities for rental housing, financed under an agreement with the Commonwealth Government; and fourth is the development of the National Health Service.

THE SOCIAL SECURITY SERVICES

Social security cannot itself free men from the fear of want, because it does little about the basic standard of living, which depends upon total production. No amount of redistribution of incomes will cure a really severe depression, should one occur. Social security is a redistributive process, so it depends for its success upon there being sufficient to redistribute. A very poor country has little scope for schemes of redistribution.

A definite price has to be paid. To allow the spread of security everyone must agree to pool part of his income and let the government spend it for him. People who might think they could provide for themselves, or people with low risks (for example young healthy workers) have part of their income removed from them to benefit others who are more likely to suffer illness, unemployment and so on. This is a redistributive process which has, no doubt, net benefits in welfare, but not necessarily net benefits for each individual; and it does mean that the government invades private life and private financial arrangements for an end which, however good for some, is less so for others. However, there is no doubt that, consciously or unconsciously, people have decided to pay the price of social security.

Social security systems then, may be regarded as any form of organization of a general character designed to ensure income security for all, or a substantial proportion, of the community. They take the form of compensation to persons for lack of income from their own efforts or from those of their breadwinner, and also of health services designed to restore the sufferer to full earning capacity and to prevent him and his dependants from incurring undue costs for maintenance of health. The Australian social security system covers most of the income hazards to security, but on the health side the structure is still being developed.

The principal social security services are now provided by the Commonwealth through the Department of Social Services([1]). Most of these services involve a means test, that is, to obtain them the applicant must show that his income and/or property do not exceed a figure laid down by legislation. Two services, child endowment and maternity allowances, are free of means tests and available to all. The means test services are designed to meet a need which must be proved; it cannot be assumed. Child endowment and maternity allowance, however, are given on the assumption that certain expenditures have to be made, and that people require to be compensated for

---

([1]) By 1956-57 the Commonwealth was paying to 554,000 aged and invalid pensioners an estimated £109 m. p.a.; to 45,000 widows pensions totalling £8.9 m. p.a., while a total of 153,000 weekly unemployment and sickness benefit payments was made at a cost of £4 m. p.a. In that year, over 1.3 m. families received child endowment in respect of 2.96m., children at a cost of £57m. p.a., and 217,000 mothers received maternity allowance at a cost of £3.5m. p.a. Total "Social Security" expenditure was £183.5m.

them. The means test probably originated with the idea that economic relief from the State should only be given in cases of proved economic need, and that in general it should be discouraged. In present-day Australia there has been a movement away from this idea. However, the cost of complete abolition of the means test is very great, and governments in the past have retained it for certain services according to considerations of financial and political expediency.

(a) *Age and Invalid Pensions* may be treated together. Age pensions are given at 65 for men and 60 for women. Invalid pensions are given to persons permanently incapacitated for work or permanently blind, who must have become so during residence in the country([2]). Residential qualification for an age pension is 20 years, and for an invalid pension five years. British citizenship is required. The weekly pension is the same for both([3]) and is equal for men and women. There is an allowable income which pensioners may receive without reduction of income, but over that figure the pension is reduced by the amount of the excess; that is, earnings over the allowed amount are in effect taxed one hundred per cent., and beyond a certain income no pension is paid. A full double pension is paid for married couples both eligible, and they may receive extra income where there is a dependent child.

The means test for property disregards the value of the claimant's home, if he lives in it, and furniture and effects, and surrender value up to £750 of life insurance policies; the effect of other property is to cause a progressive reduction of the pension. If other property worth more than £2,250 is owned, no pension is payable. The income and property of a husband and wife are deemed to be half their combined means, even if only one is a claimant.

Invalid pensions are not granted before 16 years of age; a degree of incapacity for work of 85 per cent. or more attracts pension; but the payment is ostensibly for permanent incapacity for work; and a less degree of incapacity or a temporary total incapacity does not render a person eligible for partial or temporary pension. The income test for blind persons is more liberal. Where any invalid pensioner has dependent children, he may have some additional income for each child and still draw a full pension. In addition, the wives and children of invalid pensioners get special allowances. Age pensioners who are permanently incapacitated may receive wife's and child's allowance. An age pensioner over 70 years of age is deemed to be permanently incapacitated and eligible for wife's and child's allowance unless there is evidence to the contrary.

The Act requires pensioners to be of good character; they must be "deserving" of a pension, and age pensioners must not have deserted husband, wife or children. These provisions are now almost nominal. They are survivals of an age when it was felt that relief should be given only to the "deserving" poor.

([2]) This condition is waived if the claimant has resided in Australia for not less than 20 years.

([3]) The present rate (1958) is £4 7s. 6d. a week plus 10s. a week supplementary pension for single pensioners (or married pensioners, where only one is in receipt of a pension and the other is not in receipt of an allowance), who pay rent and are entirely dependent on their pensions.

(*b*) *Unemployment and Sickness Benefits* are equal in amount, but have remained at a lower level than age and invalid pensions, probably because there has been but little call upon the benefits in the post-war period of high employment. Unemployment benefit is payable to a person between 16 and 65 (60 for women) who is unemployed, is capable of undertaking suitable work and has taken reasonable steps to obtain such work. A person previously self-employed can obtain benefit if he is now ready to take employment. A married woman may not draw sickness benefit if it is reasonably possible for her husband to support her, even if she has been in regular work.

Sickness benefit is payable where the person is temporarily incapacitated for work by reason of sickness or accident, and must be supported by the certificate of a medical practitioner. Additional income up to £2 per week may be earned before benefit is reduced. Property is not taken into account. Lower rates are payable for unmarried claimants under 21.

(*c*) *The Unemployment and Sickness Benefits Act,* 1944, also introduced a *"Special"* benefit which is given to a person who by reason of age, physical or mental disability or domestic circumstances, or for any other reason, is unable to earn a livelihood, is not qualified to receive sickness or unemployment benefit, and is not in receipt of an age, invalid or widows' pension or a service pension. The benefit has been applied among other cases, for persons of pensionable age temporarily unemployed but not wishing to apply for age pension, and to migrants required to take a course in civics or English; but the total paid out is small.

(*d*) *The Tuberculosis Act,* 1948, is an excellent example of the use of public funds to combat a specific public health hazard, because tuberculosis is a highly communicable disease. The Act introduced special higher rates for tuberculosis sufferers provided that they agree to refrain from working, and to undergo the prescribed treatment from time to time, and generally conducted themselves in the best interests of the campaign against tuberculosis. The allowance is continued, subject to the means test, until there is no further need for treatment, or the sufferer is no longer infectious and therefore no longer a public health hazard, or there is no immediate danger of relapse if tuberculosis allowance is withdrawn.

(*e*) A fourfold classification is adopted for the purpose of *Widows' Pensions,* according to the age of the widow and the dependency of children; and women may be classified as widows for receipt of benefit if their husbands are imprisoned or inmates of hospitals for the insane, or if they are divorced or deserted; even *de facto* "wives" are in some circumstances eligible for the pension. In brief, a widow does not get benefit below 50 years of age unless she has dependent children. If she is in necessitous circumstances, she may receive benefit for 26 weeks after her husband's death, whatever her age. The level of benefit depends upon the classification of the widow, and the provisions with regard to permissible income and property also vary; the Class A widow (a woman who has the custody, care and control of one or more children) may have considerable property (excluding home and furniture) and still receive a pension.

(*f*) *Funeral Benefit* is confined to the funerals of age or invalid pensioners, or those who would have been eligible for pension. It amounts to £10 or the cost of the funeral, whichever is the less.

(*g*) *Child Endowment* is a scheme of quite a different nature. It is available for all children under 16 years of age who are permanent residents. There is no means test. The benefit, which is paid to the mother([4]) every four weeks, is required to be applied to the maintenance, training and advancement of the child. The rate of benefit is 5s. weekly for the first child, and 10s. weekly for each subsequent child. The benefits may be paid by cheque, by order books encashable at post offices or banks, or by credit to bank accounts.

(*h*) *Maternity Allowances* are the oldest Commonwealth benefit after invalid and age pensions, coming into operation in 1912. Benefit is now universal, being paid without means test for all births. The amount varies, the minimum being given where there are no previous children under 16, with rises where there are three or more such children, and extra for each child at multiple births. It is available to all permanent residents, regardless of nationality.

(*i*) Another contribution to the growing array of social security services is *Hospital Benefit,* whereby the Commonwealth subsidizes the fees of hospital patients. The scheme has varied according to the Government in power, the Chifley Government when introducing it requiring the States to provide free treatment in public wards of hospitals, that is, to give up collecting fees, in return for a hospital benefit of 6s. (later 8s.) per day in respect of every patient ordinarily resident in Australia. But the Menzies Government terminated that scheme, replacing it under the Hospital Benefits Act, 1951, by a basic payment of 8s. per day for all patients, plus 4s. per day for all patients who are members of an approved Hospital Insurance Organization([5]). The scheme is being progressively extended to all patients; for example, patients in approved private hospitals who are members of a hospital insurance organization which pays from its own funds at least 6s. per day get the Commonwealth benefit of 12s. per day, making a total of 18s. The present Commonwealth Government encourages the extension of voluntary hospital insurance coverage, though this so far falls a good deal short of complete community protection.

(*j*) *Health Insurance.* In addition to hospital insurance, the Commonwealth Government now also subsidizes voluntary insurance against medical expenses. This takes the form of supplementation of insurance payments by private insurance organizations, covering the expenses of medical consultations and operations. Specialist consultations are covered, but not dental or optometrical services or appliances.

(*k*) *Pensioner Medical Service.* A service of a different kind is provided to age, invalid, widow and service pensioners, and to their dependents, subject to a not severe means test. They receive free general practitioner medical service and free pharmaceutical benefits. Persons receiving tuberculosis allowance and their dependants are also eligible. The medical practitioners are paid by the Government on a fee-for-service basis.

(*l*) *Free Drugs.* There is no general pharmaceutical service, but so-

([4]) It is also payable to institutions caring for children, a father with the custody of his children following separation or divorce, etc.

([5]) In 1957 the additional Hospital Benefit payable to insured persons entitled to receive benefit from a private organisation of 16s. a day or more was increased from 4s. to 12s. a day.

called "life-saving" drugs are supplied free to all persons, whether insured or not, on prescription from a medical practitioner.

(m) *Home Nursing.*—A recent addition to the list of National Health Service benefits was provided by the Home Nursing Subsidy Act, 1956. Grants are made from the National Welfare Fund to non-profit organizations to cover the salaries of nursing sisters visiting homes as district nurses. The subsidy covers any expansion of their activities. A new organisation commencing operations will receive half the salary of each nurse employed.

The scheme has two purposes. It will save hospital beds and it will cater for persons who do not wish to go to hospital for various reasons. Hospitals are short of beds, and home nursing is economical. Many persons, especially older ones, are happier being treated at home. Moreover, the district nurse can give valuable help in the field of preventive medicine by instruction in general health matters, nutrition, food habits, etc. There are real advantages in sending a nurse into the home rather than sending a patient into hospital.

(n) *Workers' Compensation.*—Treatment in this Chapter of the protection given by law to the worker suffering injury or disease while about his employer's business must be inadequate, for two reasons: the matter is the subject of separate State laws which, whilst similar in principle, differ greatly in detail; and over the years the law has become technical and complex, if not, as Sir John Cockburn put it, "a happy hunting ground for the pettifogging lawyer". Compensation to workers suffered from being introduced before the idea of insurance was popularized. It remains cast in its original mould of a legal contest between employer and worker. The worker is dependent upon his ability to prove his case in a law-court; but in Great Britain the whole procedure has been changed, and replaced by a social insurance scheme which awards pensions from the State to injured workers.

Workers' compensation in Australia is based on the pioneer British Act of 1897, and its principles are still largely the principles of that Act. Constitutionally the power of the Commonwealth to legislate on this subject is limited to its own employees and territories and to seamen.

For the rest, the State Acts establish a right of civil claim by the worker on the employer, enforceable by litigation if, as is often the case, agreement cannot be attained by negotiation. From 1902 to 1918 all the States passed legislation on similar lines. In the years which have followed amendments have often been an annual event, without fundamentally changing the original principles, except that industrial diseases are now compensable. An employee is entitled to compensation if he suffers an injury as a result of his employment, irrespective of whether he or another employee is guilty of negligence. Compensation is only given for reduction in earning capacity. Where death results compensation is given in the form of a lump sum payment to the dependants, not as a pension. Where total incapacity results the compensation is a weekly payment of a percentage of the average weekly earnings before the injury, with a weekly maximum limit; in cases of partial incapacity a weekly payment is made, depending upon the degree of incapacity. The Acts cover persons working under a contract of employment, with a maximum limit of weekly income varying from State to State. Casual workers are mostly excluded.

The major disappointment of the Act has been the mass of litigation to which it has given rise. The Australian States have made insurance against the liability to pay compensation compulsory on employers. The insurance companies have unlimited funds to fight law suits, and an interest in winning all suits which may involve matters of principle. This has turned an apparently simple scheme into a legal jungle. The States have tried to help by establishing special workers' compensation tribunals, part of whose function is to enlighten employer and worker on their rights and obligations.

The Australian schemes are now ripe for scrutiny. There are several objections to present arrangements. One is the lack of uniformity between States. More important are the high cost, uncertainty and general inappropriateness of the schemes, which rely upon lump sum payments when regular weekly pensions would be more suitable. Cost of administration is also unduly high. The schemes tend to worsen industrial relations by turning an industrial hazard into an occasion for antagonism between employer and worker.

There are two possible ways out. One is to adopt the Canadian method of setting up a tribunal as the insurer, which is generally responsible for the welfare of the worker suffering injury, and to which the employer pays premiums. The other is to adopt the British system, transforming the scheme into a social insurance. The British National Insurance (Industrial Injuries) Act, 1946, swept away the 1897 system and substituted a social security benefit, financed by weekly contributions from workers and employers. The difficulty about the introduction of a scheme on social security lines in this country is the Commonwealth's lack of power. It would be possible for the States to refer to the Commonwealth the necessary power; but such a move will not come until the subject has been discussed and aired at some length. There has been no full-length study of the various schemes, nor any apparent realization of the legal bog into which they have descended.

Relief Activities.—Most States now confine their relief activities to persons in destitute circumstances not eligible for some form of Commonwealth benefit, and especially to women with dependent children. In many cases they supplement Commonwealth benefits, where these are felt to be inadequate; and they provide benefits for people awaiting determination of claims for Commonwealth benefit. States such as New South Wales maintain an active organization for coping with disasters such as floods or fires.

As the volume of their responsibilities diminishes and they find themselves left with the intractable core of social problems, the States, in varying degrees, have tended to develop the family casework attitude to their clients. It is a criticism of Australian social services that they have tended to lay undue stress on money payments, and that a monetary payment has too often been regarded as a sufficient solution for problems of social maladjustment; but this attitude is changing.

Queensland's example is typical. It confines its relief to persons ineligible for Commonwealth benefits ([5a]), and refuses benefit to all persons fit for work, referring them to the Commonwealth Employment Service (where they may, if eligible, receive unemployment benefit). But in its Depart-

---

([5a]) With some exceptions, e.g., the Relief Assistance Branch of the Department of Labour and Industry will pay relief to a woman awaiting payment of widows' pension.

ment of Health there is a senior social worker, whose duties have included both health and welfare work, including advice to mothers, assistance to women during confinement, and arranging conveyance to, and admissions to, hospital; another feature of her work is the care of unmarried mothers and deserted wives. This work in other States is often the duty of the child welfare authorities.

In New South Wales, which is frequently the leader in welfare matters, the social welfare services of the Department of Child Welfare and Social Welfare are based on the family casework principle, and are "designed not merely to extend help by way of actual benefits but to alleviate the problems of distress from a practical angle and to adjust as far as possible the circumstances causing distress . . . .; where a case has been included in the special Social Welfare class . . . . the interest and care of the Social Welfare Branch is not relaxed whilst the need for help and advice continues".

The task of the social caseworker is to facilitate a healthy adjustment by the individual and the family to life as a whole. The problems faced, being social, psychological and spiritual as well as economic, cannot be solved by economic means alone, or even by the provision of free State services, whatever their form. Sympathetic and skilled attention and treatment for personal problems are also necessary. The more complicated becomes the society, and the greater grow its demands on each person, the stronger is the likelihood that some persons will fall below the general standard, and will have to be assisted.

Some payments of a relief nature continue to be needed. All States grant assistance to women on whom children are dependent, such as unmarried mothers, widows, deserted wives, and wives whose husbands are in prison, or sick, or unemployed. Commonwealth pensions are supplemented where there are dependent children. The example of Western Australia may be taken. This State provides relief payments as supplements to Commonwealth social service benefits or otherwise, under five categories: invalid and age pensions, widows' pensions, non-pension rate, sickness benefit, unemployment benefit. There is a scheme of "unit" payments whereby assistance varies according to the size of family. At October, 1958, figures, a widow applying for supplementary benefit from the State might receive 12s. 6d. for her first child, and 15s. for successive children, so that if she had eight children she could receive from a combination of State and Commonwealth benefits 355s. (Commonwealth widows' pension 162s. 6d., child endowment 75s., and 117s. 6d. from the Western Australian Child Welfare Department. which administers all relief payments). The basic non-pension rate (for people not entitled to Commonwealth benefits) was 67s. 6d. plus 30s. for the first child and 15s. for successive children. Sickness and unemployment benefit are somewhat higher, owing to the recent increase in Commonwealth benefits.

The New South Wales authorities continue to operate an extensive relief system, which includes the State organization for the relief of major disaster. The scheme is interesting for the extent of its decentralization; there are special officers of the Department of Child Welfare and Social Welfare in several parts of Sydney, in the Wollongong area, and on the northern coalfields, and officers go out from these centres to many localities throughout the State. The State continues to issue so-called Food Relief and Cash Benefit, but only in cases where an applicant is in need pending payment of Commonwealth assistance, or is ineligible for Commonwealth assistance. The Child Welfare Department subsidizes Commonwealth pensions where children are involved.

Unlike Western Australia, New South Wales does not supplement Commonwealth unemployment benefit; it provides an amount roughly equivalent in cases where the applicant, for some reason, is ineligible for the Commonwealth benefit. The essence of the State's relief is that it is available without delay; and this is, perhaps, an implied criticism of the Commonwealth's benefits, which are apparently somewhat slower to operate. Apart from money payments, if the applicant is in immediate need an interim food order is issued; but before regular relief is instituted a house visit is usually made by an experienced Social Welfare Officer.

New South Wales gives several other benefits in appropriate cases. Additional milk is given for expectant and nursing mothers and young children. Special foods are given for infants and for persons suffering from malnutrition or in ill-health. Medical attention and medicine is provided through approved medical practitioners and pharmacists for relief recipients. A winter and summer distribution is made of supplies of clothing and footwear to cash benefit recipients. Baby outfits are provided to expectant mothers in poor circumstances. There are free issues of blankets. Free spectacles are provided to persons in indigent circumstances. A wide variety of surgical aids is supplied to indigent persons. Hearing aids are given to similar people. Free transport is provided in special cases, including transport to and from hospital. Persons under Court order for eviction are given cash assistance to move and to find themselves fresh accommodation. Assistance is given for funerals. And, most important from a financial viewpoint, a supplementary children's allowance is paid to widows in receipt of Commonwealth Widows' Pensions.

In addition to cash benefit, there is another benefit known as Special Cash Assistance, which can take the form of supplementation of small incomes, lump sum payments, or purchases on behalf of a family. Special help is given by way of cash grants, clothing, bedding, food orders, tents, household effects, etc., to families rendered destitute by fire, flood or other catastrophe. Similar services are available in other States, to a greater or less extent; and they provide a valuable, if not so costly, addition to the basic Commonwealth services.

Social Security: The Policy Issues

As we have seen, there are three principles operating in the finance and administration of Australian social security services. Most services operate under a means test; child endowment and maternity allowances are universal and free from restrictions as to means or contribution; while the Menzies Government's encouragement of voluntary health insurance introduces a third element. The merits of these principles are best discussed against the background of the main types of social security system.

Many countries have adopted for their basic social security structure some variation of the principle of social insurance pioneered by Bismarck in Germany and extended by Great Britain. Strictly speaking, the insurance principle is incompatible with the application of a means test. In theory a member of a social insurance scheme receives his benefits as a result of the payment of regular contributions. The amount and duration of his benefit is dependent on his contribution record. An applicant for unemployment benefit, for example, has to show not only that he is involuntarily out of work, but also that he has a good record of contributions and has not exhausted the period of benefit to which these contributions entitle him. An applicant who has had a long spell of unemployment will find himself, sooner or later, refused benefit.

The special advantage of social insurance is that the applicant suffers no inquisition into his income or property; it is sufficient to prove that he is out of work, or sick, or the like. The principle is also supposed to have the financial advantage of keeping expenditure actuarially related to funds specially collected for the purpose. But the limited nature of the benefit and the limited extent of the coverage of social insurance mean that it does not provide a complete protection for the community, especially in time of economic stress which is precisely when social security is most needed. At such times many people are excluded from benefit, and some other means must be found to protect them. In the emergency of the Great Depression a second tier was added to the British scheme, the National Assistance service. The National Assistance Board provides benefits, at practically the same level as national insurance, to everyone in need, whatever his condition and whatever the cause. It is also used to supplement national insurance benefits for those who find them insufficient for their needs[*].

Thus Britain has established an exceptionally heavy and complex social insurance administration, involving an unprecedented programme of national book-keeping, since contributions have to be calculated in relation to income and pay-outs related to "entitlement". Yet it finds its system does not cover all cases. The major needs in a social security system are a universal coverage; adequate benefits; a method of finance which is adequate to meet all demands on the system though easy to collect and not too burdensome on any class; and finally reasonable simplicity of administration. The linking of contributions and benefits in social insurance makes sure that people pay up, but their contributions are insufficient to pay for all the benefits needed at all times.

A variation on the insurance principle is the encouragement of voluntary insurance for health purposes. The general plan is to assist and subsidize the development of voluntary organizations which will provide health cover for their members. A start has been made in Australia with hospital and medical insurance, as described above. The Scheme is similar to the discarded Approved Society principle in the pre-Beveridge National Health Insurance Scheme in Britain, and the inoperative 1938 Australian Act modelled on it. Costs of administration of such a scheme are high and coverage not complete. But it may well be the best which can be obtained in present circumstances. Ever since 1938 Commonwealth Governments have been negotiating, without success, with the medical profession for a

[*] There may of course be a case for supplementary assistance in special instances, even under a scheme like the Australian one. The 1958 Budget has recognised this, at least in part, by introducing a form of supplementary assistance at the rate of 10s. a week, to relieve hardship and improve the circumstances of single pensioners (and married persons, where only one is in receipt of an allowance), who pay rent and are entirely dependent on their pensions.

national health service. In the meantime a less than full scheme is better than no protection at all. The danger is that a partial scheme may prove a barrier to a full scheme later on, because of the special interests it has engendered.

If the insurance principle be discarded, we are left with schemes of benefits paid according to fixed rates and for unlimited periods, and not linked actuarially to specific contributions by the individual. The financing of such schemes is relatively simple, coming from the general revenues of the government, sometimes also from a special ear-marked tax. Such a system is free of contribution conditions, but if it is also free of means test, it is the most costly of all, since it provides benefits universally, simply upon proof of the event against which society offers protection—additions to the family, widowhood, invalidity, old age, sickness, unemployment, and so on. It is easy to administer, does not deter people from working or saving, and is preferable on all counts except its high cost.

The desire to limit this expense, along with the principle that available social assistance should be confined to those who really need it, has given rise to the means test which in practice is applied to most of the benefits paid under non-contributory, non-insurance social security schemes.

For the means test there is something to be said, despite its unpopularity. It is the system which confines benefit to those who really need it, and ensures that no one really requiring help goes without. The means test is the device used to determine (1) the existence of need as defined by law, and (2) the amount of benefit necessary to relieve that need. Under a means test system no more is taken from the taxpayers or contributors than is necessary to relieve need as defined by law. There is practically no taking of money by the exercise of the sovereign power of the State to give to persons who are not in need.

But while the means test is cheaper and less burdensome, it is disliked. It is felt to be damaging to people's dignity to have their affairs inquired into by public officials. The system savours of "charity", of discrimination between rich and poor. To qualify under the means test seems to some people an admission of economic failure in life. On the other hand, it is thought to discourage saving, to encourage dishonesty by the concealment of assets or income, and in the case of the aged, to deter people from working who would otherwise wish to continue. Again, the means test has to draw a line somewhere between those who qualify and those who do not, and there are bound to be anomalies and discontent in the borderline cases. Finally, the administration of the means test requires many officials and elaborate records.

To sum up, social insurance involves much book-keeping and does not cover everyone all the time ; State-assisted voluntary insurance is only a short-term expedient and in any case is only applicable to certain classes of social security ; while an uncompromising system of universal benefits paid out of general taxation is very expensive. At present, for example, to wipe out the means test on age pensions would double their cost.

On balance the writer's view is that perhaps the best social security scheme in terms of present needs is one of universal allowances paid for out of a fund refreshed by special ear-marked tax. The New Zealand and Canadian schemes which embody this principle would therefore repay study. Only a country which can afford high taxation can introduce such a scheme. Its benefits ought not to be invariable, but subject to changes upward or downward as national prosperity varies. Its effects upon willingness to work are still problematic. And its introduction would have to be timed carefully; a time of active inflation would be less auspicious for commencing it than a period of relative stability. A good deal more work and thought is needed before a really suitable scheme can be evolved.

THE WELFARE SERVICES

Bad social conditions affect everyone. No single individual, however rich or powerful, can create for himself an entirely favourable environment if the society around him is brutish, ignorant, poor, violent and sick. He cannot insure himself and his children against disease or the danger of physical attack. He cannot get unlimited pure water, fast and frequent transport, efficient hospitals equipped for research, first-class university teaching, good radio programmes, except on the foundation of an educated, prosperous mass society. Compare the lot of a Persian nobleman and an American middle-class businessman.

It is easy to see what the modern welfare State has done to change the conditions of life. It is more difficult to explain how and why the change has come about. What conditions have favoured the development of the social services? It must be a combination of opportunity, need and demand. The opportunity was provided by the simultaneous growth of knowledge and of wealth. The new knowledge came in the fields of medicine, human psychology and social problems of all sorts. Lister, Pasteur, Freud and a hundred others contributed to the new science. Another form of science also provided the means to ever-increasing wealth, from the days of Watt and the steam engine to those of Rutherford, Einstein and the atomic energy pile generating the promise of limitless electricity. The need came from the unhappiness of men, caused by disease and maladjustments of all kinds. The opportunity came with the development of political democracy and its insistent demands for government redress of popular grievance or social ills. Now no political party could survive which did not offer an ever widening programme of social welfare, whether in pensions, health, education or housing.

In Australia the States administer the social welfare services, and the influence of State Governments is therefore very wide. The quality of State administration—for example in child welfare, education, probation of criminals and prison administration—is very variable, and much good would flow from research on the various State administrations and a comparison of their differences. The States control education and most aspects of public health (including hospitals and mental health, maternal and child welfare and nutrition); regulate the conditions of work in factories and otherwise protect the worker; undertake housing and slum clearance; endeavour to reform the criminally minded adult and the delinquent child; relieve those who fall through the net of Commonwealth social security protection; administer workers' compensation (partly a social security function); and undertake such special functions as the anti-tuberculosis campaign and the provision of home helps. The Commonwealth also administers one welfare service, rehabilitation of the unfit, and its work in public health, education and nutrition involves close collaboration with State health authorities.

Public Health

Like education, public health was an established function well before federation. The nineteenth century was the time of the discovery of the main facts about the propagation of disease, and the application of this knowledge to the prevention of ill-health, especially in cities. The first health legislation was that of New South Wales, which for a good time applied also to the other colonies; but the New South Wales legislation was fragmentary, and the first full-scale public health legislation was the 1854 Victorian Health Act. Public health administration has always been one of the major activities of local authorities, more or less under the supervision of the State.

The public health activities of the States are now directed, in the broadest sense, to the maintenance and improvement of the physical and mental health of the community. They fall under eight main heads:

  (i) Environmental sanitation, including the limitation and suppression of infectious and preventable diseases (such things as control of sewers and other waste, ensuring cleanliness of streets and dwellings and other buildings, ensuring purity of water supply, etc.);

  (ii) control of food and drugs, poisons, etc.; control of killing of meat;

  (iii) control of infectious disease (compulsory notification of disease, vaccination and immunization, etc.);

  (iv) maintenance and control of hospitals;

  (v) maintenance and control of mental health institutions and administration of legislation with regard to mental health;

  (vi) responsibility for the special measures with regard to the health and welfare of mothers and babies, including baby health clinics, ante- and post-natal clinics, and other measures;

  (vii) responsibility for the operation of bodies regulating the professional groups in medicine—medical practitioners, nurses, pharmacists, opticians, and several others;

  (viii) administration of the special campaigns for the eradication of disease, such as the campaigns against tuberculosis and venereal disease, and maintenance of special clinics and institutions for this purpose.

The administration of public health shows an unusual pattern. In the two most populous States the administrative head of the controlling Department is a civil servant, and all the public health activities of the State are concentrated in the one Department of Health or Public Health. But the professional aspects of the work are recognized by the appointment of a senior medical officer, who is also head of a long-established health board. This has statutory duties in relation to sanitation and control of disease, especially as concern the duties of local authorities. In both cases, also, there is a Hospitals Commission, a statutory body, very largely autonomous, which supervises the operation and finance of hospitals, although these are not nationalized even public hospitals generally operating under independent charter.([7])

At first the established constitutional functions of the Commonwealth in relation to health were restricted to quarantine. But now it is has expanded its health functions in many directions. It maintains large hospitals for ex-servicemen. It administers the Commonwealth Serum Laboratories in Melbourne, which produce a wide range of biological and therapeutic preparations; it conducts health laboratories throughout Australia; it administers the School of Public Health and Tropical Medicine attached to the University of Sydney and the Australian Institute of Anatomy; it assists the National Fitness movement, mainly by means of selective grants to the States; it takes an interest in pre-school children, and in the nutrition of school children, sponsoring the Milk in Schools scheme; it assists in campaigns against cancer, venereal disease and tuberculosis; and (as indicated above) it is introducing, by degrees, a national health service, of which the first steps have been the provisions of a comprehensive medical and drug service to pensioners and their dependants, subsidies for hospital patients in the States, and subsidies to voluntary insurance against hospital and medical expenses. Most of these functions are administered by the Commonwealth Department of Health, with considerable decentralisation from the Director-General of Health in Canberra to his State Directors.

The nature of State administration may be illustrated by an examination of Victoria, which has the longest history of central administration of health. The 1854 Act provided for appointment of a Central Board of Health and local boards of health; appointment of officers of the Central Board, and of Medical Officers of Health and other officers by the local boards; and gave wide powers to the boards, including construction of drainage and sewers, oversight of sanitary conditions, control of food and noxious trades, provision of hospitals for contagious or infectious diseases. The boards were empowered to take action against an epidemic. For its time this was a most advanced Act. The central board still exists, and is now called the Commission of Public Health.

The first Department of Public Health in Victoria was established in 1889. After several changes of form a 1943 Act effected an administrative simplification by creating a Ministry of Health "to promote the health of the people of Victoria", which "serves as a central co-ordinating Health Department for the whole of the State, to supervise and correlate the manifold and diverse operations of State Medicine as they are initiated by Parliament."([8]) The duties of the Minister of Health are to take such steps as may be desirable to secure the preparation, effective carrying out, and co-ordination of measures conducive to the health of the people.

The Secretary is the permanent head of the Department for administrative purposes. It includes four main branches. The Chief Health Officer is head of three of them—The General Health Branch, Maternal and Child Hygiene Branch and Tuberculosis Branch—and a Mental Hygiene Authority is in

---

([7]) Queensland operates a system of free public hospitals through the Department of Health and Home Affairs, and 54 district Hospitals Boards. The work of State Departments of Health is outlined in the *Commonwealth Year Book*, see, e.g., 1956 ed., pp. 515-518.

([8]) *Health Bulletin*, Victoria, Jan.-June, 1946, p. 2275.

charge of the Mental Hygiene Branch. The Commission of Public Health, through the General Health Branch, oversees local health services, deals with infectious and industrial diseases, undertakes research and publishes reports and prepares regulations and model by-laws. The Government Medical Officer is responsible to the Secretary. The Hospitals and Charities Commission and various professional boards, although responsible to the Minister, do not come within the framework of the Department.

Wherever possible the Department works through local municipal councils or organisations sponsored by them. While the government bears the whole cost of treatment of infectious disease it uses municipal services in carrying out preventive measures such as immunization against diphtheria, "Salk" vaccination, etc., and reimburses councils half the nett costs involved in providing those services. The Department makes capital grants towards the cost of erection and establishment of infant welfare centres, kindergartens and old people's clubs and gives maintenance subsidies towards the running of those activities, play-centres, ante-natal services and home help schemes.

The Hospitals and Charities Commission was set up in 1948. It was preceded by a Charities Board created in 1923. It administers the Hospitals and Charities Fund and generally oversees the hospital and ambulance services of the State. It is the source of finance for public hospitals and charitable institutions and provides about three-quarters of capital expenditure on hospitals and approximately two-thirds of their maintenance income. The original intention was that the Fund should supplement where necessary the receipts of hospitals from other sources, but as in other States and other countries, the diminution of public charity and the growth of costs have caused the hospitals to lean more heavily on public funds. Victoria has not nationalized its hospitals; the Commission does not own public hospitals, its control being exercised through the grants made from the Hospitals and Charities Fund. Each public hospital is a corporate body conducted by a Committee of Management appointed principally by contributors to the funds of the hospital. The Commission's activities extend to the subsidy of benevolent homes, children's homes, and many philanthropic and benevolent associations.

Basically the functions of the health administrations in the other States are not dissimilar. New South Wales lacked a general Public Health Act until 1896, but health legislation goes back to the first part of the century, and public hospitals and mental hospitals were established early. Amongst the special activities of the New South Wales Department of Public Health may be mentioned the Division of Industrial Hygiene, a pioneering body established in 1923 and concerned solely with occupational health problems. Its first work included the investigation of silicosis, the control of atmospheric conditions in textile mills, and an examination of the incidence and control of lead poisoning. Its function was epitomized by Mr. Justice Piddington: "The principle to be followed is not that unhealthy conditions be allowed to continue and palliative sought in reduced hours or a solatium in increased wages, but the organized service of medical and engineering knowledge ought to be employed to abolish the unhealthiness of the condition."

Other sections of the New South Wales Department of Health include (a) the Division of Epidemiology, created to enable the department to play an effective part in the intensive study and control of infectious diseases; (b) the School Medical Service, first established in 1913-14, which operates mainly in the field of preventive medicine, and examines children two or three times in the course of their primary or secondary school career; (c) the School Dental Service, with its travelling clinics examining and treating children; (d) the Consultative Council for the Physically Handicapped, constituted to take over and extend the work of the Consultative Council for Infantile Paralysis. This body concentrates on after care of patients suffering from poliomyelitis, but also undertakes vocational training of physically handicapped persons.

The Commonwealth Government is also engaged in the work of rehabilitating the handicapped. Rehabilitation is seen as "the restoration of the handicapped to the fullest physical, mental, social and vocational usefulness of which they are capable". This scheme started in 1945 as part of the treatment of convalescent ex-members of the Forces not eligible for Repatriation benefits, and was extended in 1948 to certain categories of disabled civilians, mainly pensioners and sickness beneficiaries, and T.B. sufferers. The intention is to expand it to all classes of the community where a remediable disability is a substantial handicap to satisfactory employment. There is now a Rehabilitation Branch of the Commonwealth Department of Social Services.

It was an astonishing and rather perverted judgment which gave Australia in 1909 a protection for confirmed invalids, but no sickness benefit and no medical treatment for them. The history of legislation can be searched in vain for a more gratuitous invitation to permanent invalidism. A person whose earning capacity was impaired got no benefit unless he could persuade a doctor to certify him totally unfit; so there was a perpetual temptation to become and to stay unfit—not to take the effort to make use of whatever capacity to work remained. The new scheme changes this. Benefit continues during rehabilitation, and is even increased when the training stage is reached. The process of rehabilitation is divided into treatment, vocational assessment and training, and employment. Medical treatment is first given, followed by treatment, where necessary, in Rehabilitation Centres. These are Commonwealth institutions (except in Tasmania) where facilities exist for occupational therapy, physiotherapy, remedial exercises and pre-vocational training. After that, vocational training is given for new occupations, in the light of assessment for suitable employment. Finally, employment is found suitable to the disablement and the capability of the disabled person through the Commonwealth Employment Service and its District Offices.

Mental Health

Mental health in Australia has traditionally been the direct responsibility of State Health Ministers. In New South Wales, for example, the State mental hospitals are administered by the Division of Mental Hygiene of the Public Health Department, through the Inspector-General of Mental Hospitals[a]. However, in Victoria a statutory authority, the Mental Hygiene Authority, was established in 1951 to take charge of the Mental Hygiene Branch, and plan improvements in treatment and accommodation. It consists of three members of whom one, an expert in psychiatry, is chairman.

[a] A new Mental Health Bill (announced in Aug., 1958) will make him Director of State Psychiatric Services.

The Commonwealth Minister of Health arranged some years ago for a survey of Australian mental health facilities, and the resulting report (the Stoller Report, published in 1955) revealed many deficiencies. In particular, most State laws, including those of New South Wales, were said to be out-of-date, concerned with committal and custody rather than voluntary admission and treatment. There was also a grave shortage of accommodation and staffing. Some difficulties are attributable to the fact that mental institutions have increasingly needed to cater for the aged, and also for mental defectives, two groups many of whom would not need to be admitted if better community services were available.

The appraisal made in the Report was that the immediate shortage could only be made good by providing 10,000 beds at a cost of £3,000 each—a capital expenditure of £30m. The Commonwealth Government therefore proposed, and the States accepted, a new Agreement, whereby capital expenditure by State Governments could be accelerated. An amount of £10m. was made available on the basis of the provision of £1 by the Commonwealth for every £2 spent by the States. It was recognised that at best this dealt only with the physical side of the problem, but this was judged to be the most urgent need. In New South Wales, a committee appointed by the Minister of Health has recommended more up-to-date legislation in the mental health field.

The Tuberculosis Campaign

State and Commonwealth Governments are collaborating closely in an attack on tuberculosis. Australia has always had an unusually low tuberculosis rate, but it is possible with present knowledge to go close to wiping it out. So the campaign has been developed on two fronts: special benefits to patients willing to undergo treatment, and Commonwealth grants to States to expand their diagnosis and treatment facilities.([*])

The plan involves a good deal of oversight of State administration by the Commonwealth. The agreements provide that the Commonwealth shall pay all capital costs and maintenance costs over the amount spent by the State in 1947-48. So the approval of the Commonwealth has to be obtained for all State capital works. The Act requires the State to appoint a full-time medical Director of Tuberculosis. The Commonwealth has persuaded the States to agree to inspection of their institutions, and through its own Director of Tuberculosis to offer advice to the States on additions and improvements to their schemes. Administration of the allowances scheme involves the Commonwealth Department of Health, responsible for overall direction, the State Directors of Tuberculosis as medical referees, and the Commonwealth Department of Social Services, as the assessing and paying agent.

Education

Education, whether public or private, got off to a slow start in Australia, and by the middle of the nineteenth century more than one-half of the children in New South Wales were said to be receiving no education at all.

([*]) See E. A. Dundas, "The National Campaign Against Tuberculosis", *Pub. Admin. (Sydney)*, XI, June, 1952.

By slow degrees, and principally between 1872 and 1890, the States set up government departments under Ministers to control primary education and to institute compulsory attendance at school. Today over three-quarters of the children are enrolled in the State school system, the bulk of the remainder attending Roman Catholic schools. With minor exceptions all State education is free.

To an outstanding degree the educational system is marked by the centralism common in Australian administration, local authorities having no place at all in the system. State systems are notably alike. Each is independent, federation having made no difference in State educational responsibilities. At the head of each State service is a Director of Education. The teachers are responsible to the Department which he controls, and which selects, trains, disciplines, places, classifies and promotes them. There are separate branches dealing with primary, post-primary and technical education[10] under officers responsible to the Director. The Department exercises discipline by means of inspectors who have charge of a district and visit the schools regularly.

Attendance at school is compulsory at 6, and continues until 15 in New South Wales, 16 in Tasmania, and 14 in the other States. At secondary level super-primary, technical, commercial, domestic science and High School courses are given. The High School courses are integrated with the requirements of the University system of each State. In New South Wales, a special division of Research Guidance and Adjustment provides a highly skilled service, involving counselling and casework, to assist children towards better educational adjustment.

The Commonwealth plays no part in primary or secondary education, but it has an important influence in tertiary education, in two ways. It gives benefits to students, and it subsidizes all Universities through ear-marked grants to the States. It has a Commonwealth Scholarship Board; and it has appointed an Australian Universities Commission to advise it on its general policy with regard to universities. Commonwealth scholarships relieve students of all normal fees and expenses, and in the case of a smaller proportion who can meet a means test, also provide a living allowance. Nearly half the University students, amounting to 3,000 new entrants a year, were benefiting by this scheme in 1957. All courses given by Universities may be taken, and some diploma courses at technical colleges and other professional courses.

The Commonwealth provides supplementary income to Universities, normally on the condition that their combined income from State grants and fees reaches a stated minimum. This is to avoid the possibility of the States withdrawing any part of their subsidies because of Commonwealth support. Increasing demands have caused further pressure to be exerted on the Commonwealth Government to increase its assistance to the States. The Commonwealth responded by appointing a Committee of Inquiry into

---

[10] In New South Wales there is a separate Technical Education Department with its own Director.

Australian Universities, to make recommendations for the future, which reported in September 1957.[11]

But if the plight of the Universities is severe, those interested in State primary and secondary education are making free play with the word "crisis". The combination of rising educational standards, increased birth rate and heavy migration has pressed heavily on State resources. Popular response to this situation is to turn to the Commonwealth Government for specific grants to State education. The Commonwealth responds by pointing to the undoubted State responsibility in the field, saying that the annual tax reimbursements are for the States to spend as they see fit, and that it is giving all it can afford. There is no doubt that direct earmarked grants to education would further imperil the States' already weakened independence. The question to be solved is how to preserve the States and at the same time relieve the acute needs of their educational systems.

Two fields in which the Commonwealth Government finds itself increasingly interested are the education of the aboriginal natives of Australia and the training of Asians under the Colombo Plan. Under the Colombo Plan Technical Co-operation Scheme over 750 students were in Australia by the end of 1956, studying a wide variety of subjects at tertiary level; many other Asian students were paying their own way at Australian universities and colleges.

Physical Education

The overseas development of interest in physical fitness met a response in Australia in 1938, when a Commonwealth Council of National Fitness was established to effect collaboration of Commonwealth, State and local authorities in a National Fitness Campaign. The Council meets at least annually, and there are active State Councils. The Commonwealth gives grants to the States on the recommendation of the central Council for purposes of organisation, and to six Australian Universities for lectureships in physical education. The National Fitness Act 1941 gave the Commonwealth Council statutory existence, and it continues in active work, giving advice and providing machinery for the expenditure of Commonwealth funds.

New South Wales in 1938 appointed a Director of Physical Education within the Department of Education, and he organizes a Physical Education and National Fitness Branch. In the general community, the New South Wales National Fitness Council encourages the work of local governments, sports and youth organisations, and gives grants-in-aid to local authorities for an extended physical recreation programme on a £ for £ basis. The work done includes development of play centres (especially in vacations), and of youth hostels, and leadership training, and, among other things, swimming schools.

[11] See Committee on Australian Universities, *Report*, Sept. 1957. It recommended a large increase in Commonwealth grants and the creation of a permanent committee to advise the Commonwealth government on the needs of the universities.

Housing and Slum Clearance

Traditionally Australian emphasis is on the virtues of ownership, and until the 1939 war nearly all the considerable government housing activity took the form of assistance for home purchase. This was wise enough, but ignored the fact that Australia possesses a severe slum problem. To deal with this problem several of the States by 1939 had legislation, more or less adequate, for slum clearance and rental housing. The wartime housing shortage and a realization of the gap in Australian social provision owing to the absence of a rental housing programme led to the signing of the Commonwealth and State Housing Agreement of 1945. Like the Tuberculosis Agreement it involved the Commonwealth in financing and subsidizing the States, and in overseeing the development of their programmes. Administration is through the Commonwealth Department of National Development and State Housing Commissions.

The Agreement was conceived as a social measure, the principal emphasis being upon the provision of low-cost housing for workers on modest incomes. A scheme of rental rebates was put into force, the principal being that a family at basic wage level should be required to pay only one-fifth of its income in rent. If the economic rent was higher than this, a rebate was to be given. The Commonwealth paid three-fifths and the States two-fifths of losses incurred as a result.

The Agreements were renewed in 1957, but a change of Commonwealth Government brought a different approach. The new Agreements delete all reference to rental rebates, the main benefit to the States being a concessional interest rate. The States are at liberty to continue the rebate scheme if they wish to do so. Greater emphasis is placed on home ownership, a substantial and increasing proportion of the moneys lent by Commonwealth to States being passed on to co-operative building societies or similar bodies to assist their members to buy homes. Very little slum clearance has so far been possible under this scheme, because of the pressure on accommodation. For the same reason, it has been necessary to offer housing to anyone in need, whatever his income. Apart from alleviating the shortage, the Agreement, which produces over 10,000 houses a year, has provided houses in expanding industrial areas and in the country.

The Commonwealth Government has a direct administrative interest in housing in two ways: by the construction of homes in its own Territories and by lending money to eligible veterans under the War Service Homes scheme. In recent times it has been lending £35m. each year on long terms and easy interest rates. Demand for this facility exceeds the funds available.

The development of public opinion on housing is most interesting. Before the 1939-45 war, while both States and Commonwealth assisted home purchase, and some States were taking an interest in slum clearance, there was no public disposition to regard governments as ultimately responsible for the housing of the people. Four factors have changed the public view. First is the housing shortage. Second is the full employment doctrine and the view that governments, particularly the central government and the central bank, cannot allow appreciable unemployment to develop in any field. Third is the migration programme and the emphasis on housing for migrants, but also on the need to house the existing population before migrants are accommodated. And fourth is the heightened and perhaps unique Australian emphasis on home ownership.

All these things lead the public, the politicians and the spokesmen of the building industry—employers and workers alike—to place on governments the duty of making money available for housing. And although the constitutional position has not changed, and in consequence the Commonwealth Government has quite limited powers in this field and the States, although they have larger powers, have no set responsibilities in law, the Governments vie in accusing each other of dereliction of duty should housing activity fail, and by implication they accept a joint responsibility for ensuring that the people are properly housed.

Protection of Workers

Wages and working conditions are the two main considerations of the worker. In Australia the community steps in to regulate both. Direct State legislation on minimum wages was an early activity, and vestiges of it still remain. But the bulk of activity in this field has long been the prerogative of courts or commissions of conciliation and arbitration and of wages boards.([12])   These bodies fix wages, and also play a considerable part in establishing working conditions. The States have, since the late nineteenth century, also regulated conditions of work (normally through Departments of Labour or Departments of Labour and Industry) by means of Factories and Shops Acts, which have laid down minimum standards for lighting, ventilation, sanitary conditions, and so on.

Emphasis in recent years has shifted, especially since the establishment of the Commonwealth Department of Labour and National Service in 1940, to more positive measures to raise the welfare of the workers, including provision of canteens and rest rooms. An interesting development, typical of later attitudes, was the establishment in New South Wales, under a 1942 amendment of the Factories and Shops Act, of a Factory Welfare Board designed to attack and secure the elimination of sub-standard conditions and of all other factors in industry detrimental to the physical and psychological welfare of the worker. The Board, which consists of the Chief Inspector of Factories as Chairman and a representative each of workers and employers, is concerned with the environment in which the worker spends his working hours, with particular reference to lighting, ventilation, cleanliness, safeguards for health, prevention and treatment of accidents and provision of welfare facilities. It encourages social and cultural activities amongst factory workers. Its statutory powers enable it gradually to improve accommodation, health, and safety measures for workers in factories and other occupations.

Child Welfare

Child welfare is one of the most constructive spheres of State welfare activity. Most of the now small relief disbursements of State Governments go to women with young children through the child welfare machinery. But money payments are only one aspect of this work.

([12]) See K. F. Walker, *Industrial Relations in Australia,* 1956, Ch. II, for a short account of these.

The New South Wales Child Welfare Department[18] has in recent years made outstanding progress, and has a very wide field of administrative responsibilities. According to its Annual Report for 1947-48, "This Department is the most important single agency operating in the State for the welfare of children and young persons. Its activities include the fields of neglect and dependency of children, the treatment of those who show signs of delinquency, adoptions, unsatisfactory school attendance, licensing of homes for young children apart from their parents and the licensing of children who may be permitted to undertake various forms of street trading and employment. Within its framework the Child Welfare Department embraces functions and responsibilities which in other parts of the world are either left to the goodwill of the individual or to an embarrassing number of agencies, or which are simply not dealt with at all or to the same degree as in this State."

The Department may underestimate the value of voluntary effort, which is less developed in Australia than in some other countries. It regards itself primarily as a social agency: "It is unfortunate, but perhaps unavoidable, that because of its existence as a governmental body, the Department is regarded merely as an authoritarian institution. Its role as one of the leading social agencies in the community is not always appreciated. Departmental officers, trained social workers, are not confined in their work within strict statutory limits."

The Child Welfare Department grants monetary assistance to mothers in need ; it looks after children who, for various reasons, come within the fostering care of the State ; it acts as a skilled agency in arranging the legal adoption of children ; and it is responsible for all aspects of juvenile delinquency. Section 27 of the Child Welfare Act empowers the Minister to grant an allowance for the support of a destitute child or young person to a mother, a single woman who has adopted a young child, or a father. Juvenile offenders[14] may be examined by Children's Courts administered by a special magistrate, which have power to deal with juvenile offenders up to eighteen years of age. But the first emphasis is on building up the family and on skilled preventive work, for which the technique of family casework is used. There is a well-developed probation service, staffed by trained probation officers, into whose care the Court frequently commits offenders. If the child is committed to an institution he is visited monthly by his probation officer, who watches progress at the school and prepares his home for his eventual return, provided it can be brought up to a reasonable standard.

Children may come into the care of the State either because for some reason their parents or guardians cannot care for them, because they are neglected, or because they have committed an offence. The Department

---

[18] This became the Department of Child Welfare and Social Welfare in 1956, when the Social Welfare Branch of the Department of Labour and Industry was amalgamated with it.

[14] In Victoria, the Barry Committee reported in July, 1956, on juvenile delinquency. It recommended a Youth Authority with wider powers than the present Victorian Children's Welfare Department, an extension of the work of children's courts and probation officers, and that the State should establish its own institutions for wayward and problem children and not leave this burden mainly to voluntary denominational organisations.

prefers where possible to place children in foster homes "because it is considered that such a placement allows a child to enjoy a home, school and social life, very little different from normal." An allowance is paid to the foster parent and the Department meets educational, medical and dental expenses. The foster homes are carefully supervised. But if the children are unsuitable for placement, or if placement in foster homes cannot be arranged, they go first to special depots where they are built up physically and an atmosphere of security is induced. Later, they go to a specialized Departmental home for training. There are institutions, ranging from a home for mothers and new babies to homes for juveniles approaching maturity.

In its attitude to its work the Department expresses the constructive nature of the welfare approach. It has wide powers, but hesitates to use them, preferring to influence rather than compel. "It is only when all preventive and ameliorative action has failed that the Department invokes the law which it administers." (1948-49 Report.)

Some States are considerably less advanced in this field. There are still parts of Australia where, for example, there is no probation service, few trained social workers employed, and little use made of foster-homes, so that dependent children who cannot be adopted have to be cared for in institutions.

Prisons and Probation

How does the Australian system of judicial punishment show up in the light of modern penal theory? On the whole, not well. New South Wales has made some progress, both in prison administration([15]) and in the establishment, since 1951, of an adult probation service on a full-time basis; but other States seem to have made little progress in recent years, though changes are foreshadowed. New South Wales, for example, has a system of classification of prisoners both before conviction and on entry, while the Victorian system until recently was almost rudimentary. Prison classification committees are set up, including, as well as the Deputy Comptroller of Prisons, an education officer, trades supervisor, and psychologist-secretary, with medical and psychiatric opinion as necessary. The committee tries to match the offender and the institution. But the treatment is simple. It is not felt that much can be done for short-sentence prisoners; for those with sentences of twelve months or more something can be done. Treatment is based on self-discipline, vocational treatment, physical building up, education and proper use of leisure. There is certainly no general application of psycho-analytic techniques, and no spectacular results are claimed.

New South Wales is also experimenting with a new form of prison. In the past there have been two categories of penal institution: the "maximum security", and the "open establishment". Classification has indicated the need for an intermediate type, and for this purpose a special Training Centre has been developed on the site of the old Berrima Gaol, where a systematic attempt is being made to reclaim social offenders and turn them into valuable citizens.

([15]) An account of the N.S.W. prison system is given in *Social Service*, Nov.-Dec., 1954.

But it is better not to have to treat people in prison if it can be avoided, and it is from this angle that the recent extension of the New South Wales probation system offers some real hope. Australian probation in the past has been mainly for young offenders, there being few trained professional probation officers for adults. But in 1951 the New South Wales Government set up a full-scale probation system, based on professional principles of case-work, which applies to adults under the age of 30 and to all first offenders. This Adult Probation Service, within the Attorney-General's and Justice Department, is distinct from the supervision of persons released from prison on parole, who are the responsibility of Parole Officers of the Prisons Department.

The work of the Service falls into three parts—

    (i) pre-sentence report ;

    (ii) supervision of persons released on probation ;

    (iii) assistance to probationers to restore themselves as self-respecting members of the community.

In each case referred to the Service, Officers trained in social casework techniques are required to furnish reports, which are available for the consideration of the Judge. The report is designed to give as full a background as possible, and it deals with family and living situations, character and reputation, home circumstances, financial position, employment record, intelligence, education and training of the accused, interests, activities and associates, religious attitude, health history (physical and mental) of the accused and his parents and family, so as to assess the environmental pressures on the individual. The Judge takes the report into account in deciding his verdict, though it in no way fetters his discretion. If the accused pleads or is found guilty, the Judge may have recourse to it to assist him in determining what the sentence will be, or whether the person will be likely to respond to the opportunity if released on probation and committed to the care of a Probation Officer.

The Officer in this connexion is an agent of the Court, and while he continues to exercise his social work skills and attitudes, he must ensure that the conditions imposed by the Court are complied with ; he has no discretion to overlook breaches, but must report them to the Court. But probation, in the words of Sir Leo Page, is "an attempt to do lasting good to the character of an offender", and the underlying principle "is the real control over the life and conduct of the probationer which the order of the Court gives the probation officer for the period for which the order remains in force." With the implementation of this plan Australia has begun to fall into line with Britain, other Commonwealth countries and the United States, which have for a long time placed special stress on probation as a constructive alternative to prison.

Adult probation services now exist in Victoria, South Australia and Tasmania as well as New South Wales. A Probation and Parole Service was established as a branch of the Victorian Penal Department in 1957, which deals both with the usual functions of adult probation (pre-sentence reporting and supervision) and also with assistance to prisoners on release, and supervision and guidance while on parole license. Until this new service was created, New South Wales had the only organised parole system. Its parole officers work closely with voluntary bodies in the field, through a series of Civil Rehabilitation Committees.

Legal Assistance

Several States have in recent years given legal assistance to persons in restricted circumstances, both in defending criminal cases and in actions in civil courts. In New South Wales a Public Defender was first appointed in 1941, and a Public Solicitor in 1944. Under the Public Defender system Counsel has been appointed whose sole duty is to appear for indigent persons. The principle adopted is that no person through lack of means should be without representation at his trial on a criminal charge; and in appropriate cases indigent persons are represented on appeal also. Accused persons committed for trial on indictable offences are given a written notice showing the details of the legal aid plan. The Public Defender may act himself, or some other counsel or attorney may be appointed. Special attention is paid to cases where the condition of the accused is felt to merit representation, such as young accused, persons unfamiliar with Australian jurisdiction, aboriginals, and persons who, through lack of education or inferior intelligence, cannot put their cases without assistance.

The Attorney-General decides whether the services of the Public Defender shall be made available, but the Public Solicitor himself decides whether his services or those of his assistants shall be placed at the disposal of the applicant. Income and capital owned are taken into account in deciding eligibility for assistance, the income limit being somewhat above the basic wage. The Public Solicitor will represent clients in the courts, and he also gives free legal advice to eligible persons. The Public Solicitor may appear in cases himself, and there is also a panel of private solicitors and barristers ready to act, or to investigate and report on cases.

The Public Solicitor "differs much from the private practitioner in that he is called upon to render a specific social service. A large number of his clients need help badly, not only in the sense that they lack the means to obtain redress for their legal grievances, but because they are, through disabilities such as age, ill-health, lack of business knowledge or the language difficulties or inexperience of migrants, at a great disadvantage when involved in legal troubles. Much of the Public Solicitor's work which does not reach litigation level can be described not unaptly as of a clinical order. The test is that people leave his office feeling clear where they were confused, confident when they are insecure, and even though the verdict is pessimistic at least certain where they stand."[16]

Welfare of Aborigines

The States pay special regard to the welfare of aborigines. There are Aborigines' Boards charged with their welfare, and the work is usually carried out from mission stations and reserves where the aborigines are encouraged or required to live. Perhaps 20,000 full-bloods and 10,000 half-castes, or rather less than half the total, live in supervised camps.

Administration of native welfare is of a strongly paternalistic nature. The New South Wales Aborigines Welfare Board, which may be taken as

[16] N.S.W. Pub. Solicitor, *Report,* 1951-52.

typical, is a statutory body, with official representatives and two aborigines on it. This body exercises general supervision and care over all the aborigines and all matters affecting their care and welfare, and it has to protect them against injustice, imposition and fraud. It provides aboriginal children with primary education and apprentices them; it maintains Stations and Training Schools, and supervises entry and exit from Aboriginal Reserves; it provides relief, blankets and clothing; it controls entirely the movements of aborigines on reserves, and decides when they may be released from supervision; it may obtain a Court order giving it full control and custody of an aboriginal child, if it is satisfied that such a course is in the interest of the physical and moral welfare of the child; it may take charge of the wages of an aborigine; and it has many other powers.

The ultimate aim now is the gradual assimilation of the aborigines into the economic and social life of the community, and this involves encouragement of agriculture, technical training for youth, organizing of adult and juvenile employment, and provision of adequate housing. Free medical service is available to all needy aborigines and attempts are made to improve diet. In general, of course, the picture is one of a people in tutelage. The goal of full membership of the white community is still a long way off.

One problem which has caused a good deal of public concern is the payment of Commonwealth social service benefits to aborigines. The Commonwealth pays benefit in appropriate cases to aborigines exempted from State control, but does not give benefit where aborigines are still under control and presumably not assimilated to white conditions. Aboriginal natives may receive age pensions, for example, if the States, who have control over their welfare, have granted them exemption from the control laws. In States where exemption is not provided for, they may receive pensions if they are considered, by reason of character, standard of intelligence and social development, to be suitable persons to receive pensions. Unfortunately, these provisions mean that many aborigines are debarred from receiving pensions while they remain on the special State settlements, where they may have lived in comfortable houses for long periods and where they have their friends and relatives. This is a thorny administrative problem, but it is strictly one of administration, not of policy.

One cannot help feeling that this is a bureaucratic dilemma which could be resolved by some constructive imagination. With Commonwealth, States and public opinion all in agreement that at least some more, if not all, aborigines are entitled to benefit, it would seem that some way out could be found to give benefit to aborigines without asking them to leave their reserves. Of course, a true nomad could hardly be expected to obtain an age pension, giving him a higher living standard than he has ever enjoyed; but the settled aborigine, who has worked and paid taxes, is thought by many to be entitled to benefits, wherever he lives. In the face of general Government goodwill in this matter, the failure to find a solution is surprising.

CONCLUSION: ADMINISTRATIVE PATTERNS

As we have seen, by and large, the Commonwealth administers the social security services and the States the social welfare services. This arrangement has its justification in the impersonal nature of social security and the more personal character of social welfare. But the arrangement has its drawbacks. Social security and social welfare should be interdependent parts of a broadly conceived social policy. In Australian social administration two tendencies may be discerned; centralization of activity which some argue could be undertaken locally, and a disproportion between functions and finances. This means that the Federal Government undertakes activities which the States could perform and the States are unwilling to make fuller use of local authorities. Federalism in Australia is still operated too much as a system of rival governments each supreme in its sphere, instead of a working partnership. Some of the most interesting and vital work being performed arises when the Commonwealth takes the initiative, lays down general policy lines, and leaves administrative policy to the States. Two outstanding examples are the anti-tuberculosis campaign and the housing scheme. In each case finance and guidance come from the centre, but the States are the principals and take full responsibility for detailed administration.

The States are reluctant to entrust the local authorities with responsibility, arguing that they are unfit to take it. This may be a circular argument, since local authorities must continue to lack ability and experience until they are entrusted with responsibilitiy. In those rather rare cases where responsibility is devolved, such as maternal and baby welfare, the results are satisfactory. There is a strong case for a measure of devolution in educational administration, which is quite exceptionally centralized. The possibility of direct devolution from Federal Government to localities should not be ruled out; and the States could apply more to the localities the principle of conditional grant, so successful (in the cases of housing and tuberculosis) as between the Commonwealth and themselves. For example, the Victorian State Government has recently agreed to subsidize certain work for old people through local councils.

Somewhat similar remarks may be made about the relationship between the States and voluntary organizations. This chapter has concentrated on the work of public agencies, but this should not be taken as implying that the work of voluntary social service bodies, still the pioneers in some fields, is regarded as unimportant. They fill many of the remaining gaps in State provision, and operate many homes for children, old people, and other groups in need of special care. They are now being put in a position to co-operate more fully with one another through bodies such as State Councils of Social Service and Old People's Welfare Councils; there is also a new trend towards giving them increased public financial aid for certain purposes. The 1954 Aged Persons Homes Act makes Commonwealth grants available (since 1957 on a "two pounds for one pound" basis) to voluntary bodies running homes; and the State Governments also make contributions. As mentioned earlier in this chapter, grants are also now available to non-profit organisations for a number of other purposes.

Future developments in the social services will no doubt stress the welfare aspect. To take the example quoted above, the care of the aged, at present a neglected function. is essentially a matter for personal, humane service,[17] and hence specially suited for local administration. But policy guidance and financial help might well come from the centre. "Welfare is partly a matter of humanity backed by thought and planning."

---

[17] See B. Hutchinson, *Old Age in a Modern Australian Community*, and R. I. Downing, *Raising Age Pensions: A Five Point Programme*, 1957.

Chapter Six

LOCAL GOVERNMENT

RUTH ATKINS

Local government in Australia has always been primarily an administrative arrangement devised by colonial and then by State governments to deal with specific local tasks. At no stage has there been any general demand for local self-government, nor have the conditions ever been favourable to its easy growth. The influences that fostered equality and uniformity in Australian life generally did not encourage strong local government. We do not find, as we might in parts of Britain, or the United States, or in some of the cities of Europe, any long history of local independence or survivals of special privilege, distinctive organization, sources of income, or responsibilities. Once established, the local council has sometimes become the focus of local pride, the leader of local development. But the characteristic feature of local government development in Australia has been the attempt by higher governmental authorities first to persuade and then to require local groups to accept financial and administrative responsibility for certain tasks.

Even though each State has its own system of local government, the uniformity of style throughout Australia is noticeable. There are differences between States[1] in the titles used, terms of office, and so on but the similarities are more important than the differences. In each case the State Government directs and controls local authorities in a most detailed way, e.g., through the Department of Local Government in New South Wales. What they may or must do does not vary strikingly from State to State. The practical possibilities involve the same fairly narrow range of essential housekeeping tasks, roads, sanitation, garbage, street lighting, protection of food supplies, and much the same possible excursions into welfare and cultural activities. Money is raised in much the same ways in all States, and the same financial difficulties and general problems appear. Where a model was used, it was in all cases the British one and this helped to encourage similarity in organization, procedure and rules in all States. The council system, terms and titles used, procedure at meetings, electoral methods, financial rules, etc., are all modelled on the English system. "Rating" is on a different basis, but the general idea of a real property tax based on official valuations is the same. Much the same historical, social and economic forces affected each colony. As a result we see the same three stages in the growth of each local government system.

---

[1] The Road Boards of Western Australia are the equivalent of Shire Councils in New South Wales. In three States (and in Sydney) the Mayor or President is directly elected; in N.S.W. and Queensland, elections are triennial; elsewhere one-third of the council faces election each year.

First, there was paternalistic control from Britain with some abortive attempts to transfer something of the English government system to the colonies; then with growing self-government came a scattered development of local authorities, again on the English pattern and with little public support on one hand or official recognition of special problems on the other. By 1905, when the basic principles of the New South Wales system were finally established, each State had developed a general system of incorporation and local authorities had become generally recognized as a third level of government.

There are some areas, for example, the Western division of New South Wales, which are sparsely settled and where the constitution of shires has not proceeded far. The Northern Territory in 1957 had no local authorities, though the Municipal Council of Darwin was being reconstituted after a twenty-year gap, and the Minister for Territories promised further developments. Canberra, the national capital, has no elected council. Its affairs are administered by the Commonwealth Department of the Interior with the aid of a local advisory committee, though there are some demands for a locally elected council. But otherwise the local council is a familiar part of the Australian scene. In the whole of Australia there are 914 local authorities (excluding bodies of the "county council" type). In New South Wales there are 97 municipalities, including 17 cities, 133 shires and also 46 county councils,([2]) second-tier authorities representing a group of neighbouring councils and concerned with electricity supply, water, noxious weed destruction or some other service for the whole area. This has been an interesting and successful development, which is discussed below. Some shires in New South Wales have minor authorities within their boundaries— urban committees for some of the townships and villages, with delegated powers.

These councils are composed of elected members—for example, the 2,115 aldermen and shire councillors of New South Wales (who include 398 serving as "delegates" to county councils). There are also the permanent officials, town and shire clerks, engineers, health officers, planning officers and so on, with their appropriate professional organizations, one of the concerns of which is the status and prestige of their profession. From these groups come valuable practical proposals concerning local government in general. Moreover, local authorities often have representation on other bodies. In New South Wales they are represented on such bodies as the Board of Fire Commissioners, the Metropolitan Water Board, and on advisory committees of various kinds. Local authorities' representatives sometimes complain that State Governments have neglected opportunities of giving representation to local government on housing commissions or electricity authorities. Whether or not the complaint is justified, it is still true that local government spreads in this way beyond the ordinary elected council.

But for the greater part of this survey we must concern ourselves with the core of the local government system—the local council. As we noted,

---

([2]) These are 1957 figures. Changes are frequent, usually reducing the number of councils by amalgamation. So, since December, 1956, the Municipality of South Grafton has been amalgamated with the City of Grafton. Three Counties were proclaimed in September, 1957.

what these councils may or may not do depends on State laws and ordinances. In some States they have limited powers of local regulation, but in New South Wales they do not even make by-laws (the State makes "ordinances", the councils may make rules filling in the details). Their functions are less obviously important than in Britain where education, housing, police, and many welfare activities are to a considerable degree the responsibility of local authorities. Their financial independence is far less than, say, in the United States of America, where a variety of local taxes are levied. In their dependent and controlled position, local councils are probably less powerful and significant in Australia than in any other part of the British Commonwealth.

This situation is explicable in terms of Australian history and conditions. It is foolish to bemoan the fact that local government was not set up and developed differently here. Moreover, we should not delude ourselves into believing that only in Australian local government are there difficulties. Almost everywhere that local authorities have in the past been of some importance—in Britain, South Africa, Canada, the United States, and on the continent of Europe—the cry is the same. "Real local government is being destroyed; its problems are neglected, it is starved of funds; few people are interested in participating." It looks as if there are some general causes contributing to weaknesses in local government here and elsewhere. It seems, for instance, that the present trend (one associated with "democratisation") is towards uniformity and away from special local privilege, or disability; towards the centralizing of responsibility and the provision of more and more things on a wider national or state basis rather than to the increase of local responsibilities. Moreover, in our interdependent world it is no longer easy to decide what is a local matter.

It should be emphasised that local government, if it is to be more than the local administration of central decisions, means local differences and local responsibility. It means that some areas will to an extent be better off, and some worse off, according to local capacity to pay and according to the quality of local efforts. One other general point needs to be made. Strong local government cannot be taken for granted as an end in itself. There is no certainty that, for example, having education as a local responsibility is better than having it under a central government. Better for local government, perhaps. But better for education? We should need to look at the whole pattern of government before we could decide. We should not take it for granted that we are at a disadvantage. It may be so. But it is misleading to assume that the British or some other system of local government is a perfect model which Australia has unfortunately failed to copy. If we notice, for example, that fire prevention and control are the affair of a State board in New South Wales and some other States, we should think not only of local authorities being kept out of an important field, but of citizens being spared some of the confused boundary disputes and problems of co-operation that we can read about in some areas of the United States.

Even if local government in Britain or elsewhere seemed to have advantages, some of the conditions are unique and not easily reproduced. Local government in Britain is the second, not the third level of government. Local authorities, at least the more important ones, deal directly with Whitehall and Westminster. Their position is not complicated by dependence on State governments, themselves in an uneasy financial relationship with a Federal government. Some of the larger local authorities in Britain are more comparable with our State governments([a]) than with municipal Councils. The London County Council deals with a population greater than that of any one Australian State, concentrated in an area less than that of Metropolitan Sydney. No wonder its activities are of national importance or that its budget and policy will sometimes allow for imaginative experiment. Local government in England also has behind it a long, varied and sometimes colourful history. This gives it dignity, makes for local pride, encourages research and writing, provides a store of experience and example to be drawn upon. But we cannot create a new past for ourselves. We cannot give Perth a medieval origin or Brisbane a centuries' old accumulation of municipal property or put the City of Sydney in the unique historical position of the City of London.

Nor is it certain, if our aim is good government, that we should wish to do so. The past virtues of English local government can be just as much exaggerated as the present ones. Instead of deploring the fact that the early attempts (in the 1840's) to reproduce "the British system" were half-hearted and unsuccessful, we might rather regard Australia as fortunate in that the real adaptations from Britain were postponed until the model itself was rebuilt. British local government in the early nineteenth century was a bewildering confusion of overlapping authorities—municipal corporations, parish and vestry authorities, Turnpike Trusts, Highways Trusts, Sewers Commissions, Health Boards, and so on—and few of these had any general electoral basis. Local self-government existed in the sense that local rather than national minorities were powerful in local governing bodies, not that the local community as a whole had any chance to participate. Some areas can, of course, point with pride to achievements of local governing authorities at various stages in their long history, including the early nineteenth century. The point here is simply that there was really no effective British "system" of local authorities when the beginnings of local government were made in Australia. One theme in the history of government in Britain over the past 100 years has been the endeavours of the national government to develop some general system of effective local government, to impose national standards and general rules on a confusion of jealously independent and often conflicting authorities. That some few of these local authorities were enterprising and efficient is true but not relevant here.

The tremendously important achievements in British local government have been in the development of these national standards, in administrative techniques and organization, in practical ways of meeting problems which any local authority might face. As part of a Parliamentary system which is a British heritage—and sometimes an important export—local government in Britain is comparatively well-documented, its history well explained, its problems much discussed. These are the reasons why cadets in Government Administration in Thailand are sent to study Local Government in Britain, why a British expert (Sir John Maud) was invited to investigate

---

([a]) Alan Davies (in J. W. Leeper (ed.), *Introducing Victoria,* 1955, p. 295), makes the comparison the other way, pointing out the "likeness to the range of powers exercised by English County Councils" in the activities of the Victorian State government, and indicating that they are now both creatures of the nation-state.

and report on city government in Johannesburg, why the Sudan a few years ago invited a British expert to advise on developments in local government there—and why "the British System" can be a source of valuable information and example to Australia. None of these seekers of advice expect to reproduce it. What they have wanted has been help from British practical experience in meeting problems arising in their own systems.

So we should recognise that the circumstances which moulded British local government (long history, varied experience, closely settled relatively stable communities) and those which have helped to give it, comparatively, political strength (its position in a unitary state, as the second level of government) are not easily reproducible, and that to regret their absence in Australia is a futile occupation. Britain's most effective contribution to modern local government is in details of administrative organization, and much of this, as will be seen, has been transferred here.

Developments to 1900

It should have been clear at once that conditions in Australia were not favourable to development of local government on the English model. Concentration of population, stability of settlement, local tradition were naturally lacking. In this new country scattered settlements were spreading tentatively from coastal bases. The developmental tasks were enormous, much too great to be financed by tolls or rates which were even inadequate for local tasks in nineteenth century Britain—and there some at least of the provision for roads, bridges, drainage, and so on, had already been made. It is just possible that an imaginative policy might have established local government even in these adverse conditions. The Governors and the British authorities were anxious to see some local authorities develop. But there is no sign that they realised the way in which the job was made harder by the special conditions of new colonies.

The first stage in local government in Australia was an attempt to reproduce something on the style of English Highways Trusts and Municipal Corporations—to persuade local citizens to take responsibility for providing roads, streets and bridges in the few main towns. Perth had a Town Trust in 1838, Parish Road Trusts were begun in New South Wales in 1840, Adelaide had the first elected municipal council in Australia in the same year ; Sydney and Melbourne were incorporated in 1842.([4]) In spite of some excitement in Melbourne at the first council elections (December, 1842) there was at this time little demand for or enthusiasm about these developments. Most schemes "reflected the desire of the Home Authorities to lessen the cost of such services [roads, etc.] to the Imperial Government." ([5]) Local groups could scarcely be expected to share this desire. The new authorities sometimes found their legal powers insufficient for the

---

([4]) On Sydney, see C. H. Bertie, *The Early History of the Sydney Municipal Council,* 1911. Sydney was also proclaimed a city in 1842, Melbourne in 1847. The first Sydney Council had wide powers. The 1850 Act reconstituting the 1842 scheme, with amendments, contained penalties for refusing the office of alderman, a significant inclusion not legally removed till 1879.

([5]) J. R. Johns, "Development of Local Government in Western Australia", *Pub. Admin. (Sydney),* VIII, Oct.-Dec., 1949.

enforcement of the payments on which their work depended. Even when government grants were made they were too often related to population or income, seldom to the special needs of an area. Those who were elected or appointed to these new Councils, Boards or Trusts, and the staff they employed, were inexperienced in the work of local authorities and sometimes bewildered even by the matter of meeting procedure.

In the late 1830's, a general scheme for local government had been suggested as part of proposals for granting colonial self-government to New South Wales. It was proposed to divide New South Wales into large areas, whose councils would elect the Legislative Council. This came to nothing, owing to local opposition. But in 1842, when New South Wales was granted representative government, the act also provided for a system of District Councils, constituted at the discretion of the Governor, which were to have important responsibilities. Beginning in 1843, twenty-nine District Councils were established but apart from Parramatta none accomplished anything and the system was quietly abolished. This was partly owing to the Legislative Council's fear that the original scheme of making it subservient to the districts would be revived (the plan was, in fact, resurrected briefly in 1847). But there were other difficulties. The population was too scattered, the inhabitants either indifferent or hostile, often ready to evade or refuse rate payments to an authority they had not asked for. The duties, and especially the financial responsibilities of councillors, were not clearly defined.

Most local authorities faced serious difficulties in the early years. A Select Committee which investigated Sydney's Council six years after its formation recommended its abolition. It was, in fact, disbanded in 1854 and replaced by an appointed Commission. Though this Commission is reported to have made valiant efforts to improve streets and health facilities in Sydney its difficulties soon became so grave that three Select Committees in turn reported on its activities, and it was replaced by another elected Council in 1857. In Melbourne the City Council was saved from very early financial disaster by a private loan, and the wise use made of this seems not only to have given Melbourne a good civic beginning but to have been an example encouraging other Victorian urban areas to establish local authorities. In Perth the early Town and Road Trusts met with many difficulties, partly because their financial arrangements were badly planned and partly because local citizens were reluctant to use the powers given to them to form these Trusts.[6] Six years after the formation of the Perth Town Trust it "practically ceased to function" and in 1856 it "was again without finances or labour to carry on local works.[7] The Adelaide corporation was declared defunct in 1843, but re-established in 1851.[8] Hobart Council was established in 1852, Brisbane in 1859.

It was in Victoria that local government first moved from this tentative stage to something more vigorous and extensive. Settlement was expand-

---

[6] In Fremantle, the Government Resident tried in vain on several occasions to get a public meeting to form a Town Trust. The enabling legislation was passed in 1838; Fremantle formed a Town Trust in 1848.

[7] J. R. Johns, *op. cit.*

[8] D. Pike, *Paradise of Dissent: South Australia,* 1829-1857, 1957, pp. 240, 245, 462.

ing rapidly after the discovery of gold and the comparative success of Melbourne's Council set the example. In 1854 the Municipal Constitution Act created the system of permissive incorporation which was to be the characteristic second stage in each of the colonies before Federation. Under this Act municipalities could be formed by petition of householders to the Governor-in-Council if the area was no more than 36 square miles and the number of householders not less than 200. Similar Acts were passed in Tasmania and New South Wales in 1858, in South Australia in 1861, in Queensland in 1864, and in Western Australia in 1871. The formation of road boards and municipalities proceeded fairly rapidly in Victoria and there was sufficient interest in these local authorities for a Royal Commission to review their working in 1862. Its findings were mainly favourable and its suggestions (e.g., a property qualification for electors) were put into effect fairly rapidly. Two important Acts were passed in 1863, including one to transform suitable road districts into shires. The 1874 Local Government Act consolidated these with some amendments. By 1875 the general pattern of a system of local government had been firmly set in Victoria and most areas of this State were incorporated for local government purposes well before 1900.

In the other States, developments were slower and more difficult, though some vigorous experiments were made. The Municipalities Act of 1871 in Western Australia not only set up the City Council of Perth but extended the functions of municipal corporations to include the licensing of vehicles, slaughterhouses and markets, the regulation of markets, to permit the establishment of gardens, recreation areas, libraries, museums and so on. Between 1871 and 1905 there were forty-three municipalities formed in Western Australia, whereas only eight town trusts existed in 1871. In 1878 and 1879 Queensland made provision for a general system of local government, with cities, towns and divisional boards (later shires). South Australia, which had had road districts since 1852, re-organized them into the present units in 1887. In Tasmania a considerable number of special areas for different services developed (as in New Zealand), but in 1906 the whole island was divided into municipalities.

In N.S.W. the Municipalities Act of 1858 was the answer to requests for Parliamentary assistance to country towns for roads and streets. It allowed the establishment of a municipality on petition of only fifty householders of any city, township or rural district. Councils of these municipalities were empowered to provide not only roads, bridges and homes, etc., but water supply, sewerage, public hospitals, and gardens. Thirty-five areas took early advantage of this legislation, the first municipalities established under it being Randwick and Wollongong. Further development was complicated by challenges to the legality of the constitution, rating powers, or policy of these new councils. The constitution of one council in the Shoalhaven area was declared invalid by the courts,(°) after a bitter local

(°) cf. F. A. Larcombe, *History of Local Government in N.S.W.*, (unpublished M.Ec. thesis, Sydney University). This Shoalhaven story is a fascinating one. It seems to have been a struggle by one group to set up a council area which would include all the land of a wealthy landowner named Berry so that rate payments by him would finance the general development of the area. Berry not unnaturally objected—but this pressure is characteristic of early local government schemes.

fight. It took considerable prodding by councils and citizens before the New South Wales government at last introduced further legislation in 1867 which cleared up some of the difficulties, added some new functions, and made some alterations to the franchise. This Act divided municipalities into boroughs and municipal districts, the boroughs being the populous centres, and municipal districts being proposed for the less settled areas. The next generation saw a considerable though gradual increase in the numbers of councils and the area incorporated, some real efforts on the part of governments to encourage development and some examples of practical achievements.

There were 29 municipal councils in 1865, 74 in 1876, 157 in 1890, 192 by 1900. In 1880 the Country Towns Water and Sewerage Act enabled the colonial government to construct the necessary works (or sometimes to lend money to councils for this purpose) and then to hand them over to the council when completed. In 1884 loans were authorised for gas works; in 1888, for building town halls and council chambers. Considerable use was made of these powers, and others. The memorials of this time can be seen in the solid town halls,[10] council chambers, parks and gardens in some country towns and metropolitan areas. This is the period of the Centennial Hall additions to Sydney Town Hall and of the Queen Victoria Markets, both large scale expenditure for their time. In a few places, at this stage, conditions were more favourable to local government than formerly. In some prosperous settled urban communities, still comparatively isolated and independent because of poor transport, local residents were kept pretty much in their own locality for entertainment, societies, sport, etc., and hence were sometimes led to concern themselves with civic matters.

But in spite of some evidences of energy in local government most of the rural areas were unprovided for in New South Wales, which lagged behind Victoria, Queensland and South Australia in this respect. Only a few relatively prosperous areas had adequate funds, and there was considerable reluctance among property owners to accept the responsibility of paying local rates for development which they hoped might be financed from general government funds. Moreover, 192 was a large number of municipal councils when the area incorporated was less than one per cent. of the State's area. Many of the municipal areas were too small, too sparsely populated and hence had insufficient revenue to develop facilities properly.

We should not ignore the importance of political factors. Since local authorities were neither generally established nor powerful, active political groups did not find them worth much attention. In Britain in this period (c. 1880-1900) and later, the new Labour and Socialist groups fought some of their battles first on the smaller fields of local government. Municipal socialism was a quite important issue; national party groups were strongly interested in some local elections. But in our comparatively open society, reforming groups were not likely to spend their energies on local contests

---

[10] Many of those in the Sydney area are depicted in Morton Herman, *Victorian Architecture in Sydney*, 1956.

when they could move with greater ease into the wider political struggle.([11])
Development remained haphazard and half-hearted in New South Wales
until the State government decided on a major reorganisation in the first few
years of the new federation.

DEVELOPMENTS AND PROBLEMS SINCE 1900

At the turn of the century State governments were dominant and confident. New developments were in the air. A federal government had
just been formed to carry out certain jobs which the States "found it
inconvenient or impossible to administer adequately themselves". State
governments also recognised the need to delegate to local authorities some
of the powers which they found it "inconvenient or politically embarrassing
to administer themselves".([12])

For example, between 1898 and 1902 a whole group of New South Wales
Acts—Commons Regulation (1898), Dairies Supervision (1901), Cattle
Slaughtering (1902)—named local councils as the appropriate authorities
to appoint inspectors, issue licences, control standards and sometimes to
administer the Acts in detail. But local authorities had not yet been universally established even in the comparatively well-settled areas of the State.
There had been talk for a long time about possible extensions. But public
interest was not strong and government policy was vacillating.

The real development of a general system of local government in N.S.W.
followed the passing of the Local Government (Shires) Act, 1905, and
the Local Government (Extension) Act, 1906. The Shires Act tackled
the problem of the sparsely settled rural areas by empowering the government to divide into shires the whole of the State outside the City of Sydney,
existing municipalities, and the Western Lands Division, and to compel the
incorporation of those shires for certain specific tasks. It was expected that
the State government would have to subsidise the shires because they were
to take over jobs of roadmaking and maintenance, etc., which were beyond
their financial powers and which had formerly been a State responsibility.
The functions of these shire councils, it was hoped, would be extended
gradually.

The 1906 Act repealed the permissive system of 1867 and 1898 and laid
the basis for a general municipal system with a detailed statement of rules
about the formation, procedure, financial organization and functions of these
councils. At the time of the passing of these Acts the aim was stated in
wide and generous terms as being "to provide for the perfectly natural and
free growth of the local governing body in powers, functions and respon-

---

([11]) It is often made a virtue of the British Labour Party that they recognised the
need for an apprenticeship in local politics before entering the national
field. But first, this was largely making a virtue of necessity. Conservative and Liberal strongholds were fairly well defended—the Labour
Party in Britain had to wait till 1945 for a majority national government,
whereas the Australian Labour Party was in power much earlier. Secondly,
local politics were more attractive to British reforming groups because the
issues to be fought out there were sometimes important. For example,
Labour's struggle for adequate unemployment benefits was fought partly
in local councils.

([12]) R. S. Parker, *Highlights of Local Government Legislation in N.S.W.*, 1956,
p. 6.

sibilities *pari passu* with the needs caused by growth and development of the district and the State".([13]).

Confident plans were also announced to concentrate "all local administration in one local authority", at some future date, by handing over to city, municipal or shire councils many of the functions then performed by harbour trust, fire board, traffic commissioners, etc., as well as some jobs done by State departments. These hopes were not fulfilled. The story has rather been one of declining prestige and financial strength in State governments and of consequent disabilities suffered by local authorities dependent on these. So discussion of local government problems in these years tends to be preoccupied with grievances. The story of the past half-century in local government is often presented as one of injustice, neglect, decline.

However, concentration on the disabilities of local government is likely to obscure the fact that very significant achievements in local government, especially in local government administration, have been made in the twentieth century. First, the local government service is now a highly organized institution. Qualifications have been laid down for the various important officers of local councils, and training schemes to provide the bases for these qualifications have been developed. Professional associations ([14]) have been formed and their regular meetings and conferences have played an increasingly important part in setting standards, encouraging technical developments and in providing spokesmen in negotiations with the State authorities.

Some functions have been lost to State departments and commissions, but several new ones have been gained. In matters of community welfare and entertainment the local council is now, in many areas, far more important than it was even twenty years ago. Libraries, community centres, art exhibitions and collections, baby health centres, these and many similar services are becoming common in the case of at least the larger councils.

Some local government supporters may deplore the "uniformity" that is enforced by the State Government, the increasing number of detailed returns to be sent in, the uniform system of accounting and checking which must be followed and so on. But on the credit side it must be remembered that these techniques of supervision and checking have aimed at and largely achieved certain minimum standards of service and of accountability throughout the whole system of local authorities. This has been, and could only be, a gradual achievement. Moreover some local authorities have by now been established long enough to have developed both in efficiency and in local reputation. The breakdowns, the occasional scandal that is headlined, the petty stupidities that occur in any popularly elected group (and perhaps in any group) should not prevent us from recognising that a great deal of patient public service has been given and much real development achieved with limited means. One of the reasons for the petulance and dissatisfaction frequently noted in defenders of local government is that they

---

([13]) Carruthers, 2nd reading Speech, N.S.W. Legislative Assembly, 1905, cited in R. S. Parker, *Highlights of Local Government Legislation*. p. 7.

([14]) e.g., in New South Wales, the Local Government Auditors Association, Local Government Clerks Association, and the Institute of Local Government Engineers. The Local Government Association and the Shire Association of New South Wales represent councils.

feel themselves to be a part of a potentially effective and efficient machine which for one reason or another is not given a chance to develop its potentialities. And, of course, just to make things more exasperating, so many Australians assume without any testing of evidence that "it is all a racket".

The Area Problem

The question of the appropriate area for the provision of various services is a recurring one in local government, especially in Australia, where the average size of local authorities (in terms of population served) is low. For example, early councils were concerned with individual water supplies for their area. But it was soon recognised that satisfactory provision sometimes required a larger area of operation. It is clear that the local area, even if its boundaries have been drawn carefully to include a fairly distinct and recognisable "community", of a certain minimum number, and so on, may not necessarily be the appropriate and most efficient area for various technical services. A comparatively satisfactory garbage disposal service was more within the range of a small and not wealthy municipal area when the main equipment was some carts to take rubbish to a "tip" or a "dump". But what happens at the stage where proposals are being made to have large amounts of rubbish transported in covered, specially designed, trucks to large-scale incinerators or disposal plants? Many existing council areas may well be too small to afford such modern equipment. What then should be done?

We might hope that the councils themselves would agree on some common scheme and on an allocation of costs or benefits. But this is not easy for them to do unless, at least, some other authority is encouraging and directing their negotiations. Should we then form a separate garbage authority to do the job for all the neighbouring councils? And if so, form it from representatives of these councils? Or by election from the area? Or by a combination of these methods? Or perhaps, since the areas are admittedly too small for efficient garbage disposal services, should we amalgamate the areas and councils concerned? But then, will the new area serve adequately for all other local activities? Are there some functions for which a relatively small unit is essential? These are not just academic questions. Many of the recent developments in local government follow from just this sort of problem arising, and from each of the solutions mentioned having been tried.

The place where it is often first obvious that provision of services over more than one local area is desirable, is in a growing metropolitan area. The Metropolitan Water Sewerage and Drainage Board, first established in Sydney in 1880,([15]) represents one solution to this problem, the setting up of a special metropolitan authority for a task which may continue to be the responsibility of individual councils in many country areas. A Water Board was set up for the Newcastle area in 1892, the Hunter District Water Board, which added sewerage to its functions in 1907. Another example of a special authority for metropolitan control is the Metro-

---

([15]) The Board's members were not appointed until 1888. Five of its present membership of seven are elected by aldermen and councillors of the local areas concerned.

politan Meat Industry Board, set up in 1915 to control slaughtering and the sale of meat in the County of Cumberland. Its members were appointed by the State and contained no municipal representation. A similar body in Newcastle was elected by Council members until the Great Newcastle Council took over this function in 1937. The control and supervision of dairies and of milk distribution was placed under a Milk Board for the Sydney and the Newcastle districts in 1931. These were mainly schemes directed at the special needs of the two great metropolitan areas. As other places become metropolitan centres, e.g., the Wollongong area, the same problems arise. Some way has to be found to provide a uniform and co-ordinated service on a large scale especially for certain technical services.

One other common solution has been the setting up of a special State-wide authority. In New South Wales, the Main Roads Board (later the Department of Main Roads) was set up in 1925, for the whole State, to control finance and direct a large proportion of the road-making within each council's area. Local councils do much of the actual work as its agents or under its supervision.[16] The Fire Brigades Act of 1909 provided for Fire Districts comprising groups of local council areas. The Board of Fire Commissioners controls fire brigades in these, local councils retaining the responsibility in some of the less populous areas. In the case of some smaller fire brigades, the council supervises the organization and the commissioners pay for most of the equipment.

The Housing Commission is another State-wide authority. There are some who would like to have seen local authorities, as in England, become the chief government housing authorities. That this did not happen is partly because council representatives could not agree on an acceptable scheme, partly because State governments have seldom shown themselves ready to use local authorities as their agents in this way, and partly because the general tendency in Australia is to favour the uniformity that comes from a single authority. House-building by councils has never been common. Sydney Council erected low-rented dwellings between 1914-27; but has not repeated the experiment.

A slight variation of this State-wide conformity is seen in the Electricity Authority (1946) and the Electricity Commission of New South Wales (1950). The Authority has wide powers to formulate proposals affecting the electricity undertakings of councils—for example, to fix the forms and bases of charging and the maximum prices for electricity supplied in bulk. The Electricity Commission has power to generate, purchase and supply electricity, and supplies electricity in bulk through inter-connected transmission networks. The distribution of electricity to the public is almost wholly in the hands of local government in New South Wales (in 1957, 92.4 per cent. of consumers in the State were supplied by local governing bodies, compared with about 25 per cent. in Victoria). In other States most (in Tasmania, all) consumers are supplied by State boards or commissions.

The New South Wales Electricity Authority has recently made pro-

---

[16] See H. M. Sherrard, "Main Roads Administration in New South Wales," *Pub. Admin. (Sydney),* XV, Sept., 1956.

posals([17]) for the amalgamation of local electricity undertakings, including the present county councils, into thirty-three new county districts. There is an obvious and difficult problem here of balancing advantages and disadvantages. Some local councils can put up a good case. They have supplied electricity efficiently and cheaply. Their own area would probably gain little by the change. There would, however, be benefits in the near future to some other areas, if the new proposals were adopted; and perhaps some long-term benefits to the whole area in cheaper electricity supplies. However, local government representatives are naturally disturbed at the tendency to remove electricity undertaking from direct council control even when the undertaking has been successful.

It is interesting that the Electricity Authority proposes the adoption of the "county council" form. At least, in this kind of organization, the local councils retain some direct interest in the electricity undertaking. County councils have been one of the more fruitful attempts in this period to solve the problem of providing services over a wider area than that of one authority.

Two early New South Wales experiments with bodies constituted on county council lines were the Newcastle Abattoirs Board (which began operations in 1916) and the Richmond River Water Hyacinth Board. From 1905 to 1915 representatives of four councils and six shires in the latter area tried out schemes to deal with the water hyacinth pest in some co-operative way. At last a body representative of the various councils was elected, and, with the blessing of the Minister for Local Government, went on, with the aid both of government subsidies and funds from the constituent councils, to do this work. The 1919 Local Government Act made use of the successful experiment and not only formalised the arrangements already working among the Richmond councils, but outlined a general scheme for the formation of county councils for any joint project (within, of course, the regular powers of local government) which local councils might decide upon. Developments at first were slow. It was left to the councils themselves to initiate and finance any such scheme. After twenty-five years there were only a dozen county councils in the State. But from 1943 onwards great developments have occurred in this type of authority. By June, 1957 there were 46 county councils in N.S.W. and three others were about to be proclaimed. There is also, as we have seen, a proposal to create a number of additional county councils for electricity supply.

Some local government supporters see in county councils the greatest hope for the future of local government because they provide a second-tier authority, representing the local councils concerned, for specific tasks, while still retaining existing councils for local services. But some of the increase has followed the decision to allow the Minister of Local Government to initiate, even to compel, the formation of such councils. If this power is used indiscriminately against the desires of the local councils concerned, it is not likely that county councils will remain the "greatest hope" for future local government. They will become simply another compulsory administrative device.

([17]) N.S.W. Electricity Authority, Apr., 1957, *Report on the Organisation of Electricity Supply.*

A county council has a specific purpose. Normally it can carry out only those functions which the constituent councils delegate.([18])   The members of a county council, termed "delegates," are usually elected from and by the participating councils. Sometimes, as with the Sydney County Council, the constituent authorities are grouped into electorates, the representatives being chosen by and from each group. Funds are raised either by a (limited) county rate through the area, or by a levy on each council, and by government subsidy. Payments are not necessarily equal. An attempt is usually made to consider relative benefits received.

The functions of the forty-six County Councils in New South Wales are as follows:—

Function.	Number of County Councils.
Electricity Supply	24
Electricity and control of noxious weeds	1
Electricity, flood control and aerodromes	1
Electricity and aerodromes	2
Electricity and coalmining	2
Electricity and water supply	2
Abattoirs	1
Noxious plants and pest removal	8
Water supply	3
Town and Country Planning	2

There is one way in which the development certainly has helped local government. It has given the opportunity for working in wider fields to many aldermen and councillors; and this has a good effect on the council members themselves and also on their appreciation of the problems which affect their own locality.

All these developments mentioned so far followed recognition that for one purpose or another, the usual local area is too small a unit. It is not surprising then that another development has been the attempt to make those local areas themselves larger. Amalgamation has been a regular feature of local council development. Departmental policy has pretty consistently favoured reducing the number of councils, and increasing the size of the areas they control. The cry from the official side is always "these traditional areas are too small for efficiency; money could be saved, better staff employed, better equipment used if, for example, South Grafton Municipality amalgamated with Grafton City, if Woollahra and Vaucluse were made one unit, if East and West Maitland were joined, and some neighbouring areas also, to form Maitland City, if the boundaries of Parra-

---

([18]) Generally, county councils depend upon a delegation from the majority of councils concerned in the county districts. The exceptions to this rule are the constitution of county districts under section 12 of the Electricity Development Act pursuant to a recommendation by the Electricity Authority and also the constitution of county districts for the purpose of the supply of gas. Legislation is planned at the time of writing to enable county councils for flood mitigation and abattoir purposes to be constituted without the concurrence of the majority of councils.

matta City were extended to include the dormitory areas nearby." (All the proposals just mentioned have actually been put into effect.) [19]

Against amalgamation there is always the natural reluctance of any council group to think itself redundant; there is the appeal to local pride and tradition; the long-standing jealousies of neighbours; a sometimes justifiable fear that haphazard amalgamation will destroy what little sense of community and local loyalty manages to develop; the objection of the more favoured area to accepting the disadvantages and underwriting the finances of a less prosperous neighbour. Occasionally the resistance to amalgamation is strong enough to be successful. In the Sydney area Hunter's Hill, for example, was able to resist moves to unite the area with Ryde. It can point with pride to an old map showing the same boundaries for the early "village" as for the present municipality.

The fact that areas are often too small and that amalgamations are common, adds to the insecurity of local authorities. The basis of local government has not been determined satisfactorily enough to remove this constant threat of annihilation from the smaller councils, and their suspicion that larger councils may be predatory empire-builders. Local authorities and their representatives are likely to oppose every amalgamation that is suggested. The Chairman of the Royal Commission on Areas (1946) mentions in his report that almost every local government witness resisted suggestions for amalgamation on the grounds that "Local Government, as we know it, would be destroyed."

But, in spite of all this, a great many amalgamations have been successful and a great many citizens have welcomed the improved services that have usually followed the increase in area. This prompts the suspicion that what people want out of local government is largely a matter of effective local services and that they readily accustom themselves to being members of a large unit if these services improve.

Metropolitan and Planning Problems

The great metropolitan area is a special modern phenomenon, in all countries and under all economic systems. Only modern transport and technology makes it possible. Its problems have not yet been solved anywhere though some Great Cities have made more gallant attempts than have others.[20]

Like London, New York, Bombay, Moscow, Buenos Aires, Manchester and Los Angeles, Sydney and other Australian capitals have experienced certain characteristic metropolitan developments in the last fifty or sixty years. These include:

(i) the linking of formerly separated suburban and outlying areas into a fairly continuous built up area and the consequent blurring of old local boundaries;

---

[19] A number of recommendations on these lines were made in New South Wales by the Royal Commission on Local Government Areas in the County of Cumberland, *Report*, 1946.

[20] See W. A. Robson (ed.), *Great Cities of the World*, London, 1954. It includes a chapter on Sydney, by F. A. Bland. cf. J. D. B. Miller, "Greater Sydney, 1892-1932", *Pub. Admin. (Sydney)*, XVI, June and Sept., 1954.

(ii) an increasing movement of people through and across the whole area in search of entertainment, open spaces, beaches and so on, and to visit one another ;

(iii) the growth of dormitory suburbs and a situation where thousands (or millions) of people journey to the commercial and industrial centre.

Another characteristic feature is that a larger and larger percentage of the population concentrates in this metropolitan area. In the United States about thirty-five per cent. of the population lives in fourteen large metropolitan areas of over one million people, with New York having eight million. In Britain seventeen million people, forty per cent. of the population, are in London and five other cities. In Australia the capital city of each State has half or more than half the State population and the percentage is growing. What is peculiar to Australia is the dominance of one city in each State. But the developments are similar everywhere.

This concentration of numbers and this urban sprawl over nearby areas leads to great transport problems, and problems of uncontrolled building development and the ruin of the countryside near the metropolis. These problems and the proliferation of special authorities attempting piece-meal solutions have led, on many occasions, to the consideration of some governing body for the whole of the area. Most of such proposals have come to nothing. The problem is complicated in Australia by the weight of the capital cities in their States. For example, the State Government which has left greater Sydney's local government in the hands of a mass of different authorities, state and local, is itself located in Sydney and (some would say) dominated by Sydney. A greater Sydney Council would include over half the population of the whole State and might be something like a "State within a State." It is perhaps significant that the one capital which has acquired a unified and fairly strong local authority is Brisbane, the relative weight of which in terms of population in its own State is least.

In Sydney, the rival merits of a single metropolitan authority or of some kind of "federal" body were canvassed busily at the turn of the century, encouraged by dissatisfaction with the existing state of affairs, charges of corruption in the Sydney City Council and discussion of the newly established London County Council (1888).([21]) Legislation was promised in 1902, but did not appear. In 1912 a bill providing for a convention to plan Sydney's government was introduced, delayed by the Legislative Council's opposition, and dropped. A Royal Commission for Greater Sydney was appointed in 1913 and its findings resulted in a Greater Sydney Bill in 1915. Had this been passed the Sydney area would have been divided into an inner and an outer zone, the inner one being the full responsibility

---

([21]) Sidney Webb was in New South Wales in 1898, giving lectures on municipal government in Britain and especially on the London County Council, for which he was a devoted worker. An interesting work of the period is:—
J. D. Fitzgerald, *Greater Sydney and Greater Newcastle* (Sydney, 1906). "The municipal government of Greater Sydney is hampered by every disadvantage which divided control can bring . . . . It has 41 councils, nearly 500 aldermen and 41 staffs . . . . It has built 41 costly Town Halls; it has 41 separate debts . . . .; it has 41 different health problems, met and solved in different ways . . . ." Fitzgerald was later the first Minister for Local Government.

of the Greater Sydney Council, the outer zone retaining the old councils but having the more important general functions—electricity, roads, e.g.—run by the metropolitan authority. This Bill also failed.

When the Sydney City Council was dismissed for corruption and inefficiency (especially with regard to its electricity undertaking) in 1927, the non-Labour government which took this action announced plans to work out a greater Sydney scheme to take over from the temporary appointed Commission. A Parliamentary Committee's scheme of 1929 proposed a Greater Sydney Council to deal with electricity, main roads, fire brigades, national parks, airports, town planning, transport, health and some other functions. As Minister for Local Government in the Labour Government of 1931, McKell sponsored a scheme somewhat on these lines and including provision for a parliamentary franchise, payment of members and a reduction of councils in the county of Cumberland from 68 to 27.[22] Existing municipalities opposed the amalgamations, there was opposition, especially from the Legislative Council, on the franchise and payment proposals—then the depression raised more urgent problems and hastened the collapse of the government which had proposed it. The question of Greater Sydney government lay dormant up to and during the war.[23]

Since the war the problems that caused the schemes to be considered have become acute, and some of them have been tackled, but in a slightly less ambitious way. In New South Wales, Newcastle has had a Greater City Council since the mid thirties, Wollongong since 1947. In Sydney the hurdles seem too difficult. There never has been agreement on just what is sought. When the proposals have been developed in detail there have been violent differences of opinion about the form of such an authority and its powers. Existing councils have feared and resented being abolished or over-ridden. They have feared especially the possible concentration of power in the City Council. Each time a bill has been sponsored, it has become the battleground for other political fights. One is inclined to feel, for example, that a Labour government really anxious to start the scheme might have compromised on the then thorny issues of franchise and payment of members, and hoped for later changes. Or that the non-Labour government might have taken advantage of the 1927-28 situation of the City Commission and tried out the scheme they were talking about. But always these proposals have collapsed.

In the later years of the war planning and development schemes were in the air, and once more a State government decided to concern itself with the government of Sydney. But the approach now was more piecemeal. In 1945 a Royal Commission[24] was appointed to consider Local Government areas in the County of Cumberland and make proposals on boundaries and

---

[22] Department of Local Government, 1930-31, *Report*, p. 2; and schedule 10 of the 1931 Bill.

[23] In 1935 a joint authority for electricity was established, the Sydney County Council. It distributes electricity over an area of 329 square miles, with a population of about 1.25 m. See also pp. 106-107.

[24] cf. Royal Commission into Local Government Areas in the County of Cumberland, 1946, *Report*. It consisted of: Mr. Justice Clancy (Chairman), Mr. Havilland (of the Local Government Dept.) and Mr. Storey (Mayor of Drummoyne).

areas.   An enormous amount of interesting evidence was collected but its work was very inconclusive. The terms of reference were so narrow, the assumptions and attitudes of the Commissioners so dissimilar that in the result three quite separate and very different recommendations were made. The one favoured by the government was Mr. Havilland's scheme—a curious proposal for eight cities in the metropolitan area. Strong opposition came from the local authorities concerned. Most of the scheme was shelved. All that did happen was an amalgamation of areas that reduced the number of metropolitan councils from 66 to 39.

While this investigation was going on, another attempt was being made to deal with control and supervision of at least one problem that was obviously "metropolitan" in scope—the problem of land use, development and planning. In 1944([25]) the Cumberland County Council scheme had been proposed. In 1945 the Council was established with the duty, first, of drawing up a master plan for the whole of Sydney—to zone areas for future land use, plan parks and open spaces (and for this purpose, necessarily to suggest restrictions on land use) and new roads and streets and bridges. It operates over an area of more than 1500 square miles. The problems, of course, have not been solved by the Cumberland County Council. A vast amount of work has been done in surveys, estimates of future growth, "green belt" planning, schemes for arterial roads and traffic diversion. But every proposal made by the Council must necessarily involve some restriction and perhaps hardship. Every modification made to meet protests or accede to the Minister's requests or to fit in with plans of other departments weakens this authority and encourages a nibbling away of the general structure of the plan. It is probable that the legislation setting up the Council has real weaknesses. There are those who believe that the Council has too small a staff to do the detailed and patient surveys which would allow it more fully to anticipate the possible objections, and that it has too little authority—is too subject to possible political and departmental control—for it to be able to resist the pressures put on it. We cannot go into the Council's work in detail here.   But, whether the Cumberland County plan works out as some people hope, it is important that at last some authority is concerned to study the problems and collate the information about this area. If the Council had done nothing else it would need to be remembered as a practical educator, a constant reminder to Sydney's citizens of the dilemma they are in—the dilemma involved in the fact that, if nothing is done officially to control land use, this in itself means enormously important decisions are being made with no-one seeing the problem as a whole. What happens now in the development of Sydney must at least be against a background of knowledge.

The Cumberland County Council was not the only planning authority set up. There is a somewhat similar organization for the Newcastle area, and elsewhere individual councils have been encouraged to appoint plan-

([25]) At first the government proposed an appointed body. It was only after intensive campaigning by the Local Government Association that the government yielded to their request to have the members of the Council of this planning authority indirectly elected from the councils in the area. On its work, see D. Winston, *Sydney's Great Experiment*, 1957. It consists of ten Councillors elected by the municipal and shire councils of the area.

ning officers, develop plans for their area and submit them for public approval or objection—and then for ministerial approval and gradual implementation. In some of the provincial cities of New South Wales this development has been very interesting. This is the first time that such comprehensive studies have been made of these towns—of their streets and buildings, topography, traffic, commercial flow, and so on. Whether a local authority adopts or not the plan which the council's planning officer has prepared and displayed, at least future development will proceed against this background of awareness. In the course of preparing detailed studies of what building and land use is being projected by all the varied organizations—the Education and Main Roads Departments, Post Office, Electricity Commission, churches, banks, commercial groups and so on—that have some claim on a town's building area, a planning officer becomes to some extent a liaison officer, a co-ordinator, the source of all the knowledge which would never have become available otherwise. Town planning schemes, where they have been established, have put the council in the position of being general directors of local development.([26])

Metropolitan Problems in other States

In Victoria, Melbourne has had a history rather like Sydney's, with a series of bills which "all foundered at earlier or later stages on the rocks of apathy and the hostility of entrenched interests."([27]) The Melbourne and Metropolitan Board of Works (1890) representing councils of the metropolitan area, was given similar functions to those of the Metropolitan Water, Sewerage and Drainage Board in Sydney. It levies its own rates. Some attempts have been made to extend its functions. A "unificationist" Bill was passed in 1951, but narrowly defeated in the Legislative Council. It provided for the Board of Works and the thirty metropolitan councils to be incorporated in a new Greater Melbourne Council. As in the case of Sydney, the potentially most fruitful development has been in the field of town planning. The Board of Works was asked to prepare a plan in 1949, and in 1954 the State government passed legislation making the Board "the continuous planning authority for the metropolis". In 1956 a further step was taken when it was made the responsible authority for metropolitan highways, bridges, parks and foreshores.

The other capitals are smaller, and their problems perhaps less pressing.([28]) Queensland is the only State where plans for a truly unified "metropolitan" authority have come to anything. In 1925 the Greater Brisbane Council assumed the responsibility for an area of 375 square miles, in which all other local authorities were abolished. It was also given wide general powers to govern its area. The Greater Brisbane Council, in addition to

---

([26]) i.e., outside the Cumberland and Northumberland County areas—though even there, councils individually have town planning responsibilities under the County Council's general supervision.

([27]) A. F. Davies "Local Government in Melbourne," *Pub. Admin. (Sydney)*, XIV, June, 1955, p. 66. This article contains a good discussion of the merits and demerits of various schemes.

([28]) On Perth, see *Plan for the Metropolitan Region of Perth and Fremantle, 1955*. The metropolitan area round Adelaide, with a population of about 500,000, contains 21 separate local authorities. See S. B. Hart, "Town Planning and Metropolitan Adelaide", in R. J. Best (ed.), *Introducing South Australia, 1958*.

assuming the powers of local authorities in the area, took over from ad hoc state agencies such as the existing Metropolitan Water Supply and Sewerage Board, the Brisbane Tramway Trust, etc. The scheme was part of a more general "greater local authority" policy initiated in 1915 and which resulted in the creation of several other "greater" cities in Queensland, though its impetus failed before the policy could be extended generally to local authorities in that State. A recent development is the creation of the Town of South Coast by a union of tourist resorts and their hinterlands.

Regionalism and New States

In some states there has been a mild amount of interest in the creation of "regional" authorities. In New South Wales the Cohen Royal Commission on new States recommended in 1925 a series of indirectly elected district councils, whose functions were to include a number then undertaken by State agencies, e.g., most public works. No action was taken on these proposals, but there has been some revival of interest in them lately.[29] During the war, a Regional Boundaries Committee divided the state into seventeen "regions," based on various geographical, economic and social factors and advisory Regional Development Committees were established, representing local councils, State departments and others. They were to prepare schemes for the development of their regions; but their work has not on the whole come to much. Some similar developments have occurred in other states, e.g., Victoria. There has been some regional decentralization of State government activities—for example, in New South Wales, the Area Offices of the Education Department, the Regional Supervisors of the Department of Agriculture and the District Offices of the Child Welfare Department, Housing Commission and Soil Conservation Service. Towns like Newcastle, Wollongong, Bathurst, Lismore and Wagga are coming to have quite a number of regional officers with duties in the surrounding area. But this is not, of course, local government.

The "regional" movement in New South Wales derived some of its initial impetus from the New States Movement,[30] which has been more vigorous there than in other States, though there have been some similar proposals in Queensland. The New State movement has many influences behind it —hostility of the country for the city; irritation felt in some areas at Labour Party control of State government; a belief that the rural areas could develop better as independent units; a hope that, by forming New States, the predominance of the great metropolis would be destroyed and a more satisfactory spread of population achieved.

During the nineteen-twenties a proposal for the formation of a New State of New England (in the northern area of New South Wales) actually came before the Legislative Assembly, and the Commonwealth Government indicated its willingness to accept the New State if it were formed. But

[29] The Local Government Association of N.S.W., has proposed a system of indirectly-elected councils with responsibility for large-scale works, housing, education, roads, etc., financed by government grants.

[30] The best short survey of this is by R. S. Parker, in *New States for Australia*, Australian Institute of Political Science, 1955. The paper also includes some details of administrative decentralisation in New South Wales.

that was a non-Labour concession to Country Party desires; and no further action was taken.

The Commonwealth Constitution requires the consent of the Parliament of the existing State affected before a new one can be formed; and no State government is likely to surrender willingly any area rich enough to be an independent State. So there are many difficulties in the way. However, the movement has had enormous political value for the areas where it is strong. It has drawn attention to their needs, encouraged the spread of electrical power, the decentralization of education and so on. The New State movement includes among its supporters some members of city, municipal and shire councils in the area concerned. But generally, local government supporters appear to distrust the movement's proposals, though they sympathise with the grievances which have prompted them.

THE COUNCIL SYSTEM

It is difficult to talk in general terms about what local authorities do as they vary so much in area, population and income. In New South Wales, a provincial city council like Albury has a total staff of 179 with a salaries and wages bill of £167,312 for the year. Eighty-eight of these are concerned with providing electricity, water and sewerage and with running the municipal abattoirs. A municipality like Warren, however, has a total staff of only seven and a salaries and wages bill of £5,151. Excluding Sydney and Newcastle, the municipalities and cities in New South Wales vary in area from one square mile to more than 500, in population from under 1,000 to 135,000, in resources from under £1,500 to more than £200,000 a year. Three shires—Lake Macquarie, Warringah and Sutherland—have total staffs of 264, 386 and 409.[31] But Murrumbidgee shire has a total staff of fifteen, of whom eleven are construction workers, and a salaries and wages bill of £16,604. More than half the 133 shires have an administrative staff of under ten (including office assistants) whereas the few large shires have an administrative staff of thirty to sixty, or even more in one or two cases.

Thus some councils are the controllers of large and varied administrative organizations—while others are concerned only with minimum responsibilities, say, country roads and, perhaps, some prevention of noxious weeds and some health supervision. It is essential that these wide variations should be remembered. If an area is sparsely populated and its rate income low, the chances of its having a local authority that can provide a variety of services are slight.

Elections for New South Wales councils are on a parliamentary franchise, together with an owner, ratepaying lessee or occupier franchise and are held in December every three years. Voting is compulsory and, though this has not been strictly enforced, the numbers voting in local elections have increased considerably over the past ten years. Compulsory voting in State and Federal elections is so generally accepted that only a small minority worries about this extension of compulsion to local government. Some members of local councils deplore this and blame it, and the pro-

---

[31] 1956 figures, from annual returns in Local Government Department, N.S.W.

portional representation system which is also general, for the increase in "party" organization and voting in local authorities.

The major political parties are sometimes, but by no means universally, the chief contestants at local elections. The principal cities, especially capital cities, in any country are likely to be prizes that no national party will ignore. But even for the Sydney City Council the contest is by no means simply between Liberal and Labour, and the existence of purely "local" competing groups does have its effect. In the ordinary municipalities, shires and provincial cities there has been some increase, so it is claimed, in "party politics" but there are still quite a number of places where candidates do not even form groups for election purposes, but simply stand as individuals.

If party organization is essential for the proper working of State and Commonwealth governments, it is difficult to see at once why it should be opposed in local government. And it is possible to discover local authorities—suburban as well as rural—where there are strong differences in party allegiances among the members of council without this preventing effective co-operation on local matters. But this is rare. Experience of strong party divisions in a municipal or shire council has been generally unfortunate. Party organization in the State or Federal sphere is directed at capturing power and deciding policy in one governing body, the Federal parliament or the State parliament. But local elections are not contests for one local governing body, or even for a collection of nearly identical authorities, but for hundreds of different ones. There are, of course, some common issues, but there are many more specific to each area. Too much concentration on national (or State) party affiliations is therefore almost certain to distort things and to make the councils battlefields for contests on national or State issues to the detriment of local concerns.

Once elected a councillor or aldermen finds himself[32] with certain duties. He becomes responsible, as do his fellow councillors, for the activities of the council and its staff, especially for the custody and proper control of the funds at their disposal. He must accept certain rules designed to prevent the enrichment of himself or his family directly through council policy—or to safeguard him from suspicion of this—rules requiring declaration of any interest in a contract, or abstention from voting in some cases. Neglect of these rules may bring a challenge from another member of council, from a local citizen, or some action from the Local Government Department. The proper working of a local council system requires a vigilant check against the possibility, or the suspicion, of personal profiteering. But the checking is sometimes lax. Councillors who know one another well may sometimes feel that obedience to formal rules and strict procedure is scarcely necessary among friends. Sometimes vigilance can develop into petty obstruction. Sometimes it is not easy to know what obligations a member of council has, and there are frequent requests to legal advisers associated with e.g., the Local Government Association, for information on real or hypothetical cases of this kind:

> "Councillor Jones has a son who requested the paving of a footpath in his street. This was rejected, Councillor Jones abstaining. Now

---

[32] himself or herself. There are (1958) forty-two women councillors and aldermen, and a woman has been mayor in several municipal areas.

in the course of the regular programme of works, Council is faced with deciding between paving M— Street (Where Jones, jnr. lives) and another street. May Councillor Jones vote?" (The answer was that he could.)

Responsibility in matters of finance is one of the main matters to be faced by all members of the council. There are strict rules about the passing of accounts, authorising of expenditure and so on. Members of the Finance Committee have a special responsibility but a failure at any stage by council members to ensure that the rules are obeyed may render them liable to surcharge.([33]) Aldermen and councillors have been held liable for surcharge for allowing disbursements that have not been properly authorised or for authorising expenditure which councils should not properly undertake. The Local Government Department, through its annual reports, inspectors' reports and special bulletins endeavours to enforce conformity to its pattern of financial procedure. But sometimes it has a difficult task.

As individuals, therefore, members of councils who are interested in their jobs and want to safeguard themselves, must "learn the rules". The council as a whole, too, has certain things it must do, many things which it may do and some things which are expressly forbidden. There are obligations on a council concerning how it conducts its business, how its staff is appointed and employed, the reports it must furnish, as well as, of course, the jobs it must do.

One of the first duties of a council is to elect a mayor or president (save where he is directly elected by the voters, as in Sydney). It should also decide formally on a time and place of regular council meetings. Omitting this may make possible a challenge to the legality of decisions at a particular meeting. A Finance Committee and a Works Committee must be formed. Most councils form other committees also, though there are some where no separate committees are formed, where the whole council is Finance Committee, Works Committee, Parks Committee and so on. This is not favoured by the Department of Local Government which prefers the more business-like concentration of effort made possible by separate committees.

In the ordinary business of the council the rules and procedures are minutely laid down. Certain records must be kept and duly confirmed. As these constitute the legal record of council decisions and the authority for its servants' actions, neither minute books nor rate books may be destroyed for twenty years. The most detailed requirements are laid down concerning financial powers and procedures—the making as well as the levying of rates, their collection, the separate funds to be used, the publishing of accounts and so on. They must send in regular returns to the Department of Local Government (on staff, salaries and wages, rates levied, income

([33]) For example, where a council left the conduct of affairs almost completely to the town clerk, issued blank cheques, failed to see that purchases shown had actually been made, and so on—with the result that the town clerk absconded with £7,000—the council members were surcharged, that is, ordered to pay certain sums in recompense. Even in this quite obvious case, however, it proved difficult to get more than a token amount from each alderman.

generally, etc.) However small the council, however poor, the same regular returns are required. This is one reason why the smaller local authorities may seem to consist almost entirely of administrative staff. The Department of Local Government depends on the checking of these as a way of seeing how effectively each council is working. Over the years enough material is piled up in the Department to enable inspectors of accounts and other officers to see where the trouble-spots are and to judge whether satisfactory work is being done.

If they suspect that all is not going well they may send an inspector to the council, with powers to investigate accounts and the general working of the authority, and also to recommend changes. In extreme cases of inefficiency or malpractice he may recommend the council's dismissal and its replacement by an administrator. About twelve such appointments have been made in New South Wales since 1919, not a large number in a State of more than two hundred and thirty councils. The Local Government Department usually tries gentle persuasion, almost too patiently, before it takes the drastic step of dismissing a Council. Some such occasions are preceded by press "revelations", local citizens' protests or by information sent to the Department. But as a rule the inspection staff in the Department will have been aware of weaknesses and will have been warning and advising for a long time in the course of routine visits and enquiries.

In 1952 newspapers in Sydney printed the story that members of a local council[34] were alleged to have used council vehicles for their private use, and for the private journeys of their wives, to have built houses for themselves with council labour and equipment, and generally to have used their Council position for open private gain. It was not so readily revealed that the Local Government Department had been issuing warning after warning to this Council for their failure to keep proper accounts, especially for their failure to insist on payments due from members of council for work done on their behalf. And when another council was dismissed in 1954 there was the same history of patient reproach and warnings by the inspectors of accounts. Here the charge was mainly concerned with the refusal of councillors to carry out the proper supervision and restraint of one of their engineers in buying materials and selling electrical goods.

But the appointment of an administrator is not necessarily because of corruption. In one recent case a council in financial difficulties was declared a defaulting area because the resignation of a number of aldermen left it without a quorum. It was eventually made the centre of a newly created shire.

When an administrator is appointed he is, in law, the council and directs policy, deciding on rates and giving instructions to the staff. He even holds council "meetings"—i.e., he goes through the formalities of announcing decisions in the council chambers on regular occasions, and the public have the right to be present and to learn what is being planned. The administrator has the right to do anything he considers necessary—within a coun-

---

[34] The council was eventually dismissed, though it defended its actions vigorously. One feature of this incident was a public resolution in support of the council. Admittedly it was at an "organized" meeting, but still it casts a strange light on public concern for local government.

cil's powers, of course—to set the authority's organization and development on the right lines again. But the dismissal of a council is rare.

In all these local authorities the council officially controls policy while an administrative staff, headed by the town or shire clerk, is the permanent organization which carries out council decisions. The town or shire clerk is usually the key figure in any local council. He is in effect the general manager, he controls the staff and usually has considerable powers of appointment for any but the senior positions. The clerk sets the tone for most councils. An efficient and knowledgeable clerk can be a powerful influence. Of course the final word is with the council. It must authorise his action and can refuse to accept the advice of its clerk, engineer or any other officer. But councillors are busy men, and their council work is part-time and unpaid, so they often rely enormously on the efforts of their clerk.

The appointment of an engineer is also required, though it is possible for his services to be shared between two or even three small local authorities who could not separately afford a qualified engineer. Most average-sized councils now would also have a health officer and buildings inspector. Planning officers are now becoming quite common in New South Wales.

As we have seen, for most purposes local councils are under the supervision of the Local Government Department. But they are agents for a number of other government departments. A great deal of the engineer's work is concerned with roads, where his staff is largely doing work on behalf of the Main Roads Department. The health inspector, though responsible to the council, has most of his duties laid down by law and by the numerous regulations and decisions of the State Board of Health.

If councils have sufficient money, if they are energetic, and if they have support for their policies, there are many things, beyond their basic responsibilities, which they may do. They must be responsible for paving and lighting streets—they may in addition provide garden plots, weather shelters and many other possible improvements. They must deal with cleansing and with garbage disposal—but they may do this more frequently and more effectively than is legally required ; and so on. New South Wales councils have powers covering the provision of libraries, public markets, playgrounds and sports arenas, art galleries or collections, children's clinics, even community hotels, and many other services. There are also activities which councils may subsidise, as well as those which they may provide directly. In certain rural areas they may subsidise medical nursing and ambulance services, welfare centres, hospitals and kindergartens. Examples of every one of these activities can be found in some areas in New South Wales. The factors which decide whether any of these powers will be used and whether the local authority will become something more than a local provider of roads, pavements and drainage are principally these: how far the area has already been "developed" (i.e., how much really costly new work in street-making, etc. has to be done) ; how acceptable their policies are to local ratepayers ; how much money they can raise. Money and local support are the crucial factors.

Local Authorities and Finance

Lack of finance is one of the main brakes on the activities of local government. As will be seen from Appendix V, the nominal powers of local authorities in a state such as New South Wales are in fact fairly wide. But the actuality is often different, as few councils feel that they can finance large expansions into new fields without increased aid from State governments.

The revenue of local councils is derived from four sources: rates on local property, income from trading undertakings, grants from the state government, and local licences and fees.

Australian local authorities are very dependent on revenue from rates. In contrast with the United Kingdom, grants from higher authority are relatively small. In England and Wales (1953-4) grants represented 42 per cent. of total local government revenue, excluding income from trading undertakings. In Australia, the equivalent figure (1955-56) was 17 per cent. State grants are mainly for roads, though there are sometimes other subsidies for special purposes, e.g., baby health centres, libraries. The percentage of grants to total revenue has fallen since before the war, when it was about a quarter, and included large sums for unemployment relief work. The other sources of revenue are normally of minor importance, at least as a net contribution to general income.[35]

Local Authorities Ordinary Services, Revenue and Expenditure, 1955-56 [36] *(£m.)*

	N.S.W.	Victoria	All States
Revenue—			
Rates	24·03	15·37	56·66
Licences	0·49	0·09	0·78
Sanitary, etc., services	2·82	1·23	6·68
Council properties	2·38	2·28	6·56
Street construction	1·38	1·04	3·28
Government grants (mainly roads)	8·26	0·69	16·58
Business profits	..	0·29	0·33
Other (including fees and fines)	1·78	0·63	3·76
	41·14	21·62	94·63
Expenditure—			
General administration	2·72	3·33	9·13
Debt services	4·23	1·84	10·72
Roads, streets, bridges	20·10	7·60	41·08
Council properties	5·16	4·25	13·89
Sanitary, etc., services	3·51	1·85	7·50
Street lighting	0·95	0·42	1·90
Health administration	0·77	0·90	2·23
Other[37]	3·50	1·38	8·26
	40·94	21·57	94·71
Loan expenditure	6·10	3·09	15·23

[35] In Western Australia the proceeds of vehicle registration represent an important source of income.

[36] Figures supplied by Commonwealth Bureau of Census and Statistics. For Queensland, they relate to 1953-54, the latest year available. More detailed statistics for New South Wales are given in Appendix II.

[37] Including fire and hospital grants and some payments to roads boards.

Local Authorities Business Undertakings (£m.)

	N.S.W.	Victoria	All States
Revenue—			
Water and sewerage—			
Rates and charges[38]	2·52 ⎱	0·12	5·57
Grants, etc.	0·69 ⎰		1·76
Electricity and gas—			
Rates and charges	44·20	9·22	60·69
Grants, etc.	1·26	0·14	1·80
Other	2·64	0·51	6·65
	51·31	9·99	76·47
Expenditure—			
Water and sewerage	2·36	0·12	6·36
Electricity and gas	43·52	9·14	60·33
Other	2·56	0·54	6·97
	48·44	9·80	73·66
Loan expenditure	9·57	1·14	16·59

Local authorities' current expenditure in 1955-56 represented about 11 per cent. of expenditure by all public authorities (federal, state and local). This compares with about 15 per cent. before the war. In relation to state expenditure, current expenditure on local government services has remained fairly constant.

(£m)	State expenditure from consolidated revenue	Local current expenditure
1938-39	128	37
1955-56	541	168

But this is minor when compared with the relative decline of both state and local government in the face of mounting federal expenditures. Local authority loan expenditures have declined relatively to the states— they represented about one-third of state gross loan expenditure on works in 1938-39, and only about one-sixth in 1955-56.

The most important item of local expenditure (ignoring the self balancing items of electricity), is on roads and streets.[39] The next two are on upkeep of council properties—including parks, gardens and recreation facilities, and sanitary and garbage services. When the expense of these and one

[38] The "rates" involved were mainly for water and sewerage in N.S.W. (£2.00m) and Tasmania (£0.56m).

[39] In 1956, 40.6 per cent. of the total expenditure (excluding expenditure from Loan Funds) on roads in New South Wales was financed from local rates. See *Survey of Local Government Finance (Summarised Statement)*, Local Government Association of N.S.W., p. 13. The equivalent figure for U.S.A. and Canada is about one-fifth, as there road-user taxes bear more of the burden.

or two other items have been met, there is not much left over for the newer health and welfare services.

Rates on local property form the chief source of local authority income. There may be a number of rates—a "general rate" which must be levied, special rates for certain purposes (e.g., water, library) and loan rates for repayment of borrowing. In some states limits are imposed on rating. but in New South Wales there is no maximum general rate.

Councils may also raise loans for capital works, but the total amount depends on Loan Council allocations, while the distribution of the amount allocated is a matter for State government decision. It is one grievance of local authorities that no representative speaks for them at the Loan Council, and that when loan funds are reduced, it is almost always local government that suffers most in proportion. But even if greater allocations were made loans still have to be repaid, and this requires rate levies.

Councils do sometimes engage in trading activities, e.g., electricity supply, markets. In New South Wales they are strictly limited in what they may do with any profits made. Ministerial policy insists that trading operations should, as nearly as possible, cover costs only, passing benefits back to consumers rather than making profits and using them to reduce rates. Some representatives of local authorities in New South Wales have tried to have this policy altered, pointing out that in Victoria, for example, councils are permitted to use profits from these as additions to their general funds. (In fact the amounts involved are usually small as the scope of municipally-owned business undertakings is not great.) This has been strenuously opposed by the Department of Local Government in New South Wales.

Rates are normally levied on either the unimproved capital value of land (U.C.V.), i.e., site values, or on the annual value of improved land, i.e., rental values. The former is the main basis of rating in New South Wales and Queensland.([40]) It involves the payment of a tax based on the estimated amount which the land owned would fetch if it were to be sold without the buildings, etc., on it. One of its merits is held to be that it makes owners put their land to full use (or sell to someone else who will). Its adoption by New South Wales and Queensland in the early part of this century was regarded as a "progressive" reform—rating by annual value was the English system. The fact that U.C.V. disregards the actual use made of a given site can cause some hardships. Site value revaluations are harder and more costly to make than improved value reassessments; and obsolete valuations distribute the rate-burden unfairly between individuals. Dissatisfaction about rates is also linked with methods of valuation. Since councils are required to levy uniform rates over their areas the more recently valued section of a shire or municipality may find individual rate bills much higher than those for similar blocks which happen to have come under an earlier valuation. One council near Sydney recently tried to meet this

([40]) Western Australia uses both systems; this is true to a small extent in a number of states, though "annual value" is still the main basis in the others. In South Australia and Victoria some local authorities have changed to the unimproved capital value system. In some cases in New South Wales rates may be levied on "improved" values (i.e., land and buildings).

problem by differential rating—but this is forbidden and the Department of Local Government eventually forced the council into altering its policy.

It has been claimed that dependence on rates puts the burden of local services wholly on the property owners, whereas a great many services provided by councils benefit the whole of the local community. While local authorities were concerned almost exclusively with property development— streets, lighting, cleansing, sanitation, etc.—payment for these by property-owners only could be defended (so runs the argument). But, as councils are asked more and more to take social welfare and cultural responsibilities the financial responsibility should be shared more widely. Rates have been increasing in recent years. In New South Wales between 1946 and 1955 the average rate (on unimproved capital values) rose from 4.61d. to 6.95d. in the pound, and rate revenues from £6.08m. to £23.8m.

Even if we do not believe that rate levels have reached "the limit of what the property-owner can bear" we might still agree that some more just arrangement might be one where all residents contributed something, on the basis of ability to pay. Against this it is argued that many owners can pass on the cost of their rates through rents and other prices and that therefore all local residents are indirectly made to pay rates. However, there is something in the argument that a more direct payment might be a stimulant to local interest. In other countries, especially in continental Europe and America, local authorities have many special local dues to supplement their "rate" or property taxes. Chicago taxes entertainments and motor vehicles, Rome gets funds from a long list of taxes on such items as domestic servants, rent receipts, dogs, coffee-making machines (to name only a few). New York City has a sales tax and a tax on businesses, sixty per cent. of Moscow's income is derived from the profits of local industries. In some places a local income-tax, or a local sur-tax on the national income tax, is collected for the local authorities.

The British local government system is more dependent on property rates than those in continental Europe or in America. But its rate income is supplemented by central government grants in a way that has not yet been adopted in Australia. If, therefore, Australian local authorities need greater financial resources than rates provide, and if it is agreed that they should be supported by more than the local property-owners, then the most prac- ticable solution seems to be increased grants from the States. Some have even pressed for grants from the Federal Government. It is not likely that a grant of special taxing powers would now be made to New South Wales local authorities. It is just as unlikely that such special local taxes would be accepted in our increasingly uniform society. They would in any case not provide any equitable solution of the problem of special needs. The only policy which might gain acceptance seems to be something on the lines of British grants-in-aid.

In Britain, the central government has for many years followed a policy of making grants-in-aid to encourage special developments, which has also been used to a certain extent in Australia. But in Britain this system is used more extensively, and there is also a growing practice of making Exchequer Equalisation Grants—i.e., supplements to the general income of local authorities where there is special need. To work out a satisfactory formula for making such grants was a complicated and difficult task. But a formula was developed and has been in use for years. A real attempt was made to take into account variations in population, age distribution, income, and thus develop a measure of relative needs. With the British experience to assist us, and with the experience of the Commonwealth Grants Commission, it would not be impossible to work out some scheme of grants that would give assistance where it was most needed.[41]

Even if there were available to local authorities in New South Wales some share of the "common pool of taxation" the problem of fair allocation would not be easy. Some areas are wealthy and well-established with most of their developmental tasks—paving, lighting, sewerage, garbage disposal—adequately dealt with. In such areas, with probably a high average rateable value of land per head of population, and maintenance rather than development the main task, a comparatively low rate may provide effective local services and allow for some local experimentation. In other places it may be difficult to decide whether more efficient planning of activities and careful use of available finance might not have had better results. But in some areas at least (the outer suburbs of large cities for example, and in some provincial towns) where rapid expansion is occurring and enormously costly facilities are demanded in a short time, even a comparatively high rate may bring insufficient return for effective tackling of the jobs. Those who urge that government grants should subsidise such development are in effect urging that these developments are not just a local problem, that it is justifiable to claim that the more fortunate areas should contribute through taxation to them.

Another financial grievance of local authorities is the problem of non-rateable land owned by Federal and State departments and commissions, churches, schools, etc. There is a considerable list of exemptions from general rating where the Crown is owner or where some special religious, charitable or educational purpose is involved. These exemptions affect some areas much more seriously than others, but in all areas it means that some developments, say, a Housing Commission scheme,[42] cause quite serious loss of rate revenue at least for the time being. Local authorities here have unsuccessfully reminded State and Commonwealth departments that the British government in similar circumstances makes considerable ex-gratia payments in lieu of rates.

Finance is then the crucial problem of local government. Not all councils are in difficulties. But it is true that most of them face enormously increased costs for the basic services for which councils are responsible at the same time that more health and welfare responsibilities are being added to councils' tasks. Representatives of local authorities claim that council income is drawn from too restricted a source, and that since local rates as they stand are inequitably based, great increases in them are likely to make for greater injustices. They assert that difficulties in the Federal system—especially in finance—make the position of local authorities worse than it was some years

---

[41] The British Government announced plans in February, 1957, for replacing most specific grants by a general exchequer grant to local authorities, based on a formula which takes account of varying needs.

[42] Housing Commission homes are, of course, rateable once they are occupied, but from the time the land is reserved for this purpose until there are residents, the council's revenue suffers.

ago. For all these reasons their spokesmen hope to bring attention to their problems by making submissions to current discussions of Federal-State taxation arrangements and general constitutional problems.

Conclusion—Local Government and the Public

Two contrasting pictures are often presented of local government in Australia. Euthusiasts, conscious of departmental control, financial problems and public neglect, conjure up a vision of a noble giant, tied down by rules and restrictions, capable of moving mountains if only State governments and public opinion would recognise its true worth and provide adequate resources. Opposed to this is the press and popular caricature—a Hogarthian gallery of racketeers and their shady "deals". The ordinary citizen does not necessarily believe this of his own council. But popular talk and press comment constantly imputes the worst motives to local councillors.

Neither of these pictures is, of course, a true one. And there is a third often left out altogether—the picture of a large number of administrative units, varying enormously in size and resources, but almost always discharging with reasonable efficiency a great variety of essential jobs—road making, street cleaning, garbage disposal, supervision of health regulations in food, cleanliness of shops and hotels, etc., maintenance of certain general standards in building, prevention of disease, and so on. Most of the functions of local authorities are essential tasks which would need to be carried out by some governmental authority if the "local council" were not in control. And it cannot be assumed that the local council system, generally, does not provide a more effective service than would come from a completely state-directed organization. It is often assumed that local councils, shire councils in particular, are so restricted in their functions that it is difficult to imagine a real interest being taken in their work by councillors. But this, I believe, is false. It is like the intellectual's assumption that all repetitive mechanical jobs must be boring and frustrating. Shire councillors are principally concerned with roads. But roads are of enormous importance to most shire councillors. The difference that can be made by the sealing of a road to the commercial and to the social development of a country area is a very important one.

Moreover, local authorities provide a great variety of other local services of a slightly less utilitarian kind in which local choice and local effort can play a considerable part. Under the New South Wales Library Act, a continuous expansion of council-controlled libraries has occurred.([48]) There is at least one council with a municipal orchestra, quite a number of metropolitan councils have or are developing community centres, or are building municipal shopping areas, some councils have art shows and art competitions, some have child centres, one or two in the country have even experimented with community hotels. Where there is a range of permissive

---

([48]) One hundred and twenty-eight councils now have library services under the Act, about half operating a library jointly with other councils. There are 6 regional library services. Ten councils have mobile library services. Of the regional services, those run from Albury and Tamworth are widest in operation, the Upper Murray Regional Library serving 11 councils and 60,000 people, the Namoi Regional Library serving 14 councils and 67,400 people.

powers for local authorities this means that the locally elected council can, if it has public support, experiment in a number of ways. And, counter-balancing the occasional failure, there is a quite impressive list of areas where the local council has become the focus of local enthusiasm, the leader of local community effort.

Some at least of the suspicion of local government is really an expression of dissatisfaction about policies which, quite legally and properly adopted, may involve decisions most distasteful to some groups and individuals. If we favour municipal housing schemes we may deplore the defeat of one council group which recently began such a scheme. If we are interested in local libraries we may think that only the narrowest commercialism would prevent support for such a development. But decisions to oppose such schemes need not be dishonest or corrupt. The standard of honesty and of responsibility is at least as high among members of councils as in the society in which they work. If they are sometimes parochial, narrow minded, interested in commercial developments first and in cultural activities perhaps last—are they singularly unrepresentative of their constituents?

For those who are dissatisfied with local council policy, one long-term remedy is, of course, to seek election or to support those whose proposals are more acceptable. Of course, in local councils, as in State and Federal Parliaments, the enthusiastic newcomer is often tamed (a) by finding that decisions are by majority, of which he may not be one, (b) by realising that council time and money are not as elastic as he had imagined. But even if the citizens' interest is too spasmodic and short lived for him to seek election to council, there are some local and customary remedies which he may use.

In the first place, he has the legal right of access to certain information. He may attend council meetings, he may have financial statements produced for him, some items—e.g., the making and levying of a rate—must be published in certain ways and there are formal ways of lodging objections. In practice, very few local residents ever do attend council meetings, or keep themselves informed on council activities. Very often the only thing about councils of which they are aware is their rate notice. This is another reason why local government is so acutely aware of financial problems. Those councils which want to be judged not simply by rate levels but by value-given-for-rates find it necessary to build up public support by more direct publicity and propaganda than is possible through dependence on citizen enquiries.

One shire in the Riverina, lacking a newspaper which services the whole area, has over the last few years issued a regular bulletin to all ratepayers. In fact, this has proved much more satisfactory than are local press reports which tend to overstress any dramatic argument and are most unlikely to provide the full and detailed programme and information which the bulletin carries. Already, the officers claim, the scheme is paying dividends in reducing the number of enquiries and in enlisting greater public support through understanding. Many councils are now taking similar steps.

A ratepayer, of course, has a right to more than information. If he opposes a project which the council is undertaking there are some circum-stances where he may seek an "injunction to restrain". A more customary method, where anyone wishes to make objections, is to get some member of council to act as spokesman. Many council members will accept this responsibility (as a member of Parliament may, in asking questions) even if they are not in sympathy with the particular request.

There are open to local citizens, too, all the usual political methods of deputations, letters, meetings, petitions, and so on. The charge of public apathy is justified if we think of lack of interest in local elections, of the general ignorance of councils' achievements, of the few who consider becoming candidates for membership of councils. But councillors and council officers do not as a rule feel that the local public is unaware of and indifferent to what the council is doing. Most of them are bombarded with requests and complaints. In fact, they must often pray for a little apathy for a change.

If the actions of a whole council are felt to be unsatisfactory, local citizens can petition the State department for an enquiry and there have been cases where a petition has been made for a council to be dismissed. The Department, as was shown earlier, is in the position of inspector and supervisor of local authorities and treats with respect well-supported complaints from local groups. But opposition to and, of course, demands for specific or general policies need to be organized and continuously pressed. If citizens are interested and if they will take the trouble there are many opportunities for encouraging a local authority to do certain things, or for restraining them from doing others.

If citizen participation is not strong, is this a thing to be deplored? The assumption is often made that local government is so obviously the basis of our "self-governing democracy" that the claim scarcely needs defending. If the idea is developed it is argued that local government is historically the basis of democracy and that it is the only "truly democratic" government because it allows for wide participation. Now, we have already disposed of the claim that local government was in the past in Australia a vigorous form of self-government, from which it has now declined. The contribution of local government to the "democratic" tradition even in Britain was not one of wide participation. Local authorities till almost this century were in the hands of local privileged minorities. They did act as restraints on central power. But local authorities here have never been independent in that sense. In fact, local authorities in New South Wales now are more effectively part of the general political system than they were fifty years ago. But the second claim also has to be looked at sceptically. It assumes a simple identification of democracy with direct participation when those who claim to be democratic now would be more likely to stress liberty of protest, on one hand, and equality of opportunity on the other, as being at least as important as claims to participation.

But even taking this over-simplified view of what is democratic it would be fairly easy to show that the democratic tradition has not depended here in any important way on local authorities. Self-government, self-determination, responsibility for political decisions—these can be developed in a number of ways. Since local authorities here are, and always have been, largely the administrative tools of State government, the politically active may try to press their claims by participation in State or Federal politics. Or, indeed, by working through any of the numerous associations and organisations which may present claims at any level of government. Enthusiasm and interest in local councils may wane not because democracy is dying, but because even those interested in participation may choose other avenues for their activities.

It is a pity to make too extravagant claims. Local government is not quite the giant depicted by its enthusiastic supporters, nor are the restrictions as irksome and regrettable as is sometimes implied. Local councils do provide a vast amount of voluntary unpaid service to local communities of which they are a part. Their work is probably in general more effective and competent than the cynical public believes, or even deserves. But a great deal of what is important in council work comes from the services of trained professional staff working to codes([44]) that apply throughout the State. Their first duty is to provide and supervise certain essential services, and to raise the money for them. If, in addition, a local council becomes a focus for local pride and provides an opportunity for co-operation and community development, then virtue is added unto it. But we should not expect greater miracles from locally elected councils than we would from State or Federal Parliament.

([44]) Codes that, incidentally, local elected groups would not have been likely to develop themselves. In this, of course, they are little different from other elected groups. Parliamentary decision is the means, but seldom the initiator, of administrative reform and development.

Chapter Seven

THE FINANCE OF GOVERNMENT

R. C. GATES

This chapter is concerned with government revenue and expenditure: their composition, the procedures to which they are subject, and their effects on the community. Since virtually all the activities of governments require some expenditure on administration, even if no other financial transactions are directly involved, the study of the nature and effects of revenue and expenditure could cover a very wide field. Usually, however, the subject-matter of public finance is limited to those areas and aspects of government activity in which the financial element is predominant. It may be further defined by drawing a distinction between fiscal measures and direct measures. The former comprise the acts of government revenue raising and spending. the financial transactions of governments. Direct measures embrace all the other rules by which governments exercise control over the disposition of income and the use of resources: licensing, zoning, rationing, wage fixation, price control, etc. It is with fiscal measures that this chapter is primarily concerned.

GOVERNMENT AS A SECTOR OF THE ECONOMY

As a first step in studying the nature and effects of government financial transactions, it is useful to have a general picture of the place of government in the structure of the economy. Such a picture is provided by the technique of classification known as social accounting. The owners of the assets of the economy are divided into three sectors: flesh and blood *persons,* together with many of the voluntary associations in which they pool their expenditure ; *corporations,* such as limited liability companies ; and *governments.* These three sectors operate the productive enterprises of the economy, including farms, professional practices, factories, shops and plumbers' businesses.

Out of the enterprises there comes a flow of goods and services. Part of the flow is sold to the rest of the world outside the economy, part to the personal sector and part to governments. The payments received in return by the enterprises are known respectively as foreign credits, personal consumption and government expenditure. The part of production which is not sold in this way is added to the stocks of the enterprises in the form of fixed capital (land, buildings and equipment) and inventories (materials, goods in process and goods ready for sale). Such additions, less sales out of stock, are termed gross business investment. They may be treated as being purchased by the owners of the enterprises, not for consumption but as a way of holding assets ; for the owners will have met the expenses incurred in their production. Thus there are four components of the total expenditure of the economy. Their estimated

G 78713—7   K 5805

magnitudes for the Australian economy in three representative years are set out in Table 1. The figures for investment there are confined to privately owned enterprises: because of the lack of separate estimates, investment by government enterprises is included with other government expenditure.

TABLE 1

NATIONAL EXPENDITURE AND REVENUE

	1938-39	1946-47	1956-57
	£m.	£m.	£m.
Personal consumption	642	1,069	3,501
Gross private investment	122	279	978
Government expenditure	174	405	1,170
Foreign credits	163	330	1,116
Total expenditure	1,101	2,083	6,765
Foreign debits	178	366	977
Business taxes	147	303	982
Gross personal factor income	707	1,296	4,454
Gross corporate saving	69	118	352
Total revenue	1,101	2,083	6,765

The rest of Table 1 shows what happens to the proceeds of the expenditure. A part goes to the rest of the world as foreign debits, or payments due for the supply of goods and services to the economy. What is left may be called the *gross national revenue*. Governments take the first slice in the form of business taxes, which include the gross profits of government business undertakings. Some revenue is retained and saved by corporations, chiefly in the form of undistributed company profits. The largest part, however, goes to members of the personal sector as a payment for their productive services: wages and salaries for the services of labour, and rent, interest and dividends for the services of capital. We may include here also the profits of unincorporated enterprises, such as individually owned farms and professional practices, such profits being a composite payment for the services of the owners' labour and capital.

The estimates in Table 1 are derived mainly from figures published annually in the federal government budget paper, *National Income and Expenditure*. Being based on statistical data of varying completeness and reliability, they are for the most part rough approximations.

The national revenue and expenditure account shows the share which accrues directly to governments out of the revenue of enterprises. In addition, however, governments take part of the income of the personal sector in the form of personal taxes. These two sources of government income appear in Table 2, in which the transactions of all three levels of Australian government (federal, state and local) are consolidated into a set of accounts for the government sector of the economy. Government outlay consists not only of expenditure on goods and services, which appeared in Table 1, but also cash benefits, which are transfers of government income to the personal sector in payment of child endowment, age pensions, etc. If outlay exceeds income, there is a deficit in the current account, which means an increase in government liabilities or a decrease in government assets. The capital account shows what part of the deficit is financed by net borrowing and what part by running down cash balances. A surplus on current account would have opposite effects.

TABLE 2

THE GOVERNMENT SECTOR ACCOUNTS

	1938-39	1946-47	1956-57
Current Account			
	£m.	£m.	£m.
Business taxes	147	303	982
Personal taxes	33	167	443
Cash deficit	24	26	35
Gross income	204	496	1,460
Government expenditure	174	405	1,170
Cash benefits	30	91	290
Gross outlay	204	496	1,460
Capital Account			
Decrease in cash	?	7	—6
Borrowing less repayments	?	26	91
Funds available	?	33	85
Cash deficit	24	26	35
Lending less repayments	?	7	50
Funds used	?	33	85

Governments are able to purchase goods and services to a value greater than their share of the total revenue of the economy only if people elsewhere in the economy refrain from spending a corresponding part of their shares. This happens when the personal sector saves (refrains from consuming) some of its current income; or when companies do not distribute all their profits as dividends. It also happens, in effect, when the economy has a balance of payments deficit; for that means that the rest of the world is not using all its current revenue from the economy to buy the economy's goods and services. Such acts of saving are also necessary to permit enterprises to add to their physical capital out of current production and thus to increase their productive capacity. Saved income is lent through the capital market, where governments do their borrowing (see pp. 226-232 below).

In Table 2, government expenditure on current account includes expenditure on public works and on new fixed capital for government enterprises.

Since these classes of outlay largely result in the creation of assets in a manner similar to that of private investment, they might alternatively be regarded as expenditure on capital account. Measured roughly, they amounted in 1938-39, 1946-47 and 1956-57, respectively, to 33 per cent., 21 per cent. and 39 per cent. of government expenditure on goods and services. If they were removed from the government current account, the combined deficit shown there would be converted in each of the three years to a sizable surplus.

It may be calculated from Table 1 that the share of governments in the *gross national expenditure* on goods and services (which excludes purchases by the rest of the world) increased between the pre-war and post-war financial years from 18½ per cent. to 23 per cent., but had fallen again by 1956-57 to 21 per cent. In this comparison, expenditure includes payments of interest on government debt, which, it is often argued, are not a part of the community's expenditure on goods and services, but a mere transfer of income from taxpayers to bondholders. Since the real (as opposed to the money) burden of government debt interest was greatly reduced by the post-war inflation, the exclusion of such expenditure for the purposes of the comparison virtually eliminates the decline between 1946-47 and 1956-57 in the share of governments in gross national expenditure: the percentages become 13½ per cent. for 1938-39 and about 19 per cent. for both the post-war years. A similar picture is presented by government employment (including the employees of government business undertakings, but excluding members of the defence forces), which grew over the eighteen-year period by 83 per cent., while private employment (excluding rural and household domestic employment) increased by 60 per cent.

Table 2 shows that the increase in government purchases of goods and services was paralleled by a similar movement in transfers of income to the personal sector, which grew from a little over 3 per cent. of the gross national expenditure in 1938-39 to about 5 per cent. in 1946-47 and 1956-57. On the revenue side, business taxes, at 16 per cent. of the gross national revenue, were of much the same relative size in 1956-57 as before the war. Personal taxes, on the other hand, had increased from 3½ per cent. to 7½ per cent., and in 1946-47 were above 9½ per cent.

The composition of government income and outlay in the same three years is shown in greater detail in Tables 3 and 4. The division between the federal government, on the one hand, and the state and local governments, on the other, serves to indicate some of the significant differences in the nature of their activities, as well as some of the changes which have occurred since 1939 in their relative financial positions. The finances of the two mainland federal territories are included with state and local government finances in Table 4, although they, in fact, form part of the budget of the federal government. In consequence, Table 3 shows only the net cost of the territories, or the excess of territorial expenditure over territorial revenue. The figures are drawn from the official estimates of *National Income and Expenditure*, supplemented by some subsidiary calculations.

The federal income tax (known legally nowadays as income tax and social services contribution) is the successor to the separate federal, state and territory income taxes which existed until 1942 (see pp. 220-221 below). It is levied on both individuals and companies, and company profits which are paid as dividends are taxed in the hands of both the company and the individual shareholders. Income is measured net of the expenses incurred in earning it. Some sorts of income (such as educational allowances and certain classes of income from mining) are exempt, and others receive special treatment. Individuals are allowed deductions from income for dependants, medical expenses, contributions to life assurance and super-annuation funds, etc. The tax on individuals is progressive: that is to say, the rate of tax per pound of income is greater the larger the income, rising to two-thirds of that part of an individual's yearly income which exceeds £16,000. The tax on companies has only a slight element of progression, in that the first £5,000 of income is taxed at a lower rate than the remainder.

TABLE 3

FEDERAL GOVERNMENT INCOME AND OUTLAY

	1938-39	1946-47	1956-57
	£m.	£m.	£m.
Company income tax	4	54	216
Customs duty	31	46	69
Excise duty..	16	56	217
Sales tax	9	36	126
Entertainments tax	..	5	..
Land tax	1	4	..
Pay-roll tax	..	14	49
Other indirect taxes	5	8	9
Gross trading profits	5	6	9
Rent and interest	1	5	23
Business taxes	72	234	718
Personal income tax	8	154	404
Estate and gift duty	2	5	15
Cash deficit	1	— 11	— 180
Gross income	83	382	957
Defence	13	57	183
Gross capital formation ..	5	13	78
Repatriation	3	18	15
Immigration	..	..	10
Development of resources	..	4	15
Subsidies	3	36	17
Interest	12	47	31
Other goods and services	7	56	66
Government expenditure	43	231	415
Age and invalid pensions..	16	29	109
War and service pensions	8	16	50
Child endowment ..	..	20	57
Unemployment and sickness benefits	..	2	4
Hospital and medical benefits	..	4	40
Other cash benefits	1	19	26
Grants to states	15	59	244
Net cost of territories	..	2	12
Gross outlay	83	382	957

TABLE 4
STATE AND LOCAL GOVERNMENT INCOME AND OUTLAY

	1938-39	1946-47	1956-57
	£m.	£m.	£m.
Company income taxes	12	..	..
Stamp duties	3	5	21
Liquor licences	1	2	7
Motor taxes	7	8	34
Entertainments taxes	2	3	9
Land taxes	1	1	12
Local government rates	14	17	64
Other indirect taxes	3	4	22
Gross trading profits	27	21	65
Rent and interest	5	8	30
Business taxes	75	69	264
Personal income taxes	18	..	..
Death and gift duties	5	8	24
Federal grants	15	61	256
Cash deficit	23	37	215
Gross income	136	175	759
Gross capital formation	53	72	378
Law and order	6	7	34
Education	12	19	93
Health and welfare	10	14	67
Development of resources	3	4	21
Subsidies	..	1	1
Interest	41	40	108
Other goods and services	6	17	53
Government expenditure	131	174	755
Unemployment relief	5	..	..
Other cash benefits	..	1	4
Gross outlay	136	175	759

The federal estate duty is also progressive, rising to a maximum of 27.9 per cent. on estates of £500,000 or more. It is levied on the value of a person's net assets at his death. Gift duty, at the same rates, was introduced in 1941 to discourage people from dispersing their property in order to avoid the progression of the rates of income tax, estate duty and federal land tax. (The land tax was abolished in 1952.)

The customs duty is essentially a means of protecting Australian manufacturing industry, although duty is imposed on a number of items mainly for revenue purposes. The duty is partly *ad valorem* (a fraction of value) and partly specific (a fixed sum per unit of quantity). There are three classes of rates: the British preferential tariff on goods from the United Kingdom, Canada and New Zealand; the intermediate tariff for countries with which trade agreements have been concluded; and the general tariff. The federal customs department also administers the excise duty, which is levied on Australian-produced liquors, tobacco products, coal, matches, petrol and playing cards. The rates are specific, and in some cases are related to the rates of customs duty on the goods of the same kind. The sales tax is administered by the federal taxation department, which also has charge of the income tax and most other federal taxes. Its rates are *ad valorem*. Some goods, such as building materials, equipment for use in primary production, scientific and educational goods, drugs and most food-stuffs, are exempt, and others are subject to special rates above or below the general rate of 12½ per cent. Sales tax also falls on imports.

The federal pay-roll tax was introduced in 1941, to provide part of the finance for the new child endowment scheme, which was itself intended to avoid the need of a general increase in wage rates. At present it is paid by employers at 2½ per cent. of the part of their wage bill which exceeds £10,400 per annum. It is levied on state and local governments as well as on private employers, since the federal constitution only prohibits the federal and state governments from imposing taxes on each other's *property*. The other minor federal business taxes include wireless licence fees (which might be treated as mainly a personal tax) and the stevedoring industry charge, which is levied on waterside employers and is used to provide benefits for their employees. There are also a number of taxes on the production or export of primary products, notably wool and meat, which are used to promote sales, research, etc.

Although the general structure of state taxation is much the same in each of the states, the systems differ a good deal in some details. In Table 4 death and gift duties include succession duties levied on inheritors. Stamp duties are payable on documents ranging from cheques and receipts to transfers of land. Motor taxation consists of fees for the registration of vehicles and for the licensing of motor dealers, motor drivers and motor transport services. The entertainments taxes consist mostly of taxes on betting at horse and dog races. Land taxes are now levied by all the states, a general land tax having been introduced in New South Wales in 1956. They are assessed on the unimproved capital value of land, except in Western Australia, where the value of improvements (buildings, etc.) is also taxed. Local government rates are also generally assessed on the unimproved value of the land within each local area, although other bases are used. Other state and local taxes include miscellaneous licence fees, court fines, taxes on lotteries in the two states in which they are privately operated, and the proceeds of government lotteries, after paying prizes, in three others. Parts of these miscellaneous levies might alternatively be treated as personal taxes, if appropriate estimates were available.

Gross government trading profits, in Tables 3 and 4, consist of the excess of current revenue over current operating expenses for all government business undertakings except housing authorities and banks, whether the profits were retained by the enterprise or paid to the treasury of the parent government. In calculating the profits, no deduction has been made for contributions towards interest on the government debt incurred to equip the enterprises, nor for the depreciation of their fixed capital. If these two items (which represent the value to the community of resources used in the enterprises) were deducted in full, the combined profits would be converted into large losses. Rent and interest received are shown separately from trading profits in the tables, although they are of a similar nature.

They include the rental revenue of government housing authorities, net of operating expenses.

Federal grants to the state governments, and net federal expenditure on the territories, appear as outlay in Table 3 and as income in Table 4. When the accounts of all levels of government are consolidated, as in Table 2, they disappear, just as transfers of revenue from one federal fund to another do not appear in Table 3. For the same reason, Table 4 does not show as state government outlay, or as local government income, state grants to local authorities, which amounted to about £6 million in 1938-39, £3 million in 1946-47 and perhaps £18 million in 1956-57.

The outlay half of both tables includes a sub-total for aggregate government expenditure on goods and services, as distinct from transfers of income. Gross capital formation consists of expenditure on public works and on additions to the fixed capital and inventories of government business undertakings.   No deduction is made for the offsetting depreciation during the year of existing physical assets. The item, development of resources, includes the annual expenditure of agriculture, forestry and mines departments, and some government expenditure on scientific research.   In the federal government account, the item, other goods and services, is inflated in 1946-47 by the inclusion of £39 million in gifts to the United Kingdom government and to international relief organizations, which might alternatively have been treated as international transfers of income.

It will be noted that the two main items in the federal government's outlay are defence and cash benefits (including pensions).   In the case of the states, the major items are capital formation and interest on the government debt, both of which are attributable largely to investment in public utilities and other government business undertakings.

FISCAL POLICY

The economic effects of government financial transactions fall into three classes: quantitative, allocational and distributional. *Quantitative effects* are those exerted on the general level of economic activity and on the size and money value of the national production.   They include effects on the level of employment, on the rate of growth of the economy, and on the balance of payments with the rest of the world. *Allocational effects* arise when the pattern of production, or the allocation of resources between alternative uses, is different from what it would be if there were no government transactions.   This is clearly the case when the community spends co-operatively and compulsorily, through the government, on projects which it would not have undertaken to the same degree on a private or voluntary basis.   But there are also allocational effects when taxation or government outlay causes particular prices or rates of income to change, and people in consequence alter their spending or working habits. Finally, there are *distributional effects*. Government transactions affect the distribution of income between rich and poor, between smokers and non-smokers, between families and single people, between residents of different areas, between young and old, and so on.   Much of this influence is direct, through personal taxes and cash benefits; but also much of it arises because government transactions indirectly affect relative prices and rates of income.

Where such effects are intended by the government concerned, we may speak of quantitative, allocational and distributional *policy*, and, in the case of financial transactions (as opposed to direct controls), sum them all up in the term, fiscal policy. However, many of the economic effects of government transactions are not foreseen or intended, but are the incidental results of the pursuit of other aims of policy. Attempts to secure full employment and rapid economic growth, primarily through fiscal means, have been a major but unintended cause of the post-war price inflation in Australia. This in turn has led to a redistribution of income in favour of those whose rates of income have more than kept pace with the rise of prices, and against the less fortunate who live on superannuation pensions, government loan interest and similar receipts, or who hold assets of fixed money value. (Universities and other endowed institutions have been major sufferers.) Since this redistribution of income is partly between classes with different spending habits, it may be assumed to have affected the allocation of resources. Redistributions of income also have a bearing on the size of the national production through their influence on levels of expenditure.

The core of quantitative (sometimes called macro-economic) policy may be summed up in the objective, "full employment without inflation". The definition of full employment is the subject of some dispute. It is generally agreed that there must always be some unemployment, for there are always people who are looking for their first jobs or moving to new places and new jobs. Changes in the structure of the economy in fact usually require some continuous movement between occupations, industries and places. The question at issue concerns the permissible level of such unemployment. It arises chiefly because policy is subject to the additional constraint, "without inflation".

In principle, almost any desired level of employment is not difficult to secure: it is simply a matter of achieving the right level of total expenditure (or "effective demand") in the economy. This may be done by adding to government expenditure, and by reducing taxation and increasing cash benefit payments to enable the private sector to spend more; or, where a reduction is required, by the reverse processes. Each such rise or fall in the level of expenditure, by increasing or reducing people's incomes, causes further rises or falls, and so on (the "multiplier effect"). It may also cause enterprises to spend more or less on investment, so as to adjust their productive capacity to the new rates of expenditure. Thus only a small initial impulse from the government may produce quite large effects on the level of employment.

In practice, two sorts of difficulties arise. One concerns the timing of the fiscal changes: economists are not yet able to say with confidence and soon enough how much government action is needed and when it should be taken. The other difficultiy is more fundamental. If the employment target is set too high, it can be achieved only by creating a situation of excess demand, where government and private expenditure add up to more than the total supply of goods and services at current prices. The result is price inflation, both from the demand side, because of competitive bidding for scarce resources of labour and capital, and from the cost side, because wage increases are more strongly canvassed, in the names of prosperity and need, at a time when employers have a less pressing constraint to resist them.

If full employment is defined as the highest level of employment compatible with general stability of prices, then it cannot be interpreted in terms of a fixed maximum percentage of unemployment. There are two main reasons. Firstly, the percentage level of employment at which sectional shortages of labour begin to cause wages costs to rise will depend on how well the labour supply is adapted to the economy's needs, and this varies from time to time with the rate and type of structural change in the economy and with other factors. Secondly, the less unemployment there is, the more the necessary marginal mobility of labour must be achieved by offering higher wages where additional labour is needed; and the scope for doing this without raising prices depends on the rate at which labour productivity is increasing, which again is a variable factor. Definitions of full employment which are couched in terms of a relationship between the number of vacancies and the number of people seeking jobs are generally more satisfactory on the first count, but are still of limited value.

In the Australian economy, the attainment of price stability is made more difficult by the importance of international trade. Even if internal costs are kept stable, rises in the prices of imports may still lead to cost inflation. Likewise, higher world prices may produce increases in export earnings and consequently in effective demand. At the same time, if the structure of the economy becomes geared to a higher rate of imports than its foreign earnings can sustain, import restrictions become a necessity, at the cost of accentuating the internal excess demand and possibly creating sectional unemployment by depriving some industries of imported supplies.

The federal government's assumption of primary responsibility for quantitative economic policy dates from the war period. In 1945 a special statement, *Full Employment in Australia,* was issued, setting out the government's intentions for the ensuing time of peace. The history of such policies, through the initial period of post-war reconstruction and up to the present day, has been one of decreasing reliance on direct measures and increasing reliance on fiscal measures. This was to be expected: the direct controls (rationing, licensing, price fixing, etc.) cost the economic machine something in efficiency; and the constitutional powers under which they were imposed arose mainly out of the war-time paramountcy of the requirements of military defence. The general tendency is subject to one notable exception, namely, the restriction of imports by licensing. This lies within the peacetime powers of the federal parliament. It has also been intended, though perhaps not destined, to be of short duration. It represents, at least in part, an unavoidable alternative to stricter limitation of internal demand, possibly coupled with some freedom in rates of exchange with foreign currencies.

To achieve internal stability, it is necessary to alter, fairly directly and rapidly, the level of the gross national expenditure. For practical and political reasons, it is difficult to make large and sudden changes in the level of government expenditure on goods and services; and decreases in the amount of payments of cash benefits are also subject to political restraint. Thus the main burden of stabilization policy falls on taxation. The weight of federal taxation was increased greatly during the war, in order to reduce private demand as government expenditure bore progressively more heavily on the full employment output of the economy. For a similar reason, it has remained since the war at levels well above those of pre-war years.

As will be seen below (pp. 220-221), the uniform income tax was introduced in order to make the taxation system more effective in this direction, as well as to restrict the income available to the state governments for their expenditure. The personal income tax offered a much larger scope for increases than any other tax, and such increases in turn had a more direct effect on the rate of private expenditure. Thus while company income taxes (federal and state combined) increased between 1938-39 and 1946-47 from £16 million, or a little over 1½ per cent. of the gross national revenue, to £54 million, or 3 per cent., personal income taxes rose from £26 million to £154 million, or from less than 3 per cent. to 9 per cent. The increase was achieved partly by very much heavier taxation of the large incomes. But the scope for increased revenue is inevitably greater at the lower levels, where the large numbers of incomes lie. Their rates, too, were raised a good deal, and at the same time the exemption level was reduced. In 1938-39, for a person without dependants, it had stood at £250 per annum for the federal income tax and £156 for most of the state taxes. Since 1943-44 it has remained at £104; but this has had a progressively smaller value in real terms as inflation has proceeded, and £104 in 1956-57 might be counted as equivalent to £35 or less in 1938-39 prices and only about £45 in 1943-44 prices. The war also saw the general adoption of the system of collecting tax from employees by instalments, and the later development of a pay-as-you-earn system for all taxpayers except companies. Besides reducing evasion and making tax rates seem less severe, these systems greatly increased the effectiveness of the personal income tax as an instrument of quantitative policy, for any change in rates could now have an almost immediate effect on the disposable incomes of the majority of taxpayers.

During the war, reliance was also placed on increases in other forms of taxation; but the scope for such increases was more limited. The result was that between the pre-war and post-war financial years personal taxes (including death and gift taxes) increased from 18¼ per cent to 35½ per cent. of the total tax revenue (including gross government trading profits, etc.) of Australian governments. There were some large fluctuations in later years, but by 1956-57 the proportions appeared fairly stable at about one-third personal taxes and two-thirds business taxes. Of at least equal significance is the large increase in the relative dependence of the state governments on federal grants. This development has inevitably made the level and the direction of state expenditure more subject to the control of the federal government, and consequently more amenable to federal fiscal policy. There has been a parallel change in the field of government borrowing. These matters are explored further in the last two sections of this chapter.

Despite the growth in the means of fiscal control, it cannot be maintained that quantitative economic policy has achieved more than moderate success. Certainly unemployment has been virtually eliminated. But the general level of prices, which by 1946-47 had risen by only about a third since before the war, had by 1956-57 increased to nearly two and a half times the 1946-47 level. The growth of real output has been steady and in some instances spectacular. But there have been recurring balance of payments crises. Perhaps the main reason for the patchiness of the results is that the four strands of policy are not fully compatible with one another. It is doubtful whether it is possible to have so little unemployment (about 1¼ per cent. of the employee population in 1956-57, compared with perhaps 12½ per cent. in 1939 and more than 25 per cent. in 1933) without price inflation, and without so interfering with the mobility of labour as to reduce significantly the rate of economic growth. It is equally doubtful whether government expenditure could be sustained at the post-war levels, and inflation at the same time avoided, without a greater restriction of private demand than has been politically possible. There have, however, been contributory difficulties, such as the need for re-equipment, both private and government, after the war; the export boom which came with the Korean War; and the adherence, until at least the end of 1951, to the war-time policy of very low interest rates, which encouraged investment expenditure and government borrowing and discouraged saving. In brief, it seems fair to say that the conflict of policies has been resolved mainly at the expense of the objective of price stability. This was perhaps to be expected. One reason is that inflation has distinct advantages with regard to the burden of the government debt (see p. 231 below). Another, of greater importance, is that it reduces the need to resist increases in the money value of sectional incomes, which are unaccompanied by corresponding increases in production.

Government policy on the allocation of resources has been determined largely by the rate of growth of the economy, which has required the devotion of large amounts of resources to provide additional physical capital. The government component of this capital accumulation, and the means used to achieve it, are considered briefly in the final section. To encourage a greater rate of private investment, two major fiscal measures have been used: special initial depreciation allowances, which enable an enterprise to deduct a large proportion of investment expenditure from income for tax purposes in the first year (and consequently smaller proportions in the later years) ; and agreements with the United Kingdom and the United States governments for the avoidance of the double taxation of investment income paid abroad. The *direction* of private investment has been influenced by special income tax and sales tax treatment for capital outlay in farming and mining enterprises, etc. ; by the payment of bounties on tractor production ; and less directly by the multitude of other fiscal measures which make some expenditures and productive activities relatively more profitable, and others relatively less.

The pricing and investment policies of government enterprises play an important part in the allocation of resources. Government transport undertakings provide a good example. The costs of using labour have risen relatively to the costs of using equipment throughout the economy, partly because of shorter working hours coupled with increases in the quantity and quality of capital, and partly because of the effects of inflation, government controls and other factors on the distribution of the revenue of industry. Transport is a heavy user of labour, and its money costs have therefore risen more than those of other basic industries. At the same time there are serious political difficulties in raising the prices charged by government transport undertakings, even when other prices rise. They must therefore be subsidized. The gross profits of government business enterprises in 1956-57, in Tables 3 and 4, incorporate as a negative component a combined loss on the rail, tram and bus undertakings of all governments of £8 million ; and this is without including in costs any item for interest on the community's capital employed in the undertakings, or for annual depreciation of physical assets.

As in the case of subsidies paid to private enterprises, these losses mean that the community is receiving particular goods and services for less than their cost of production. In effect, the same expenditure is enabled to buy a larger bundle of resources in one form than in another. In allocating his income between alternative uses, the individual will spend more than he otherwise would on the bundle for which he does not have to pay the full cost. His total satisfaction may thereby be increased; but that of the community as a whole is reduced, for resources are diverted from one use to another although, given a free choice, the community would prefer to have what they could produce in the former use. This may, of course, be a matter of deliberate policy, as when the production of certain medicinal drugs is subsidized because the community, in its collective voice, declares that more resources should be employed in their production than the community, considered as a collection of individual spending units, would choose to employ.

Government finance affects the distribution of income in many ways. The *impact* of an item of government income or outlay may be defined as falling on the person or institution who is at the paying or receiving end. If the net impact of total government income and outlay differs between individuals, then, in one sense, a redistribution of income has occurred. But it is well known that the burdens of taxes and the benefits of government outlay do not always rest where they first fall. In other words, they may be shifted through changes in the prices which people pay and receive for goods and services and for the labour and capital used to produce them. When all such effects have been measured, the resulting distribution of burdens and benefits may be termed their *repose*. In practice, however, it is not possible to carry the measurement so far. Instead, we may talk about the *incidence* of fiscal items, and give incidence a definition which lies within our field of vision.

For personal taxes and cash benefits, incidence may well be identified with impact; for, no matter how a person's decisions about earning, spending and saving are affected by these budgetary items, the great bulk of the burden or benefit which he directly bears also rests finally and ultimately with him. Here, indeed, is the most powerful fiscal influence on the distribution of income in the community. Personal taxes are heavily progressive with income, which means that they take a much larger proportion of a large income than of a small one. Cash benefits, on the other hand, being based on need, tend to be regressive, accruing in greater measure to those with small incomes. The increase in the weight of taxation and the shift of emphasis in government revenue towards personal taxes, which have been examined above, have made the tax system as a whole a stronger agent in redistributing income from rich to poor. Cash benefits, too, have shown an increase, from just over 3 per cent. of the gross national revenue before the war to just over 5 per cent. after. The increase is a good deal larger than might appear at first sight, for the community is generally much more prosperous than it was before the war, unemployment has been greatly reduced, and the need of assistance for individuals is correspondingly smaller. The biggest change in the scope and scale of benefits came during the war, when the federal government assumed responsibility for almost all classes of payment. The real value of benefits as a whole has remained fairly constant during the post-war inflation. As the war also put the personal income tax completely in the hands of the federal government, it may be said to have made that government virtually the sole agent of direct income redistribution in Australia.

Business taxes are by and large regressive with income. They fall to a great extent on the purchasers of goods and services, through their effects on prices; and usually the smaller a person's income, the larger the proportion of it which he spends on goods and services. It should be mentioned, however, that the increase in company income taxes (just over $1\frac{1}{2}$ per cent. of the gross national revenue before the war, 3 per cent. in 1946-47 and $3\frac{1}{2}$ per cent. in 1956-57) has reinforced the effect of inflation and direct controls in reducing the share of income going to the recipients of rent, interest and dividends, who are not always among the poor. Government expenditure on goods and services also tends to be regressive, constituting a larger proportionate supplement to the income of the poor than to that of the rich. Thus the increase in government purchases during and since the war is likely to have increased the extent of the downward redistribution of income.

Effects on the distribution of income are not, of course confined to vertical redistribution between rich and poor. Other measures of need, such as size of family and amount of sickness, operate to attract redistribution through income tax allowances, cash benefits and government expenditure on health, education, price subsidies, etc. The distribution of income between classes and regions is also affected by allocational policy: if, to encourage or discourage particular uses of resources, subsidies or business taxes are applied, so that price becomes divorced from cost, there is a redistribution of income between users and the rest of the community. More generally, geographical redistribution occurs when a government raises proportionately less taxes, and spends proportionately more, in poorer areas. It also occurs on a large scale through the system of federal grants, to which attention is given below (pp. 217 and 221-225).

THE GOVERNMENT ACCOUNTS

Although it is useful to consolidate government transactions into a single current account and a single capital account, as has been done above, the accounts actually used by governments are by no means as simple. Broadly speaking, government transactions at both the federal and the state levels are carried on through three different funds, for which separate accounts are kept. These are the consolidated revenue fund, the loan fund and the trust fund. Their transactions for 1956-57 are summarized in Tables 5 and 6. Receipts and payments are recorded almost exclusively on a cash basis, which means that they show for each year moneys actually received and paid by the treasury on behalf of the government during the year. This differs from the accrual basis normally used in business accounting, where the accounts for a year record moneys which become due to or by the business, whether they are actually paid during the year or not. Thus in the accrual system, debts are recorded as revenue or expenditure in the year in which they are created; and in the cash system, in the year in which they are discharged by payment.

The *consolidated revenue fund* receives most of the taxes and other ordinary revenue of the government, and is used to meet the expenditures voted by parliament annually in the appropriation act, as well as the charges covered by standing appropriations (see p. 211 below). In some cases these items include the trading revenue and expenditure of large government business undertakings: for example, the federal post office and most of the government railways. In New South Wales the transactions of three major government business undertakings (railways, tram and bus services, and the Sydney Harbour Trust) are recorded in separate accounts, but are subject to the same accounting and parliamentary procedures as the items in the consolidated revenue fund, and are therefore commonly amalgamated with them for statistical purposes, as in Table 6.

TABLE 5

THE FEDERAL GOVERNMENT ACCOUNTS FOR 1956-57

Consolidated Revenue Fund

	£m.		£m.
Personal income tax ..	403·7	Public debt charges	72·2
Company income tax	216·6	Defence services	188·4
Customs duty	68·6	Capital expenditure ..	107·8
Excise duty and sales tax ..	343·2	Social service benefits ..	223·9
Other taxes	66·6	Business undertakings ..	97·7
Business undertakings ..	99·8	Territories	16·1
Territories	2·5	Federal grants	244.1
Other revenue	110·8	Other expenditure	166.8
		Surplus	194.8
Total revenue	1,311·8	Total expenditure ..	1,311·8

Loan Fund

	£m.		£m.
Borrowing abroad	17·4	Loan to Qantas	3·9
Public treasury bills	—15·0	War service farms	8·0
Trust fund treasury bills ..	20·2	State housing	32·2
Other trust fund loans ..	36·1	Surplus to trust fund ..	14·6
Funds raised	58·7	Funds spent	58·7

Trust Fund

	£m.		£m.
Balance from 1955-56 ..	818·4	Payments during year ..	821·1
Receipts during year.. ..	907·1	Balance to 1957-58 ..	904·4
Total receipts	1,725·5	Total payments ..	1,725·5

Money borrowed by the federal or a state government is paid into its *loan fund*. Borrowing has generally been used by the state governments to meet expenditure of a capital or developmental nature. The division of expenditure between the consolidated revenue fund and the loan fund has also, however, depended largely on the availability of funds from the two sources, especially since the end of the war. Most of the federal borrowing has been for war purposes, and federal expenditure on developmental projects or on the expansion of government business undertakings is normally met from current revenue.

TABLE 6
THE STATE GOVERNMENT ACCOUNTS FOR 1956-57

Consolidated Revenue Funds

	£m.			£m.
Taxes	84·0	Public debt charges		85·8
Federal grants	200·8	Social expenditure		207·1
Business undertakings ..	214·3	Business undertakings ..		208·8
Other revenue	77·8	Other expenditure		82·2
Deficit	7·0			
Total revenue	583·9	Total expenditure ..		583·9

Loan Funds

	£m.			£m.
Borrowing abroad	1·3	Railways		29·5
Loans from public	97·7	Water and sewerage ..		20·3
State trust fund loans ..	1·1	Electricity supply		27·6
Federal trust fund loans ..	59·7	Public buildings		40·8
		Other uses		41·6
Funds raised	159·8	Funds spent		159·8

Trust Funds

	£m.		£m.
Balance from 1955-56 ..	148·6	Balance to 1957-58 ..	155·6
Net receipts during year ..	7·0		
Total receipts	155·6	Total payments ..	155·6

In addition to the records of the consolidated revenue and loan funds, both the federal and the state governments maintain a number of special accounts, in which certain transactions are recorded separately. Some of these refer to moneys which the government holds in trust for outside individuals or organizations, such as unclaimed prizes in state lotteries and the deposits required of trustee companies. Others deal with public funds which have been appropriated for particular purposes and which may be spent in future financial years without further parliamentary appropriation. The moneys covered by these two classes of accounts are commonly referred to as the *trust fund.* In New South Wales the accounts are divided into the Special Deposits Account, which is concerned with moneys of both types, and the Special Accounts, which relate to funds coming into the trusteeship of the Public Trustee and of some officers of the Supreme Court.

Some state government revenues are paid directly into the trust fund, without passing through the consolidated revenue fund. For example, the governments maintain separate road funds, which receive directly the proceeds of all or part of their motor taxation (except in South Australia) and of federal road grants, such revenue being "ear-marked" for the specific purpose of road construction and maintenance. The federal government pays its cash social service benefits out of the National Welfare Fund ; but although this was initially financed by the proceeds of the pay-roll tax and of a supplement to the personal income tax, known as the social services contribution, it has since 1952-53 merely received an annual appropriation from the consolidated revenue fund equal to the expenditure on benefits.

As moneys standing to the credit of the trust fund are not usually separated from those in the consolidated revenue and loan funds, all forming in effect part of the one banking account, trust fund balances may be drawn on temporarily to cover a deficit in the operations of the other funds. The federal government invests a large part of its trust moneys in its own government securities (most of which are issued on behalf of the states), as an alternative to borrowing from the public and the banks. These and other aspects of the trust funds are considered further below.

The accounting records of local governments are naturally simpler than those of their parent governments, for the range and size of their activities are a good deal smaller. Their transactions may be separated fairly readily into those of ordinary services and those of business undertakings. The latter are concerned mainly with water supply and sewerage, electricity and gas supply, transport services and abattoirs, although some local governments also run hotels, cinemas, quarries, ice works, etc. Ordinary services cover the expenditure of the authorities on activities (such as general administration, garbage services, and roads, parks and other public works) which are not run on commercial lines, although direct charges may be made to the public for some of them. A distinction may also be drawn between expenditure on revenue account, out of the proceeds of local taxation, fees and charges and state government grants ; and on loan account, out of borrowed funds.

The transactions of Australian local governments for the financial year 1955-56 (1953-54 in Queensland, 1955 in New South Wales) are summarized in Table 7. The figures cover a total of 912 authorities in the six states. Ordinary services are accounted for on a cash basis, except in New South Wales, where an accrual basis is used. As might be expected, the accrual system is employed generally for local government business undertakings. In many cases, however, costs do not include any provision for the depreciation of fixed capital, while on the other hand they do sometimes (especially in New South Wales) include payments to sinking fund for the ultimate redemption of debt.

The relative merits of the cash and accrual systems of keeping public accounts have been the subject of controversy. The purpose of the accrual system is to show the true outcome of the year's operations as they affect the net assets of an undertaking. It therefore requires some estimation in connection with items of revenue and expenditure which are not finalized by cash receipts or payments during the year, but remain as debts due to or by the undertaking. In the case of governments, this estimation may be of three kinds. Firstly, it is necessary to remove from the record of cash transactions items relating to past years, which merely discharge existing claims and obligations, and to bring in newly created claims and obligations in respect of which actual payment has not yet been made. Secondly, sums previously owing to the government (for example, advances for land settlement) must be written off or written down when there is a significant reduction in the prospect of collecting them. And finally, an attempt may also be made to apportion capital expenditure between the years over which the assets will last, by means of charges to the annual budgets for depreciation. In all of these cases, there may be a wide scope for the exercise of judgement on the part of the administration. The cash basis, on the other hand, results in firm, verifiable figures. It is therefore to be preferred where accountability is the primary consideration. Moreover, it enables the accounts for the year to be prepared and presented with the minimum delay, and the net result of the year's operations to be known immediately the year has ended.

TABLE 7

THE LOCAL GOVERNMENT ACCOUNTS FOR 1955-56

Revenue Accounts—Ordinary Services

	£m.		£m.
Taxes	57·4	Public debt charges	10·7
Charges for services	18·9	Works and services	70·2
State grants	16·6	Other expenditure	13·8
Other revenue	1·7		
Deficit	0·1		
Total revenue	**94·7**	**Total expenditure** ..	**94·7**

Revenue Accounts—Business Undertakings

	£m.		£m.
Water and sewerage ..	7·3	Water and sewerage ..	6·4
Electricity and gas	62·5	Electricity and gas	60·3
Transport	3·3	Transport	3·7
Other services	3·4	Other services	3·2
		Surplus	2·9
Total revenue	**76·5**	**Total expenditure** ..	**76·5**

Loan Accounts

	£m.		£m.
Loans from public	30·4	Ordinary services	15·2
Loans from states	2·5	Business undertakings ..	16·6
		Surplus	1·1
Funds raised	**32·9**	**Funds spent**	**32·9**

In practice, the great bulk of government outlay is paid as it becomes due. In this respect, therefore, the results achieved under the cash system are not much different from those which would flow from the accrual basis. In the case of taxes, where the final liability is not always so soon determined and discharged, the estimates of cash revenue for the ensuing year are normally accompanied by estimates of the ultimate effect in later financial years of proposed legislative changes. Similar supplementary statements might be used to indicate the estimated change during the past year in the totals of all debts due to and by the government. The desirability of separating capital expenditure from the budget and replacing it with annual charges for depreciation is by no means universally accepted, even apart from considerations of accountability ; and again, equivalent information may be given in supplementary accounts.

Local government is in a rather different position. Since the basis of local real property taxes is fixed and known within very narrow limits, it is not difficult to estimate the revenue accruing in respect of a particular year.

Given the small scale of operations and the restricted range of ordinary services, it is likewise fairly easy to account for expenditure as accruals rather than payments. The revenue resources of local authorities are limited and are capable of little variation from year to year. Their financial management must therefore be directed partly towards avoiding too great a growth in the annual burden of their expenditure, and too heavy an incidence of expenditure in any one year. For these reasons, there is much to be said for the further step of making annual financial provisions for the depreciation of non-business fixed assets, both to spread the cost of renewals evenly over the years and to ensure that more capital is not built up than can be adequately maintained and replaced. These ends are at present met in part, but only in part, by the requirement that loans must be redeemed by annual contributions to sinking fund over a set peroid.

Important questions of principle are also raised by the *classification* of the items in the government accounts. Broadly, there are two alternative bases, the functional and the administrative. The former classifies expenditure according to the objects served (and hence is sometimes termed "objective"), and revenue according to the economic nature of the transactions which create the liability of the public to pay. This sort of classification has been followed in Tables 3 and 4 (pp. 195 and 196). The administrative basis classifies receipts and payments according to the branch or agency of the government involved, and, within each, divides expenditure between salaries, office supplies, rent, etc. (the subjects of the expenditure, whence the description as "subjective").

The classifications actually used vary in their details, but generally follow the administrative basis for both consolidated revenue and loan funds. This constitutes a recognition of the primary importance of accountability, for which, indeed, the form of the accounts was developed. But the scope and size of government have so changed that it is almost equally important to have accounts cast in a form which indicates effects on the general level of economic activity, and on the allocation of resources and the distribution of income. Some such accounts are, in fact, provided in the official estimates of *National Income and Expenditure;* but their form and content are sufficiently divorced from those of the budget proper to make them a poor guide to decisions on immediate questions of fiscal policy. Parliaments nowadays also want to know how much particular activities of government cost, in order to decide whether they ought to be maintained at their present level, expanded or contracted. The administrative basis provides this information only in a very general way, for the activities of many departments and branches are both large and diverse. There have been some experiments in the state parliaments in presenting alternative, functional classifications of expenditure alongside the formal accounts. Such classifications are also made, in very broad outline, for federal, state and local governments, in the annual bulletin of the federal bureau of statistics on *Finance,* and it is from that source that the figures in Tables 5, 6 and 7 have been largely derived.

It will be clear that a number of issues are involved in the form of the government accounts, and that the outcome is necessarily a compromise between the different ends to be served. The nature and implications of those ends are considered in the course of the next section.

BUDGETARY PROCEDURES AND SAFEGUARDS

Out of the long history of government in Britain, the House of Commons has emerged as the supreme law-making body, and as the creator and controller of the executive government, largely because it has asserted its claim to the power of the purse. (The history of the Australian federation, outlined in the next section, is one of many other examples of the tendency of political power to rest in the hands of those who hold financial power.) Thus the supremacy of parliament is founded on the general rule that no charges may be imposed or revenue spent by the government without the express approval of the legislature.

The federal parliament and the parliaments of all the states except Queensland are bicameral. The lower house in each case is dissolved and re-elected at intervals no greater than about three years (five years in Tasmania), the franchise embracing all adult citizens with a few exceptions. Each of the upper houses is constituted so as to provide a greater continuity of membership than in the lower house; and in some cases the franchise is more restricted. In order to preserve the financial supremacy of the lower, or "popular", house, various restrictions are placed on the power of the upper house to amend financial legislation. The federal constitution provides that the Senate may not originate or amend proposed laws imposing taxation or appropriating revenue for the services of the government. The Senate may, however, reject such laws altogether, in which case the constitutional provisions for dealing with a deadlock between the two houses may be invoked. In each of the states, "money bills" must originate in the lower house. But except in New South Wales, where the Legislative Council has virtually no control over bills appropriating revenue for ordinary services, the upper houses appear to possess considerable constitutional power to delay the passage of financial legislation.

The federal and state constitutions follow the British tradition that the initiative in financial matters must come from the executive. This is achieved by requiring that proposals to levy taxes or to appropriate revenue can only be considered in parliament if they are recommended by the Queen's representative, which means, effectively, by the cabinet. Thus the body of ministers is able to present a comprehensive financial programme, with the assurance that it will not be upset by proposals for additional expenditure.

The budget is presented to parliament annually, usually several months after the beginning of the financial year. It takes the form of a speech, made by the treasurer (the minister of finance), which outlines the government's financial achievements and proposals and which is supported by financial statistics of the previous year and estimates of revenue and expenditure for the current year. A sample page from the latter will be found in Appendix III. In recognition of the responsibility which the federal government has assumed for maintaining the general level of economic activity, it has become customary for the federal treasurer's budget speech to include an analysis of the state of the economy and its prospects.

The procedure of parliament is much the same at both the federal and the state levels. After the estimates of expenditure for the year have been considered and voted on, item by item, in the lower house, government expenditure of the total amount is authorized by an appropriation bill. A similar procedure is then followed in the upper house, and the bill finally becomes law by receiving the governor-general's or governor's assent. Budgeting is done on a cash basis, and any parts of appropriations not spent by the end of the financial year to which they relate automatically lapse. This strict annual control does not, however, extend to moneys which have been appropriated to trust accounts; and the financial authority of the legislature is thereby undermined.

In order to provide for the services of government during the early part of the new financial year, until the appropriation act has been passed, the federal parliament passes a supply act, authorizing the government to continue spending on the various items at the rates approved for the previous year. In New South Wales the executive is permanently authorized by act of parliament to spend for a period no greater than the first three months at the rate approved for the previous year, expenditure for a further period being authorized, if necessary, by a supply act. The other states follow procedures similar to those of the federal and New South Wales parliaments. Some items of expenditure, including the salaries of judges, interest and amortization charges on the government debt and almost all social service benefits, are appropriated by separate acts of parliament which do not require annual renewal; and thus they do not come within the scope of the estimates and the appropriation act. Unexpected requirements in excess of the amounts approved by parliament are covered by a lump sum provision (the treasurer's advance) in the estimates and the appropriation act; or by supplementary appropriations made during the year; or, in some cases, by illegal expenditure which is submitted for parliamentary approval in the estimates of the following year.

Taxation legislation and other provisions for collecting revenue are normally of a continuing nature, like that of the standing appropriations mentioned in the previous paragraph. The proposals put forward in the annual budget are therefore confined to amendments of the rates or of the law relating to liability. An exception exists in the case of the rates of the federal income taxes on individuals and companies, which are customarily re-enacted each year, although the rates of the previous year continue in force until a new act is passed. In order to preserve the right of the federal Senate to amend non-monetary measures, the constitution provides that laws appropriating revenue for the annual services of the government shall deal only with such appropriation, and that laws imposing taxation shall deal only with the imposition of taxation; and, to prevent one tax being "tacked" to another, it further provides that each of the latter shall deal with only one tax. Thus the rates of each federal tax are prescribed and levied by a law separate from that which determines who is taxable and prescribes the method of assessment. In New South Wales, provisions "tacked" to a supply or appropriation bill do not become law unless the upper house passes the bill.

In the formation of financial policy, the treasury (department of finance) occupies a key position. Towards the end of each financial year, it calls for estimates of revenue and expenditure, from all the departments of government, for the ensuing year. The estimates of expenditure are examined critically, and particular items may be eliminated, and others returned for revision. At the same time, the need and possibility of variations in revenue are explored. Thus the treasury takes responsibility for preparing an integrated financial programme, which is expressed in the treasurer's budget speech and the supporting statements.

The position of the treasury is not, however, as strong in Australia as in the United Kingdom ; and this applies especially to the states. Perhaps the main reason is that links between the treasury and the other departments at the policy-making level are more limited and less continuous, so that there is less prior consultation in forming plans for expenditure, and conflicts have more frequently to be fought in the cabinet instead of being settled beforehand. A contributing factor may be that the Australian treasuries do not control the staffing of the public service: sizes of establishments, appointments, rates of pay and conditions of work for all but the highest grades of employees are normally in the hands of a separate public service board or commission. Nevertheless, the treasury's voice in cabinet is a strong one, and it has the largest single say in the size and composition of the budget.

The financial planning of the state governments is hampered by their heavy dependence on the federal government for revenue grants, and by the need to have their borrowing programmes approved by the Australian Loan Council and the funds raised or provided by the federal government (see the next two sections). Expenditure is partly contingent on the size of grants and loan raisings, and this has in the past created an element of uncertainty in the states' budget estimates. For example, the size of the income tax reimbursement grant, which is the largest single source of state consolidated revenue, was until recently commonly determined at a con-ference of federal and state ministers after the beginning of the year to which it related. The situation has, however, been improving in this regard ; for the conference was held in June of 1955 and 1956, in May of 1957 and in June of 1958.

The range and magnitude of the federal and state budgets, and indeed the size of the parliaments themselves, are such as to make full and effective parliamentary examination of financial proposals extremely difficult, if not impossible. Nevertheless there are complex procedures directed towards this end, and much attention has been given to the possibilities of improve-ment.

The rules of formal parliamentary debate, as embodied in standing orders, place fairly strict limits of duration and frequency on speeches. To allow greater scope for useful discussion (though originally, in the United King-dom House of Commons, to obtain greater freedom from royal supervision), each house conducts much of its financial business in committees of the whole house, under a chairman instead of the speaker or other formal presiding officer. The treasurer's budget speech is delivered and debated in committee of supply, and the estimates of expenditure are discussed in detail and adopted by resolutions in the same committee. In committee of ways and means, the government puts forward resolutions concerned with the imposition of taxes and other revenue raising devices, and with the appropriation of moneys from the consolidated revenue or loan fund to meet the expenditures approved by committee of supply. When these have been formally adopted by the house, it instructs the government to prepare (as if it had not already done so!) and bring in the necessary appropriation and taxing bills.

Once the appropriation act and the revenue raising measures have been passed, the largest part of formal parliamentary control over the public purse has been exercised. This is especially so in the case of appropriations to trust funds, whose expenditure escapes much of the subsequent reporting machinery. But in any case, having approved the budget, parliament may probe and complain, by means of the question and the debate on adjournment; but it cannot usually change its mind.

Control over the execution of the budgetary programme rests with the treasury and the auditor-general. If the first major function of the treasury is to prepare the government's financial programme, the second is to ensure that the departments conform to it. The latter function is served largely by making the treasury the accounting centre of the government; and by requiring that, with some exceptions, revenue should be paid into and expenditure met out of a single banking account which is under treasury control. Unlike other public servants, the federal and state auditors-general are directly responsible to their respective parliaments and, although appointed by the governor-general or governor, can only be removed from office at the request of parliament. The treasury may not draw on the public account, from time to time, to meet the expenses of government, until it has obtained a governor-general's or governor's warrant, and such a warrant requires the certificate of the auditor-general that the expenditure has been authorized by parliament and has not already been drawn for. It should be noted, however, that this requirement is not always complied with in practice, as in the case of the annual excess expenditures of the New South Wales government, which are recorded as "unauthorised in suspense" and submitted for parliamentary validation in the appropriation act of the following year.

The actual revenues and expenditures of the year are set out in the annual budget papers, and details of expenditures are also shown against the corresponding items in the estimates for the new year. The formal and complete financial report of the government to parliament comes later, however, in the form of the public accounts, which are also called the treasurer's statement of receipts and expenditure. Parliament requires that these be certified as correct by the auditor-general, and accompanied by his annual report. This report, always a long and detailed document, discusses the results of the financial year, and draws the attention of parliament to violations of the laws dealing with public finance and to inefficiences of accounting administration. Although the report usually receives little attention in parliament, its contents are often given salutary publicity in the press, and the criticisms and suggestions of the auditor-general carry a good deal of weight within the administrative machine.

The concern of the auditor-general is primarily with the financial honesty of the administration, although he also often reports on examples of wasteful methods of doing things, and makes suggestions for changes in accounting procedures and controls. To supplement his work in the latter two directions, and to extend it to some consideration of whether particular government uses of resources are warranted by the results, parliaments sometimes adopt the device of the public accounts committee. This is a select committee of parliament: that is to say, one comprising only some of the members of one or both houses. Such committees operated in the federal and Victorian parliaments until 1931, when they were abolished as part of the reduction in administrative expenditure which was expected (mistakenly, hindsight tells us) to assist recovery from the economic depression.

The federal committee was reconstituted in 1951, with members drawn from government and opposition sides of both houses. To the end of 1957, it had made thirty-five reports, most of which were concerned with the activities of particular departments and agencies of the federal government, or with aspects of government financial procedure. They covered such diverse topics as the administration of the sales tax, the purchase and disposal of equipment by the Joint Coal Board, the functions of the Department of National Development, the form and content of the financial documents presented to parliament, and the decisions of the treasury on the committee's comments and recommendations. Although the committee's reviews of operations, coming usually well after the event, may have the appearance of shutting the stable door too late, it seems likely that the expectation of such reviews, and the publicity which they have attracted, act as a deterrent to the waste of resources, in much the same manner as the certainty of audit limits their misappropriation. The Victorian committee was re-established in 1955, and has commenced to operate along the same lines as the federal committee. Its members are drawn from the lower house of parliament only.

The New South Wales lower house has had since 1902 a public accounts committee, which is charged with reporting to parliament on two sorts of matters: expenditure made by the government without parliamentary sanction or appropriation; and questions relating to the public accounts which have been referred to the committee by a minister, the auditor-general or the Legislative Assembly. In its former function, the committee necessarily operates every year, but its reports are no more than an uncritical record of unauthorized expenditure from consolidated revenue and loan funds. In the latter, it has been completely inactive for lack of the power to initiate investigations without reference, and the desire to seek any such reference.

The federal parliament also makes use of a joint standing committee on public works, whose duty is to enquire into government proposals for capital expenditure in advance of their consideration by the legislature. Although the committee is not usually critical in its reports, it has on occasion secured revision of the government's proposals. New South Wales once had such a committee, but it disappeared in 1930.

If parliament has the will to exercise effective financial control, the extended use of select committees, especially to examine the various parts of the estimates of expenditure, appears to offer a useful means. In the case of revenue proposals, the formal procedures of debate ensure almost as much informed examination as other limiting factors permit. What is lacking (apart from freedom from some of the restrictions of predetermined party attitudes) is supplementary information on the sorts of economic effects which were considered in the second section of this chapter. On the expenditure side, however, more serious difficulties are met; and it is clear that the pivotal point of control of financial policy and performance lies in the form of the government accounts.

One of the barriers to effective parliamentary consideration of the estimates of expenditure is the mass of detail which they contain, although there are also some large items which leave a good deal to the discretion of the executive. (Parliament may well prefer not to have to scrutinize separately a proposal to spend £5 on tea money in one branch of the government; but it may look for some breakdown of £15 million which is merely stated to be for military arms and mechanization.) But whether there is less or more detail is not as important as the manner in which the estimates are arranged. Given the limited time available for debate, and the size of the debating body, there is an inevitable tendency towards a concentration of the discussion on a few items from which government or opposition may seek to extract political capital, and the hasty passage of the rest. If there is any remedy, it seems likely to be found in a form of accounts which encourages parliament to set the estimated cost of particular sorts of government activity against the benefits to be derived from them, at least with regard to marginal changes.

For this purpose, a functional classification of expenditure, of the kind mentioned in the previous section, is needed. Provided that the cash basis is retained, it seems doubtful that the accountability of the government to parliament would be weakened by casting the accounts in this form rather than relegating the functional treatment to a supplementary statement. The problems of apportioning common expenditures are already successfully overcome in both the federal and state budgets, where the expenditure of one government agency is partly charged to others; and the federal Commissioner of Taxation now publishes in his annual report a statement of the cost of preparing income tax assessments and a division of the total cost of his office among the various taxes (including in both cases an estimate of the rental value of premises owned by the federal government).

For a wider picture of the effects of fiscal operations on the economy through the level of activity, the allocation of resources and the distribution of income, additional information is required. In particular, government transactions need to be presented as part of a scheme of social accounts. This is in fact done in the official estimates of *National Income and Expenditure,* which are presented to parliament annually with the federal budget. The estimates, however, lack a link between the government sector accounts and the government accounts as they are presented to the various parliaments. As the latter at present stand, a formal reconciliation would be too complex to assist materially in parliamentary discussion of fiscal policy.

The difficulty arises in part from the use of a completely functional classification of transactions in the social accounts. Of greater importance, however, is the comprehensiveness of the latter, as compared with the scope of the actual government budgets. The use of a *consolidated* revenue fund was originally intended to bring the whole range of government transactions before parliament for annual review and approval. The federal constitution provides, for example, that "all revenues or moneys raised or received by the Executive Government of the Commonwealth shall form one Consolidated Revenue Fund, to be appropriated for the purposes of the Commonwealth in the manner . . . imposed by this Constitution". But "appropriated" does not mean "spent", and moneys may be passed through the consolidated fund and then held in the trust fund. The constitutional requirement, moreover, does not cover loan raisings, so a separate loan fund may be maintained. The state governments are subject to no such constitutional mandate, and much of their revenue is paid directly to trust funds. In consequence of the division of accounts, surpluses and deficits in government transactions for the year may be kept out of the budget proper by allowing rises or falls in extra-budgetary funds, and the over-all result may be ascertained only by a laborious amalgamation of accounts. Also, the financial programme on which parliament and the electorate pass judgement may be incomplete in important details of size and composition.

Although financial authority is vested in the federal and state parliaments, much of it is delegated to subsidiary agencies of government. One class of these, namely local government authorities, has its own system of representative legislatures. The procedures of accounting and of financial control at the local level are similar to those of the parent state governments, although naturally somewhat simpler. Perhaps the major difference is that, in the absence of any institution such as the state cabinet (though this lack may well be remedied ultimately by the growing intrusion of the party system), financial and other proposals are prepared by council committees, of which the finance committee is perhaps the most important. Outside fairly narrowly defined limits, local government borrowing, taxation and expenditure are subject to the approval of departments of the state governments; and in many respects, such as the administration of building and health regulations, the councils might be considered as agents of their parent governments rather than as legislative bodies possessing their share of political power.

The other class of agencies, to which both the federal and the state parliaments delegate some of their financial power, is that which is often referred to as semi-governmental authorities. These boards, commissions, etc., may be created to administer government business undertakings, or to carry out particular spending or regulatory functions of government. At one end of the scale, they are characterized by freedom to borrow in their own names; to receive and spend revenue without its passing through the consolidated revenue fund or being subject to the normal machinery of government budgeting; to employ staff and determine the conditions of employment without the intervention of the public service staffing authority; and to exercise all these powers with only the most limited and general influence from the government of the day. In practice, some or all of these freedoms are absent or at least curtailed, and the semi-governmental authority merges at the borderline into the department of government proper. It must be noticed, however, that much of the revenue and expenditure of government agencies is not subject to direct treasury control or to parliamentary appropriation, is accounted for on an accrual basis, and does not appear in the annual budget papers. (This question is further explored in Chapter 4.)

FINANCIAL RELATIONS BETWEEN GOVERNMENTS

Wherever there is more than one level of government, the problem of intergovernmental financial relations arises. In its simpler form, it is a matter of allocating fields of revenue between the different levels of government in such a way that each may raise enough to cover its expenditure needs. But if, as often happens, practical or constitutional difficulties prevent such an allocation, the more complex problem of intergovernmental transfers of revenue arises. Australian experience since 1900 is rich in these two fields, especially the latter. It is therefore worth devoting some space to an account of it.

In brief, the history of the Australian federation has been characterized by a continuous growth in the functions and the practical power of the federal government, and an accompanying decline in the relative importance of the states. This development has been hastened by the exigencies of two world wars and a great depression; but it seems certain that it would have occurred, albeit more slowly, even in much less unsettled circumstances. It has been possible mainly because of the superior powers enjoyed by the federal parliament in matters of finance.

The federal constitution, which became effective at the beginning of 1901, reserved some powers exclusively for the federal government, and placed many others under the concurrent jurisdiction of the federation and the member states. Some actions were prohibited to both levels of government. All residual governmental powers remained in the hands of the states. On the financial side, the federal parliament was given exclusive authority to levy customs and excise duties, which had previously provided the states with the main part of their revenue. At the same time, there passed to it the responsibility for expenditure on services such as defence and posts and telegraphs. In all other fields of taxation, the powers of the federal and state parliaments were made concurrent; but the constitution provided that, in the event of inconsistency between federal and state laws, the former should prevail. The federal parliament was empowered to grant financial assistance to any state on such terms and conditions as the parliament thought fit. It was also given the exclusive right, with some minor exceptions, to pay bounties on the production or export of goods. The federal powers to levy taxes, to pay bounties and to regulate some branches of trade and commerce were not to be exercised so as to give preference to any state or part of a state. Both the federal and the state parliaments were prohibited from placing restrictions on trade, commerce and inter-course among the states.

In return for the loss of their customs and excise revenue, the state governments were given the right, during the first ten years of the federation, to receive three-quarters of the revenue of the federal duties. In addition, the constitution provided that for at least the first five years after uniform duties were introduced (that is to say, until 1907), all the surplus revenue of the federal government should be paid to the states. As there was some doubt whether the continuance of these payments was compulsory or merely permissive, the federal parliament took care, after 1907, that there should be no surplus, by appropriating excess revenues to trust funds for the building up of naval defence and the payment of the newly-introduced age and invalid pensions. By 1900, general income taxes had appeared in three of the states (then colonies), and dividend taxes in the three others; and during the first ten years of federation the states turned increasingly to this source of revenue.

In 1910 the federal parliament substituted for the three-quarters (or "Braddon clause") payments an annual grant of twenty-five shillings per head of population, thus effecting a reduction of nearly 30 per cent. in the total grant to the states, and making it roughly equal to their own taxation collections. During the Great War the federal government entered the fields of death duties and income tax alongside the states, the former in 1914 and the latter in 1915. It has remained in these fields ever since. A federal entertainments tax was introduced in 1917, but was abolished in 1933 to increase the scope of the states for raising revenue to meet their depression needs. The inflation of the Great War and post-war periods reduced the real value of the per capita payments until they were about one-third of the size of the states' taxation revenue.

During the 1920s the state governments found it increasingly difficult to borrow overseas to finance their developmental expenditure. They therefore explored the possibility of co-ordinating their borrowing programmes; and, indeed, an advisory loan council was created in 1923, on the representations of the federal government, and operated until 1929 with varying success. At the same time, active consideration was given to the reallocation of taxation fields between the federal and state governments in such a way as to eliminate the need for grants and to remove the irritations and inefficiencies of overlapping jurisdictions. There being firm state opposition to all new federal government proposals in these directions, the federal parliament in 1927 asserted its superior financial power by repealing the per capita grants legislation, and thereby forcing the state governments to accept the Financial Agreement. This subjected the annual borrowing programmes of both federal and state governments to the approval of a joint body, the Australian Loan Council, consisting of a representative of each of the governments (see also the discussion at pp. 230-232 and in Chapter 8). The federal government was given sufficient voting power to enforce its will with the support of only two of the six states. It took over the administration of existing state debts and future state borrowing, and guaranteed the liability of the states to their bond-holders. The per capita payments were replaced by an equal, but fixed, annual contribution towards the states' interest liability. A sinking fund was established, with the federal government bearing one-third of the compulsory basic contributions on existing state debt, and one-half of similar contributions on future state borrowing. In 1928 the constitution was amended to enable such agreements to be entered into with the full force of law; and in 1929 the federal parliament passed legislation which brought the Financial Agreement within this provision. Until then it was carried out voluntarily.

The economic depression of the early 1930s forced the states into large budget deficits. The federal government, however, was able to meet its expenditure by increasing the rates of its existing taxes and imposing a general sales tax. By the financial year 1938-39 the situation had changed little. In that year the state budgets showed a combined deficit of £4 million. State taxes yielded £50½ million. The main federal grants totalled £15½ million. This included £9 million paid under the Financial Agreement; £4½ million in federal aid roads grants; and £2 million in special grants to assist the budgets of the three less populous states. The grant for the construction and maintenance of main roads was one of a series that had been made annually since the financial year 1922-23. Special grants had been paid to Western Australia since 1910-11, Tasmania since 1912-13, and South Australia since 1929-30. Since 1933-34 they had been assessed by the Commonwealth Grants Commission, to which further reference is made below.

Some of the more important developments in federal and state government revenue and expenditure since before the Second World War are reflected in Table 8, where a few key items are shown as percentages of the totals in each year. The table relates generally to the consolidated revenue funds. In the case of the states, however, the revenue and expenditure totals on which the percentages are calculated include a number of state taxes and federal grants which are paid directly to trust funds, instead of passing through the consolidated accounts. It should be noted, also, that both the federal and the state totals include large amounts of revenue and expenditure of those government business undertakings which are conducted within the budget. The figures have been built up from several different sources, and are intended to indicate trends rather than to present exact budgetary information.

One of the more interesting developments relates to payments of cash benefits. Both the federal and the state percentages here are based on total benefits actually paid from consolidated revenue and trust funds, rather than on appropriations from consolidated revenue; but the difference is generally small. Before the war the constitution had empowered the federal parliament to grant only war pensions and age and invalid pensions (though maternity allowances were also paid), and other social service benefits were provided, on a low scale and within a limited range, by the states. State expenditure on cash benefits was, in fact, concentrated on unemployment relief, and the minor assistance in other directions was given largely through voluntary organizations which were well placed to assess the need of the recipients. In 1941, under its overriding defence powers, the federal parliament introduced a system of child endowment payments, which was initially financed, so far as the children of employees were concerned, by a pay-roll tax payable by employers. During the remainder of the war, many other federal cash benefits were added, including unemployment and sickness benefits and allowances for students. In contrast to the common state approach of supplying the greatest needs on a case by case basis, the federal provisions were of the blanket kind, applying equally to all who satisfied the general conditions of eligibility. To achieve the same degree of assistance to the most needy cases, the latter system had necessarily to spend very much more on benefits than the individual approach.

In 1946, after an adverse judicial decision on the validity of the federal benefits in peace-time, the government proposed an amendment of the constitution. The amendment was accepted by the electorate, voting in a referendum, and thus the federal parliament received concurrent power with the states to pay virtually all cash social service benefits. With the entry of the federal government into this field during the war, and the decreasing requirement of any sort of unemployment relief, the states had confined themselves even more to special cases of need. The table reflects this development. It also indicates a steady growth in the proportion of state expenditure devoted to goods and services for social purposes: health and welfare services, education, and law and order. Although much of this growth derives from an increase in real terms, part of it is only relative: for the post-war inflation reduced the burden of debt service (sinking fund contributions and interest) steadily from 23 per cent. of total expenditure in 1945-46 to 11 per cent. in 1952-53, despite a very large expansion in the debt of the states; and this, of course, meant an increase in the percentage of expenditure devoted to other purposes. That federal expenditure on cash benefits should be a smaller proportion of total federal budget expenditure since the war than before it, despite the great increase in the coverage of the benefits, is a reflection of the growth in other forms of federal outlay, especially defence services (8 per cent. of expenditure in 1937-38, 21 per cent. in 1952-53, and 17 per cent. in 1956-57). The percentage for cash benefits in 1950-51 is unusually high because of the heavy incidence of war gratuity payments in that year.

TABLE 8

CHANGES IN FEDERAL AND STATE GOVERNMENT FINANCE

| | Federal Budget | | | | State Budgets | | | |
| | Revenue % | | Expenditure % | | Revenue % | | Expenditure % | |
	Income Taxes	Commodity Taxes	Cash Benefits	Federal Grants	State Taxes	Federal Grants	Cash Benefits	Social Expenditure
1937-38	11	63	28	19	35	11	4	20
1938-39	13	60	27	17	36	11	4	20
1939-40	15	59	24	14	36	10	4	20
1940-41	29	49	19	10	35	9	3	20
1941-42	37	40	19	7	35	8	2	19
1942-43	48	32	16	14	15	23	1	18
1943-44	54	28	15	13	12	26	1	18
1944-45	57	26	15	13	12	27	1	19
1945-46	55	29	18	13	14	28	1	20
1946-47	48	32	21	14	15	32	1	22
1947-48	50	32	21	14	15	31	1	23
1948-49	49	30	20	14	15	32	1	24
1949-50	48	32	21	17	15	36	1	25
1950-51	54	26	25	15	15	38	1	26
1951-52	54	30	17	16	15	38	1	27
1952-53	53	26	20	18	15	38	1	28
1953-54	52	31	23	20	15	37	1	28
1954-55	50	32	24	20	16	37	1	30
1955-56	50	32	25	20	17	37	1	30
1956-57	47	31	26	22	18	38	1	30

Without doubt the most important change which has occurred in the federal structure since the 1930s is the introduction of uniform income taxation. The federal income taxes on individuals and companies had originally been superimposed on the existing state taxes. Eventually the federal and state income tax administrations were amalgamated in each state. But it proved impossible to secure full or lasting agreement on uniformity of assessment legislation; and as the national economy became more integrated, the multiple legal requirements involved an increasing waste of resources. The Second World War brought further problems. Mention has already been made (p. 201) of the great expansion of federal taxation, and especially the personal income tax, which was needed to free resources for the war effort. By the beginning of 1942, the government had come against the barrier of the state income taxes.

The essence of the problem was that the weight and structure of the rates of these taxes differed greatly from state to state. In introducing the federal income tax in 1915, parliament had waived its right of priority in concurrent fields by permitting state taxes paid to be deducted from income before federal tax was assessed on it. This, of course, made the federal tax bear more heavily on taxpayers in the more lightly taxing states, and so helped to reduce the disparities in the combined rates. Parliament was prevented from going further in this direction by the constitutional prohibition against discrimination in the rates of its taxation. With the practicable weight of taxation at each income level thus limited by the combined taxes in the most heavily taxing state at that level, many people were left with surplus income to spend, after paying state and federal taxes, to the detriment of war requirements. Moreover, because the revenue of the state governments was benefiting from the war-time growth of employment and private incomes, they were reaching a position where they could make increasing demands on resources for their own purposes.

After unsuccessful attempts to solve these problems by negotiation, the federal parliament in 1942 passed legislation which had the effect of forcing the states out of the income tax field. This was done by the use in combination of three constitutional powers. The parliament imposed new uniform rates of tax roughly equal to the sum of the existing federal and state rates, and at the same time required that the federal tax be paid before any state tax on incomes. It also offered the states fixed annual grants equal to their former income tax collections, on the condition that they did not impose a tax on incomes. And under the very wide federal defence powers, the tax administrations of the five states which had previously collected both federal and state income taxes were requisitioned to the federal public service. When three of the states challenged the legislation, the High Court upheld its validity. The states then agreed to a federal proposal for a similar scheme for their entertainments taxes.

The effect of the uniform income tax scheme on the sources of federal and state revenue may be seen clearly in Table 8. Federal commodity taxes there consist of customs and excise duties and sales tax, but do not include the special taxes on the production or export of primary products. The state taxes include those which are paid directly into trust funds (for example, for road works). The same applies to the federal grants, of which by far the largest component since 1942 is income tax reimbursement.

While the war lasted, the states, with a necessarily restricted scope for expenditure, found the reimbursement grants generally sufficient for their current needs; and some of them built up fairly large budget surpluses. At the same time, however, they accumulated formidable arrears of capital development and maintenance, especially in their railway systems.

At the end of the war, the federal government announced its decision to place the uniform income tax scheme on a permanent basis. The state governments protested, but collaborated in drafting a new system of reimbursement. The war-time scheme had given proportionately smaller grants to those states which had formerly levied less severe income taxes. Under the new scheme, which commenced in the financial year 1946-47, the distribution of the total grant among the states was to be modified progressively over a period of ten years, at the end of which the grant would be allocated in proportion to the populations of the states, with adjustments in favour of states with sparser populations and with larger proportions of children of school age. The total of the annual reimbursement grant, which had previously been a fixed sum, was to be adjusted each year for increases in population and in average wages paid per person employed in Australia.   However, this formula for determining the total grant proved quite inadequate to meet the needs of the states during a period of price inflation.   In each year since 1946-47 the federal government has found it necessary either to amend the formula (as in 1947 and 1948) or to pay large amounts of supplementary financial assistance for recent changes, see Appendix II.

The state governments have frequently criticized the uniform income tax system on the ground that it infringes their financial independence and responsibility.   In 1953, however, when the federal government announced that it wished the states to resume imposing their own income taxes, they showed reluctance to accept this obligation.   Certainly such heavy dependence on federal grants as at present exists provides a useful excuse for their failure to do all that their electors demand, whether or not they would be prepared to do it if they were able to raise most of their own revenue.

Perhaps the strongest criticism has come from the government of Victoria, which before the war levied a relatively light income tax; and in 1956 it filed a new judicial challenge of the constitutional validity of the system. It was joined at the hearing by the government of New South Wales.   The judgement of the High Court was delivered in August, 1957.   The court unanimously confirmed the constitutional power of the federal parliament to make grants to the states on the condition that they did not impose a tax on incomes.   But at the same time, by a majority of four justices to three, it declared invalid the legislative provision which purported to give the federal income tax absolute priority of collection over any such state tax.   The judgement seems to have little immediate significance. The federal government is prohibited by the constitution from discriminating between states in the rates of its taxation.   Thus, unless at least the three more populous states agree to impose their own income taxes, any state which does so will thereby place a disproportionate burden on its citizens; for they will still have to meet a federal tax sufficient to provide reimbursement payments for the other states.   As with other major changes in the federal system (especially the Financial Agreement of 1927 and the social services amendment of 1946), it seems clear that the initiative lies with the federal government.   It should perhaps be added that, chiefly to increase the independent revenue resources of the states, the federal parliament in 1952 abolished its land tax, and in 1953 its entertainments tax.   The states were generally slow to take advantage of the resulting opportunity to extend their own levies.

The federal grants at present paid fall into three classes: block transfers of revenue made necessary by the imbalance in the apportionment between federal and state governments of sources of taxation and outlets for expenditure; supplementary grants to the weaker states, which constitute in effect an interstate redistribution of revenue, since they are financed by taxes levied on the citizens of all states; and payments made on the condition that they are used for particular objects of expenditure. In the financial year 1956-57, the states received £244 million in federal grants, and acted as the agents of the federal government in spending a further £16 million. Of the former total, £174 million was paid in tax reimbursement, of which £19½ million was provided as a supplement to the formula amount. The contribution towards interest and sinking fund payments on state debt had become relatively insignificant at £12 million. These two grants fall into the first category. £18½ million was paid in the annual special grants to South Australia, Western Australia and Tasmania. The grant for road works totalled £31½ million. This and the remaining £8 million of payments belong to the third category, which may be called tied grants.

The major criticism of the system of *block grants,* as exemplified by the tax reimbursement payments, is that it violates a fundamental principle of democracy: the recipient governments become financially responsible to the donor rather than to their own electors. The validity of this proposition depends in part of the size of the grants. It is significant, therefore, that the federal grants proper in 1956-57 totalled well over twice the states' own taxation revenue, whereas before the war the yield of state taxes was more than three times the total of federal grants. (This development may be contrasted with the relative constancy of the grants as a percentage of federal government expenditure: see Table 8.) There is little doubt that the scope for heavier state taxation in the ordinary sense is severely limited: indeed, the state governments have perhaps a relatively greater opportunity of raising additional revenue by increasing the prices charged by their business undertakings. Any large increase in their expenditure must depend on additional federal grants, or on loan finance (which is considered in the next section). Thus they have to justify their additional expenditure proposals, perhaps even the current levels of their expenditure, before the federal government rather than before their own legislatures and electorates. Likewise, any reduction in their expenditure needs may well be balanced by a reduction in the federal grants, so that there is not necessarily the incentive or the opportunity for the state legislator or elector to weigh marginal items of expenditure against the corresponding marginal tax burdens.

These problems may be overcome without the complete abolition of block grants. Two things only are required: that the total and the distribution of the grants should be entirely beyond short-term political negotiation; and that there should be sufficient marginal scope for variations in the states' own revenues to enable them to increase or reduce the pressure on their citizens' pockets as they vary their outlay. The first condition can be met only if the second operates; for experience since 1946 has demonstrated the futility of fixing block grants by formula unless the recipients have room for manoeuvre in their independent revenue resources.

There are various possibilities of increasing the scope of state taxes. The Royal Commission on the Constitution, appointed in 1927, was unanimous that the states should be given the constitutional right to levies of the sales tax type, which they are denied by the prohibition of state customs and excise duties (this recommendation was subject to exclusive federal power in the case of goods for the time being subject to customs duty, so that the states could not nullify the policy of protection). New South Wales had a pay-roll tax from 1927 until 1933. The federal estate and gift duties are not an essential instrument of national fiscal policy, although they contribute to the redistribution of income through their effect on capital ownership. Finally, there is no insoluble economic, legal or administrative problem in concurrent federal and state income taxes, based on income as assessed for federal purposes, and collected by the federal taxation department. The rates for each state might be expressed as a proportionate supplement to a standard federal scale, leaving the determination of the degree of progression to national policy. If the system applied only to individual incomes, the difficulties of apportioning taxable income among the states would be minimized.

Some discrimination between states, on the basis of need, is implicit in the tax reimbursement and Financial Agreement payments, and in some of the tied grants. Indeed, nondiscrimination on one ground (for example, population) may necessarily involve discrimination on others (for example, area, and the contribution of state citizens to the federal revenue). It is arguable that the block grants should be distributed on a simple basis of population, leaving all other measures of relative need to be incorporated in the assessment of discriminatory *supplementary grants*.

Payments of the latter type, the so-called special grants, are made each year to South Australia, Western Australia and Tasmania. Since 1933 they have been assessed by the Commonwealth Grants Commission, an advisory body of three members appointed by the federal government. Out of its experience there came early a statement of the principles to be followed, and its standing is such that its recommendations have never been amended by federal government or parliament, although the federal treasury itself participates in the commission's hearings to put the counter-case to that of the claimant states.

The commission rejected, as a basis of assessment, any direct measurement of the supposed disabilities arising from federation, or of relative poverty of natural resources, or similar factors. It chose instead to rely on the measurement of budgetary need: a state government is entitled to a special grant sufficient to enable it to function at a standard not seriously below that of the other states. The commission "corrects" the budgetary results of the six state governments, to bring them to a roughly uniform basis. Then it adjusts the deficits of the claimant states to eliminate any part arising from differences between them and the non-claimant states in some major budgetary items. (These are currently the level of expenditure on social services, the severity of state taxation, and the budgetary impact of the financial results of government business undertakings.) The resulting adjusted deficit becomes the amount of the recommended grant, subject to some reduction if the non-claimant states have also experienced budget deficits. Payment for each year is made during the year, on the basis of a preliminary estimate with some reduction for safety. A final, adjusting payment is made two years later.

The success of the Commonwealth Grants Commission has given rise to suggestions that it or a similar body might be charged with assessing the amount and distribution of a more general supplementary grant, whose purpose would be to add to the block, per capita payments a necessary element of discrimination based on need. Against this it is argued that the commission has depended heavily on the existence of three non-claimant states, whose budgets might be used as a standard of reference. To incorporate all recognitions of relative need in a single grant would be to reduce the number of non-recipients to one. It seems fair to say, however, that the commission's methods have been developed in response to a particular requirement, and are capable of as much variation and development as changing circumstances may demand.

The spending powers of the federal parliament are limited by the constitution, which the electorate has shown a marked unwillingness to amend. In many instances the parliament has overcome this limitation by the use of its power to make conditional grants to the states. Thus in 1948, when the electorate refused to amend the constitution to empower the federal government to control prices and rents in peace-time, the state administrations were persuaded to impose such controls by a federal guarantee to pay the expenses involved. Virtually all the *tied grants* are of this general nature. They include payments to the state universities, subsidies to meet the cost of long service leave for employees in the coal mining industry (financed by an excise duty on coal), and contributions towards capital expenditure on mental institutions and on the campaign against tuberculosis.

Such payments may be regarded as primarily a means of securing the provision of particular services at a uniform national standard, independent of the financial resources of the different states. It may be argued that some of these services, such as the construction and maintenance of inter-state roads and the provision of flood and bush fire relief, are proper charges on the incomes of taxpayers throughout Australia, rather than of those who reside in the states where the expenditure is made. In most cases, however, the objects lie clearly within the sphere of responsibility of the states, and federal assistance is necessary chiefly because of the limit to the states' financial resources. The danger arises that the federal government, in providing the finance, will also, explicitly or otherwise, prescribe increasingly the details of the expenditure, at the cost of some of the adaptation to local conditions, the experiment and the competition which are a major justification of separate state legislatures and administrations.

Since the end of the war there have been two important examples of spending authorities set up by the federal parliament in co-operation with the states. The first of these, the Joint Coal Board, was established by federal and New South Wales legislation in 1947, to continue the control exercised by the federal government, under its wartime powers, over the production, distribution and price of coal. The second, the Snowy Mountains Hydro-electric Authority, which dates from 1949, is a purely federal body ; but it was established in consultation with the governments of New South Wales and Victoria.

Although less important by most standards, the financial relations between state and local governments raise questions similar to those discussed above. The organization and finances of local government authorities have already been considered briefly in previous sections, and are treated more fully in Chapter 6. Their main sources of revenue for ordinary services are taxes, fees and grants from the state governments. The taxes consist of real property rates, which amounted to £56½ million in 1955-56, and licences, which provided only about £800,000. Fees for services yielded a further

£19 million, and state grants £16½ million. Of the latter, £12 million **was** for road construction and maintenance. The state grants constituted about one-sixth of the authorities' non-business revenue in 1955-56, which may be compared with one-quarter before the war. During the intervening period, there has been a significant increase in their activity in the provision of social and cultural amenities, and in consequence they have canvassed their need of a broader basis of local taxation or a greater share in the revenues of the superior levels of government.

The scope for independent local taxation is limited by the economic effects of differences between areas in its weight and incidence, and by the problems of delimiting jurisdictions. Sales and even income taxes have been used in some countries. But the desirability of a truly *local* base is recognized in the almost universal adoption of real property taxes, which have the further advantage of charging to property owners the expenditures which maintain and improve the value of their assets. As the activity of local authorities broadens, however, this last point loses some of its force. Of other possible taxes, those on entertainments seem to come closest to satisfying the requirements. Apart from the general question of allocating revenue resources between the different levels of government, there is also the problem of disparities between localities in the balance of resources and needs. This is met in part by the weighting of state grants in favour of authorities in country districts, and similar devices, although there is not in Australia any thorough-going system such as the United Kingdom exchequer equalization grants. The devolution of functions from the state governments is also accompanied by some provision of tied grants, especially in the case of road works.

LOAN FINANCE

Some aspects of government borrowing and of the transactions of the loan funds at the federal, state and local levels have been considered in previous sections of this chapter. But the topic occupies such an important place in the finance of Australian government as to warrant further and more extensive treatment.

There are four major sources from which governments may borrow: the banking system; the public outside the banking system; the rest of the world; and the accumulated balances of the governments' own trust funds. Most borrowing in Australia is done by the sale of long-term securities, or government bonds, which entitle the holder to a fixed periodic interest payment (usually around 5 per cent. per annum), and to the return of his capital at some stated future time which may be only one year or more than ten years distant. The federal and state governments also borrow from the banks by the issue of treasury bills, which mature at the end of three months and carry a lower rate of interest (at present 1 per cent. per annum). Interest in this case is allowed by selling the bills at a discount: that is to say, at less than they are to be redeemed for. In addition, the federal government uses treasury bills as well as long-term securities to borrow from its own trust funds. As much of the treasury bill issue is normally replaced by further bills as it matures, it constitutes a "floating debt". Parts of it may occasionally be "funded" by redemption out of the proceeds of long-term loans. Some temporary finance is also secured from the banking system by means of overdraft. Since the bank deposits of the various government funds are usually treated, in effect, as belonging to the one account, the government does not incur any interest charge if it merely overdraws one fund to the extent of the credit balance in another. Finally, there are miscellaneous items of government debt, in the form of subscriptions received in advance for future loans, and savings certificates and other securities of small denominations such as are commonly issued in war-time.

The forms and sources of government borrowing suggest some answers to the question: Why do governments borrow? The first reason, though quantitatively the least important, is to cover temporary excesses of expenditure over revenue. Government expenditure tends to be spread fairly evenly throughout the financial year, except for some variation towards the end either to avoid exceeding the amount voted by parliament or to use up that amount if spending has lagged unexpectedly. Revenue, on the other hand, is often seasonal. This is especially true of the major source, the income tax. Even in the case of the instalments deducted by employers from wage and salary incomes, some three-fifths of the actual payments to the government occur in the second half of the financial year. Instalment deductions, however, account for only about 30 per cent. of total income tax revenue. The remainder, which consists mainly of tax on company incomes and on individual incomes other than salaries and wages, is heavily concentrated towards the end of the financial year, so that, of income tax revenue as a whole, less than 30 per cent. is collected in the first six months, and less than 50 per cent. in the first nine months. Temporary finance is therefore needed.

The second reason for government borrowing is to secure command over resources additional to those available within the government's jurisdiction. When the economy is fully employed, borrowing at home cannot, of course, create additional resources, although it may help in the diversion of some from private to government use. But if funds are raised abroad, foreign exchange is made available to purchase more goods and services than the current oversea earnings of the economy would permit, and thus the government is able to spend more without reducing private purchases. The additional flow of imports need not be used directly by the borrowing government: it may, instead, be merely an indirect offset to the extra government demand on local resources. The large oversea borrowing of the state governments during the 1920s constituted mainly such an offset, although part of it was used to finance imports of machinery, etc., for government business undertakings. The federal government's borrowing abroad since the end of the Second World War has been of a different kind. It was not undertaken primarily because the federal government wished to use more resources without reducing the purchases of the rest of the economy: rather was it intended to supplement the private flow of funds from abroad, as a source of foreign exchange to offset the excess of the economy's imports over its exports.

Government borrowing overseas has its analogue within the economy. When a state or local government issues a public loan, it draws partly on national resources outside its own boundaries, and to that extent is able to use more goods and services without restricting the amounts used by its citizens. As with oversea borrowing, the justification of this procedure is that the additional expenditure, which it makes possible now, will confer benefits outweighing the future disadvantages of the payment of interest and the repayment of capital. Borrowing by business enterprises for the purpose of expanding productive capacity, and by individuals who wish to spend a part of their future income in advance, depends on similar comparisons of expected benefits and costs. Reasons will be suggested below for thinking that governments sometimes underestimate the real costs; and it might equally be argued that they tend to overestimate the benefits. Moreover, when all the state governments are borrowing from each other's citizens, the command over interstate resources which each secures will tend to be nullified by similar lending in the other direction.

Government borrowing within a fully employed economy is essentially a means of reducing the private command over resources to release them for government use. Thus it stands alongside taxation as an instrument of quantitative economic policy (see above, pp. 199-200) ; and this is the third reason for its existence. But it is generally less efficient than taxation for this purpose. Increases in the weight of *taxation* (except perhaps those which bear mainly on people with very large incomes) tend to have a direct and fairly immediate effect on consumption expenditure, and a more delayed but equally powerful effect on business investment in inventories and fixed capital. Even so, private expenditure may not be reduced by the full amount of the extra tax revenue raised: people meet tax increases partly by reducing saving rather than consumption, and this gap will not necessarily be fully closed by the accompanying drop in investment expenditure, for business enterprises may substitute bank and other credit for the missing saving. In the case of government *borrowing,* the reduction in consumption is likely to be very much smaller, and there may be little reduction in investment. Thus an increase of a given amount in government expenditure requires to be offset by a much larger amount of borrowing from the public. Borrowing from the banks, or from government trust funds, may be almost completely ineffective in releasing additional resources for government use. It is therefore to be recommended, as a substitute for taxation, when the economy is underemployed and effective demand needs to be stimulated.

The important conclusion which flows from the previous paragraph is that the transfer of funds, which takes place when governments borrow, bears only a very loose and uncertain relation to the corresponding transfer of resources. Borrowing often appears easier than taxation as a means of financing government expenditure. If the availability of finance is thought to indicate an equal availability of resources, there is a danger that too much expenditure will be undertaken, with a consequent creation of excess demand, leading to price inflation.

There remains a fourth major reason which is often advanced to justify government borrowing. This is that it throws part of the burden of paying for capital expenditure on to the future generations of taxpayers who will enjoy part of the benefit. This is clearly so in the case of foreign loans. For borrowing within a full employment economy, however, the argument is true only in a very restricted sense. If the burden of paying for public works is interpreted in real terms, as a sacrifice of part of one's current ability to purchase goods and services for consumption or business investment, then clearly the burden falls on those whose purchases are necessarily limited while the resources are being used by the government; and as soon as the works are completed, the drain on resources ceases and no real burden remains. There is, however, a *financial* burden which may be passed on to future generations through loan finance. If government expenditure is financed by borrowing, the resources which the government uses are given up voluntarily, in return for the promise of repayment and of an additional annual interest payment. To meet the interest and repayment, taxpayers in future years must generally be forced to part with more of their purchasing power than would be required from present taxpayers if loan finance were not used.

Perhaps the most obvious instance where a government may prefer to impose a greater burden of taxation later, rather than a smaller one now, is that of a large, non-recurring expenditure. In such a case, financing from current taxation might require so great an increase in its weight as to cause a serious dislocation of the economy. A greater aggregate burden of taxation, spread over a number of years, might on the other hand have only a negligible effect on productive activity. This reasoning lies behind some local government borrowing. It has little relevance when the government expenditure involved is of much the same magnitude from year to year.

Australia has a long tradition of government borrowing for public works and similar purposes. Up to 30th June, 1957, the total loan expenditure of the state governments, net of recoveries, amounted to some £2,450 million. £660 million of this was for railways, and the other major purposes included electricity supply, water supply and sewerage, public buildings, and land settlement. State public works have not been financed exclusively out of the loan funds, however; nor have loan moneys always been used solely for that purpose. Much capital expenditure, especially for road works, is met out of current revenue. On the other hand, more than £90 million of the total of loan expenditure mentioned above was devoted to making good deficits in the revenue accounts of the state governments. Moreover, with few exceptions, receipts from the sale of crown lands have, from the earliest colonial times, been treated as current income and applied to meet the ordinary expenses of government.

Since the end of the Second World War, the state governments have made especially heavy use of loan finance. Perhaps the chief reason has been the need of large-scale developmental expenditure, which is traditionally financed by borrowing. Since 1945, the Australian population has increased at an average annual rate of 2.3 per cent., of which nearly two-fifths has been due to net immigration. The resulting requirement of additional social capital, in the form of transport services, water and power supplies, schools, hospitals, etc., came on top of a post-war backlog in such expenditures. In recent years, the largest outlay has been on electricity and gas development, with roads next in importance and railways third. The heaviest capital expenditures of the federal government since the end of the war have been on defence equipment, war service homes, and the development of post office services. Unlike the state expenditures, they have been financed almost entirely from current revenue.

A brief summary of the public debt in 1939, 1947 and 1957 (1956 for local governments and statutory corporations) is presented in Table 9. Debt due abroad has been converted to Australian currency at the rates of exchange ruling at the relevant dates. The decline since 1939 in the importance of oversea debt is very apparent. So, too, is the scale of the post-war borrowing of the state governments and their subordinate agencies. The

figures do not, however, give a clear indication of the changes in debt owed
to the public within Australia, for they include government securities held
by government trust funds and other debt due from one level of government
to another. At 30th June 1956 federal and state public debt redeemable
in Australia amounted to £3,568 million. £402 million of this was on account
of federal treasury bills, of which a total of £252 million were "internal"
bills, that is to say, bills held by federal trust funds. Of the other federal
and state securities, federal, state and local governments and statutory
authorities held £655 million, and an additional £53 million were held by
government pension and provident funds and commodity marketing boards
and stabilization funds. Finally £740 million of long-term debt was due to
the Commonwealth Bank and its savings bank subsidiary. The total debt
of local governments and statutory corporations at 30th June 1956 included
£18 million owed by the former and £446 million by the latter to the
state governments.

TABLE 9

GOVERNMENT DEBT

At 30th June	1939	1947	1957
Federal Government			
	£m.	£m.	£m.
Due in Australia	218	1,755	1,746
Due abroad	226	112	233
Total debt	444	1,867	1,979
State Governments			
Due in Australia	485	568	1,822
Due abroad	519	456	378
Total debt	1,004	1,024	2,200
Local Governments and Statutory Corporations			
			(1956)
Due in Australia	227	256	1,187
Due abroad	38	32	25
Total debt	265	288	1,212

Reference has been made above (p. 218) to the Financial Agreement, under
which government borrowing is authorized each year by the Loan Council,
a body with constitutional authority, consisting of representatives of the
federal and state governments. Borrowing for temporary purposes is expressly excluded from the main provisions of the agreement, and it does
not cover federal borrowing for defence purposes or borrowing by local

governments or statutory corporations. In the case of the last two classes, however, proposals to borrow £100,000 or more in a year are submitted to the Loan Council by the state governments, by virtue of a "gentlemen's agreement", and the amounts and terms of such loans are thus decided along with those of state government loans proper. A more limited control is also exercised over the total amount to be borrowed in loans of less than £100,000. Borrowing by local governments and statutory corporations is in any case normally subject to the approval of their parent state governments.

Both federal and state loans are raised by the federal government, and federal securities are issued for them. By reason of its superior voting power in the Loan Council, and of its responsibility for actually raising the funds, the federal government is able to exercise a strong influence over the total of state borrowing and over the conditions on which the loans are issued. This control has been made greater by the survival until 1952 or later of the war-time "cheap money" policy, and by the post-war inflation, both of which have contributed to a scarcity of loan funds. In 1951-52, of a total of £197 million raised by issues of federal bonds in Australia, £160 million was subscribed by the federal government itself from trust funds, which were largely the result of federal revenue surpluses. This practice has been continued in subsequent years: the amount was £99 million out of £140 million in 1956-57. In consequence of the control thus exerted by the federal government over the borrowing programmes of the states, the proceedings of the Loan Council have become similar to those of the Premiers' Conference, at which the quantum of the supplementary tax reimbursement grant is decided. The state governments invariably ask for more than they expect to be allowed to raise, and attribute their failure to spend all that their electorates would like to the strictness of the federal government. Within the states, however, the allocation of the total proceeds of loans among competing projects is entirely a matter for the respective governments and parliaments, and one in which the federal government has shown in recent years no desire to intervene.

Alongside the limitation of state borrowing, there have existed since the war some factors making loans an attractive source of finance to the state governments. Until recently these included artificially low interest rates. They have also included (and perhaps still do) the effects of inflation on the real burden of debt charges for interest and repayment, which are fixed in money terms. For example, although the public debt of the states more than doubled between 1946 and 1956, debt charges fell during the same period from 25 per cent. to 15 per cent. of total expenditure out of their consolidated revenue funds. A part of the latter movement must, of course, be attributed also to the growth of the economy in population and production, which has progressively widened the revenue base of governments and thus incidentally provided an additional incentive to borrow against future revenue.

A further reason for the attractiveness of loan finance lies in the provisions of the Financial Agreement relating to the redemption of state loans. The agreement provides that new borrowing by the state governments shall be redeemed over a period of fifty-three years by annual contributions of ½ per cent. to the National Debt Sinking Fund. However, only one-half of each annual contribution is to be paid by the borrowing state, the remainder being contributed by the federal government. The fund is administered by the federal National Debt Commission, and forms part of the federal government trust fund. Moneys paid into the sinking fund are not accumulated, but must be used to repurchase or redeem state loan securities. Repurchased securities are cancelled, and the state pays during the remainder of their original currency, in addition to the normal sinking fund contributions, an amount of 4½ per cent. per annum as a substitute for interest.

The federal government also contributes to the sinking fund in respect of its own public debt. Similar repayment obligations are imposed by the state governments on borrowing by their local authorities and statutory corporations; but the states do not normally contribute towards these sinking fund payments. Exceptions to the latter rule are to be found in cases where the state treasuries have assumed complete liability for part of the accumulated debt of their business undertakings, especially the railway systems. A similar effect arises out of the recoupment from the state budgets of losses on current business operations.

The capital account of the government sector of the economy was presented in a very abbreviated form in Table 2. Some further light was thrown on the sources of loan finance by the summaries of loan fund transactions in Tables 5, 6 and 7. The picture may now be completed by reference to the government capital account for 1956-57 as it appears in the official paper on *National Income and Expenditure*.

The combined deficit of federal, state and local governments on current account is estimated at £35 million, which is made up of a federal surplus of £180 million and a deficit of other governments amounting to £215 million (see Tables 3 and 4, pp. 195 and 196). In addition, the governments made net advances to the rest of the economy totalling £54 million, of which £49 million was for housing. Net sales of existing real assets (including houses) yielded £4 million. Thus they needed to raise a total of £85 million from other sources on capital account.

In the same year, local governments and statutory corporations borrowed £66 million from the public by the issue of securities, net of redemptions and government puchases of existing securities. Federal bonds, totalling £140 million after redemptions, were issued in Australia on behalf of the state governments; but at the same time government holdings of such bonds, in place of cash in trust funds, increased by £107 million, making the net raising from outside the governments £33 million. This was further partly offset by a net redemption of £15 million of the issue of treasury bills held by the banks. Net borrowing abroad from the International Bank and from the public in the United States yielded £6 million. Other sources of borrowed funds provided £1 million. The total raised was thus £91 million. As this exceeded the total used by £6 million, government holdings of cash and bank deposits increased by the latter amount.

The government cash balances are thus the final buffer which absorbs the net effect of transactions on current and capital accounts. In the previous two years they had fallen by £59 million, and by the end of 1955-56 they had in some cases been close to the working minimum. Running down cash balances has much the same economic effect as borrowing from the central bank: it permits government expenditure without limiting (indeed, often stimulating) private expenditure.

But the state of the government bank account is only one among a multitude of indicators of the economic effects of government transactions. More than sixty years ago the British economist, Bastable, drew attention in his *Public Finance* to the need of scientific study as a basis for judging the merits of possible state actions. He added:

> "More particularly is this true at present in consequence of the great expansion of the functions of the State, which is partly due to— and which in turn increases—the complicated structure of modern societies. . . . The many indirect results of financial processes must be considered before we can either understand their operation or fairly judge their merits ; but to trace the action of economic forces in their effects on the highly developed systems of modern industrial societies is a task of considerable difficulty, not to be accomplished without the aid of general principles and careful reference to former experience."

Though the study of public finance has developed significantly since the 1890s, Bastable's plea is at least as relevant today.

Chapter Eight

COMMONWEALTH-STATE
ADMINISTRATIVE RELATIONS

A. J. A. GARDNER

The Commonwealth Constitution itself, apart from a provision for the transfer of certain departments from the States to the Commonwealth,[1] makes little reference to administrative arrangements. But the effect of the setting up of the Commonwealth political structure was the addition of another administrative organization to the six existing separate administrative organizations of the federating Colonies. Each of these seven administrative organizations, being engaged in the administration of policies or programmes determined by separate legislative bodies, each of which exercises independent power within its own sphere, is self-contained and independent of the others. Many people still imagine that the States and the Commonwealth determine their policies and carry out their administration with little or no reference to one another. This is far from the truth. Necessarily, as we shall see later, their administrative organizations have many points of contact both at ministerial and at administrative level. The Constitution at federation, however, provided no formal machinery for consultation between them or for joint action on common policy, though some sections of the Constitution expressly envisage co-operation, for example, concerning railways (section 51, xxxiv) and prisons (section 120).

Although there have been few formal amendments made to the Constitution since its adoption, nobody would claim that the federal system as it is today operates in the same way as it did originally or that there has not been a tremendous change in the balance of power between the Commonwealth and the States. The pressure of changing political and economic forces has been exerted hardly at all through amendment of the Constitution but through the legislatures and the administration. The formal or legal approach to the division of powers in the Constitution is not adequate, therefore, in the study of Commonwealth-State administrative relations. What is required is an examination of the devices and techniques developed within the administrative structure, whether as a result of constitutional amendment or not, in response to changing social forces, and a discussion of how administration really operates under our federal system. Further, while a discussion of Commonwealth-State political and financial relations is outside the scope of this chapter, the interrelation of politics, finance and administration makes it impossible to deal with administrative relations without taking some account of the political and financial background.

The most noticeable feature of the operation of the federal system since 1900 has been the growth of Commonwealth political power compared with that of the States. This marked increase in the centralization of political

[1] Australian Commonwealth Constitution Act, sec. 69.

power has many causes, the most important of which are the financial supremacy of the Commonwealth based on the working of the Financial Agreement of 1927 and the Loan Council, the use of the Commonwealth Bank and the introduction of the Uniform Taxation scheme in 1942; the exercise by the Commonwealth of the defence power through two world wars, particularly the Second World War; and the general trend of High Court decisions. The extension of Commonwealth political power into new fields has had a corresponding influence on Commonwealth administrative activity.

The 1929 Report of the Royal Commission on the Constitution listed instances of entry by the Commonwealth Parliament upon fields of legislation which were not expressly assigned to it by the Constitution.([2]) Some of the items listed were:—

"(6) The Commonwealth has no power to legislate with respect to industrial conditions, but by virtue of its power to legislate with respect to conciliation and arbitration, it has set up a Court which may in part override State laws and fix standard wages and hours.

(7) The Commonwealth may impose conditions on loans made to States and so influence State administration. . . .

(8) The Commonwealth may influence the method of administration of the States by making grants, subject to conditions as to the manner in which the money granted shall be expended. The most conspicuous instance is the roads' grant, . . ."

In 1901 there were only seven Commonwealth departments (see Chapter 3). By 1939, though others had come and gone, there had been only four permanent additions—Prime Minister's (1911), Health (1921), Commerce (1925), Civil Aviation (1938). The number rose rapidly during the war, and by 1956 there were twenty-five full departments. The following are examples of fields where new or largely new Commonwealth activities have developed:—

(1) Coal—Joint Coal Board.

(2) Education—Commonwealth Office of Education.

(3) Employment—Commonwealth Employment Service.

(4) Exports—Departments of Primary Industry and Trade.

(5) External Affairs—domestic implications of international discussions.

(6) Industrial Services (e.g., food services, personnel practices and industrial training)—Industrial Services Division of Department of Labour and National Service.

(7) Health and Social Services—Expansion of functions to include, e.g., hospital benefits, pharmaceutical benefits, medical services, assistance to States in relation to tuberculosis, child endowment, unemployment and sickness benefits and rehabilitation of physically handicapped persons.

(8) Housing—Commonwealth-State Housing Agreement.

(9) Mining and Mineral Resources—Bureau of Mineral Resources (geology and geophysics).

([2]) pp. 86-87.

(10) Primary Industries—Australian Wool Bureau and Bureau of Agricultural Economics.

(11) Secondary Industries—Industries Division, Department of Trade.

(12) Shipping and Shipbuilding—Australian Shipbuilding Board, Australian Coastal Shipping Commission and Australian Stevedoring Industry Authority.

(13) Transport and Rail Unification—Machinery for co-ordination of all transport activities through a Council representative of the Commonwealth and States.

(14) Irrigation and Power—Snowy Mountains Hydro-Electric Authority.

Many of these activities were introduced as war-time necessities, but one feature common to nearly all has been capacity for survival and it appears that they have become permanent additions to the Commonwealth administrative organization. Moreover, in the field of economic activity, some of the most important powers are, under the Constitution, shared between the Commonwealth and the State. It is in this field that some of the most urgent and difficult problems confronting government in Australia lie. Examples are: taxation, borrowing, banking, the regulation of commerce, the prevention and settlement of industrial disputes, social services, national development and control of business undertakings.[2]

The sharing of powers, particularly economic powers, in face of the emergence of nation-wide problems in defence and in the economic and social fields and the development of new attitudes to standards of social services throughout Australia, has made vitally necessary the development of techniques and procedures of co-ordination between the Commonwealth and States and between the States themselves. The points of contact between Commonwealth and State administrations in fields of administrative activity which are now being shared or which are closely allied offer just so many potential points of conflict, irritation and duplication of effort. With the expansion of Commonwealth activity, as exemplified above, these points of contact have been multiplied very rapidly. Indeed, much of the history of administrative relations between the Commonwealth and the States consists of the gradual evolution of institutions, devices and procedures supplementing the formal arrangements of the Constitution and intended to facilitate consultation and complementary action to meet common problems. Closely associated with this has been the desire to avoid overlapping and duplication of administrative effort.

As might be expected, there is no fixed pattern discernible in the techniques and devices by means of which co-ordination is sought. They include formal and informal agencies at ministerial level or at administrative level, formal or informal agreements, grants-in-aid, conferences between ministers or between departmental officers, seconding of officers, exchange of information and day to day contact between ministers or between officers engaged in the same field of administrative activity. A brief account of some of these developments is given in the following sections.

---

[2] See Sir Douglas Copland, "The Impact of Federalism on Public Administration" in G. Sawer (ed.), Federalism: an Australian Jubilee Study, pp. 136-137.

CO-ORDINATION AT MINISTERIAL LEVEL

(i) *The Premiers' Conference*([4])

Even before federation the Australian self-governing colonies found it necessary to send political representatives to intercolonial conferences to discuss matters of mutual concern and common interest. Since federation, conferences of State Premiers have been called at frequent intervals. The first, held in November, 1901, was called by Edmund Barton, the Prime Minister of the Commonwealth and, under his chairmanship, all States, except Western Australia, met to discuss such matters as the acquisition of State properties for Commonwealth purposes, quarantine, lighthouses and postal arrangements between the Commonwealth and the States. Each State attending was represented by the Premier and a Minister. The next conference was held in May, 1902, under the Chairmanship of the Premier of New South Wales. Western Australia and Tasmania were represented by Ministers and the other States by their Premiers.

For some years the Premiers' Conferences were called on the initiative of the States themselves and were confined largely to the State Premiers, although a Commonwealth Minister was often present for at least some of the sessions, and the Prime Minister was sometimes present by invitation. Even when the Commonwealth Government took the initiative, the State Premiers and Ministers met privately outside the main conference. In 1908, the government of New South Wales undertook to provide a secretariat which would act as a link between successive conferences, and Holman (N.S.W. Premier from 1913 to 1920) tried to establish his State's leadership of their proceedings.

Up to 1919, the conferences followed this pattern. The Commonwealth took the opportunity given by the Premiers' Conferences to discuss matters of common interest with the States but, as a rule, did not take the initiative in convening the meetings. From that year onwards the practice developed, with some exceptions, of the Commonwealth arranging the conferences,([5]) the present position being that a conference may be called by the Commonwealth Prime Minister either on his own initiative or at the request of a State Premier. The State Premiers often hold informal meetings between themselves before meeting together with the Commonwealth in the main conference. Representation at the conferences varies. The Commonwealth is represented by the Prime Minister, the Treasurer and, where appropriate, by the Minister concerned with any important item to be discussed. Each State is represented by its Premier, usually its Deputy Premier or Treasurer (in some States, the Premier also holds the Treasury portfolio) and, sometimes, an additional Minister.

Since the setting up of the Loan Council, the conferences have been held in conjunction with meetings of that Council. There is now at least one conference a year but further conferences are sometimes called if it is

---

([4]) K. N. J. Bernie, "The Premiers' Conferences", *Pub. Admin. (Sydney)*, VI, Dec., 1947, gives an account of the development of the Premiers' Conference up to 1930.

([5]) Since 1929 the name "Premiers' Conference" (which strictly applied to a meeting of State Premiers summoned by one of them) has dropped out of official use. The meetings are always referred to as "Conference of Commonwealth and State Ministers".

necessary to deal with special problems between the annual meetings. Thus, in addition to the June 1956 conference, where the main topic was the annual allocation of tax reimbursements to the States, conferences were held in August and November of that year to continue the discussion of uniformity in wage policies and means of stabilizing costs in Australia which was initiated at the June conference.

While the value of these conferences in the discussion of mutual problems is generally recognized, doubts are frequently expressed as to their effectiveness as a means of ensuring uniform action by the States even after agreement has been reached. It was suggested to the 1929 Royal Commission on the Constitution, however, that the failure of the Senate to act as a States House gave the Premiers' Conference added importance at a time wher the financial relations of the States and the Commonwealth were undetermined and were about to come before Parliament or the people for reconsideration.[6] The Report of this Commission in a later section made this comment:—

> "Witnesses who had attended one or more conferences on behalf of their respective States said that the value of these conferences could not be judged from the presence of the same item on successive agenda papers. The conferences may not be successful as instruments for having proposals passed into law, but they have considered or formulated agreements between one or more States which have been or are being carried into effect. In a great number of instances recommendations or resolutions of a conference have not been carried out, but, in many instances, suggestions have been made which have brought about legislation on the part of the Commonwealth or of one or more States.
>
> The conferences have paid most attention to two topics—the financial relations of the States and the Commonwealth, and the problem of industrial relations."[7]

During the depression years of the thirties, the Premiers' Conference became an important means of securing necessary co-ordination in economic policy between the Commonwealth and the States, and the States played an influential part in the determination of that policy. Since the introduction of Uniform Taxation by the Commonwealth in 1942, however, the question of the size of the tax reimbursements to the States has come to overshadow the whole of the proceedings. The present situation is commented on by Sir Douglas Copland as follows:—"As with other aspects of Commonwealth-State relations, this useful working arrangement between the several governments was dealt a severe blow by the imposition of uniform income tax in 1942. Although a wide range of topics continues to be discussed at the meetings, the size and distribution of income tax reimbursement grants have tended to dominate the discussions, which have often been held in an atmosphere of domination by the Commonwealth and recrimination by the States, with the worst possible consequences for co-operative administrative action on other points of mutual concern."[8]

---

[6] Royal Commission on the Constitution, *Report,* 1929, p. 46.

[7] *ibid.,* p. 181.

[8] *op. cit.,* p. 139.

(ii) *The Loan Council*(°)

The Loan Council was formed in 1923, without statutory authority, as an agency for the co-ordination of public borrowing by the Commonwealth and the States. The Financial Agreement of 12th December, 1927, between the Commonwealth and the States, defines the powers and functions of the Loan Council. After this agreement had been approved by the Commonwealth and the States, the proposed law for the alteration of the Constitution was submitted to the electors at a referendum and approved by the required majorities. The amendment to the Constitution, one of the few important amendments since Federation, introduced section 105A into the Constitution which, among other things, gave the Commonwealth power to make agreements with the States with respect to the public debts of the States. The financial agreement was validated under section 105A by the Financial Agreement Validation Act, 1929, and the Loan Council thus given statutory authority.

The Loan Council consists of a representative of the Commonwealth and a representative of each State, in practice, the Commonwealth Prime Minister and the State Premiers. On every question for decision by the Loan Council, the Commonwealth has two votes and a casting vote and the States one vote each. The Commonwealth and the States are required to submit to it a programme setting forth the amount it is desired to raise by loans for each financial year for purposes other than the conversion, renewal or redemption of existing loans or temporary purposes, and also the amount required for the conversion, renewal or redemption of existing loans. Each programme must state the estimated total amount of such loan expenditure for the year, and the estimated amount of repayments which will be available towards meeting that expenditure. Any revenue deficit to be funded is to be included in the loan programme. Commonwealth loans for defence, and a few other items (see pp. 230-231), are not subject to the agreement.

If the Loan Council decides that the total amount of the loan programme for the year cannot be borrowed at reasonable rates and conditions it must decide the amount to be borrowed for the year, and may by unanimous decision allocate that amount between the Commonwealth and the States. If the Loan Council cannot reach a unanimous decision, the Commonwealth is entitled to borrow at least one-fifth of the amount to be borrowed and each State is entitled to an amount which bears the same proportion to the balance of that amount as the total of the net loan expenditure of the State during the preceding five years bears to the total net loan expenditure of all States during the same period. The Commonwealth is to arrange for all borrowings including borrowings for conversion, renewal, redemption or consolidation of existing loans, and to issue Commonwealth securities except where the Loan Council by unanimous decision has decided that a State may borrow money outside Australia in the name of that State.

Under the agreement the Commonwealth and the State public debts are combined and the Commonwealth is, for 58 years, to pay £7½ million towards the interest payable by the States, the States paying to the Com-

---

(°) For a more detailed account see C. G. Headford, "The Australian Loan Council—Its Origin, Operation and Significance in the Federal Structure" in *Pub. Admin.* (*Sydney*), XIII, March, 1954.

monwealth the balance of the interest due. A joint sinking fund is established under the control of a National Debt Commission which acts as the agent of the States in connection with payments due to bondholders.

Because of the allocation of voting power, the trend has been for the Loan Council to be dominated by the Commonwealth. Even if the Commonwealth is outvoted by the States, as happened in 1952, it is clear that the Commonwealth by reason of the financial power of the Commonwealth Bank, can retain its dominating position.

The Loan Council machinery was designed to settle global borrowing totals and had not up to 1958 made possible any fixing of priorities for public works. During the Second World War, a National Works Council, representing Commonwealth and States, was set up to co-ordinate public works policy. Although the Council fulfilled its purpose during the war, it did not seem effective subsequently and has not met since 1953. It developed a "shelf" of public works, in case of post-war unemployment, though in its later years this was not kept up to date. However, there has continued to be a Co-ordinator-General of Works, in recent years attached to the Commonwealth Treasury, who advises the Loan Council on Commonwealth and State Programmes with an eye on the resources available to meet them.

(iii) *The Australian Agricultural Council*[10]

The necessity for co-ordinating agricultural policy throughout the Commonwealth led, in 1934, to the establishment of the Australian Agricultural Council. The Council now consists of the Commonwealth Minister for Primary Industry, who is Chairman, the State Ministers for Agriculture, and any other Minister who is concerned in the agenda, e.g., the Commonwealth Ministers for Trade and Territories. The stated objectives and functions of the Council throw interesting light on the nature of the co-ordination required in this field between Commonwealth and State authorities. They are, therefore, quoted here in full as they appear in the Sixth Report of the Rural Reconstruction Commission, 1945:—[11]

"(a) generally to promote the welfare and development of agricultural industries ;

(b) to arrange the mutual exchange of information regarding agricultural production and marketing ;

(c) to co-operate for the purpose of ensuring the improvement of the quality of agricultural products and the maintenance of high grade standards ;

(d) to ensure, as far as possible, a balance between production and available markets ;

(e) to consider the requirements of the agricultural industries in regard to organized marketing ;

---

[10] See F. O. Grogan, "The Australian Agricultural Council", *Pub. Admin. (Sydney)*, XVII, March, 1958.

[11] p. 86.

(f) to promote the adoption of a uniform policy on external marketing problems, particularly those pertaining to the initiation of intra-Empire and international agreements ;

(g) to consult in regard to proposals for the granting of financial assistance to agricultural industries ; and

(h) to consider matters submitted to the Council by the Standing Committee on Agriculture."

The Council is assisted by a Standing Committee which comprises the permanent heads of the Commonwealth Departments of Primary Industry and Trade and of the State Departments of Agriculture, representatives of the Commonwealth Departments of Health, Treasury and Territories and the Chairman of the Commonwealth Scientific and Industrial Research Organization, or his nominee. This Committee, in addition to advising the Council, is charged with advising, and securing the co-operation of, Commonwealth and State Governments on research and quarantine matters.([12]) In the year 1955-56, the Council met once, the Standing Committee three times.

The majority opinion in the Sixth Report of the Rural Reconstruction Commission credited the Council and the Standing Committee with only partial success, attributing the partial failure to a number of reasons including the infrequency and irregularity of meetings, the tendency for schemes to be framed by Commonwealth officers not always fully versed in the conditions and then to be forced on the States, insufficient time given for consideration of proposals, the tendency to hold back information and the lack of authority of the State representatives to reach agreement on at least the principles of the plan to be adopted. These views were contested in 1952 by Mr. J. G. Crawford, Secretary of the Commonwealth Department of Commerce and Agriculture (now Secretary of the Department of Trade) who stated that much of the criticism had then lost any force that it had during the war years and that a partnership had been developed. Mr. Crawford commented as follows:—

"I have felt in our recent meetings we are getting nearer a co-operative organization in the field of administration. We are settling down to the job of trying to work out the answers to food and agricultural policy without indulging in name calling. . . . In agriculture we have enjoyed a very great advantage in recent years in comparison with other fields of policy in that we have had an established piece of machinery for Commonwealth-State collaboration."([13])

(iv) Conferences of Ministers

In addition to the formal arrangements described above, which may be regarded as examples of permanent machinery for co-ordination at ministerial level, conferences are held from time to time between Commonwealth and State Ministers, or between State Ministers only, for specific purposes. Among the most important of these are the annual conferences of State Health Ministers. The Ministers are accompanied by their permanent

([12]) Rural Reconstruction Commission, 6th Report, 1945, pp. 86-87.

([13]) J. G. Crawford, "Administrative Aspects of Food and Agricultural Policy", Pub. Admin. (Sydney), XI, Sept., 1952, p. 106.

heads and, a more recent practice, by some of the heads of various services within the Department of Health. The matters discussed fall into two main groups—those which are of interest to two or more States (for example, the poliomyelitis immunization campaign, control of radioactive and thera-peutic substances, training of nurses and suggestions for reciprocity in the registration of optometrists) and those where an approach to the Common-wealth is considered desirable or necessary (for example, matters relating to finance for mental hospitals, including payment of medical benefits to patients, old age pensions for patients and the inadequacy of the Common-wealth capital grant, and for hospitals). The Commonwealth Minister of Health has been invited to all conferences of the State Health Ministers but does not always attend. He attended the 1957 conference but it was his first appearance for a number of years.

Other important fields in which conferences of Ministers have been and are held from time to time are finance, housing and transport. A major topic of discussion at the 1957 conferences on both housing and transport was the need for the provision of additional finance by the Common-wealth. The State Housing Ministers at their 1957 conference also publicly expressed their dissatisfaction at the failure of the Commonwealth Minister responsible for housing to attend the conference despite an invitation to do so. During the late forties and early fifties, periodical meetings of State Prices Ministers provided the means for policy co-ordination in the administration of price control by the States, but, in 1952, there was evidence that co-ordination had weakened and when, later, most States abandoned price control, the conferences naturally were discontinued.

Co-ordination at ministerial level is extended and supplemented by co-ordination at administrative level. Some examples of this are given in the succeeding section. Many of these forms of co-ordination, of course, represent the projection into administration of agreements reached, in the first place, in political discussions. Some instances where this is neces-sary are—where neither State nor Commonwealth has enough power to act alone in some field, where special Commonwealth financial aid is sought for some particular project or field, or simply where more effective execu-tion is possible through joint action. Some of these devices are as much aimed at improving co-operation between the separate States as between State and Commonwealth.

It might be appropriate here to mention an example of joint action through legislation and regulation arising out of a constitutional limitation on powers. No general power in respect of civil aviation has been conferred on the Commonwealth and, although the Commonwealth has power to make laws with respect to international air services and to air services within a Terri-tory and (subject to section 92 of the Constitution) to make laws regarding interstate air services, the legal power in respect of intra-state services is vested in the States and not in the Commonwealth. Each State has provided by legislation that the Commonwealth Air Navigation Regulations as applic-able to the Territories are to apply to air navigation within the State. "So far as intra-state air services are concerned, the operation of Common-wealth legislation is dependent upon the willingness of the States to incor-porate the Commonwealth legislation into their own law. In recent years (mostly since 1950) various States have amended their originally uniform

Acts or related transport legislation, so as either to restrict the Commonwealth to legislation covering safety factors or to make compliance with State requirements an obligation concurrent with Commonwealth requirements."[14] There are other cases of complementary legislation, e.g., in the field of agricultural marketing, usually following some formal agreement between the two sides.

CO-ORDINATION AT ADMINISTRATIVE LEVEL

(i) *The Joint Coal Board*[15]

The Joint Coal Board is another example of co-operation between the Commonwealth and a State where neither government had sufficient power to do all that was considered necessary. The Board was established under Coal Industry Acts passed by both the Commonwealth and the New South Wales Parliaments in keeping with an agreement between the two governments on the regulation and improvement of the coal industry in New South Wales. The members of the Board, which consists of a chairman and two other members, are appointed by agreement between the Governor-General of the Commonwealth and the Governor of New South Wales. The powers of the Board include:—

". . . the taking of such action as, in the opinion of the Board, is necessary or desirable—

(*a*) to ensure that coal is produced in the State in such quantities and with such regularity as will meet requirements throughout Australia and in trade with other countries;

(*b*) to ensure that the coal resources of the State are conserved, developed, worked and used to the best advantage in the public interest;

(*c*) to ensure that coal produced in the State is distributed and used in such manner, quantities, classes and grades and at such prices as are calculated best to serve the public interest and secure the economical use of coal and the maintenance of essential services and industrial activities; and

(*d*) to promote the welfare of workers engaged in the coal industry in the State."[16]

(ii) *The Australian Aluminium Production Commission*

The Aluminium Production Commission was established by the Commonwealth and Tasmania in 1944 to produce ingot aluminium. The Commission consisted of four members, including the Chairman and Vice-Chairman.

---

[14] Commonwealth Parliamentary Joint Committee of Public Accounts, 24*th Report*, on Department of Civil Aviation, pp. 6-7 and App. 1. See also G. Packer, "Airways", in J. Wilkes (ed.), *Australia's Transport Crisis*, pp. 160-161.

[15] See T. H. Kewley and Joan Rydon, "The Joint Coal Board", *Pub. Admin.* (*Sydney*), VIII, June-Sept., 1949, p. 58.

[16] *ibid.*, p. 61. In 1956 its activities were in decline. But it was still operating a number of mines through subsidiary companies, trying to promote coal exports, running a workers' compensation scheme, spending £150,000 on welfare, awarding university scholarships, etc.

There were two representatives of the Commonwealth, one of whom was Chairman, and two representatives of Tasmania, one of whom was Vice-Chairman. The members were appointed by the Governor-General of the Commonwealth, those members representative of Tasmania being nominated by the Governor-in-Council of that State.

This arrangement continued while the Commonwealth and Tasmania shared equally the cost of the Commission's activities. The increasing cost of the project led, in 1952, to the assumption by the Commonwealth of the greater proportion of the financial burden and a consequential alteration in the composition of the membership of the Commission in 1953. The Commission now consists of five members appointed by the Governor-General, of whom four, including the Chairman, are Commonwealth representatives and one the Tasmanian representative, the latter being appointed on the nomination of the Governor-in-Council of Tasmania.

(iii) *The River Murray Commission*

The Commission consists of four Commissioners representing the Commonwealth and the States of New South Wales, Victoria and South Australia. The Commonwealth representative presides at all meetings of the Commission.

The work of the River Murray Commission is based on the River Murray Agreement which was ratified in 1915 by the River Murray Water Act in the Parliaments of the Commonwealth and the States of New South Wales, Victoria and South Australia, and amended since from time to time. The Agreement, which the Commission is required to put into effect, provided for the construction of works and the allocation of water between the three States concerned. The Commission is not a constructing authority, its responsibility being to arrange for the construction of works by existing State authorities.

(iv) *The National Health and Medical Research Council*

In 1925, the Commonwealth Government appointed a Royal Commission to inquire into, and report upon, public health as a matter for legislation and administration by the Commonwealth in conjunction with the States where necessary, and with respect to a number of other detailed matters. This Commission, amongst other things, recommended the establishment of a permanent Federal Health Council and set out recommended functions for such a body. Following the adoption of this recommendation by a Conference in 1926 of Ministers of Health of the Commonwealth and States, a Federal Health Council was set up in the same year, consisting of the Commonwealth Director-General of Health as Chairman, two other officers of the Commonwealth Department of Health and an officer from the Health authority of each State, with the following functions:—

> "To advise the Commonwealth and State Governments on health questions generally, and as to measures which should be adopted for the co-operation of Commonwealth with States, and of States with States, and for the promotion of uniformity of legislation and administration, where advisable, in matters concerning the health of the people."[17]

[17] First Session of the Federal Health Council of Australia, *Report*, 1927, pp. 3-4.

Experience in the working of this Council led, in 1936, to the setting up of a new body, the National Health and Medical Research Council, with revised membership and functions, to replace the Federal Health Council.

The membership of the National Health and Medical Research Council consists, at present, of the Commonwealth Director-General of Health, who is Chairman, and two other officers of the Commonwealth Department of Health; the chief administrative medical officer of each State; one representative each from the Federal Council of the British Medical Association, the Royal Australasian College of Surgeons, the Royal Australasian College of Physicians and the Australian Dental Association; an obstetrician representing the Australian Regional Council of the Royal College of Obstetricians and Gynaecologists; a representative of the Australian Universities having Medical Schools; and a layman and laywoman appointed by the Commonwealth Government.

The functions of the Council are as follows:—

"To advise the Commonwealth and State Governments on matters of Public Health legislation and administration and on any matters concerning health, medical and dental care and medical research;

To advise the Commonwealth Government as to the expenditure of money specifically appropriated as money to be spent on the advice of this Council;

To advise the Commonwealth Government as to the expenditure of money upon medical research and as to projects of medical research generally;

To advise Commonwealth and State Governments upon the merits of reputed cures or methods of treatment which are from time to time brought forward for recognition."[18]

The Council has appointed a number of committees to deal with specialized aspects of its work such as medical research, industrial hygiene, maternal and child welfare, nutrition and control of infectious diseases. Persons with expert knowledge, not necessarily in the employment of Commonwealth or State Governments, may be attached to these committees.

(v) *The Snowy Mountains Hydro-Electric Authority*[19]

Although the Snowy Mountains Hydro-Electric Authority is a Commonwealth body, its inclusion in the story of co-ordination is justified by the extent and degree of Commonwealth-State co-operation involved in its establishment and operations.

Joint action began in 1946 when Ministers of the Commonwealth, New South Wales and Victoria, with their technical advisers, met to discuss the future of the Snowy waters. Preliminary investigations carried out by the

---

[18] Thirty-Third Session of the National Health and Medical Research Council, *Report*, 1952, p. 4.

[19] This summary is based on the *Annual Reports* of the Snowy Mountains Hydro-Electric Authority, an explanatory booklet issued by the Authority in January, 1953, the *Final Report* of the Technical Committee, May, 1950, and the Principal Agreement (Sept., 1957) and Supplemental Agreement (Dec., 1957) between the Commonwealth, New South Wales and Victoria.

Commonwealth as a result of this conference were assisted by New South Wales and Victorian government agencies. A Premiers' Conference in 1947, after consideration of the report of the Commonwealth preliminary investigations, recommended further investigation and a Technical Committee was set up composed of two representatives each from the Commonwealth, New South Wales and Victoria together with a third representative from New South Wales to advise on behalf of that State in connection with the more technical electrical power aspects. The Technical Committee's Reports were considered by conferences of Commonwealth, New South Wales and Victorian Ministers. The recommendations in the First Report were approved in February 1949 and those in the Second Report in July 1949. To give effect to the proposals, the Snowy Mountains Hydro-Electric Power Act 1949 was passed by the Commonwealth Parliament (relying on the defence power) and the Snowy Mountains Hydro-Electric Authority was established on 1st August 1949. The Technical Committee made its Final Report in May 1950.

Pending the settlement of the final terms of an Agreement between the Commonwealth, New South Wales and Victoria concerning the generation and disposal of power and the provision of water for irrigation, the responsible Ministers of the three Governments set up an Interim Advisory Council composed of three Commonwealth, two New South Wales, and two Victorian representatives. The functions of the Interim Advisory Council included—

(i) the making of reports on the nature, order, sequence and rate of construction of works of the Authority and on matters affecting the States in respect of the diversion, storage and release of waters by the Authority, the generation, transmission, allocation and use of electricity generated by the Authority and catchment areas ; and

(ii) advising on the co-ordination of works by the Authority with works by the States for the generation and transmission of electricity and irrigation, on the allocation of electricity to the Electricity Commissions and on the principles to be applied by the Authority in the allocation of expenditure in determining its cost of production.

The Principal Agreement, signed in 1957[20], provides for a Snowy Mountains Council with a Chairman and Deputy Chairman appointed by the Commonwealth, two members each from New South Wales and Victoria, and two representatives of the Authority. It is to report and advise on the rate of construction, diversion, storage and release of waters, electricity generation and use ; and, subject to any directions from the Commonwealth Minister, to direct and control the operation and maintenance of the permanent works of the Authority. The generating stations will in due course be manned by the two State Electricity Commissions. So when the scheme is complete, the Authority itself will simply operate and maintain the dams, tunnels, etc.

Many State government agencies have assisted with technical advice and with the design and construction of works associated with the Snowy scheme. The New South Wales Department of Public Works has undertaken the

[20] Both Agreements have since received the legislative sanction of the Commonwealth, New South Wales and Victoria.

design and construction of Adaminaby Dam. Examples of other State bodies which have given assistance are the New South Wales Department of Main Roads, Water Conservation and Irrigation Commission, Electricity Commission, and Forestry Commission; the Victorian State Rivers and Water Supply Commission, State Electricity Commission and Forests Commission; and the Snowy River Shire.

(vi) *The Australian Apprenticeship Advisory Committee*

In December 1955, following a Commonwealth-State Enquiry into apprenticeship matters throughout Australia, Commonwealth and State departmental officers (all States being represented except Western Australia) met at the invitation of the Commonwealth to discuss those parts of the Report of the Enquiry which affected the Commonwealth and the States. The departmental officers' conference recommended that there should be constituted an Australian Apprenticeship Advisory Committee with the following functions:—

(a) To consider and make recommendations in respect of all aspects of apprenticeship, other than wages and industrial conditions, including matters arising from the Report of the Commonwealth-State Apprenticeship Enquiry;

(b) to arrange for the conduct of basic research in matters affecting apprenticeship, etc., and for the compilation of necessary statistics of apprenticeship and other labour market information bearing on apprenticeship;

(c) to provide an information service for the circulation of ideas, information and overseas developments concerning all aspects of apprenticeship, among the various Apprenticeship and Technical Education Authorities;

(d) to propose trades which should be considered as apprenticeship trades;

(e) to disseminate information for bringing about better understanding of, and arousing public interest in, apprenticeship's role in the training of skilled workers.

The conference recommended, further, that the Committee be composed of two representatives of each of the States (being senior officers who would cover the technical training and industrial aspects of apprenticeship) and representatives of the Commonwealth Department of Labour and National Service and Commonwealth apprenticeship and technical training authorities with power to co-opt additional members as necessary.

The establishment of the Committee was approved by the Commonwealth and State Governments and the first meeting of the Committee was held in February-March 1957, the Commonwealth and all States being represented.

(vii) *Atomic Energy*

A Commonwealth-States Committee for the Exchange of Information concerning the Peaceful Uses of Atomic Energy was formed in 1955. The State representatives at the first meeting were mainly drawn from State Electricity Commissions, with one or two engineering and public works experts. The committee is mainly designed to see States are kept fully informed.([21])

(viii) *Other examples of Co-ordination*

The above examples of co-ordination at administrative level by no means constitute an exhaustive list of the formal arrangements. For example, agreements relating to housing, war service land settlement, rail standardisation and certain health activities have not been dealt with separately. But the seven instances described above will serve as a sample of formal methods in operation.

As well as co-ordination through organized agencies or based on formal agreements, there takes place a large measure of consultation and co-ordination arising either in conferences held from time to time to deal with specific problems or from day to day contacts between Commonwealth and State officials in the same administrative field. Working arrangements are often agreed upon at this level. The Report of the Royal Commission on the Constitution refers to co-operation in the following fields([22]):—Health, including quarantine, laboratories and industrial hygiene ; railways ; fisheries ; navigation ; forestry ; taxation ; mining ; soldier settlement and immigration. This Report also mentions the arrangement, then in existence, under which the Commonwealth and the States worked together for the collection of income tax. In all States, except Western Australia, where the Commonwealth collected State income tax on behalf of the State, the State Income Tax Office collected both Commonwealth and State Income Tax. This arrangement has, of course, disappeared since the Commonwealth monopolised the income tax field. There have been a few other instances of the use of State officers or bodies by the Commonwealth, especially in the judicial field. Commonwealth and State Statisticians for long co-operated in the collection of statistics.

Since the Report of the Royal Commission, consultation and co-ordination have grown as increasing contact and nation-wide problems have made the need more pressing, and instances could be multiplied of administrative fields where such developments have taken place. Close contact is maintained in a number of areas of administration, for example, by the Public Service Commissioners' Conference (held every two or three years and which has done useful work on problems of overlapping), conferences of treasury officers, heads of Labour and Industry Departments, joint consultative committees or conferences in such fields as electric power, water supply, transport and roads([23]) and the National Mapping Council. The Departments of Labour Advisory Committee is concerned with methods of co-operation and the formulation of agreed technical standards in such fields as industrial hygiene, safety and welfare and in exchanging information on labour affairs generally. The administration of the Colombo Plan illustrates another aspect of co-operation of the States with the Commonwealth. The States have responded readily to Commonwealth requests for assistance

---

([21]) See Australian Atomic Energy Commission, *Fourth Annual Report*, 1955-56, p. 54.

([22]) Royal Commission on the Constitution, *Report*, 1929, chs. XVII, XVIII.

([23]) See H. M. Sherrard, "Main Roads Administration in New South Wales" *Pub. Admin.* (*Sydney*), XV, Sept. 1956, pp. 212-213.

in the provision of lecture courses and inspections of State administration in selected fields to enable the training of administrative officials from South East Asian countries within the scope of the Plan. The States have also seconded officers to help in the technical planning and direction of developmental projects in Colombo Plan countries.

There is also the daily reference between Public Service authorities on all kinds of subjects from arbitration to personnel practices. It frequently happens that one Board or Commission will act as an agent for another on matters which cannot be effectively dealt with otherwise because of problems of time and distance. For example, in matters of recruitment, the Public Service Board of New South Wales may ask the Public Service Board of Victoria to interview, or to appraise the qualifications of, a Victorian resident who has applied for a position in New South Wales. The co-operation between Commonwealth and State Statisticians referred to above has been extended further and, under legislation passed in 1956 by the Commonwealth Parliament, the Governor-General is authorised to enter into an arrangement with the Governor of a State "with respect to the collection and publication of statistics, and the supply of statistical information for the purposes of both the Commonwealth and the State" and this agreement may include the transfer of State employees to the Public Service of the Commonwealth, so that even integration of statistical services is possible if the State agrees.([24]) Although some of the committees mentioned provide a means by which each party keeps its eye on the other, they do help to foster a spirit of co-operation and mutual education.

The Commonwealth by the device of grants to the States for particular purposes, has been able to exercise a growing influence in fields, often outside the constitutional powers of the Commonwealth, where, although the detailed administration is left to the States, the Commonwealth wishes to secure uniform nationwide standards of service. Instances where the Commonwealth is providing money but where the State is carrying out the detailed administration, are to be found in the administration of public health and social services ; in agriculture, where State administered improvement schemes for the dairying and tobacco growing industries and extension services are receiving Commonwealth financial support ; in war service land settlement ; and in housing. The Commonwealth Government has been able, for example, to promote the campaign against tuberculosis, and to provide milk for school children, by providing money for these purposes to the States. In connection with the making of grants by the Commonwealth to the States, the special position of the Commonwealth Grants Commission should be mentioned. While the financial activities of the Commission are not within the subject matter of this chapter, it is appropriate here to point out that its investigations and reports have had an important influence on the co-ordination of accounting and budgetary methods in the claimant States, and the integration of various aspects of their administrative activities with over all national policy.([25])

It must not be supposed from the account of the various devices intended to achieve co-ordination that all have been successful. Evidence is not

([24]) Statistics (Arrangements with States) Act, 1956, sec. 5.   Statistical services were largely amalgamated in 1957.

([25]) e.g. Commonwealth Grants Commission, *Third Report*, 1936, ch. IX.

lacking to show that in both the legislative field and in the administrative, results have sometimes been disappointing.([26])

DUPLICATION AND OVERLAPPING

Duplication and overlapping between Commonwealth and State administrative activities are always possible in a federal system where many powers are "concurrent" and where Commonwealth powers have been capable of wide extension by, for example, the use of the defence power and by the centralization of financial strength. As the activities of the Commonwealth or of the States expand, and points of contact on administrative boundaries are thus added to, the possibility of duplication and overlapping becomes greater. It is this feature which becomes a point of attack for critics of the federal system. Professor Greenwood, for example, claims as instances where duplication has occurred between the Commonwealth and the States, death duties, land tax, income tax, industrial arbitration, savings banks and the collection of statistics; and, as examples of collision, the application of Federal awards to State enterprises, such as railways, and divergent policies of development.([27])

Because of the recognition by both Commonwealth and State ministers and administrators of the existence of this problem, detailed investigations have been made from time to time of the extent to which duplication and overlapping have occurred so that remedial action could be taken. Such investigations, however, have shown that real overlapping is extremely difficult to isolate for correction, and that much of what may seem at first sight to be duplication or overlapping is more apparent than real. Although it may appear, sometimes, that the Commonwealth and States are providing the same service or administering the same controls, the fields of activity are, on examination, often found to be so arranged that the services are either complementary or cover different areas of administration. Abolition of one department or section would in such instances merely mean that its activities would be taken over by the other authority without any decrease in staff. The existence of separate Commonwealth and State public works agencies has been quoted as an example of duplication of function. There is no particular evidence, however, that they overlap in the sense that great economies would be possible if they were combined. They are mostly engaged on different tasks.

The Report of the Royal Commission on the Constitution, 1929, did, incidentally to its main task, touch briefly on the question of duplication and overlapping.

The impact of the depression in 1931 brought the question forward as a live issue in connection with press and other agitation for retrenchment of public services and reduction of the number of administrative agencies.([28])

([26]) e.g. Royal Commission on the Constitution, *Report,* 1929, pp. 169, 171, 181, 186.

([27]) G. Greenwood, *The Future of Australian Federalism,* p. 108.

([28]) S. R. Davis, "The Problem of Overlapping and Duplication between Commonwealth and State Public Services in Australia", *Pub. Admin. (Sydney),* X, Sept.-Dec., 1951. See also extracts from *The Age,* 18th August, 1931, and *The Herald,* 18th August, 1931, quoted by J. C. Westhoven in "Some Thoughts on the Organization and Administration of Public Services in Australia", *Papers and Proceedings of the Victorian Regional Group of the Institute of Pub. Admin.,* Vol. 1, No. 4.

Public and political pressure of this sort led to the appointment of a Commonwealth officer, J. C. Westhoven, by the Commonwealth, to investigate, in collaboration with the States, the problem of duplication and overlapping between Commonwealth and State services. When Mr. Westhoven was later appointed as Commonwealth Public Service Arbitrator, he was succeeded by J. S. Duncan, also of the Commonwealth Public Service. To facilitate the investigation, it was agreed that D. D. Paine, then an officer of the Victorian State Treasury (Taxation Branch), later Chairman of the Victorian Public Service Board, should work with Mr. Westhoven and Mr. Duncan on behalf of all States.([29])   The reports on this investigation were never published, but Dr. Davis, who had access to the result of the investigation in South Australia and a summary of recommendations made in each State, states that the investigators concluded in respect to South Australia that "the field within which overlapping and duplication of Commonwealth and State services may exist is much more limited than may be popularly assumed".

The conclusions which Dr. Davis considers may be drawn from the report on South Australia are:—

"In the first place, the investigation revealed the existence of serious overlapping and duplication in three instances only (Commonwealth and State representation in London ; savings banking ; and the administration of inheritance and land taxes), and minor duplication in two cases, the publication of trade statistics and the maintenance of coastal lights by the Commonwealth and State maritime services.   Secondly, the report emphasised the considerable degree of co-operation which had been established in most of the examined services between the Commonwealth and State authorities to eliminate, or obviate, the possibility of overlapping and duplication (electoral administration, agricultural research, inspection of primary products, purchase of stores, and certain maritime services, etc.).   Thirdly, the investigation found that in almost every service, irrespective of the absence of overlapping and duplication, there was room for further economies through closer co-ordination between the Commonwealth and State authorities (tax administration, purchase of stores, etc.).   Fourthly, the report disposed of the loose view that a simple consolidation or merger of Commonwealth and State services would necessarily result in any significant economies.   And, finally, it emphasised the importance of treating each inter-service relationship as an unique administrative problem to which no preconceived ideas of Federal-State relations readily applied."([30])

Mr. Westhoven, himself, in an address to the Victorian Regional Group of the Institute of Public Administration on 17th September, 1931, made this comment:—

"The general impression of an elaborate Commonwealth Public Service framework—duplicating the State framework—has been dissipated and with it the expectation that large savings are possible.   In its place we see more clearly that it is only in small and comparatively minor sections that duplication really exists."([31])

([29]) In stating that Mr. Westhoven succeeded Mr. Duncan, Dr. Davis has reversed the correct order. He also omits reference to the State representative.

([30]) Davis, *op. cit.*, pp. 508, 509.

([31]) Westhoven, *op. cit.*, pp. 8, 9.

In 1951, the question of administrative duplication and overlapping was again the subject of examination by officials of the Commonwealth and State Public Services. Following an exchange of detailed reports, information and comments on the subject between Commonwealth and State Departments through the Public Service Boards or Commissioners, a conference was held to ascertain the extent to which there was avoidable overlapping between them, and in the interests of economy, to make recommendations for its elimination. At this conference, which met in Sydney on 27th and 28th February, 1951, the Commonwealth was represented by the Chairman of the Commonwealth Public Service Board and each State was represented either by the Chairman of the State Public Service Board or the State Public Service Commissioner according to the constitution of the authority for personnel control in the particular State.

This conference was valuable as a medium for the exchange of views. Again, there does not appear to have been any detection of many specific instances of serious overlapping. As a result, however, some adjustments were made in administrative activities between the Commonwealth and States. For example, the States took over the administration, on behalf of the Commonwealth, of the Commonwealth Scholarship Scheme and the Adult Migrant Education scheme. At the conference it was agreed that: "It is the unanimous view of all the State Commissioners that there is overlapping of functions and unnecessary employment of officers by the Commonwealth in the Education field. The Commissioners regard education as being singularly a State function and they consider that the bulk of the work of the Commonwealth Education Service could be undertaken by the States with comparatively small additions to existing staffs."[32]

As a result of similar investigations carried out in particular fields since 1951, much has been done to eliminate such cases of overlapping as have been revealed. A good recent example of this is in the field of labour inspection. Informal co-operation between Commonwealth and State inspectorates has existed for some years, but now formal machinery has been created for co-operation between, and some integration of, the inspectorates. By agreement between the Commonwealth and any State, Commonwealth inspectors may be invested with certain of that State's powers of inspection and the State's inspectors with Commonwealth powers, so as to avoid, wherever possible, the necessity for dual inspection. This arrangement has already been introduced in several States, its introduction being accompanied by reciprocal training of the inspectors concerned. It does not, however, cover the whole field of labour inspection, even in those States in which it has been introduced. The scheme was formulated by the Departments of Labour Advisory Committee to which reference has already been made above.

It appears, then, that the investigations that have been made have not been able to point to fields where extensive duplication or overlapping is occurring. This may indicate that there is no serious duplication or overlapping. On the other hand, it does not remove the uneasy feeling in some State administrative circles that duplication and overlapping might be present but concealed in the ramifications of administrative processes, for example, in those fields where the Commonwealth is providing money for State

---

[32] See Queensland Public Service Commissioner Report, 1951-2, p. 39.

administered activities and, therefore, imposing detailed supervision over the way in which the money is being expended.

Since the discussion on this topic has been in somewhat general terms, the point should be made that the possibilities of duplication and over-lapping vary from State to State according to the extent to which any particular State had previously developed its own activities in administrative fields now shared with the Commonwealth.

PROBLEMS, REMEDIES AND TRENDS

From the point of view of public administration, two very significant features are noticeable in the working of the federal system in this country since its establishment. The first is the rigidity of the written Constitution, the second is the changing character of Commonwealth-State administrative relationships. Apart from the rare amendments introduced by referenda, the Constitution is still as it was in 1900. In the same period, the economic and social situation in Australia has changed beyond recognition. The significance of this for the administrator is that the impact of the adjustments required to meet changed circumstances has been felt mainly in the field of his responsibility. Within the federal system provided by the Constitution and within the degree of flexibility permitted by trends in judicial interpretation of the Constitution, the administrator has had the task, subject, of course, to agreement at the political level, of developing administrative agencies and procedures capable of dealing with new problems as they arise.

Assessment of the value of the techniques and devices evolved is not easy. So much depends on the political approach of the assessor. The unificationist is, by virtue of his political philosophy, impatient at such methods and would expect, by concentrating political power in the hands of the Commonwealth, to render most of them unnecessary. In his view, under the federal system, co-ordination of State action with Commonwealth is either impossible or so difficult as to be not worth the effort. Professor Greenwood, for example, maintains that:

> "Superficially, therefore, the record of co-operation in Australia seems to be an imposing one. However, a deeper probing reveals that actually it is far otherwise because, while there has been co-operation between governments in the sense of continual communication and discussion of vital problems, the results which have flowed from these contacts have been meagre and unusually disappointing. The test by which the principle of co-operation must stand or fall is the speed and efficiency with which it secures action upon problems of major significance. Measured by such a standard, the record of co-operation is seen to be dilatory and ineffective."([*])

This view is often accompanied by the belief that if the Commonwealth were given greatly expanded political powers, decentralized administration would follow as a corollary. Experience does not support such optimism. On the other hand, there is the view that the division of power in our federal system is a necessary safeguard against too great an encroachment on the rights of the citizen by a central government vested with dominant

---

([*]) Greenwood, *op. cit.*, p. 299.

political power and that the problems raised by this division of power can be solved by co-operation between the Commonwealth and States. This view, too, places stress on the diversity of resources, population, economic conditions, habits, outlook and interests in the various parts of Australia. The majority report of the Royal Commission on the Constitution, 1929, has this to say on the subject:—

"We are aware that the division of powers must lead to some inconvenience and has often been found irksome by Ministers both in the Commonwealth and State Parliaments. But this difficulty may be diminished by a re-adjustment of powers in the light of the experience of the past 28 years, and it has been diminished to a very large extent by co-operation. If there had been further co-operation between the States and the Commonwealth, it is probable that the impression of the Constitution as an almost inflexible instrument would not have been formed. This conclusion appears to be supported by the history of the last constitutional amendment, but apart from the power of amendment the inconvenience attributable to a division of powers has been greatly diminished by co-operation in administration, e.g., in health, in fisheries, in navigation, and in the control of railways, as well as by the operation of certain Commonwealth instrumentalities which work in conjunction with the States and are supported by the revenue or the credit of the whole of the Commonwealth."([34])

The administrator in Australia, whether he likes it or not, is working within a federal system and with reference to a particular division of powers made in the federal constitution. The electors have demonstrated by referenda on many occasions that they are not disposed to centralize political powers in the Commonwealth in peace time. Attempts to adjust functions by obtaining the reference of matters by the States to the Commonwealth under section 51 (xxxvii) of the Constitution have not proved any more successful.([35]) It is probable, then, that techniques of co-ordination will always be necessary and that what is required to improve the co-ordination of Commonwealth and State administration is the encouragement within the federal political system of a disposition to consider administrative activity in terms of the most appropriate administrative level. This is particularly true in relation to new activities. What is necessary here is the development of the practice of consultation before a new administrative agency is established; consultation on the most satisfactory level for administration and on the possibility of using some already existing administrative organization. As most of the new administrative agencies established during and since the second World War have been set up by the Commonwealth, the weight of the criticism on failure to make the fullest use of existing agencies has, naturally, been directed against the Commonwealth.([36]) Certainly had

([34]) p. 241.

([35]) See, e.g., K. C. Wheare, Federal Government, pp. 248-250; Post War Reconstruction—A Case for Greater Commonwealth Powers, 1942, pp. 99, 100; and R. Anderson in R. Else-Mitchell (ed.), Essays on the Australian Constitution, pp. 115-116.

([36]) For example:
"While incursions by the Commonwealth Government into certain fields of administration, hitherto the sole preserves of the State, have been largely directed by the necessities of the War, the tendency towards duplication by

(continued on next page.)

such a practice been followed more frequently there would have been fewer charges of duplication and overlapping and less irritation over encroachment and over the recruitment of trained staff by new Commonwealth agencies from State agencies already in the same field. Allied with this is the view expressed in many quarters that there should be greater facilities to ensure that the more intimate local knowledge and the resources and information at the disposal of State administrative agencies is used to the fullest extent by the Commonwealth to avoid the setting up of additional Commonwealth research agencies engaged on the collection of the same kind of material. Here the solution appears to be a more adequate exchange of information and a greater readiness to use information already available.

Duplication does not necessarily have to exist to give the Commonwealth a measure of control over functions which have been constitutionally those of the States. Despite the fact that the constitution does attempt to divide Commonwealth from State powers, there is nothing to prevent the Commonwealth from appropriating funds and spending money on anything it wishes, even though it may have no power to legislate on the subject.

All Governments at all times are confronted with the need to undertake certain essential tasks. The States, being chronically short of funds, are unable always to proceed with these tasks immediately. In these situations it is often the policy of the Commonwealth to finance the project, entrusting its actual execution to the State, subject, of course, to the Commonwealth's being satisfied with the way the job is being done. In these circumstances, the relationship between the Commonwealth and the State is not always that of partnership, but rather of principal and agent or employer and employee, and this is probably almost as dangerous from the State standpoint as a direct encroachment by the Commonwealth on State functions.

There is no doubt that, where a particular problem requires uniform action over the whole of Australia, effective action will be much more likely if the necessary power is in the hands of the Commonwealth. The exasperation of the Commonwealth official faced with the task of persuading reluctant States into agreement on a common policy or on a joint administrative programme can easily be imagined, particularly when it is realized that State political boundaries do not always conform to the most appropriate Commonwealth administrative areas. "The organisation of the great majority of Commonwealth departments has been based, not on considera-

---

the Commonwealth of existing State administrative organization and services is becoming more evident.

In some instances, State organization is being profitably utilized to implement Commonwealth policy under conditions where powers are temporarily vested in the State authority. In others, new Commonwealth administrative organization has been set up and superimposed on existing State services to achieve, during the War, regulatory control in certain spheres of activities.

Only where Commonwealth control is so exercised through properly coordinated Commonwealth and State services is efficient and economical administration assured.

The position in regard to the maintenance of dual administrative organizations, involving the question of the disbandment of Commonwealth organization temporarily created during the War, will undoubtedly be a major matter in post-war considerations."

(Victorian Public Service Board, *Report.* 1942-3, p.8.)

tions of the efficiency of each department as a nation-wide concern, but on the almost primitive idea that each department must have a head at the centre of government with sub-heads in each of the States."([37])

However, a point that must not be overlooked by administrators at the centre is that uniformity of State administration is often less desirable than diversity. It is easy to fall into the error of pursuing uniformity for its own sake or because it makes for greater convenience of administrative arrangements. Due allowance must be made for different conditions and requirements in each State. There seems to be a strong body of opinion that, even in those activities where the Commonwealth has confined itself to setting standards of performance and providing the necessary finance, scrutiny and control by the Commonwealth is far too rigid and detailed. The numerous statistical statements and detailed returns required from State Departments administering schemes financed by the Commonwealth have on many occasions been the subject of critical comment.

The multiplicity of contacts made between the Commonwealth and the States in the administrative field resolves itself into contacts between individual officers whether in person, by telephone or by correspondence. Personal relations are most important factors, then, in setting the atmosphere for administrative consultation and co-ordination between the Commonwealth and the States. The attitude of Commonwealth and State officials to each other will depend, in part, on the concept each group has formed of the other, whether based on reality or not. The Commonwealth official is sometimes apt to regard the Commonwealth administration as the superior partner and to forget the true nature of the relations between the Commonwealth and the States under the federal system. The reaction of the State official to this treatment is naturally one of resentment, especially where he sees what he believes to be attempted Commonwealth intrusion and interference in fields which, hitherto, have been regarded as proper to State administration. When this resentment is accompanied by the suspicion that the Commonwealth official may be influenced by expansive tendencies or by the desire for self-aggrandisement by "empire-building", the way to co-operation is not likely to be easy. In the background, too, lurks the spectre of finance. Where the relationship is such that the Commonwealth is providing the necessary finance, the attitude of domination and superiority can be too readily reinforced.

Dominating the whole field of Commonwealth-State administrative relations is the overwhelming superiority of the financial strength of the Commonwealth. Through it the Commonwealth has been able to influence increasing areas of State administration. The future pattern of administrative relations will undoubtedly, be conditioned largely by the trends in financial relations. If, for example, it became possible for the States to impose their own income tax once again we might well see a lessening of this influence. If present arrangements continue, it is probable that Commonwealth direction and supervision will grow in strength and extent. Perhaps it is not entirely beyond reasonable conjecture to consider the possibility that the determination of the annual amount of the tax reimbursement for each State could lead through the necessity for the justification of requests by the State

---

([37]) Professor K. H. Bailey, in G. Sawer (ed.) *Federalism: An Australian Jubilee Study*, pp. 167-168.

Premiers to the imposition of conditions as to the objects of expenditure, and thus to even greater control over the relative importance and activities of various sections of State administrative frameworks.

So much has been said in this section on the points of irritation and conflict that the impression might be left that the techniques and devices adopted to achieve co-ordination have been unsuccessful. Such a conclusion would overlook those activities, and they are in the majority, in which Commonwealth and State officials are co-operating in a spirit of mutual understanding and good will. In fact, over recent years, there appears to have developed a much greater appreciation of the necessity for co-operation and co-ordination at the administrative level.

The primary object of this chapter has been the examination of administrative aspects of Commonwealth-State relations. In consequence, perhaps, these may have been given too much emphasis at the expense of the political or legislative aspects. For example, no reference has been made to the important influence on co-ordination of the political composition of the Commonwealth and State governments at any particular time. It is as well, therefore, to stress the point that in reality politics and administration are intimately linked. For this reason, too, reference should be made here to the care required in passing judgment on what is often referred to in discussions on Commonwealth-State relations as the "efficiency" or the "adequacy" of the administrative structure. Broadly, "efficiency" in public administration, correctly defined, means the achievement of the desired objective with the least possible expenditure of manpower and other resources. The term "inefficient" is frequently applied to the administrative structure in Australia not with this meaning but because of disagreement with the objectives sought. In other words, there is a confusion of means (public administration) with ends (politically determined objectives). What, then, appears to be criticism directed at the administrator proves, on analysis, to be the expression of opinion on a political issue.

Chapter Nine

ADMINISTRATIVE LAW

R. Else-Mitchell

The growth of a substantial body of administrative law in English-speaking countries can be traced to the economic and social developments of the last century. A hundred years ago their governments had much less concern with economic and social matters such as the regulation of trade and industry, the conduct of public utilities or the maintenance of labour standards; they left those matters to the enterprise of the individual and contented themselves with declaring rules of general conduct and maintaining the courts as tribunals in which matters of private right could be litigated and determined. The trend to greater government intervention was manifested originally by legislative regulation in the form of Acts of Parliament which were enforced in the courts in the accepted way; but it was soon found that resort to established judicial procedures was inadequate. The complexity and variety of the situations which had to be met, the need for flexibility in the application of a pre-determined policy, the delay, expense and lack of expertise so characteristic of judicial procedures and the need for primary regard to be paid to social factors and the public interest, all contributed to the inability of Parliament and the courts to give full effect to these new trends and to cope in detail with new problems. The solution was therefore found in the conduct of the necessary activities and functions by administrative authorities—government departments, public corporations and local authorities.

The function of these executive and administrative authorities was to prescribe rules of conduct within the scope of the policy laid down by Parliament in legislation; this entailed the exercise of law-making functions under delegated authority. Secondly, the need for flexibility involved those authorities having the power of making decisions with respect to individual cases; this entailed the exercise of discretions and was a form of adjudication. Thirdly, in some cases, a power was conferred or a duty imposed upon those authorities to engage directly in a particular field of activity; this entailed the making of contracts and the performance of acts which infringed both public and private rights and thus raised a new question of legal liability because the executive authorities represented the Crown and for historical reasons were not bound by statute nor subject to the ordinary processes of law.

These three aspects indicate in broad outline the content of administrative law in its present state of development and will be discussed in this chapter under the headings:—

(1) Delegated Legislation;

(2) Administrative Adjudication; and

(3) Legal Liability of Administrative Authorities.

DELEGATED LEGISLATION

The vast increase in delegated legislation can be traced directly to a variety of factors, all of which are related to the character of our parliamentary institutions. First, the time of Parliament has been largely occupied in modern times in debating and determining issues of social and economic policy. Secondly, the growing influence of social and economic considerations has demanded legislation on a wide range of new topics and situations and so has increased not only the number of laws but their individual bulk. Thirdly, the complex nature of these new topics and situations has made it impossible for Parliament to discharge its duty by laying down a few simple and comprehensive rigid rules. Fourthly, Parliament has not the expert knowledge in matters of a technical character to enable it to work out the detailed scheme of all laws. Fifthly, in cases of emergency such as war, disease and famine, the parliamentary process is too slow to take effective action. In the result Parliament has neither the time nor the equipment, and its processes are not adequate, to enable it to undertake the formulation in detail of every necessary law; it must content itself with declaring the policy or outline of legislation and empowering some administrative authority to prescribe the machinery by which and the circumstances in which that policy is to be implemented. This has been achieved by conferring power in the Act on a Minister or other authority to make regulations, orders, rules or by-laws which when made are forms of "delegated legislation". Sometimes, as in recent years in Australia by the National Security Act, 1939, and the Defence Preparations Act, 1951, power is conferred to make regulations which in turn may authorize the making of orders and the giving of directions; this entails a double delegation of power and any orders so made or directions given are further distinguished as sub-delegated legislation.

Delegated legislation may take a variety of forms. In England Orders in Council and statutory rules of general application are usually made under Acts of Parliament in pursuance of ministerial or departmental authority but there may also be orders, warrants, rules and ordinances; in addition by-laws of particular application in specified localities may be made by local authorities. In Australia Acts of the Commonwealth Parliament mainly authorize the making of regulations by the Governor-General in Council, but Acts like the National Security Act, 1939, contemplate the making of regulations under which power is granted to a Minister to make orders or give directions having the force of law. In the States regulations are generally made by the Governor in Council or by special authorities such as the Railways Commissioners. Local government legislation generally authorizes the making of ordinances or by-laws by the Governor in Council, and the local authorities also may have powers of regulation and control which enable them to make rules or by-laws of limited application in their own districts.

Although it is almost universally recognized that delegated legislation in some form is inevitable in modern democratic communities there has for many years been strong criticism of this form of legislation. The most vocal critics have undoubtedly been Lord Hewart who, in a book published in 1929, included it as part of *The New Despotism;* and Sir Carleton Allen, who has trenchantly attacked such legislation in two books, *Bureaucracy Triumphant* and *Law and Orders.* Foremost in the criticism of delegated legislation is the charge that it is undemocratic because a Minister or other authority can promulgate legislative measures without their being approved by elected representatives in Parliament. Though this is basically true, the argument loses a lot of its force when it is realised that, generally speaking, all such measures must be laid on the tables of both Houses of Parliament and can be disallowed by resolution of either house; any charge along these lines is in reality a reflection on Parliament for its failure to supervise the measures which are placed before it.

It is also said that delegated legislation tends to concentrate power in the hands of executive authorities who treasure power for power's sake, and that this is gradually reducing the citizen to a state of serfdom in which he is governed by laws made in secret by officials who are responsible to no-one. This argument, which has been emotionally developed by Allen and by F. A. Hayek in *The Road to Serfdom,* overlooks the central feature of responsible Cabinet government, namely that every Minister is liable to account to Parliament for the acts of his department and subordinate officials; it does possess some force in relation to sub-delegated legislation because the chain of responsibility may have too many and remote links. Finally, amongst the chief criticisms of delegated legislation is the claim that it frequently abrogates the rule of law and precludes the courts exercising control over the authority which makes such legislation. This objection is based on a few exceptional cases and is more apparent than real.

A more moderate approach to the whole subject of delegated legislation has been made by C. T. (now Sir Cecil) Carr, formerly Counsel to the Speaker of the House of Commons and whose experience in the field of legislation and administration has been immense. His first work on the subject, published in 1921 under the title *Delegated Legislation,* is a minor classic and despite the lapse of thirty years its views still command respect. Carr propounded five safeguards which he considered would prevent or minimise the abuse of delegated legislation and which many later authors have accepted in principle. They are these:—

(1) The delegation of legislative power should be delegation to a trustworthy authority which commands the national confidence.

(2) The limits within which the delegated power is to be exercised ought to be definitely laid down.

(3) If any particular interests are to be specially affected by delegated legislation, the legislating authority should consult them before making its laws.

(4) There should be publicity of delegated legislation.

(5) There should be machinery for amending or revoking delegated legislation as required.

These points are worth considering in more detail in relation to the prevailing position in England and Australia.

(1) No-one would deny the importance of the requirement that power should be delegated only to a trustworthy authority commanding the national confidence. It would be opposed to the principle of all our representative institutions to allow the delegation of power without limit to persons of bodies who might exercise it for ulterior purposes or who could not be made responsible to Parliament for any abuse of power. In general, therefore, it

is difficult to object on this ground to the exercise of delegated legislative power by the Executive Council or by any other similar body consisting of Ministers, or even by individual Ministers of the Crown ; so too the power of representative bodies such as municipal and shire councils, which are subordinate legislative authorities elected by ratepayers or householders, is unobjectionable. But the process of sub-delegation is opposed to this concept because the power to make laws becomes exerciseable by an authority which is not directly responsible to Parliament or to any body of electors.

Recent illustrations of the lengths to which sub-delegation may go and of the dangers which are involved in such a process are to be found in the regulations made during the Second World War under the National Security Act 1939 in Australia and the Emergency Powers (Defence) Act 1939 in England. The latter Act was responsible for many instances of "five-tier" legislation, namely, the Defence Regulations made under the Act, orders made under these regulations, directions given under the orders, and licences issued under the directions. In Australia the process of sub-delegation is rare in peace time but during times of war it has been regularly practised, though not to the same lengths as in England. Regulations under the National Security Act 1939, for instance, often did no more than to set up a separate legislative and administrative system with respect to some very general topic, such as "prices", "rationing", "food control" and to pass the power of legislation to some person or body which was not necessarily a part of the governmental system and could therefore be only remotely controlled by the appropriate Minister of the Crown.

Further objections to the sub-delegation of power have arisen from the absence of any specification of the method of exercising the power. This has left the way open to legislation by informal documents such as "circulars", "rulings", "instructions" having legislative effect but no legislative form. In England the same tendency has been evident in post-war years, and the practice of legislating by "circular" has come in for some severe comments by the courts. In one case in 1948[1] the Court of Appeal described as "really monstrous" and "almost incredible" the action of Ministers in delegating power under the Defence Regulations by circulars to local authorities empowering them to requisition private property ; the whole matter savoured of such secrecy, even to the reluctance of the local authority to produce the documents under which it exercised its powers, that the court branded it as "an example of the worst kind of bureaucracy".

It is not easy to prevent the sub-delegation of authority unless some specific provision is included in the Act which empowers the primary delegation. In matters of private law the maxim *delegatus non potest delegare* precludes an agent or delegate from further delegating his authority. Although this has been held to apply in the field of public law,[2] the terms of most Acts permit of delegation by a Minister, if only for the purpose of enabling his departmental officers to issue any necessary instruments in his absence. Provisions of this sort, framed in wide terms, often had the effect during the Second World War of authorizing a delegation to persons not

---

[1] *Blackpool Corporation v. Locker* (1948) 1 K.B. 349.

[2] *Allingham v. Minister of Agriculture* (1948) 1 All. E.R. 780. *Manton v. Brighton Corporation* (1951) 2 K.B. 393; Fox and Davies, Sub-Delegated Legislation, 1955, 28 *A.L.J.* 486.

under a Minister's direct control. By this means power found its way into the hands of men of business and commerce who occupied positions as "controllers" or members of a board in which they were not subject to the ordinary disciplinary process of the administrative hierarchy.

The courts have been astute to limit the right of sub-delegation by subordinate authorities and have seized on even minor indications in an Act of Parliament to confine power to the hands of the primary repository. Thus it has been held that the Municipal Council of Sydney cannot delegate to its Town Clerk its general power to control and regulate the use of premises and nuisances thereon,([3]) and also that the Council cannot delegate the power to levy a rate or make by-laws.([4]) In Victoria the Supreme Court has for similar reasons restricted the right of a Shire Council to delegate its power to manage and control a town hall.([5]) In New South Wales a recent amendment to the Local Government Act, 1919 (Section 530A) has extended the power to delegate, but the wisdom of this provision is open to doubt.

(2) The second of Carr's requirements, that the limits of delegated power should be definitely laid down, acts as a safeguard because it enables the courts to protect the citizen against any excess or abuse of power by the application of the doctrine of *ultra vires*. Before considering how this is achieved it should be mentioned that all law-making bodies other than Parliament are classed as subordinate or non-sovereign. In England Parliament has complete sovereignty and no Act of Parliament can be set aside or annulled in the courts; since the Statute of Westminster, 1931, all Dominion Parliaments are in a similar position; but in a federal state, such as Australia, where the powers are distributed between the Commonwealth and the States, each has sovereign power only within its own sphere of activity. Any legislative power which is granted by an Act of Parliament to any other law-making body is not sovereign but is subordinate in its character and, in consequence, the courts can scrutinize its exercise and determine the validity of any such exercise. The grounds on which they will do this are that it is beyond power, or in some circumstances is unreasonable or uncertain.

Delegated legislation is *ultra vires* and invalid when it exceeds the powers granted by the Act of Parliament to the subordinate authority. This naturally entails an examination of the legislation in the light of the powers granted. It follows that the wider the grant of power the less possibility there is of holding any subordinate legislation to be invalid. But a grant of power, even in absolute terms, will be construed by the courts as limited to the specific purposes for which the Act was passed and will not authorize extraneous matters. In Australia the regulation-making powers conferred by Commonwealth and State Acts usually refer to specific matters which are mentioned in the Act or must necessarily arise thereunder; in addition it will be frequently found that a general power is conferred to make regulations or by-laws "prescribing all matters which by this Act are required or permitted to be prescribed or as may be necessary or convenient to be prescribed for giving effect to this Act".

([3]) *Municipal Council of Sydney v. Herman* (1948) 65 W.N. (N.S.W.) 265.
([4]) *Bailey v. Municipal Council of Sydney* (1927) 28 S.R. (N.S.W.) 149.
([5]) *Morrison v. Shire of Morwell* (1948) V.L.R. 73.

It might seem that a provision in these terms gives extremely wide powers to the subordinate authority, but a series of decisions in Australia has imposed important limitations on its scope. One recent decision related to Section 164 of the Excise Act, 1901-1947, which was in the terms quoted above and under which regulations had been made penalizing any failure in the safe keeping of excisable goods.([6]) In holding the regulation to be invalid six judges of the High Court said:

> "A power expressed in such terms to make regulations enables the Governor-General in Council to make regulations incidental to the administration of the Act. Regulations may be adopted for the more effective administration of the provisions actually contained in the Act but not regulations which vary or depart from the positive provisions made by the Act or regulations which go outside the field of operation which the Act marks out for itself. The ambit of the power must be ascertained by the character of the statute and the nature of the provisions it contains. An important consideration is the degree to which the Legislature has disclosed an intention of dealing with the subject with which the statute is concerned.
>
> In an Act of Parliament which lays down only the main outlines of policy and indicates an intention of leaving it to the Governor-General to work out that policy by specific regulation, a power to make regulations may have a wide ambit. Its ambit may be very different in an Act of Parliament which deals specifically and in detail with the subject matter to which the statute is addressed. In the case of a statute of the latter kind an incidental power of the description contained in sec. 164 cannot be supposed to express an intention that the Governor-General should deal with the same matters in another way."

An examination of cases in which the High Court has held regulations and orders to be invalid on the ground that they are beyond power shows that, except in time of war or other emergency, it has been careful to limit the delegated power to the "filling in of the outline" of the Act. Even during the war the supervision it exercised over regulations and orders did not impede major matters such as universal manpower control, but invalidated minor regulations relating to such matters as the admission of students to universities, factory lighting standards, and orders regulating the manufacture, or fixing the prices, of some individual products. The power of the courts to hold delegated legislation beyond power is a control of an important and salutary character.

The courts will also on occasions resort to the doctrines of uncertainty and unreasonableness to hold delegated legislation to be invalid. These doctrines, which originated in England in the field of local government, purport to require that a by-law to be valid must "have two properties—it must be certain, that is, it must contain adequate information as to the duties of those who are to obey and it must be reasonable."([7]) These doctrines provide most unsatisfactory criteria to determine validity. There are decisions which reject unreasonableness as a ground of invalidity,([8]) while others treat it as a branch of the doctrine of *ultra vires* on the basis that an unreasonable by-law or regulation will not be regarded as a *bona fide* exercise of power ; and there is at least one decision of the High Court upholding the validity of a by-law which required an impossibility.([9])

([6]) *Morton v. Union S.S. Co. of New Zealand Ltd.* (1951) 83 C.L.R. 402; cf. *Shanahan v. Scott* (1957) Argus L.R. 171.

([7]) *Kruse v. Johnson* (1899) 2 Q.B. 91.

([8]) *Williams v. The Melbourne Corporation* (1933) 49 C.L.R. 141.

([9]) *Footscray Corporation v. Maize Products Ltd.* (1943) 67 C.L.R. 301.

The doctrine of uncertainty was often invoked during the Second World war as a ground for declaring subordinate legislation invalid. But the view has been expressed by a learned author that this doctrine had a false foundation and that the legal decisions relied upon to support it were either cases where invalidity followed for some other reason or were wrongly decided.([10]) This view has received some judicial recognition but it seems that delegated legislation may be held invalid on the ground of *ultra vires* if it imposes a duty by standards which are not capable of ascertainment.([11])

By way of contrast with the doctrine of *ultra vires* and the desirability of defining the limits of delegated power, it should be mentioned that some Acts of Parliament confer power to make regulations in terms which attempt to preclude any challenge to their validity by the courts. One device, more common in England than Australia, is to provide that the subordinate authority (not Parliament) may by order amend the Act. This is known as the "Henry VIII clause" and was so "named after that monarch in disrespectful commemoration of his tendency to absolutism".([12]) Needless to say, this device has few supporters and the United Kingdom Committee on Ministers' Powers in 1932 recommended that it should be abandoned in all but the most exceptional cases. It is nevertheless found in a limited form in a Commonwealth Act, the Re-establishment and Employment Act, 1945, which authorized the Governor-General to make regulations "providing for the repeal or amendment of or the addition to any of the provisions of this Act" (Section 137).

A second device which has been resorted to is for the Act to declare that "any regulations or by-laws made under this Act shall have effect as if enacted in this Act". The House of Lords has said of such a provision([13]) that it operates to give delegated legislation the effect of statute law and to remove its validity from the scrutiny of the courts. This view was only expressed incidentally as an *obiter dictum* and its authority has been doubted by the English Court of Appeal.([14]). Provisions of this type will be found in a few Commonwealth and State Acts, notably in Queensland.([15]) The courts in Australia have not in general treated them as precluding enquiry into the validity of a regulation though cases can be found in which this view has been taken. As recently as 1950 the High Court, in considering a regulation under the Post and Telegraph Act, 1901-34, did not regard its hands as tied by the section which declared that regulations should have effect "as if they were enacted in this Act" and

---

([10]) Sugerman, "Uncertainty in Delegated Legislation" (1945) 18 *A.L.J.* 330.

([11]) *King Gee Clothing Ltd. v. The Commonwealth* (1945) 71 C.L.R. 184; *Canns Pty. Ltd. v. The Commonwealth ibid.* 210.

([12]) C. K. Allen, *Law and Orders,* 2nd edition, p. 198.

([13]) *Institute of Patent Agents v. Lockwood* (1894) A.C. 347; C. K. Allen, *Law and Orders,* 2nd edition, pp. 295-300.

([14]) *R. v. Minister for Health; Ex parte Yaffe* (1930) 2 K.B. 135; (1931) A.C. 494; the House of Lords did not deal with this aspect of the case, see C. K. Allen, *Law and Orders,* 2nd edition, Appendix 3.

([15]) Diseases in Plants Act of 1929; Grazing Districts Improvement Act of 1930; Heavy Vehicles Acts of 1925 to 1931; State Transport Act of 1932.

embarked on a discussion as to its validity on other grounds.([16]). There are other statutory provisions in various forms which attempt to secure the validity or *prima facie* validity of delegated legislation ; a novel one, contained in the Local Government Act, 1934 (South Australia), precludes any attack on the validity of a by-law if a certificate is given by the Crown Solicitor that it is within the competence of the authority to make it.([17]) Despite criticisms, there is much to be said for such a provision so long as the power is vested in responsible law officers of the Crown.

(3) The third safeguard advocated by Carr, that particular interests who are specially affected by delegated legislation should first be consulted, involves practical difficulties. It is often essential that legislation, whether by Parliament or some subordinate authority, should come into operation forthwith so as to prevent steps being taken to evade its effects. Notable instances of such legislation are revenue and taxation laws, for which Parliament has evolved a special procedure. It is seldom that a positive obligation is cast upon a legislative authority to consult interests affected, though some Acts in these terms can be found in England. Nevertheless it is a general practice for departmental officers to consult trade and other sectional interests with respect to proposed legislation. Even Sir Carleton Allen has refuted the claim that "delegated legislation is made in the dark without conscientious effort to understand the nature of the subject-matter and the scope and effect of the ordinances when made".([18]) There are, of course, in England and Australia various bodies which, from time to time or continuously, carry out investigations to determine precisely what steps should be taken by a legislative or administrative authority ; the Australian Tariff Board is a notable example.

An obvious method by which the views of the interests concerned will be known is to give prior public notice of intention to make regulations pertaining to a particular subject and to make draft copies of the proposed regulations freely available. This procedure was formerly provided for in England by the Rules Publication Act, 1893, but that Act did not apply to orders nor to any rules certified to be urgent. Its piecemeal character deprived it of real value and in 1946 it was superseded by the Statutory Instruments Act, 1946, which has abandoned the requirement of antecedent notice. Under this Act a statutory instrument must be laid on the table in both Houses of Parliament and can be annulled by resolution within a period of forty sitting days. To assist the operation of this procedure, every copy of a statutory instrument must indicate on its face (*a*) the date when it came or will come into operation ; and (*b*) the date upon which copies were laid before Parliament or a statement that such copies will be laid before Parliament. This procedure affords an opportunity for representations to be made by interested parties to their parliamentary representatives or the Minister concerned, but in the absence of any objection the measure will come into force. The essence of this system is to cast the onus of objection on to someone affected who will take steps to stir the

---

([16]) *Brebner v. Bruce* (1950) 82 C.L.R. 161; see also cases noted in Australian Digest and Supplements *sub tit.* By-Laws and Regulations [15].

([17]) Norman, "Invulnerability of Local Government By-Laws in South Australia" (1949) 22 *A.L.J.*, p. 509.

([18]) C. K. Allen, *Law and Orders*, p. 198.

parliamentary machine into action. It is too much to expect members of Parliament to look at instruments for themselves ; they are too numerous and technical and, in any case, members cannot spend all their time perusing regulations and orders. However, the Select Committee on Statutory Instruments sits regularly to review all instruments which are laid before Parliament and draws the attention of the House to particular instruments.([19])

In Australia there was formerly provision for prior notice of Commonwealth regulations. In 1916 this was superseded by a requirement now contained in Section 48 of the Acts Interpretation Act, 1901-19, that all regulations made under Commonwealth Acts be laid before each House of Parliament within fifteen sitting days, failing which they will be void and of no effect. Notice of intention to move a resolution of disallowance may be given within a further fifteen days after tabling in the house and if the resolution is carried at any time thereafter the regulation is deemed to be repealed. This provision has advantages over the English Act in that it makes tabling in both houses a condition of validity and allows a greater opportunity for disallowance. In England the annulment must be carried within the prescribed time, but in Australia it is sufficient if it is carried at any time provided that notice has been given within the prescribed period. On the other hand the Australian provision does not apply to orders but in practise, except during emergencies, all Commonwealth delegated legislation of any consequence is effected by regulation ; moreover Acts envisaging legislation by means of orders, rules or by-laws have often expressly extended the requirement of tabling to all orders, rules and by-laws which are of a legislative character.

In the Australian States there is no uniform procedure with respect to checks upon delegated legislation. South Australia, Western Australia and Tasmania have general Acts which are similar to the Commonwealth Acts Interpretation Act. In New South Wales and Queensland it has been the practice to embody similar sections in each Act which confers power to make regulations ; this procedure is also followed in Victoria but no power of disallowance is conferred in that State. There is no general provision or practice in the States requiring antecedent notice of delegated legislation but in some instances such a procedure is mandatory where a local authority proposes to exercise compulsory powers such as the acquisition of property.

The charge has frequently been made that the obligation to table regulations in Parliament is an empty formality which results in their becoming effective by default, and many writers have urged the re-introduction of the requirement of antecedent notice and publicity. With due respect to these writers such a course would not only be too cumbersome but could not apply comprehensively to all forms of delegated legislation, if only because some measures must not be made public before becoming law ; nor could such a course be justified on the ground that consultation with interests affected is desirable. No doubt commercial, industrial and land-owning interests who seem to be the subject of most delegated legislation today would prefer to have the opportunity of being consulted beforehand. No doubt too, anyone who is prejudically affected by any restriction or control would like to be consulted on the question whether he should be affected,

---

([19]) A. H. Hanson, "Select Committee on Statutory Instruments, 1944-1949", 27 *Pub. Admin. (London)*, 1949, p. 278.

to what extent and by what method; even the convicted criminal would like to be in this position, if only to remonstrate with the hangman. But the real point of consultation surely is that the authority should not legislate in ignorance of the problems of a particular trade or activity, rather than that it should ascertain the desires of the persons engaged in that trade or activity. If proper investigations are made by competent administrative officers the decision as to the necessity for any legislation, delegated or otherwise, must ultimately rest with the administrative authority or with Parliament. Moreover, in these days when all sections of industry and employees are highly organized into trade associations and unions, and pressure groups of every type are ever watchful for any infringement of their rights, it seldom happens that the persons affected do not make full representations to the responsible authority, if not before, at least very promptly after, any legislation comes into force.

(4) It would be of the essence of tyranny to deny the force of Carr's fourth point that there should be publicity of delegated legislation. Yet in England, America and Australia there are instances—some very notable—within quite recent years of laws having been made without any notice to anyone and without any publication at all; and in some of these cases the authority responsible has gone gaily ahead with penal proceedings for the enforcement of the law. In England this occurred during the First World War with orders of the Food Controller; a prosecution for breach of one such order was dismissed by the King's Bench Division on the ground that the order did not become effective until it became known and was not like an Act of Parliament which received publicity during debate and came into effect forthwith.([20]) Much the same thing occurred during the Second World War and even more recently, in *Blackpool Corporation v. Locker*,([21]) instruments which operated as a sub-delegated legislation had not been published and were produced to the court only with reluctance by the authority concerned; this attitude received well-deserved condemnation from the Court of Appeal, whose comments have already been quoted.

In the United States of America the "Hot-Oil Cases" in 1934 revealed a similar state of affairs to that which existed in England before the Statutory Instruments Act.([22]) In these cases proceedings for the enforcement of restrictive oil regulations broke down when it was disclosed that the regulations had never been published and counsel for the oil industry stated that the only copy he had ever seen of the regulations "was in the hip-pocket of some government official". This incident of the "Hip-pocket Law", as it was later termed, resulted in the immediate passage of the Federal Register Act of 1935 which required all delegated legislation to be published in full in the Federal Register, a publication similar to the official gazettes in Australia and other countries. The Register, however, has achieved the objective of "recording" legislation rather than giving it publicity because of the tremendous mass of regulations it now contains.

([20]) *Johnson v. Sargent* (1918) 1 K.B. 101.

([21]) (1948) 1 K.B. 349.

([22]) *United States v. Smith* 293 U.S. 633; *Panama Refining Company v. Ryan, ibid.*, 388; Lavery: "The Federal Register and the Need for its Reform (1948) 29 *Chicago Bar Record* No. 7; 2 The Lawyer and Law Notes (1948-9) 1. The same position arose in Canada in *R. v. Ross* (1945) 24 *Can. Bar. Rev.* 149.

The Commonwealth and States of Australia have largely avoided the irregularities which England and America experienced, as the official Commonwealth and State Gazettes have been used consistently in conjunction with Government printing offices for notifying the promulgation of and publishing regulations, orders, rules and by-laws. But although Commonwealth regulations must be published or notified in the Gazette the same requirement does not necessarily apply to orders. In illustration it may be mentioned that many orders of legislative character made during the Second World War never saw the light of day; some regulations under which power was given to make orders expressly contemplated non-publication and declared that this should not affect their validity. This practice was expressly disapproved by the Regulations Advisory Committee set up by the Commonwealth Government in 1944 to review and make recommendations with respect to the large volume of National Security Regulations. However, the recommendations of that committee were ignored when the Defence Preparations Act 1951 was passed a few years later.

The requirement of publicity is not adequately satisfied by merely providing, as many of the laws do, that regulations or orders "shall be published in the Gazette". This is important as a means of recording the instrument in accurate and permanent form but it does not necessarily bring its terms to the notice of the public. This is nowhere better illustrated than in America where the Federal Register, after the lapse of less than twenty years, now contains a mass of regulations and indecipherable amendments which the lawyer, let alone the average man, cannot readily comprehend. There is a real need for every piece of delegated legislation to be accompanied by a memorandum explaining its effect in simple terms and for more official handbooks, pamphlets and advertisements setting out in concise language the purport of regulations which affect members of the public.

(5) The final requirement recommended by Carr is that there should be machinery for amending and revoking delegated legislation as required. This involves two factors, first, that there shall be flexibility, and secondly, that there shall be some means whereby objectionable features can be readily removed. In England, as Carr points out, some authorities can exercise their powers only with the approval of a superior official: for example, by-laws of railway companies formerly required the approval of the Minister of Transport. This had the advantage of securing some supervision and uniformity in the by-laws of different companies, but it also had the disadvantage that an objectionable by-law could only be repealed or modified by a procedure involving reference to and approval by the Minister with consequent delay. It might be said, of course, that if adequate supervision is exercised when a law is made, the need for amendment or repeal can never be urgent. This would be best achieved by the setting up of some central body to review and report to Parliament on all delegated legislation, a course which was recommended in the 1932 report of the United Kingdom Committee on Ministers' Powers.

Nothing was done to implement this recommendation until 1944, when a Select Committee on Statutory Instruments was established. The reports of this committee were responsible for the passing of the Statutory Instruments Act in 1946. The Act and the supervisory powers of the committee now operate as an important safeguard in ensuring that all delegated legislation is reviewed by a competent independent body before the lapse of the period allowed for annulment after tabling in Parliament.([23]) The Committee's terms of reference authorize it to draw the attention of the House to any statutory instrument on any of the following grounds:—

(a) that is imposes a charge on the public revenues ;

(b) that it is made in pursuance of an enactment containing specific . provisions excluding it from challenge in the courts ;

(c) that it appears to make "unusual or unexpected use" of powers confered by statute ;

(d) that it purports to have retrospective effect without specific statutory sanction ;

(e) that there appears to have been unjustifiable delay in the publication or in the laying of it before Parliament ;

(f) that there appears to have been unjustifiable delay in notifying it to the Speaker under the provision of the Statutory Instruments Act relating to instruments which have come into operation before tabling in Parliament ; and

(g) that for any special reason its form or purport calls for elucidation.

The Committee has had a salutary effect on the form and substance of delegated legislation and the number of instruments which it has found occasion to report to the House has steadily declined ; there is no doubt that the mere existence of a body of this character itself operates as a substantial check on any excess or abuse of power in delegated legislation.

It is in this respect that Australia sadly lags behind England. Regulation-making bodies in Australia usually have full power to amend or revoke regulations so as to achieve flexibility but neither the Commonwealth nor any State has any permanent machinery for the review of delegated legislation. There have at various times been committees appointed by the Commonwealth with functions of this character but they have not had the necessary powers or organization to enable them to be fully effective. The nearest approach to the English Select Committee is the Standing Committee of the Senate which has for many years performed general functions of reviewing and reporting upon regulations ; but it has not had the staff and facilities to deal adequately with the large volume of regulations and orders, especially those made after the passing of the National Security Act.([24]) There is obviously much room for further progress in active parliamentary control of delegated legislation, and it behoves the Parliaments to exercise this control for they are just as responsible for any abuses which are manifested by delegated legislation as the administrative authorities themselves. Not only have they sanctioned the delegation of powers with gay abandon over a long period of time, but they have failed to exercise the supervision which was contemplated by the procedure for tabling regulations and orders. If Parliament keeps a watchful eye on the administrative bodies from which regulations and order emanate there would be far less cause for alarm at the growth of delegated legislation. This element is of as much import as all the safeguards which Carr

---

([23]) Hanson, *op. cit.*

([24]) F. A. Bland. *Planning the Modern State.* 2nd ed., 1945, pp. 12-14.

advocated in 1921 and to which he added the qualification that "if Parliament and the public are reasonably vigilant the safeguards should be adequate".([25])

This review of delegated legislation has been made on the lines of Carr's five *desiderata* in a practical rather than purely theoretical way because it is evident that no Utopian ideal can ever succeed in this field without a wholesale revision of our parliamentary and governmental institutions. But if administrators are conscious of the dangers which any delegation of power involves and take steps to adhere in principle and not merely give lip-service to the safeguards those dangers should be reduced to a minimum. Recruitment and training of administrators to ensure that they have a consciousness of their part in the governmental system and a sense of their responsibility to the people through the ministerial head of their department may well mean the difference between a workable system of delegated legislation and one which will break down under its own weight.

ADMINISTRATIVE ADJUDICATION

Professor W. A. Robson wrote in 1927 that "one of the most striking developments in the British Constitution during the last half century has been the acquisition of judicial power by the great departments of State and by various other bodies and persons outside the courts of law".([26]) The nature of this development must be examined against the historical background of English institutions, in which the King's courts were with minor exceptions the only bodies having power to make decisions which affected the personal or proprietary rights of the individual. The criminal courts enforced laws for the protection of person and property with no other aid than the executive which apprehended offenders and brought them to trial; the common law, chancery and other courts determined matters of private right arising out of contract, property and otherwise in accordance with established rules of law and equity, modified in small measure by Acts of Parliament. In this setting most disputes, claims and rights were determined by the courts in accordance with accepted judicial methods and, subject to imperfections in the substantive law, there was a right to resort to the courts in every case.

The trend towards government control of trade, commerce and industry gave rise to legislation on a wide range of subjects. The variety and complexity of the situations which arose could not be dealt with by one uniform and permanent legislative measure, and decisions on how the law applied in individual cases had to be made by some one—who better than a governmental agency which knew the policy of the legislation? Moreover, the fields into which such legislation penetrated were, because of their social content, quite foreign to the courts, and the remedies which were called for were alien to established judicial processes. Finally, considerations of time and cost made judicial procedures unsuitable for the determination of matters which had to be settled informally, quickly and at a minimum of expense. So a tendency developed to give the power of decision on individual cases in certain fields to administrative authorities or tribunals. The prin-

---

([25]) *Delegated Legislation,* p. 41.
([26]) *Justice and Administration Law,* p. xxviii.

cipal types of decision involved in Australia have been classified by Fried-mann as follows:—([27])

(i) Regulation of industrial conditions—industrial arbitration, terms and conditions of employment, etc.

(ii) Disciplinary tribunals for the public services—terms and conditions of service of Crown and semi-government employees.

(iii) Award of pensions, allowances and other state grants—pensions to discharged servicemen, public servants and others, workers compensation, etc.

(iv) Supervisions of social conditions affecting the community—regulation of buildings, health and sanitation, factory conditions, theatres, rent control, etc.

(v) Licensing of occupations involving special skill or public responsibility—medical, dental and other professions, electrical contractors, estate agents, money-lenders.

(vi) Supervision over trade, commerce and transport—marketing of primary products, licensing of distributors of primary and other products, licensing of transport operators, etc.

(vii) Assessment of taxes, rates and duties—income and other taxes, valuations for rating purposes, etc.

(viii) Legal protection of industrial property—patents, copyrights, trade marks, etc.

(ix) Compensation for interference with private property rights in the public interest—town and country planning, valuations of property acquired by public authorities.

(x) Various matters of State policy—surcharge of public and semi-governmental officers.

The machinery set up by legislation to make decisions relating to these widely divergent subjects does not follow any single or general pattern: the determination of conditions of employment is effected chiefly by conciliation or arbitration; the assessment of compensation for acquisition of property and the determination of liability for rates and taxes is on some occasions exercised judicially and on other administratively, subject to appeal to a court; supervision of social conditions, trade and commerce and the licensing of occupations is generally achieved by a system of licensing or registration, or by prohibition *sub modo,* with provision for the consent or approval of an administrative authority. Just as there is no single pattern in the machinery, so there is no uniformity in the character of the functions which the appropriate tribunal or authority exercises.

It is clear that all decisions by administrative authorities that affect the rights of the individual cannot be made subject to the courts. Attempts have been made to distinguish certain types of decision termed "judicial" and/or "quasi-judicial", which it is held impose some obligation to follow certain rules, e.g., to hear both sides, not be biased, and so on; while other types of purely "administrative" or "ministerial" decision are properly left to the discretion of the authority concerned. But all attempts to make such dis-

---

([27]) *Principles of Australian Administrative Law,* pp. 87-95.

tinctions water-tight have broken down, and "there is no authoritative definition of the respective qualities of governmental acts"([28]) which will place them in one category or the other. It is clear that in the case of some administrative decisions that affect individuals the best check is Parliament. The administrative authority may, for instance, be carrying out policies which cannot be defined in ways which would make it possible for a court to say whether a particular decision was necessary to its achievement, or simply an arbitrary piece of unfairness. (This is true, for instance, of some town-planning decisions and licensing activities.) The test in practice is often one of convenience ; some decisions cannot be subjected (or subjected much) to judicial procedures because they need to be taken quickly, cheaply, flexibly ; others require special types of expertise that an ordinary court cannot command ; others seem inextricably bound up with "policy". There is a sense in which each type of case has to be considered on its merits.

In discussing methods of judicial control of administrative authorities, we should first mention the prerogative writs of mandamus, prohibition and certiorari which superior courts in England and Australia can issue to supervise the exercise of jurisdiction by inferior tribunals. These writs, and independent proceedings for a declaratory order or injunction, are the main weapons for controlling the irregular exercise by administrative authorities of their powers and functions.

(1) The writ of mandamus can be issued to compel the performance of a legal duty by any person, corporation or inferior tribunal whether in respect of "judicial" or "ministerial" functions. By this means public officials and authorities can be required to perform duties cast upon them, but they cannot be controlled in the exercise of a discretion. If however an authority has so acted that its decision is not a real discharge of its duty, the writ of mandamus will require it "to determine the matter according to law". A further limitation on the writ of mandamus is that it will not be issued to Ministers of the Crown or other public officials in respect of duties owed by them to the Crown or performed on its behalf. This is discussed further below.

(2) The writ of certiorari is available to control the judicial acts of inferior courts and the exercise of judicial or "quasi-judicial" functions by any administrative authority. It is therefore not available where an authority has a merely ministerial duty or function to perform. The effect of the writ of certiorari is to require the whole of the proceedings to be transferred to the court issuing the writ. If it appears from the record of proceedings that there has been any excess of jurisdiction or error of law, the court will quash the proceedings and remit the matter for reconsideration on proper lines. The wide scope which is afforded by this procedure in connection with proceedings before administrative authorities makes it a most useful and summary method for ensuring that such authorities act within their powers and according to proper standards of natural justice.

(3) The writ of prohibition is similar in many respects to certiorari but can be availed of merely to prevent or "prohibit" proceedings which are beyond the jurisdiction of an inferior court or administrative authority which is obliged to act according to judicial or quasi-judicial standards. Like

---

([28]) Scott, "Administrative Law" (1948) 26 *Can. Bar Rev.* 274.

certiorari also it can be used to ensure that proceedings are conducted by the inferior court or authority in conformity with principles of natural justice.

(4) Proceedings for a declaratory order or injunction may be maintained against administrative authorities which are not purely judicial in character. This jurisdiction is still in a formative state but is clearly available where there is an infringement of some public right which causes special damage to an individual or where rights of property have been prejudicially affected by some exercise of power which is *ultra vires*.([29]) In Australia there is a wide scope for this remedy in proceedings in the High Court against the Commonwealth and States and officers of the Commonwealth in matters where legislative or executive action is claimed to be in excess of the powers respectively allotted to the Commonwealth and State Parliaments by the Constitution.

Apart from these general remedies it will sometimes be found that a right of appeal to a court is granted by an Act to "any person aggrieved" by the decision of an administrative authority. This may have the effect of entitling the court to re-hear the matter *de novo* and to give any decision which it thinks proper, substituting its own exercise of discretion for that of the administrative authority ; but, unless the Act indicates otherwise, the court will generally take the view that its only function is to supervise the exercise of the authority's own power and to decide whether it was entitled on the material before it to reach the conclusion which it did. The Privy Council, in a Canadian appeal against a taxation decision of the Minister for National Revenue, adopted a view somewhere between these two extremes and laid down the following rules:—([30])

(*a*) The onus is on the appellant to show that the Minister's decision should not stand.

(*b*) The court cannot interfere with the Minister's discretion unless he acted in contravention of some principle of law or his decision was manifestly against sound and fundamental principles.

(*c*) The power of the Minister must be exercised "according to the rules of reason and justice ; according to law and not humour ; it is not to be arbitrary, vague and fanciful, but legal and regular".

(*d*) If the Minister has properly exercised his powers in conformity with these rules the court will not substitute its opinion or exercise of discretion for his.

(*e*) The court is entitled to have before it all the material which was before the Minister when he made his decision.

In the light of this review of the various procedures which are available by way of supervision over or appeal from administrative authorities some attempt can be made to indicate the principles which the courts insist should be followed by those authorities in the conduct or determination of matters before them. These are naturally minimum requirements because in each case the Act constituting the authority may impose duties of a higher charac-

([29]) W. H. Friedmann, "Declaratory Judgment and Injunction as Public Law Remedies" (1949) 22 *A.L.J.* 446.

([30]) *Minister for National Revenue v. Wrights Canadian Ropes Ltd.* (1947) A.C. 109.

ter. In many cases as, for instance, industrial arbitration courts, workers' compensation tribunals, land and valuation courts, marine courts and the like, the authority is constituted as a court and pursues strict judicial methods involving evidence on oath, cross-examination of witnesses, rules of evidence and a formal judgment on matters of law and fact. Other authorities have a remarkable similarity to courts, particularly some of the tribunals relating to the licensing of professions and the Commonwealth taxation boards of review; these bodies pursue a formal hearing procedure similar to that adopted in a court of law but their functions are not necessarily judicial. At the other end of the scale some of the licensing and trade supervisory authorities do not conduct formal hearings but deal with applications and matters on the basis of correspondence, written or oral statements or reports and communicate their decisions by letter, usually without reasons, to the person concerned; this informal procedure, however, does not necessarily mean that these bodies are under no obligation to act in a judicial manner.

The basic conditions which any of these authorities must observe, in the exercise of functions which are not held to be purely ministerial, are simple but are designed to ensure just and fair treatment. First, it must act in accordance with the Act under which it is constituted and not exceed the powers conferred on it. Secondly, it must hear both sides, though an oral hearing is not necessary; this usually .neans that the person affected must be given an opportunity to make representations and present any facts which he considers will help his cause. Thirdly, it must not be biased nor have any interest in the subject matter; this does not preclude an authority which has formulated a plan or scheme from itself determining objections to it, provided that the determination is made in good faith. Fourthly, where the matter involves a charge against the person affected, for example, where it is sought to cancel a licence on the ground of misconduct, he should be informed of the charge. Fifthly, provided the above rules are followed there is no necessity to observe the procedure of a court or any particular procedure. Where on the other hand an administrative authority is performing a function which is held to be purely ministerial these rules have no application but the authority is nevertheless bound to act within the scope of its statutory powers and must not be influenced by bad faith or irrelevant motives.

Having noticed the remedies which are available to review the decisions of administrative authorities and the procedure which such authorities should follow, it may be of profit to look at some instances of the exercise of supervision by the courts on various grounds relating to jurisdiction or power, procedure and irrelevant purpose.

(1) *Jurisdiction or power*: (*a*) An industrial authority had power under National Security Regulations to increase the wages of coal miners if it was satisfied that there was an anomaly in the wage rates in the industry; it made an award under this power although there was in fact no anomaly and its award was set aside on prohibition by the High Court on the ground that it was made without jurisdiction. The judges of the court held that the industrial authority could not give itself jurisdiction by an erroneous determination of a fact on which its jurisdiction must be founded nor upon its own mistaken opinion of the meaning of the regulations under which it was constituted.([81]) (*b*) A shire council proposed to raise a special loan

---

([81]) *R. v. Connell* (1944) 69 **C.L.R.** 407.

to acquire land for the erection of a community hotel but failed to take a poll of ratepayers which under the Local Government Act was a condition precedent to raising the loan. The court, on the application of the owner of the land to be acquired, restrained the council from proceeding with the scheme unless a poll was first taken and held that two remedies were available to achieve this end: the council could be directed by mandamus to hold the poll, or any person whose rights were specially affected, such as the owner of the land to be acquired, could obtain an injunction against its raising the loan without first holding the poll.([32])

(2) *Procedure*: (a) The Liquid Fuel Board cancelled the licences of certain dealers in liquid fuel on the ground that they had committed breaches of the regulations but for which they had not been prosecuted; an injunction was granted against enforcing the cancellations on the ground that no opportunity had been given the dealers to be heard in their own defence before their licences were cancelled.([33]) (b) The cancellation by the Chief Secretary of a pharmacist's authority to sell drugs was set aside on an appeal to the District Court under the appellate procedure prescribed by the Police Offences (Drugs) Act, 1927-1945 (N.S.W.) on the ground that the pharmacist had not first been asked to show cause against the cancellation and given an opportunity of being heard.([34]) (c) The Victorian Supreme Court restrained by prohibition the cancellation of licences of public vehicles where the holder of the licences was not allowed to be heard in his own defence although he had been called upon to show cause why the licences should not be cancelled.([35])

On the other hand, the High Court has refused an injunction to an importer whose licence for the importation of certain goods was cancelled without any prior notice and without giving him the opportunity of being heard. It was held that the minister in granting or cancelling a licence was performing a purely ministerial act which did not require him to act in a judicial or quasi-judicial manner.([36])

(3) *Purpose*: (a) The Municipal Council of Sydney was restrained by injunction from giving effect to a decision to resume lands in the City of Sydney because it was proved that its real purpose was not to widen the streets or effect improvements but to resell the land at a profit.([37]) The same decision has been reached with respect to the acquisition of land by councils constituted under the Local Government Act, 1919 (N.S.W.).([38]) (b) The High Court in an action for a declaratory order set aside a Minister's decision that consent to the sale of land under Land Sales Control legislation would be given only if the purchaser invested a certain sum of money in Commonwealth Bonds, because that imposed an extraneous and collateral condition.([39]) (c) On the other hand, the Court of Appeal in

([32]) *Blanch v. Shire of Stroud* (1947) 48 S.R. (N.S.W.) 37.

([33]) *The Commonwealth v. Horten Jamieson* (1945) 19 A.L.J. 410.

([34]) *Cutcliffe v. Baddeley* (1946) 63 W.N. (N.S.W.) 84.

([35]) *R. v. City of Melbourne* (1949) V.L.R. 257.

([36]) *Election Importing Company v. Courtice* (1949) 80 C.L.R. 657.

([37]) *Municipal Council of Sydney v. Campbell* (1925) A.C. 338.

([38]) *Minister for Public Works v. Duggan* (1951) 83 C.L.R. 424.

([39]) *Shrimpton v. The Commonwealth* (1945) 69 C.L.R. 613.

England upheld the decision of a local authority granting a Sunday picture theatre licence subject to the condition that children under the age of fifteen years should not be admitted to any Sunday performance. In previous decisions on similar Acts it had been held that such a condition was extraneous.([40]) (d) The New South Wales Supreme Court on an application for a writ of mandamus held that the Water Conservation and Irrigation Commission was not entitled to refuse to approve the transfer of an irrigation farm to an Italian because its proper function was to ensure that farms were held by competent farmers irrespective of nationality. The High Court reversed this decision and held that the personal qualities of a transferee were matters for the sole determination of the Commission.([41])

These illustrations show that the various remedies which the law provides can on occasions be most effective checks on administrative excesses ; many other decisions of a similar character could be quoted. It is nevertheless difficult to gauge the overall extent to which the courts have been successful in controlling the decisions of administrative authorities. Critics like Lord Hewart and Sir Carleton Allen have been free in the use of expressions such as "administrative lawlessness" and "bureaucracy" and point to a few cases like those cited above, where an administrative authority's discretion has been overruled or it has been castigated by the court for abuse or excess of power ; but these are the very cases which prove the effectiveness of judicial control. By way of contrast no-one troubles to make a count of the thousands of cases in which there has been fair dealing and no dissatisfaction has been expressed with the decision of an administrative authority other than that which invariably flows from an adverse decision. In the absence of statistics of administrative decisions it is obviously absurd to point to a few individual cases to prove that administrative adjudication is predominantly bad or predominantly good. Likewise, although effective control has been exercised by the courts in a number of reported decisions, its total value as a check on administrative excesses is difficult to determine. Indeed students of administrative law seem to be unable to agree on any uniform conclusion as to whether the courts have been able to control administrative authorities.

Useful contributions to this subject made by Canadian writers in recent years suggest that the confusion and fine distinction between judicial, quasi-judicial and administrative powers and functions have been used by the courts to extend their control and that in the last fifty years this has been achieved particularly by (1) an increase in the class of discretions which the court is prepared to control, (2) the inclusion of procedural error in the class of facts which deprive the authority of jurisdiction, and (3) the evasion by the courts of sections of acts which apparently purport to deprive them of their power to review. These factors were felt to justify in 1942 the conclusion, repeated in 1948,([42]) that "In the development of administrative law, judicial review of administrative adjudication has become a commonplace with respect to matters of law, of jurisdiction, of adequacy

([40]) *Associated Provincial Picture Houses Ltd. v. Wednesbury Corporation* (1948) 1 K.B. 223.

([41]) *Water Conservation and Irrigation Commission v. Browning* (1948) 74 C.L.R. 492.

([42]) Scott, "Administrative Law", 26 *Can. Bar Rev.*, 1948, 275-6.

of procedure, of procedural fairness, and even of the question of sufficiency of evidence. The finality of administrative determinations has in a real sense, and this regardless of statutory provisions, been dependent on judicial approval". On the other hand Friedmann has observed([43]) that the tendency to strict control by the courts has "been checked by more recent decisions which indicate a definite return to judicial restraint and a refusal to interfere with the proper sphere of administrative and executive discretion through the excessive use of prerogative orders". Elsewhere he says of the post-war decisions in England that they "show a definite awareness of the danger of judicial interference in administration and tend to restrict the meaning of 'quasi-judicial' ". S.A. de Smith has taken a similar view and said that "the judges have moved with the times and that in recent years the courts have shown greater readiness to give effect to the social purpose of collectivist legislation".([44]) This tendency is nowhere better manifested than in a judgment of Lord Greene who said in relation to the functions of the Minister for Health under the Housing Act, 1936 (Eng.) : ([45])

> "Every Minister of the Crown is under a duty, constitutionally, to the King, to perform his functions honestly and fairly, and to the best of his ability ; but his failure to do so, speaking quite generally, is not a matter with which the courts are concerned at all. As a Minister, if he acts unfairly, his action may be challenged and criticised in Parliament."

What Parliament can do in such circumstances if it is inclined is well illustrated by the recent Crichel Down case in the United Kingdom, in which arbitrary administrative interference with the rights of an individual resulted in a Committee of Inquiry, the resignation of a Minister and some drastic measures of administrative reorganisation involving two government agencies.([46])

There is perhaps no field of law in which so many diverse views are held as in the field of administrative adjudication. But there is no student who does not see the necessity for some re-organization or co-ordination of the authorities which are entrusted with the power to determine questions affecting members of the community in their trades, businesses, professions and everyday lives. Robson and Jennings have long urged the establishment of a special system of administrative courts rather than an extension of judicial control of administrative authorities by the existing courts. Sir Carleton Allen has now come to the conclusion that this is the better view, provided that an appellate administrative tribunal is also established as a judicial body.([47])

This problem of how to achieve some measure of administrative justice has been squarely faced in the United States of America and, since the

---

([43]) *Principles of Australian Administrative Law*, 81, 84.

([44]) Recent Constitutional Trends in England, 1 *Annual Law Review*, (W.A.), 1950, 445.

([45]) *B. Johnson & Co. (Builders) Ltd. v. Minister for Health* (1947) 177 L.T. 459; cf. *Election Importing Co. v. Courtice* (1949) 80 C.L.R. 657.

([46]) See C. J. Hamson, "The Real Lesson of Crichel Down", and D. N. Chester, "The Crichel Down Case", in *Pub. Admin. (London)*, xxxii, *Winter* 1954.

([47]) Foreword to Siegart: *Government by Decree*, xiii; C. K. Allen, *Law and Orders*, 2nd edition, p. 396.

comprehensive reports of the Acheson and Benjamin Committees in 1942, the Administrative Procedure Act 1946 has been passed to establish a uniform system of procedural rules for all administrative tribunals. In England the Committee of Ministers' Powers as long ago as 1932 made recommendations for the improvement of the position and propounded several principles to achieve a measure of administrative justice.([48]) They were—

(1) That the courts should retain a supervisory power where authorities exceed their statutory powers or act without jurisdiction.

(2) That authorities should observe the rules of natural justice that—

(i) a man may not be a judge in his own cause;

(ii) a party should have the right to be heard and should be informed of the case against him; and

(iii) reasons for the decision should be given.

(3) A right of appeal to the courts should be allowed on questions of law.

These recommendations have not been implemented but they would provide a working basis for any improvement short of a complete overhaul of our institutions and the establishment of a system of administrative courts.

LEGAL LIABILITY OF ADMINISTRATIVE AUTHORITIES

Many of the problems of administrative law arise from ill-defined distinctions in power and function. The nature and extent of the legal liability of administrative authorities likewise depends on distinctions which though of a different character, are equally ill-defined. The character of an administrative authority may be distinguished not only by the nature of the powers it exercises or the functions it performs, but also by its status as a part of the Crown or as an independent authority. Thus there is a basic difference between departments of the Crown, "Ministries", on the one hand and independent corporations established by statute on the other. The legal consequences of this difference are of fundamental importance and call for separate consideration. The device of incorporation which is now commonly resorted to in establishing public authorities is not the sole criterion of status, although it is true that the independent authorities which are not identified with the Crown are almost invariably corporations constituted by or under an Act of Parliament.

Historically, the King as the reigning monarch was the origin of all governmental power whether legislative, executive or judicial. The conflicts of the seventeenth century with Parliament and the courts deprived the monarch of the great bulk of these powers and nowadays the only remaining powers and functions of the King are of an executive character and are exercised in accordance with ministerial advice. But the historical position of the King is responsible for two modern rules, first that the Crown is not ordinarily bound by legislation and, secondly, that legal proceedings cannot be maintained against the Crown in the courts.

([48]) Many of these principles have been reaffirmed by the Report of the United Kingdom (Franks) Committee on Administrative Tribunals and Inquiries, 1957, which also proposes the establishment of a standing council on Tribunals to supervise the constitution and procedure of such bodies.

In earlier times these rules occasioned little or no hardship because the functions of the Crown were limited to the basic matters of government which are carried out by one agency, namely the executive government. In modern times, however, the importance of the rules has been magnified. The extension of the field of governmental activity and the multiplication of laws and authorities have made it impossible to avoid conflicts with and infringements upon public and private rights.([49])

(1) The cardinal rule is that the Crown is not bound by an Act of Parliament except by express mention or necessary implication. This rule does not involve any denial of the competence of Parliament to bind the Crown but, unless it specifically declares that purpose, or the nature of the Act necessarily requires that result, the Crown and all its agencies will remain unfettered by the statute. Express mention naturally leaves no doubt as to the position but "it has not always been easy to determine when the Crown is bound by necessary implication". Halsbury's *Laws of England* suggests that necessary implication will follow *inter alia* where statutes are made (i) for the public good, (ii) for the suppression of wrong, (iii) to protect gifts and inheritances, or (iv) to maintain religion, education or charity. These classifications were formulated over three centuries ago in a vastly different social and economic setting and it is doubtful how far they should be accepted under present conditions. Recent decisions of the courts in Australia and abroad appear to indicate a tendency to restrict the cases in which the Crown will be bound by necessary implication and to show a refusal to treat "the public good" and the "suppression of wrong" as expanding concepts which would embrace the economic and social legislation of the modern democratic state. Thus in *Province of Bombay v. Municipal Corporation of Bombay*([50]) it was held by the Privy Council that the Bombay City Council's compulsory powers of requiring owners of streets to lay drains could not be asserted against the Province of Bombay which was the owner of a street, on the ground that the Province was a part of the Crown and was not bound by the Act of the City of Bombay, although it was obviously in a modern sense an Act "for the public good". A similar result has ensued in Australian courts in recent years, particularly with reference to legislation protecting tenants against ejectment which has been held not to bind the Crown in the absence of any express provision in the Act.([51])

The rule exempting the Crown from the binding force of legislation would not be likely to give rise to any serious problems or anomalies if it were limited to purely governmental functions and agencies of the Crown; but it applies to all agencies of an executive or administrative character which represent the Crown and even to some of the new public corporations which are constituted by statute. Since many of these agencies and corporations are engaged in trading and other non-governmental activities and are owners of property, it is evident that conflicts must arise with Acts of

---

([49]) Public rights in this sense are rights arising under Acts of Parliament for the benefit of the whole or a section of the community; private rights are chiefly those which arise from contract, the ownership of property or the personality of the individual.

([50]) (1947) A.C. 58.

([51]) *Minister for Works (W.A.) v. Gulson* (1944) 69 C.L.R. 338; *Wynyard Investments Ltd. v. Commissioner for Railways* (1955) 93 C.L.R. 376.

Parliament as well as with other governmental or administrative agencies. Thus in recent years the courts in Australia have devoted much time to considering the status in relation to the Crown of such bodies as the N.S.W. Forestry Commission, the Victorian Forests Commission, the Rural Bank of New South Wales, the Victorian Grain Elevators Board, the Railways Commissioners of the States, the South Australian Electricity Trust and the N.S.W. Housing Commission. No uniform result has been reached in these cases and the courts still manifest a tendency, despite modern developments, to extend the "shield of the Crown" to trading enterprises. The basic principles which govern the character of a body as a part of the Crown have been stated by the Supreme Court of New South Wales on more than one occasion[52] as being whether the particular body is:—

(i) (a) a branch or department of the Government—a mere agent of the Government, or

(b) a body which, though independent of the Government, performs functions which are inalienable governmental functions, e.g., the administration of justice ; in which cases it does represent the Crown ; or on the other hand:—

(ii) a body independent of the Government with independent powers and discretions of its own ; in which case it does not represent the Crown. If the body is really a governmental agency the fact that it can sue and be sued does not alter its status ; nor does the fact that it is incorporated or engages in trading. If the body is really independent of the Crown, it is immaterial that it discharges public functions or that its profits must be devoted to the benefit of the public or its receipts paid to public revenue.

Friedmann has trenchantly criticised this approach[53] and has made a plea for a more limited interpretation of the concept of the Crown and the restrictions of the privileges and immunities attaching to incorporated authorities and administrative agencies.[54] Some of the consequences which flow from the status of a body if it is part of the Crown show the force of this criticism. The Housing Commission in New South Wales, which has been held to represent the Crown, is engaged throughout the State in constructing cottages, flats and other buildings which in the main are let, but may also be sold, to people in need of accommodation. But because of its status as a governmental agency, the Housing Commission is not obliged to comply with the ordinances and building standards prescribed by the Local Government Act, 1919 (N.S.W.) and is free from all incidental obligations such as submitting plans for approval.[55] Whether this has resulted in abuse or not is beside the point. So long as municipal and shire councils are recognized by legislation as the local building and planning authorities, the efficient conduct of local government and the proper plan-

---

[52] *Ex parte Graham; Re Forestry Commission* (1945) 45 S.R. (N.S.W.) 382.

[53] The Shield of the Crown (1950) 24 A.L.J. 275.

[54] Public Welfare Offences, Statutory Duties and the Legal Status of the Crown (1950) 13 Mod. L.R. 24.

[55] *North Sydney Municipal Council v. Housing Commission of N.S.W.* (1948) 48 S.R. (N.S.W.) 282; but for other purposes the Housing Commission has been held not to possess the immunities of the Crown: *Housing Commission v. Imperial Paint Manufacturers Ltd.* (1956) 73 W.N. (N.S.W.) 358.

ning of an area require that their dictates should prevail in these matters. The courts have also, by denying the application of landlord and tenant legislation to certain public authorities on the ground that they represent the Crown, placed such authorities in a privileged position and enabled them to eject tenants who would otherwise have been entitled to the benefit of this protective legislation.

A further complication is introduced into this problem in Australia by the co-existence of Commonwealth and State governments in the same geographical field. It has been said frequently that the Crown is one and indivisible but the Crown as an integral part of both Commonwealth and State governments may have a dual capacity. This has given rise to the question whether, if the Crown is mentioned in an Act, it will be bound in right of the Commonwealth as well as in right of the States. This result may follow if the Act gives no indication of the capacity in which the Crown is mentioned, but references in the Act to matters which are relevant to the Commonwealth or a State alone may be availed of to limit its binding force to the Crown in one or other, but not both capacities.([56]) This difficulty has been avoided by Acts such as the Bankruptcy Act, 1924-1946 (Cth) and the Companies Acts of the various States which contain express provisions to the effect that they "shall bind the Crown as representing the Commonwealth or any State".

(2) The immunity of the Crown from the ordinary processes of law originally extended to all actions. This immunity was strengthened in the law of torts by the theory that the King could do no wrong, which was held to preclude the Crown being liable for the act of its servants or agents even when, in later years, appropriate proceedings were available in which the Crown could be sued. It has long been recognized that this is an anachronism and from time to time provision has been made allowing redress in limited classes of case. The procedure of petition of right to the King was first allowed in England in cases where a subject was deprived of property, the petition being referred to the court for trial in the same way as an ordinary action. Subsequently in 1860 this procedure was extended to a wider range of subjects, including claims under contract for damages or otherwise and compensation for injury to or interference with a subject's property by the Crown. This extension, for the reason mentioned above, did not allow any action for tort, and it was not until 1947 in England that legislation was passed to permit of such actions being brought. The Crown Proceedings Act of that year has, subject to certain exceptions, placed the Crown in the same position as an ordinary subject for the purpose of being sued for any cause of action whatever, but a judgment against the Crown cannot be enforced by ordinary methods of execution ; if it requires payment of money the judgment creditor must normally await the appropriation of moneys by Parliament but a procedure laid down under this new legislation facilitates moneys being made available.

In Australia the position of the Crown in legal proceedings must be considered separately in relation to the Commonwealth and the States. The Commonwealth Constitution provides specifically for the High Court having jurisdiction in actions against the Commonwealth and States in certain circumstances and enables laws to be made with respect to these matters by

---

([56]) *City of Essendon v. Criterion Theatres Ltd.* (1947) 74 C.L.R. 1.

the Parliament. The Judiciary Act, 1903-1948, which was made under this power, provides expressly for actions being brought against the Commonwealth in tort or otherwise in the High Court or the Supreme Courts of the States, and for this purpose the Commonwealth is liable for the acts of its servants and agents in the same way as if it were a private person. The States have also, in the main, abolished the old limitations on actions against the Crown, but the procedures involve the clumsy petition of right or the appointment of a nominal defendant to represent the Crown ; Victoria alone retains the archaism that the Crown is not liable in tort. It should be noted that both Commonwealth and States are still free in general from proceedings for the execution of judgments, the attachment of debts or other moneys and some incidental proceedings. Moreover, it must be remembered that these procedures and privileges are not restricted to the Crown in the sense of the executive government but apply to all authorities which may, for the reasons discussed earlier, be deemed to be governmental agencies which are within the "shield of the Crown".

There are some other matters which are relevant to this general topic of the privileged position of the Crown and which can be conveniently summarized here: (a) The historical position of the Crown conferred priority on Crown debts over other debts ; this was formerly of importance in the administration of bankrupt estates and the liquidation of companies but the Bankruptcy Act, 1924-1946, and the Companies Acts in the various States have abolished this priority ; however, some Commonwealth Acts have since re-created this priority in the case of certain taxation and other liabilities. (b) The Crown cannot be made liable for any criminal proceedings and a public authority which represents the Crown is in the same position. Normally, as Dicey puts it, this will not excuse a servant of the Crown from personal liability, but in Australia the High Court has refused to hold a servant of the Crown guilty of an offence where the acts constituting the offence were done in an official capacity and although the only consequence would have been the imposition of a fine.[57]. This decision is a serious impediment on the enforcement of statutes which lay down some general rule of social conduct which the Crown is also obliged to observe, and threatens to create problems of Crown immunity in a different form. (c) Servants of the Crown and its agencies at common law could not have any enforceable rights arising out of their offices because their employment has been held not to arise from contract.[58] This doctrine applies to members of the armed forces, police officers and some other public officials. However, employees of administrative authorities are engaged under Acts of Parliament which confer express power to make contracts of employment or establish special tribunals for the determination of rights of employees.

It remains now to consider the legal position of administrative authorities which are not within the "shield of the Crown". These authorities are for the most part, if not entirely, corporations which derive their existence from an Act of Parliament giving them a corporate existence, conferring powers and imposing duties. Most of the trading enterprises associated with the Commonwealth and State governments in Australia and many of the public utilities will be readily identified as falling into this category. Since

---

[57] *Cain v. Doyle* (1946) 72 C.L.R. 409.
[58] *The Commonwealth v. Quince* (1944) 68 C.L.R. 22.

these corporations are not within the "shield of the Crown" they are bound by all Acts of Parliament in the same way as ordinary citizens and they do not share any immunity from legal proceedings. In both England and Australia they have in consequence been held to be fully liable in the courts for any cause of action in the same manner as any private corporate body except in so far as the Act under which they are constituted confers special protection or rights ; sometimes, for example, the liability of transport bodies for damages for personal injury has been limited to a specified sum of money. On the other hand a statutory corporation may incur additional liability because of the powers or duties it is authorized or directed by statute to perform.

The mere fact that an authority performs some act under statutory powers does not exempt it from all liability for damage. If it acts negligently or otherwise violates the rights of a member of the public it may be made liable in damages by the person affected and in certain cases restrained by declaratory order and injunction ; in like manner it will not be allowed in the performance of a statutory power to create a nuisance unless that is the inevitable result of the exercise of the power. But where the authority is directed by Act of Parliament to carry out some work, so as to impose a duty as distinct from merely conferring a power, different considerations may apply depending upon the purpose of the work and the general nature of the duty ; if the duty is of an overriding public character it may be held to exclude any claim for injury to private rights on the ground that such rights are presumed to be negatived by the Act itself in imposing the duty.([59]) These matters make it difficult to formulate any general principle concerning legal liability for acts done under statutory duty. However, it would seem that the trend of the law is in favour, first, of treating a statutory power as implying or carrying with it a duty not to act negligently or otherwise in a manner which will violate private rights, and, secondly, of regarding a statutory duty as not exonerating the authority from all consequences arising from the performance of that duty.

No discussion of the liability of public authorities would be complete without reference to the anomalous position of highway authorities, which are exempt from the consequence of non-feasance but are liable for misfeasance. Hence a highway authority, even if it is under a statutory duty to maintain roads, cannot be liable for the failure to repair them no matter how shocking their condition—this is non-feasance ; but if it undertakes the task of constructing or repairing a road and performs the work negligently it will incur full liability—this is mis-feasance. The reason for this unsatisfactory position derives from the history of local government in England in the eighteenth century and a full discussion of its origin and development will be found in the judgments of the High Court in *Gorringe v. The Transport Commission*,([60]) where the Commission as a highway authority was excused from liability for damage occasioned by the collapse of a culvert which had fallen into disrepair.

It should be added in conclusion that the whole question of the status and legal liability of administrative authorities, whether they are within the

---

([59]) See the graphic analysis made by Friedmann: Statutory Powers and Legal Duties of Local Authorities (1945) 8 Mod. L.R. 48-9.

([60]) (1950) 80 C.L.R. 357.

"shield of the Crown" or not, requires rationalization in three directions. First, the artificial rules which are applied to determine the status of an authority as a part of the Crown or an independent body require review in the light of their diverse functions and the fact that they frequently possess trading powers which enable them to compete on an unequal basis with private enterprise. Secondly, there is a need for the clarification of the legal effects of an exercise of statutory duties and statutory powers on a uniform basis, related to the social character of the duty or power and the nature of the acts performed. Thirdly, the provisions of Acts which confer special privileges such as limiting the liability of certain authorities to a specified sum of money or fixing an unduly restricted period of time for actions being instituted should be reviewed and either repealed or reduced to a uniform basis.

CONCLUSION

Is it possible in the present state of development of administrative law in England and Australia to assess its part in our governmental system and its impact on our representative institutions and accustomed liberties? Debate on these matters has ranged far and wide and vastly divergent views have been expressed by students in England, America and Australia.

Some conclusions are nevertheless almost beyond controversy. First, the resort to delegated legislation and administrative processes has enabled governmental institutions to cope with the emergencies of two world wars; secondly, it has facilitated measures of social reform and given effect to the growth of collectivist ideas; thirdly, the privileged position of the Crown and administrative authorities at common law or by statute has assisted in the establishment of some great public undertakings which may have been beyond the capacity of private enterprise; and above all the development of a body of administrative law has lent to our democratic institutions a flexibility without which they could not have dealt with the new problems which have accompanied the advance of civilization and economic and social progress. On the other hand the development of administrative law has involved sacrifices and not a little expense. It has in one way or another resulted in the whittling away of much of our liberty and freedom of action; secondly, the substitution of departmental determination of anonymous origin for judicial decision has resulted in a weakening of respect for and confidence in governmental institutions; thirdly, the vast increase in cost of administration cannot pass unnoticed when such a large proportion of the population is engaged in various forms of public administration; finally, the centralization of power which has resulted from the growth of administrative authorities is a potential danger because of the ease with which a non-democratic faction, wedded to one of the "isms", could assume complete control of the whole political and economic life of the community.

The key to the future does not lie in the abandonment of all the techniques and processes which have been described in this chapter nor in the adoption of inflexible constitutional guarantees such as the "due process of law" clauses of the Constitution of the United States of America. Instead of any such revolutionary change which might prove of doubtful value, experience and caution alike suggest the adoption of safeguards within the framework of the existing system and along the lines discussed elsewhere in this chapter. As Professor Stone has observed,([a]) in preference to arresting existing trends in administrative law it would be more promising if effort were directed to "two main constructive tasks. The first is to ensure an adequate level of understanding and social responsibility among officials. The second is to devise appropriate checks on official action, with adequate expertise at all levels, right from the parliamentary control of policy down to the provision of easy, cheap, quick and impartial consideration of the grievances of individual citizens."

([a]) Province and Function of Law, 592.

PART II

PUBLIC SERVICE MANAGEMENT

INTRODUCTION

The Australian public services are the product of a series of reforms that began with the 1859 commission of enquiry in Victoria, and the decisive events in which were the 1895 New South Wales and 1902 Commonwealth Public Service Acts. The effects of these are discussed below by Mr. Bourke and Mr. Curtin. Broadly they set a pattern for the public services with three main elements: (1) central control by Public Service Board or Commission, (2) recruitment from school by competitive examination, (3) promotion by a combination of seniority and merit. It is a pattern which is not without interesting variations, and one which has never extended itself to anything like all positions. But it has been the norm, departures from which, however numerous, have been felt to need special justification.

The extent of control by Public Service Board varies; over the public service proper (i.e., those employees who come under the Public Service Acts) it is greatest in New South Wales, perhaps least in the Commonwealth. On the other hand, most Commonwealth employees are part of the Board-controlled service, while most State employees are the servants of statutory corporations and other bodies, many of which are partly or wholly independent of the public service authorities of their State.

Recruitment is in theory at the bottom, and from school; only the Commonwealth has recruited any sizeable number to non-technical positions from the universities. All the same, there are many who have entered the services in other ways—as professionally trained lawyers, engineers, scientists of various kinds, as ex-servicemen with preferential treatment, or as "mature recruits" when the supply of schoolboys showed signs of drying up.

Merit is in theory (and quite often in practice) the primary basis of promotion, discussed by Dr. Scarrow and Mr. Howitt. But seniority has a way of creeping in, and the best test of merit is sometimes taken to be the possession of a "symbol of proficiency", a certificate or diploma. A well-developed appeals system in most parts of Australia imparts a certain caution to promoting authorities.

Changes in the public service since this basic structure was established have mainly been the result of wars. The First World War produced a series of Royal Commissions on public service problems. The second produced no comparable reports;[1] but had perhaps more important permanent effects, at least on the Commonwealth service.

The Commonwealth Public Service consists of four main divisions. The First and Second Divisions (a select group of 361 officers in 1957, earning from £2,000 to £6,000 a year) contain the most senior officials, responsible for advising Ministers on policy and for operating the major sub-divisions of departments. The Third Division (29,000) includes their main administrative and clerical subordinates, and represents a very wide spread from

---

[1] For the Commonwealth, the Bailey Committee reported on promotions; and the Pinner Committee made some unpublished recommendations on post-war readjustment of the public service. The Commonwealth Government has recently appointed a Committee on Recruitment.

fairly senior officers to routine clerical workers. It also includes most "professional" public servants—accountants, architects, surveyors, and so on (see Appendix IV). The Fourth Division, much the largest in numbers (over 50,000), again includes a fairly mixed bag of typists, postal workers, skilled artisans, attendants, and others. Outside the regular divisions, there are about 70,000 "temporaries" and "exempt" employees, who can be dismissed at any time.

In theory appointments to the two top divisions are normally made by promotion from the Third—the three are treated as a unity. Australia has not, like the United Kingdom, an "administrative class" at the top of the service, recruited primarily from the universities direct. The contrast is not, however, as great as it seems at first sight. Nowadays half the British "administrative class" is filled by promotion from below, though promotees are not very well-represented in the strategic policy-forming positions. In the Commonwealth, many of the more senior officials (and some strategically well-placed ones) are now graduates, and a fair number have been appointed direct from outside. Over 200 members of the two top divisions have university degrees or diplomas and about 150 were recruited from outside the service.[2] There are at least the beginnings of an "administrative" class in Canberra. Canberra itself, it should be added, contains under 10,000 of over 200,000 Commonwealth employees; there are almost as many in some States as there are State public servants, in post offices, customs, military establishments, employment and social service offices and so on.

The State public services have certain features in common. In all of them, there is one administrative-clerical range of positions, to which entry is normally on the basis of school-leaving examinations. New South Wales has five divisions: special (the departmental heads), professional, clerical, general and educational. Victoria has four: first (departmental heads), administrative, professional, and technical and general. South Australia has four, like the Commonwealth ones. In both Commonwealth and States, the divisions are less significant than the many "grades" within divisions —Commonwealth and New South Wales systems of grading and classification are described below by Dr. Scarrow and Mr. Howitt, and are broadly typical of other Australian systems. Promotions in most States are made, subject to appeal, by the Public Service Board or Commissioner, on the recommendation of departments. In this and other respects, State boards tend to have more power than the Commonwealth Board.

But behind these formal similarities between States, lie some important differences. There is clearly bound to be a great difference between a great machine like the New South Wales service, and that of Tasmania, "one in which everyone knows everyone else . . . . and (where) one of the Public Service Commissioner's worries must be that so many decisions involve his

---

[2] Figures based on an enquiry by Mr. S. Encel. About 6,800 (27 per cent.) of the Third Division had educational qualifications higher than secondary (over 40 per cent. of them obtained after entry) and of these 3,600 were graduates, roughly half in Arts, Economics, Law and half in Science, Engineering, Medicine, etc. See *Sample Survey of Third Division of the Commonwealth Public Service, 31st July, 1956* (mimeo).

friends."(³)   A small service has the advantage of intimacy; on the other hand it is more difficult for it to have, say, specialised training facilities of the kind discussed by Mr. Derwent and Mr. Parker; it may be harder for it to attract first-class talent; or to resist pressures from outside.

Mr. Parker in his chapter in Part I, discusses some of the differences between Commonwealth and State functions, and concludes that they have been exaggerated; in particular, he discredits the notion that most Commonwealth departments (as is often alleged) are remote from the citizen and from bread-and-butter routines. However, there is still some difference in atmosphere between the two. In the States more of the senior men "have come up through the ranks of the service, which many of their Canberra counterparts have not done; they are somewhat older than the men in Canberra, and they possess fewer academic qualifications".

It has been said that they think of themselves as "more dependable than the brilliant Johnny-come-lately in Canberra".(⁴)   This may be something of a myth; there is in fact a not dissimilar view held by some Commonwealth departments of others; but the feeling is certainly there. They feel themselves to be concerned with more down-to-earth activities, and more immediately answerable if things go wrong. Mr. Parker's comments on the greater ease with which constituents' claims and grievances can be pressed in the States suggest that these latter feelings correspond to reality.

The State services are also on the whole of a "stabler" character; not that the States have not developed their functions, even in the period of rapid Commonwealth growth.   But new developments have generally been the slow outgrowth from old and well-established tasks, though there are some important exceptions in the field of public enterprise.   There has been nothing comparable to the war and post-war revolutions at the Commonwealth level, from which wholly new departments have sometimes emerged, or the balance of power shifted quite rapidly from one to another. Perhaps the most interesting change in the State services is their increased "professionalization".   For example, in one State between 1939 and 1953, while clerical-administrative numbers increased by 36 per cent., the professional and semi-professional grades increased by about 140 per cent.(⁵)   This is partly due to the mechanisation of clerical work, but mainly owing to the increasing demands of technical services, water schemes, public works and so on.

However, Commonwealth and State services still have many characteristics and problems in common, some of which are discussed in the chapters that follow.   In particular, the Australian public services share a tradition of integrity and of concern for the impartial conduct of the business confided to them which is taken for granted even by their bitterest critics; and the transcendent value of which we begin to appreciate only when we come across a service overseas, or an individual officer at home, that lacks them.

(³) C. J. Hayes, "The Administration of State Public Services", *Pub. Admin.*, (*Sydney*), XV, June, 1956, p. 125.

(⁴) "Our Administrators—I", *Sydney Morning Herald*, 12 Oct., 1957.

(⁵) See Report of South Australian Public Service Commissioner, Dec., 1953, pp. 8-9.

Chapter Ten

MANAGEMENT AND CONTROL
OF THE PUBLIC SERVICE

J. O. A. BOURKE

Present-day methods of managing and controlling the public service in the English-speaking democracies are largely a product of the nineteenth century, though a few of them go back much earlier. They may be summarised as follows: firstly, the leaders of the administration are responsible to Parliament. This is usually provided for nowadays by putting each department under a Minister, who is a member of Parliament and also in charge of the administrative activities confided to his care. There is an attempt to draw a clear line between such Ministers, who are "politicians", and their subordinates, who are "officials"—or "public servants" or "civil servants". The Ministers collectively form the Government, which depends for office on commanding majority support in Parliament; and so we have "responsible government".

Secondly, the officials are full-time employees appointed to perform the prescribed duties of an "office" or, as we would more usually say, a "position". Each position, and the duties and powers that go with it, is (as its very name suggests) part of a unified system. The efficiency of this system depends on (*a*) the arrangement of positions in relation to one another, that is, a structure of powers and duties well-calculated to achieve the aims of the administration. We might call this *the problem of structure* ; (*b*) getting the right individuals into the right positions and motivating them to do their best in those positions, which might be called *the problem of personnel*. The two cannot really be separated from one another, and both are part of the task of organization and management.

Finally, modern public services have tended to develop specialized organs to ensure that the problems of organization and personnel are looked at as a whole. It is with the development of some of these that this chapter will be mainly concerned. Their growth has resulted from the belief that the public service is more than a collection of servants of different Ministers, but an organization with problems of its own, common to many departments.

THE NINETEENTH CENTURY

The British Background

So far as English-speaking countries are concerned, we may conveniently date the beginnings of modern management and control of the public services in the 1780's. The British House of Commons listened to Edmund Burke in 1780 with some practical effect when he argued([1]) "That all juris-

---

([1]) Speech "Of Economical Reform".

dictions which furnish more matter of expense than advantage to justice or political administration . . . . that all public estates which are more subservient to the purposes of vexing, overawing and influencing those who hold under them . . . . than of benefit to the revenue . . . that all offices which bring more charge than proportional advantage to the State . . . . ought to be abolished" and "that it is right to reduce every establishment, and every part of an establishment, (as nearly as possible,) to certainty ; the life of all order and good management".

So began a period of administrative reform, mostly initiated by William Pitt, which laid the foundations of the structure we know today both in the United Kingdom and Australia. Cabinet leadership was established, which meant that although much was still left to individual departments, they were also expected to work together more as a unified whole. Centralised control of the budget and finance was increased, with more effective control of departmental spending. Some attention began to be given to a logical division of functions between departments and within departments. A century after Burke's speech most of the essentials of a modern organization had been achieved and the Australian colonies had in the main followed British practice.([2])

But attention was also beginning to be paid to the problem of personnel. Whereas Burke and Pitt fixed attention on the need for good management of "public offices", other reformers emphasised that a consideration equally fundamental was the quality of the holder of the office. Macaulay in his proposals for the reform of the Indian Civil Service (1833) suggested a device to give practical form to this thought—competitive recruitment by written examination. Twenty years later, both the thought and the device were incorporated by Sir Stafford Northcote and Sir Charles Trevelyan in their "Report on the Organisation of the Permanent Civil Service"([3]). By now it was clear that the administrative business of a great modern state, with power over and duties towards all classes, not only within the realm but in all quarters of the globe, could not complacently be left to job-men, subject only to the indifferent and spasmodic supervision of Parliament.

Introducing their theme, Northcote and Trevelyan wrote: "It may safely be asserted that, as matters now stand, the Government of the country could not be carried on without the aid of an efficient body of permanent officers, occupying a position duly subordinate to that of the Ministers who are directly responsible to the Crown and to Parliament, yet possessing sufficient independence, character, ability, and experience to be able to advise, assist and to some extent, influence, those who are from time to time set over them."

The Commissioners' Report was the impulse that launched the modern civil service. They repudiated the traditional system root and branch: "Admission into the Civil Service is indeed eagerly sought after, but it is for the unambitious, and the indolent or incapable, that it is chiefly desired. Those whose abilities do not warrant an expectation that they will succeed in the open professions, where they must encounter the competition of their

---

([2]) For some examples, see R. S. Parker, "Public Administration as the Study of Bureaucracy", *Pub. Admin.*, *(Sydney)*, XV, March, 1956, p. 31.

([3]) The report is reprinted in *Pub. Admin.*, *(London)*, XXXII, Spring, 1954, pp. 1-16.

contemporaries, and those whom indolence of temperament, or physical infirmities unfit for active exertions, are placed in the Civil Service, where they may obtain an honourable livelihood with little labour, and with no risk ; where their success depends upon their simply avoiding any flagrant misconduct, and attending with moderate regularity to routine duties."

"The general principle, then, which we advocate is that the public service should be carried on by the admission into its lower ranks of a carefully selected body of young men, who should be employed from the first upon work suited to their capacities and their education, and should be made constantly to feel that their promotion and future prospects depend entirely on the industry and ability with which they discharge their duties, that with average abilities and reasonable application they may look forward confidently to a certain provision for their lives, that with superior powers they may rationally hope to attain to the highest prizes in the Service, while if they prove decidedly incompetent, or incurably indolent, they must expect to be removed from it."

To secure this result, they recommended:

(1) That competitive examinations under a central Board for the service as a whole should replace the patronage of heads of departments.

(2) That there should be a division of the service between those concerned with intellectual work and the more mechanical side of administration.

(3) That promotion should be generally by merit.

(4) That when a post had to be filled, the candidate should be chosen from those successful at the open examination.

(5) That the examinations should be held periodically at stated times.

(6) That there should be a period of strict probation for the successful candidates.

(7) That consideration be given to a system of inter-departmental promotion.

The proposals met with a most mixed reception. John Stuart Mill and Benjamin Jowett were enthusiastically for them, others jeered that Wellington and Nelson could not have passed the prescribed examination. There were distinguished public servants who feared centralized control, as well as those who supported it.

By an Order in Council dated 21st May, 1855, the Government opened the door for the adoption of the main principles of the Report ; the order set up a Board of three Commissioners "for conducting the examination of the young men proposed to be appointed to any of the junior situations in the Civil Establishments". Candidates could not be admitted to probation in such appointments without a certificate of qualification from such Commissioners, whose duty it was, before granting the certificate, to satisfy themselves of the age, health and character of the candidates, and to ascertain that they possessed the requisite knowledge and ability for the proper discharge of their official duties. But the candidates were still nominated by departments, and nine out of ten appointments were still not made competitively. The grip of patronage was further loosened by a decision in 1859 that no person thereafter appointed should be deemed to have served in the permanent civil service (and consequently be entitled to a pension) unless he had been admitted with a certificate from the Civil Service Commissioners.

In 1860 a Select Committee on Civil Service Appointments recommended open and unlimited competition for junior posts. Open competition carried the day by another Order in Council in 1870. Except for situations to which the holder was appointed directly by the Crown, some professional positions largely in the Home Office and the Foreign Office, and positions filled by promotion of persons serving in the same department, open competitive examination, followed by certification by the Civil Service Commissioners, was made the sole method of entry into the civil service. The Order was followed by Treasury regulations dividing the Service into two. Recruitment to the Higher Division came to be confined largely to graduates. There was at first no provision for promotion between divisions, the then Chancellor of the Exchequer (Robert Lowe) believing it undesirable to promote owing to the need for persons with "a superior style of education" in the higher posts. A civil servant, he thought, should be content with what he is and not try to get higher. Thus began one of the chief subsequent causes of friction in the Service. This disqualification was finally removed after the First World War, in 1919. In fact, 13.5 per cent. of First Division positions were already filled by promotion between 1892 and 1911.

Later Orders in Council provided machinery for incorporating the principles that characterise the British Civil Service and which have made it an exemplar for other public services. "Their aim was to prevent the waste of public funds and to abolish patronage and corruption. They were designed to establish honesty and efficiency and equality before the law as the basis of public service. Injustice and inefficiency would together be removed by moulding the central administration on the three ideas of the career open to talent, of economy through the division of labour and the careful checking of expenditure, and of a professional service. The means were to be the grading of the Civil Service according to the work done, with recruitment to grades by relation to the educational system ; entry by open competition presided over by independent persons removed from political or corrupt influence ; and the unification of the service under Treasury control. To these was later to be added the principle of fair conditions of employment to be secured through the Whitley system of recognised channels of negotiation and adjudication."(⁴)

There does not exist in England an independent public personnel authority, responsible both for recruitment and for supervision of the "establishment" of government departments, that may be recognised as the counterpart of the well known Australian instrument of public service control—the Public Service Board. Owing partly to the circumstances of their evolution as a congeries of departments and boards each under a Ministerial head and each entitled to recruit its own staff, the departments of the English civil service today still retain some independent staff authority, but their "global

(⁴) H. R. G. Greaves, *The Civil Service in the Changing State*, 1947, p. 14.

manpower budget"([5]) is ordained by the Treasury and their choice of occupants for these positions is restricted to those who have passed the examinations prescribed by the Civil Service Commissioners, which examinations in their turn must be approved by the Treasury. This is partly due to the historical accident that the Treasury was already a department with great power and influence in England when the civil service was reformed.

The civil service of England is therefore under Treasury control; the "Head of the Civil Service" is a title held by the Permanent Secretary of the Treasury, and this officer is responsible for approving staffing requirements as well as the money to pay the salaries; also "The Treasury may make regulations for controlling the conduct of His Majesty's Civil Establishments, and providing for the classification, remuneration, and other conditions of service of all persons employed therein, whether permanently or temporarily."([6])

Whether vesting the control of the civil service in the Treasury produces a body of administrators best suited for the many-sided purposes of modern government has been questioned by many critics. While all admit that an uncontrolled public service quickly becomes gargantuan and bureaucratic, some believe that the Treasury as the financial conscience of the government is necessarily more concerned with safeguarding economy than with building an able service.

If it is true that in the past the British Treasury as the financial watchdog scared many a department off making innovations, all the recent evidence points to knowledgeable and effective co-operation on its part. Its sponsoring of Organisation and Methods sections in departments, its training of Establishment Officers, its undeniable success in maintaining high standards in recruitment, in official and financial conduct, must be favourably acknowledged. Its supervision may be (as in fact it must be) strict; but in recent years it has not been repressive, while its creative work has been admirable and stimulating.

By 1870, therefore, the principles of modern public service were accepted in England. The most important of the principles was the recognition of the principle of *control* itself. The English political genius had early recognised the need to control its ruling institutions, had brought the King and his Ministers within Parliament, and in turn made Parliament more responsible to the electorate, but until the nineteenth century it was not as clearly seen that a new ruling institution—a permanent civil service—equally must be held accountable. This is not to say that the nineteenth century English reforms clearly established the modern principle of a "responsible bureaucracy"; but they did deny that affairs of the Ministers' servants were the concern only of the Ministers, and affirmed that control of the civil service based on criteria of efficiency and economy was essential. Until some such affirmation was made, the role of the modern public service board could not be conceived.

([5]) For a good short account of modern Treasury control of establishments, see Sir Thomas Padmore, "Civil Service Establishments and the Treasury", in W. A. Robson (ed.), *The Civil Service in Britain and France*, 1956, pp. 124-138.

([6]) Order in Council of 22nd July, 1920.

Early Administrative Development in New South Wales

Until 1823 the machinery of government was controlled entirely by the Governor, who was directly responsible to the Secretary of State for the Home Department, and later to the Secretary for War and the Colonies. The Governor incorporated in his person all legislative and executive functions. "He was an autocrat, wielding the widest powers, answerable to no criticism but that of the Minister in England."([7])   Senior officials were appointed by the Secretary of State in England. The Governor appointed all other civil officers.

Until the grant of responsible government in 1856, the principal civil officer was the Colonial Secretary, who was the chief adviser to the Governor. The position grew from that of Secretary to the Governor. The first holder of this post was Andrew Miller (January to June, 1788). He was followed by David Collins (from 1788 to September, 1796) who set the office on its feet. The title of Colonial Secretary was first officially used in 1821 by Goulburn, who on 30th June, 1820, had been commissioned as "Secretary and Registrar of the Records of our Territory called New South Wales". For the last thirty years before responsible government there were only two Colonial Secretaries, McLeay and Deas Thomson, both very efficient administrators.

William Balcombe, the first Colonial Treasurer, was appointed in 1823, and the Sydney Gazette of the 27th May, 1824, announced that payments would be made at the Colonial Treasurer's Office, O'Connell and Bent Streets. Some months later another significant civil appointment was made under the Governor. On 8th November, 1824, William Lithgow was appointed Auditor of the Colonial Revenue of New South Wales "in order that he may have the entire financial state of the colony under his eye"; and on 20th September, 1825, regulations for the guidance of financial officers were issued stating that "quarterly returns of monies received and expended were to be furnished, all vouchers to be taken in duplicate, and to be successively numbered, care to be taken not to blend sums received or disbursed under different sources of revenue or heads of expenditure".

John Oxley had been appointed Surveyor General in 1812 and by 1826 was directly in charge of a Surveyor General's Department—though the Governor was still advised on land policy by the Colonial Secretary. A Department of Public Works and Department of Roads and Bridges existed from 1826, the former being called Engineer Department in 1826 and 1827. Departments also developed to deal among other things with Police, Post Office, Customs, Gaols and the Harbour.

With the coming of responsible government and the intense economic and social growth following the discovery of gold, the responsibilities of the infant executive rapidly expanded. In 1856 the Department of Lands and Public Works was established; by 1859 separate Departments of Lands and Public Works were formed. In 1874 the administration of "mines generally" was transferred to a new Department of Mines.

On 14th October, 1824, Governor Brisbane had appointed the Reverend Thomas Reddall Director General of all the government public schools of New South Wales, at a salary of three hundred pounds a year, "to enable

---

([7]) Ernest Scott, *A Short History of Australia*, p. 63.

the nominee to bear up against the heavy expense of making continual tours of inspection to all the straggling schools of this extended territory". The appointment was short-lived. However, by 1848 a Board of National Education had been incorporated, and in 1866 the administration of primary education was committed to one governing body, the Council of Education, a board of five members. By 1880 Sir Henry Parkes' historic Public Instruction Act ensuring "free, compulsory and secular" education placed its administration under a Minister and a Department of Public Instruction. To these, Departments of Agriculture and of Labour and Industry were added in the 1890's.

Thus by the late nineteenth century a system of departments had emerged not widely different in essentials from the one that we know today. The major structural change since then has been the great growth in agencies of the board and commission type, beginning with bodies like the Railway Commission (N.S.W., 1888). Indeed, it is an ironical comment on the subject of this chapter that just as the first effective moves were set on foot to co-ordinate the personnel of the departments, a new type of agency began to emerge, the staff of which were often to be exempted from the controls provided for by the Public Service Acts.

Problems of the Unreformed Civil Service

While the story of the emergence of the new departments tells no new tale to one who has studied the development of similar devices of government in England during the nineteenth century, the emergence of the principles for the recruitment and management of its infant public service did not follow entirely the pattern laid down in the older country, and in one instance—the creation of an independent statutory public personnel authority, the Public Service Board—radically departed from it.

Before 1856, all senior appointments were made by the Secretary of State, and most of these were sent out from England, having obtained their appointment by political or personal influence. There was a dearth of talent in the Colony, and governors were hard put to it to find suitable staff for the more junior posts. Sometimes they brought a secretary with them on first arriving in the Colony; sometimes they secured local appointees for senior vacancies and sought the Secretary of State's approval. All Colonial Secretaries from 1820 to 1856 were, however, appointed from England.

Governor Macquarie unashamedly appointed emancipists to civil vacancies and did what he could to attract ability and character, irrespective of origin, to government employment. One must not imagine, nevertheless, that most of the civil servants of the Colony would merit any higher praise than Northcote and Trevelyan gave to their counterparts in the English system. "I remember a Colonial Treasurer flitting from the colony; I remember a Curator of Intestate Estates running away from the colony; I remember one or two High Sheriffs defrauding the colony; . . . . Corruption was then gross and outrageous."([8])

([8]) The Hon. John Robertson, to the Select Committee of the Legislative Assembly to inquire into the civil service, 1872-73, *Minutes of Evidence*, para. 51, p. 3.

The coming of responsible government emphasised the need for an effective civil service. Ministers were required to nominate their departmental staffs and were plagued by their friends and constituents to admit them to office and to promote and protect them once admitted. Consequently, they acquired at the one stroke an army of officials of poor education and sometimes worse sobriety and a host of disappointed supplicants, who raged against an over-manned and over-paid public service in which they had been denied asylum. Attempts to reduce the size of the service brought screams from those already in the "tart-shop". As a correspondent wrote to Sir Henry Parkes: "I think it must be admitted . . . that since we have employed the principles of popular representative institutions there have been many offices created and appointments made merely for interestedly political purposes. Many useless offices must now exist—possibly some incompetent officers in the service."(⁹) When we read that one of the terms of reference of the 1884 Commission of Enquiry into the efficiency of the Civil Service was the "extent of drunkenness" in the service, we are not left in doubt as to one explanation of incompetence.

The correspondence between Sir Henry Parkes and the Chief Justice in 1868 throws sufficiently strong light on the condition of the service at that time.

"If the public service is to be raised in efficiency and economy, the considerations that ought to be forced on men in office—whoever they may be —are:

(1) What does the public require in the situation for which this salary is paid?

(2) Who is the best man to do what the public require? So long as we consider the interests of the applicant before the interests of the Public in filling situations, so long will the Public who pays be badly served . . . In my judgment the time is come when the Public Service of this Colony ought to assume the character of a profession and only young men ought to be received into it who should have a 'fair field' to work themselves up through the varifying ranks of official employment."(¹⁰)

Parkes clearly saw the root causes of inefficiency in the civil service and a way out—but his ideas of reform lay fallow for twenty years until they were resolutely applied in New South Wales by Mr. G. H. (later Sir George) Reid in the Public Service Act of 1895.

It could still be argued, in the days before disciplined party machines had emerged and governments were often formed from loosely associated groups of M.Ps., that patronage was necessary in order to buy support in the Legislative Assembly. "Parliamentary (or as it is fancifully called, Responsible) Government is necessarily to some extent . . . . a government by corruption . . . Pass a stringent Public House Act—or try to do so—such as shall really restrain largely drunkenness and you will not be Colonial Secretary six months. Appoint the sons and nephews of a sufficient

---

(⁹) *Parkes Correspondence*, V. 19, pp. 204-207, 20 May, 1872.

(¹⁰) Sir Henry Parkes to Sir Alfred Stephen, 30 May, 1868. *Parkes Correspondence*, V. 35, pp. 160-166.

number of members of parliament to be clerks of Petty Sessions, or Waiters in the Customs or something on the Roads or in a Light House, and you will command votes for the Session, probably for two."[11] Similar arguments were used in England a few years earlier, and went on being used in the United States much later.

Victoria had been the first colonial government to seek a path out of this morass. It appointed in 1859 a commission of enquiry under the chairmanship of R. Grice, "to enquire into the clerical strength and efficiency of the several departments of the public service and to report on such improvements in the organisation of the same, by way of consolidation or otherwise as may . . . . promote efficiency and economy."

The commission commented in its report: "The radical defect of the present condition of the Civil Service is the total absence of any general rules. There is no rule as to appointments ; no rule as to promotion ; no rule as to dismissals ; no rule as to leave of absence ; no rule as to superannuation. There are few defined degrees of rank ; there is no uniform correspondence between salary and duty, and there are variations in salary between officers of equal rank who perform similar duties."[12]

The report went on to stress that nothing like an integrated civil service had yet been achieved. "Although according to the theory of our Constitution the civil service is a uniform body under the control of the Governor assisted by a council composed of the political chief officers of the various departments into which the service is divided, yet from the absence of any formal regulations, the service has practically become fragmentary and is split up into small departmental subdivisions each of which regards itself as distinct from even kindred offices." It recommended that "as a first step to remove these anomalies, and to restore to the service its natural and lawful unity", a proper system of classification should be adopted.

Keen though the insight of the 1859 Victorian Commission was into the defects of the civil service, its recommendations did not tackle the gravest defect—appointment on ministerial nomination. They were embodied in an Act of 1862, which provided for ministerial appointment after a qualifying (non-competitive) examination which was left optional. The Act also permitted appointment without examination of "persons of known ability". Through this loophole all the good intentions of the Act escaped.

Another Commission (under the chairmanship of A'Beckett) followed in 1870, the complaints of all nineteenth century civil service enquiries again finding voice in its report.[13] The service was over-staffed, ill-organised, bred to duplication and circumlocution, stuffed with nondescript temporary clerks. However, this Commission is significant because it was the first to envisage the establishment of a public personnel authority to stand between the service and the ministers and to provide for some more continuous oversight than busy politicians had the time, mood or talent to enforce. It based one of its findings on a recommendation of a civil

[11] Sir Alfred Stephen, Chief Justice, to Sir Henry Parkes, 31 May, 1868. *Parkes Correspondence*, V. 36, p. 148.
[12] Victoria, Royal Commission on the Civil Service, 1859, *Report*, pp. 10-11.
[13] Victoria, Royal Commission on the Public Service, *Report*, 1873.

service commission that had reported on similar difficulties in the Civil Service of Canada in 1868. The Canadian legislation of the same year had provided for a Civil Service Board comprising deputy heads of departments (some fourteen permanent heads) to (1) frame and publish regulations concerning examinations; (2) to examine candidates; (3) to issue certificates of qualification; (4) to report to the Governor in Council any case where there had been departure from the rules and regulations of the Act; and, a most pregnant suggestion, to whom the Governor in Council might "refer such questions as he may think fit connected with the administration of the service, including questions connected with the efficiency and welfare of such service."

This Canadian example was strongly commended by the A'Beckett Commission. "It might be found desirable to give to this Board very much the character of a permanent public service commission, in which case it should be assisted by a Secretary, and furnish yearly to the Parliament reports as to the Public Service" (para. 111). The A'Beckett Commission sought to extend the responsibility of the Audit Commissioner "to make reports as to the condition of the Public Service . . . to the Chief Secretary, pointing out all matters relating thereto that seem to demand special attention, and that they should also offer suggestions for simplifying the work of departments, and for lessening the cost thereof, wherever they discover in the course of their examinations, an opportunity for improvement" (para. 112). Finally, the Commission recommended "that an officer, or more than one if necessary, to be called an Inspector of the Public Service, be appointed by the Governor in Council, for the purpose of inspecting from time to time, and at least once a year, all the public departments and reporting thereon" (para. 113).

The Commissioners presented their report in 1873, but the Victorian Government took no effective action until 1883, by which time, the supernumerary service (those employed "temporarily" to avoid the restrictions of the existing legislation) had increased sixty per cent., while the civil service proper had decreased twenty-five per cent. Many who had passed the examination prescribed in the 1862 Act were never appointed.

Other Colonies, following the Imperial Act of 1859 providing pensions for those permanently employed in the civil service, copied its main provisions—Tasmania in 1860, Victoria in 1862, Queensland in 1863, New South Wales in 1864 and in 1873, and Western Australia in 1871 and 1885. Queensland in 1863 passed a wider act providing rules for classification, promotion and dismissal, extending it in 1864, but repealed it in 1869, finding "the system of superannuation and other allowances . . . burdensome to the finances of the Colony without being advantageous to the public service", as the preamble to the repeal legislation puts it.

New Zealand provided a retirement act in 1858 and followed it in 1866 with "an act to organise and regulate the Civil Service of New Zealand"— the most comprehensive of this generation of public service laws. Section 10 provided that "the first class officers at the seat of government shall form a board to which all appeals shall be referred before they are submitted to the Governor in Council". Ministers of the Crown were empowered to refer to the board "such questions as they may think fit connected with the administration of the Colony . . . or other questions connected with the efficiency and welfare of such service . . . the Board to have power and authority to summon and examine witnesses and to call for and obtain papers".

South Australia, by a Civil Service Act of 1874, prescribed that youths between sixteen and eighteen who wished to be appointed to the classified division of their service should be required to pass a prescribed examination. But there were no teeth in the legislation, as the examination was not competitive and there were no restrictions placed on the entry or retention of temporary employees.

In 1872 the New South Wales Legislative Assembly had appointed a Select Committee to inquire into the Civil Service, following a petition to Parliament asking that a Civil Service Bill be introduced. The Select Committee recommended that a bill should be brought before Parliament as soon as possible with general provisions for the proper classification of the service; for the examination, probation and appointment of candidates; for the promotion of civil servants; for the mode of dealing with offences; for the granting of leave of absence on some uniform basis; and for the retirement and superannuation of officers.

No legislative action was taken to give effect to the Committee's recommendations. There was no public indignation; no ministerial alarm. The mood of the times, engaged with land laws and the bitter issues of free trade, was well reflected in the comment of the Select Committee discussing the need for open competitive examinations: "As it would interfere with the prerogatives of Ministers, trench on the time honoured custom of political patronage, weaken private interest, and render it difficult for members of Parliament and other influential persons to procure situations in the Government offices for their relatives or constituents, it will scarcely meet with general approval."[14]

"Thus, up to 1883, while lip service was paid in Public Service legislation of some States to the principle of open competition for recruitment, none of the Acts was ever strictly enforced. Patronage had too strong a hold and the Acts did not provide for independent control of the Public Service."[15]

THE FIRST PERIOD OF REFORM (1883-1914)

Slowly the legislatures and their dominant executives were introduced to the idea of abdicating patronage in the interests of a "protected" public service supervised by an authority protected in its turn from the importunities of political pressure.

Victorian Public Service Act, 1883

Victoria in 1883 passed a Public Service Act which embodied most of the main principles of modern public service recruitment and control.

According to its preamble, the Act purported "to abolish all patronage with respect to appointments and promotion in the Public Service, and to establish a just and equitable system in lieu thereof which will enable persons

[14] N.S.W. Select Committee of the Legislative Assembly to inquire into the Civil Service, 1872-73, *Report*, sec. 5, p. 9.
[15] R. S. Parker, *Public Service Recruitment in Australia*, 1942, p. 24.

who have qualified themselves in that behalf to enter the Public Service without favour or recommendation other than that of their own merit and fitness for the position". The Act went on to provide for a Public Service Board of three members appointed by the Governor in Council, and prescribed that no new appointment should be made except on the request of the permanent head of the department to the Minister, a certificate of the Public Service Board having first been obtained that such an appointment was required. The Act also provided that no vacancy should be filled by the appointment of a person not in the service without the Board's certificate that there was no person available and fit in the public service to be promoted or transferred to fill such vacancy.

Competitive examinations were provided for entrance to the lower classes of the clerical and industrial divisions, and a qualifying examination for promotion from the lower to the higher classes of the clerical division. But a back door was left unlatched. "A clause reserving temporary appointments to Ministers completely destroyed the authority of the Board, and when the financial crisis of 1890 provided the excuse for retrenchment, the Board was side-tracked, and Victoria relapsed into indifference to public service problems from which it has scarcely yet been roused."[16]

New South Wales Public Service Act, 1895-1902

Where Victoria had squandered its opportunity, New South Wales went forward resolutely. The prime impulse once again was a resounding denunciation by a Royal Commission. "There is a popular assumption that the Civil Service of New South Wales is both overmanned and overpaid, that it includes a number of incompetent or inefficient officers: that its modes of procedure are more or less antiquated: that the economical and rapid despatch of public business is not its main object; that favoritism prevails in many quarters: and that it is a means of providing employment for relatives and friends of political adherents . . . the assumption is not without justification."[17]

The Government, embarrassed by the excesses of their own liberality and plagued by rising administrative costs, gladly grasped the device suggested by the Royal Commission of a full-time "independent Board of Commissioners, three in number, to be chosen for their reliability, probity and administrative capacity", and before the end of the year in which the Commission presented its report, a new Public Service Act was passed.

Its main provisions were:

(1) A full-time Board of three[18] Commissioners to control the service.

(2) Systematic grading and classification of all offices.

(3) Salaries to be determined upon the basis of the value of the work performed.

(4) Open competition for admission to the service—by separate competitive examinations for entrance to the professional, clerical and educational divisions.

---

[16] F. A. Bland, *Government in Australia*, Introd., p. xiii (A considerable rousing has occurred since this was written in 1943).

[17] N.S.W., Royal Commission on the Public Service, 1894-95, *Report*, pp. 29-30.

[18] Raised to four in 1955.

(5) A superannuation scheme.

(6) Regulation of temporary employment.

Resolute and far-reaching as these provisions were, they went little further than to incorporate the best principles of control of departmental recruitment that had been in the air since the publication of the Northcote-Trevelyan reforms.

What was not realised in earlier legislation both in Great Britain and Australia was that the problem of controlling the new civil service went beyond the question of suitably staffing the separate departments. At first it was taken for granted that inefficiency and waste were simply the unkempt children of patronage; but they did not disappear on the waving of the wand of competitive recruitment. And separately efficient departments did not make a co-ordinated public service. However, almost unconsciously, with the introduction of the terms "economy" and "efficiency" the legislation of 1883 and 1895 had fashioned an instrument and enunciated a principle that in the next century was to be used to integrate the departments under the Public Service Board into a better balanced machine of government. Section 9 of the 1895 New South Wales Act provides that: "as often as is necessary to carry out the directions and provisions of this Act, and ensure the establishment and continuance of a proper standard of efficiency and economy in the Public Service, the Board shall, as far as practicable, personally inspect each department and investigate the character of the work performed by every officer therein and the manner in which such officer has performed his duties, and the efficiency, economy and general working of such departments, and may, for such purpose, examine the permanent head of such department and such other witnesses as may appear to the Board to be necessary".

The implications of this section were, and continue to be, enormous. Was the Board responsible for managing the Service or was it to ensure that it was well managed? If the first, then what had happened to the principle of Ministerial responsibility? If the second, could the Board prevail against the Minister who insisted that issues of management were inseparable from considerations of policy?

The 1895 Act was replaced by the consolidating Act of 1902 with little alteration to its main provisions, and this Act today is the principal instrument of public service control and management in New South Wales.

The Commonwealth Public Service Act, 1902

Benefiting by the experiences of the States and their problem eased by the fact that they were fashioning a new service without any of the embarrassments of entrenched privilege,([19]) the Commonwealth Parliament passed its Public Service Act in 1902. The Act vested complete control of the service in a single commissioner, appointed for seven years and eligible for re-appointment. The Commonwealth service was divided into four divisions, first, embracing Heads of Departments; second, embracing other

---

([19]) However, by section 84 of the Constitution officers in departments transferred from the States retained their accrued rights as State officers. For some of the consequences, see V. Subramaniam, "The Integration of the Commonwealth Service", *Pub. Admin. (Sydney)*, XVI, June, 1957.

very senior officers; third, covering the lower and middle grades; fourth, covering all manipulative, industrial and minor clerical grades. Admission to the service was to be by open competitive examination and promotion was to be from "below"; greater regard was to be paid to merit than to seniority.

The Commissioner was required to make recommendations to the Governor-General regarding management and improved methods of work and in an annual report to the Commonwealth Parliament "to recommend changes and measures necessary for improving the method of working of the public service and especially for ensuring efficiency and economy" (section 11). To assist the Commissioner in the administration of the Act and the discharge of his responsibilities, power to appoint inspectors was given (section 8).

The Second Reading debates in the House of Representatives disclose how far the prudence of legislators had progressed. Sir John Quick, while confessing([20]) that "political patronage had proved an utter nuisance", went on to say: "But while not desiring to exercise patronage or influence of any kind for political considerations, we should inflexibly resolve that we will see that the public service is properly manned and equipped, and that its business is conducted with efficiency and satisfaction to the whole community. The question is how far this result can be obtained by transferring not only political patronage but power and control from responsible ministers to unresponsible boards." Deakin agreed that it was "confessedly an intricate problem; how to control a public service by means of statutes and yet be enabled to fuse into it something of the spirit and energy which are obtained in private business affairs". He hoped that the Commissioner and his inspectors would prove "watchdogs of the public, Parliament, and the Minister".

By the turn of the century, therefore, several of the States and the Commonwealth had developed coherent public services in which many liberal and some democratic principles had found fruition. Patronage had been effectively scotched and the legislative and public consciences had been awakened to the necessity of establishing and maintaining an effective, honest and equalitarian service. While it is clear that the state had not yet forseen all its problems and responsibilities as the largest single employer, the "civil" service had been transformed into the "public" service and was well on the way to being recognised as an essential institution of statecraft. Finally, Australia had evolved a device of public service control—the Public Service Board—which was to prove a most resourceful instrument in the future.

([20]) *Com. Parl. Deb.*, I., 1257-58, 19 June, 1901.

THE AUSTRALIAN PUBLIC SERVICE BOARD IN THE
TWENTIETH CENTURY

The passing of the Commonwealth Public Service Act in 1902 and of the New South Wales Act in the same year placed their two public personnel authorities in the van of the management and control of Australian public services in the twentieth century.

Other states had passed about the turn of the century legislation setting up public service boards or commissioners (Queensland, 1889; Tasmania, 1900; Western Australia, 1904; South Australia not until 1916). Later legislation eliminated some loopholes in these early statutes. All this legislation presented common features, although not unexpectedly there were differences in the degree of "independence" accorded the new agency. All purported to remove appointments to the civil service from the caprice of patronage; all provided for the posts in the permanent sections of the service to be filled only on the recommendation of the public personnel authority([21]); in all, recruitment was confined almost exclusively to youths under twenty-one selected after an open competitive examination; promotions were to be from within and transfers were to be facilitated; seniority as a principle of promotion was eschewed and merit was enthroned; rules regarding all kinds of leave were codified and a special group of offences was created calculated to keep the public servant of the new century obedient, sober and politically anonymous. Salaries were to be commensurate with service and with the duties of the position, which were to be fixed by the board after a process of classification; superannuation schemes were provided in the public service legislation or in associated statutes. Each public service board was required to report annually to Parliament any breaches or evasions of its Act, particularly in the matter of appointments to or promotions within the service without its authority. Finally, the boards or commissions were obliged to investigate the work in all public departments under their control and to "indicate the changes and measures necessary in their opinion for improved working".([22])

The record of Australian public service boards in the fields of recruitment, classification, promotion and discipline has been a successful one and most boards today are concerning themselves with developing training and welfare schemes as well. Some of their achievements in these fields will be presented in other contributions to this book and cannot find a place in this chaper, which must now confine itself to an account of the way in which the public service boards of the Commonwealth and of the States have discharged their unique function of acting in Deakin's phrase "as the watchdogs of the public, Parliament and the Minister".

Problems of Public Service Management

Once you have evolved a public service as distinct from a number of public servants gathered together in a number of public departments, you are confronted with an ever-growing range of problems. Certain of these

---

([21]) In the case of heads of departments, most executive governments (and particularly the Commonwealth Government) reserve some right to make their own appointments. See p. 346.

([22]) N.S.W. Public Service Act, 1902, sec. 12.

problems are obvious but none the less difficult, for instance, personnel problems construed narrowly as staff problems, e.g., recruitment, training, remuneration, discipline, conditions of service, transfer, promotion, grading, superannuation. In Australia, these problems are definitely the responsibility of the public service boards, although it is important to remember that in the States and to a lesser degree in the Commonwealth, many public personnel are not subject to the authority of the Public Service Board. This point is discussed further below.

Next, there are problems in which the central issue is the department itself rather than its individual staff members. For instance, the problem of establishment, i.e., just how many officers and of what kind a department should be given to get on with its job. Again, in this category, fall all the problems of management. For instance, what is the best type of organisation, what are the best methods and procedures for getting the work done, is morale good or how can it be improved, what type of financial control should be imposed?

Then there are problems that inevitably followed in the wake of the creation of the public service boards, problems that high-light the relation between the public service board as "controller" and the departments as the "controlled", problems of the administrator who has to get the job done and who has not a free choice of tools; and on the part of the public service board, the nice problem of controlling the service without "governing" it. Ever present in this context is the Minister charged with his own constitutional responsibility for the practical and political performance of his department.

Finally, there are the problems of the Public Service Board itself, how it should be designed for its tasks, the implications of its responsibilities, its relations with the Executive Government, i.e., the Cabinet of the day. It must not be forgotten that while the government may have vested in the Board responsibility for the staffing and control of the public service, it never intended to wash its hands of public service problems, nor indeed would it by public opinion be allowed to do so. Cries that the public service is over-manned or bureaucratic are meant for the ears of the government just as the service organisations press on their ultimate employer, the Premier, their demands for higher pay, shorter hours, equal pay for women. And if we may be permitted a postscript, there still remain over the large questions of the role of the public service in the state itself—is it becoming bureaucratic, is it invading the functions of the judiciary, is it dreaming dreams of dominion over private enterprise, is it fast forgetting that it is a "public service" and becoming a "state within a state"?

Politics and administration are intermingled; together they comprise government, and the administrator must consciously and continually subordinate himself and his wishes to those of the democratically elected government. True, he serves the state, but he must obey the Minister, and through the Minister, the Parliament and the People. In proportion as he understands and accepts democracy, has a feeling for its institutions and respects its tough enterprise and independence, will an administrator be creative and successful. If he neglects these considerations or is ignorant of them, he will confuse career with function and strut a stage he is expected to grace.

As already stated, all Australian public employees are not subject to the public service acts. In the Commonwealth about one-quarter are excluded. There is considerable variety of provision as between States. Queensland's public service acts have a wider coverage than other States,([23]) but even there over half the State employees are excluded. In New South Wales, the figure is nearly three-quarters, and in most other States the percentage excluded is even higher. In New South Wales employees of the authorities dealing with: railways, main roads, road transport, police, water and sewerage, maritime services, etc., are not subject to the Public Service Act. The largest exclusion is that of railway employees. This is accounted for partly by the fact that some State agencies were already well developed before strong public service boards appeared, and their controllers (or their employees) have not relished the prospect of losing their autonomy. In other cases, the Government has evidently considered that the individual agencies concerned could be trusted to operate their own recruitment and promotion policies and look after their own efficiency, and that this has even some advantages over control through a central public service agency. This has been claimed for many public enterprises. Statutory corporations are mostly empowered to appoint their own staffs, and also have some freedom to determine wages and conditions, on the ground that business enterprises should have some freedom from the rules of the ordinary government department. However, there has been, of recent years, a "tendency to bring methods of recruitment and conditions of employment more into line with those applying in the regular public service", as Mr. Kewley remarks in his chapter ; and terms and conditions of service are now often subject to the approval of the Public Service Board.

However, such agencies have still greater freedom in personnel matters than the ordinary government department, which sometimes envies them for this reason. The case for more independence has been stated as follows:— "The Department's staff is appointed by the Department itself, and members of the staff make their careers within it ; they have thus an undivided loyalty . . . It also creates a personal relationship between management and officers of a somewhat closer nature than might otherwise exist".([24]) The case is strongest where an agency's work differs so much from that of other agencies, that it must employ a highly specialised personnel. In the general run of departments the advantages of some centralised control have been more evident. The natural desire of a departmental head for greater freedom is sometimes supported by that of outside groups closely associated with its work, who hope thereby to make it more responsive to their needs. Teachers have often been prominent in moves for greater independence in personnel matters for Departments of Education. (In Victoria a different device has been used: to make teachers' salaries and promotions the responsibility of a separate Teachers' Board.)

In Australia a considerable degree of permanency attaches to the tenure of positions on Public Service Boards, and this has been thought necessary to protect their independence and to preserve continuity of policy. In the

([23]) In 1950 their scope was widened to cover the salaried staff of a number of statutory corporations. See C. J. Hayes, "The Administration of State Public Services," *Pub. Admin. (Sydney)*, XV, June, 1956, p. 121.

([24]) H. M. Sherrard, "Main Roads Administration in New South Wales", *Pub. Admin. (Sydney)*, XV, Sept., 1956, p. 202.

Commonwealth, members are appointed for five years, but are eligible for re-appointment, and in New South Wales, members hold appointment until 65, as does the Queensland Commissioner. In Victoria this is true of the Chairman, the other two sitting for three years, with their term of office renewable. In most other States the Commissioner is appointed only for seven years, but is eligible for re-appointment. Commissioners are nearly always from the public service. The present Chairman of the Commonwealth Public Service Board, for instance, is a former Secretary for External Affairs. The Chairman of the New South Wales Board has served in the State public service for the whole of his career. The Victorian Commissioner was previously the Chief Parliamentary Draftsman of his State.

There has been pressure at times for the Commissions to include staff representatives, but this is still unusual. One of the three Victorian Commissioners is a staff representative, and the same is true of the South Australian Board (but the latter has only limited powers).([25]) There are at present demands for staff representation in Queensland and Western Australia. It has been argued that a Board tends to have more prestige than a single commissioner (but that is mainly a question of the personalities involved) ; that it makes continuity of policy easier (but a break in policy may sometimes be desirable) ; and, as mentioned above, that it enables some specialization. So one may have board members specially interested in a particular service (say, education or social services), in organization and methods, legal questions, and so on. It also enables, if it desired, some "representative" element to be introduced. In 1955, the N.S.W. Public Service Act was amended to increase the number of Board members from three to four, one of whom was to be an officer of the service who had been "trained as an educationist and who had been directly concerned with teaching or administration of education." The first appointee after the amendment had been a recent president of the N.S.W. Teachers' Federation.

The New South Wales "experiment" may be considered as an attempt either to create a "functional" board or a "representative" board. The Teachers' Federation in the State had for years strongly urged the removal of the activities of the Education Department from the jurisdiction of the Public Service Board and the creation of an Education Commission with direct representation of the Association. However, the statutory specification did little more than formalise the convention, observed for the most part since the early nineteen twenties, that one of the board members be an officer of substantial experience in teaching or in educational administration. A similar convention has been that an officer with considerable experience in public finance should be appointed. Both conventions have been rather closely observed by the Government in making appointments to the Board. A "functional" board drawn from members of the service with adequate experience does ensure to a considerable degree that the Board is a knowledgeable one, and having regard to the volume and complexity of the decisions it must take, no Government in its senses would deliberately refrain from ensuring that it has a competent board.

([25]) It fixes salaries for permanent staff, recommends the creation of new offices and (with an independent person replacing the Commissioner) hears promotion appeals. On most other matters (e.g., recruitment, promotion, efficiency of the service) the Public Service Commissioner acts alone.

A "representative" board is not necessarily an incompetent board; it is open to criticism solely on the ground that the principle of selection by representatives is an invalid one, and its assumptions if blindly observed would go far towards destroying the efficacy of any board. The assumption of the case for a representative board is that the members of the board will or should obediently respond to the interests of the group they allegedly represent, that, in short, they are delegates. But no body with the heavy responsibilities of Australian public service boards can win the desired respect of its servants and of its masters, if it accepts allegiance to anything but its own best judgment. In proportion as that judgment is informed by long experience in the councils of employers or employees, or more strictly speaking, in the fields of negotiation and arbitration, will the decisions of the board be wise and acceptable.

The notion that a properly designed Public Service Board should (like an Arbitration Tribunal) consist of an "impartial" Chairman, an "employer's" representative and a "staff" representative, is quite widespread. Where members of Public Service Boards function, as they do in some States, as salary fixation or promotion appeals authorities, the analogy with arbitration seems more plausible.[26] However, the tendency has been to remove these functions wholly or partly from the Public Service Board's discretion; and in its central function of controlling recruiting, training, and other personnel questions, there is a very strong case for keeping any flavour of "representativeness" from the Board's personnel.

A related problem is that of the relations between the Chairman of the Board and other members, if any. As we have seen, there have been experiments with both Boards of three or more members and single commissioners. The Commonwealth originally had the latter, but now has a Board of three. Victoria has a similar Board. New South Wales has a Board of four, but the Chairman may overrule his colleagues. South Australia has a single Public Service Commissioner, who for certain purposes sits as Chairman of a Public Service Board of three. The other States have a single Commissioner at the time of writing, but there is strong pressure for change in both Queensland and Western Australia.

There has been widespread recognition of recent years in countries such as the United States of the value of concentrating execution of policy and the control of day-to-day administration of personnel matters in the hands of a single person; and of regarding the task of the other commissioners as aid in formulating policy, rule-making, and in any appellate functions of the Board. If the position of the Chairman is made strong enough in relation to his Board, there can then perhaps be less objection to a representative of employees being included among the Board members. The important point to recognize is that a Public Service Board nowadays is a major administrative arm of Government, and that its policies need to be applied no less single-mindedly than in any other field of public activity.

---

[26] Promotion appeals in three States are normally heard by a special board, with a judge or magistrate as chairman, and with representatives of the public service agency and the staff as the other members. In Tasmania the Public Service Commissioner is chairman. In Victoria and South Australia the Board itself hears appeals; but in the latter an independent Chairman takes the place of the Public Service Commissioner.

Creating an Integrated Public Service—The British Background

As contrasted with English practice, where the financial, establishment and organisational controls are vested in the Treasury (leaving, of course, the directive authority of the Minister untouched) the Australian departments subject to their Public Service Acts must acknowledge (and somehow satisfy) at least three matters:

(*a*) the Minister who expects them to get the job done in a way that will redound to his own and his party's credit;

(*b*) the Treasury, which must be persuaded to find the funds for new staff, even after the Public Service Board has agreed they are essential;

(*c*) the Public Service Board, with its vast authority to help or hinder what (in the department's eyes at least) is necessary expansion.

It is no consolation to the permanent head in this predicament to reflect that no man can serve two masters, much less three; and it speaks much for the good sense of the three authorities concerned that, except in rare instances, each has respected the other's function and they have combined happily to make the system work and (it may fairly be said) work well.

As we have already seen, the New South Wales and the Commonwealth Boards were instituted as virtually independent staffing authorities and it was expected that they would be preoccupied with recruiting and running the staff side rather than with the less clearly seen problem (at that time) of checking over and improving the whole machine of government administration. Yet it was just on this last point that the New South Wales and Commonwealth as well as other Australian public service boards were trenchantly criticised in the first twenty years of their performance.

The British government long ago established the tradition of employing a Royal Commissioner or a Select Committee of Parliament to satisfy itself from time to time that its civil service was not falling short of the high standards implicit in its nineteenth century reforms and was successfully taking the strain of the new functions forced upon it by war, post-war and depression emergencies.

The Playfair Commission of 1874-75, following the indication of the Order in Council of 1870 that the British Treasury should assume powers over staffing, recommended the creation of an advisory committee of permanent heads to assist the Treasury in securing a measure of uniformity in organisation and co-ordination of departmental functions. The Ridley Commission in 1886-1889 recomended appointment of a permanent consultative committee consisting of four heads of departments and a representative of the Civil Service Commission to "entertain all questions affecting establishments . . ., all proposals for increased expenditure, and . . . to review periodically all offices, with the object of ascertaining whether any reduction can be made in the number of the staff, or other economies effected".[27] The MacDonnell Commission of 1912-15 recommended that there be created within the Treasury a new division charged with the general supervision and control of the civil service and particularly "to carry out

[27] E. W. Cohen, *The Growth of the British Civil Service*, 1941, p. 153

inquiries and investigations into any matters connected with departmental administration and methods of working".([28])

None of these recommendations was fully adopted and they "were made in the face of explicit opposition from the Treasury which maintained its traditional attitude that the principle of ministerial responsibility would be violated were departments compelled to adopt a form of organisation or an administrative policy against their will. World War I provided an escape, and the recommendation was disregarded."([29])

In the later stages of the war, criticism of the deficiencies in the departmental structures broke out afresh; the Haldane Committee, reporting in 1918 on the "Machinery of Government" (note the recognition of the problem in the title) held existing departmental insularities up to scorn, and strongly recommended the setting up within the Treasury of a special section dealing with Establishments, such section to collaborate closely with departmental officers. The Bradbury Committee in the next year (1919) recommended a detailed structure for the new Division. To these continuous and authoritative proddings the Government in 1919 responded by appointing the necessary senior staff to the Treasury to permit the Establishments Branch to function, and by allocating to it a few specialists in office machines and methods. The critics were mollified, not silenced. The Tomlin Commission of 1929-1931 expressed its dissatisfaction with what had been achieved in the matter of departmental organization and urged the Treasury to embark upon a systematic overhaul of the machinery of government irrespective of whether they received proposals for increased expenditure or not. Some more recent British developments are discussed by Mr. Grainger later in this book. The theme has not yet been exhausted in England; but turning to the Australian scene we find that similar stocktaking of public service controls has produced almost identical criticisms.

THE SECOND PERIOD OF REFORM

The 1914-18 war provoked a new series of enquiries into the Australian public service. Between 1914 and 1928 no fewer than twelve Royal Commissions or Select Committees surveyed their management. Public services had been growing in numbers and seemingly in authority. Ministers and public alike were alarmed by fears of bureaucracy. Business men big with commercial success persuaded governments that all that was needed "to stop the rot" was to enlist their talents and run the public service on business lines. Commercial and industrial interests complained that there was too much government in business and too little business in government. Dunning's memorable resolution that the "power of the Crown has increased, is increasing and ought to be diminished" was revived and directed against the swollen wartime departments.

New South Wales

The first service to feel the pressure was that of New South Wales. Mr. G. M. Allard, a prominent Sydney accountant, was appointed by the Fuller

([28]) Cited in F. A. Bland, "Personnel Management in England", *Pub. Admin. (Sydney)*, IX, March 1950, p. 189.
([29]) Bland, *loc. cit.*

Government in August 1917 to "inquire into the administration, control, efficiency and economy of the Public Service of New South Wales" and more particularly "as to the methods adopted in making appointments, permanent or temporary . . . the training of officers and their promotion", the adequacy of remuneration, the numbers employed, "and as to what increase or reduction should be made . . . having due regard to efficiency and economy"; "as to the sufficiency of the regulation and control of the Public Service", and the administration of the Public Service Board.

Allard turned to his task with a will to reform and a flair for exposing complacency. He was provocative. "Several remarkable parallels may be drawn in connection with Public Service conditions as they existed prior to the Royal Commission of 1895, and the time of the present Royal Commission. Popular assumption is much the same as to the overmanning of the Service; political and other patronage is still alleged to exist; temporary officers are numbered in their thousands; while it is a general article of faith that there is room for greater efficiency and better economy throughout."[30]

Criticising the proneness of the Board to rely upon the permanent heads and the passive influence of the regulations to ensure efficiency and economy, the Commissioner said: "There is not a shadow of doubt that the responsibility for economy in the Public Service rests with the Public Service Board itself", and he went on to revive and restate the intent of the 1895 legislation. "The powers and duties of the Board under section 9 have not been varied or modified in any way by subsequent Acts affecting the Public Service; and it stands clear and unanswerable that the Public Service Board is the body responsible for the efficient and economical running of the several departments of the Service as much now as ever it was."

"There does not appear to be the slightest doubt that the Public Service Act of 1895 contemplated a continuous and close supervision of the Public Service by a Board specially selected for individual capacity. It was not only a matter of re-organising the Service and putting an end to conditions that had made of it a public scandal; but it was the expressed function of the Public Service Board so to administer the Service that those conditions should not recur. It was only to be expected that the Public Service of a young and rapidly developing country—the social legislation of which had a direct trend towards government control of public activities—would expand; and the obligation was put upon the Board by the Public Service Act of ensuring that such expansion should be consistent with the requirements of the State, having constantly in view economies to be effected by the adoption of improved business methods."[31]

Yet he was constructive: he recommended that (1) the term of office of the three existing members of the Public Service Board be determined; (2) a chief commissioner and two assistant commissioners be appointed, to hold office until they reached sixty-five years of age, unless previously removed by vote of both Houses; (3) that an inspectorial staff of three to five officers be appointed, to whom the Board should delegate their powers of inspection; (4) that the Board establish training classes to assist officers

---

[30] N.S.W. Royal Commission on the Civil Service, 1st *Sectional Report*, 1918, p. xv.

[31] *Ibid.*

preparing for the various grade examinations; (5) that there be only one door of entry to the permanent staff of the public service, and that by qualifying examinations; (6) that the Board have express power under the Act to terminate the services of any officer for whom suitable employment could not be found, or who had passed the limit of useful service.([32])

The New South Wales Public Service Board from 1919

Amending legislation in 1919 incorporated the best of Allard's thinking, and since that date the New South Wales Public Service Board has actively maintained a tradition of independence, enquiry and economy. Its inspectorial staff has never been allowed to languish in terms either of numbers or capacity, and on more than one occasion, the Board has been utilised by the government of the day to investigate the administration of some activity not subject to the Public Service Act.([33])

The New South Wales Board is statutorily in the most independent position of all Australian Boards. Its members are appointed till 65 and when holding an enquiry have the power of a royal commissioner. Appointments to "all public offices under the Government" are vested by the Constitution in the Governor with the advice of the Executive Council; and the same section provides that such appointments shall be subject to the provisions of the Public Service Act and of all other enactments relating to the appointment of officers. In the absence therefore of express statutory enactment to any other effect, all appointments to government offices are subject to the Public Service Act.([34]) Appointments under the Act are absolutely controlled by the Board. The Act provides that entrance examinations shall be held for admission to the various divisions of the public service and that the Board shall hold such examinations; that no person shall be admitted to the public service of the State unless he has successfully passed the prescribed examination; that the appointment in the first instance is on probation only for a period of six months or longer if the Board directs, and may be confirmed or cancelled by the Governor thereafter, but only on the recommendation of the Board in either instance. No appointment of any person not already in the service (i.e., a person from "outside" in the smug jargon of the "insiders") to any permanent office or position can be made except at the instance of the Board, or upon a written request of a minister or his permanent head; and in each instance the Board must give a certificate that such an appointment is required. In giving such certificate, the Board must state that there is no person in the public service fit and qualified and available for such appointment. Vacancies are filled from within the service on the recommendation of the Board, having regard to the fitness and seniority of all officers eligible. The Board may dismiss or reduce officers in status and salary for disciplinary offences, and may retire officers found permanently unfit to discharge the duties of their office.

([32]) *Op. cit.,* pp. xcvi-xcviii.

([33]) For example, in 1952 the Board was asked by the Premier to investigate the staffing of the administrative sections of the New South Wales Transport Department, which was being criticized at the time on the score of its costs and operating efficiency.

([34]) Such enactments are, of course, quite numerous, as is indicated above.

So far as the statute can make it, the control of the Board over appointments to the service is watertight. Equally complete are the Board's powers to manage and control the "service". The Act gives the Board power to make regulations for the classification of the service, its officers and their work ; for the assignment of work ; for promotion, transfer and exchange of officers ; for the recruitment and control of temporary employees: for the grant and control of leave ; for the control of stores ; and generally for the "maintenance of discipline, order, economy and efficiency in the service". Finally, the Board is required to report annually to parliament "on the condition and efficiency of the Public Service, and of its proceedings and indicate the changes and measures necessary in its opinion for improved working methods", and "the Board shall in such report draw attention to any breaches or evasions of this Act which may have come under notice".

The N.S.W. Public Service Act in resolute hands, is an effective defence against undue influence in public appointments: and in equally resolute hands, it can be a powerful weapon against waste, corruption, mismanagement and inefficiency within the Service.

The Commonwealth

To resume the account of commissions of enquiry into the Australian public services, one cannot help being struck by the large degree of legislative insistence in the golden age of public service legislation (1880-1905) that the public service boards occupy themselves with ensuring economy, good management and efficiency in their public services, and the small measure of achievement by the boards in these fields.

The First Annual Report of the Commonwealth Public Service Commission (1904) under the heading of "Circumlocution" promises better things: "There is of course a certain degree of unavoidable delay incidental to the formal procedure that must necessarily be observed in every government department or extensive commercial or banking institution—a delay, however, that is capable of considerable minimisation by the simplification of such procedure: and, as far as I am able by regulation to simplify procedure, this will be done" (page 17). The Commissioner (D. C. McLachlan) returned to the theme in his Second Annual Report and after quoting instances of money saved by not filling vacancies in redundant positions, he writes: "By zealously pursuing the policy of close scrutiny, I hope in the course of time not only to check unjustifiable attempts to swell the number of hands in departments, but also, by keeping staffs down to the lowest limits, to compel officers to look round for simpler and more up to date method of carrying out their work" (page 40).

But while the spirit of the crusading Commissioner was not weak, the surplus flesh of the growing public service proved stronger, and by 1912 the theme of efficiency by admonition had disappeared from the annual reports of the Commonwealth Commissioner. Eight years later the theme reappears, and this time dominantly, in the Final Report of the Economies Royal Commission (1920). "Our investigations have convinced us that large economies are possible under a system of management which should give closer attention to organisation and systematisation and with a system of continuous and far-reaching inspection in all departments which will bring to the light of publicity all evidence of extravagance and inefficiency . . .

the maintenance of reasonable economy in governmental expenditure cannot be secured by means of investigation carried out by fits and starts, and though specific errors may be put right temporarily, no lasting benefits can be insured by such means as against continuous supervision and criticism."

The Commission recommended that a permanent Board of Management for the public service be set up to report directly to the Government, leaving to the departmental heads under the minister the responsibility for "selection, appointment, reward and punishment" (page 20).

In the same year Mr. D. C. McLachlan had presented the government with a comprehensive report on the Federal service. McLachlan was ideally equipped to report. He had been a permanent head in the New South Wales service before Federation. He was the first Commonwealth Public Service Commissioner and was in that office for fourteen years. He recommended the amalgamation of the separate services of the Commonwealth under one public service act with control by a commissioner; the repeal of the Arbitration (Public Service) Act which had resulted in "disloyalty, extravagance and reduced efficiency" and the vesting in the Public Service Commissioner of sole power to fix salaries and conditions: a general reclassification of the service; the determination of promotions and transfers by permanent heads (instead of by Commissioner and Governor-General as previously); new provisions as to disciplinary action including a board of appeal; provisions to deal with incompetent or ineffective officers by reduction or dismissal; regulation of sick leave on a more equitable and economic basis; restriction of temporary employment; and a review of allowances.

The Commonwealth Public Service Act, 1922

Armed by advice from the Economies Commission and McLachlan, the Government introduced a new Federal Public Service Act in 1922. The principal features of the new Act, involving departures from conditions established under former legislation were: a board of commissioners (three members constituted in lieu of a single commissioner, with a term of office of a maximum of five years in the first instance, and eligible for re-appointment); disposal of excess officers by transfer or retirement from the service to be determined by the Board instead or by the Governor-General as previously; classification of the service into four divisions in accordance with the importance and character of the work: provision for appeals against classifications; power to grant or refuse annual increments of salary to be vested in the permanent head of the department with right of appeal to the Board; appointments to the service to be made by the Board and where such appointments were probationary to be subject to confirmation by the Board instead of by the Governor-General as previously; aggrieved officers to have right of appeal against promotions and transfers; the permanent head to deal with disciplinary cases and decide punishment, including recommendation for dismissal, with a right of appeal to an Appeal Board; provision for summary dismissal by the Board, after an inquiry and hearing, of officers directly fomenting or taking part in a strike which interfered with or prevented the carrying on of any part of the public service or utilities of the Commonwealth; incompetent or inefficient officers to be transferred to other positions or dismissed; recruitment of temporary employees to be vested in the Board and not as previously in departments; and important and far-reaching duties imposed on the Board to devise means for effecting economies and ensuring efficiency.

The last mentioned provision (section 17) is so important in Australian public service board reform as to justify quoting in full. It has been embodied in principle and in some cases in the same language in the Public Service Acts of Queensland, South Australia and Tasmania. It spells out in specific terms the kind of responsibility implied in section 9 of the New South Wales Act, "which section is practically the keystone of the legislation" (Allard). It reads: ". . . the Board shall have the following duties:—

(a) to devise means for effecting economies and providing efficiency in the management and working of Departments by
   (i) improved organisation and procedure ;
   (ii) closer supervision ;
   (iii) the simplification of the work of each Department, and the abolition of unnecessary work ;
   (iv) the co-ordination of the work of the various Departments ;
   (v) the limitation of the staffs of the various Departments to actual requirements, and the utilization of those staffs to the best advantage ;
   (vi) the improvement of the training of officers ;
   (vii) the avoidance of unnecessary expenditure ;
   (viii) the advising upon systems and methods adopted in regard to contracts and for obtaining supplies, and upon contracts referred to the Board by a Minister ; and
   (ix) the establishment of systems of check in order to ascertain whether the return for expenditure is adequate ;
(b) to examine the business of each Department and ascertain whether any inefficiency or lack of economy exists ;
(c) to exercise a critical oversight of the activities, and the methods of conducting the business, of each Department ;
(d) to maintain a comprehensive and continuous system of measuring and checking the economical and efficient working of each Department, and to institute standard practice and uniform instructions for carrying out recurring work ; . . ."

At the last moment, however, the Government regretted its generous delegation of authority (and opportunity) to its instruments. The final subsections of section 17 provided that if departments failed to give effect to the Board's decisions, and in the event of the Board still being of the opinion that its decisions should be implemented, it was to report the matter to Parliament. A sadder example of the Lord giving and the Lord taking away, of Parliament keeping a dog and doing the barking itself, could with difficulty be found—unless we look at the conflicting jurisdictions in salary fixation blithely conferred by the same Federal Government on the Public Service Arbitrator and the Commonwealth Public Service Board.[85]

---

[85] A bad example that was not lost on the New South Wales Government when it gave concurrent jurisdiction over salary fixation to its Industrial Commission and its Public Service Board. See Chapter 14.

Although the teeth of the section were loosened, the Board might still have done effective work in the departments had its inspectorial staff been commensurately increased to cope with the new tasks. Owing, perhaps, to the limited tenure of its Commissioner (five years), or to other factors which now there is little opportunity to establish, the Board remained a supervising rather than a controlling authority until the post-World War II years. Then the Government, faced with lowering public opinion, stupendous numbers in wartime departments obstinately clutching the cores of the sweets of temporary office, and an unparalleled expansion in the machinery of Federal Government, considerably increased the inspectorial and auxiliary staffs and a rejuvinated Commonwealth Public Service Board has now entered energetically upon the tasks presented in section 17.

Other States

Public Service legislation in Victoria lagged behind that of New South Wales and the Commonwealth both in spirit and resolution. There was in that State for a long time a reluctance on the part of the Government to vest any real powers in their public service commissioners or to give them a tenure of office substantial enough to destroy the diffident attitude to change and responsibility which the insecure incumbent develops.

The original Commission of 1883 (see above) became a part-time body in the eighteen-nineties. In 1902, when renewed interest in public service reform followed Federation, control was vested in a single Public Service Commissioner. This arrangement lasted until 1941, when the present Public Service Board was established.

An amending Act in 1912 reinforced section 14 of the main Act (1890) providing that the Commissioner "may at any time, and shall whenever requested to do so, investigate the efficiency, economy, and general working of each department and report to the minister the result of such investigation", by permitting the appointment of inspectors, and made it clear that the public service commissioner could make recommendations to the Governor in Council as to the result of inspections. The 1917 Royal Commission on the Victorian Public Service found that "an Inspector" had been duly appointed but "it was found necessary to transfer his services to another department" and "that the results of the amending legislation were not what might have been anticipated".

Wallace Ross in his excellent report on the Victorian Public Service (1927) emphasised to the government who commissioned him that theirs was the responsibility to forge the tool of reform. "The Public Service Commissioner should be made responsible for the efficient and economical working of the Service and his power should be a real one." He clearly saw the central issue, that the size of public services is largely proportionate to the amount of government business and that the staff of government departments is large and the manner of working wasteful because the executive government, which is ultimately responsible, does not bother itself over the growing profusion or arm some independent authority against it. He reported (par. 210): "Under the present system the administration of each Department is vested in the permanent head, subject to the minister. But there is no co-ordinating authority, or any official whose definite responsibility it is to devise means for effecting economies and providing efficiency in the management and working of departments . . . Here it may be pertinent to state what the terms economy and efficiency involve. There may be a tendency to confuse what must be considered as two very distinct matters, viz. (*a*) economy of the government's policy and activities, and (*b*) economy of the Service appointed to carry out such public policy and activities. In respect of (*a*), the Public Service Commissioner would generally have no voice, though in certain matters . . . it is highly desirable that he periodically review the effect of these policy decisions and make recommendations to the government regarding any desirable changes, but in (*b*) his control as to efficiency and economy should be complete, and his recommendations thereupon the last word in staff administration." The words were those of Mason Allard (see below, p. 324).

Ross concluded that the Commissioner's power to effect economies he considered desirable was practically nil, though theoretically it might be thought to be reasonably wide, and he gave instances of his comparatively limited powers being restricted by executive action. A cabinet subcommittee existed dealing with a number of administrative functions in connection with public service control, thus cutting across the Commissioner's responsibility.

It was not until 1946 that the Victorian government, provoked by decades of public as well as public service resentment over Cabinet interference in the Commissioner's recommendations, granted a substantial increment of independence. The Victorian Public Service Act, 1946, established the virtual independence of the Board, giving it complete authority in the making of appointments, and independent power in the matter of fixation of salaries and wages, and prescription of annual increments. The Board's determinations in these matters are subject only to disallowance by Parliament by resolution of both Houses. Absolute powers are reserved to the Governor in Council in regard to the prescription of conditions of employment relating to hours of duty, discipline and conduct of officers, and leave of absence. The power to create new offices is also reserved to the Governor in Council.

The same gap between the theory and practice of "efficiency inspectors" disclosed by Mason Allard and Ross was noted in Queensland by J. D. Story in his 1919 Report on "The Classification of Officers of the Public Service".[36] Story reported that section 18 of the Queensland Act prescribing annual inspections was "practically inoperative. Even in the head offices, a searching detailed inspection of the work of the office, and of each officer is seldom, if ever, made by the chief administrative officials. I am certain that the public service suffers through the lack of systematic and searching inspection of the work of its officers . . . an effective system of inspection should assist towards maintaining efficiency and economy throughout the service."

The Queensland Public Service Acts vest supreme control of the public service in the Governor in Council. They require the Commissioner to submit for consideration of the Governor in Council reports and recommendations on any matter required to be dealt with by the Governor in Council in terms of these Acts. Where matters arise concerning a particular department, the reports and recommendations are submitted through the departmental minister. Where reports and recommendations concern more

---

[36] Queensland P.P. 1919-20, I, pp. 45-805.

than one department or concern the administration of the public service generally, they are submitted to the Governor in Council through the Premier. If the Governor in Council does not approve, he may remit to the Commissioner for reconsideration. The Governor in Council must have due regard to the report and recommendations of the Commissioner. The Queensland legislation does not impress as giving its Public Service Commissioner the degree of independence that encourages fearlessness, although the last Commissioner achieved exactly this reputation.

ECONOMY AND EFFICIENCY

Since the period of misgiving, public service boards in Australia have been left alone to their own devices. Public zeal for public service reform in any institutional sense has seemingly waned. The device of a public service board, headed by one or more commissioners with substantial security and independence, and responsible for appointing and managing the public service in conformity with undisclosed criteria of "economy and efficiency", is widely adopted in Australia and largely respected.

At the same time daily charges are made (and believed) that Australian public services are overmanned and ill managed: wild accusations are made that governmental employment is the greatest single cause of under-production. Suggestions follow that something like a purge of the public service is long overdue. Statistics of public service growth are sedulously publicised to condition the public mind to accept the public servant as the source of his present discontents. A representative reaction was that of the President of the Australian Council of the Employers' Federation when shown statistics that Federal government employment had increased 207.6 per cent. since 1939:— "A bloated public service, grossly overstaffed in some departments, is sucking the life blood from Australia . . . the fact that one person in four in Australia is a government servant maintained by the other three persons must cause deep misgiving to everyone with the welfare of the country at heart."[77]

That on this argument, housewives, mothers, school children, the sick the aged must equally be indicted as parasites, we will not pause to It is enough to emphasise that while public services are being attacked on the question of their size, they must prove their efficiency and the soundness of their organisation. They are rather prone to take their virtues for granted. When the British governing class in the middle nineteenth century was faced with the problem of founding a new civil service that was honest, efficient, and equitably chosen, they hit upon the open competitive examination as the most reliable tool. Using this tool, there is no doubt that they fashioned a loyal service, representative of the products of the various levels of the national system of education. The preoccupation of the British, Australian and American civil services with the recruitment problem is an understandable one, when we reflect that most of the evils of their earlier services stemmed from policies of patronage which negated sound recruitment. But the tradition of the public services of the last hundred years, and particularly the view that to obtain an able public service one simply needs to recruit a well-educated one may not

[77] *Sydney Morning Herald*, 3rd Nov., 1951.

hold so good in the next fifty years. The Australian public are not likely to tolerate complacency on the part of a public service that is little better educated than its masters. And public criticism of the service, ill informed and vindictive though it often is, focusses on just this assumption that the service, because it is efficiently recruited, is therefore efficient.

While it may be consolation to the philosophic public servant to reflect that he receives many blows meant for his political masters, and that if the service is oversized, it is no more than the measure of governmental plans and ministerial ambitions, the problem of making a modern, complex public service effective is a challenging one. Public support of the service is indispensable to its function in the modern social service state. Alexander Hamilton, writing in the *Federalist* (No. 70), stated this requisite as follows: "The ingredients of safety in the republican sense are first, active dependence on the people; secondly, a due responsibility", and over a century and a half later the Congress of the United States made the same point that the ultimate objective is to ensure accountability to the people in an "Act creating a Commission on Organisation of the Executive Branch of Government", the first Hoover Commission.

The first two assumptions of public service management—that the service should be a career one and chosen independently of any political influence—are now so widely accepted as to be beyond debate; the third—that the public service board is the apt and only instrument for ensuring efficiency and economy in the service—is one that brings forward for discussion many issues.

The first is the least satisfactory of all—what exactly are "economy and efficiency"? They have stood as admonitory twins since the nineteenth century when public service legislation was actuated by a desire to retrench the public service as a cure for its ills, real and imagined; and one may suspect that in the political vocabulary of public service reform, efficiency was synonymous with economy, and economy with frugality.([38])

Efficiency and economy are not self-explanatory terms: much less are they self-evident formulae which can be applied to relieve the public pain in all circumstances. They are statements about an organization or, what amounts to the same thing, about the methods and objectives of an organization. We are all prone to define "organization" in terms of "efficiency" and vice versa. We say—"that place is run efficiently, it must be well organized", or "that store is well organized: it must be pretty efficient". In both cases, we are describing results we are satisfied with, but we have no very clear ideas how these results are brought about. In other circumstances, we say about a governmental venture, a state tileworks or transport system: "Look at the Government making a hash of that business—too many bosses, too much interference—no organization. How can it be efficient? Governments never make a go of anything. They have no right to be in business!" How much clear thought upon organization and efficiency prefaces such outbursts, which is a common way of thinking about state utilities, can be imagined.

([38]) There have always been more enlightened views. "We have always felt that the real want of the country was not cheap service, but good service." (Royal Commission on Victorian Civil Service, *Report,* 1859.)

Organization is a method of dividing work up to get it done. Work in a governmental structure consists of tasks and responsibilities allocated to a position whose occupant is responsible for the satisfactory performance of those tasks and satisfactory discharge of those responsibilities. Organization is not an end in itself; it must be a means to an end. These ends in government are as varied and complex as the multitudinous functions of government itself. They range from the total mobilisation of a society for war to the protection of wild flowers, from the licensing of dogs to help for an under-developed area at home or abroad. So we must start with ends; shortly we must decide what we want to do and then we go about doing it.[39] We cannot start with any absolute ideas about organization and efficiency, first, because there are none and secondly, because it would not get us anywhere. The assumption that there are golden rules of organization that operate and produce results in a vacuum is the defect of a certain type of literature on "efficiency" (usually with a capital E).

"Efficiency" is a treacherously simple term. It is a quality of something; the quality of effectiveness. Whether we find this quality or not depends upon what effect or effects we are looking for. Consequently we expect that a process or organization will achieve certain effects before we call it effective. These expectations are called "criteria". We can readily agree that the criteria of one kind of organization can differ from the criteria of another, e.g., a retail organization is judged according to groups of criteria—those held by its managers, by its shareholders, by its customers, by its competitors, by the taxation department. And the emphasis placed on the criteria differs from group to group: the customers want quantity and quality of stock, reasonable prices, "service"; the management wants labour stability, loyalty, responsiveness to management policies; the shareholders want dependable profits; the competitors want fair competition, and so on. These criteria are not mutually contradictory but different judges of efficiency are looking for different things.

Efficiency and Economy in the Public Services

As we have already seen, legislators have pinned their high hopes of achieving efficiency and economy in public services by charging their public personnel authorities with the responsibility for ensuring it. But in relation to what ends are their means to be employed? Are the criteria of efficiency and economy in non-public organizations to be those for public organizations?

The criterion of efficiency is most easily understood in its application to commercial organizations that are largely guided by the profit objective, viz., balance sheet efficiency, being the minimisation of cost and the maximisation of income, since money is a common denominator for the measurement of both output and income, but even here there are non-money objectives, for instance personnel work.[40] Such a criterion of efficiency cannot be

---

[39] cf. Leonard White, *Trends in Public Administration*, 1933. "When we say 'efficiency' we think of homes saved from disease, of boys and girls in school prepared for life, of ships and mines protected against disaster. We do not think in terms of gadgets and paper clips alone, and when we talk of economy, we fight waste of all human resources, still much too scanty to meet human needs." (p. 11).

[40] H. A. Simon, *Administrative Behavior*, 1945, pp. 172-173.

applied to a non-commercial organization such as a state education department or a commonwealth repatriation department, although hectoring press critics continually resort to it. A sub-leader writer on the subject of Public Service Reform recently complained "that it would be uncandid to deny that the 'system' operates against the development of the qualities and procedures requisite to success in private enterprise." Here is a complete confusion of ends that one could pity without pausing to correct, were it not characteristic of the continual complaint of publicists that the public service is "costing too much" or "spending too much".

Government is not intended to serve the same ends as business or public servants to satisfy the same motives. Management problems in the public service are not solely those of lowering costs or speeding services. Even in private enterprise, these ends may not be as important as the need to raise the quality of the product. The responsibilities, and consequently the difficulties, of government are much more complex. Government is the authority which the people of the nation expect to determine their common obligations, assure their common rights, provide common services, and to act in all things in their common interest. While efficiency in private enterprise is often achieved by arbitrary methods, government cannot afford to be efficient in any sense that would involve hurt to the rights of others in the community.

There is no spectacular solution to this problem of public service reform. Thoughtful public servants agree that its procedures should be simplified, its staffs better trained, and its prose pruned, but, mindful of the cult of "efficiency" in totalitarian societies, they cannot in the light of the trusts given them by the public agree that these and other reforms should be lightly purchased at the cost of the democratic freedoms they serve.

Accordingly some substitute for the money-making criterion of efficiency must be found for the public services. Employing the principles we have already stated, we must go back to our objective and construct indices that measure the degree of attainment of this objective. In the educational field, for example, a number of indices suggest themselves:—

> (a) the number of school age children provided for by the system and the ratio of this number to the total number of children of school age ;

> (b) the coverage of the system, e.g., how far children in the country receive the same educational services as children in the city ;

> (c) the prestige of the system—among parents, among employees, among educators, among the children themselves ;

> (d) the cost per head to the population of the educational service and how this cost compares with the cost of comparable educational service in other similar communities ;

> (e) the size of classes and the ratio of teachers to classes ;

> (f) the type of facilities, e.g., buildings, equipment used and how they compare with those facilities in other systems costing no more ;

> (g) what proportion of the states' resources is devoted to this purpose as compared with public health, or, say, maintenance of public order? And in the outcome is this ratio of resources justified? Is the State getting value for "its money"?

These (and other indices) are an attempt to set standards, the attainment of which can be measured to some extent against cost, i.e., the proportion of the State's resources employed for a given effect. In general, our criteria of efficiency in these services are:

(a) is this service justifying the expenditure of the proportion of the State's resources being devoted to it?

(b) are the best results being obtained for the expenditure of a given sum of money?

The answers cannot be in terms of money, and never of profit, and they cannot be absolute ; for the problem of comparison between competing objectives of government expenditure remains.

In the discharge of their responsibility for efficiency and economy are public service boards to follow their quarry into the realms of government policy? This is the no-man's land of public administration. Our system of "parliamentary bureaucracy" (as Professor Wheare has called it) neatly divides executive responsibility between Parliament and its ministers on one hand and the permanent public service on the other. Ministers propose policy, parliament approves, and the public service carries it out. No one pretends that it works out exactly like that, and many will concede that public servants "suggest" policy for ministerial approval. Be that as it may, such discussions confine themselves to the process of the making of present policy. A large part of the problem of public service management is how to assess the efficiency and economy of a department of state patiently administering policies that are the vestigial remains of the policy-making of yesteryear. Should public service boards, if they frankly believe that these policies are no longer serving any "felt need of the times" recommend to governments that they drop them? Theoretically all Australian public service boards possess the power to report to Parliament or to the Executive on the condition and efficiency of the public service, and of its proceedings, and to indicate the changes and measures necessary in their opinion for its improved working. Conceivably any public service board could utilise this opportunity to suggest to Parliament how its policies could be changed to give better administrative results. Apart from suggesting repairs or reinforcements to public service statutes, there is no record of any Australian public service board so indulging itself. Possibly they hearken to Mason Allard's dictum. "The question arises as to what the terms efficiency and economy involve within the meaning of this section (i.e., section 9). There is a tendency on the part of many to confuse what should be considered as two very distinct matters, viz: (1) the economy of the Government's public policy and activities ; and (2) the economy of the Service appointed to carry out such public policy and activities. In respect to (1), the Public Service Board would have no voice or control, but in (2) its control as to efficiency and economy should be complete."(⁴¹)

The primary responsibility for efficiency and economy in governmental organization lies where the good sense and constitutional genius of the British peoples have always placed it—in the responsible ministers. Theirs is the responsibility of deciding on what services and obligations the public revenue shall be expended, and how much on each. Should too little be

_____
(⁴¹) *1st Sectional Report,* 1918, p. xxi.

spent, or too much, and that not wisely, they must answer in their place in Parliament. Little more needs to be made of this issue than was succinctly said by Sir John Quick in the House of Representatives when the first Commonwealth Public Service Bill was being debated. "I cannot see why a Public Service Commissioner can more effectively wield political power than a responsible minister."[42]

Nevertheless, the Australian Public Service Boards are justifying Deakin's hope that they could be "the watchdog of Parliament, of the Minister, of the people". The old fashioned virtues of honesty, integrity, prudence and industry are still needed and rewarded in the service of the people, and public service boards are the custodians of these virtues. Whatever economy and efficiency may or may not mean, they are not empty platitudes but can be transformed by a vigilant system of inspection into homely virtues that can, and do, save many hundreds of thousands of pounds of the taxpayer's housekeeping bills.[43]

All in all, the public service boards of Australia impress as being very much awake to their responsibilities and as rigorously discharging them. When we reflect that they are self-dedicated to their tasks and operate largely on fields where press and public opinion is vindictive where it is not indifferent, and where governments alternate between treating their servants as stalking horses or mendicant poor relations, we can conclude that the traditions of a capable, honest and selfless service are in good hands.

---

[42] *Com. Parl. Debs.* I, 1258, June, 1901.

[43] The Annual Reports of Public Service Boards on the whole make impressive reading. To take one example, the high rate of mechanisation of accounting and other clerical procedures is peculiarly an achievement of these **authorities.**

Chapter Eleven

RECRUITMENT

P. W. E. CURTIN

Recruitment is the first step towards a good public service. The main tasks are to find the right tests of competence ; to prevent favouritism, that is, avoid selection on grounds unrelated to efficiency ; and to get a fair share of able candidates by recruiting from all the main sources and not missing any out. Efficiency is a complex criterion, for the needs from bottom to top of the service have to be taken into account by the recruiting of people ultimately to fill posts at all levels. So a good recruitment procedure depends on a good system of classification and must be linked to training and promotion.

Possibly more has been written about recruitment than any other topic in public administration. The reason is that here as in other countries, recruitment is well recognised as one of the primary factors in a public service. It is primary in importance, for to some extent, the State is as its officials are ; and it is primary in origin, for like all other modern services, the present Australian public service is the product of a long campaign to reform the system of recruitment. The whole growth of the public service has been closely related to the movement to replace patronage, political or personal, by the merit principle, and improve the competence and qualifications of public officials.

There have been three, or perhaps four, stages in the history of recruitment to the Australian public services:—

(a) A stage of personal appointment unchallenged until the 1850s.

(b) A stage of haphazard but persistent challenges to patronage by the principle of open competition—from the 1850s to the 1880s. During these decades, open competition established itself as a valid principle of entry in men's minds but not in fact. It was paid the compliment of lip-service but not practised on any scale.

(c) The stage of open competition from the 1880s to the present day (though not starting so early in all colonies).

Future writers may trace a fourth stage from the First World War, when, with the system of open competition firmly established, men's minds turned more deliberately to the task of building a competent service fitted to its present-day tasks.

As in other countries, the later stages overlapped the earlier. A form of limited competition still controls recruitment for a few important posts, and qualifying examinations give entry to some subordinate posts. A few of the highest posts, mainly in government authorities outside the service proper, are on occasion filled by nomination or patronage, under the jealous scrutiny of Parliament and the public service. In some States, temporary public servants enjoy privileges not shared by other citizens. Open competition, however, is the normal method, departure from which has to be justified under the Public Service Acts.

One principle, the co-ordination of recruitment with the educational system, was lacking in Australia right up to the eve of the First World War. After a fairly slow start, secondary education achieved some momentum in those great years, the early 1910s, and the public service thereupon began "gathering the natural fruits of the educational system of the country in its various stages as they mature"([1]) by adopting the State educational examinations for entry to the clerical and administrative divisions. The Commonwealth has also begun to gather the fruits of the third stage, university education, by direct entry after graduation for administrative work.

The Australian public services are linked through the Victorian Acts of 1862 and 1883 to the United Kingdom Northcote-Trevelyan Report, to which they owe a great deal. The same forces were at work in both countries, but progress towards the modern public service was delayed by Australia's social immaturity and the slower impact of utilitarian social philosophy. Australian reformers, especially the invaluable and versatile Professor W. E. Hearn of Melbourne, helped to make up the leeway beginning as early as the 1850s.([2])

It was in Victoria, under Hearn's persistent but perhaps somewhat doctrinaire advocacy, that the main principles of modern public service recruitment and control were first established. The Victorian Public Service Act of 1883, consolidated in 1890, was passed when legislators had learned from experience that the sweets of patronage were as nothing to the wolfish appetites of their constituents for civil service posts. The aim of the Act was "to abolish all patronage" in appointments or promotions. The legislature created an independent Public Service Board and incorporated the principle of open competitive examinations for entry to the lower classes of the clerical and to the non-clerical divisions, to be reinforced by a qualifying examination for promotion from the lower to the higher classes of the clerical division. In practice, the Board was weakened by a clause reserving temporary appointments to Ministers (see Mr. Bourke's chapter). New South Wales followed in 1895, after an 1884 Act had been stultified by the absence of a full-time controlling board and by weak provisions for temporary employment.

The 1895 Act provided that separate competitive examinations should be held for entrance to the professional, clerical and educational, but not the general division. In its *First Annual Report*, 1896, the Board claimed that the Act "absolutely abolished" all patronage whether of the political heads of departments or of the higher officials. The 1895 Act was replaced by the consolidating Act of 1902, the basis of existing public service legislation in New South Wales.

When the new Commonwealth of Australia turned to study State legislation, it found the principles of open competition embodied in the legislation of most States. The Commonwealth Public Service Act of

---

([1]) United Kingdom, Royal Commission on the Civil Service, *Fourth Report,* 1914, p. 29.

([2]) Victoria. Royal Commission on the Civil Service, 1859, *Report.*

1902, modelled on the New South Wales and Victorian legislation, adopted the same principles, under (it is worth recording) Alfred Deakin's careful guidance. Section 67 of the Commonwealth Constitution had provided that until legislation should be passed to regulate the public service of the Commonwealth, all new appointments were to be made by the Governor-General in Council. This provision held from 1st January, 1901, to 31st December, 1902. The Commonwealth Public Service Act came into force on the 1st January, 1903, and its main provisions were subsequently carried over into the Public Service Act, 1922-1957, and still govern the Commonwealth service.[a]

Until 1912, even positions like labourer were to be filled under the examinations system, but as the principle of open competition took root, this kind of position could be safely exempted from the system. After 1922, temporary employment was placed more firmly in the hands of the Board, although during the Second World War, control was qualified by the need for speed. It has not yet been regained over the swollen temporary service.

The Commonwealth began with unified control; the States were less fortunate, for railways, water and other services were usually in separate hands. Then, especially in the nineteen twenties, when the public corporation was being hailed, perhaps prematurely, in Australia as in the United Kingdom, as the great twentieth century discovery in political science, new bodies began to be established outside the Commonwealth public service. Lately there has been some reaction against the independent staffing of these bodies. For example, in the Commonwealth, from about 1947, legislation setting up new authorities has either placed the staff under the Public Service Board or required the authorities to seek the approval of the Public Service Board to terms and conditions of employment. Authorities which need this approval are the Australian Wheat Board, Commonwealth Scientific and Industrial Research Organisation and Snowy Mountains Hydro-Electric Authority. The Board's control is over salaried officers, not wages staff, except in the Commonwealth Scientific and Industrial Research Organisation, where the control extends to temporary and casual employment. The Board has also accepted responsibility at the request of the Government for the conditions of employment of some commodity authorities responsible to the Minister for Primary Industry, such as the Australian Egg Board or Australian Wool Bureau. The aim is to achieve consistency in conditions of service so as to reduce variations in pay and in hours and conditions of employment in Commonwealth employment as a whole. A further responsibility of the Board is to decide how persons are to be selected as officers by the Snowy Mountains Hydro-Electric Authority, or as officers and employees by the Commonwealth Scientific and Industrial Research Organisation.

Whether unified or not, the Australian services are all in theory career services of the United Kingdom type. That is, young people are recruited

[a] An exception is the separate public service of the Australian Territory of Papua-New Guinea. The Ordinance makes provision for a Public Service Commissioner, but under the Papua and New Guinea Act, 1949, appointments are still in the hands of the Minister.

direct from the schools—and to a limited extent from the universities also—by educational examinations (not practical tests based on work and experience). The emphasis is not on prior achievement or technical abilities, but rather on education and intelligence. The only exceptions are in positions calling for special skill or some maturity, and these exceptions are limited and well scrutinised.

The system pre-supposes, and this is its second characteristic, a careful classifying of the service to create a number of career hierarchies, or classes of positions, or ladders, up which the more promising officers may move throughout their public career by promotion from the lowest post in each hierarchy. That is, a career service presupposes a vocation with prospects of regular advancement for the successful. So educational standards are related to the whole range of positions within each class and not only to the position of entry. This type of service stands in contrast to the traditional United States service made up of a collection of separate positions to be filled in accordance with acquired technical qualifications for each particular job.

The English had seen in open examinations the means of abolishing patronage and at the same time selecting the fittest. Open competition was regarded as a positive principle of achieving efficiency by attracting able officials. So the United Kingdom established its administrative class drawn from a developed university system, and was careful to co-ordinate entry to the lower posts with the other stages of the educational system. The double aim was an efficient service free from patronage. In Australia, the main emphasis was on abolishing patronage and preventing favouritism; people felt that efficiency would look after itself, once equality of opportunity was achieved, irrespective of the educational standards set. Some hoped that once political influence was removed, enough able men would become candidates without any firm steps being taken to attract them, and there was in any event faith in the law of averages producing good candidates from among large groups.

Attention turned slowly to positive standards and special competence. The examination system, a useful enough expedient for eliminating the personal factor in choice, was accepted with relief without much scrutiny of its power to improve standards of administration. It ensured broad equality of opportunity and guaranteed some standard of education and character. Fortunately, the system was open to improvement and could be put to better use as the civil service was called to greater tasks.

It may be asked whether the Australian public services have achieved the primary objective of abolishing patronage. The task is still with us, for in government as elsewhere no dangers are finally averted. The stakes are greater now owing to the increased scope and the greater ambitions of the modern state.

The active party member is naturally irked by any limitations on the power of his government. With the permanent service safeguarded by competitive examinations, he is now particularly sensitive to dismissals of temporary employees. He may be inspired by friendship or he may be anxious to avoid trouble for his party. Ministers, especially chief ministers, naturally show a greater sense of responsibility than the average private member. They know more and are helped by the warnings of public service commissions and permanent heads at their elbows. In one or two administrations, ministers, conscious of their heavy political responsibility for the administration of departments, may on occasion want to assume personal responsibility for the internal structure of their departments, and even, at times, for actual appointments or promotions, particularly to the higher offices of their departments. The general impression, however, is that interference has not been significant, except on occasion in a weak department, or at times over some forms of temporary employment. Although some cabinets may have imagined that they had the power to issue general directions to public service commissions, the principle of no patronage has held firm in essentials. This is so whether we are thinking of positive patronage over appointments or promotions, or negative patronage leading to the rejection of someone for appointment or promotion.

This chapter will be concerned largely with the recruitment problem in departments with staffs subject to the Public Service Acts. However, it has been indicated above there are now many public bodies outside the "public service" proper and these constitute more than two-thirds of public employment in Australia. Some of their problems are discussed in Chapter 4. Many now adopt similar recruitment methods to those of the general public service authorities, sometimes better methods. However, it is in this sector nowadays that political and personal influence on recruitment is most likely to make itself felt, as periodical criticism of the nature of appointments to some of the numerous statutory boards suggests.

EXAMINATIONS AND CLASSIFICATIONS

The examination system of the Commonwealth and States can only be broadly outlined here. It reflects the separation of the services into two broad categories, the Clerical—Administrative Divisions (including the special professional), and the rest. In the Commonwealth, these are called the Third and Fourth Divisions; advancement is by promotion within the Third Division and from it to higher administrative and professional posts in the Second and First Divisions, without further examination. The Fourth Division is separate, transfer upwards to the Third Division being by clerical examination. There are some differences in title and composition in New South Wales and the other States. For example, shorthandwriters and office assistants are included along with clerks in the Clerical Division, but these must pass clerical examinations before being transferred as Clerk. There is also a separate Professional Division in some States. The Educational Division, which in New South Wales comprises forty per cent. of the public service, is under control of the Public Service Board in that State, as in Queensland.

The divisions are subdivided into several career groups, each with its own career ladder or pyramid, resting on examination qualifications. For example, in the Commonwealth Fourth Division, the industrial or technical and the sub-clerical (office routine) positions form distinct groups, as do the clerical or administrative posts and the established professional positions in the Third Division. Again, the groups may be further divided, e.g., clerical assistants and typists are sub-groups of the sub-clerical group. There is thus a tendency away from a linear recruitment and promotional structure towards comparatively distinct careers for groups and sub-groups with different educational qualifications (either possessed on recruitment or subsequently obtained) ; entry or advancement being limited to the group or sub-group until further examinations are passed.

Recruitment, however, remains fairly general and career lines are not highly specialised. None of the Australian services has introduced the specialised career ladders of the United States of America, with fragmented lines of promotion based on limited experience. The only exceptions are industrial posts and some established professional posts in all services. Each group, or sub-group, for example typists, is usually recruited separately from both inside and outside the service, but sometimes officers advance from one sub-group to another by promotion.

Examinations are generally educational examinations controlled by the Commonwealth and State Boards, usually for appointment to the particular service as a whole, not to any one department. The Boards usually allot the successful candidates according to the needs of departments, paying regard (some think not enough) to the desires and ability of the new officer. Appointments are nearly always made to the first salary range of the lowest class of each division or group within a division. Examinations are held yearly, or more often, for each type of position, open to all British subjects of the prescribed age. The upper age limit has been low, usually under 21 for clerical work, but in the Commonwealth and New South Wales, where special efforts have been made since the war to encourage the recruitment of adults with some experience, age limits have been higher.

HISTORY OF RECRUITMENT SINCE 1900

The history of recruitment is of current importance for it has affected the present size, composition and quality of the services. As space is limited, the emphasis will be on recruiting for clerical and administrative work.

For the first appointment examination in April, 1903, the Commonwealth followed the system operating in New South Wales and the other States. It is not possible now to identify the standard, for it was a special service examination, often held in the middle of the school year, and consequently not linked to any definite stage of the school curriculum. The Commonwealth examination was Australia-wide ; State examinations were confined to each State.

Fourth Division officers could apply in competition with outsiders, but in the Commonwealth from 1909 on, separate examinations were usually held for insiders and outsiders. At first, only officers of two years standing were eligible to sit, but later this time limit was abolished. With time, the standard, too, was somewhat relaxed for officers. The Postmaster-General's Department has recruited most of its higher administrative officers from the internal examination ; other departments recruit mainly from the external examination.

In the earlier years, the Commonwealth held its own in competition for recruits with other employers and recruited many good people from all types of schools, private and public. The needs of departments were quite small in the 1900s ; for example, the Commonwealth recruited 10 at the start from both examinations in the larger States, the numbers rising to 50 or so as the First World War approached. The States needed more recruits than the Commonwealth and New South Wales, for example, from time to time found it hard to obtain junior recruits. Owing to adverse economic conditions, no entrance examinations were held in 1904 or 1905, and special classes, formerly held for the service examination in schools, languished. The lag in recruitment continuing, recourse was had to the recruiting of temporary employees. Then in 1912, the Board devised, but without much success, a second type of examination for ages 21-30 years. Through powers conferred on the New South Wales Board in the 1895 Act and the amending Acts of 1910 and 1915, many of the temporary employees were made permanent without examination. (In 1918, the Board also extended to temporary employees the right to compete at grade examinations, referred to in the next paragraph). By 1924, however, the Board was able to report with relief that the number of temporary clerks had decreased and that the call for "the passing of Acts such as Public Service (Temporary Officers) Acts of 1910 and 1915 is not likely to recur".

After appointment, recruits in the Commonwealth as in the States, before attaining the adult salary, had to pass a simple advancement examination (in some States there were a series of examinations) in subjects related to their work like précis and letter-writing, and departmental legislation, along with practical questions about the work of the various branches. This examination came to an end in the Commonwealth in 1911 when the Government decided that every adult should get the adult salary, but the examination continues in the States. In New South Wales, the service was divided into a higher and a lower series of grades in the clerical and professional division with limits fixed by the Public Service Act. Then in 1935, the Act was amended to introduce a higher grade barrier. Grade examinations were prescribed, the first to advance beyond the 6th year, the second beyond the 10th year rate, and the third from the lower to the higher grades. A university degree entitles the officer to exemption from this "Higher Grades" examination.

After some uncertainty, it became settled policy in the Commonwealth from 1914 to exclude girls from the examinations, but they were admitted again in 1949. From 1915, competitive examinations were held in New South Wales for the appointment of girls as junior clerks (New South Wales held an entrance examination for women as early as 1899). Boys, however, are preferred there as in other States, partly to obtain greater stability of staffing and partly because of prejudice.

As secondary education developed, the States turned to tap the State educational examinations, at first the Intermediate, but later the Leaving examination as well. The first use of the Leaving Certificate was made by New South Wales in 1913 and by Victoria in 1921. The Commonwealth was thinking of adopting the same examination, but there was thought to be the difficulty that State educational standards varied, while examinations were required by the Commonwealth in each State at broadly the same standard.

The 1914 War interrupted planning. Caught unprepared, the Commonwealth, as the government responsible for the direction of the war, suffered severely in recruitment as in other fields of policy. In 1915, the Commonwealth Government decided to suspend, while the war lasted, appointment examinations for male persons of military age. The Public Service Act was amended to grant preference to "returned soldiers" (that is, those who served abroad) among successful candidates at examinations, and also to raise the maximum age limit to 25. The Act was further amended in 1917 to provide a form of preference for returned soldiers which by interpretation became, mainly through government influence, exclusive and absolute, even over junior recruits. Returned soldiers who passed the examination for appointment were given priority over all other candidates at the same examination, irrespective of the order of merit. Second, the Act provided for appointment on evidence of educational qualifications, usually the Junior or Intermediate, without any further examination. Third, and most important, the Board was empowered to confine candidature to returned soldiers, who, upon passing, retained their eligibility for appointment until the age of 50 years.

In New South Wales, the Government suspended permanent appointments for youths from January, 1917, to early in 1919. In the meantime, candidates qualifying by examination were employed temporarily. In the Commonwealth some examinations were held with an age limit of 25, open to servicemen and others, while in 1917, 1918 and 1919 the Intermediate or Junior examinations were adopted for recruiting in New South Wales and Queensland. From 1918-1922 the Commonwealth examinations were confined to ex-servicemen whether from inside or outside the Service. The standard was broadly the Intermediate or somewhat lower.

The recruiting of juniors then stopped in the Commonwealth. In the 16th Report, 1921, the Acting Commissioner lamented a principle "which will prevent the addition to the Service of a percentage of youths adaptable to training, whose presence is a necessity for the future well-being of the Service". The Service should, he thought, be "enriched by recruits possessing a good standard of education and of an age rendering them particularly suitable for training".[4] Undeterred, Parliament embodied the Government's existing preference provisions in the new Commonwealth Public Service Act of 1922. Guided or influenced by the government, the new Board of three Commissioners allowed regular junior recruitment to remain in abeyance but in its Second Report had misgivings about "the complete exclusion from appointment of youths about to enter on their career in life". No special examinations were held by the Board after 1922, exservicemen qualifying through the Intermediate Certificate.

The only break in the policy of excluding youths came when, on the transfer of departments in 1928, posts could not be filled in Canberra. Examinations were accordingly resumed for appointment as clerk for Canberra only. Later in 1929, in its Sixth Report, the Board felt that as the number of qualified returned soldiers had been reduced it could resume examinations at Intermediate standard, and also prepare to appoint a few graduates (see next section on graduate appointment). This tentative new start lapsed, however, as the economic depression deepened.

The effect of the suspension of normal recruitment for eighteen of the thirty years of the Commonwealth Service (1915-1933) was shown by the Board early in 1933. After a series of parliamentary questions by an Opposition member in this year, it prepared a case for the government in support of proposals to resume normal recruitment of juniors. From 1903 to 1918, it pointed out, 1,364 youths had been appointed from outside the

Service and 1,199 transferred from the Fourth Division, a total of 2,563. (These were mainly appointed before 1915.) Over the next fourteen years, 1918-1932, in the words of the Board, there was "an almost total exclusion from the Third Division of that select class of educated youth which in previous years formed the major source of recruitment". From 1918-1932, youthful recruits from outside the Service had dropped to 49 ; transfers from the Fourth Division produced 699 (including returned soldiers from the service) ; while 1,031 returned soldiers had been appointed from outside the Service, a total of 1,779.

The Board pointed to the amendment of the Public Service Act of 1917 as the primary cause of the drop in the entry of youths. A secondary cause from 1929-1933 was the falling off in departmental activities during the economic depression. The depression had reduced the demand for staff by the re-organisation and amalgamation of sections. The economic upset had been a calamity for the Board, which had hoped "the position would normally have adjusted itself before a more serious situation had developed". Besides, the intake from appointment and transfer examinations alike had been almost entirely of adults and older people. In central departments in 1916, there were 1,385 officers ; the average age was 31 years and slightly more than half were under 30. In 1932, the number of officers in the central departments had increased to 2,049 ; the average age had jumped to 41 and only 1/20 or 105 officers were under 30 years of age.

Youths, barred from service in the Commonwealth, flocked into the State services. In 1926, the New South Wales Board reported "great improvement in junior recruitment", a position sustained until entrance examinations were suspended in the depression year of 1930. Again, as the Commonwealth Board pointed out in 1933, 110 youths had been admitted to the smaller service of Victoria in the past five years, as compared with 49 in the whole period of 14 years in the Commonwealth. The Board expected "the most prejudicial effect in probably from 5 to 15 years", that is from 1938-1948, when as senior positions became vacant, "the field for replacement must necessarily become limited and as a whole, inferior".

At this time, 1933, the Board proposed to re-open competitive examinations for youths from outside the service and also hold internal transfer examinations. It saw a chance of clearing the list of returned soldiers and of absorbing those who might freshly qualify. The government concurred in the Board's proposals but said that the standard of the examination should be the Leaving.

In that year 173 appointments were made, subject to returned soldier preference which remained absolute with concessional entrance at the Intermediate standard, except that juniors were at last admitted to examinations. In the next year, the Board abolished its own separate examinations for outside candidates and with the help of the universities or Education Departments adopted the Leaving as the annual examination. The transfer examination for Fourth Division officers, "the Service clerical", was retained ; some have questioned the need for this sub-Leaving examination now that the Leaving is available to all, but it has apparently taken root in the service. As the Board pointed out in its 12th Report, school candidates are thus enabled to pursue their studies for the Leaving Certificates in all States and, at the same time, qualify for appointment to the public service without interrupting their school courses. Thus the Board had co-ordinated its senior entry examination with the examination system for the reasons suggested by the U.K. Macdonnell Report in 1914. "The principal aim to be kept in view in recruiting the Civil Service (towards which examinations are a necessary though somewhat fallible means) is to obtain the best results of the regular educational system which is in actual operation . . . the most valuable elements in education are those formative influences which help to mould and develop character. Such influences form no part of a cramming institution, the main object of which is to surmount or evade the difficulties of an examination with the smallest expenditure of time and trouble."[5]

Examinations for appointment and transfer continued in the Commonwealth and States up to the early years of the Second World War. The States usually accepted both Intermediate and Leaving candidates while the Commonwealth sought its recruits at the Leaving standard. In these years, State and Commonwealth alike usually attracted more successful candidates than they appointed and many good officers were lost through lack of boldness and foresight, especially in 1937-39 when another war loomed.

In the Commonwealth, recruitment to the permanent staff was suspended during the middle and later years of the Second World War but was quickly resumed after the war and has continued to this day, subject to a new form of universal preference for ex-servicemen embodied in the Re-establishment and Employment Act, 1945. This Act applies equally to the whole community, to private as well as to public employment, and to States and Commonwealth alike, in practice and in law. It is thus much wider in scope than the preference of the 1914-18 War and consequently less onerous to the Commonwealth.

In 1949, the Commonwealth decided to open all its examinations, including those for clerical and administrative work, to women as well as men. In this, it was following belatedly the practice of modern public services overseas. In its earlier years, the Commonwealth had admitted women to the examinations and indeed some women clerks had been taken over from the State services, but from 1909-49, the Commonwealth, as mentioned above, had confined examinations, apart from examinations for assistants and typists, to males. Women must still retire from the permanent service on marriage and this rule clouds their prospects of promotion from the beginning.

Unfortunately, the state of full employment in the economy as a whole has combined with developments in the educational system, to reduce the number of young recruits to the services, Commonwealth and State, especially Leaving entrants. For example, in 1950, less than 3 per cent. of the clerical and administrative staff of the Commonwealth service were aged 19 years and under, as compared with 9 per cent. in 1939, itself a low figure.[6]

---

[5] United Kingdom Royal Commission in the Civil Service, *Fourth Report,* 1914, p. 35.
[6] In 1956, only 18 per cent. of the Third Division had entered on the results of the Leaving examination. Another 18 per cent. had taken the special clerical examinations for Fourth Division, temporaries, etc., 31 per cent. were ex-service, 27 per cent. had been exempted from examination for various reasons (e.g., professional and technical appointees from outside). See *Sample Survey of Third Division of Commonwealth Public Service,* 31st July, 1956 (mimeo).

The lag in recruitment has resulted in the use of new methods, such as better publicity and more discriminating selection, and some efforts have been made to raise the prestige of public employment by fostering a career system attractive to able men and women. Before the Second World War, recruitment procedure was usually confined to advertisements in the Commonwealth Gazette, supported by perfunctory notices to schools. The public services usually got the number they wanted and numbers were what counted. There is still some room for improvement in recruiting methods.

GRADUATE RECRUITMENT FOR ADMINISTRATION

While the public services accepted the Junior or Intermediate and the Leaving examinations, they were slow to co-ordinate entry with the next stage of the educational system, university graduation. University education in fact preceded State secondary education, though the masses participated more slowly. Yet only in the Commonwealth after much argument was the graduate able to enter the administrative service direct from the university. Some States were already recruiting university graduates for technical posts before the First World War, but no State service has yet made any special provision for graduates for clerical and administrative work, though New South Wales, Victoria, and other States grant liberal study leave (as does the Commonwealth) to allow their officers to graduate while in the service. New South Wales did consider graduate recruitment in 1911 when the Board prepared draft regulations for the government. The recommendations were deferred, however, until the Royal Commission of Enquiry reported. The Allard Report recommended that graduates should be admitted([7]) but nothing came of the proposal until it was revived from 1938-41 in the form of full-time study leave after entry.

The first move to force the door for the graduate came in 1925. In August of that year, Sir John Monash, Vice-Chancellor of the University of Melbourne and Chairman of the Standing Advisory Committee of Universities, submitted to the Commonwealth Public Service Board a resolution of the Committee "that it is highly desirable in the interests of the Commonwealth, as well as of the more capable youth of the different States, that for the higher positions in the Commonwealth Public Service a university education or its equivalent should be required". This went beyond a request to open the Commonwealth Service to graduates; it was a proposal for an administrative class confined to graduates. The Committee hopefully saw no hardship for juniors already in the service, as it would be open to them to obtain a university degree. The universities offered to co-operate with the Public Service Board to effect the new policy.

However, a specially trained administrative class on the English model has never become a serious issue in Australia. Apart from the influence of democratic sentiment and dogma, the early customs and traditions of the

---

([7]) *First Sectional Report,* 1918, p. lxii. "It is essential that provision shall be made for the admission of students who have graduated . . . in specified subjects suitable as training for a Public Service career . . . at a salary higher than that of candidates admitted on lower qualifications; and as soon as they demonstrate fitness and gain a knowledge of departmental duties, practice, and procedure, should reach a status in accordance with their higher qualifications."

public service were well-established before the Australian universities and public secondary education became national institutions. Four Australian universities were indeed founded in the nineteenth century: Sydney in 1850, Melbourne in 1953 (coeval with the first report on the Victorian Public Service), Adelaide in 1874, and Tasmania in 1890. Queensland and Western Australia followed in 1909 and 1912. However, it was not until Australian youths from all classes poured into the universities under the Commonwealth Reconstruction Training Scheme and the Universities Assistance Scheme from 1941 onwards that the universities became democratic communities. So it was perhaps natural that the Australian public services, should set about the gradual task of recruiting and training their administrative cadres in their own way. "The archetypal career in the public service would, in these circumstances, be one 'From telegraph messenger to Director-General', and despite many changes since these early days, the archetype has not been destroyed."[8]

The classical case for the administrative class is stated by the United Kingdom MacDonnell Commission. In administration, the Report points out: "the duties range from the simplest routine work to the highest intellectual effort with gradation in between . . . It is generally admitted that such difference in function must involve a corresponding difference of agency. The powers of those who are fitted to discharge the highest functions would be wasted if diverted to the simplest; the capacity best suited for the simplest duties would be inadequate for the more difficult. The fundamental principle, therefore, of the public service organisation should be division of labour. This principle has been laid down by every important Commission or Committee which has enquired into the subject, and we desire to reaffirm its soundness at the outset of our recommendations. With the lapse of time, the principle has become not less but if possible, more potent, because the importance of the Civil Service has increased in recent years in a manner which calls for special remark."[9]

Since (the argument is) modern administration demands, in addition to administrative experience a trained and educated mind, the administrative class should be composed of graduates selected by competitive examinations meant to single out some of the best products of the universities. They should be recruited straight from the universities and then given further training as cadets for their career. This corps, offering attractive career opportunities to highly trained individuals, will attract men (and women) who would not otherwise be likely to enter the public service.

Even the modified proposal that a more or less separate career group should be developed to staff the higher administrative posts, but recruited from inside as well as from outside the service, which corresponds to present British practice, has attracted little support in Australia. Professor F. A. Bland from time to time advocated in the press and in his other writings a similar compromise with democratic sentiment, as did R. S. Parker in his *Public Service Recruitment in Australia* (1942). Parker pressed for a clearly defined "administrative cadre" but had an open mind on the means of recruitment, with a certain emphasis on university education.

---

[8] S. Encel, "The Commonwealth Public Service and Outside Recruitment", *Pub. Admin. (Sydney)*, XIV, No. 1, March, 1955, p. 30.

[9] *Fourth Report*, 1914, p. 28.

Moulded by different traditions from those inspiring the United Kingdom, the Commonwealth service was not to be taken by storm by the Universities Committee in 1925. The Board could see little in the Committee's plea for graduate recruitment to the administrative division. From that year on it made a feature in its annual report of measures taken "in accord with a general policy of co-operation with universities and other education agencies", for the recruitment and training of public officers. In 1927, the Board told the Committee that it had appointed twelve university graduates from outside the service as engineers in the Postmaster-General's Department. The Committee showed interest but was not impressed; it had administrative positions in mind. (A technical cadet engineering scheme for the Post Office, entered from the Leaving and involving some university training, had already been launched by the Commonwealth in 1925. Some of the States had been earlier in the field with this form of recruitment, as is indicated in Chapter 16.)

In the next year, 1928, the Board established, with university co-operation, a free-place scheme to help officers undertake university courses. Pioneer officers studying under the scheme found the atmosphere of the service inimical at the beginning. The Board was also taking an interest in proposals to establish a Diploma of Public Administration at the universities. Next year, the Committee, now the Conference of Universities of Australia, in renewing representations to the Prime Minister, confined itself to a plea for the regular entry of graduates, but added that certain posts, including those which required training in economics and statistics, should be limited to graduates. (This second suggestion was widely adopted in the service after 1939, as we shall see, not so much as a recruitment but as a promotion measure.) The Board was fully alive, it said, to the desirability of securing the best qualified persons for appointment to positions of clerk in the Commonwealth Service—adding that recruitment might in future be by means of the Leaving and Intermediate examinations. The Board went on to say that when recruitment was resumed, it "would favourably review the reservation annually in each State, of a fixed number of positions of Clerk to be filled by university graduates".[20]

Later in the year, as part of its abortive endeavour to re-open junior recruitment, the Board actually invited applications from university graduates for appointment as clerk in the Commonwealth Public Service, but confined to Canberra, then starting on its career as the seat of government, and, as always in the future, short of recruits. Appointments were to be made at the commencing salary of £300 per annum and the entrants were to get credit in seniority for three years in the Third Division of the Service. Three appointments were to be made and the Board promised to consider calling for applications regularly each year.

In its 1929 report, the Board of the day explained its policy on graduate recruitment. "From time to time, the universities had advocated that the Commonwealth Service should offer careers in clerical positions to a restricted number of graduates in order to furnish a nucleus of officers in training for the higher executive and administrative posts. The Board has

[20] Earlier in the same year, the Report of the British Economic Mission had said "our enquiries lead us gravely to doubt whether the system followed in Australia sets out to attract the best available talent."

always appreciated the increased efficiency which would ultimately result.
. . . The strengthening of the service . . . would assist in building up a
reserve for filling the higher departmental positions, without interfering with
the advancement of officers within the service who may demonstrate their
fitness to undertake the high responsibilities of office."([11])

On taking over from the Bruce-Page Government in October 1929, the
Scullin Labour Government immediately interested itself in appointments
to the service. A short time before Labour came into power, examinations
for telegraph messengers had been replaced by a system of personal selection. This obscured the issue whether the recruiting of graduates represented
a departure from "the ideal of equal opportunity, free from all suspicion
of patronage, to all applicants for entrance to the Public Service of the
Australian democracy", as one influential member of the Labour Party
expressed it on departmental papers.([12]) Any idea of graduate recruitment
was put into cold storage.

There the matter rested until 1932 when another body, the Headmaster's
Conference of Australia, discussed graduate recruitment with Mr. Bruce,
then marking time as Assistant Treasurer in the new Lyons non-Labour
Government. The Public Service Board, while admitting its concern for
recruitment to executive and administrative offices, did not think the time
ripe "owing to the number of surplus officers to be placed and the returned
soldiers".

Then in August, 1932, the Universities Conference renewed its campaign
by submitting to the Commonwealth Government proposals for the annual
appointment of some graduates to the Second Division of the Commonwealth Public Service. The University Association of Canberra intervened,
seeing that the Conference, in insisting on appointments to the Second
Division, had got on the wrong track again. This Association was a small
influential body, the main aim of which was to develop a university in
Canberra, and meanwhile, to improve the standard of university education
at the Canberra University College. It was a knowledgeable body.([13])

In March, 1933, the Association wrote to Sir John Latham, Acting Prime
Minister and Attorney-General of the Commonwealth, as follows:—

"The Council of the University Association of Canberra respectfully
recommends to the Government of the Commonwealth that increased
opportunities should be afforded for the admission of graduates of
Australian Universities to the Commonwealth Public Service and that
the Commonwealth Public Service Act be amended by the addition
of a provision to the following effect:

"Whenever it is proposed to hold an entrance examination in connection with the Third Division, the Public Service may, notwithstand-

---

([11]) Public Service Board, *Report,* 1929, p. 21.

([12]) cf. W. K. Hancock, *Australia,* 1930, p. 120 of 1945 ed. "Democratic sentiment
applauds the sound argument that every office boy should have a chance to
become a manager, and perverts it into a practical rule that no one shall
shall become a manager who has not been an office boy."

([13]) Its Chairman at this time was the Solicitor-General of the Commonwealth,
Mr. (later Sir) George Knowles, and members included the former Solicitor-
General, and eminent public figure, Sir Robert Garran, and Mr. H. F. E.
Whitlam, who was to become Commonwealth Crown Solicitor.

ing anything contained in the Public Service Act, invite applications from persons who are graduates of an Australan University and may appoint any of such persons who are not more than twenty-five years of age, without examination, and if the Board thinks fit, without probation, and the number of persons to be appointed shall be, as nearly as practicable, ten per cent. of those appointed during the prescribed period of eligibility of those candidates who are successful at the entrance examination and are not officers of the Public Service.

"Any graduate so appointed shall be appointed at such commencing salary as is prescribed having regard to the age of the appointee and his qualifications."

The Public Service Board now expressed serious doubts whether the service needed graduates or could provide enough scope for their talents. It knew that the Public Service Clerical Association, in harmony with the then general sentiment of the service, had up to that time opposed the admission of graduates. In September, 1933, however, the Cabinet, after considering the views of the Board and of educational organisations, including the Canberra University Association, approved the principle of the admission of university graduates to the Commonwealth Service. It authorised an amendment to the Commonwealth Public Service Act, as proposed by the Association, but embodying important suggestions by the Board that the Act should limit the commencing salary to the maximum salary of the class to which successful candidates at the normal entrance examination may be appointed, i.e., the lowest clerical scale in the Service; and that the number of graduates admitted should not exceed 10 per cent. of normal clerical appointments in the year.[14]

The Labour Party opposed the bill; and the Public Service Clerical Association protested against the proposal, considering that except in certain professional and other special positions, university education should follow and not precede appointment to the service. The Association pointed out that there were already 600 persons in the Commonwealth Service who possessed academic and professional qualifications of various kinds, the majority of whom had secured their qualifications after appointment to the service. The Association considered that only the assurance of rapid promotion would induce a university graduate to enter and remain in the service. This view reflected the sentiment of the service and perhaps of the Australian people at this stage.

This graduate entry has commended itself to the service as a common sense way of co-ordinating recruiting with the third stage of the educational system. It has become part of the established routine, the more easily as it lessens the need for exceptional outside recruitment, while the graduate starts off on the same footing as clerks, though with a somewhat higher salary than the younger Leaving entrant has reached at the same age.

Twelve graduates were selected in the first year, the number varying from five to eleven in later years, until the scheme was suspended by the war in 1941. In the early years, the Board tended to place the graduates in head

---

[14] As embodied in sec. 36A of the Public Service Act, the ten per cent. is of positions to be filled, not actual appointments; so the Board can appoint more than 10 per cent of graduates if there are not enough candidates for all vacancies.

office positions. This was mainly in Canberra, on work in Departments such as External Affairs, the Bureau of Census and Statistics or Taxation (especially the legal section). Many turned to general administration, and when the scheme was revived after the Second World War the recruiting of graduates expanded eightfold, spreading through the service in each State, but with the graduates still finding their best chances in head office work.

Many good men are discouraged from entering a service when they must begin on the clerical ladder; some graduates have not come up to the mark; but in general they have taken their place in the service and proved valuable recruits. Already several permanent heads ([15]) and many Second Division officers have come from the graduate entrants, as distinct from other graduates who have entered the service from outside later in life, as indicated in the next section. Nearly all the pre-war graduates have risen to senior positions and the post-war entrants are now making their way in the service, along with those who have taken their degree after entering the service. These may be assisted by free places for part-time study, but on the whole they are not doing as well as the graduate entrants.

Now that more young men and women are going on to universities, it is inevitable that more public officials will be recruited in this way. This increase in graduate recruitment fits in well with the expansion of policy-forming and other higher administrative work of the central staffs in the Commonwealth service. With experience many departments are learning how to handle graduates; though they have something still to learn in this respect.

A related development is the growth in research positions for which university training is required. These research posts, which resemble positions of Assistant Principal in the United Kingdom service, in that the occupants help with higher administrative work, were pioneered by the Commonwealth Statistician just before the Second World War. They have multiplied since, until now most central departments have similar posts in their establishments, whether or not the word "research" is used in the title. The junior posts represent in some departments a kind of administrative cadetship to afford graduates training in the more difficult aspects of administration. It is an obvious means of adjusting the classification system of the service to the graduate method of recruitment under Australian conditions. Some see a natural tendency for the general run of graduates to join the rest of the service on executive and clerical work, while a minority will concentrate on administrative work proper.

Resembling these posts, but in the form of an administrative traineeship, was the External Affairs cadetship introduced when Dr. H. V. Evatt was Minister for External Affairs. From 1943, the cadetship was the main method of recruitment to the diplomatic branches of the Department of External Affairs. Before the Second World War, the Department had relied upon the direct intake of university graduates—nine officers had been so recruited between 1934 and 1939. This graduate recruitment was suspended

---

([15]) In other fields of government, there is some interest in observing that of 16 Ministers in 1939, 5 were graduates, as compared with 10 out of 20 in 1951. Among ordinary members of the Commonwealth Parliament the percentage of graduates rose from 10 per cent in 1939 to 18 per cent in 1951.

by the war, just when the needs of the Department were increasing with the opening of Australian diplomatic posts in Washington, Ottawa and Tokyo. In 1943 the Department, with the approval of the Public Service Board, decided to recruit batches of young men and women for training before advancement as third secretaries. Entry is now confined to graduates,[16] and the term "cadet" was dropped in 1955.

There are some who would like to see this type of scheme extended to other departments which require similarly trained officers. The argument is that higher administrative work in the present-day Commonwealth service calls as naturally for an administrative cadetship as the pre-war service demanded the introduction of graduate recruitment. On this view, an administrative cadetship is the only way now open to attract more of the best graduates to the service for training in the higher administrative work now confronting the Commonwealth service. Some of the departments, however, who have been able to attract and use the best Honours graduates, at least in Economics, are satisfied with the present graduate scheme.

SPECIAL RECRUITMENT FROM OUTSIDE THE SERVICE[17]

Even when modern public services have fully accepted the principle of competitive examinations, exceptional appointments from outside the service may be allowed on occasion to fill gaps. Properly, that is, sparingly, used, this method can raise the standard of the service at the margins; abused, it can reopen the door to patronage and "backdoor" entry. If made to higher posts, the outside appointments cut into the chances of promotion of those already in the service unless the appointees develop new work, as of course they often do. Too many exceptional appointments can endanger the morale of the service.

The positive and negative aspects of this form of entry were well illustrated at the birth of modern public service recruitment in Australia. "Although we believe that in the civil service as at present constituted," the Victorian Royal Commission reported a century ago, "there is sufficient talent efficiently to supply all vacancies that may for years occur, yet it is possible that cases may arise in which it will be desirable to place in some important office a person unconnected with the service. . . . The existing civil service have a right to preference but no monopoly. We are, therefore, of the opinion that notwithstanding the general rule of promotion, Your Excellency-in-Council should have power to deviate from that rule, and to make initial appointments from without. . . . But a statement of all such appointments and of the specific reasons which led to the departure from that rule, should, as soon as practicable, be laid before both Houses of Parliament. . . . The force of public opinion, even independently of Parliamentary control, will be sufficient to ensure only such a guarded use of the discretionary power as is consistent with the spirit of the entire system."[18]

So much for the theory. The 1862 Victorian Act allowed the appointment without examination of "persons of known ability". The opportunity for

---

[16] Originally these External Affairs recruits underwent a formal university course after entry, but now they attend individual courses as required.

[17] For a fuller discussion, see S. Encel, "The Commonwealth Public Service and Outside Recruitment", *Pub. Admin.* (*Sydney*), XIV, March, 1955.

[18] Victoria, Royal Commission in the Civil Service, 1859, *Report,* p. 13.

patronage was made use of so enthusiastically that by 1882 only 1,703 persons had been appointed to the service under competition as compared with 15,843 exceptional entrants. Things have been better ordered since. It is interesting to trace developments. The Victorian Act of 1862 had merely provided that wherever it is expedient to secure a person of known ability, and to place him immediately in the higher classes of the civil service, the Governor-in-Council may appoint such person although there may be in the lower classes of the service officers competent to perform the duties. The 1883 Victorian legislation was more cautious, providing that whenever there is no person qualified for an office in the First or Professional Divisions, the Governor-in Council may appoint some person outside the public service, but only if the Board certifies that he is qualified for the office. This provision was repeated in the 1890 Consolidated Act. The present Act provides for outside appointments in all divisions where there is no fit applicant in the division. In practice the Victorian Board does not make outside appointments to the higher administrative vacancies as it has always held that there are fit candidates already serving; but it does make some outside appointments to the higher classes of the Professional Division.

A similar provision to that of the 1883 Victorian Act was included in the 1884 New South Wales legislation, while the 1895 Act went further and provided that appointments to the special, professional or educational divisions should not be made unless the Board had reported whether there was any person in the service able and available to fill the post. The reports had to be laid before Parliament. This provision was repeated in section 36 of the 1902 New South Wales Act.

In South Australia, the rule until 1950 was that no appointment could be made from outside unless no-one already in the service was "as capable as" the outsider. This has been changed to the requirement that the appointee "has sufficient superiority of qualifications and aptitude for the position . . . to justify his appointment in preference to" a serving officer. The Public Service Commissioner has said that this may lead to "inbreeding and a decline in efficiency."[19]

Under the Commonwealth Act of 1902, appointments could be made to a vacancy in the administrative and professional divisions without examination if the Commissioner certified that there was no officer as capable of filling the position. The appointments were to be made by the Governor-General, on the recommendation of the Commissioner, upon a report from the Permanent Head. A copy of every recommendation, report and certificate was to be laid before Parliament within seven days. The provision was "largely used for the admission of specialist professional officers for whom the normal system of entry requiring an elementary education did not provide; but in those early days, as later, their marked superiority . . . had caused them to be transferred quite soon to purely administrative positions."[20]

In his Royal Commission Report in 1920, Mr. D. C. McLachlan, thinking that the service had benefited from the provision, recommended that it

---

[19] South Australia, Public Service Commissioner, *Report* dated 24 Dec., 1953, p. 6.

[20] Encel, *op. cit.*, p. 32.

should be continued for the Third Division, if the Government adopted the Commissioner's proposal to amalgamate the professional and clerical divisions, into a Third Division. This, he felt, would afford the government "a much wider field for the recruitment of the service by the appointment of persons with special and distinctive qualifications." The provision, he thought, should be used only in exceptional cases, and in no case where a vacancy could be adequately filled by an officer from within the service. The Act of 1922 followed this recommendation. (A similar, but simpler, provision is included for the Fourth Division.)

The provision in the Act (section 47) was clearly intended only to cover exceptional cases and is hedged round by the legislation with special safeguards to ensure great deliberation and adequate parliamentary control.[21] First, there has to be a "special case" where it is desirable in the public interest to appoint an outside person. Second, the Board must obtain a report from the Permanent Head, and then certify that in its opinion there is no officer available in the Commonwealth service who is as capable of filling the position as the person to be appointed. Third, a copy of every recommendation, report and certificate has to be laid before both Houses of Parliament. Moreover, the Board has established a special procedure to protect the claims of permanent officers. Under this, vacancies open to outsiders must be advertised in the Commonwealth Gazette (unless otherwise approved by the Board) as open to persons both in and out of the service. Applications are then examined by the department and if the Permanent Head favours the selection of a person from outside the service, a committee consisting of the Commonwealth Inspector and a representative of the department reviews the applications and sees all persons inside the service who, on the face of their applications, have the qualifications for the job. A joint report is forwarded to the Board through the Permanent Head, who bases his recommendation in it. The Board makes its decision on these reports.

There is a corresponding provision in the Commonwealth Act (section 44) providing for the appointment of officers from the State services, but without the special safeguards for parliamentary control. The State public services have been an important source of Commonwealth public servants ever since federation; and since the war accusations of pirating have been fairly common.

Appointments under section 47, and transfers from the States under section 44, have naturally been closely watched by the public service staff associations. These have a legitimate interest in the rights of their members and their vigilance is sustained by the sentiment of the service as a whole. Constant vigilance is indeed the price of freedom from patronage, but some feel that the associations have perhaps been a little undiscriminating in their opposition to some appointments under the section—in reaction perhaps to the tendency of some departments to use the sections freely in the early post-war years. Outside appointments have in fact never been uncommon in the Commonwealth service, and "during the period 1901-1939 less than half the senior officers originally appointed under provisions of the Public Service Act were recruited through the regular examination

---

[21] Appointment is to a particular position; but once appointed, promotion to any other vacant position is possible.

channels."([22]) The others came from outside, or from the States; often they were professional officers promoted to senior administrative positions, e.g., lawyers or engineers.

After the war, the expansion of the Commonwealth Service and the greater variety of administrative tasks, added to the deficiencies in pre-war recruitment, clearly called for some outside appointments. Both sections were used for the first three or four years after the war to strengthen the higher administration, chiefly with persons, mainly university trained, who had proved their ability in temporary employment during the war, and indeed developed much of the work in the Commonwealth on which they were to be used permanently. By 1953, 14 out of 29 members of the First Division were in fact drawn from outside appointees. The sections have been used more sparingly during the past few years for general administration. On the other hand, great use is still made of them to appoint technical and professional officers both in the Commonwealth and the States where, by general admission, the technical services would have broken down but for these appointments. In the service, as elsewhere, the post-war years have seen a great expansion in technical and scientific work and the traditional methods of recruitment to the service are still imperfectly adapted to the new work. More generally, it remains to be seen whether the quality of present entrants into the lower divisions is such that future reliance on outside recruitment can be small. Much will depend on making positions there attractive to a proportion of good university graduates.

Competition with the outside world for scientists and engineers has been keen since 1945. The demand has been met in three ways: (i) the development of traineeships and cadetships—see Mr. Derwent's chapter, (ii) the recruitment of graduates with experience outside the service, (iii) special recruitment overseas. In New South Wales, for example, vacancies for the Professional Division are advertised inter-state and overseas where necessary; and use has been made of the Commonwealth migration programme to try to attract engineers, architects, medical officers, survey draftsmen, and so on.

All this has been a response to practical needs, and not based on any settled theory, such as is advocated in some writings on public administration, that a door should be opened from time to time to a few men and women in their early thirties, carefully chosen after mature experience of other walks of life, so as to enliven, diversify and enrich the services. In fact, some of these persons have come into the Commonwealth service under sections 44 and 47 and as ex-servicemen, but not through any conscious adoption of the principle of mature-age recruitment. In general, fewer have entered the settled State services from outside, though some States have admitted mature recruits to clerical positions to compensate for lags in junior recruitment.

Under the Commonwealth Act of 1902, no special provision was made for selection for the highest departmental office of Permanent Head, apart from the general provision for promotion or appointment to the administrative division. As the Commissioner said in his Report in 1920, "As a

---

([22]) H. A. Scarrow, *The Higher Public Service of the Commonwealth of Australia*, 1957, p. 101.

general rule, vacancies which may occur in the Administrative Division are filled by the promotion of officers from within the service, although the law permits of appointments from outside on report to Parliament, should the circumstances justify such a course." The Commissioner recommended that provision should be made in any new Act that, in all appointments or promotions to the proposed new First Division, the Commissioner should submit a recommendation to the Governor-General, "seeing that the filling of the highest positions in the service should, above all others, be free from any suspicion of outside influence."[23]

The 1922 Act as passed by Parliament provides two things. First, all "appointments and promotions" in or to the First Division are to be made by the Governor-General on the recommendation of the Board—the First Division consists mainly of permanent heads. Second, notwithstanding this, "appointments" (not "appointments and promotions") to any position of permanent head may be made by the Governor-General without reference to the Board (section 54). In practice permanent heads are selected by Cabinet after reference to the Board, and normally from within the service.[24]

The procedure differs in the States. In New South Wales, the general rules. for the filling of senior vacancies (which provide for appointment by the Governor on the recommendation of the Board) and for the appointment of outsiders under section 36 apply. Victoria provides for reference to the Board and further prescribes that no appointments shall be made of an outsider as permanent head unless the Board reports that there is no officer in the Public Service fit to be appointed to the office.[25]

From time to time, there have been keen differences of opinion in some States between Government and Commission on the appointment of permanent heads before compromises have been reached on the filling of these critical offices.

CONTINUITY IN RECRUITMENT

The Commonwealth service, and to a lesser extent the States, have suffered severely in Australia's short history from economic and military disturbances, aggravated by mistakes of policy. Two wars and the economic depression have disrupted normal recruitment, and now the source of youthful recruits has failed in both the Commonwealth and the States to respond to increasing government responsibilities. The decline in recruits in the Commonwealth is to some extent a result of discontinuous recruitment, for parents lost the habit of looking to the Commonwealth service as a career for their children. The States and the Commonwealth have also found themselves in competition with each other for recruits. More general factors have been: depres-

---

[23] pp. 49-50.

[24] "The bearing which such appointments would have on the efficiency of the service is obvious . . . and the Government has approved the suggestion of the Board that it be given the opportunity of submitting its views before such appointments are made." Commonwealth Public Service Board, 24th Report, p. 6.

[25] In practice only the Director of Education has been appointed from outside the "public service", as defined in Victoria. He is appointed from the teaching service.

sion birth-rates; full employment, which has lessened the advantage in security of the public service; greater competition from industry and trade, where there have been expanding opportunities for the clerical-administrative worker, and there is less obligation to maintain salary systems based on consistency of rewards; and expanding facilities for further education. Many public authorities have been especially short of recruits in the professional fields, e.g. engineers, architects, agricultural and veterinary scientists, draftsmen.

It was noticed above how the Commonwealth Public Service Board in 1933 had fears for the future of the service. In its *Bulletin* for March-April, 1951, the present Board published an article on the unbalanced age structure of the Commonwealth service. This confirmed the worst fears of the Board. "The two top Divisions of the service contain less than 5 per cent of all permanent officers but they consist of good men, not easily replaced . . . only three of the twenty-eight First Division officers are under 52 years of age and only fifty-seven of the 306 Second Division officers are under 50."

The writer saw the most critical problem in the clerical and administrative group. "There is a small percentage, less than 3 per cent of the 1950 Clerical and Administrative staff, who are juniors 19 years of age and under. In 1939 over 9 per cent were in this group and this was far less than an ideal figure. Secondly, the graph shows the high concentration of officers in the 25-29 age groups, reflecting the influx of returned servicemen after the 1939-45 World War. The similar high concentration of the 1939 age structure around the 40-44 and 45-49 age groups which represents recruitment of ex-servicemen after the 1914-18 War, re-appears in the 50-54 age groups of the 1950 structure as a relatively smaller concentration in the larger total. Thirdly, there is a sharp drop in the 1950 distribution at the 40-44 and 45-49 age groups. This is a legacy of the non-recruitment of youth in the twenties."

The article points out that ideally the age distribution of a career service might taper evenly from a high percentage in the younger groups towards the small proportion of experienced men who will hold the few senior positions. "Experience is acquired not simply from length of service but by a progression towards greater responsibility which places capacity continuously under test. This progression will tend to be blocked when large numbers in older groups are in the path of promotion . . . wastage from retirement can be expected to be very high in the next few years in view of the high proportion of clerical and administrative officers in the 50-54 and 55-59 groups and of Second Division officers who are now over 50." The *Bulletin* expected strain to appear in higher administration from a lack of experience among those who will move up into the senior positions. "Thus . . . nearly 10 per cent of the present clerical and administrative staff, those aged 50-54, will be due to retire between 1960 and 1965, and the next most experienced group aged 45-49 is not in sufficient numbers to fill much more than half of their places. Promotion will be accelerated right through the 40-44 groups but here too the Service is short."

It is arguable that the age distribution of senior Commonwealth officials in 1951, troublesome as it appeared at the time, has in the outcome had some advantages. It has, for example, allowed time for the development of young men and their entry into higher positions.

Some steps have been taken since then to improve recruitment. A sample survey of the Third Division, as at 31st July, 1956([28]) showed 5 per cent aged 20 and under, and 40 per cent between 31-40. Seventy per cent of officers have been employed for ten years or less. The position as regards school-leavers could ease temporarily, during the next few years, as larger numbers will be coming on to the labour market. But the time is nevertheless due for a thorough review of recruitment practices in both Commonwealth and States, and it is to be hoped that the recently-appointed Commonwealth Committee on Recruitment is a first step in this direction.

([28]) See *Sample Survey of Third Division of the Commonwealth Public Service* (mimeo).

Chapter Twelve

CLASSIFICATION AND PROMOTION IN THE COMMONWEALTH PUBLIC SERVICE

HOWARD A. SCARROW

Many of the more significant changes in the Commonwealth Public Service since its creation in 1901 have centred on policies of classification and promotion. The legislative provisions and administrative practices relating to these policies have been of great concern to the staff and official side alike, and as a result the Service has acquired some of its most distinctive features. The following survey is intended to outline the evolution of the classification and promotion system and to suggest some of the problems which have arisen.

CLASSIFICATION

Like other Commonwealth countries, e.g. Canada and South Africa, the Federal Government in Australia has adopted a classification scheme under which each post is separately graded. Although the phraseology of the Public Service Act is rather ambiguous on this point, in practice it is the position—identified by a detailed statement of duties and an appropriate title—which is the object of classification, rather than the individual officer. The theory of position classification should not conceal the fact that often, particularly at the higher levels, an officer's merit can determine the classification of his position; and in the External Affairs Department the system actually operates in such a way as to give diplomatic officers a personal rank much the same as in the British or United States Foreign Service. Nevertheless, the entire administration of the Service is based on the assumption that the "position" is the basic unit of classification.

Divisional Classification

Each position in the Public Service is classified in two ways, by Division and by salary scale. The Public Service Act, 1902, separated the Service into four Divisions: Administrative, Professional, Clerical, and General. To be included in the first were all Permanent Heads and Chief Officers (the head departmental officers in each State), and also persons recommended by the Commissioner. The Professional Division was to comprise officers whose duties necessitated "some special skill or technical knowledge usually acquired only in some profession or occupation different from the ordinary routine of the Public Service". The composition of the Clerical and General Divisions was to be left to the discretion of the Commissioner.

The Public Service Act, 1922, introduced two significant changes in the divisional classification. The first was an amalgamation of the Professional and Clerical Divisions. In his Royal Commission *Report,* D. C. McLachlan stated that numerous anomalies had resulted from the distinction between

"Clerical" and "Professional". Officers were to be found in the Professional Division "whose duties could not even on the most liberal interpretation be considered as professional in character".([1]) They had been so classified in order to overcome the examination barrier or age restriction, in order that higher salaries might be paid, or because it was considered "injudicious" to classify them in the Administrative Division. Rather than recommend that the composition of the two Divisions be more closely regulated, McLachlan questioned the justification of distinguishing between them. The original purpose of the separation, he reasoned, had been that the conditions of entrance to the two Divisions had not been the same. The Act had prescribed separate entrance examinations to the Professional, Clerical, and General Divisions; and appointment without examination, under certain special circumstances, was allowed only to the Administrative and Professional offices. In the opinion of the former Commissioner conditions of entrance to both the Professional and the Clerical Division should be identical, viz., normally by competitive examination; and appointment without examination to positions requiring special skill and training should be allowed to both the Professional and the Clerical ranks.

The second departure from the original divisional classification scheme was the abandonment of descriptive nomenclature in favour of numerical designation; for McLachlan had argued that the old titles (Administrative, Clerical, Professional, and General) had given rise to "an irritating distinction of 'caste' ".([2])

In line with his recommendation, therefore, the Public Service Act, 1922, separated the Service into First, Second, Third, and Fourth Divisions. The First Division was to include "all Permanent Heads of Departments and such other officers as the Governor-General determines". The Second Division was to be composed of "officers who, under officers of the First Division, are required to exercise executive or professional functions in the more important offices of the Service". The composition of the Third and Fourth Divisions was to be left to the discretion of the Public Service Board. In fact, however, McLachlan's recommendation that the Third Division represent an amalgamation of most former Clerical and Professional Division officers was adopted; and the Fourth Division continued to cover the manual and manipulative grades (mostly in the Post Office).

Two points may be noted in connection with the altered system of divisional classification. The first is that the First Division is now far more exclusive than the former Administrative Division. Although it is evident from his Report, and also from the wording of the Act, that McLachlan had not anticipated this result, the policy of the newly formed Public Service Board was to confine the First Division almost exclusively to heads of Departments. Formerly, in addition to Permanent Heads, the Administrative Division had included the Deputy Postmasters-General and the Collectors of Customs in each State, the Commonwealth Statistician, the Chief Electoral Officer, and certain other senior officials.

Of greater significance is the fact that justification for divisional classification has now largely disappeared. Where formerly the Divisions were

([1]) Royal Commission Report, pp. 36-37.
([2]) Ibid.

of use in connection with recruitment methods, the abandonment of Professional and Clerical Divisions in favour of Second and Third Divisions substituted a classification based on the importance of the work for one which had been based on the nature of qualifications required. Thus with the exception of the barrier separating the Third and Fourth Divisions, recruitment methods and divisional classifications are no longer related. Within the range of positions embraced by the First, Second, and Third Divisions —including Permanent Heads at one end of the scale and base grade clerks on the other—competitive examinations are conducted solely for entrance to the latter, and non-examination appointment is allowed to each.

Apart, then, from separating the Fourth Division from the rest of the Service the present divisional classification serves little practical use. The First Division does little more than reinforce the exclusiveness of officers already singled out by their designation "Secretary" or "Permanent Head". Second Division status can denote positions ranging from the Deputy Secretary of the Treasury, to a Medical Officer in the Health Department, or a relatively junior departmental representative stationed in Hobart; and the salary classifications of officers in the Third Division—even non-professional officers—are sometimes higher than those in the Second Division. Indeed, a single schedule of salary scales applies to both Second and Third Division officers. All that can be said, therefore, is that the First, Second, and Third Divisions provide a convenient designation for officers in rather broad and overlapping salary and occupational groups. And although these Divisions are usually said to equate roughly with the British Administrative, Executive, and Clerical Classes, they form a single pyramid, rather than three separate ones. The absence of qualification barrier, combined with the emphasis on filling higher positions by promotion from below, render them useless as recruitment and promotion aids.

By June, 1956, the permanent officers of the Service were classified as follows: ([a])

First Division	..	..	..	..	30
Second Division	..	..	..	..	331
Third Division	.	..	..	..	28,857
Fourth Division	..	..	..	..	56,042
Total	..	..	..	..	85,260

Classification Within Divisions

Under provisions of the Public Service Act, 1902, classification within Divisions was based upon numerical or alphabetical designation. The Clerical Division, for example, was divided into five classes (a "Special" Class was added in 1911), and the Schedule of the Act prescribed the minimum and maximum salary as well as the amount of annual increment appropriate to each. It was a workable arrangement, distinguished by its clarity and simplicity.

([a]) Public Service Board, *Thirty-second Report*, 1955-56, p. 31. There were also 18,922 temporary employees and 49,418 "exempt" employees.

As the service grew larger and more complex, McLachlan became increasingly dissatisfied with this feature of the Public Service Act. The number of classes were insufficient and the salary scales too rigid. In his report, consequently, the former Commissioner recommended an increase in the number of classes, smaller salary ranges for each, and automatic annual increments—a system intended to reflect more carefully the worth of each position and to relieve the heavy burden on administrative officers in granting discretionary increments.

In general, the new Public Service Board accepted the principle underlying these recommendations, and the new legislation opened the way for a reclassification of the Service. Nevertheless, the Board departed from McLachlan's proposals in one important particular. Rather than adhere to the former system of numerically designated classes, it abandoned class designation completely and simply classified each position by salary scale.[4] Moreover, it was the policy of the Board to draw extremely minute distinctions between the value of positions, to classify each individual position as an independent unit, and to eliminate classes of positions altogether. When it commenced its reclassification of the Service, the Board attempted to extend the principle of minute evaluation to its ultimate limit. Later, however, it modified its policy, and from all the dismembered units of individual classification there emerged a relatively fixed number of standard salary scales, most of them covering a five-year span. [5] The determinations by the Public Service Arbitrator appear to have been largely responsible for this retreat, since the original scheme rested on a precarious positional relativity easily upset by a single award.[6].

There remain, however, several problems associated with the present method of classification. The first results from the large number of short and overlapping salary ranges. Because of the limited opportunity offered in a particular position, officers are constantly striving to seek promotion to a new position classified with a higher—although sometimes almost insignificantly higher—maximum salary. The weekly Commonwealth *Gazette,* which contains notifications of vacancies, is zealously scanned by officers searching for promotion opportunities. The time consumed in applying and, if unsuccessful, in appealing, results in frequent disruption of work. The successful applicant, moreover, sometimes spends only a few months in the new position before being promoted to yet another. Thus the rate of turnover assumes significant proportions, and what little experience the officer can gain in a particular line of work is soon lost. The system also results

---

[4] Thus the "Fifth Class Clerk" under the 1902 Act became "Clerk £90-324."

[5] The number of salary scales has recently totalled about thirty for the Second and Third Divisions. This number is not exhaustive, however, for certain positions are classified at salary ranges not represented in the standard list.

[6] In its 1929 *Report* (pp. 5-6) the Board complained: "Unfortunately much of the work performed in the classification has been rendered nugatory by determinations made during the past year under the Arbitration (Public Service) Act . . . . The scheme of classification, laboriously brought to completion by the Board after some years of patient research and inquiry, has been varied by the Court in important details with further increased cost to the Commonwealth and with a disturbance of previous relativity of officers which must affect the stability and contentment of the Service."

in situations in which a valuable officer can virtually blackmail the head of his Department into recommending reclassification of his position in order to prevent his seeking promotion in another section of the Service. Finally, from the administrative side, the work and expense involved in the constant movement of staff results in overburdening the Board and departmental administrative officers with a maze of detailed tasks. Most of these objections were admitted by the Board in its 1947 *Report*. In reply, however, the Board stressed that "stagnation" must be avoided and that capable officers should quickly be able to adapt themselves to various types of positions.([7])

A second difficulty resulting from classification by salary scale is also apparent. Originally it was intended that the worth of each position was to be expressed in meaningful terms of monetary units. In periods of currency instability, however, it becomes impossible to maintain the correlation. During the depression of the 'thirties, when all Public Service salaries were reduced under the terms of the Financial Emergency Act, the prescribed salary scales lost their significance and became mere descriptive designations. More recently, as Australia has experienced a violent inflationary spiral and all salaries have been increased with each rise in the basic wage, the amount of actual salary paid to an officer has become considerably more than that indicated by the salary range attached to his position. Margins awarded by the Public Service Arbitrator have further increased the discrepancy. By 1951 the relationship had become so completely distorted that special legislation was enacted which attempted to bring the "standard" into line with the "actual". The major purpose was to present the Public Service to potential recruits in more favourable terms. Yet even after 1951 there were significant rises in actual salaries, so that by 1955 another salaries adjustment act was necessary to raise again the standard salary labels.

The third problem associated with the present classification scheme is that the system, as it has evolved, necessitates continuous review by the Public Service Board so that proper and consistent relationships between positions may be maintained. Some review is always necessary; but the present scheme makes it a more complicated and frequent affair. Since 1945 a portion of this task has been assumed by Classification Committees constituted under legislation enacted in that year.([8]) Established at the request of the public service associations, these committees are composed of one representative of the Public Service Board (who acts as chairman), one from the department concerned, and one from the appropriate staff association. They conduct classification reviews in selected areas referred to them for advice and make recommendations to the Board. The Board has not been relieved of its primary responsibility for classification, however, and it is continually being solicited by Departments to grant higher classifications to positions in their establishments. Just as individual officers scan the

---

([7]) Public Service Board, *Twenty-third Report*, 1947, p. 10. Accelerated promotions have been partly caused by the shortage of officers in the post-war service. In conditions of stability, this movement would be much less.

([8]) These committees made their contribution during the period 1945-50 when practically every Department underwent a complete reclassification. Their use is now more limited. In effect, the committees take the arbitration process one step backward by getting the employee associations to approve classifications before they are formally registered.

Gazette for possible promotion opportunities, so the Permanent Heads or administrative officers watch for reclassifications, which are notified in the same publication. Any alleged discrimination against their Department is usually met by appeals to the Board. A flow of correspondence or series of discussions with the Public Service Inspector then ensues, all with the object of determining which position or type of position is of greater value. The weakness of the system is most sharply revealed when Departments request reclassification of positions for the sole, yet very legitimate, reason that the occupant has proved himself to be of greater worth than is allowed by his salary classification. Usually the request is couched in terms of increased responsibility which has accrued to the position, but the real reason is often that the one occupant imparts to the position an importance which it would not possess when filled by another officer. The system allows of no redress short of a complete position reclassification with all the consequent administrative work involved. Finally, it has been observed that at the higher levels the differentiated salary ranges foster "an unnecessarily and dangerously competitive element in some officers' approach to policy problems".[9]

McLachlan had foreseen some of these difficulties and had recommended that provision be made for officers occupying certain positions "to advance through two or even three classes irrespective of the occurrence of vacancies and without formal reclassification of office".[10] Since the war the Board has partially adopted this principle by attaching to some positions, especially those at the more senior levels, relatively broad salary scales. On the whole, however, the system remains a rigid one. The Board's attempt at a simplified scheme for the Second and Third Divisions, which was introduced with the revision of margins following the Metal Trades decision,[11] was lost in the following decisions of the Court and the Arbitrator, which related margins to the salary scales previously existing. This may remind us that the arbitration system is another hindrance to simplicity, which makes it harder to effect the needed classification of all positions to a defined simplified plan, with a prime concern the efficiency of the service.

PROMOTION

Because Australia has followed neither the British model of an Administrative Class nor the United States example of direct appointment from outside the service, the quality of its higher public service is determined to a large extent by the policies adopted in bringing through the ranks the officer who begins his career in a subordinate position. Thus in Australia the machinery governing promotion performs a role no less important than that regulating initial recruitment. It is not insignificant that the sole major inquiry into the Commonwealth Public Service since 1919—and the only major inquiry which has resulted in a thorough investigation by a repre-

---

[9] Canberra Research Group, "Commonwealth Policy Co-ordination," *Pub. Admin. (Sydney)*, XIV, Dec., 1955, p. 208.

[10] *Report*, p. 43.

[11] See Commonwealth Public Service Board, 31*st Report*, 1954-55, pp. 18-19, and 32*nd Report*, 1955-56, pp. 24, 26.

sentative group of interests—was the Bailey Committee investigation of 1944 into "Systems of Promotion and Temporary Transfers".([12])

Methods of Promotion

Methods of promotion may be classified broadly into three major categories: (*a*) promotion by competitive or qualifying examinations; (*b*) promotion from a list of eligibles restricted to officers possessing particular qualifications; and (*c*) promotion determined solely by the personal discretion of the promoting authority.

(*a*) In the Commonwealth Service promotion examinations are held only for Fourth Division positions.([13]) During the operation of the 1902 Act nine examinations were held for Clerical Division officers to qualify for advancement beyond a certain salary figure within the Fifth Class clerical grade. The main object of the examinations was to achieve some measure of uniformity in the qualifications of officers who had been taken over from State public services. By 1910, however, the practice had ceased, and no attempt has been made since to examine Third Division officers for their capacity for advancement. In the opinion of the Bailey Committee, under the present classification scheme, and indeed "under any circumstances," examinations "could have only a limited place in determining fitness for promotion".([14]) The Committee, therefore, did not recommend their wider use.

(*b*) The 1922 Act empowered the Board to erect qualification barriers and prescribe conditions of minimum and maximum salary for selected positions. The qualification barriers governing promotion or transfer have been applied mostly to positions requiring scientific or technical qualifications, such as those of architect, engineer, medical officer, geologist, etc. Among positions requiring training of a more liberal character the following may be mentioned: Audit Inspector, Grade 1; Education Officer, Grade 1; Vocational Guidance Officer, Grades 1 and 2; and Research Officer, Grade 1. An officer cannot be promoted or transferred to one of these positions unless he possesses the required qualifications.

Determinations governing commencing salary and conditions of salary advancement *within* certain positions have been made by both the Board and the Public Service Arbitrator. Although these too relate mostly to technical positions, they embrace on the non-technical side positions of Assistant Research Officer and External Affairs Officer, Grade 1. The conditions governing these positions specify a fixed minimum salary which shall be paid if the occupant possesses certain qualifications and make that salary the maximum which shall be paid to the unqualified officer. Other determinations, such as those applying to various grades of taxation officers, lack the minimum salary clause and simply erect a salary barrier.

([12]) *Report,* Committee of Inquiry into Systems of Promotion and Temporary Transfers, 1945. The Committee was composed of representatives of the Public Service Board, employee associations, and certain Departments. Its chairman was Professor K. H. Bailey, then Professor of Public Law at Melbourne University.

([13]) Apart from a few minor Third Division positions in certain Departments.

([14]) *Report,* p. 12.

(c) With the exception of these positions which have been singled out by the Board, selection for promotion to any position in the Third or Second Division is determined solely at the discretion of the promoting authority.([15]) The basis upon which selection is to be made, as spelled out in both the 1902 and 1922 Public Service Acts, is "relative efficiency" or, in the case of equal efficiency, "relative seniority". To date the only challenge which has threatened the principle of promotion on merit was the legislation enacted in 1945 which, on the recommendation of the Bailey Committee, provided for the promotion to certain minor manipulative positions in the Fourth Division of the most senior efficient officer.

The Public Service Act defines efficiency as meaning "special qualifications and aptitude for the discharge of the duties of the office to be filled, together with merit, diligence and good conduct". The Bailey Committee devoted considerable attention to the wording of this section, recognising the criticisms which had been raised by the officers, on the one hand, and Permanent Heads, on the other. From the viewpoint of applicants for vacancies, it was contended that the Act discriminated against the officer who had demonstrated high efficiency and general capacity yet who, in relation to competing applicants, could claim little or no experience with the type of work to be performed in the vacant office. The Committee, however, was of the opinion that the instruction memorandum defining efficiency which had been issued by the Public Service Board was sufficiently comprehensive in discounting experience as opposed to general capacity and aptitude.([16]) Moreover, it refused to attempt to define by law a precise formula for determining efficiency.

In contrast, the Committee did recognize the need for a modification of the Act as applied to the duties of a Permanent Head in selecting officers for promotion to the higher executive posts in his Department. In these cases, the Committee reasoned, "the promoting authority ought to be able to make the selection with some regard for future contingencies as well as for immediate requirements." The Committee recommended, therefore, that the Permanent Heads in making promotions "within a defined limited range of more senior posts" be allowed "and indeed required" to take into account qualifications of the applicant in relation to prospective vacancies in higher posts within the Department.([17]) Although legislation enacted in 1945 granted to the Board the power thus recommended, no action has yet been taken in defining the "range of more senior posts".

([15]) The practice of selecting officers for promotion on the results of periodic rating reports has been adopted only in certain sections of the Postmaster-General's Department and in one or two other Departments. The Bailey Committee, although recognizing the wide use of rating reports in public services throughout the world, was impressed by "the volume and severity of the criticism levelled against the system" and thus did not feel justified in recommending its general introduction. The Committee stressed, however, that its negative conclusion was to be regarded as tentative. See *Report of Committee of Inquiry*, p. 14; and below pp. 454-5.

([16]) An extract from the Board's memorandum is reprinted in the Committee's *Report*, pp. 9-10.

([17]) *Report*, p. 11.

Promoting Authority

One of the most significant innovations resulting from the recommendations of the McLachlan *Report* was the transfer from the central personnel authority to the Permanent Heads of the power over promotions. Under the legislation which had been in effect since 1902, the Public Service Commissioner, after a report from the Permanent Head, had recommended to the Governor-General the officer to be promoted. Under this system, McLachlan stated, excessive delays had occurred in filling vacant positions, and expense and inconvenience to Departments had resulted. Moreover, the time of the Public Service Inspectors had been largely absorbed in dealing with promotions and transfer, thus militating against their usefulness in other directions. In McLachlan's opinion, the heads of Departments had come to acquire a clear conception of the principles which would govern the promotion of officers and therefore, subject to certain safeguards, should be entrusted with the promotion power.([18])

The far-reaching implications of the McLachlan recommendation were recognized by Parliament, and consequently a large proportion of the debate over the Public Service Act of 1922 centered around its incorporation in the draft legislation. The House of Representatives proved particularly adamant in its objection and was able to force an amendment which returned to the Public Service Board authority over promotion and transfer. It was not until 1924 that the McLachlan recommendation was enacted into law.

Final responsibility for promotion, however, was not entrusted to the Permanent Heads. All promotions were to be provisional and subject to appeal to the Board. Under provisions of the 1902 Act an officer could make similar appeals to the Commissioner, but since the Commissioner himself, through the Governor-General, was the promoting authority and since promotions when published in the *Gazette* were final, not provisional, this safeguard seems to have amounted to very little. With the passage of the 1924 amendment the review power of the Board acquired added importance not only as a result of the new authority given to the Permanent Heads, but also from the practice of the newly constituted Board of gazetting all provisional promotions.

The Bailey Committee considered the question of whether Permanent Heads should assume final and complete responsibility for all promotions. It acknowledged and considered the arguments advanced for complete departmental control, but concluded that the drawbacks which would result from any change in the existing system would far outweigh any advantages which might be gained. The Committee observed that to insist on departmental autonomy would cut directly across that section of the Public Service Act (section 17) which imposes on the Board responsibility for exercising critical oversight of departmental activities, methods, and utilization of staff. Moreover, in the opinion of the Committee, inter-departmental promotions implied the existence of an outside promotion authority, "at any rate at the reviewing stage", which can impartially determine the claims of officers throughout the Service. Finally, it was recognized that "strong staff dissatisfaction" would result from any attempt to abolish centralized

([18]) *Report*, p. 26.

review of provisional promotions. For these reasons the Committee strongly recommended the retention of the system of divided control.([19])

Investigation by the Committee, however, revealed that although most Permanent Heads were satisfied with the working of the appeal machinery, a few, together with a large majority of the staff associations, were not. The associations alleged that the Public Service Inspectors investigating an appeal could easily allow their decision to be influenced by a hesitancy to challenge the judgment of an officer of higher official status, and in order to preserve harmony between the Board and the Department concerned would be prone to support the Department's decision. It was stressed that inquiry into an appeal was one which should be settled through quasi-judicial inquiry by a board or committee.

As a result of these representations the Bailey Committee recommended that the claims of appellants be heard before a three-man committee made up of one representative of the Department, one from the appropriate staff association, and one—the chairman—appointed by the Public Service Board, but not subject to direction by any person or authority under the Act. In cases where all appellants were located within a single State and the salary of the position did not exceed a certain level the decision of the committee was to be final. In other cases, the committee was to make a recommendation to the Board which would have final authority.([20])

These recommendations were incorporated into legislation enacted in 1945, and promotion appeals committees were subsequently established in each State and in Canberra. The legislation marked one of the most fundamental innovations in Commonwealth Public Service administration since 1922. Combined with the present system of classification, the new machinery offers wide opportunity to those who would improve their rank. As already suggested, however, the costs in terms of unproductive man hours and organizational instability run high.([21])

Australia has long been looked upon by the outside world as a trail blazer in social and political experiment. Innovations in the realm of public administration form a significant part of this total picture, as the Public Service Arbitration Act of 1911 clearly illustrates. The promotion appeal system appears to have added another chapter to this tradition.

([19]) *Report of Committee of Inquiry,* p. 19.

([20]) This provision was inserted to prevent injustices from arising from varying standards of judgment adopted by committees in different States, and to prevent difficulties in cases where the officers involved were of higher status than those on the committee. In fact, however, the committee's decision is nearly always final, where only one State is involved.

([21]) The number of promotions challenged by appeal has averaged about 3,000 each year, or 30 per cent of the total. About 17 per cent of these appeals are successful.

McLachlan considered the question of promotion appeal boards and strongly advised against them. In his opinion the future administration of the Public Service was too serious a matter "to be prejudiced by endeavours to obtain theoretical justice." *Royal Commission Report,* p. 48.

Chapter Thirteen

ARBITRATION AND STAFF RELATIONS IN THE COMMONWEALTH PUBLIC SERVICE

Leo Blair

In Australia we have now become so accustomed to the idea of statutory and compulsory arbitration that we tend to forget that this is not the only way of settling industrial disputes—using the word "industrial" to cover also public service employment of all kinds, Federal, State and local.

In fact, of course, once a dispute has arisen between an employer and his employee, there are broadly three ways in which it can be settled. First, by the trial of strength—strike, lockout, "go slow", "work to rule" or wholesale dismissals are examples of this kind of action. Second, by negotiation between the parties, with or without the aid of a third party, for example, conciliation or mediation ; and finally, by the decision of a third party, i.e., arbitration.

The striking contrast between Australian and British industrial relations is that in the former case, the primitive stage of all-out trials of strength was (legally, at any rate) superseded by the intervention of the state and the establishment of compulsory arbitration machinery. In Britain, on the other hand, the development of industrial relations has been almost entirely non-legal, the emphasis being on "collective bargaining"—the bargaining of organisations of employers on the one hand, with, on the other, similar organisations of employees. The result is usually a collective agreement which will lay down the conditions of work within the particular industry concerned until such time as a new agreement is drawn up.

In the field of government employment, the same contrast is apparent. In the United Kingdom Civil Service employer-employee negotiations are carried on through the medium of the Whitley Council system.([1]) This was established in 1919 and provides for continuous contact between representatives of the "staff" and "official" sides of the service, at local, departmental and national level.([2]) It is important to appreciate that this system

The author wishes to acknowledge the assistance received from the Arbitration Section of the Commonwealth Public Service Board, from whom permission was received to use numerous documents prepared by them. The section on arbitration is reprinted with minor amendments from the Spring, 1956, issue of *Public Administration* (*London*) and the Editor's permission to reprint is gratefully acknowledged.

([1]) On the British Whitley Council system, see E. N. Gladden, *Civil Service Staff Relationships*, 1943; H.M. Treasury, *Staff Relations in the Civil Service*, 1955; and D. Houghton, "Whitley Councils in the Civil Service", in W. A. Robson (ed.), *The Civil Service in Britain and France*, 1956.

([2]) In Britain the Treasury carry out the staff functions which in Australia would be within the purview of the Public Service Board. Senior civil servants within each department together with certain Treasury representatives are the "official" (or employer's) side; other civil servants chosen by their colleagues within the departments are the "staff" (or employees') side.

is entirely extra-legal in the sense that no legislation is involved, nor will the courts of law recognise as binding any of the decisions of the Whitley Councils. This is of little practical importance, however, as the long-standing tradition of acceptance of Whitley agreements by both sides is sufficient to ensure strict compliance.

By contrast the system of staff negotiation in Australia, though it has developed some informal machinery, is closely regulated by statute. And the historical development of this system is an interesting commentary on the growing power of the public service employee during the twentieth century.

The closing years of the last century were, for Australia, a period of economic distress and industrial unrest. It is not surprising, therefore, that when the Commonwealth was established in 1901, the Constitution Act provided that the Federal Government should have powers to make laws with respect to "conciliation and arbitration for the prevention and settlement of industrial disputes extending beyond the limits of any one State." (Section 51 (xxxv).) High hopes were placed on what Alfred Deakin called "the authority of independent minds" as the key to industrial peace. For Labour, Hughes spoke of arbitration as "the coping-stone of civilization". By an Act of 1904, the Conciliation and Arbitration Court was empowered to determine industrial disputes and to make awards governing wages, terms and conditions of employees in industries as defined in the Act. But, as defined, the word "industry" did not apply to the Federal Public Service; public servants were thus denied access to the Court. The Public Service Commissioner was the sole authority for determining salaries, hours and conditions generally in the public service.

Naturally, the 1904 Act had a profound influence on public servants, who now desired to benefit from this new approach to industrial relations. Public service staff associations were formed and in the Report of the Public Service Commissioner for 1904 the question of the recognition of these is raised. As the following extract suggests, there was a certain disinclination on the part of the "official" side to allow much scope to the new bodies:

"Since taking office I have gladly granted recognition to three Associations whose avowed objects, if strictly adhered to, will, I feel, greatly contribute to the social, intellectual and ethical advancement of their members; but the caution cannot be too early given that as soon as any attempt is manifested by an Association of stepping beyond the limits of its legitimate and acknowledged functions, so soon will difficulties arise. Subject to the due observance of this premonition, I shall always be prepared to receive suggestions, through the proper channel, in regard to matters affecting the Service upon which an Association may be competent to express itself, it being recognised that in the administration of an extensive Service there are necessarily matters respecting which suggestions are often invaluable. In this connection I cannot do better than quote an excerpt from a communication conceding recognition to one of the Societies referred to: 'The Commissioner will be pleased to receive suggestions from the Association in regard to matters they are competent to express themselves upon, and he is glad to learn that there is no desire to countenance any movement or agitation calculated to harass those in administrative authority. All communications intended for the Commissioner should be addressed to me, and they should deal only with matters concerning the Public Service as a whole or classes of officers. Strong objection would be taken to the Association interfering in individual cases, as there is ample provision in the Public Service Act and Regulations in that respect.' ".([2])

By means of the newly formed staff associations, therefore, there was a certain amount of agitation to obtain for the public servant the right to have his claims heard and determined by the Arbitration Court. It is not easy to estimate how widespread this attitude was in the public service; certainly some public servants were against being brought under the Conciliation and Arbitration Act.

Nevertheless, discontent was strong in the service, particularly in the Postmaster-General's Department, which employed some three-quarters of the total number of public servants. In 1910 a Royal Commission had reported adversely on the administration of, and the general conditions within, that department. It would seem that this report, together with the protestations of the staff associations, gave the final impetus to some form of public service arbitration, and in 1911 the Arbitration (Public Service) Act was passed.([4])

Under this Act employees of the public service of the Commonwealth were deemed to be employees in an "industry" within the meaning of the Commonwealth Conciliation and Arbitration Act, 1904: hence with power to form associations and to gain access to the Arbitration Court. The new legislation vested authority in the Arbitration Court to make awards, whose contents need not be restricted to the specific claims made or to the subject matter of the claim, but which might include anything which the Court thought necessary in the interests of the public or the service. Such awards could not be challenged or appealed against in any other Court. Awards had to be laid before both the House of Representatives and the Senate, and could not come into operation until thirty days had expired from the date of tabling. The Court was empowered to make an award which was not in accord with a law or regulation of the Commonwealth relating to salaries, rates of pay or conditions of service. When laid before Parliament, an award of this nature was to be accompanied by a statement as to the laws or regulations with which it was not in accord. If either House of Parliament within thirty days passed a resolution of disallowance the award was not to take effect.

With the passing of the 1911 Act, therefore, public service associations operated under substantially the same conditions as other industrial trade unions. The first award was made in 1913 in favour of the Australian Postal Electricians' Union. In 1916 came the first award covering clerical officers in all departments.

([3]) Public Service Commissioner, *Report,* 1904, p. 54.

([4]) For a fuller account of this Act and its working, see E. E. Crichton, "The Development of Public Service Arbitration—I", *Pub. Admin. (Sydney),* XV, June, 1956.

This innovation in public service practice had wide repercussions and in 1916 the Public Service Commissioner expressed doubts as to its effects on employees, particularly with regard to mobility: "Since my appointment as Public Service Commissioner one of the objects which I have constantly kept in view as desirable of attainment, was the establishment as far as possible of uniform conditions for the Service as regards privileges, practices and principles of administration. The establishment of uniform conditions has simplified the work of administration and has also made for the mobility of the Service, a very important factor in the organization of large Departments such as the Postmaster-General's. The measure of uniformity and mobility, which has been secured as the result of past efforts, is in danger to some extent of disintegration as the result of the Court's awards, and it is in connection with these matters that my chief concern lies."([5])

After outlining four awards made by the Court, the Report goes on: "In these four awards three different methods of dealing with the one matter have been laid down and in other matters which are apparently identical as affecting different classes of officers, dissimilar conditions are prescribed. In regard to . . . mobility . . . it may be stated that in the positions which are considered to be closely related to one another . . . uniform limits of salary had been adopted, and consequently officers could be transferred from one of the positions . . . to another without alteration of status or interference with their existing seniority. This arrangement was convenient . . . and facilitated the filling of vacancies and the movements of staff generally. Under the awards, barriers are to some extent imposed which tend to restrict the free interchange of officers. Cases have already occurred which illustrate the difficulties . . . which arise when officers desire transfer from 'award' positions to 'non-award' positions."

Apart from these objections by the Commissioner, there were also complaints from the staff associations. It was alleged that, because of the very large demands made upon the Court by industrial employees, there were inordinate delays in the settling of public service claims. Certainly so much of the Court's time was taken up with the determination of actual or threatened disputes in industry at this time that the public servant was forced into the background by the pressure of the more urgent industrial questions. The objection was put forward by some staff organisations that the conditions and nature of work in public service were radically different from those of private employment, and it was suggested therefore that a separate tribunal for public service matters only should be set up, which by specialising in this way would become expert in determining conditions appropriate to the public service. But the public service seems to have been divided on the issue, and many supported the existing system.

In 1918 the Federal Government commissioned Mr. D. C. McLachlan (the former Public Service Commissioner) to inquire into, and report upon, the various Acts relating to the administration of the public service, particularly as to their effects upon management and working.

([5]) Public Service Commissioner, *Report*, 1916, pp. 49-50.

His report was trenchant in its criticism of the general state of the public service, and in particular of the Arbitration (Public Service) Act of 1911. He considered that the procedure was costly, 'ime-wasting, piecemeal, productive of anomalies and inconsistencies, and oî discontent. "I have carefully watched the effect of this modern feature of Public Service employment since the first award was made in 1913 and have no hesitation in saying that while it may have worked to the personal advantage of some officers, it has not tended to foster that zeal, sense of discipline and proper recognition of responsibility to constituted authority which is necessary for the maintenance of a well-ordered and efficient service. I am also satisfied that true work values can only be determined by an intimate knowledge of . . . the class of work under consideration . . . Further, while the object of arbitration is to secure a contented service I am doubtful, to say the least, whether it achieves that end. An organisation goes to arbitration in the knowledge that they have everything to gain and nothing to lose, and if the judgment does not give them all that they seek . . . the feeling of disappointment engendered must have a disturbing effect upon them as a body of officers . . . Public service arbitration has proved a most costly matter . . . representation of the Commissioner and the Departments has involved heavy expenditure because of the necessity for bringing witnesses from other States to give evidence and in paying salaries of those witnesses and other officers in attendance at the Court . . . The salaries and expenses of executive members of associations appearing in the Court also form a serious item of expenditure."(°)

McLachlan thought that the aim of most of the public service unions had been to establish a dead level of mediocrity. He recommended that the Act be repealed and that final power to determine salaries and other general conditions of employment should reside with the Public Service Commissioner.

But the government of the day, having accepted the principle of arbitration, was not going to return to the idea of absolute control of the public service by the Public Service Commissioner. The result of its consideration of the McLachlan Report was the passing of the Arbitration (Public Service) Act, 1920, which, with amendments, is still the basis of arbitration in the public service. It came into force on 31st March, 1921, and provided for the appointment of a Public Service Arbitrator with power to determine wages and conditions of employment for public servants who were now removed from the jurisdiction of the Commonwealth Court of Conciliation and Arbitration. No appeal was permitted from the decision of the Arbitrator, a provision which was, however, modified in 1952.

Thus from 1904 to 1913 Commonwealth public servants had no right to go to arbitration, although this right was given to private industrial employees. From 1913 to 1920 public servants had the right to be heard by the Conciliation and Arbitration Court, taking their place with the industrial organisations and subject to the same treatment. From 1920 the Public

---

(°) Royal Commission on Public Service, *Report*, 1920, pp. 12-13.

Service has had its own Arbitrator with, since 1952, a means of appeal from his determination to the Conciliation and Arbitration Court.[7]

The Arbitrator

The Public Service Arbitrator is appointed by the Governor-General, for a term of seven years, renewable, and may be removed from office only by an address from both Houses of Parliament. He is required, by section 13 of the Commonwealth Public Service Arbitration Act, 1920-55, to act upon "equity, good conscience and the substantial merits of the case, without regard to technicalities or legal forms, and shall not be bound by any rules of evidence, but may inform his mind in such manner as he thinks fit". In practice procedure during public hearings is substantially that of an ordinary court of law.

As in the 1911 Act, any determination made by the Arbitrator must be laid before Parliament and does not take effect until 30 days have elapsed from the date of tabling; where his determination is not in accord with "the laws of the Commonwealth and the regulations made thereunder," he is required to submit a statement showing the inconsistency and such a determination may be disallowed by resolution of either House within 30 days.

The Arbitrator is not restricted to matters which are the subject of the claim before him and if he considers it to be in the interest of either the Public Service or the public generally, he may include in his determination any matters which are in his opinion necessary. His decision, when given, is binding on all parties, provided, of course, it is not disallowed by Parliament. Legally it is possible for the Arbitrator to make awards with regard to public service employment which conflict with those made by the Arbitration Court in similar cases in industry (Commonwealth Public Service Arbitration Act, 1920-55, s. 22 (1)). Since, however, an appeal now lies to the Court from the Arbitrator, it is not likely that any major differences would go unchallenged by the Court. Nevertheless it is common for the Arbitrator in individual cases to prescribe minor conditions which do differ from those made by the Court. In any salary or wage award made by the Arbitrator there are two elements: (i) the basic wage, with any cost-of-living adjustments—this is determined by the Arbitration Court for employees generally and is normally accepted by the Arbitrator; (ii) the "margin" for skill or work value, additional to the basic wage, which is determined solely by the Arbitrator.

Procedure

The basic power of the Arbitrator is provided for as follows: "The Arbitrator shall, subject to the provisions of this section, determine all matters submitted to him relating to salaries, wages, rates of pay, terms or conditions of service or employment of officers and employees of the Public Service" (section 12 (1)). Then it is provided that: "Any organisation shall be entitled to submit to the Arbitrator by memorial any claim relating

---

[7] For the history of public service arbitration since 1920, see E. E. Crichton, "Development of Public Service Arbitration"—II and III, *Pub. Admin.* (*Sydney*), XV, Sept. and Dec., 1956.

to the salaries, wages, rates of pay, or terms or conditions of service or employment of members of the organisation" (section 12 (2)).

It is worthwhile observing that the word "organisation" is defined by section 3 of the Commonwealth Public Service Arbitration Act, 1920-55, as "an organisation within the meaning of the Conciliation and Arbitration Act, 1904-1950". This means, therefore, that any organisation which has been registered under the Conciliation and Arbitration Act may submit claims to the Public Service Arbitrator in respect of its members who are officers or employees of the Public Service. Thus, a claim may be submitted, on the one hand, by a body like the Administrative and Clerical Officers' Association, the members of which are all public servants; on the other hand, the organisation concerned may have in its membership employees of outside industry as well as public service employees, for example, the Transport Workers' Union of Australia. Any determination made in the latter type of case, of course, is restricted in its application to those members of the organisation who are public servants.

The memorial is the type of claim which seeks a completely new determination covering, say, salaries or conditions of service. It can be lodged only by an organisation and not by the Public Service Board or a departmental employing authority. The reason for this is simply that the Public Service Board has the power to prescribe by regulation matters affecting salaries and other conditions of service and thus there is no need for it to approach the Arbitrator in the first instance. With the memorial it is usual to submit an explanatory memorandum setting out briefly the main reasons why the claim is being lodged.

The Arbitrator must allow the Board or the Ministers concerned an opportunity of replying to the claim, and their "answers" must be lodged within 14 days of the date when the memorial was filed with the Arbitrator. In the event of there being no objections to the claim, the Arbitrator may proceed at once to issue a determination in favour of the claimant organisation. Where, however, an answer is lodged within the prescribed period objecting to the claim made by the organisation, copies of these answers are forwarded to the organisation concerned. Again, it is the practice to accompany the answer with a statement setting out concisely the grounds on which objection is based. With this and the explanatory memorandum from the organisation which accompanied the memorial, the Arbitrator is in a position to appreciate the main points at issue in the dispute.

The Act places great emphasis on the settlement of disputes by negotiation between the parties. During the second reading debates the Attorney-General said: "Every endeavour should be made to arrive at the settlement of any dispute by conciliatory methods before entering the tribunal which is to be created under the Bill."[8] And even after negotiations have broken down and a claim has been lodged, the attempt to secure a settlement by conciliation is not given up.

When the memorial and answers have been lodged, the Arbitrator "shall call a conference, to be presided over by himself, of representatives of the organisation and of the Board and of any Minister who has lodged objections

---

[8] *Com. Parl. Debs.*, XCIII, p. 4202. Some 80 per cent of the awards are made by consent of the parties after negotiation.

to the granting of the claim . . ." (section 12 (5)). This conference is intended to play a very important part in the negotiations; as was said by the Minister who piloted the Bill through the House of Representatives: "Under this measure, when the issues have been arrived at, the first step taken is the calling of a conference. . . . The desire is to settle disputes so far as possible by these conferences . . ."(*) At the conference, therefore, agreement on some, or even all, of the points in dispute may be reached. For example, the subject of the particular claim may have been fully considered by the Arbitrator in a recent case. On this being pointed out to the parties, they might agree to accept the Arbitrator's previous decision on the specific matter covered. At these conciliatory, or so-called "statutory", conferences the public is not admitted.

If all the issues are settled by agreement at the conference (including an agreement simply to let the Arbitrator decide) the Arbitrator may then make a determination, otherwise the next step is the hearing of evidence. This takes place in public, and where the facts of the claim are not in dispute the hearing may be limited to the presentation of arguments by representatives of the organisation and of the Public Service Board or a Minister. As a rule, however, sworn evidence of the facts is given at the public hearing and normal court procedure with regard to evidence is followed. The respective cases are outlined and cross-examination may take place, this stage being closed by a summing-up by each side.

With regard to the representatives engaged in the public hearing, the Public Service Arbitration Act, 1920-52, provided: "No person or organisation shall in any proceeding under this Act be represented by counsel or solicitor." In 1955 the representative of a staff association (one of its full-time officers) was found to be a qualified lawyer. This raised a rather difficult point. Was he arguing the case *qua* union representative or *qua* lawyer? The issue has been settled by an amendment to the Act which provides, in effect, that in all proceedings before the Arbitrator([10]) either party may be represented by someone who is legally qualified, so long as he is either a member or officer of the organisation which he represents or an officer of the Public Service Board or of the department involved in the proceedings.

At the close of the public hearing the Arbitrator will invariably reserve his decision and before discussing the actual judgment it might be worth while to sum up, briefly, the information available to the Arbitrator to assist him in giving consideration to the conflicting claims. He will possess:

    (a) oral evidence of the witnesses called at the public hearing;

    (b) information contained in documents and other exhibits produced in the case;

    (c) details of any agreements arrived at by the parties, e.g., at conference stage;

    (d) information obtained by personal inspection of the work performed by the individuals on whose behalf the claim is being made;

(*) *Com. Parl. Debs.*, XCIII, p. 3689.
([10]) In proceedings on reference or appeal to the Court or the Chief Judge, leave may now be given for legal representation.

(*e*) any other information which he may obtain in accordance with section 13 of the Act.

With regard to this last source of information it need not be emphasised that the Arbitrator will be wise to ensure that all interested parties know how he has informed himself.

When the Arbitrator issues his decision, it may be, and in other than "consent" determinations invariably is, accompanied by a statement of the reasons upon which the decision is based; the provision also appears that "subject to this Act, a determination of the Arbitrator shall come into operation upon the expiration of a period of thirty days, or of such longer period as the Arbitrator specifies in the determination, *after the determination has been laid before Parliament*" (section 21 (1)) [my italics].

Thus, in theory at least, the principle of parliamentary control over public expenditure is safeguarded. During the thirty-day period any member may move that the determination be disallowed and on a resolution of either House to that effect the determination will not come into operation. There have been very few cases where such disallowance has been resorted to—it is not intended that Parliament should set itself up as a court of review on the merits of the determinations of the Arbitrator as to the facts of any particular case; rather, the idea is that if it is not in agreement with the principles on which the decision has been arrived at, Parliament may exercise its right to disallow the determination. The criterion appears to be that if it is difficult to raise the money to pay any large increases in salary which have been awarded by the Arbitrator on the merits of the case, then Parliament can by its veto prevent the additional demand on the Treasury.

This point was put very clearly by the then Attorney-General when he introduced the 1911 Arbitration (Public Service) Act: "It would be most undesirable that any Court, Tribunal or person outside the Parliament should be permitted to fix, without supervision or regulation of any sort whatever, any rates or conditions of employment that it thought fit for public servants of the Commonwealth irrespective of the ability of the Treasurer to pay them or the country to find the money."[11] Capacity to pay has not been accepted by the Arbitrator as a valid criterion in his own determinations.

So much for the way in which the decision of the Arbitrator is arrived at. Before going on to examine subsequent events mention might be made of what is known as an "application to vary". This occurs where an existing determination is in force and the staff organisation concerned or a Minister whose staff is affected or the Public Service Board desire to have the determination varied in some way. The procedure followed is much the same as that outlined above, except, of course, that the application to vary is not confined to staff organisations, unlike the memorial claiming a new determination.

When the Arbitrator has made his decision he will then forward a copy to all the interested parties. Under sections 21-22 of the Act he must also **forward a copy to the Prime Minister and to the Attorney-General together**

(11) *Com. Parl. Debs.,* LXIII, p. 4883.

with a statement of any laws or regulations with which his determination may be in conflict.

On promulgation of the determination the Public Service Board normally forwards copies to all departments whose staffs will be affected by the award, indicating where necessary any salary adjustments which may be required or changes in general conditions of service which may have to be made as soon as the determination takes effect. These instructions are meant to enable the departments to implement correctly the provisions of the determination and, since the Board's representatives will have been present at all stages of the negotiations, conference and public hearing, the Board is in a good position to advise on the contentious points.

At the same time as it forwards the determination, with explanatory instructions, to the departments, the Board dispatches copies of the instructions to the interested staff organisations. This enables these organisations to raise immediately any points concerning the Board's instructions with which they may not agree. Negotiations follow, and if these are unsuccessful and no agreement can be reached on how the determination of the Arbitrator is to be implemented, application may be made to the Arbitrator who "may give an interpretation of any determination made under this Act" (section 15F (1)).

The party submitting the application for interpretation will set out the clauses in respect of which the interpretation is desired, the interpretation which the employing authority has placed on these clauses and the interpretation placed on them by the organisation. A copy of these submissions will, of course, be sent to the other party to the dispute. No answers need be lodged, and the matter proceeds direct to a public hearing where the points in dispute are argued before the Arbitrator. Generally, the facts of the case are admitted and all that is necessary is for the differing viewpoints to be presented by the representatives of the disputants. After hearing the parties, the Arbitrator gives his interpretation. As an interpretation is merely explanatory of a determination already in existence there is no need for it to be tabled in Parliament.

Appeals and References

In 1952 the Federal Government examined the various statutes relating to arbitration, both industrial and public service. The main result for the public servant was that certain rights of appeal from decisions of the Arbitrator were now allowed. Application for leave to appeal may, of course, be made by the Public Service Board, a Minister or a staff organisation affected by the decision. Leave to appeal will not be granted unless the Chief Judge of the Conciliation and Arbitration Court is of the opinion that the matter of the appeal is of such importance that it is in the public interest that leave should be given. The appeal is heard by the Full Court (i.e., not less than three judges) and "upon the hearing of an appeal under this section the Full Court may—(a) admit further evidence and (b) direct the Arbitrator to furnish a report to the Full Court with respect to such matter as the Full Court specifies, and shall (c) make a determination confirming, quashing or varying the determination under appeal, or (d) make a determination dealing with the subject-matter of the determination under appeal" (section 15c (5)).

In addition to this provision for appeal, the 1952 amending legislation provided for reference direct to the Full Court without any prior adjudication on the part of the Arbitrator: "Upon application by (*a*) the Board, (*b*) a Minister affected by the claim or application, or (*c*) the organisation by which the claim or application was submitted to the Arbitrator, the Arbitrator may, if he is of the opinion that a claim or application made to him under this Act, or a matter arising out of such a claim or application (including a question whether a term of a determination should be a common rule of the Public Service or of any branch or part of the Public Service), is of such importance that the claim, application or matter should, in the public interest, be dealt with by the Full Court, and subject to the concurrence of the Chief Judge, refer the claim, application or matter to the Full Court" (section 15A (1)). If the Arbitrator refuses to grant an application to refer direct to the Full Court, an appeal against his refusal lies to the Chief Judge of the Court.

It should be noted that in these proceedings the Full Court has the same powers, duties and obligations as though it were the Public Service Arbitrator. It exercises jurisdiction under the Public Service Arbitration Act and not the Conciliation and Arbitration Act and its decisions on appeal or reference must, therefore, be tabled in Parliament before they can have effect.

An important recent case in which a successful appeal by the Public Service Board was made against a determination of the Arbitrator was the so-called Public Service Margins Case.([12]) The bringing back of the court into public service arbitration may have some advantages in securing more uniformity as between the public service and outside occcupations. But it adds to the time and cost involved in cases. It is also possible that the court may once again become the effective determiner of public service conditions, as it was before the 1920 Act.

Informal Machinery

The great expansion of the Commonwealth Public Service and the consequent increase in the volume of claims have tended to produce delays in the hearings by the Arbitrator.

Many staff organisations now see fit to approach the Board with a view to seeking agreement on as many issues as possible at the one time. There is no specific authority for this informal discussion but it saves considerable time and appears to work to the satisfaction of both the Board and the staff organisations. In some cases complete agreement is reached between the Board and the representatives of the staff association ; in other cases the agreement may be partial. In the former case the association representatives submit a claim to the Arbitrator in terms of the agreement reached with the Board and, since no objection is lodged by the Board, the Arbitrator can at once issue a determination. In the event of an agreement on some points only, the staff organisation will lodge a claim on the matters remaining at issue and this will be challenged by the Board in the usual manner.

([12]) For an account of this, see E. E. Crichton, The Development of Public Service Arbitration—III, *Public Admin. (Sydney)*, XV, Dec., 1956, pp. 331-332.

Naturally, in making these agreements with staff associations the Board must be very careful to ensure that no embarrassment is caused to the Arbitrator. Many claims may not lend themselves to this method of negotiation, and the Board will frequently refuse to enter into informal discussions with a view to a "consent" determination. Nevertheless, the informal "agreement" procedure seems to have resulted not only in a saving of time for the Arbitrator but in a gain to the members of the staff organisations concerned since there is less delay in implementing conditions which have been informally agreed.

Another result of the greatly increased pressure on the Arbitrator was the appointment in 1949 of an assistant to help the Arbitrator in deciding claims. This assistant presides over conferences and the public hearings but, while he has the power to make recommendations to the Arbitrator, only the latter can make the actual determination.

The Future

The principle of arbitration is now firmly entrenched in the practice of the Australian public service, and this, in effect, makes for dual control over many aspects of Public Service employment. On the one hand, the Public Service Board may make regulations setting out the rules governing, for example, leave, salaries and allowances; on the other hand, the Public Service Arbitrator and ultimately, in some cases, the Arbitration Court will make awards and determinations which will greatly affect Public Service administration.

There have been strong criticisms of the idea of arbitration in the Public Service and it has been contended that the public servant is *sui generis* by virtue of the nature of his work and that the usual principles governing industrial and commercial employment do not, and cannot, apply. It has also been maintained that arbitration adds to the number of separate jurisdictions determining pay, the decision of each of which may react on the other in a "leap-frogging" fashion. (In particular, this raises doubts about the wisdom of the Arbitrator hearing claims from unions mainly concerned with members outside the public service). There is sometimes concern with the way in which decisions may affect administrative efficiency, e.g., by hindering rational classification and promotion systems.

But, although considerable dissatisfaction may be voiced about the existing system of arbitration, it is extremely unlikely that any move to abolish it will take place in the foreseeable future. It is a question of balancing the need for the public servant to feel that he is being justly treated against the necessity of maintaining an efficient system of Public Service control. That a system of arbitration independent of the Public Service Board may lower efficiency in this respect is not easy to deny; that it contributes much to the feeling that justice is being done is equally evident.

Employer-employee Relationships([18])

The Commonwealth Government has come to appreciate the value of good employer-employee relations. Side by side with the cautious statement of 1904([14]) may be placed the following from the 1951 Training Handbook of the Public Service Board (p. 38):—

"Representative organisations are afforded every facility from the administration, and you are advised to join your service association. It is now widely recognised that organised staff associations are a help not only to individual public servants but also to the departments and the Service as a whole. The worth and method of participation by the staff in management are among the more recent discoveries in administration."

Though there are no Whitley Councils in Australia, staff associations play an important part in the service. Their activities in relation to wage and salary arbitration, and promotion appeals, have already been mentioned above. Staff organisations also "have easy access to the Board by deputation and this process is freely used".([15]) But apart from furthering the interest of their members in these ways, they have also recently sought to participate in the general management of the service. A not untypical statement is the following:—

"Officers who have served for any length of time in employee organisations have acquired a wide knowledge of the Public Service and have a definite contribution to make to the administration. It will be found that they have not lost their capacity for forming sound decisions or of judging a case on its merits . . . the appointment to the Board of a representative of the employees would ensure that questions bearing on the welfare of officers and employees would be fully considered when matters affecting their employment are under consideration."([16])

Opinions may differ on the value of having a staff representative on a Public Service Board. However, there are certainly areas where staff associations can do much. In 1945, largely because of representations made by the Chairman of the Commonwealth Public Service Board, a Joint Council was created to further co-operation. This is an advisory body, but one with considerable influence; and apart from its direct influence it is a means of allowing its members to become familiar with one another's problems. The

---

([18]) For a fuller treatment, see L. Blair, "Employer-Employee Relationships in the Federal Public Service of Australia", *Pub. Admin. (London)*, XXXV, Spring, 1957. Staff associations are registered by the Industrial Registrar. More than one can represent the same kind of staff, the criterion being the convenience of the employee. The main clerical unions are the Administrative and Clerical Officers' Association (with a membership of 16,900 in 1956), the Federated Public Service Assistants' Association and the Federated Clerks' Union. The activities of A.C.O.A. may be studied in its official organ, the *Federal Public Service Journal*.

([14]) See above, pp. 360-361.

([15]) Commonwealth Public Service Board, 32nd *Report*, 1955-56, p. 9.

([16]) F. L. Hedges, "Role of Public Service Staff Associations in Public Administration", *Pub. Admin. (Sydney)*, V, December, 1945, p. 358.

Joint Council has fourteen members, six departmental representatives (normally senior administrators), five nominated by the High Council of Public Service Organisations, two by the Postal Workers' Union ; and a Public Service Board Chairman. The Australian Postal Workers' Union is given separate representatives because it is the only large Public Service Association not affiliated to the High Council. Staff associations or departments can submit to the Board any matter which they consider to be of general interest in relation to the service ; it then lies with the Board to refer these matters to the Joint Council. It does not normally deal with pay structure. The Council reports back to the Board. It meets for two days at a time every few months, but also works through sub-committees (normally the chairman and two from each side). A sub-committee was, for example, recently appointed to study compensation legislation.

There are a number of other fields in which the staff and its associations are active, e.g., staff welfare and social amenities. Some departments have clubs or elected committees representing employees, but provision varies greatly. Public servants may appeal against punishments "on the ground of innocence . . . or excessive severity of punishment" to Disciplinary Appeal Boards, consisting of a chairman (who must have the qualifications of a magistrate), an officer of the department, and an officer from the appellant's own Division of the service. The latter are elected in each State every three years. The appeal board may confirm, annul or vary the punishment. Staff representatives also play an important part in departmental suggestions committees, training committees, and occasionally in management advisory committees. The Advisory Committees on Management of the Department of Customs include elected members of the staff and, as well as considering and recommending on suggestions by officers, have also from time to time considered wider aspects of departmental policy, for example, staff reporting.

Chapter Fourteen

PROMOTION, SALARIES AND CLASSIFICATION IN THE NEW SOUTH WALES PUBLIC SERVICE

E. W. HOWITT

The existence of an efficient and contented staff in any organisation, and particularly one so wide and complex as the public service, depends to a large degree on wisely-planned systems of pay and promotion. Nothing is more calculated to engender dissatisfaction than the absence of uniformity or proper relationship between the remuneration of officers in different sections of the public service. No less important is the need to encourage ability and to avoid the destruction of incentive which is inherent in a system of promotion by seniority alone.

As a result of the work of two Royal Commissions in New South Wales in 1895 and 1918, the present legislation has been designed to achieve both these objects, while retaining adequate recourse to appellate tribunals for officers who may feel aggrieved by a decision which adversely affects them.

Promotion

The New South Wales Public Service Act, while instituting a system of seniority, nevertheless directs that, in making appointments, seniority is to be subordinated to "special fitness", defined as "special qualifications and aptitude for the discharge of the duties of the office to be filled." This was the broad principle recommended by the 1895 Royal Commission on the Public Service and first embodied in the Public Service Act of the same year. In 1956-57 there were 843 promotions, of which 432 were not in accordance with seniority.

New South Wales makes more use than many public services of the qualifying promotion examination. The Professional and Clerical Divisions are each subdivided (by section 48 of the Public Service Act) into two series of Grades, namely, the "Higher Grades" and the "Lower Grades". Section 50 provides that no person shall be eligible for promotion to the Higher Grades of the Divisions in question unless he has passed the examination prescribed by the Board as preliminary to admission to those Grades. The examinations, usually referred to as the Higher Grades Examinations, are prescribed by Regulation—Regulation 122 in the case of Clerical Officers and 126 in the case of Professional Officers. Other examination barriers are created in the Clerical Division by Regulations 116 and 119 and in the Professional Division by Regulation 124. A prime requisite for an officer wishing to be considered for promotion beyond certain salary points is that he shall have qualified by passing an examination. The aim of the Higher Grades Examination is twofold. It aims at assessing the professional competence of the officer and the breadth of his experience. In the case of the professional officer the main emphasis of the examination is on his technical competence. In the case of the clerical officer it is on his breadth of experience. All Higher Grades Examinations, however, incidentally provide evidence of the candidate's capacity, industriousness and interest. Of the Lower Grades Examinations, the first is more concerned with subjects and topics associated with the day-to-day duties of officers within the Department. The second examination is designed to provide a broad knowledge of the Service and the functions of government.

Section 47 of the Act provides that all promotions in or appointments to the Special Division, which comprises the most senior administrative officers shall, as far as practicable, be from the Special Division or the Higher Grades of the Professional or Clerical Divisions, or from the Educational Division, and shall be made with regard to special qualifications and aptitude, as well as to seniority in grade or duration of service, seniority again being subordinated to considerations of special fitness.

Under Section 49 of the Act, internal promotion is to be made—

    (1) by the appointment of an officer of the "Department"([1]) in which the vacancy occurs, regard being paid to the relative seniority and fitness of the officers of such Department; or

    (2) of an officer from any other "Department" whom, on the ground of seniority combined with fitness, it seems desirable to appoint.

As already indicated above, the important principle embodied in the Act is that in all cases seniority must be subordinated to "special fitness".

For the purpose of filling any positions that may become vacant, section 49 (i) of the Act enables the Board to draw upon the entire service. Naturally, officers in the department in which the vacancy occurs have the advantage of a knowledge of the activities of the department, its legislation and policies, and for this reason most positions are filled by internal promotion. Where, however, it appears that there is no person in the department who fully meets the requirements of the position, applications are called by circular throughout the service, and if necessary by simultaneous advertisement in the daily press. In deciding between conflicting applicants from inside and outside the public service, regard must be had to sections 35 and 36 of the Act which assure preference to candidates from inside the service who are fitted, qualified and available for appointment.

Where applications have been called to fill a position they are considered by the Board upon a recommendation from a Selection Committee which interviews applicants whom it regards as eligible. The Board is enjoined by the section to make its recommendation "on the ground of seniority combined with fitness" but, because officers in different departments as

---

([1]) Regulation 56 defines "Department" for the purposes of this section (and also Section 49A) as normally meaning certain categories of officers within a Division or Divisions grouped together on a common seniority list.

defined in Regulation 56 are not on a common seniority list, seniority is only relative and again "fitness" becomes the paramount consideration.

However, the real difficulty in such cases arises when an officer from another department is chosen to fill a vacancy. Not being an officer of the department to which he is to be appointed, he has no place on any seniority list in that department. Consequently, unless he is placed on the seniority list below all officers in that department, a right of appeal against the appointment is given by the Crown Employees' Appeal Board Act (see below) to every officer in that department whose seniority is affected.

Again, though far less frequently, such a situation may arise where it is necessary for the Board to place in a department an officer who has become surplus to the establishment of another department. (See sections 9 (2) and 15 of the Public Service Act.)

Promotions Committees

Section 49A of the Public Service Act provides that where a recommendation to the Board is made for the filling of a permanent position in any department by the promotion of an "officer other than the officer of that department who is next in order of seniority for such promotion" the Board shall refer such recommendation to a Promotions Committee. It is important to note that the section requires automatic reference to the Committee even though no protest against loss of seniority has been made by any officer proposed to be passed over for appointment. The Promotions Committee consists of the Permanent Head of the Department or his nominee, an officer's representative, nominated by the appropriate association of employees, and a third member, appointed by agreement between the other two members, or failing agreement, by the Board. It is required "to enquire into the claims for the promotion in question of all officers proposed to be passed over".

Before making its decision on the promotion, the Board is required to take the Promotions Committee's report into account and, if so requested, to interview the officer's representative in support of the claims of anyone whom it is proposed to pass over. The requirement of reference to a Promotions Committee is limited to the filling of positions carrying a salary of £750 per annum or less, unless the Board otherwise decides. As a matter of practice, the Board refers proposed promotions to Promotions Committees in all cases where the salary attached to the position to be filled is normally within the equivalent of the lower grades in the Clerical Division. The terms of the section are supplemented by Regulations 51-55.(²)

Appeals to the Public Service Board

By section 19 of the Act, a right of appeal is given to an officer who is dissatisfied with any decision of the Public Service Board, either particular or general, in regard to seniority or grade affecting him, as well as salary and the classification of the work performed by or assigned to him. The

---

(²) For a comment upon the delays resulting from the operation of this section, see the Report of the Public Service Board for the year ended 30th June, 1955, p. 44.

appeal must be lodged with the Board within 30 days of the decision and must include the grounds of appeal. Many appeals are made under this section and an officer is given the opportunity to state his case personally to the Board and, if he so desires, to be represented and to call witnesses in support of his appeal.

Crown Employees Appeal Board

In 1944 the Crown Employees Appeal Board Act was passed giving to persons employed under the Public Service Act, and also those employed by the authorities named in a Schedule to the Act, certain rights of appeal against decisions of the Public Service Board or the employing authority as the case may be. The Appeal Board consists of a Chairman, who is a Judge of the Supreme Court or of the Industrial Commission or is a person eligible for appointment to such offices, together with a representative of the employing authority nominated by that authority and an employee's representative nominated by the employee association concerned. It should be noted that, in contrast to the Commonwealth appeals system, the Chairman is not drawn from the Public Service Board. Again, the New South Wales Board is "open" and allows legal representation ; a Commonwealth Promotions Appeal Committee hears appeals *in camera* and no one is allowed legal assistance.

A right of appeal is given (under section 10) to any officer who deems himself adversely affected by a decision or determination of the Public Service Board concerning the "promotion or appointment to any permanent office of an officer other than the officer who according to the rules governing promotion in the particular service is next in seniority for the promotion or appointment". No appeal lies where the salary attached to the office to be filled exceeds £2,500 per annum or where the office is in the Special Division.

Notice in writing is to be given to officers affected as soon as practicable after the decision and an appeal must be lodged within 30 days of the service of such notice. It is important to note that the right of appeal to the Appeal Board is alternative to any right of appeal granted by law or award to any other authority or tribunal (including the officer's employer) and if an officer elects to exercise one he is debarred from exercising the other (section 10 (4)). A decision or determination against which an appeal may be lodged cannot be carried into effect until the expiration of the time granted for lodging an appeal and, if an appeal is lodged, until the appeal is determined.

The effect of these statutory provisions is to give the utmost consideration to an officer whom it is proposed to pass over for promotion. On the other hand, the result is that promotion for many officers is greatly delayed, particularly where there is need to refer the recommendation to a Promotions Committee and an appeal is subsequently taken to the Appeal Board by one or more officers whom it is proposed to pass over. The position is often complicated when appeals have been lodged against one decision of the Public Service Board and some or all of the officers affected by such decision are also affected by a later decision in relation to another promotion. It is at least open to question whether in the long run such elaborate machinery is in the interests of the efficiency of the public service.([2])

Promotions appeals generally arise from the statutory requirement that seniority shall be subordinated to considerations of special fitness. It is therefore appropriate to say something more of the history of this provision and the interpretation placed upon it by tribunals, particularly as it has also been adopted, although not always in the precise form in which it appears in the New South Wales legislation, in all other States of the Commonwealth. For example, in Victoria provision is made by statutory regulation that in determining the claims of officers for promotion consideration shall be given first to the relative efficiency of officers, "efficiency" being defined similarly to "fitness" in the New South Wales Act. In the event of an equality of efficiency of two or more officers, consideration is then to be given to relative seniority.

The wording of section 49 in the 1902 Act followed that of section 42 of the 1895 Act. As enacted in 1902, paragraph (a) under subsection one reads:—

"(a) any officer of the Department in which such vacancy occurs (regard being had to the relative seniority and fitness respectively of the officers of such Department) *if it appears that such appointment would result in the duties of such office being more efficiently performed than by selecting an officer from any other Department*; or"

The words in italics were omitted by Act No. 10 of 1929 (section 7 (1) (d) (i)). By the same amending Act the words "In all cases seniority shall be subordinated to considerations of special fitness" were inserted at the end of subsection one.

The meaning of the expression "special fitness" in subsection one in the light of the definition of "fitness" as "special qualifications and aptitude for the discharge of the duties of the office to be filled", has been considered by the Crown Employees Appeal Board on numerous occasions. That Board has rarely found any officer to possess "special fitness" except in relation to the possession of particular academic qualifications, for example,

---

([2]) A recent comment by the Public Service Commissioner of South Australia on the not dissimilar appeals system operating in that State is apposite: "Probably the principal complaint against present practice is that it tends to favour the appellant. As much of the evidence is now given in the presence of all parties, there is a disinclination on the part of heads of departments and other senior administrative officers to make statements in open session derogatory to individual officers. The impressions built up over years of association with officers are impressions only and often cannot be proved by factual evidence. A head of department may be prepared to say that in his opinion A is a better officer than B, but if he is to be called upon to prove his statement in the presence of both A and B he is inclined to express no opinion at all. It is often contended that if a statement cannot be proved it should not be made, but every executive officer knows that he can usually express a genuine preference although it may be incapable of evidential justification." (*Report* on the Efficiency of the South Australian Public Service, 1954, p. 5.)

possession of qualification of Solicitor has been held to be special fitness
for promotion to the office of Stipendiary Magistrate.

The particular difficulty is in the use of the word "special" in relation to
fitness, which itself is defined as "special qualifications and aptitude for
the discharge of the duties of the office to be filled". The amendment in
1929 appears to be clumsy, but it is suggested that full significance could
be given to the phrase "special fitness" if "special" is regarded as meaning
"superior". The latter is an adjective often adopted by the Crown Employees'
Appeal Board, usually in circumstances where it has found that an officer
possesses such superior fitness to that of an appellant that on the balance
the seniority of the latter is clearly outweighed. Although the Appeal Board
has in fact distinguished "special" and "superior" fitness, it is suggested
that such distinction is in fact unreal.

Two types of situations arise under section 49, that is, under paragraph (a)
and under paragraph (b) in subsection (1). So far as paragraph (a) is
concerned, the "contest" for a position is between officers in the same
"Department" for a vacant position and the Board is required to make its
recommendation having regard to the relative "seniority and fitness" of the
officers of the Department. The concept of the total sum of the seniority
and fitness of each officer must, according to the section, be weighed against
the sum of those factors possessed by each other officer. In point of fact,
however, the determining factor is normally the "fitness" of the selected
officer for the position, compared with the "fitness" of the other officers.
This would clearly appear to be in accordance with the spirit of the section
which requires seniority to be subordinated to *considerations* of special
fitness, not (as is often claimed) to special fitness.

It is interesting to note that in the Tasmanian Public Service the rule is
that in selecting an applicant for promotion regard must be had to the
relative efficiency of officers and it is only in the case of equality of
efficiency that relative seniority is considered. Officers who are not selected
have a right of appeal to the Classification and Appeal Board on the grounds
of superior fitness only. "Efficiency" there is construed to mean "any
special aptitude and qualifications for the discharge of the duties of the office
to be filled, together with merit and good and diligent work".

In Western Australia an unsuccessful applicant may appeal to the Promotions Appeal Board on one of two grounds, either—

(a) superior efficiency to the person recommended; or

(b) seniority and equal efficiency to the person recommended.

The definition of "efficiency" is the same as that adopted in Tasmania.

In Queensland and South Australia also the legislation provides that in
determining the claims of officers for promotion, consideration is to be given
first to relative efficiency and in the event of an equality of efficiency of
two or more officers then to relative seniority. Here again the definition
of efficiency is in substance the same as that of "fitness" in New South
Wales except that "merit, diligence and good conduct" must also be considered. In both States there is a right of appeal which can only succeed on
grounds similar to those in Western Australia.

In Victoria all appointments except those of Permanent Head are made by the Public Service Board. The Permanent Head is required to recommend the applicant whom he considers most suitable and an appeal lies to the Board on similar grounds to those prescribed in South Australia and Queensland, the definition of "efficiency" also being the same.

The adoption of similar provisions in this State would seem to resolve the difficulties which the Appeal Board has found to exist.

Salaries and Classification

The public service in its broadest sense includes all those persons who are employed directly by the Crown, or by some person or authority on behalf of the Crown. Section 47 of the New South Wales Constitution Act, 1902, vests the appointment to all public offices in the Governor, with the advice of the Executive Council. The section, however, by express provision makes the exercise of this power subject to the provisions of the Public Service Act, 1902, and of all other enactments relating to the appointment of officers which were in force at the time of the passing of the Constitution. In any case, therefore, where the appointment is one which is made under and subject to the Public Service Act, the terms and conditions of employment are regulated by the Act. By a proviso to section 47 this does not extend to minor appointments which by any Act or by order of the Governor-in-Council are vested in heads of departments or other officers or persons.

Under its original commission, the New South Wales Public Service Board was solely responsible for the determination of the salaries and gradings of the officers and employees of the public service. "One of the arguments advanced for the creation of an independent Public Service Board was that it would introduce system into the fixing of salaries for officials . . . Salaries and work values were to be brought into line not only within departments but as between different departments."[4] The Board thus came to fix salaries without reference to Parliament, which, however, reserves the right not to provide money for increases or (as in 1932) to impose cuts. Nowadays, the Board is required to review salaries every two years.

Various limitations on the Board's power have since developed, though they have left it still the most important determinant of pay and service conditions.

First, the legislature has seen fit to vest in certain statutory authorities the sole right to select and to appoint the officers and employees necessary to carry out its functions. In such cases the statute provides, either expressly or by necessary implication from the words used, that appointment is not to be under and subject to the Public Service Act. In New South Wales the Public Service Act applies to most State Government Departments as well as to a number of statutory authorities such as the Housing Commission of New South Wales, the Forestry Commission of New South Wales and the Government Insurance Office. These authorities, however, have a limited right to engage casual employees.

The largest group of employees not employed under the Public Service Act are those under the Ministry of Transport, viz., persons employed by

---

(4) F. A. Bland, *Government in Australia,* 2nd ed., 1944, Introd. p. xxiv.

the Commissioner for Railways, the Commissioner for Motor Transport, and the Commissioner for Government Transport. Other persons not subject to that Act include those in the service of the Water Conservation and Irrigation Commission, the Maritime Services Board of New South Wales, the Metropolitan Meat Industry Board and the Milk Board. However, many statutory authorities confer regularly with the Public Service Board with the aim of reaching some uniformity of salaries and working conditions with Public Service Act employees.

Another limitation has been the growth of arbitration as a means of settling disputes about pay. New South Wales passed an Industrial Arbitration Act in 1901. As in the case of the Commonwealth, public servants were not at first affected. Commonwealth public servants obtained access to arbitration in 1911. By 1935 all Australian public services except Victoria and Tasmania had in some measure given public servants access to arbitration machinery. The history of the New South Wales provision is fully dealt with later in this chapter in connection with the classification of positions.

The position in New South Wales is that industrial tribunals([5]) (constituted under the Industrial Arbitration Act, 1940-55) have the same power to fix rates of pay and conditions of employment for employees of the Crown not employed under the Public Service Act as they possess in relation to employees in private industry. In respect of persons employed under the Public Service Act, however, the Industrial Arbitration Act restricts their powers principally to fixing the lowest rate of pay for work, for overtime, holidays or other special work and to declaring what deduction may be made from the wages of employees for board or residence. This is an important restriction because not only does it leave in the hands of the Public Service Board the function of determining proper rates of pay as distinct from minimum rates but it also gives that Board the exclusive power to determine the wide range of conditions for which provision must be made in a service as large as that of New South Wales. These include such matters as hours of duty, annual holidays, sick leave, and travelling allowances.

An increasing number of classes of officer are now also covered by Agreements between the Board and employees' associations, and over ninety per cent. of the salaries in the service are now determined in this way.

Developments since 1895

The Public Service Act, 1895, required the Public Service Board to make a complete review of the grading of the service as soon as possible after its appointment, and the Act prescribed that regrading should thereafter be at intervals of five years. The first grading of the service was in 1896 and quinquennial regradings followed in 1901, 1906 and 1911. The long intervals between regrading, however, were found to be unsatisfactory. For this

---

([5]) There is an Industrial Commission of up to 12 judges, any 3 of whom may exercise the jurisdiction of the Commission or the Commission may delegate its powers and functions to a single judge. A public service case may be heard by a Conciliation Committee, a single judge of the Industrial Commission or by a full bench of the Commission either originally or on appeal.

reason and also to provide for the association of heads of departments and branches with regrading, the Public Service (Amendment) Act, 1910, authorised a system of Departmental boards responsible for determining the salaries of all officers (excepting Under Secretaries and heads of branches, for which the Public Service Board remained responsible).

Each Departmental board consisted of three members. The Chairman was a member of the Public Service Board, the other members being the Under Secretary and the head of the particular Branch employing the officers whose salaries were being reviewed. No regular grading periods were fixed, the Departmental board meeting as and when necessary to determine the salaries of officers applying for consideration.

If the decision of the Departmental board was not unanimous, provision existed for the member of the Public Service Board acting as Chairman of the Departmental board to refer the case to his two remaining Public Service Board colleagues for consideration. The officer concerned also had the right to appeal to the Public Service Board which was empowered to vary, rescind or confirm the original decision. However, if the Public Service Board's decision on appeal (i.e., to the two remaining members) was not unanimous, the case was referred for final determination to a tribunal consisting of the same two members of the Board plus a District Court Judge.

The Departmental board system functioned for nine years. There were, however, serious objections to its operation. The system did not, for example, ensure a periodical revision of each officer's work. The review occurred on application or when a promotion involved seniority. Despite the fact that a member of the Public Service Board acted as Chairman of each Departmental board, there was a lack of uniformity in the Departmental board's decisions. Moreover, there was a want of finality in that an officer who appealed unsuccessfully against the decision of a Departmental board, could immediately apply again to the Departmental board for a new hearing. Other objections were the undue demands placed upon the time of Public Service Board members and on permanent heads in hearing and determining cases and the interminable delays which occurred in dealing with cases and in notifying officers of results.

The Public Service (Amendment) Act, 1919, ended the activities of Departmental boards and provided for the constitution of salaries committees and the determination of remuneration by such salaries committees or by the Board, as the latter might determine. In the same year, the Industrial Arbitration Act was amended to grant employees under the Public Service Act access to the Industrial Courts, which had jurisdiction extending to all officers in receipt of wages and salaries up to £525 per annum. Comprehensive claims in respect of the professional, clerical and general divisions of the service were lodged in the following year, and in the period 1920 to 1922 many awards were made by the Court.

The Arbitration Act was amended in 1922 to exclude employees under the Public Service Act from the Arbitration jurisdiction. Right of access to the Court was, however, again conferred on employees under the Board's jurisdiction in 1926 and the jurisdiction was extended to officers and employees receiving up to £750 per annum. Following an amendment to the Industrial Arbitration Act in 1940, jurisdiction of the Court was extended to fix rates of wages up to £1,000 per annum. Jurisdiction was further extended to £1,750 in 1951, to £2,000 in 1953, and above £2,000 in 1957.

In 1922, the Public Service Act was amended to make provision for the Board to enter into Agreements with an association or organisation representing any group or class of officers or employees as to salaries, fees, allowances and grades (Section 14B) and to constitute Salaries Committees to make a biennial review of the grades and salaries of officers in receipt of salary not exceeding £525 per annum. The Salaries Committees consisted of three persons, at least one member representing officers or employees.

The reports of the Salaries Committees were submitted for the Board's concurrence and, if the Board were in agreement, the officers were informed accordingly. Where the Board disagreed, the amending Act provided for a reference of the case to a new Appeals Tribunal consisting of a District Court Judge sitting with two Members of the Board. In addition, any officer not satisfied with the determination of the salary had the right of appeal to the Board or to the Appeals Tribunal.

In its report for the year ended 30th June, 1923, the Board pointed out that although comparatively few appeals were made to the Tribunal (nine out of every ten applicants electing to appeal to the Board) it was emphatically of the opinion that its final authority in salary matters should be restored. The Board considered that one effect of the amending Act in this regard was to take away a great deal of the power necessary to enable the Board effectively to maintain efficiency and economy.

The Public Service (Amendment) Act, 1929, confirmed the Salaries Committee system previously authorised, committee determinations being subject to approval or variation by the Board. At the same time, the special Appeals Tribunal was abolished. But, subject to Awards determined by the Arbitration Court, the final determination of salaries, etc., became again the sole responsibility of the Board, as had been the practice from 1896 to 1922.

Thus it will be seen that a number of avenues have come to exist permitting the valuation of work and the fixation of the salaries and wages of persons employed in the Service, whether by Salaries Committees, by determination of the Board, by the Arbitration Court, or by Agreement between an appropriate employees' association and the Board.

Agreements and Grading Committees

In 1945, the practice of fixing salaries by Agreement under section 14B of the Public Service Act was beginning to develop, and from that time a rapidly increasing number of classes of officers have been covered by these Agreements. Where an Agreement is made under this section fixing the salaries of a group or class of officers, the salaries committees contemplated by section 14A of the Act do not operate.

Under section 14B of the Public Service Act the Board may enter into an Agreement with an association or organisation representing any group or class of officers and employees as to salaries, fees, allowances or grades and may by regulations prescribe the salaries, etc., so agreed upon. Such an Agreement is binding not only on the Board and the association or organisation signing it but also on all officers and employees in the class or group covered by the Agreement whether they are members of such association or organisation or not and no such officer or employee has any right of appeal from the terms of such Agreement.

This is interpreted to mean that where an Agreement is concluded, the Board is not required to carry out the biennial review of salaries contemplated in relation to officers and employees covered by the Agreement. The Board, however, has varied the terms of an Agreement during its currency where it is satisfied that valid grounds exist for doing so. Nevertheless it has always insisted that any variation of an Agreement during its currency should be only by the consent of the parties to it. The Board has also taken the view that it may increase the salary of an individual officer where circumstances so require during the currency of an Agreement.

The Industrial Commission has recognised the sanctity of these Agreements. Although it has held that the existence of a current Agreement made pursuant to the section does not affect the jurisdiction of tribunals under the Industrial Arbitration Act to make an award covering the same group or class of officers and employees, such jurisdiction should be exercised only in "special and exceptional circumstances".

There is much to be said in favour of this method of salary fixation because, although it may be true that there is some "give and take" by the parties, an Agreement frequently represents more accurately the combined views of the parties to it. The overwhelming number of officers and employees whose associations have adopted this method would seem to be a good indication of its popularity.

Over 90 per cent. of the salaries in the service are now determined by Agreements made under section 14B, and most of them provide specific scales of salaries in respect of the various classes of positions existing in the Service, and in some cases the actual work content of the various grades is specified. In the course of the negotiations, representatives of the Board and of the associations review the salaries for the various classifications and grades, and frequently too the work appropriate thereto is reviewed.

Notwithstanding this opportunity for review of work classifications, certain Agreements specifically provide for the constitution of Grading Committees empowered to consider the grading of positions referred to them by the Board and to make recommendations to the Board as to the reclassification of the position. It is customary for such Agreements to provide for reference of cases to the Grading Committees only in the event of a substantial alteration of duties or an anomaly. The Agreements provide that in all cases the Board shall have the final decision on the grading. Even in cases where there is no express provision in an Agreement for the constitution of a Grading Committee, the Board has agreed to constitute a Committee to deal with individual cases arising under the Agreement.

In respect of the salaries not covered by Award or Agreement, the Board still makes determinations every two years as required by the Act.

The Industrial Commission

While power to determine the salaries of Public Servants is vested both in the Industrial Commission and the Public Service Board, the Industrial

Commission has authority to determine only minimum rates whereas no such restriction applies to the Public Service Board. In its judgment in *In re Crown Employees* (*Clerks, Professional, Public Trust Office and Lands Department*) *Award* (1929 A.R. 135 at 137) the Commission said that "the duty of the Conciliation Committee and of this Commission (is) to form its own independent judgment as to the proper salaries to be awarded, applying the same principles as it would in the case of any other employer. There is nothing in the Industrial Arbitration Act to suggest that different principles are to be applied, and we can see no reason for treating an application for an Award to cover persons employed under the Public Service Act in any way differently from any other application made with a view to having rates prescribed for any other classes of employees, or (assuming the power) for individual employees."

At page 138, the Commission continued: "the Committee's duty is clear, namely, to consider the work required to be performed by any officer holding the position in question, and in the exercise of its discretion and in the light of evidence as to such work, to assess what is regarded as a fair and proper rate of remuneration as a minimum which should be paid to any individual carrying out those duties."

The Board and Classification

Not being required to fix what are strictly minimum rates within the meaning of the term as used in the Industrial Arbitration Act, the Public Service Board determines rates appropriate to positions, taking into account not only work value but other considerations. Consequently, the salaries paid are generally in excess of the rates which would, strictly speaking, compensate officers for the grade or type of work actually performed.

Broadly speaking, there may be said to be two general classes of gradings in the service. One class comprises career scales divided into grades, and promotion from grade to grade is dependent not on the precise value of the work actually being performed at any particular stage, but on length of service combined with satisfaction of certain requirements for promotion prescribed by Agreement, regard being had, in determining the scale, to the increasing value of the work falling to be performed by the officer as he progresses.

The second class comprises officers performing duties in respect of which a specific grading is allotted appropriate to work value. While it is true that in these cases also the rates determined by the Board or by Agreement are not minimum rates and take into account factors other than the value of the work performed, they are, nevertheless, referable in substantial measure to the value of the work undertaken. It is within this class that a Grading Committee functions, it being required to consider and recommend whether specified duties should be placed in a higher or lower grade or should remain in their existing grades. Officers normally serve a number of years on an incremental scale before moving into graded positions. There is a certain body of work in most fields of activity for which a specific salary is not fixed, since any part of the work may be performed by an officer at any stage within the scale. The principle on which the salary is fixed is that the maximum salary of the scale is determined by reference to the best class of work comprised within the scale.

The Industrial Commission, in considering the question of incremental scales in 1939, said:—

"It is common ground that it would be impossible to assess individual minimum salaries for all of the positions in the Public Service held by male clerical officers, and that the only practicable method of remuneration, up to a point, is by an incremental scale of salaries. But a salary scale under which an officer gets annual increments, subject only to compliance with examination requirements, good conduct and proper performance of duties, quite apart from the nature of the work he has to do, is not an ideal method of prescribing minimum rates, and should not be employed longer than is necessary. As soon as it is reasonably possible, rates of pay should be related to the work actually being done. The Commission thinks that for the officers concerned, a scale should be awarded covering the earlier years of an officer's service when he is generally engaged on simple clerical work and during which period he can, as a rule, be given, from year to year, work of increasing value."

In an organisation as large as the public service, there is inevitably a great volume of work which does not readily lend itself to classification within a rigid set of grades, and, as already stated, service within grades is usually preceded by service on an incremental scale. The argument against the Industrial Commission's view that as soon as it is reasonably possible the salary rates should be related to the work actually being done, is that many people would prefer a lengthy scale with assured salary progression such as one commonly finds in the case of bank and insurance offices. The objection to this is that it tends to stifle ambition and incentive. In practice, the system in the New South Wales Public Service has worked satisfactorily and the short incremental scale of ten years for clerical officers has meant rapid promotion to classified positions for officers with comparatively short service.

As early as 1929 the Industrial Commission itself pointed out that the Public Service Board and the special tribunals (e.g., Salaries Committees) constituted under the Public Service Act have jurisdiction to consider the nature of the work performed by members of the Public Service and to prescribe not merely the minimum rate of pay which is proper for classes of employees or for positions but the actual salary appropriate for each officer in that service.

In dealing with the jurisdiction of the Conciliation Committee the Commission said:—

"As regards the rate which it is proper to award for any particular position, that will depend upon the duties required to be performed by an officer in that position. For the purpose of determining what those duties are it is, of course, material to ascertain what work is in fact performed by the officers holding those positions, and it is also material to know what qualifications those officers have. But the fact that a particular officer holds special qualifications which are not necessary for the efficient carrying out of the duties of the position, such, e.g., as the acquisition of a degree or diploma, etc., or a long experience, or some individual aptitude, is no ground in itself for awarding a rate higher than would otherwise have been awarded for that position, though these may add to the value to an employer of the individual occupant of the position. The Committee's duty is clear, namely, to consider the work required to be performed by an officer holding the position in question, and, in the exercise of its discretion and in the light of the evidence as to such work, to assess what it regards as a fair and proper rate of remuneration as a minimum which should be paid to any individual carrying out those duties."

The jurisdiction of the Board is therefore at least co-ordinate and in some respects wider than that of the industrial tribunals. For example, the Board has frequently granted to officers an enhanced salary progression because of the lack of promotion available to them in their particular field of work, where the tribunals would be limited to fixing a flat rate of pay. In other cases long service is recognised by the grant of a similar scale with increments after, say, five and ten years service. Again the Board has granted a special salary to officers possessing certain academic qualifications which, though not necessary to the performance of their duties, render them better qualified to carry out such duties.

Federal Awards

It is necessary to mention the incidence of Federal Awards in the public service although comparatively few officers and employees are covered by such awards.

To establish the jurisdiction of the tribunals constituted under the Commonwealth Conciliation and Arbitration Act, 1956, it is necessary that there exist an industrial dispute extending beyond the limits of any one State. There is considerable doubt as to the extent, if any, to which the jurisdiction of these tribunals may be exercised in respect of employees in the public service engaged in carrying out the executive, administrative and judicial functions of government. The question arises whether such employees are engaged in "industry". The only awards so far made binding on the State of New South Wales in respect of employees under the Public Service Act are those which have been made in settlement of disputes concerning the wages and conditions of tradesmen and other manual workers.

Staff Associations

It will be clear from the above that employee associations have been playing an increasing part in decisions on questions affecting public servants. Regular conferences between staff associations and the Board are now a permanent feature of the administration of the service. Apart from this the Board's senior officers are in daily contact with the various unions concerning matters affecting the service. During the year 1956-57, 48 conferences were held by the Board with various employee organisations. In New South Wales the largest unions operating in the public service proper are the Public Service Association of New South Wales (formed in 1899 and with 14,644 members in 1955,(°), and the New South Wales Teachers' Federation (formed in 1915 and with 17,423 members in 1955). There are separate associations for professional officers, police, fire brigade employees and so on—and, of course, for railway employees and industrial workers generally.

Employee associations are naturally mainly concerned with pay and conditions, although there is a growing tendency for them to seek consultation on matters of administration. Some have at times pressed for a larger voice in the service, extending to representation on the Board itself. There is nothing to prevent Australian staff associations from affiliating with outside bodies, though generally a majority of their members have been opposed to any links that might indicate political bias. The Public Service Association's own rules forbid its members to take part in strikes.

In this regard it might be noted that section 99 of the Industrial Arbitration Act renders illegal any strike by Crown employees.

Conclusion

It is noteworthy that while governments have differed on the question of whether persons employed under the Public Service Act should have access to the ordinary industrial tribunals, no government has seen fit to entrust to such tribunals the task of determining all the conditions of employment of such persons. Successive governments, no doubt, have recognised the wisdom of leaving such matters to the Public Service Board, whose members not only have had lengthy training in the public service but have also an intimate knowledge of its day-to-day problems.

Industrial unions representing employees have at various times sought to have the restriction on the jurisdiction of the industrial tribunals removed, principally on the grounds that the employees have no independent arbiter to which they may have recourse to settle disputes relating to conditions generally. The gravamen of the objection is really that the Public Service Board is not an independent body, but the employer.

The clear intention of the Public Service Act, however, is that the Board itself should be independent of political control. It seems that while the legislature intends that the measures which a representative government should decide to carry out remain a matter for that government, the task of ensuring that the departments implementing those measures shall be supplied with an adequate and efficient staff properly remunerated should be a matter for an independent authority.

(°)See report of Industrial Registrar, 1955. The official organ of the Public Service Association in N.S.W. is *Red Tape* (monthly) and there are similar journals in other States, e.g., *Victorian Public Service Journal*.

Chapter Fifteen

ORGANISATION AND METHODS

K. E. GRAINGER

It might be thought that investigations into organisation and methods by independent specialists are solely the province of management consultants operating in industrial and commercial fields. It is not generally known that practically every large public service today has specialised units actively and continuously taking stock of the management aspects of departmental administration, and acting in the capacity of independent advisers. In fact the very nature of government administration forces the development of this activity to an even higher degree than is generally found in private enterprise. In a public service where turnover and profit margins are not applicable, an organisation and methods investigation does not begin its operations on the evidence of inefficiency thrown up by a profit and loss account. Management efficiency may fall off undetected unless a constant watch on performance is kept, using other criteria.

It is remarkable how interest in O and M studies has intensified throughout the world in the last few years; most countries with well-developed government administrations have established O and M units; publications dealing with various aspects of management, public and private, have increased greatly in number; at the international level the United Nations Organization has taken an active interest in fostering the administrative efficiency of public authorities; through the International Institute of Administrative Sciences and its Committee of Administrative Practices, various studies of administrative management are proceeding and closer liaison between practising O and M officers of the various nations has been developed.[1]

This may be regarded as an outgrowth of the "Scientific Management" movement which was pioneered in the field of private industry by such men as Taylor, Gilbreth and Fayol, and has now developed into the systematic and objective study of all aspects of administration. Its present increased acceptance and application in governmental administration, however, can be attributed in large part to the impact of the last world war with its unparalleled problems of organisation and development of manpower and material resources; and generally to the considerable extension of governmental activities which has occurred over comparatively recent years. The tendency for the activities of government to become wider in scope and more positive in objective, not merely regulatory but operational, and the multiplication of the contacts between the official and the private person,

---

This chapter is based on a paper originally prepared for the Royal Institute of Public Administration (N.S.W. Regional Group) in 1953.

[1] See, e.g., T. D. Kingdom, *Improvement of Organization and Management in Public Administration*, International Institute of Administrative Sciences, 1951. This is a comparative study, based on answers to questionnaires circulated to various countries.

has forced greater attention to the problems of public administration. It was no doubt an appreciation of these problems which led to the formation of O and M officers (or Divisions of Administrative Management or similarly titled offices) in the Public Services of Great Britain, the United States, Sweden and Belgium and later in those of many other countries.

The principles and practice of "O and M" are not new to public administration—

"what is new is that public administration has entered a period that calls for a new approach and that this has now become generally recognised ; and that what has been developed in other fields under other names ("Management Engineering", "Research and Planning", "Scientific Management", "Operational Research") has been adapted to the particular problems and requirements of public administration under the title of Organisation and Methods."(²)

The Public Service Acts of the Commonwealth, of several Australian States and of New Zealand have for many years required Public Service Boards to take such steps as may be necessary to ensure the efficiency of the services under their control. Section 17 of the Commonwealth Act, for instance, gives the Board wide responsibilities for effecting economies and promoting efficiency in the management and working of departments. It requires the Board to do this by improving organisation and procedures, by simplifying work, co-ordinating the activities of departments and ensuring the use of staff to the best advantage. Readers who look up this detailed Section may be interested to see how completely the essential elements of modern O and M practice were recognised when it was adopted in 1922. But the basic objective was also expressed in the original Commonwealth Act of 1902, in the N.S.W. Act of the same year which is still in force, and it can be traced back to the pioneer Victorian Public Service Act of 1883.

I hasten to point out that the responsibility for Service efficiency does not rest on the Boards alone and that the chief officers of departments have a corresponding responsibility.

In discharging their responsibilities the Commonwealth and other Public Service Boards have maintained a continuous system of measurement and check of the work of departments and a critical oversight of organisation and operating methods. Over recent years, the Commonwealth Board has endeavoured to extend and intensify its own and departmental activities in this field, and since 1948 has progressively been developing special sections now generally known as "O and M".

Other Australian Public Service Boards and Commissions have, in their several ways, developed investigating sections to help them in testing and improving the administration of departments, but the degree of development of the O and M type of unit, for a variety of reasons, varies between them. The views expressed in this chapter will refer mainly to the Commonwealth and N.S.W. public services, as it is with these that the writer is most familiar.

(²) N. Baliol Scott, *Report on the Introduction of an Organisation and Methods Division into the Ceylon Public Service.*

THE PURPOSE OF O AND M

I can give no better definition of what O and M offices are expected to do than that stated in the Fifth Report of the British Select Committee on Estimates (1947). It is—

> "The purpose of O and M in the Civil Service is to secure maximum efficiency in the operation of the Government's executive machinery; and by the expert application of scientific methods to organisation, to achieve economy in cost and labour."

It is, I think, important to note also that the Committee went on to say—

> "The operations of the O and M service, although not directed primarily to securing reductions in staff, almost invariably result in the more economical use of staff."

"Efficiency" in public administration may be said to depend firstly upon a full understanding and a clear statement of the end results sought by the Government; the definition of administrative policy must be firm and precise so that officers of all ranks may direct their activities appropriately to the achievement of the Government's objective. Secondly, it requires a well-designed organisation with proper distribution of functions and definition of individual responsibilities so as to ensure that the objectives are achieved expeditiously. Thirdly, the operating methods employed should be as simple and direct as practicable so that the best possible return is obtained for the time and effort, equipment and materials, expended.

Apart from factors connected with personnel, these are the main, if not the only, considerations in the problem of administrative efficiency. They ultimately place on the O and M unit a responsibility to consider and develop new and improved systems and functional arrangements and for that purpose to examine such matters as the line of organisation and the work flow, the division of labour and its related problem of co-ordination and control, the simplification of method and the maximum use of equipment, the location of facilities and office layout and lastly, but not least, the use of personnel. Competent staff can operate most effectively only if the organisation and its procedures are efficient and it is the business of the O and M unit to assist in achieving that efficiency.

The O and M unit needs to keep in mind, however, that mere improvement of the physical environment, and of equipment, methods and procedures, will not of itself guarantee efficiency, even though it is an essential means to this end. An organisation is not a machine. However well organised and equipped, employees must have a common purpose, a common understanding of the means to effect that purpose, and a common will to achieve it. The organisation must be psychologically "right". If it is not, if morale is low and co-operation is lacking, then the work of the organisation will suffer.

The development of morale and of enthusiasm for work is, however, one of the more intangible elements of management, and to this extent is outside the scope of an O and M investigation. Nevertheless, the investigator, in his talks with employees, will uncover frustrations, anxieties, and conflicts which are a consequence of inadequate personnel management rather than of deficiencies in organisation and methods. In such cases he can assist the department by informally drawing attention to the problem and can at the same time take the opportunity of "selling" the importance of the psychological aspects of management where its significance is not yet fully recognised.

THE NEED FOR O AND M REVIEWS

Having told you what "O and M" is and what its objective is, may I briefly refer to the need for these surveys and some recent results achieved?

The functions of departments and, to an extent, of branches as we find them today are very largely the result of development over the years, meeting perhaps the immediate needs of government at the time of their introduction, perhaps dictated by considerations of political or administrative expediency, and retained since without review despite changes in circumstances. Quite unrelated functions have been placed with a department or branch for reasons valid enough perhaps at the time but no longer so.

Practice and procedure have, in many cases, also developed gradually, rather on a piecemeal basis. Examination has revealed that many present operations result from the requirements of earlier administrations, serve little useful purpose today and have continued because of a conservative or unimaginative approach to the work of the department and a failure to review its operations. As in the industrial field, so too in the administrative field, techniques are constantly changing, new ideas coming forward, new processes being evolved. Processes must, therefore, be constantly and continuously reviewed and adjusted so that the administration is kept abreast of current developments and needs. As someone else pointed out— the demand for more service and for greater speed in service calls for a new treatment of old problems.

The determination of any organisation or of any procedure, nevertheless, requires careful and painstaking study and a commonsense approach ; it is not a simple *ad hoc* process. It has aptly been said—"There are good reasons why a survey of procedures in the Public Service should be undertaken. While the Service may take justifiable pride in the integrity and all-over standard of its work, charges of 'delay' and 'red tape' are made so constantly that the good name of the Service demands they be nailed by proving that what hasty critics term 'delay' is no more than the operation of reasonable care in the spending of public money, and that 'red tape' is doing necessary things in their proper order. But first we must prove such things to ourselves."

That there is urgent need for these investigations there is no doubt ; investigations so far conducted have amply proved it, and heads of departments are pressing for more and more of them to be made. In this connection, it is interesting to observe that the report of the U.S. Commission on Re-organization of the Executive Branch stated—

> "We recommend that responsibility for management research become a definite and continuing task of top management in every executive agency. We also recommend the strengthening of the Administrative Management Division of the Office of the Budget in order that Departments may receive additional assistance, guidance and stimulation in this work."

It is significant, too, that a strong endorsement of O and M in Great Britain was given by the Select Committee on National Expenditure when the country was at war and every nerve strained to ensure the maximum use of manpower resources. It was endorsed again in the immediate post-war years by the Select Committee on Estimates (1947).

The O and M units in the Commonwealth Service have brought about considerable savings in administrative costs from the objective type of study of organisation and procedure which they conduct. Their results have been achieved in various ways, and the variety is of itself indicative of the scope and possibilities of the O and M review.

For instance—

(a) Recasting and redesigning of forms in use by one division of a department gave a saving of 100 officers.

(b) Changing the work flow, and in consequence, the lines of organisation reduced the operating costs in one branch by £15,000 a year.

(c) Mechanising a large, but routine, operation in one State branch is expected to show a saving of £22,000 a year, with further economies as the new system is extended to other State branches.

(d) Eliminating unnecessary functions and decentralising activities effected a reduction of £30,000 a year in another department.

(e) Varying existing methods of collating and co-ordinating a series of documents achieved a saving of £35,000 a year.

Other illustrations could be given where the O and M survey has led to speedier handling of public business, decreased overtime and so on. Savings in many cases are difficult of estimation, but can be said already to have exceeded £500,000 a year. Possibly, however, the indirect effects of the O and M reviews, as for instance in the raising of morale and in the stimulation of management thinking, represent the greatest benefits of O and M to the public service.

The organisation, nevertheless, is still small; at the central level it will preferably remain so; and much yet lies ahead of us. Not the least of our tasks are the training of suitable officers for work of this kind and the development at all levels of a full appreciation of the responsibilities of administrative management.

THE O AND M AGENCY

The O and M agency in the Commonwealth Service is at present organised on a central and a departmental level and in this conforms to the pattern of O and M organisation in other countries. The role of each may be considered basically the same but there is a difference in approach and in emphasis.

A Central Unit

It will generally be found that the central O and M agency is placed immediately under the head of the government or in a department operating closely to him. In some countries, the central O and M agency is combined with the central personnel agency, possibly as an independent department;

in others, the agency may be placed under an existing department, frequently the treasury department.

The pattern in the Commonwealth Service conforms to the first of these arrangements while that of Great Britain comes into the second category. Let us consider each of these types of organisation a little further.

The United Kingdom Select Committee on National Expenditure of Session 1941-42 after review of the "arrangements for watching over and promoting the efficient and economic organisation of the Civil Service as a whole" accepted the attachment of O and M to the Treasury. It recommended *inter alia* that the scope of the Treasury O and M Division should be enlarged so as to cover the higher levels of organisation, that smaller departments should be periodically investigated by the Treasury O and M Division but that O and M sections should be set up in the larger departments which did not already possess them. It is of interest, too, that the Committee recommended also that:

(i) an officer of wide experience and high standing should be placed at the head of each existing departmental O and M section, and he should be directly responsible to the Permanent Head;

(ii) the recruitment of organisation officers should include both civil servants and persons with business experience; and

(iii) interchange of organisation officers between departments should be encouraged.

The Select Committee on Estimates, Session 1946-47, following an investigation of "organisation and method and its effect on the staffing of Government departments" stated—([3])

"41. The centre of O and M activities is at the Treasury. There was no evidence that the departmental O and M Branches regarded the Treasury O and M Division as being associated with the Treasury role of financial policeman. On the contrary, all the departmental and individual witnesses spoke highly of the valuable assistance and advice obtained from the Division. Your Committee recognise the need for an O and M Division which can act as a clearing house for O and M information; conduct investigations, the results of which are suitable for general application; organise training courses to improve the quality and quantity of O and M staff throughout the Civil Service; and carry out O and M work for departments without O and M Branches of their own. They recommend that this arrangement should be maintained . . .

55. Your Committee therefore recommend that:

(a) The centre of O and M activities should remain at the Treasury.

(b) The departmental officer in charge of Establishments as well as O and M should be renamed Organisation and Establishments Officer, or Organisation Officer, and his Division should be similarly renamed.

(c) Priority should be given to a continuous study of the processes

---

([3]) See Select Committee on Estimates, *Fifth Report*, Session 1946-47.

and operations in a Department, rather than to an examination of problems as they arise ; when new activities are being planned, O and M should be brought in at the very early stages.

(*d*) More attention should be given to securing O and M staff from the training of suitable officers within a Department and from among qualified men outside the Service. To this end, the status of O and M officers should be raised and the salaries, terms of employment, etc., be sufficient to attract and retain men of required quality.

(*e*) O and M should form a prominent part of the preliminary training of Assistant Principals, and a greater number of recruits, from both the Administrative and other grades, should be selected to undergo the O and M training course. No officer who has not attended the Treasury training course should be appointed to the headship of the O and M Branch in any Department. A special course should be devised by the training branch of the Treasury O and M Division, for Principal Establishments Officers."

The foregoing generally represents the policy being followed in Great Britain today. Every endeavour is being made to build up in departments trained and strong O and M branches with responsibility for continuous detailed review of organisation and operations. The central O and M staff offers an advisory service to all departments, actually carrying out the work for the smaller ones ; deals with questions of inter-departmental relationships ; maintains contact with industry and non-government management associations, thus keeping the governmental agencies informed of management techniques which may be useful to the Government ; deals with any special problems ; stimulates departmental activity and co-ordinates it where necessary.

The advisory role of the O and M unit is constantly and strongly emphasised. The O and M officer is "essentially a consultant" called by the administrative head of a department to advise on the form and practice of the organisation ; the O and M officer is not responsible for the execution of the work under review ; and so on. It follows also that the O and M branch, whether of the central agency or of the department, has no power, at least directly, to enforce the introduction of that change in organisation or in method which the branch considers desirable and perhaps essential to efficient administration. So far as the central unit is concerned, however, the fact of its attachment to an authority exercising direct controls in other avenues is no doubt significant in the overall result.

The Australian picture is coloured somewhat differently. Firstly, it should be noted that the central O and M agency is attached to a Public Service Board or Commission, which thus exercises not only those functions generally vested elsewhere in a Civil Service Commission, but also certain functions which in older countries are attached to a Treasury Department(')

(') Many arguments in favour of one or the other system have been advanced from time to time. It is impracticable to discuss them within the scope of this chapter.

The Commonwealth Public Service Board is, for instance, responsible for recruitment to the Service, the conduct and prescription of entrance and promotions examinations and determination of other conditions for appointment to the Service, fixes conditions of employment, controls promotion and disciplinary matters and so on. It also can and does determine the organisation, and thus to a material extent the procedures, of any department at any time—although the concurrence of the administrative head of the department is necessary to make this effective ; the creation and abolition of offices in a department is determined on the recommendation of the Board ; the Board may at any time enter any department for the purpose of carrying out its duties, may summon any person whose evidence appears to be material in any inspection, inquiry or investigation the Board is conducting, take evidence on oath and require the production of documents. It will be seen, too, that section 17 of the Public Service Act, to which I have referred previously, places on the Board a direct responsibility for efficient departmental management in its widest sense, but that the Board cannot of itself enforce the introduction of changes opposed by the department. The Board's "power" flows from the fact that without its sanction an organisation cannot be set up or varied. The fact that the Board is able, and indeed required, to report annually to Parliament on measures it considers necessary for the good of an efficient Service, and thus to enlist public support for its views, is an important factor in any consideration of the "power" of that authority.

The New South Wales Public Service Board is directly empowered to make, and has introduced, such changes in organisation or in method as it deems desirable in the interest of efficiency and economy of administration. It has powers similar to those of the Commonwealth Public Service Board in respect of creation and abolition of offices (although operated in a different way), recruitment, promotion, discipline, of entry into departments, reporting to parliament, etc. It constantly exercises these powers and is able to enforce co-operation in implementation. Generally, therefore, its control appears to be more positive than that of the Commonwealth Board.

It is also important to note that an investigation of organisation and of method conducted by the O and M units of these Boards, and the reports they submit, are not necessarily limited by an acceptance of existing policies. Administrative, and even governmental, policy may be reviewed in the normal course of an O and M investigation, and if revision is considered necessary in the interests of efficient and economical administration, the Board will submit its views to the head of the Government. These questions may arise in respect of inter-departmental or Commonwealth/State relationships ; they may involve consideration of the relative developments of economic and developmental services by different authorities ; or they may refer to matters peculiar to the internal administration of the one department. The role of these Public Service Boards and thus of the central O and M units in such cases is, of course, advisory but generally the prestige of the Board, its overall knowledge of departmental functions and responsibilities, and its objective approach to matters of this kind give considerable weight to the recommendations made.

While, however, the colouring may be different, the objectives are the same and there are many points of similarity between O and M in England

and in Australia. The Permanent Head of an Australian department has a direct and specific responsibility for the proper management of his department—and rightly so. The Public Service Board has made it clear that there must be no doubts in the minds of executive officers on this score. Secondly, it is accepted that no matter how carefully it has been designed, an "organisation" will not function smoothly and effectively nor a "method" give the best results without the active interest and support of departmental officers immediately responsible for the execution of the work. It is also recognised that the O and M unit does not have the executive responsibility and must accordingly "sell" its ideas. The emphasis is not so much on "power" of one or the other as it is on "collaboration". The dual responsibilities of the Board and department in effect constitute a partnership; full and frank co-operation between them is accepted as essential to the best interests of the Service.([5])

Two points may be emphasised at this stage:

(a) The personal approach of an O and M officer to his job; the attributes of tact and discretion, patience and application, imagination and flexibility of mind, common sense and judgment which he needs to bring to his work; the collaboration, the mutual respect and confidence, which needs to be developed between "inspector" and "inspected" so that the organisation suggested by the former becomes accepted by the latter as a helpful agency for promoting real efficiency; the need to avoid over-emphasis to others and particularly to himself of his own knowledge and experience and to bear in mind the thought: "Every man I meet is in some way my superior; and in that I can learn of him." (Emerson)

(b) The advantages which the detached O and M officer has over the departmental officer in the way of time to devote to the study, freedom from the personal relationships existing in a department, objectivity of approach, the chance to take an untrammelled overall view and experience gained from a number of investigations, or the disadvantages of lack of executive responsibility, of remoteness from day-to-day operations.

A Departmental Unit

The foregoing refers particularly to the role of the central O and M agency. Nevertheless, it has application also to the corresponding unit in the department. The one is complementary to the other, and joint development with continuous collaboration and consultation is essential if each is to benefit in full from the experience of the other.

The departmental, like the central, agency is not directly responsible for the task performance and must collaborate with the executive branches in the formulation of new procedures and in the preparation of organisation submissions to the Public Service Board. It is closer to the actual operating level than is the central agency and is expected to exercise the detailed and

---

([5]) Whether an O and M unit achieves its greatest effect in an advisory capacity or whether it should have power to implement its recommendations (directly or through, for instance, a Public Service Board) is not a very important question when harmonious relations exist, as they generally do in Australia.

continuing oversight requisite to efficient day-to-day management. It generally operates directly under the administrative head of the department.(*)

In the Commonwealth Service, the function of the O and M unit has, in brief, been defined as embracing:

(a) Continuous review of the organisation of each branch and section; the allocation of functions between branches and sections, staff establishments, and the like.

(b) Improvement of methods of working; the study of forms design and of their end uses, of the application and use of machine processes and office aids generally, of work flow and measurement, of delegations, of causes of absenteeism, sick leave and overtime, of office layout and furniture, the study of all matters affecting the efficient and economical performance of prescribed functions.

(c) Research in these fields and maintenance of appropriate liaison with the central and other departmental O and M units.

In recognition of the fact that the total efficiency of any department depends as much on its personnel as the plan of its organisation and procedures, the O and M unit is also, in practice, closely linked in the department with its personnel management section, particularly in its staff training and staff welfare activities.

In some departments there is, in fact, an integration of the O and M and personnel functions under the one control. This is a reflection in part of the functions of the Public Service Board, which, under the Australian pattern, has duties and responsibilities in both fields. However, irrespective of whether a grouping of all these activities in one unit is accepted as good practice, or otherwise, each of them is complementary to the other, and requires co-ordination at some point so that real administrative efficiency may be realised.

Future Development

It will be seen that the role of the O and M unit is to aid departmental management and to assist the Public Service Board appropriately to discharge its legislative responsibilities for the development and maintenance of the highest possible standards of efficiency and economy in the Public Service. The O and M unit does this through specialised study of the techniques of administrative management and the application of "scientific method" to that task.

It is, however, not enough that the review of management be left to these special units. Every section, branch and divisional head within a department must become "management" conscious. As he is carrying the burden

---

(*) It will be noted that this conforms to the practice recommended by the Select Committee in England. In Australia consideration has nevertheless been given to the alternative system whereby the O and M officer would be an officer of the Board. This system would have the merit of retaining a sense of unity with the central O and M body; encourage an inter-departmental approach to departmental O and M problems; facilitate liaison, enable experience of officers to be widened by transfer; and promote the effective dissemination of O and M practices.

of the day-to-day executive task, it is not expected that he will be able personally to devote much time to the detailed study and improvement of techniques. It will suffice if his administration is directed along appropriate lines, that he leads and stimulates the thinking of his subordinates, that he perceives avenues of investigation and that he approaches objectively all suggestions made by his subordinates or by special investigators. To this end, it is advisable to give the embryo sectional and branch heads some experience in an O and M unit during their earlier service and that the specialist O and M officers should move out to executive posts.

A development in the Commonwealth Service has been the assembly of all departmental O and M officers in a particular State and their proposed division into study groups. Members of the groups will render mutual assistance to one another in the various problems arising and will undertake detailed study assignments of particular operations of common interest. It is expected that the study groups will meet mostly outside official time in recognition of the training and experience, and of the development of confidence and knowledge, that each member will gain from discussions with those charged with responsibilities like his own. The exchange of ideas and generally the thoughts provoked from these group discussions should prove, moreover, of great value to the Service as a whole.

THE O AND M INVESTIGATION

Some knowledge of the techniques of an O and M investigation is necessary to an appreciation of the service which administrative management can obtain from O and M. The investigation is in fact very similar to that made in the industrial and commercial field by the management consultant.[7]

It can be said that there are three major steps in an O and M investigation. They are:

(a) The collection, assembling, recording and checking of facts.

(b) An analysis of the facts recorded.

(c) The construction (or formulation) of an improved organisation or work procedure.

An understanding of the task confronting him is, of course, the obvious first requirement of the O and M officer for it is only then that he can determine the appropriate method of approach to it, the order in which the examination should proceed, the extent and timing of the investigation, the possible division of the work among his assistants and so on. In other words, there must be a proper planning of the investigation.

Other preliminary steps will also be taken before the actual investigation is commenced; they involve some fact gathering, and to that extent link in with the more detailed factual investigation which follows, discovering the general line of control and the making of necessary contacts with departmental officers. At this stage, the O and M officer will, for instance, seek a full statement of functions or objectives, references to statutory or other provisions under which the department operates, organisation charts and

---

[7] For a detailed account, see H. O. Dovey, *Handbook of Organisation and Methods Techniques*, International Institute of Administrative Sciences, 1951.

duty statements, details of the geographical spread of the department, of attached agencies, approved delegations and the line of authority, information in respect of the origin and growth of the department or process and of other departments with interlocking functions. Preliminary discussions with the heads of sections, branches and divisions will moreover help the O and M officer in gaining an overall view of the aims and objectives of the department and its executives, of particular difficulties the administration may be facing and of weaknesses it is desired to correct. They also help to give perspective to the investigation, enabling it to be properly planned with appropriate break-down of the total assignment and to establish those contacts which provide the basis of future collaboration.

Because of the relationships which exist in Australia between departments and the Public Service Boards, by law and otherwise, it is not customary nor even requisite in this country to draw up a specific assignment or "charter" of investigation for the central O and M agency preliminary to the commencement of its investigation. The assignment given to the unit is in fact usually verbal and in broad general terms not limiting in any way the scope of inquiry which the unit may in its discretion deem it necessary to make. The assignment given may refer to a whole department or it may request revision of a particular operation. "The organisation and working of the Department of .... (or such and such Branch or Division)— or the materials planning and procurement practice of the Department— needs investigation—go to it."

Collecting the Facts

The collection, recording and assembly of the facts of an organisation and its work is perhaps the most onerous and time-consuming operation in an investigation. It must, however, be remembered that the "facts" must be just that, for it is upon the basis of the information obtained and its accuracy that subsequent recommendations are made. Moreover, it is upon the knowledge gained from this detailed study that the O and M officer really obtains a full understanding and appreciation of the objectives of the department; it is only by absorbing these details that he can "speak the language" of the department and give confidence in his suggestions.

The extent to which fact collection could go will be apparent. It requires the O and M officer to be selective, to discriminate between the relevant and the irrelevant. The information obtained and recorded should be such as is necessary to reach sound conclusions; it must not be too little, since in that there is danger of misunderstanding and faulty premises; it must not be too much, because that may confuse. Again, there is the necessity to discriminate between fact and assumption or belief; to obtain the rule and not what someone may believe to be the rule; to test and seek confirmation and not blindly to accept generalised statements.

The O and M officer should, therefore, endeavour to obtain his "facts" at first hand and this he may do, for example, by interviewing each officer in the organisation or in the chain of the operation. Experience will show that the officer charged with the job is best able to explain in detail what he does, what forms, records, equipment, etc., he uses and how he uses them. It brings forward information which is not recorded in a statement of duties or helps to explain an instruction; it invites ideas and suggestions for improvement; it enables the effectiveness of staff selection, training and promotion activities, as well as of the individual, to be assessed.

Experience will, however, also show, particularly where the departmental training programme is poor, that the officer may not know the purpose of his work, of the use to which it is put, what happens to it. He may know what is done but be unable to judge the necessity of doing those things. He may tell of practice but not of rule. may assume certain things and in time come to believe them to be true and may perhaps colour his information because of grievance or other personal bias. Fear lest his job be in danger, suspicion of the motives of the investigating officer, a false sense of loyalty, impatience, pride, conservatism—any of these traits may be encountered in the officer interviewed and must be overcome. Or, again, the knowledge and experience of the executive officer may offset, or even hide, a weakness in method. However, it all means that the O and M officer must be critical of the information given, actually viewing and checking the operation step by step through the organisation, returning perhaps to an earlier point for review of a phase of the operation in the light of later information, and generally ensuring that only facts are recorded.

The interviewing of officers responsible for the various tasks of the organisation combined with an examination at the same time of files actually being handled, of forms used and of records kept, demonstration of process followed, and so on is nevertheless accepted in Australian O and M practice as essential to a full understanding of the department, of its organisation, of its process and of its problems and thus to suggestions for improvement.

The techniques for securing information vary, but one which generally yields results is that of asking a series of questions beginning with "What?", "Why?", "How?", etc.:

What?—provides definitions and explanations.

Why?—relates the subject to causes, reasons.

How?—provides manner or method of achievement; combined with "many" it provides statistics.

Who?—relates the subject to persons or personal factors.

Which?—relates it to particular cases.

When?—relates the subject to time sequence.

Where?—relates it to place or position.

In summary, it can be said that in fact collection, emphasis is placed upon verification of "fact", accuracy of recording, and the adoption of a generally critical and analytical approach. The facts should normally cover the objective and purpose of the organisation or process, the arrangement or plan of the organisation and the sectional or branch relationships, the allocation of function to section and individual and the degrees of responsibility conceded, work loads and work standards, the procedures followed, the forms used and the records kept, time factors, operating costs, the state of the work, arrears, overtime, absenteeism, sick leave, geographical spread and relations with attached or other agencies with activities impinging upon the work of the organisation under review. Discretion must be exer-

cised in regard to the "quantity" of facts recorded and "quality" constantly
watched.

Analysis of Facts

During the process of fact collection some analysis will obviously con-
currently be made. Analyses made at this stage will, however, frequently
be found to be incomplete and in any case will require review before any
conclusions are drawn, when the whole of the relevant data have been
assembled.

(i) Scope of O and M Analysis

The O and M officer asks himself much the same questions as he has
posed to officers of the organisation but with a different emphasis in the
question. He must, for instance, consider the function or objective from
the point of view of its placement, of possible overlap or duplication, of
failure perhaps to use facilities elsewhere available and whether a combination or splitting-up of functions would be of advantage ; ask, "What purpose does the organisation or process serve?", in the sense of determining
whether the function or the operation is necessary, whether it is used and
is serving a useful purpose, whether it is a proper means of achieving the
objective, and whether as good a result could be achieved without it. The
provisions of a statute, rule, or order may dictate present practice and
amendment of the law may be pre-requisite to improvement.

The question "How?" leads to a study of system or method, whether
the work is being done efficiently and economically, what alternatives are
possible, whether there is a better way, that is, whether the same result
can be achieved in some easier or simpler manner, whether the forms and
records used are necessary and properly designed, whether machine application is appropriate, whether an unnecessary or too elaborate system of check
is being followed. It is in this field that some specialisation is frequently
found, the most common being that in respect of office machines and appliances which today are so numerous and diverse that special study of their
potential and application is necessary. There is now an elaborate body
of knowledge on the subjects of:

(a) The importance of, and problems associated with, forms design
and control, not only from the point of view of internal administration, but also from the aspect of public relations. This latter of
itself, with the contact points of public counter or inquiry office,
telephone and letter, form and questionnaire, and with associated
questions of "customer" needs, is a subject repaying study.

(b) Mechanisation of procedures and the use of tables and the simpler
aids.

When or how often something is done, frequencies, timetables and the
like, are often important to the functional arrangement, to the sequence
of operations (whether the operation could be done more economically
earlier or later and generally whether things are done in logical order), or
to the system followed, and must be analysed and tested with those aspects
in mind.

The question "Where?" will lead the investigator on the one hand to consider whether delegations of authority are appropriate, whether the duties and responsibilities of all employees are clearly defined, and such matters as geographical considerations, centralisation versus decentralisation ; and, on the other, to review of accommodation and office layout. Examination of accounting and correspondence records holdings will often disclose the unnecessary use of expensive and urgently needed office space.

The study during the course of the investigation of the personnel employed will indicate "the square peg in the round hole", the failure of selection, training or promotional practices, lack of supervision or appropriate definition of duties and responsibilities, irritations or other influences militating against good work performance.

Effective O and M work may thus involve a sound knowledge of:—

(*a*) Lines of authority and span of control ; optimum size of units ; criteria for good organisation.

(*b*) The factors to be considered in office layout ; standards of heating, lighting and ventilation ; the elimination of noise ; the provision of rest rooms, cafeteria and other amenities ; and, generally, the conditions under which the work is done and their effect upon efficiency.

(*c*) Personnel management and the part it plays ; its associated problems of recruitment, selection, training, duty statements, procedure manuals, job analysis, job rotation, and the like.

The analysis should always be conducted so as—

(*a*) to enable the problems and difficulties of the administration to be defined more clearly,

(*b*) to point to delays and areas which need to be corrected,

(*c*) generally to verify and test the facts on which conclusions will be based, and

(*d*) to make possible constructive suggestions for the solution of problems or the eradication of faults.

(ii) *Techniques of O and M Analysis*

In the course of his analysis, the O and M officer uses various techniques to amplify his facts, to test his ideas and to assist him generally in pinpointing causes of administrative weaknesses, of circumlocution, of excessive costs and delays.

He will, for instance, make work measurements where appropriate— measuring in selected cases the work done, the output of a group or of an individual within a particular period. A study of this kind may be of considerable importance in the review of the organisation and is, moreover, a very good guide to the determination of requisite establishment strengths. A simple illustration may suffice.

In a typing pool, for instance, the work load may be examined firstly by a measurement of typed documents ; from these linear or area measurements the number of key-strokes per document typed and an average number of words per minute per day may be calculated. Alternatively, a device known as a stroke-counter or cyclometer may be fitted to the typewriter and used for directly counting key-strokes. Investigations of this kind have demonstrated a surprisingly low output in some cases, and, as reasonable continuity of work has been maintained, have accordingly pointed to faults in supervision or in the organisation of the pool and to difficulties confronting the typists, e.g., in respect of such matters as the nature of drafts forwarded for typing, the form and content of documents typed, suitability and condition of machines, flow of work to and from typists, office layout and general environmental conditions. A low work output has, for example, been traced to faults in form design (e.g., horizontal ruling so spaced as to preclude use of the typewriter space bar, vertical ruling not coinciding with fixed carriage positions, etc.) ; to separate typing of the same information in different documents; to the use of typed memoranda when printed or roneoed forms would suffice ; to unnecessary underlining and insertion of unnecessary words in headings, etc. ; to the slanting of addresses (requiring unnecessary space bar strokes). Faults such as these could perhaps be discovered without the preliminary work measurement study, but the latter, particularly in more involved cases, points very often to the need for further detailed investigations and the directions which they should take. Again, the output of a group may be tested by a sampling, for example, of correspondence in files, of entries in a ledger, of stores issue dockets, and so on.

Work-flow and process charting has also been used extensively to throw into relief avoidable transits, stoppages, checking, etc., and to suggest means of "shortening the lines". A listing in sequence of the whole of the steps involved in a particular operation and the asking of what, why and so on of each step offers every executive the opportunity of quick review of what is being done and of the way in which it is organised. It enables him to eliminate unnecessary steps, to amalgamate two or more steps, to revise the allocation of functions to individual members of his staff and thence to reconsider the pattern of the organisation as a whole.

Again, pilot schemes have been prepared and installed on a trial basis under actual working conditions in a small section. The results of the trial are carefully tabulated and studied, "rubs" smoothed out and other adjustments made as may be necessary to provide a fully efficient new system offering advantages in time and in effort.

The O and M officer thus reaches his final conclusions from study and analysis, from observation and discussion, and perhaps by trial and error. He must avoid making changes merely for the sake of change, must subordinate theoretical to practical considerations, and must seek the simple and direct arrangement rather than the complex or ingenious. "Costs" and "convenience" are two useful measuring rods.

Conclusions and Recommendations

Recommendations which the O and M officer makes flow from the conclusions reached. They are, or should be, concise and positive and in effect summarise the action which, in his opinion, is necessary to bring about greater efficiency of administration. The recommendations offer the best solution to the problem of organisation or of procedure that can be formulated on known facts at that time but are never claimed as the "only way" ; new ideas and new needs will come forward and some adjustment will in any case be found necessary or desirable from time to time to make for continuously smooth administrative operations. The O and M officer will, moreover, have already "sold" most, if not all, of the recommendations to departmental officers during discussions; the proposals may in fact have been evolved in co-operation with them. In passing, it has been found in some cases that the executive has ideas of changes which are necessary, but lacks authority or perhaps the initiative or courage to have them made. The O and M officer assists in bringing the ideas forward and in correcting for the future the circumstances previously preventing their proper consideration. He may also stimulate initiative and infuse some greater courage —but perhaps the cure for these things lies in a change of executives.

Finally, the O and M officer is required to make his report constructive. Destructive criticism is easy to offer but is worse than useless and, unless the investigator has something to offer for improvement, is best left unspoken. If, on the other hand, the investigation shows the management to be very satisfactory in whole or in part, due credit is given to the administration.

The keynote of the O and M survey is that of co-operation with the executive. It rests on the acceptance by all officers that it is the Service, and what that word means, that counts.

Chapter Sixteen

TRAINING AND STAFF DEVELOPMENT

S. C. DERWENT

Training of some kind is necessary for the new entrant into any kind of position in the public service. The appointee to a professional or technical position, though fresh from his studies in the field, has still to be initiated into the special requirements of his branch ; most of the value of his induction period is lost if it is not recognised as a training time. Where the main criteria of recruitment are simply general educational background and intelligence or native ability, the need for training is even more obvious. Here, too, the aim of recruitment is to obtain not mature officers but young men and women capable of being trained. So much recruitment to the Australian public service is of this kind, i.e., at school-leaver level, that training is of particular importance. And because, in the absence of an administrative class, senior positions are open to all, and every officer is a potential permanent head or senior officer, the broad view must be taken of training. There is a big gap between the raw recruit and the responsible executive he may become ; and it can be bridged only by successive stages of training, each complete in itself, but designed with an eye to the possibility of the next stage.

Training has always gone on in the public services. Experience itself is training. As has been said, "In all occupations, the occupation is the best and indispensable training." The truth of this always needs emphasizing. But it is not the whole story ; and some sections of the public service have been slow to realize that experience can be supplemented in many ways that speed it up, systematize, and sometimes correct it.

The reports of Australian public service boards have for a long time stressed the importance of training. "Effective training of officers . . . is an obligation which cannot be evaded without serious danger to future administration"[1] the Commonwealth Commissioner was writing in 1911. In his next report, he drew special attention to the work of the British Postal Institutes for the training of post office workers (an example soon to be followed by the Australian Postal Institute) ; and of the New South Wales and Victorian Railways Departments, pioneers in promoting the education of their employees. Some developments followed the first World War in the Post Office and other technical departments, Commonwealth and State. But little was done in the field of clerical or administrative in-service training. At this stage, emphasis seems to have been mainly on encouraging employees to take advantage of the facilities increasingly offered in the form of evening classes by technical colleges, universities and other outside institutions. In 1928, for example, the Commonwealth began a "free place" system in Universities for selected officers.

---

[1] Commonwealth Public Service Commission, *Report,* 1911, cit. Bland, *Government in Australia,* 2nd ed., 1944, p. 184.

New South Wales had been early in the field with in-service examinations. Promotion examinations were envisaged in the 1895 Public Service Act, though it was a few years before they got going. However, in spite of these "grade tests" little practical help was given in preparing for them. Practical in-service training was limited to junior draftsmen, who were instructed in lettering, plan-drawing, etc., and to Public Library staff, who were given a series of lectures (the basis of present-day Library Board training). Some facilities were provided in 1909 for scientific "cadets", Department of Agriculture, to attend day lectures at the University and obtain degrees. Later other types of cadetships (now called traineeships) were created, but this scheme was not widely extended until just before the Second World War. The New South Wales Board, also, encouraged the officers of its service to obtain outside qualifications. In fact, early in the century it stimulated the University of Sydney and the Workers' Educational Association to provide educational facilities, originally for clerical Higher Grades students, which served as a basis for some of the University's present courses. The Department of Economics, for example, was established in 1906 partly as a result of the then Board's representations.

In spite of some developments in the inter-war period, the signs of real interest in training do not appear in Public Service Board reports until the late 1930s. The emphasis is still on external qualification. "It is the Board's policy to encourage junior officers to undertake special studies to improve their knowledge and thus to equip themselves more effectively for higher positions in the Public Service." [2] There was also some emphasis on the uses of transfer. The 1939 Report (pp. 16-17) speaks of "the Board's policy of requiring regular transfers of junior officers from one position to another, in order to widen their knowledge of the Department". It could still be written in 1941 that (for administrative officers) "positive in-service training, apart from sporadic instructions by senior officers in the immediate duties of the junior, is non-existent".[3]

The war gave an encouragement to training in many countries and spheres —including the army and industry as well as the public service. In Britain, the Report of the Assheton Committee on the Training of Public Servants (1944) was a landmark, in particular in its stress on the extension of systematic induction and in-service training. In Australia, the provision of courses for servicemen and of "refresher" courses for ex-servicemen gave in-service training an opportunity to establish itself.[4] In 1947 the Commonwealth Public Service Board requested all departments to initiate systematic plans for the training of new clerical staff. Later developments are sketched in Mr. Parker's chapter. The larger departments now have their own training officers, while in the others some officer has usually had the training function added to his general functions, usually personnel. The Board itself runs courses centrally for senior staff, and has a small expert Training Section.

---

[2] Public Service Board, *Report*, 1937, p. 20.

[3] R. S. Parker, *Public Service Recruitment in Australia*, 1942, p. 250.

[4] For a survey of the position immediately after the war in New South Wales and the Commonwealth, see H. L. Craig, "In-service Training—New South Wales Public Service", *Pub. Admin. (Sydney)*, VI, March 1947, and J. J. Betts, "Training of Commonwealth Public Servants", *Pub. Admin. (Sydney)*, VIII, June-Sept. 1949.

Recent developments in New South Wales are described later in this chapter. In most other States, while departmental heads have to see that officers are trained to do their work properly, systematic in-service training is only in its early stages; some recent developments are indicated below. In the smaller services, size makes it difficult to create adequate training schools and formalized training is still apt to be confined to "induction courses". In some services (and in many private and business organizations) there is still no officer competent to advise on training policy and practice; there is no definition of training responsibility or of the areas in which training should be carried out; and no attempt is made to ensure that the persons so constantly involved in training, the supervisors, are aware of and fitted for their critical role as trainers.

It is essential, therefore, that the administrator should recognize the need for training and make a conscious endeavour to organize and control instructional methods.

The Training Plan

Training may be carried out for:

(i) initial placement;
(ii) improved performance;
(iii) promotion or transfer;
(iv) special purposes, e.g., safety.

More than one, or all, of these reasons may be behind any particular course of training. It is natural and desirable for instance that in the design of even the most elementary training scheme, an attempt should be made to prepare the ground for later advancement and develop the best possible attitude towards the administration, the work, and, as is most important in the public service, the public; and, conversely, a course intended specifically to fit trainees for future progression will almost invariably result in an improvement in their present performance. There is no need, therefore, to attempt to place any course neatly within a given category.

What is important is the recognition by the administration of a need for training. That the need is not always fully appreciated may be shown by an examination of methods used in initial placement in the various fields of public service activity. It is generally accepted that the professional or skilled trades worker must undergo specialist training before he can take his place in the field. Courses are conveniently provided by universities and technical colleges; and it is common for employers to sponsor this training, paying fees, and sometimes living allowances.

But the need for training does not stop there, nor is it confined to these employees. All workers must be adequately trained in the basic skills and knowledge demanded by their work in its peculiar environment. Too often, employers are satisfied with the informal and usually inadequate methods by which a new employee is simply attached to an experienced worker who may, or may not, be sufficiently interested or qualified to give the necessary instruction.

A comprehensive training programme will include instructions not only on the mechanics of the job but on every item that may influence the quality of performance. In addition to giving tuition on the branch in which the employee is situated, it will deal with work of related branches, public relations, and those conditions of service that will be of interest to him in the early stages of his career.

In-Service Training

The methods used respectively by the Commonwealth and New South Wales Public Service Board exemplify two possible approaches to the problem of training new staff. The Commonwealth Public Service Board regards the induction period of the new employee as a means of ensuring his speediest possible adjustment, and as the first step in training. In the initial interview with the departmental training or personnel officer, the new employee is provided with handbooks which contain general service information and some details of the department in which he is employed.

This initial induction merges into some systematic "on-the-job" instruction, including some job rotation wherever possible, so that the trainee can gain the widest grounding in departmental functions and methods. This stage in the induction of the new employee in the processes with which he will be concerned is primarily the responsibility of the supervisor. A set procedure might well be laid down and the following steps are suggested for supervisors:—

(1) Inform the new employee of the function of the branch and its relationship to the department and the service as a whole.

(2) Explain the complete range of duties that he will ultimately have to discharge, using a statement of duties and other appropriate work documentation.

(3) Teach him the processes connected with his principal function, first by describing and demonstrating the processes and giving the reason for each; second, by requiring him to carry out each one under supervision.

(4) Instruct him, using the same method, in the remaining functions connected with his job. The number of functions or processes dealt with in one session will depend on the employee's capacity to assimilate instructions.

A later stage in the induction process, which may not take place until the officer has been in the service for six months, is the provision of lectures and discussions which supply, first a general administrative background, and then broad tuition on the procedures generally applicable to the department in which he is employed. In the Commonwealth Service, if an appropriate training unit has not been established in the department, this training is carried out at a central school under the control of the Public Service Board.

Here is a list of typical subjects dealt with at a school for new entrants to the Clerical and Administrative Division, conducted by the Commonwealth Public Service Board at Canberra (or in the States).

Government—

Principles of the Career Service.
Machinery of Government.
Milestones in the Development of the Commonwealth Public Service.

Administration—
What our Departments Do.
The Training Scheme and the New Entrant.
The Role of Service Organizations.
O. & M. in the Commonwealth Public Service.
Promotions Appeal System in the Commonwealth Public Service.
Registry and the Use of Files.
Correspondence:
    Report Writing,
    Minute Writing,
    Statistics.
Departmental Accounting Procedure.
You and Your Supervisor.

Personnel Administration—
Legislation affecting Personnel Administration in the Commonwealth
    Public Service.
The Personnel Section and You.
Organization and Classification, Salaries and Allowances.
Leave and Furlough.
Superannuation.

Your Opportunities—
Studying for Promotion.
Applying for Promotion or Transfer.
Service Publications and Library Resources.
You and Your Job.

Films and Review—
Dealing with our Public:—
    Film: "A Matter of Manners".
Effective use of the Telephone:—
    Film: "In a Manner of Speaking".
Retrospect.
Appreciation of School.

The Commonwealth Public Service Board encourages training officers to
maintain training record cards, on which a record of the trainee's progress
through the various stages of training is maintained.

The New South Wales Public Service Board, like the Commonwealth
Board, recognizes that the induction period, in addition to aiming at the
quick and effective adjustment of each new employee, should take the
initial step in training by orienting the officer with respect to the organization
and functions of his department. During the first interview with the
departmental personnel officer, an outline of the department's make-up and
activities is given to the new employee, and he is handed a brochure setting
out information on the conditions of service with which he will need to be
familiar in the first few weeks. It is usual to issue him with a departmental
brochure at one of two follow-up interviews conducted by the personnel
officer.

Training of a formal character is given to new employees in appropriate
cases, when classes are held for persons preparing for the examination under
Regulation 116—an examination which clerical officers must pass to be

qualified for progression beyond the sixth year rate of the ten year incremental salary scale. The syllabus for this course, as conducted by the New South Wales Board for its own officers, is set out below.

TOPICS

(1) *The machinery of government in New South Wales*—with particular reference to the role of the Public Service Board.

(2) *The Public Service Board*—general organization and functions—policies.

(3) *The constitution, powers and duties of the Board*—development and adjustment—pre-1884 to date.

(4) *The Inspection Section*—functions and procedures.

(5) *The Examinations Branch*—functions and procedures.

(6) *The Records Branch*—functions and procedures.

(7) *The Correspondence Branch*—functions and procedures.

(8) *The Arbitration Branch*—functions and procedures. State and Federal Arbitration systems as they relate to the New South Wales Public Service.

(9) *The Registrar's Branch*—functions and procedures.

(10) *The Personnel Section*—functions and procedures.

(11) *Leave, Allowances, Office and Officer Accommodation and Notation Sections*—functions and procedures.

(12) *Accounts and Stores Procedures*—The Board's Estimates—Office Services.

(13) *General functions and responsibilities of Departments*—with particular reference to the administration of the Public Service Board.

(14) *The preparation of correspondence and submissions.*

(15) *Public Relations.*

It will be noted that while this system does not provide the more generalized training supplied by the Commonwealth in its Central Training Schools, it fulfils the dual function of initial training and early training for transfer and promotion.

Courses for improvement of performance and promotion will naturally vary according to the needs of a particular Service; but where an entire class of officers has to be trained, it is clearly desirable that training should be carried out in related but expanding steps. As a portion of the New South Wales training system for clerical officers has shown, the complete framework will provide a useful example of this process. The full training scheme is as follows:—

......	......	Subjects
Regulation 116 examination.	For promotion beyond 6th year rate of the incremental scale.	Departmental Practice and Procedure at branch level, with the paper especially marked for English Expression. Lectures are provided by departmental officers.

Title	......	Subjects
Regulation 119 examination.	For promotion beyond incremental scale.	1. Departmental Procedure (A). which is concerned with policy, procedure, etc., in the division or department in which the officer is employed. Departmental Procedure (B), a paper on the Public Service Act and Regulations, Crown Employees Appeal Board Act, Audit Act and Treasury Regulations, and Office Organization and Supervision. 2. English Expression. 3. Principles and Practice of Government. Lectures by departmental officers in Departmental Procedure. Lectures at training centres (or by correspondence for country candidates) in Principles and Practice of Government and English Expression.
Regulation 122 examination.	For promotion beyond Grade IV.	1. Social History. 2. Economics. 3. Government (Administration). 4. Government (Political). Lectures at training centres by University and Technical College Lecturers.

This scheme aims at building up the knowledge and clerical skills demanded by an officer's departmental work, and at improving his general education as he proceeds through his career.

Although training courses such as this meet the general needs of departments so far as training for transfer and promotion is concerned, important demands are made on training facilities by newly created positions and by deficiencies in performance. We may again take New South Wales as a convenient example. In recent years the Public Service Board of that State has designed, organized and supervised special training courses for the newly created positions of parole officer, probation officer, housing officer, and public relations officer, in addition to instituting a continuous training scheme for departmental personnel officers. Courses for inquiry officers and switchboard operators were introduced to meet obvious deficiencies in performance of the people employed on this class of work.([5])

Supervisory Training

An examination of in-service training schemes leaves the impression that a great deal of attention has been given to improving the intellectual and manipulative skills at the expense of the development of the social skills which are particularly necessary in the case of supervisors. The supervisor must understand the implications of his attitude and behaviour towards his own staff in the same way as he must be aware of the implications of every

([5]) It may reasonably be expected that the South Australian Service will expand its departmental training programmes shortly after the publication of this volume, since the Commission decided in 1957 to appoint a full-time Training Officer, whose duties are associated with, inter alia, staff training, induction, counselling and examinations.

other administrative act—and this need must be emphasized in promotional training.

Despite powerful evidence of the importance of the role played by the supervisor in developing those attitudes which are most conducive to efficiency, the training of supervisors in human relations, and indeed, their training generally, is comparatively new. Courses in Supervision and Management were not introduced by the Technical Education Department in New South Wales until 1939, and Company and Government training schemes were not introduced on any large scale until after the 1939-1945 war, when the importance of training became so obvious to many employers that they arranged for classes in Supervision to be conducted on their own premises in order that they could be assured that all their supervisors attended the training sessions.

These training classes were so arranged as to ensure that supervisory staff at all levels were provided with training, and that training should not be left to the few who were interested enough to attend courses in their own time.

An examination of training courses indicates that considerable emphasis is placed on the subject of human relations, and also the techniques and practices which enable the supervisor to fill his role as planner and organizer, training officer, and one who is expected to contribute to the solution of problems involving method and procedure.

Following some research by the New South Wales Public Service Board in 1957, its departmental training classes in supervision are organized around the responsibility of supervisors, at all levels, for—

(1) The planning and organization of day-to-day work.

(2) Training.

(3) Work Method.

(4) Human Relations.

Training Methods

In the initial stages of a training course, interest might be established by revealing the findings of the Hawthorne and other experiments. While the formal lecture is often the most appropriate way to deal with this introductory material, it has been found most desirable in the training of supervisors to use the conference discussion technique, with day-to-day problems of office organization and supervision as bases for instruction. This method appears to be even more satisfactory where groups comprise those who are already employed in a supervisory capacity, because most of the group have experienced the particular problems raised for discussion, have attempted their solution, and are so able to engage quite actively, and more beneficially, in the lesson.

The conference-discussion method of teaching is regarded as most satisfactory because, although there are some basic principles underlying sound supervision, these are insufficient to cover all of the problems that may arise. Supervisors can only naturally and automatically arrive at the right method to apply in a given situation after a long process of education in human relations, based on a training system that enables supervisors to classify, systematize, and pool their experience in the human aspects of their work.

However, no matter how well conceived a training scheme may be, the results will, in large measure, depend on the effectiveness of the methods adopted. It is no less important to give careful consideration to training methods than it is to set out systematically to discover areas in which training should be given.

Such factors as the ability and experience of the trainee, the nature of the material to be taught, and the facilities available, must be carefully weighed before the precise nature of the tuition is determined on.

Public service training courses appear to lack variety. The method of presenting information most commonly used by lecturers untrained in teaching method is the simple lecture. This merely consists of telling trainees what they are required to know. It is a natural and necessary way of teaching, but is not generally adequate alone. It must be supplemented by demonstration, illustration, application and discussion, if the greatest possible impression is to be made on the student. Varying the lesson in this way not only results in increased motivation but makes the degree of "natural" learning more effective by appealing to more than one of the senses, because the trainee hears, sees, and does something.

Each lesson should be constructed so that these variations in teaching method can be most effectively used and supported by the types of instructional aids which are dealt with later.(*)

It is generally accepted that a lesson should comprise four main parts:—

(1) The introduction, which arouses the interest of the trainee by allying the lesson to be given with previous experience—often, with items already covered by the course of study.

(2) The presentation, which is concerned with explaining new ideas, skills, information and procedure.

(3) Application—or, how to apply the new knowledge given, under guidance.

(4) Testing—to check the trainee's skill and knowledge ; to determine the results of the teaching-learning situation.

Demonstration, illustration, discussion or the "Conference" technique, which encourages the greatest possible degree of student participation, may be used at any step in the lesson, although the greatest opportunity for their use occurs in the presentation step.

A special comment is required concerning the conference technique, which has considerable value in in-service training programmes. It should only be used where the trainees have experienced the problem or problems being discussed *and* some or all of them have attempted to solve the problem. Unless these conditions have been met the conference results in time-wasting chatter.

The methods used will depend upon the nature of the material taught, the capacity and experience of the students, and the instructional facilities

---

(*) Information in this section is mainly drawn from "The Instructor and His Job", University of the State of New York, State Education Department, Bureau of Industrial and Technical Education, 1945.

available. In the one lesson a number of methods may be used. In a lecture on a Records Branch, the lecturer might use a flow chart to indicate the movement of papers within the Branch and within the office as a whole, and then demonstrate the method by which papers are identified and controlled by actually making entries on registration, personal index and subject index cards in front of the group.

Application of the knowledge acquired concerning the Records Branch might be effected by organizing the class into a number of groups, each person in a group taking the part of an actual unit in the Branch. A paper might then be routed through the group, with each member taking the action that would normally be taken by the unit represented by him.

The purpose of the testing step is to require trainees to apply knowledge and perform operations which have formed the subject of a lesson or a number of lessons, without the assistance of the tutor, so that he can locate weaknesses in learning and compensate for them by additional training. Oral or written questions may be asked, or the trainee required to carry out a project which is appraised for accuracy, output, and other appropriate qualities of performance.

Flow charts and the use of items actually employed in clerical processes are only two of the many instructional aids with which learning can be facilitated. Although the instructor in clerical and administrative procedures has not the range of equipment for demonstration purposes which is so readily available to the technical college instructor, he can, if he is sufficiently interested and ingenious, devise many items which will quicken the interest and focus the attention of his students; and an examination of the material available in film libraries will reveal strips and reels relevant to almost any topic.

Training the Trainers

It is the Training Officer's concern to give general direction and oversight to all training carried out in the Department, to inform himself of the training requirements for various classes of work and to become an expert in the training methods which will give the best results for the Department.

There is no particular field of experience which would normally prepare an officer for these duties and the Commonwealth Public Service Board has instituted a training course in 1957 for Junior Training Officers to meet these requirements. The objective of the course is to equip officers for the performance of training duties in the Commonwealth Public Service and particularly to:—

(a) Outline the purpose of training and its function in the management process; explain the duties of the Training Officer, including the examination of training needs and the development of a training programme;

(b) instruct in the theory and practice of teaching;

(c) instruct in course management, syllabus and time-table planning, the preparation of training manuals and visual training aids;

(d) instruct in methods of evaluating training achievements.

The training course, of six months duration, is divided into three parts:—

PART I—Training Theory and Principles—

(a) Educational Psychology.

(b) Teaching Principles and Methods.

(c) Training Administration.

PART II—Departmental Assignments and Practical Work.

PART III—Central Workshop and Review of Assignments. Following the training periods in Departments, Junior Training Officers will be required to attend a Board's Central Training Workshop in Canberra and prepare material on training items for these sessions.

Executive Development

It is not difficult to devise a comprehensive training programme where the training needs are easily perceived. In most organizations the duties and responsibilities of positions up to the level of front-line supervisor can be defined clearly enough for the purpose of devising training programmes.

Above this level and as we proceed up the administrative scale, however, the duties and responsibilities of positions become increasingly complex, and we are more and more concerned with developing qualities rather than with the ability to carry out specialized techniques. When we come to the top executive level, therefore, we find ourselves, in designing training programmes, considering personality characteristics rather than procedures; fields of activity rather than the activities themselves.

Thus the part of a programme of executive development devoted to personnel management would be concerned with giving trainees a fuller insight into the human problems in administration, the role of the administration, and the importance of ordering their own conduct and attitudes, and a broad appreciation of the manner in which human problems could be dealt with. The course would not, however, provide detailed instruction in the design and use of the various methods of selection, staff reporting, counselling, training and the like.

The notion of executive development—a systematic attempt to foster in selected employees abilities which will enable them to become effective administrators on the higher levels—is not new. The filling of senior positions cannot be left to chance. Organizations which fill administrative vacancies by hurried, haphazard selections pay the price for doing so. The system of promotion to the higher positions simply by seniority can have an even worse result—for example, the appointment to an executive position of a man who, though an excellent technologist, completely lacks the administrative flair. Most organizations, therefore, are able to fill administrative vacancies with candidates who have been earmarked some time before, and, in one way or another, have been carefully prepared for their occupation of the positions. Generally, however, such selection and preparation has been done piecemeal in the past; seldom has it been part of the openly-avowed policy of an organization.

In recent years, with the increased recognition of the need to use specific personnel techniques in business, there has been simultaneous increase in emphasis on the need for planned preparation of employees to occupy executive positions.

Before we consider the various ways in which organizations have endeavoured to carry out such a preparation, we should try to make a general appraisal of the qualities we are likely to find in the successful executive. As we have commented, we shall find that we are dealing with rather abstract personal attributes instead of technical abilities, since administration is concerned with personalities and situations rather than detailed procedures.

If the duties and responsibilities of all the positions on an organization chart are examined, then, as the review proceeds up through the organizational structure, it will be seen that the occupants of the positions will be required to concern themselves to an ever-increasing degree with:—

(1) Matters other than the specialty on which they are initially employed. The top executive may well be described as a "generalist".

(2) Problems the solutions of which depend on a number of variables. They must not only have the intelligence and critical minds to enable them to identify the variables, but know sufficient about each variable and its significance to permit them to make a reasoned decision.

(3) The need for making decisions of a more widespread and critical character, and for the acceptance of responsibility for their consequences.

(4) The attainment of goals, the clear definition of which requires a high degree of capacity, imagination and foresight.

(5) The achievement of administrative aims through others. This demands an ability to develop, inspire and gain the co-operation of others. It also demands the quality of restraint. To become accustomed to delegating work to other people and to refrain from taking part personally in the organization of detail is frequently not an easy matter for the active executive.

(6) Co-ordinating the work of others. This function requires the executive to have a sound knowledge of the policy and working of the whole organization, and in many instances, some knowledge of the policies and practices of other organizations.

(7) The necessity to follow a persistent line of action which will be possible only if the person possesses a sound constitution capable of withstanding the prolonged and concentrated effort associated with executive work.

(8) Maintaining a high level of social and ethical standards.

(9) Making decisions which are considerably separated in time from the ends it is hoped to achieve. The executive must be occupied with the future—not just with his personal future, but with the future of his department and of the State.

Let us expand a little on only one of these items—the need to plan for the future—which is a characteristic demand in top executive positions.

Government departments, if they are to play their part, have little choice whether or not they will plan for the future. They must provide not merely for the normal, expected demands of a growing and changing community, but for the accelerated requirements caused by the developmental programmes of private organizations, which create circumstances which can be met only by adequate economic, social and technological planning.

For example, the intention of a large company to build a factory in a particular area, with prospects of rapid expansion, may soon bring about a demand for improved highway, transport and power facilities and, perhaps, an increase in population with its attendant needs for new homes, sewerage, water supply, and educational facilities. If the planning and action of the departments concerned does not keep up with that of the organization, the embarrassment that may be caused to a department or to the Government is of less real significance than the effect on the enterprise of the company itself, and the progress of development in that area of the State.

It appears, then, that the potential successful administrator must possess certain intellectual, personal and constitutional characteristics in high degree which are capable of development through training and experience into managerial skills. A successful programme of executive development depends first on sound initial selection, and then on the planning of a programme which will enable the executive trainees to develop in such a way as to meet the specifications inherent in the list above.

Programmes of executive development do not follow a consistent pattern, and a survey shows the use of a wide variety of methods, each with its own characteristic features. In some instances, management accepts full responsibility for the development of its executives, whereas in others it uses the facilities of professional and educational institutions. As would be expected, some use both internal and external training methods.

The most widely-used procedures for executive development are those which take place on the job, and the more progressive organizations ensure that their staff do not have to develop "by ear" the diverse talents characteristic of the successful executive.

Traineeships and University Studies

There has been a general, if not complete, appreciation of the value of university studies, particularly in the liberal arts, in training administrators. There is no full parallel in Australia to the British practice of recruiting extensively to the administrative service from the ranks of university graduates. However, Australian public services have recognized the value of this training by providing exemptions from in-service examinations for graduates and by providing study leave. The Commonwealth Service has gone a step farther by establishing administrative cadetships in which cadets simultaneously undergo university training, and are given the benefit of guided experience in departments. The New South Wales Board has in recent years awarded part-time scholarships, tenable at universities and technical colleges, to officers who have already shown administrative promise in their departments.

In Victoria, South Australia and Tasmania, a number of free places at the universities and technical training institutions have been granted to public servants annually for some years. In South Australia, the Government approved in 1954 of the granting of administrative cadetships; but, in the opinion of that State's Commission, there has been a shortage of suitable applicants. Western Australia has not so far taken the same attitude as other States towards the sponsoring of university studies for public servants. However, it is a pointer to the Western Australian Commissioner's realization of the importance of properly directed tertiary education for public servants that he was responsible for the establishment in 1951 of a five-year part-time course in Public Administration conducted by the Education Department, and that most of the students enrolled are public servants.

As early as the beginning of the century the New South Wales Board began to appoint professional trainees. In the earlier years, traineeships centred on the rural fields of agricultural science, veterinary science, and forestry. Since then architecture, engineering, geology, wool technology, science (for curators at the Australian Museum), rural science, social science (for work in child welfare), medicine, applied psychology, and surveying have been added. For women, traineeships have been available in social science, diatetics, speech therapy, women's handicrafts and home science (food and nutrition). Candidates are chosen by selection committees consisting of representatives of the Board, the departments, and the relevant training institutions. Their task has to be carried out carefully, because they must pick candidates who have the potential not only to complete their courses but to develop later into senior scientists or administrators.

Trainees undertake courses at the universities, the Sydney Technical College, and other institutions. Academic training is augmented by departmental experience during vacation periods, so that, for instance, a civil engineer after four years' university training would emerge as a graduate with from eighteen months' to two years' additional practical training in the profession of his choice. The traineeships provide for payment of fees on behalf of trainees and of allowances, which are supplemented by additional payments during practical training periods. Each trainee is required to complete his course and to remain in the public service for a period after graduation.

Sponsored training of this kind serves a double purpose. It helps to provide a good supply of the best available candidates for entry to the professional fields of the public service ; and it ensures that successful trainees enter on their careers as fully-fledged officers, familiar with their departments' requirements and procedures, because of the knowledge they have gained during practical training.[7]

Rotational Training

In direct contrast to the academic training provided by full-time University preparation is the system of placing officers who have demonstrated ability in specialist work in a succession of jobs, so that they are virtually forced to gain a full understanding of the policies and procedures applicable to the various sections of their organizations.

An American company described its job rotation programme as follows:—

"The men trained by this program . . . are not given lecture courses on 'How to be an executive' or 'How our system operates'. They do

[7] See *Training in the New South Wales Public Service*, N.S.W. Public Service Board, 1957.

not 'go to school'. They plunge into turbulent waters of unfamiliar jobs and teach themselves to swim. Thus a gas production expert was put into an electric power-house job; a specialist in personnel was shifted to commercial relations and sales. A systems commercial manager, whose unit put out 2,000,000 bills a month, went first to one of our electric operating departments, and then to personnel work."([8])

A common objection to position rotation plans is that periodic changes of leadership cause disturbance. Off-setting this, however, are the advantages gained by providing broad experience quickly, and placing the utmost pressure on the new leader so that he is forced quickly to develop the talents necessary for success. For example, the newly-placed head is initially at a serious disadvantage, possessing little knowledge of his new branch, and unsupported by established relationships with his immediate subordinates. He is faced not only with the necessity of learning, as soon as possible, the policy and practices and procedures of his new environment, but with the need to give special care to the handling of human relations problems in order to establish complete co-operation quickly.

Because of the frequency of promotional transfers, by way of selection, within the various Australian public services, job rotation takes place, in effect, quite often. It is by no means rare for an officer who has passed promotional examinations to be selected for a more responsible job in another department, or in a different branch in his own department. It is perhaps unfortunate that most public services are too large and heterogeneous to enable service-wide, long-term planning on this basis; but it may be noted that many public servants on the very highest levels have reached those eminences because their talent for administration has emerged following a doubtless fortuitous upward zig-zagging from department to department.

The same sort of movement within a department (and a department may be as complex in function and organization as any individual company) is a characteristic feature of public service employment. In any case, while service-wide rotational training may be impracticable, it is often possible to plan rotational placements for selected officers within a given department, with a view to developing their executive ability, in spite of the incidental difficulties (caused chiefly by problems of seniority).

The Understudy Method

This involves the assignment of promising senior staff to top-line executives whose responsibility it is to train their assistants so that in their absence, or in the event of their promotion, the assistants can assume their duties and responsibilities. Assuming that the executive to be understudied possesses the talents necessary for the position, the success of the method depends on his willingness and ability to develop the same talents in his assistant.

As with rotational training, it is possible to arrange training of this type within a particular department where promotion lines are clear, i.e., selection of the assistant is easy, and does not disturb departmental seniority. It is unlikely that there would be many examples in any Australian public

([8]) Arthur M. Whitehill, "Personnel Development: Training and Education" in *Personnel Relations*, 1955, p. 140.

service of the deliberate selection of an officer for transfer from one department to another for understudy purposes.

Multiple Management

Under this plan, initiated by an American company, McCormick & Co., Inc., in 1932, while the main administrative functions are carried out by the senior board of executives, a number of subsidiary boards also play a considerable part in management. These are: the junior board of executives, consisting of members elected from the ranks of executive, administrative and professional employees, which deals primarily with problems of administration and office management; the factory board of executives, which handles matters involving working conditions, employees' suggestions, and so on; the sales board of directors, which deals with matters connected with sales; and the institutional sales board, organized in connection with a branch plant to cater to the needs of large consumers of the company's bulk products.

While so radical a departure from the ordinary organizational structure is unlikely to be carried out in any service departments, the system has its counterpart, to some extent, in the delegation by senior executives to committees made up of lesser executives of the duty of examining, reporting on, and sometimes finally dealing with, various aspects of departmental policy. At present this practice is confined to committees dealing with regular or recurring administrative matters, e.g., suggestions committees, examinations committees, committees dealing with statutory functions of departments, and so on; but it could well be extended to cover a variety of other matters; and the selection of promising administrative officers to take their places on such committees might be of value not only in the practical formation of policy, but as a training aid.

Executive Counselling and Guided Experience

This method of training somewhat resembles the understudy system, with the difference that the general development of the trainee is aimed at, rather than his specific training for a particular job. Officers are seconded to another branch or department for a training period, during which they may be required to participate in committees, make investigations, write reports, carry out special projects, and so on. Throughout the period they have the benefit of the constant observation and counselling of one or more senior officers who, in most cases, themselves benefit from the exchange of ideas.

The New South Wales Public Service Board has used this method with some success in its own office in the training of potential executives from service departments and statutory bodies.

Central Training Schemes

A number of organizations have attempted to combine the advantages of a broad university training with instruction in subjects and methods directly related to their own activities by holding central training courses.

Although the New South Wales Higher Grades examination is aimed at preparing officers for the exercise of broad administrative techniques, the Commonwealth Service is the only one to make a deliberate attempt to train senior administrative officers at central courses. These courses are of two types:—

(a) *Lecture and group-discussion courses for senior administrative officers including personnel, general administrative, technical, scientific and professional officers.*

   (i) *Machinery of Government.*

      (a) Parliament and the Executive ;

      (b) Trends in Public Service Administration ;

      (c) Co-ordination of Policy.

   (ii) *Management.*

      (a) General, decentralisation and delegation, subordinate legislation ;

      (b) Financial management, budget system, departmental estimates and Treasury control ;

      (c) Personnel management, scope of, and the human factor in management.

   (iii) *Administrative Training.*

      (a) Departmental responsibilities ;

      (b) Training on the job, and supervisors' responsibilities for administrative training.

   (iv) *Organisation and Methods Techniques.*

(b) *Conferences on Higher Administration for Senior Executives at Assistant Secretary level.*

   (i) *Machinery of Government.*

      (a) Selected aspects of the framework within which higher executives of the Service operate ;

      (b) Policy development and its implementation ;

      (c) Allocation of functions within the Service, Cabinet and the Prime Minister's Department ;

      (d) The task of the Permanent Head, and the Parliamentary Joint Committee of Public Accounts.

   (ii) *Management.*

      (a) Managerial problems in the Service, e.g., technological changes in industry and government ;

      (b) Personnel and establishment control ;

      (c) Organisation and methods ;

      (d) Financial and monetary policy, estimates and expenditure control ;

      (e) Human relations in management ;

      (f) Comparative studies in administration, e.g., the Hoover Commission Report.

   (iii) *Reports and Review.*

      The final days of the conference are given to group discussions on the machinery of government and management, with special emphasis on the extent to which efficiency in the Service can be improved.

At the time of writing, the Victorian Service appears likely to be the next one to possess a central training unit. The Board is already proceeding to the establishment of a school, and is also considering undertaking the formal training of executives.

Undoubtedly, the most ambitious and comprehensive attempt to establish a central training school has been the British Administrative Staff College at Henley-on-Thames. A similar school, the Australian Administrative Staff College, has now been set up at Mount Eliza, Victoria. Financed entirely by contributions from Australian business institutions, and headed by Professor Sir Douglas Copland, it aims at bringing together executives of proved administrative capacity, giving them the opportunity of examining different administrative practices, and preparing them for higher responsibilities in the future. The College is fully residential and the course extends over twelve weeks. The main divisions of the course are:—[9]

1. *Introduction to Administration.*

2. *Internal Organization.*
   (*a*) Accounting and financial control;
   (*b*) Personnel management;
   (*c*) Subdivisions of the organization;
   (*d*) Delegation, control and accountability;
   (*e*) Sources of current information;
   (*f*) Organization for production—
       (i) Workshop management;
       (ii) Research and development;
       (iii) Office services;
       (iv) Management accounting;
       (v) The personnel department.

3. *External Relations.*
   (*a*) Commercial relations—
       (i) Consumers and customers;
       (ii) Purchasing;
       (iii) Sources of finance;
       (iv) Trade associations.
   (*b*) Industrial relations;
   (*c*) Public relations;
   (*d*) Relations with Federal and State Governments;
   (*e*) Relations with local authorities;
   (*f*) The State and the entrepreneur.

---

[9] Handbook of the Australian Administrative Staff College, 1957, pp. 11, 12.

4. *Establishment, Growth and Adaptation to Change.*

    (*a*) Scale of operations and size ;

    (*b*) Economic change ;

    (*c*) Technological change ;

    (*d*) Maintaining vitality.

5. *The Administrator.*

    Provision is also made for the study of biographies of some of the people who have achieved distinction in different fields of administration or public life.

The Use of Training and Educational Aids in Executive Development

Some of the training aids used by staff colleges, professional institutes and individual employers in training executives merit brief description. Most of them, of course, will be recognized as equally applicable in training at all levels.

Formal lectures may be delivered by persons within the organization or by visiting executives or specialists from universities and technical educational institutions. The method is limited by the difficulty of properly integrating the lectures where the lecturers are not regularly associated, by the often weak lecturing technique of the lecturers themselves, and by the lack of opportunity for participation by the group being trained.

Conferences.—The conference method is one of the oldest and most valid of training devices, and is a common feature in executive development programmes. Essentially, a training conference is a debate under a chairman, who expounds the problems, collates the opinions expressed, and analyses and draws out the findings of the conference, suggesting possible applications.

Seminars.—In a seminar, discussions are conducted by a chairman, following the investigation of specific aspects of a problem by small groups who report back to the main meeting which, by mutual consent, may vary individual group contributions before embodying them in the main report.

The seminar has the advantages of the conference, but is, in some ways superior to it and to the formal lecture method. It ensures a greater degree of member participation, and provides an opportunity for the give-and-take of free discussion.

Syndicates.—This method is a variation of the seminar method. Group reports are discussed at a plenary meeting, but each group report remains in its inaugural form.

The *case study* method, developed largely by the Harvard Graduate School in Administration, involves the examination, discussion and solution of "case" problems by students. Each "case" consists of the presentation of a situation which embodies one or more administrative problems worthy of serious discussion. The group might examine a plan for the building of a satellite town, critically analyse an office system, an organization, or a policy which has been a failure, or offer a solution to a problem associated with handling people, office layout, and so on.

Here, the main function of the leader is to stimulate discussion.

Role-playing is of particular value in providing students with an appreciation of human relations problems. Members of the group take the parts of various characters and dramatise a particular situation. Properly carried out, this device forces the students to consider, and usually to appreciate, the attitudes of others. Although an attempt is usually made to come to the best possible solution in a situation, this goal is subordinated to that of assisting participants to think clearly, to cultivate open-mindedness, and to learn to put themselves in others' places.

The effectiveness of most training and educational schemes depends, to a considerable degree, on the ability, skill and enthusiasm of the individual lecturers or leaders. No one particular device or educational aid can be expected to fulfil all the needs of a particular training course ; nor can it be categorically laid down that one device or aid will more effectively achieve a particular goal than another.

The selection of methods or aids must be made only after a consideration of the ideas and information it is hoped to convey, the experience and needs of the group to be trained, the responses of previous similar groups to particular methods, the facilities available, and the skill of the lecturer or leader. One working principle can be laid down quite definitely, however, and that is that the formal lecture should not be used as the sole device except where it can be established that there is no alternative to its use.

The ultimate success of any scheme of executive development depends on having the full support and understanding of management and all those who will have any influence on the scheme. To ensure this understanding, all of these people must have a complete recognition of the role that they have to play, and every attempt should be made to ensure that they play it. Training must never be allowed to degenerate into a mere formality ; it must be kept alive both to the organization and to the trainees. As soon as there are signs that those participating in training are merely "going through the motions", or that training schemes are being indulged in merely because they are "fashionable", both training methods and the reasons for training should be reviewed at as high a level as possible.

Chapter Seventeen

EXECUTIVE DEVELOPMENT IN THE COMMONWEALTH PUBLIC SERVICE[1]

R. S. PARKER

In naming this chapter I have sacrificed accuracy to brevity. "Executive development" denotes the whole art of raising the quantity and quality of people available for higher administrative work. Its most important single element is planned experience. Other vital aspects are methods of promotion and rewards for achievement. Recruitment is an inseparable consideration. Our concern here is with the specific problems of education and formal training for higher administration. The meaning attached to "higher administration" will appear in due course.

We have to consider at the outset how to determine the requirements of administrative training and education. Although administrative work is the most important of all to the efficiency of an organisation, it is the hardest of all to evaluate in concrete terms such as quantity, speed and quality of output. The training of, say, an auditor is largely determined by the technical requirements of accountancy and by the content of Audit Acts and Treasury regulations. The nature of the *work* determines the nature of the training required. Administration is much more difficult to define in terms of work techniques. What is easier is to define the administrator's *role* within the organisation, and to form a general picture of the kind of personality and qualifications appropriate to this role. Thus, administrative training and education have to be designed not so much to produce a certain kind and quality of work as a certain kind and quality of man.

THE ROLE OF THE ADMINISTRATOR

There are very many published definitions and analyses of administrative work. Selecting the main points which are common to the best statements, we may say that administrative work includes the following elements:—

(a) Assisting more senior administrators, and at the highest level responsible Ministers, in framing policies and amending them from time to time; also reporting on the execution of policy and on its results as a basis for advising policy changes or improvements;

---

[1] This chapter is based on the Report of a Study Group of the A.C.T. Group of the R.I.P.A., on "Education and Training for Higher Administrative Work in the Commonwealth Public Service". The members of the Study Group were B. C. Betts, B. Bray, K. Collings, J. C. Conway, D. R. Gothard, I. McLean, R. S. Parker (Chairman), A. Shavitsky and L. J. Trebilco. The Report was presented to and discussed by the A.C.T. Group on 27th October, 1955. It was also the subject of study and considered comment by the Commonwealth Public Service Board. This chapter incorporates the work of the Group, but as it also deals with points raised in the subsequent discussions, the writer takes sole responsibility for its present form.

(*b*) advising more senior administrators, and at the highest level responsible Ministers, on the possible ways of incorporating broad policy aims into workable plans of operation; and designing and revising appropriate forms of departmental organisation and staffing and financial arrangements to carry out such plans;

(*c*) managing and co-ordinating the activities of the various people involved in forming and amending policy and in operating accepted policies; in this work the administrator must be concerned, not only with organisation and management, but also with the staffing and financial aspects of both policy and administration.

The kinds of activity involved in administrative work are illustrated in the following summary of a detailed job analysis of actual work done by typical middle grade Administrative Class officers in the United Kingdom civil service, undertaken by the United Kingdom Civil Service Selection Board at the end of the last war:—

(1) Policy matters: discerning the more important general questions or problems arising out of the work of the branch, seeing their implications for the future as well as for the present, and for the country as a whole as well as for the department;

(2) formulating practicable and, if necessary, detailed proposals for action; foreseeing the probable results of such proposals, including their effect on public opinion;

(3) taking responsibility when required for the adoption of such proposals, and organising and supervising their execution;

(4) "paper work"—i.e., analysis of complicated material, including figures, and accurate and intelligent presentation of results; writing clear, brief, informative and acceptable letters and minutes;

(5) dealing with people inside and outside the department—i.e., discussing in committee, in conference or tete-a-tete for the purpose of reaching a decision; putting a point of view or obtaining information; managing and enlisting co-operation of subordinate staff; briefing superiors; negotiating with and interpreting the policy of the department to individuals or organisations.

Administrative work is distinguished from other kinds of work by the characteristic of "generality". The accountant may concentrate on accounts, and on the supervision of the accounting work done by officers under him. So, also, for the record clerk, or the head typist, or the research officer, or the engineer, or the ganger. They do not necessarily have to concern themselves with the validity of the policy they are carrying out, or the pay scales or promotion rules affecting their subordinates, or with the work of other branches whose work is complementary with theirs in producing ultimate service to the public. In practice, however, most officers in supervisory positions and upwards do have to consider to some extent these other matters outside their own specialism. To that extent, there is an element of administrative work in their jobs. Thus there can be no clear distinction between "administrative positions" and "non-administrative positions". What actually happens is that, generally speaking, as an officer rises in rank, at a certain stage an administrative element enters into his work, and this "administrative content" grows with increasing seniority of position.

Even the most senior officers spend some portion of their time on non-administrative work, though since they are paid to be administrators the smaller this portion is the better.

To summarise, the administrative content is that part of an executive's work which involves him in considerations of policy and of general organisation; which requires him to bring together the work of others towards a common purpose; and which makes him responsible for taking into account *all* aspects of a policy objective; organisational, staffing and financial, and for checking upon results.

These accounts of administrative work may be compared with authoritative definitions. Some are from text-book writers, some from practising administrators, some from educationists.

(a) Two by Ordway Tead:

"Administration is the comprehensive effort to direct, guide and integrate associated human strivings which are focussed toward some specific ends or aims."

"Administration is the function within an organisation which is responsible for establishing its objects, purposes, aims or ends, for implementing the necessary organising and operating steps, and for assuring adequate performance towards the desired end."

(b) Brookes Adams:

"Administration is the capacity to co-ordinate many, and often conflicting, social energies in a single organism, so adroitly that they shall operate as a unity."

(c) First Division Officers' Evidence to U.K. Royal Commission 1929:

"Administrative duties are those concerned with the formation of policy, with the co-ordination and improvement of government machinery, and with the general control of the departments of the public service."

(d) At a conference with employers in 1953 on Training Schemes for Graduates, Mr. Keith Gravell, an Assistant Secretary of the Melbourne University Appointments Board, quoted a definition of the administrator as "the person charged with the responsibility of 'originating ideas and constructively arranging for their being carried into effect'". He went on: "It is becoming more generally recognised that administration can exist as an art in itself—that a person may be able to direct experts without being an expert himself. It is often his province to act as umpire between experts, such as, for instance, the engineer and the accountant, and to co-ordinate their varied activities."

As a basis for its practical recommendations, the Study Group decided to equate "higher administration" with between two and three hundred positions in the Commonwealth service that have the highest administrative content, namely those of officers in the First Division, officers who have broader responsibilities in the Second Division, and others with similar responsibilities who may happen to be classified outside these Divisions.

At the same time, the group concluded that among these positions a broad distinction may be drawn between those in which the emphasis is on "policy-making", and those where the emphasis is on "managerial" work. The former would have a high proportion of the first two elements of administration mentioned at the beginning of this section. The latter would mainly involve the third group of elements. They require the management of a well-defined function within a stable established policy framework as in senior positions at the State level. The qualifications they require include a thorough knowledge and experience of the technical aspects of the function, and good managerial ability in the co-ordination of work and the direction and control of staff. These latter positions are so much more numerous than the top policy-making positions that many officers will find the summit of their careers in them. On the other hand, some officers who do reach policy-making rank will not have to pass much of their career in the "managerial" type of position. If this is true the distinction should be taken into account in training and educational policy.

THE QUALITIES AND QUALIFICATIONS OF THE ADMINISTRATOR

It is desirable that an administrator should have certain important qualities of character and personality, intellectual capacity, general education, and specialised knowledge and training. The first two headings have implications for selection and promotion policies, with which this study is not primarily concerned. The second two are more obviously relevant to the present inquiry. A summary of the personal qualities which seem to be important is repeated here because, like the foregoing statements on the nature of administration, it aroused interest and fairly general support in the AC.T. Group's discussion.

Character and personality. There are no generally accepted categories for defining and distinguishing types of character, so it is hoped that a general impression can be given here without raising barren argument over the details of the terms used. There should be the less danger of this in that a good administrator should have the character traits we would expect in any responsible citizen. There is more room for difference over the intangible qualities of "personality".

(a) *Personal relations.* Higher administration consists largely in dealing with other people. The administrator needs to be capable of inspiring respect and confidence ; to be able to get on well with his equals, his subordinates and his superiors ; to be interested in people ; to be emotionally mature and stable ; to be capable of leadership without exercising domination.

(b) *Integrity.* We want our higher administrator to be mentally honest ; to have the courage of his convictions ; to be loyal to his chiefs and to their policy, and also to his subordinates.

(c) *Interest.* The keen administrator should have a genuine interest in public affairs and in the history, work and future of his own department. He should have begun to think responsibly about its problems and policies well before reaching the higher ranks.

(d) *Stamina.* Higher administrative work is exacting, sometimes frustrating, often imposes physical and nervous strain. It calls for vitality, zest, enthusiasm, and powers of endurance.

(e) *Toughness and determination.* Higher administration sometimes calls for stern measures, and certain personality types are not well adapted to this kind of action.

Intellectual capacity. It should go almost without saying that a higher administrator ought to be well endowed with brains, judgment, and originality and flexibility of mind. Most of these qualities are inborn in the individual, though experience, maturity and the right education and training may sharpen them and make them more useful in meeting the practical situations of life.

(a) *Brains* or intelligence implies the ability to think independently, logically and efficiently ; to get quickly to the heart of a matter and to see the principles involved ; to think out the general lines on which a practical task should be organised and take into account the quantitative factors involved.

(b) *Judgment* means, in our view, the capacity "to weigh against each other the various factors in a policy problem, such as the opinion of the technical advisers of the department, the financial considerations involved, and the probable effect of a course of action upon public and parliamentary opinion, and to form a sound and balanced appraisal of the situation as a whole" (the words are taken from the U.K. Royal Commission evidence of 1929 already quoted). It means being able to arrive without undue delay at firm decisions which turn out more often to be right than wrong.

(c) *Originality* is necessary in any policy maker. He should be constructive and imaginative, and not merely reproduce second-hand ideas.

(d) *Adaptability* and flexibility of mind are equally important. He should not be rigid and impervious to new ideas. This does not, of course, mean undue pliability or suggestibility.

(e) *Memory* and the ability to use it selectively.

To what extent and in what ways can *education and training* contribute to the development of these qualities? In so far as they are innate, like general intelligence, comparatively little. That is why initial selection and the promotion process are so vitally important in securing an able group of higher administrators. However, some of the necessary equipment for higher administration can be developed by education and training :—

(a) A good general education at university standard, without regard to the particular subjects studied, is both an aid to intellectual development and a potential measure of mental ability. Under suitable conditions (e.g. full-time study and residence within the university) it can also help to enrich the personality and encourage flexibility of mind and outlook. University education is not the only way to produce these qualities, but it does have significance for both the selection and development of higher administrators, provided it is not assumed that every graduate has a permanent head's fountain pen in his pocket.

(b) Education to university standard in politics, economics, history and administrative law—particularly relating to his own country—is increasingly desirable for the higher administrator, and suggestions are made later of ways in which this may be combined with or added to the specialised education of professional and technical officers who may become higher administrators.

(c) Education and in-service or external training in the special field of subject matter of the administrator's own department is of great assistance, and nowadays generally available, but is not absolutely essential to the work of higher administration.

(d) Education and training in the principles and practice of public administration—that is, in governmental organisation and management methods, is highly desirable.

(e) Factual knowledge about the organisation and operation of the administrator's own department, and of the relevant other parts of the public service as a whole, is the remaining need.

CURRENT PROVISIONS FOR ADMINISTRATIVE TRAINING AND EDUCATION

The study group made a general survey of existing measures, but did not examine the working of individual courses or measures in detail. They are constantly under review and amendment by the training section of the Public Service Board and by departmental personnel and training officers. The following is a summary of progress to the middle of 1956.

A. *Training*

(1) *Induction and basic training.*—In a majority of departments the departmental training officer (or his assistant) personally receives all new junior staff, discusses the department generally and the types of work available to them. Either at this stage or later he will lend them the Public Service Board handbook *Career Service*. This gives useful information about the general structure and functions of the public service, and helps the new recruit to visualise the service as a single whole in which a variety of careers is open to him. It is also policy that the recruit should receive a handbook on the history and functions of his department. In February, 1956, nine departments had published a departmental handbook and nine others were revising an earlier issue against an outline suggested by the Board.

The Board has informed departments that basic on-the-job training should give the recruit "a thorough grounding in the work of the section, its functions and methods", an up-to-date review of the functions of the department as a whole, and in general, "all-round clerical training and experience in the department, as far as practicable", through job rotation.

After some months of service the recruit attends a New Entrant School conducted either by the department (in larger departments) or by the local public service Inspector.

The practice of assigning selected officers early in their careers as understudies to senior policy-making officers is not generally followed.

(2) *Training in supervision.*—The Public Service Board has laid down a policy on supervision training, and during 1952-53 it organised pilot courses for supervisors in collaboration with certain departments in Canberra and

the States. But this type of training was carefully considered in two papers discussed at the first Training Officers' Workshop organised by the Public Service Board in November, 1953, and the conclusion was reached that:—

> Each course must be designed for the special needs of the department. Again, each course must be small enough for active participation by all members. For these reasons, very few departments will not be able to run their own courses and so central courses will not be generally required.

The Board has adopted the view that in general training in supervision should be a departmental function ; but apart from the pilot courses already mentioned, some "courses for supervisors" have been conducted centrally, e.g., at State level by the Board's State Inspectors' offices. Supervision training can still be regarded as in the experimental stage. The plan adopted in the Board's pilot courses was modified in the "broad pattern of supervision training" outlined in a paper on administrative training published by the Principal Training Officer in *Public Administration,* September, 1954. This was the pattern followed in central supervision courses conducted by State Inspectors' offices, but naturally omitting any section on departmental policies and procedures. Some of the departments which are conducting courses of their own in accordance with the Board's policy, are Civil Aviation, Postmaster-General's, Repatriation, Supply, Army, Air, Customs, Works, Attorney-General's, Taxation, and the Audit Department.

(3) *Administrative training for technical, scientific and professional officers.*—There is a real need for this, because in the Commonwealth service officers carrying out higher administration in departments whose functions are primarily of a technical or professional nature are normally chosen from the technical, scientific or professional staff. At the same time, such people are inclined to underrate the need for trained skill in administration. The Professional Officers' Association is aware of this need, and has asked the Public Service Board and some departments to arrange for suitable administrative training for professional officers. Most senior officers in the departments concerned have had some supervisory experience before reaching higher administrative positions. Opportunity is given for some of them to attend the Board's Assistant Secretaries' Conferences. (See below.) This section is concerned with training below that level. It is entirely on a departmental basis at present:

> (a) *Postmaster-General's Department.* A professional officer in the Engineering Branch in Melbourne and also one in Sydney have been made responsible for training Engineers in management and supervisory techniques. The instruction to be given follows fairly closely the syllabus of the Management Courses given at the Royal Melbourne Technical College and the Sydney Technical College.

> (b) *Department of Works.* This department has developed a "basic administrative" training course for the professional staff. It covers the same field as the Board's Higher Administration course and uses the discussion group technique. The officers covered include architects, engineers and other professional officers from Grade 1 to Senior level. The courses are held in Melbourne, Sydney and Canberra.

(c) *Department of Civil Aviation* conducts administrative training courses for all staff including professional staff.

(d) *External Affairs.* Diplomatic staff are given brief rotation experience in the administrative sections of the department and are given some lectures on administrative routine procedures in small oversea missions.

(e) *Other Departments.* There are special courses of administrative training for professional staff in the departments of National Development, Supply, and Attorney-General. The Health Department has assessed the needs for such training and is formulating methods of meeting them. The Department of Territories holds training conferences of about four weeks at a time, for technical and professional staffs including senior officers from the Territorial Administration.

(4) *Courses for Departmental Administrative Officers.*—These were begun in 1948 and are conducted by the Public Service Board training section at Canberra. Over 350 officers have attended the courses already held. They include selected officers having a fairly high administrative content in their duties, and the age at courses held so far is between 35 and 45 years. A course lasts a fortnight, and includes about 25 officers, with so far as possible an even distribution between those with executive, administrative, professional and technical experience. It includes lectures, discussions and questions by the full group, and discussion and reporting on set projects or case studies, for which the group is divided into three or four syndicates of eight members each. Examples of projects are: Proposals for organising a specified new department; a training programme for departmental supervisors. Similar courses are beginning in Melbourne and Sydney.

(5) *Assistant Secretaries' Conferences.*—Five of these have been held at the time of writing. Those who attend are eighteen to twenty selected officers of Assistant Secretary rank or close to it, in the younger age range of this rank (40-45 years), including a cross section from head office, State offices, administrative, personnel, finance and technical and professional fields of work, and also a balance between those with lengthy service and those with less than ten years' service. The same kind of distribution is maintained within the three syndicates of six members into which the group is divided. Each conference lasts about ten days, and is set a main problem which forms its theme. Experts talk to the full group on various aspects of the problem and the syndicates discuss these, leading to a full report by the whole group on the general theme. These conferences are arranged by the Public Service Board at Canberra, and members of the Board take a full and active part in them.

In both of the last-mentioned courses, the written reports are not an end in themselves, but a means of focussing group discussion and eliciting active participation by members. In some cases discussion in syndicates is also used as a preliminary to lectures and group meetings, with the object of bringing to the fore the problems and questions in relation to the proposed subject, in which members are most interested or on which their knowledge most needs rounding out. The lectures are given by experts in the several fields, both from inside and outside the public service. Duplicated notes **are generally** distributed, containing summaries of the lectures and copies of supporting documents. Films of technical and administrative interest are shown at intervals during the course. The courses are held in the well-equipped Staff Training Centre. As a general summary of their approach it might be said that while the Administrative Staff College at Henley has contributed something to their method—syndicate discussion with rotating chairmen, production of group reports, attention to balanced composition of the group—the content is directed mostly to informing trainees about current practices, departmental functions and relationships, and only in part to inducing them to think about and analyse the broad problems and techniques involved in carrying out higher administrative duties. The reason for this is that the Commonwealth Service has grown so rapidly and many officers' careers have been so brief in the service, that even at high levels there are surprising gaps in sheer factual knowledge about central departments like the Treasury, Prime Minister's and Public Service Board and their role and relations with other departments. The courses and conferences provide an opportunity of speeding up mutual acquaintanceship, understanding and the spread of information which, in a more settled service, would naturally be acquired by officers at an earlier stage.

B. *Training and Education Combined*

(6) *Cadetships.*—The great majority of the training schemes of the cadet type are in the professional and technical fields. On the borderline of such specialist work are the cadetships for Personnel Officer, Education Officer, and for the Diplomatic Service. As in other specialist occupations in the Australian public service, these careers may lead to higher administrative work. But the only cadetship established with that end definitely in view is that for Social Services. This was introduced to provide recruits for the higher administrative positions in the Department of Social Services, with training and experience in social studies. On the same principle as in all cadetships, the cadets are recruited to the service as persons qualified to undertake the higher study in question ; they study full time for the Diploma in Social Studies, the service paying salary and fees, and during long vacations they are attached to the Department for practical training. Only two cadets have been appointed since the establishment of the cadetship in 1951. Cadetships are subject to a bond to remain in the service for a specified period after completion of training.

C. *Education*

(7) *Free and Assisted Places—Part Time.*—The conditions of the Free Place scheme include:

(a) Only officers of the Third Division who have completed their probation, and officers eligible for transfer to the Third Division, may apply, provided they have not previously received Commonwealth financial assistance for a university course (except under the Reconstruction Training Scheme) ;

(b) Free place holders are expected to take lectures outside official hours if available, otherwise leave is allowed up to five hours a week ;

(c) Free place holders are no longer required to enter a bond to remain in the public service after completing the degree ;

(*d*) There is no allowance for books, equipment, etc.;

(*e*) Free place holders may study at any Australian University including the Canberra University College, but not including the A.N.U. and the N.S.W. University of Technology.

(*f*) The courses available include Arts, Law, Economics, Commerce and Public Administration.

Since the commencement of the scheme, 247 free place holders have graduated and forty-seven Free Places were granted in 1956. The total number current is 115.

(8) *Free Places—Full Time.*—In 1952 the Board provided a small number of free places for officers who could complete a degree in one year's full time study at a university, including part-time students who hold or would be eligible for a part-time free place. This includes also study for an honours degree or for completion of a Master's degree. Fifteen of these full-time free places have been awarded and competition for them is very keen. The selection basis is that only outstanding students will be considered, and the final decision is made by determining the increased efficiency of the officer in terms of the additional advantages offered. Its most salutary effect has been to raise the standards of the degrees being taken. Formerly most part-time students were content with pass marks, but now there has been a notable increase in those taking honours courses in their individual subjects.

(9) *Short Courses in Australia.*—When officers undertake short courses, e.g., at Technical Colleges at the request of their department for departmental purposes, the Public Service Board has approved of the department meeting the full cost without prior reference to the Board, provided the cost does not exceed £20 for any one person and the time off does not exceed five hours a week. Departments are required to notify particulars to the Board as soon as the officer begins the course. Where an officer undertakes a short course of study in his own time which the department considers would substantially increase his efficiency in the performance of his existing duties, and not with a view to gaining qualifications to fit him for positions he is likely to fill by transfer or promotion, the Board will consider refunding half the fees on application, provided the cost of the complete course does not exceed £20.

(10) *Post-graduate Study.*—Under a system first instituted in 1937, but suspended at the outbreak of war until 1947, the Board may (*a*) award scholarships for post-graduate study overseas; (*b*) grant financial assistance to officers proceeding overseas for post-graduate study or experience on their own initiative. The latter class comprises mainly officers holding other scholarships, such as Fulbright awards, Carnegie grants and Commonwealth Fund Fellowships.

In practice (*a*) has been widened to include research, observation or experience as an alternative to study towards a higher degree which was obligatory at first. Such scholarships are also awarded in the scientific and technical fields. Since 1948, twenty-seven scholarships have been awarded, and financial assistance provided in about forty other cases.

COMMENTS AND RECOMMENDATIONS ON THE CURRENT PROVISIONS

A glance at the foregoing summary will show that the Commonwealth service has established most of the elements of a rounded scheme of training and assistance and encouragement to education calculated to meet substantially the requirements suggested in section III above. However, the scheme has not yet been fully implemented in all its parts; there is scope for some re-arrangement of the existing components of the scheme; the application of the scheme to certain classes of officers bears further consideration; and there are still some gaps in the structure—mostly minor but one or two of importance. And as already pointed out, no scheme of training and education can ensure an adequate supply of talent in the higher administrative ranks unless it is geared to a suitable system of recruitment, promotion and incentives. In the following paragraphs some comments are made on each aspect of the present training and education scheme, showing the basis for the recommendations made by the study group.

Induction and Basic Training

Under the current classification and promotion system, this is only marginal to administrative training. However, one or two points can be made about the present basic training process. Under present conditions systematic job rotation for training purposes is extremely difficult to carry out, owing to the high turnover in the service and to the need for transfers to meet exigencies often in other States. This may accelerate the rate of promotion, which is desirable, but in such a way as to preclude the junior from gaining balanced experience. Although supervisors often lack the inclination or the time or the capacity to organise systematic job rotation programmes, it is important that every effort should be made to put job rotation into practice, and the Public Service Board has stressed this point to departments. The Board expressed agreement with the study group's recommendation that, where job rotation schemes have been put into operation, departmental training courses should include instruction on the scheme and how it works. The Board added that it was already the case, as recommended by the group, that Board and departmental supervision training emphasised the supervisor's responsibility for job rotation, on-the-job training and the work documentation which is a necessary preliminary to supervision training.

Training in "Supervision"

The definition of a supervisor adopted at the 1953 Training Officers' Workshop was: "A person responsible for getting things done through the combined efforts of himself and others." The training officers' study report on this subject, however, drew a "dividing line between supervision and management . . . at the policy making level", and also recognised differences of level within the supervisory range. The report added that the appropriate training for this function was "that which gives the individual a grasp of particular techniques or skills: the emphasis is on practice rather than theory." These statements confirm the impression gained by a quick survey of supervision courses actually in force, that "supervision training" is in the Commonwealth service a vague term covering all systematic non-technical training between the courses for new entrants at one level and the courses for departmental administrative officers at the other. The Workshop group itself concluded that "there is no single course in supervision capable of meeting the requirements of all departments, or all categories of supervisors within a department". The study group thought that "supervision" is not a suitable term to cover all of these courses, and suggested that it be replaced by terms appropriate to each course. It is adhered to here for convenience of reference only. A more appropriate general term might be "intermediate administrative training".

Official definitions of "the general pattern of supervision training" embrace the following clearly distinguishable subjects:—

(a) Human relations in employment: selection and placement, discipline and morale, welfare, communications, relations with superiors, with other supervisors, with the public;

(b) Methods and aids for training staff under the supervisor;

(c) "Job management", including job skills, organisation and methods, work analysis, procedure statements, delegation and control, office layout, furniture and equipment, etc.;

(d) Departmental policies and procedures:

   (i) to acquaint the supervisor with the history, legislation, functions, policies and plans of the department so that he may be better able to interpret them to his staff;

   (ii) to give him a better understanding of the organisation of the department, its operating procedures (accounting, personnel, records, typing, stores, transport services), and his relationship and that of his section with the rest of the department;

(e) "Service-wide aspects of administration"—

   (i) Broad structure of the Commonwealth public service, and relationships of the department with other parts of it;

   (ii) Legislation affecting the general administration of the government and the public service;

   (iii) Roles of the Public Service Board, Treasury and Prime Minister's Department;

   (iv) Employer-employee relations, arbitration, appeals, etc.;

   (v) Current trends in the administration of the service.

It is clear that training of this kind is a departmental, rather than a central, responsibility, and that there must be a wide variety in the specific content of intermediate administration courses. However:

(1) It may be possible to give departments somewhat firmer guidance in applying the above broad pattern to their particular needs.

(2) Heading (e) in that pattern is not essentially a part of intermediate administrative training. It covers information rather than training —information which for the most part should be available to every officer early in his career, and information which requires authoritative and uniform exposition throughout the service. That is, it is more suitable for treatment in centrally-conducted or centrally-

prescribed new entrant courses (where much of it is already included). However, there is a case for including this material in "supervision" courses in the present developmental stage of training, when many supervisors will not have had the benefit of the present new entrant courses. It is also true that (*e*) (iii) and (v) have important aspects requiring treatment in higher administrative training. This connects with the next point.

(3) Some training advantages may be gained by distinguishing between "elementary" and "advanced" phases of certain subjects in the above pattern—particularly (*c*) Job Management, and (*d*) Departmental Policies (i). This suggests a simple general policy of encouraging the planning of intermediate administrative training on two levels. Training at both levels is desirable for all future administrative officers, whether destined for "managerial" or "policy-making" work. Special training and educational preparation for policy-making work is discussed in a separate section below.

It was argued by the study group that inclusion of any full treatment of "service-wide aspects of administration" in "supervision" courses should be regarded as a transitional practice to make up for gaps in the present staff's elementary training. At an elementary level this subject should be treated thoroughly in new entrant courses, on uniform lines laid down by the Public Service Board. At an advanced level, discussion of the roles of the central policy and controlling departments and of recent trends in the service should be retained in the departmental administrative officers' and Assistant Secretaries' courses.

However, the Public Service Board in its comments on the Report pointed out that there were different aspects of this topic which would have importance for officers at all stages of training, provided that the scope and presentation was varied with the experience and need of each group. The Board felt it was an over-simplification of the training problem to suggest that these "service-wide aspects" should be dealt with at only two stages. With varied treatment, this seems sound. The group's concern was to make such treatment possible by avoiding any waste of training time that might result from repeating, at different stages, factual material that could be incorporated in an explanatory manual.

The Group's specific suggestions for a broad division of intermediate administrative training into two levels were as follows:—

(The letters refer to the subjects as detailed in an earlier paragraph.)

Elementary Management Courses

    (*a*) Human relations in employment.
    (*b*) Methods and aids in staff training.
    (*c*) Job management, elementary (the more routine aspects).
    (*d*) Departmental policies and procedures, elementary.

Advanced Management Courses

    (*a*) Human relations in employment, including conference and committee techniques.
    (*c*) Job management, advanced (more intensive discussion of the principles of administration, delegation and control, co-ordination, accountability, higher organization, etc.).

(d) Departmental policies and procedures, advanced (discussing recent and pending legislation, policies and plans, and their implications for the department's organisation, procedures, and relations with other departments).

(e) Service-wide aspects of administration, advanced (roles of the Board, Treasury and P.M.'s Department, and recent trends in general administration of the service, from the point of view of their practical significance for managerial work).

The Board's observations included the following points:—

In general it may be said that in the vertical development of departmental organisation these supervision and management skills are so mingled in any position that, for training purposes, actual responsibilities and delegations must be examined to determine the needs and the content of training . . .

The assessment of needs moreover involves—

(i) A reliable system of staff reporting through which higher executives and senior supervisors can indicate the training required by subordinate staff; and

(ii) Consistent and thorough surveys and analyses of the administrative problems in Departments.

The Board has recently provided a position of Inspector (Training) on its staff to effect a more direct liaison between Departments and the Board and to give guidance to Departments in the assessment of training needs and also in the development of an appropriate training programme.

There can be no quarrel in theory with the Board's analysis and approach. But under present conditions they represent perhaps counsels of perfection. It is true that supervisory positions involve many subtle combinations of skills. The attempt to match these precisely with tailored training courses might well discourage prompt departmental action. Skills and needs may be mixed, but formal training, like all formal education, must necessarily be somewhat arbitrary in structure. The group's suggestion for a simple two-level pattern, while not for a moment implying standardised detailed content of courses nor even precisely similar levels for courses in different departments, might give departments a specific guide to action, and make it easier to hold them to account. It also sets some limit to training requirements in the experimental stage, which might be reassuring to departments. And it was thought to be realistic as an interim approach, precisely because there are not in existence as yet either "a reliable system of staff reporting" or thorough analyses of departmental administrative problems. Anyhow, it is set out here for discussion.

Administrative training for technical, scientific and professional officers

In strict logic, this is simply a part of intermediate administrative training. Special provisions of this kind are only in the exploratory stage. The following principles are worth considering in developing them:—

(a) Professional and specialist officers should get their formal administrative training in company with non-specialist officers. The building of contacts, the exchange of experience and the clash of different outlooks are in themselves valuable administrative training to both sides.

(b) As it may often not be convenient or appropriate to include professional officers in new entrant courses, it is particularly desirable to bring them into what we have called "elementary management" courses.

(c) As it is policy for "supervision" training to be tailored to the needs of individual departments, so departments may adapt some of their formal "supervision" courses to the special needs of those branches engaged in professional or technical work.

From these views it is obvious that one would endorse the present policy of including some professional and specialist officers in central courses for departmental administrative officers and in Assistant Secretaries' conferences.

Administrative Officers' and Assistant Secretaries' Conferences

These courses use an appropriate technique, which is being refined by experience, but their subject-matter is concerned much more with the managerial than with policy-making aspects of higher administration. This is inevitable in view of the interests of most of those who attend, though it will be possible to relegate some of the material to lower-level courses as more and more officers get the benefit of intermediate administrative training. Apart from this, however, the short duration and other practical limitations of these conferences are not conducive to intensive study of problems and techniques of higher administration and policy making. Further, preparation for higher policy-making work is a matter of planned experience and education as well as of in-Service training courses. Though quite small in numbers, the policy-making group of officers is so important that it should be more fully catered for in these respects than at present. The remaining sections of the report were therefore devoted specially to this group.

Training and Education for Policy-making

Since the beginning of the last war there have been great changes in the relative size and the composition of the higher administrative ranks of the Commonwealth Service. While the Service as a whole was in 1953 three times its 1936 size, the First and Second Divisions, i.e., both policy-making and managerial groups—had quadrupled. In addition, a new category of officers has been built up, in various departments, providing a career from Assistant Research Officer to Principal Research Officer. The duty of these officers (who, under Section 32 of the Public Service Act, as amended, must be graduates) is to "assemble the facts, to assist in the policy-making and policy development". The reason for these changes is the prominence given to research, planning, policy formulation and policy supervision in comparison with the past. The following comments assess the effectiveness of existing measures to secure suitably qualified officers for these new functions:—

(a) Until recently the free place scheme has been used largely for part-time study, in many cases leading to undistinguished degrees.

(b) The service did not handle graduate recruitment wisely until recently. It was only in 1948 that differential starting salaries were first offered to graduates. Once in the service, little distinction has been made between honours and pass graduates. The early years of a graduate's service often do not enable him to make proper use of his training. One quarter of the graduates appointed before the war have since resigned.

(c) In recruiting highly qualified officers whether from below as graduates or from outside, the Service has laid emphasis on certificates of professional or technical competence to the neglect of general educational preparation for higher administrative work. One critic of the Service has said that graduates succeed "commonly because they have shown ability in specialized fields, and they will, in the normal course of events, continue to specialize. Excessive specialization, like excessive routine work, is not beneficial for the development of the abilities required by the administrative official: in fact, one of the continuing problems of the Commonwealth service is that its senior officers tend to be technicians rather than administrators". [S. Encel, in *Public Administration* (Sydney), Dec. 1953, p. 230.]

Existing policies on recruitment, promotion, training and education could pay more attention to the higher administrative policy-making group in respect of the need for broad general education, avoidance of excessive routine and specialisation, advanced study of Australian political and economic problems, and advanced study of higher administration and organisation for policy-making. More specifically:—

(a) Existing provisions for post-graduate study are a valuable form of education for higher policy-making, but they are only available overseas and so do not advance the study of Australian administrative and policy problems at first hand.

(b) On the other hand, it is not desirable that graduate entrants to the Service should be required to include prescribed subjects in their undergraduate courses, such as government and public administration. At that level, these subjects should be regarded as of general educational and background value only and not as adequate preparation or training for policy-making work. An officer needs practical experience before he can benefit fully from education in the techniques of organisation, administration and policy formation. Universities can contribute to such education at the post-graduate level.

From the foregoing considerations certain principles emerge:—

(a) More effective training for higher administrative work depends on increasing opportunities for the officer of suitable abilities to gain practical experience of management and policy-making as early as possible in his career;

(b) Education for higher administration at the post-graduate level is most beneficial if undertaken on a full-time basis, and should be framed so far as possible to fit the special needs of the administrator.

As a contribution to the development of future policy-makers, the study group suggested further exploration of the use of cadetships leading to general administrative careers. One advantage of the cadetship system under present-day circumstances is that if sufficiently attractive it may secure more of the best talent by recruiting it at an earlier stage in the educational process than university graduation. This means that the government bears the cost of further education, but on the other hand this education can be directed towards the needs of the public service, and it can be combined with training and experience in such ways as to make the educational process more meaningful in terms of an administrative career. However, the group did not explore the practical problems which are important, and some of which were indicated in the Board's comment. They agreed that cadetships of the professional type now common in the service,

> tend to attract the better class of young officer, probably because of the definitive area of administrative work to which these cadet-graduates are ultimately directed. This assures the man of a career in a chosen field with systematic training to that end. In the general administrative field, however, it is difficult to specify hard and fast lines of promotion (which the Cadetship scheme would require) in view of the established promotion system.

It would be worth while to discuss and examine this idea further.

The group also felt that the "understudy" system should be developed both for administrative cadets and for other officers who show administrative promise. They felt that private secretaryships to Ministers and senior officials should be deliberately used for this purpose. Here also the Board's comments were of great relevance for future thought and action on executive development. The Board pointed out that while some departments are doing good work on these lines.

> in others this method of training is neither planned nor effectively exploited . . .
>
> The early association of future administrators with top-ranking administrators and policy makers in a Department offers obvious advantages. Nevertheless there are also disadvantages, if not dangers, in a system of understudies in that the understudy may become the "alter ego" of his chief and be too close to him to develop his own personality. "Traditional policy" is not necessarily good policy. It will be seen therefore that the planning of an understudy scheme requires very careful thought apart from questions of selection and assessment. It is agreed that in some instances the position of Private Secretary to a Minister could provide a valuable experience for potential policy makers. At present, however, selections of Private Secretaries may be made largely on the basis of personal preference of a Minister and in order that such a scheme could become effective it would seem essential that a different concept of the Private Secretaryship would have to be accepted by Ministers and by Departments.

A final recommendation of the Group was that the pattern of administrative education should include a full-time post-graduate university course of at least one year for a small number of selected officers in their thirties who show promise of attaining policy-making rank. The course should be conducted and controlled by a University, but should be specially designed and students selected in consultation between the University and the Public

Service Board. Scholarships could take the form of a full-time free place
or sabbatical year on full pay, with incremental and promotion rights
preserved. The course should be taught partly by university teachers and
partly by people with administrative experience, and should operate largely
by the seminar method. A high academic standard should be set, while at
the same time the subject prescriptions should apply the respective academic disciplines to current problems of policy in the Australian context.
Some of the subjects should be Australian government and politics, social
and economic history, public finance and public economics, principles and
practices of organisation and management, industrial and occupational
psychology and administrative law. The details of such a scheme should
be the subject of consultation between University and public service
authorities.

It may be added that this suggestion was based on first-hand knowledge
of a scheme of this kind which was begun in New Zealand in 1940, and
after a war-time suspension from 1942-1946, was resumed in 1947 and
continued to the present time. The New Zealand scheme has all the conditions mentioned above, except that the course is for two full-time university years and leads to a Diploma in Public Administration of post-
graduate standard. It has several times been subjected to careful appraisal
and review by the Public Service Commission and the Government itself,
leading to improvements in curriculum and technique but to no change
in its essential principles of operation.

There is not space here to do justice to the discussion of this proposal.
The Public Service Board agreed generally with the idea of a full-time
post-graduate course for officers of the kind the study group had in mind,
but had alternative views on the duration and organisation of such a
course, which would not conflict with its essential objectives. Secondly,
the view was expressed in the Group that formal post-graduate education
was not as useful for executive development as a period of secondment
to some extra-governmental institution, or to an appropriate government
department in a different public service, in Australia or more particularly
abroad. There is in fact no inconsistency between the two types of scheme.
The study group as already stated, was concerned only with "education
and training" and not with the whole problem of executive development.
It did not envisage that every future administrator should follow a uniform
course of education, training, experience and development, but regarded
the "pattern" of executive development, including administrative education,
as a comprehensive series of provisions, of which selected elements would
be available to individual officers in the course of their career, according
to individual background, abilities, and employment. In the wider field of
executive development the idea of secondment (including exchange of
officers between public services) is an invaluable one. And in fact there
is provision to a modest extent for exchange of Commonwealth public
servants with their counterparts in the Canadian and U.K. Civil Services.
The Board has an arrangement with the British Treasury under which
officers are exchanged between the O. and M. Divisions for periods of one
year. The Prime Minister's Department has exchanged officers with
the Cabinet Secretariat in the U.K. and the Department of Labour and
National Service and the P.M.G.'s Department also exchange officers with
their namesakes. The Canadian exchange is from civil service to civil
service with choice of Department according to priority of value.

Chapter Eighteen

PERSONNEL PROBLEMS
IN THE AUSTRALIAN PUBLIC SERVICES

S. C. DERWENT

From the earliest days of the Industrial Revolution there has been evidence of careful and conscious attempts by manufacturers to make the best use of three of the factors at their disposal in the industrial process—materials, machines and money. They have tried to economise in the use of capital, to conserve natural resources, to improve machine methods and to carry out research work which will enable a better product to be manufactured more cheaply. As a result, a high degree of precision has been attained in the handling of machine and material problems.

What of the fourth factor in the circuit of production—the human element? Is this factor as important as the impersonal ones and, if so, has it been given the same degree of consideration? It is not difficult to demonstrate that the human problems confronting management are not only as real and as complex as those which concern materials but less readily identified and much more difficult to investigate by existing research methods.

In planning the manufacture of a particular item, the manufacturer draws on the findings of research and on his own experience to predict just how materials and machines will behave in the manufacturing processes. Predictions are made in most instances with a marked degree of accuracy— for instance, he is aware of the manner in which a piece of metal will react to heat treatment or the various machine processes, and carefully selects his plant to ensure that it will enable compliance with the specifications of finish, size and performance.

The type of question which the designer and production planner ask themselves of materials and machines may equally be applied by the person whose main concern is with the management of people. The designer asks himself, "Will this piece of metal withstand the stresses induced by the machine which is made from it?" The personnel officer asks, "Is this person capable of coping effectively with the demands that this job will make on him?" The engineer asks, "What will happen if I place these two different metals in contact?" The personnel officer asks, "What will be the effect of employing this person in this particular group of people?" Similarly, the personnel officer must consider what "maintenance" measures must be used if his staff is to maintain maximum efficiency, the adjustments that must be made if the employee is to operate under changed conditions, and what will be the optimum of physical working conditions for carrying out this or that process.

That management has in many instances neglected to seek or been unable to obtain adequate answers to these questions is often evidenced by such symptoms as high staff turnover, poor individual and team performance, serious occupational maladjustment and the differences in cost of producing the same product within an industry or organization where other things are apparently equal.

This lack of consideration of the human factor in commerce, industry and government cannot be attributed merely to the apathy of individual employers; it has deeper sources, namely:—

(1) The traditional over-supply of labour;

(2) the perpetuation of a social philosophy which involved the belief that each individual had control of his own destiny and could be held personally responsible for his own good or ill;

(3) the lack of scientific knowledge concerning the nature and significance of individual differences.

Evidence that interest in the human element paid dividends was provided by the first important contributor to scientific management, Frederick Winslow Taylor. By careful selection, instruction and incentive payments, Taylor increased daily loadings of pig iron at the Bethlehem Steel Company from $12\frac{1}{2}$ tons per man per day to 48 tons per man per day. Because of the antipathy developed by organised labour towards the methods and results achieved by Taylor and his successors, such as Gantt, Barth and Gilbreth, a discussion of his activities would find little place in a treatise concerned with the promotion of good personnel relations. The methods and results achieved, however, did stress the need for the complete utilisation of all elements in the production circuit, namely, plant, material and man. Evidence to support Taylor's consideration of the human factor soon followed from the field of pure research. When Wilhelm Wundt opened his Leipzig laboratory, devoted exclusively to the scientific study of human behaviour, the first break was made with the theorising of the philosopher and current theory was submitted to the experimental methods of the laboratory.

A detailed programme of the application of psychology in industry was first formulated by a German, Hugo Munsterberg, who concluded his career at Harvard University Psychology Laboratory.[1] In 1913, in a book entitled "Psychology and Industrial Efficiency", he pointed out the importance of psychology in promoting the adjustment and efficiency of workers in the industrial situation. He outlined definite proposals for the use of tests in the selection of workers, the application of findings on learning in training industrial personnel, and the study of psychological techniques of the effects of conditions of work on motives of workers and factors producing fatigue.

Despite the efforts of Munsterberg and others, it required the stimulus of manpower shortages and war to increase the degree of attention to human problems, and even under these circumstances the principal interest was in selection, insufficient consideration being given to the problem of human relations.

Developments between the Wars

The first large-scale evidence of attention to personnel was given during the 1914-18 war, when the United States undertook wholesale psychological

---

[1] Brief reference is made to Munsterberg's work in Morris S. Viteles, *The Science of Work* (1934), pp. 46-49, and the same author's *Industrial Psychology* (1932).

testing of recruits for the armed forces. In addition, England, France, Germany and the United States used special testing methods for the selection of aviation pilots, observers and a wide range of military and civilian occupational types.

The problems of human relations which, to a large extent, had been neglected, were really made apparent by experiments carried out by the Western Electric Company at its plant in Hawthorne, U.S.A., which were aimed at determining the precise effects of varying working conditions such as temperature, humidity, lighting and the length of rest periods and of the working day.

Briefly, the company set aside a portion of the plant so that the experimental work could be carried out and observed under varying conditions without disrupting the remainder of the plant. Introduction of rest periods of varying lengths, reduction of working hours and improved illumination resulted in production increases, but there appeared to be a general upward trend which could not be readily explained by the manipulation of the other variables. This upward trend became clear when it was found that despite the removal of improved conditions the level of production was sustained. Analysis of the data revealed that a more favourable working attitude had developed in the employees because the room during the experimental period had been in charge of an observer instead of a supervisor. The observer was more ready to talk freely with them on matters that revealed their fears and dislikes, particularly those directed towards the employing company. As a result, the social relations between the workers themselves and also between the workers and the supervisors became more friendly. Not only did the group increase production, but they engaged in social activities outside the work situation, and the improvement in the social atmosphere resulted in a decline in absenteeism, which, in one instance, was reduced to one-fourth of the former rate.

Among other things, this (the "Hawthorne experiment") illustrated the importance of attitude towards work and also directed attention to the need for the better selection and training of supervisors.

Despite the significance of the findings of the Hawthorne experiment and the experience of the armed services with the use of predictive tests, a considerable time was to elapse before this new knowledge and experience resulted in the formulation of personnel policies and practices. This was, generally speaking, true of industry, commerce and government; but the government services appear to have excelled in the codifying of working conditions, and some at least used examination systems as an aid in both initial selection and promotion.

Developments during and after World War II

There was some piecemeal development of personnel work in Australian Departments between the wars, for example, in the postal service. The period was one of transition. The increasing size and complexity of departments was forcing permanent heads to realise that they must delegate to intermediate officers the direct control of staff that they had been able to exercise themselves previously. In New South Wales the 1918 Allard Commission already recognised the significance of the staff officer and the role he could play in promoting contentment and efficiency. The appointment of Assistant Under Secretaries was followed in many instances by the creation of positions such as Chief Inspector, which required general oversight of staff; but the acceptance of the "staff officer" as a specialist, particularly in human relations, was yet to come. It emerged in New South Wales just before World War II, when (1939) the Public Service Board arranged for the appointment of personnel officers in all the major departments, to act as advisers both to the permanent head and to the Board.[2] The war and manpower shortages caused this to be postponed. However, in the long run the war was a stimulus to such developments.

With the advent of World War II, governments and private enterprise were forced, as in the First World War, to devote more specialised attention to the human element in production, in a desperate attempt to maximize the effectiveness of the armed forces and civilian workers. For the first time, both in and out of the government services, officers were appointed with the special responsibility of ensuring that the same degree of consideration was given to personnel as to materials and machines. The Personnel Director appeared alongside the Production Director and the Sales Director, the Personnel Department alongside the Production Department. Jobs were analysed in an effort to place the disabled so that their disabilities constituted the least possible handicap; predictive psychological tests were used in the selection of trainees and employees, and the selection and training of supervisors began to receive the close attention suggested by the Hawthorne experiment.

There were still many gaps in practice and technique, however. Personnel practices were adopted, with considerable efficacy, in some areas, but totally ignored in others. Although the armed services used psychological tests extensively in the massive selection problems which confronted them, many organisations relied solely on the interview as a selection technique. Conversely, supervisory training produced results in industry, and attention was effectively given to all aspects of training, including the actual physical conditions; yet N.C.O.'s in the armed forces, although highly trained in technical skills, had to rely on their own capacity and insight to guide them in the handling of men and new recruits were expected to undertake complicated weapon training in a "bull ring" swept by chilly winds.

Many of the gaps have been filled today. More and more attention has been devoted to the discovery of personnel problems and the development of techniques and practices aimed at their solution. For example, the action initiated in New South Wales in 1939 for the appointment of Personnel Officers in major Departments has culminated not only in such appointments, but also in the formation of an active, creative group of Departmental Personnel Officers whose advice in personnel matters is given considerable weight by the New South Wales Board. This group has helped the Board to develop a clear personnel policy and to establish the sound practices and methods which are necessary to make it effective. During the last ten years the Board has, among other measures, developed standardised induction and exit interview procedures, issued a substantial amount of tutorial material and provided other teaching aids for officers preparing for in-service examinations, and introduced a counselling service whose function is aimed at staff development. The Commonwealth Service, too, has been

[2] See N.S.W. Public Service Board, *Report,* 1939.

active in the personnel field. Training officers have been employed in Departments, and the Commonwealth Board has designed and conducted central training courses, both for officers of their own service and for Colombo Plan trainees(³) which would do credit to the best educational institutions. An evidence of the intensified interest in personnel matters is provided by the co-operation of the Commonwealth and the States in the establishment of a Commonwealth-State Training Conference. All States were represented at the November, 1957, session. Such conferences are certain to result in the giving of greater consideration to the human element in administration.

The main problems confronting the personnel administrator are connected with the following:—

(1) selection,

(2) staff reporting,

(3) obtaining and using information about positions,

(4) human relations.

It is proposed to define broadly the nature of these problems and to indicate some of the solutions which have been adopted both in public and private enterprises.

SELECTION

Methods of selection involve the use of one or more of the following techniques:—(⁴)

(i) oral examination by an individual officer,

(ii) oral examination by a selection committee,

(iii) the use of tests of achievement, such as shorthand and typing tests, trade tests,

(iv) the use of predictive psychological tests, such as tests of intelligence and aptitude,

(v) the use of the probation period.

(i) *Interviewing by an Individual Officer*

The principal purpose of the interview is to appraise the personal attributes demanded by a position, being concerned with such things as quality of voice, appearance, attitude, interests, enthusiasm, and so on—all of which can rarely be more effectively measured by more precise means. The interview, however, should not be used to assess technical competency, ability and aptitude where standardised tests may be readily available. Practical considerations often make it impossible to use a technique other than the interview in selection.

Selection by one officer has a number of disadvantages, and, as a result, it is usually the practice to confine the activities of such a person to selecting

---

(³) The Commonwealth Public Service Board has issued a number of documents setting out details of the courses arranged for Colombo Plan Fellows. These books illustrate the effective co-operation between the States and the Commonwealth in providing training and experience for these visitors from overseas.

(⁴) "On Tests in Public Personnel Selection", *U.S. Civil Service Assembly Report*, 1943, pp. 31 and 81-85.

a limited range of occupational types where he is in possession of complete information about the nature of the duties and their physical and social setting. Thus, in a particular Public Service, selections by an individual officer may be restricted to, say, clerical staff and unskilled manipulative workers because the officer is supplied with the information that enables him to make a sound selection of clerical staff and is not handicapped in the selection of the unskilled workers because their selection presents no problems as regards assessment of technical skills, academic qualifications and personality.

(ii) *Interviewing by Selection Committee*

The committee method of selection is particularly appropriate as a selecttion method in Public Services, because it tends to inspire public confidence and permits the inclusion of one or more specialists whose capacities are related to the nature of the position for which the selection is being made. The Civil Service Assembly Committee, commenting on oral examinations, regarded three as being the optimum number of members of a selection committee, and recommended against the almost awe-inspiring committees of up to nine or ten members which appear all too frequently. The Committee recommended the following composition:—

   (i) A specialist in oral examining as chairman.

   (ii) An expert qualified in the speciality of the position, e.g., a Lecturer in Civil Engineering may be included on a committee concerned with the selection of a Research Engineer.

   (iii) A representative of the department in which the position is located, i.e., some one with a knowledge of the peculiar features of the job in its peculiar setting.

Interviewing Techniques

The effectiveness of the oral examination by an individual officer or an employing committee depends on three factors:—

   (1) The training of employment officers and committee members in selection techniques.

   (2) The extent to which precise information is available on positions and their demands on their occupants.

   (3) The extent to which the interviewer makes use of standardised tests.

The teaching of techniques of interviewing, particularly with the aid of the role-playing technique with people who, in many instances, have had some considerable experience in interviewing, shows up a number of deficiencies. Perhaps, the worst is that many of the interviews appear to proceed without any plan, with interviewers neglecting to seek obviously relevant information from the applicant for the position.

Other deficiencies are that interviewers are unable to establish *rapport,* unable to look beyond the factual content of the responses of the interviewee and lacking in fundamental information which is in constant demand during the selection interviews—for example, a knowledge of the Australian educational system.

Such deficiencies can sometimes be overcome by training. An interesting example of the sort of information that might be imparted to officers in a course on oral examining is contained in G. Munro Fraser's text on employment interviewing.[5] He describes a plan providing seven important categories under which the attributes of the individuals can be grouped, and the plan commends itself to any person engaged on selection work. The categories are:—

(a) *Physique*: Health and strength, outward appearance and manner, physical energy.

(b) *Attainments*: General education, specialised training, work experience.

(c) *General Intelligence*: The capacity for complex and intricate mental work.

(d) *Special Aptitudes*: The pre-disposition to acquire certain types of skill.

(e) *Interests*: Liking for social, intellectual, practical-constructive or physically-active work.

(f) *Disposition*: The ability to undertake a role which involves steadiness or reliability, acceptability to, or influence over others.

(g) *Circumstances*: Or the levels of expectation which the job will satisfy.

For a course of instruction to be wholly effective, it must not only provide interviewers with technical skill, but must also make an attack on the known personal deficiencies of many of the people engaged on selection work. The serious nature of these deficiencies is often only appreciated when they come under the critical fire of the trained interviewer. The more serious of these deficiencies are:—[6]

(1) Inability satisfactorily to introduce or terminate an interview.

(2) Display of irritating mannerisms.

(3) Being patronising.

(4) Making of moral judgments.

(5) Inability to appreciate that in many cases it is not what is said but rather *how* it is said that is significant.

(6) Inability on the part of the interviewer to vary his tempo of interviewing, level of expression and manner, to suit the personality and ability of the client.

When it is considered that each poor selection and every case of a selection which was not the best possible under the circumstances constitutes an immediate waste of funds, any attempt to improve on selection methods by training in technical and personal skills is well justified.

---

[5] *A Handbook of Employment Interviewing* was written by J. Munro Fraser following several years on the scientific staff of the National Institute of Industrial Psychology (U.K.), where he had been employed as a consultant in connection with higher appointments and on the training of employment interviewers.

[6] These and other hints are contained in the Department of Labour and National Service Technical Publication 17 (1945).

Information about positions can best be obtained from carefully written job specifications, which should always be made available to members of a selection committee. These specifications are written up following systematic observation of the job, and usually with the aid of a job analysis schedule. (The question of job study is dealt with in greater detail later in the chapter.) However, it would be too much to expect all significant information about a job to be contained in a job specification, and it is necessary that someone should be available who is aware of those informal characteristics, a knowledge of which is gained only by constant observation. For example, a group of workers develops an intricate informal structure, with interests and loyalties peculiar to itself and a tendency for its members to react in a unique way to the various stimuli that are present in the work situation. The extent to which a particular group will co-operate in, or resist change depends on the nature of the individuals in it, and upon the way the work situation is handled. A new employee placed within the group may, regardless of his ability to meet the standards of experience, education and proficiency laid down in the job specification, still be unsuccessful in the job on account of the effect on the group of a disparity of age, habit, or some other factor.

(iii) *Achievement tests*

Where a position calls for well-defined skills, such as typing, shorthand, or trades proficiency, it is desirable to measure these skills, where possible, with standardised tests. In the case of an applicant for employment as a shorthandwriter and typist, a test can be carried out in five minutes which will objectively determine whether she is capable of writing shorthand at, say, 80 words per minute, thereby answering the interviewer's question concerning the most critical requirement for the position. In the selection of teachers of trades, a trade test covering a large number of manual skills can supply the most important item of information required by the employing organisation.

(iv) *Psychological tests*

Psychological examining procedures are aimed at predicting levels and qualities of performance and behaviour, and consequently are of particular value in situations where there is little evidence of academic achievement or satisfactory performance in the field for which the selection is being made, and where considerable expense is involved in training. They are similarly of value where the need for an applicant to measure up to particular requirements is critical, e.g., in carrying out computing work, appreciating complex mechanical relationships, and so on. Tests are now employed unless they have been validated for the particular job for which they are used, i.e., unless they have been proved experimentally to predict job success with reasonable accuracy. Test performances, however, should not be regarded entirely as a substitute for evidence of achievement which, in many instances, is available to an employer who has been in a position to observe the individual over a long period.

Psychological examining procedures generally include a test of intelligence which gives an indication of the applicant's ability to work at a particular intellectual level, say, at professional or skilled clerical work. On this intelligence test are superimposed other tests aimed at assessing the ability of a person to deal with particular problems, e.g., those requiring good mechanical insight or verbal fluency or facility with numbers. Other tests, described as tests of special ability, are used to determine an individual's capacity to discriminate between colours, or carry out certain types of fine discriminative finger or hand movements.

Of recent years, considerable advances have been made in the assessment of vocational interests, tests of personality and examining procedures carried out by personnel administrators, psychiatrists and psychologists. The British Civil Service is using the group examining technique originally designed and used by the German army in selecting officers, and later used in the American, British and Australian forces for a similar purpose. This War Office Selection Board technique (W.O.S.B.) has been modified for civil service purposes and is used to select some members of the administrative class in the British Civil Service. Candidates are required to undergo a series of psychological tests and to take part in exercises calling for the display of particular qualities pre-determined as essential to efficient performance. During the exercise they are under constant observation by competent observers who, after making their individual appraisals, make a collective recommendation to the final selection board.

(v) *Probation period*

The final phase of the employment procedure, which may properly be regarded as an important element in selection, is the probationary period. It provides a safeguard against faulty initial selection by giving the employer an opportunity to determine whether the new employee has the capacity to solve the problems he meets in his work and to decide, with the benefit of practical evidence, whether he has the ability to adjust and apply himself. It also gives the organisation an opportunity of arranging a more appropriate placement where the officer's performance is not entirely satisfactory because the original selection has not been made entirely in accordance with his aptitudes, interests and personality.

STAFF REPORTING

One of the most vexed problems in administration is created by the need for the development of an adequate method of reporting on staff. The main purposes of staff reporting are:—

    (i) to assess at regular intervals—

        (a) the efficiency of an individual in his present job ;

        (b) his suitability for another position, e.g., a promotion position ;

    (ii) to reveal information about an individual with a view to correcting weaknesses, or to developing still further promising traits.

Mosher, Kingsley and Stahl stated the problem as follows:—

"The barriers in the way of an adequate solution of the problem of employee rating are prodigious owing both to its complexities and to the technical difficulties involved. Yet they must be faced, for the only alternative is to rely for personnel purposes upon uncontrolled subjective evaluation. Employees must be evaluated and will be evaluated, whether formally or informally, casually or periodically. The problem is to devise a method whereby these ratings will be as unprejudiced, objective and uniform as possible."[7]

The nature of the problem is more readily revealed than the solution. To illustrate the difficulties involved, the details of simple study carried out in the Applied Psychology Department, Sydney Technical College, will be related ; and it will be found that some improvements to the current methods of reporting in Australian Public Services will be suggested by the conclusions reached.

A group of students undertaking a course in Personnel Practices and Techniques, a number of them mature officers employed in supervisory positions, were asked to list the adjectives which they would use to describe the various degrees of a particular trait such as, say, capacity to get on with other members of the staff, the administration and the public. Samples of responses were:—

Student No. 1	Student No. 2	Student No. 3	Student No. 4	Student No. 5
Very poor.	Very bad.	Very poor.	Bad.	Very poor.
Poor.	Bad.	Poor.	Poor.	Poor.
Low.	Very poor.	Fair.	Average.	Fair.
Bad.	Poor.	Good.	Fair.	Average.
Normal.	Limited.	Very good.	Good.	Good.
Average.	Below			Very good.
Good.	average.			Superior.
Very good.	Average.			
High.	Above			
Superior.	average.			
Excellent.	Fair.			
	Good.			
	Very good.			
	Excellent.			
	Outstanding.			

After discussion, the following observations were made. First, different reporters have different verbal scales which differ in the number of rating points and the relative positions of the adjectives used. It will be noted, for example, that while four students used the adjective "fair", two appeared to place it below "average" in the scale and one above "average", the fourth apparently equating it with "average".

It was unanimously agreed that to ensure uniform interpretation of reports it was necessary to use the same verbal scale to describe the degrees of particular traits. It was also agreed that, for the purposes of continuing the experiment, the following terms would be used:—

Very poor.
Poor.
Average.
Good.
Very good.

Second, opinions as to the proportion of a given number of people to be placed in a particular category vary, in the absence of a prescribed frame

[7] F. Mosher, J. D. Kingsley and O. Stahl, *Public Personnel Administration*, 1950, p. 364.

of reference, with different reporters. Group members were asked what they meant by "very poor". Typical responses were, "The poorest in a particular population", "Exhibiting a degree of the trait that is lower than that exhibited by people described as possessing a poor degree of the trait." Discussion encouraged the group to seek a more specific interpretation, and it was suggested that this could be done by ascribing a certain percentage of the population to each degree. The members were then asked to write down independently what percentage of the general population they would expect to find in each category in the scale that they had set down. Examples of the responses were:—

	Student 1	Student 2	Student 3	Student 4
	%	%	%	%
Very poor ..	8	5	20	1
Poor	17	15	20	10
Average ..	50	30	20	78
Good	17	35	20	10
Very good ..	8	15	20	1

It was agreed that after selection of the scale of terms to be used, some attempt should be made either to describe the type of person that would fit into each category or to determine as a group the percentage of the population that could be expected to be found in each category. The percentages decided on by the group were:—

5 per cent.	..	..	..	..	Very poor.
15 per cent.	..	..	..	..	Poor.
60 per cent.	..	..	..	..	Average.
15 per cent.	..	..	..	..	Good.
5 per cent.	..	..	..	..	Very good.

Some of the group then observed that the rater's knowledge of the type of person to be rated might not be adequate, and suggested that a more comprehensive method of definition be sought. The alternative agreed upon was a scheme which required the rating of officers in accordance with carefully prepared phrases describing various degrees of each trait.

Suitable descriptive phrases were discussed—an example being that selected to describe the highest degree of the trait "Work knowledge"— "Exceptional knowledge of all phases of the work in which he is engaged".

The next step was to ask the group to list the traits that they would regard as important in assessing the work performance of the typical Public Service clerical officer. Except for the item of work knowledge, and a number of trait names suggesting the desirability of good address, the lists varied considerably in the number and type of the trait names listed. It was agreed that it was necessary to select a set of trait names, of common meaning to reporters, which could be applied to any particular group of employees in a clerical situation. Further discussion made the group aware of the need for the definition of the terms used. The use of definitions of this type is illustrated below.

The investigation, while simple enough in itself, provided a striking example of some of the practical problems of staff reporting, and revealed the unsuitability both of the "Yes-or-No" report, which merely states that a person is "satisfactory" or "unsatisfactory", and the prose report, which leaves the contents completely to the discretion of the reporter. The study did show, however, that even the prose report could be improved by limiting the reporter to a particular frame of reference and requiring all such reports to deal with common, defined traits and to use common adjectives in indicating the various degrees of traits.

Some early schemes for staff reporting broke down partly through failure to appreciate some of these difficulties. The first Australian attempt at the systematic reporting seems to have occurred in the New South Wales Public Service as early as 1899, when clerical officers were rated for industry, accuracy and ability. The procedure was dropped soon after, however, probably because of the scant consideration given to the ideas discussed above, and the reluctance of Departments significantly to differentiate between staff in their ratings.

In the early days of the Commonwealth service, the Public Service Inspectors made annual descriptive reports on officers, and also *ad hoc* reports on applicants for advertised positions. The system worked quite well at first, partly owing to the prestige of the first Public Service Commissioner, and also because of the small size of the service. When the power of promotion was given to departmental heads, they were left largely to their own devices (though the Public Service Board made some unsuccessful experiments with a "points" system in the twenties). Various piecemeal attempts at evaluation developed, e.g., in the Postmaster-General's Department. The staff unions were suspicious of "secret" reports. Departments mostly depended on *ad hoc* reports, and appraisals by promotion committees. However, the appeals system encouraged the development of some common criteria.

During the war the Department of Labour and National Service devised an experimental reporting form. The Bailey Committee studied the problem in 1944, with inconclusive results. It recognised the wide use of staff reports in public services elsewhere, but was also impressed by "the volume and severity of the criticism levelled against the system",[8] and did not feel justified in recommending its general introduction. It weighed the "pros" and "cons" of a periodical rating report system—it would form a continuous record, not coloured by the immediate issue of promotion, it would be a guide to training needs, might increase staff confidence and lessen appeals. On the other hand, such a system tended to become formal, not helpful in deciding the immediate promotion issue, and would be costly in a body as scattered as the Commonwealth public service.

As a result, nothing much was done until the 1950s, when several departments began to experiment with "scientific" staff reporting. In 1953 the Commonwealth Public Service Board began to study the problem, with reference to overseas schemes and those used by such Commonwealth Departments as Labour and National Service, Navy, Postmaster-General's and Civil Aviation. The Board now limited its action to suggesting the

---

[8] See *Report*, p. 14. The above account of the history of staff reporting in the Commonwealth is based on V. Subramaniam, "Evaluating Personnel Efficiency in the Commonwealth Public Service". *Pub. Admin.* (Sydney), XVI, Sept., 1957.

types of report form Departments might consider in designing their own. The New South Wales Public Service Board has done likewise.[9]

The Customs and Taxation Departments have also been developing interesting systems. The Customs scheme has been based on wide experiment and close consultation with staff and unions. It is an annual reporting system with ten main headings.[10] The report is made by branch heads, and the contents are explained to employees on application.

Differences in experience, human understanding and capacity for objective thinking among reporters, and, of course, the very nature of the material on which assessments are made, make it difficult to obtain reliable reports. It is possible, however, to compensate, by training, for the natural human limitations found in reporters. As will be pointed out in the section dealing with human relations, a course in staff reporting may well be included in a training scheme for supervisors. Such a course would aim at acquainting supervisors with the nature and significance of individual differences, with particular reference to the importance of intelligence, aptitudes and personality, and with the methods and the aims of the reporting scheme. Because of the necessity for building up a frame of reference for supervisors, it would also be necessary to discuss typical cases both before and after dealing with the system of reporting.

Who should do the reporting? Obviously, the task should be undertaken by a person who is thoroughly acquainted with the person reported on and the work situation in which he is employed. The person who generally meets this specification is the officer's immediate superior. But because of the importance of reliable reporting to the individual officer as well as to the organisation, it is not unreasonable to introduce a safeguard. One or two other senior officers who are acquainted with the person to be reported on can be required to confirm the report. They could call on the original reporting officer to justify a rating which, in their opinion, was unfair, or too flattering. The officers on whom this duty of checking the reliability of the report would naturally fall would be the Branch Head and Departmental Personnel Officer.

That the officer reported on should also be given an opportunity of commenting, particularly when the report could be regarded as adverse, is not only reasonable but essential.

When should reporting take place? The natural tendency is to require reports to be furnished regularly, say, at six-monthly or annual intervals. The time involved in reporting, an examination of the purposes for which reports are used, and the difficulty of remembering for a long time incidents to be reported on, suggest that, as a general requirement, six-monthly intervals should be the minimum period between reports, although in some cases they may be required more frequently—where, for instance, an employee is attempting to overcome a deficiency, perhaps with assistance from his supervisor, branch head or personnel officer, and it is considered desirable to report progress.

[9] See *Current Problems of Office Organisation and Supervision*, pp. 13-26.

[10] Quantity of work, accuracy, relations with others, initiative, judgment, responsibility, technical knowledge, oral expression, written expression, supervision. The Taxation Department's scheme (not yet in force at the time of writing) is for six-monthly reports, or on transfer, based on five or six basic traits.

Commonwealth Bank of Australia

C.B. 38

CONFIDENTIAL STAFF REPORT

(For use in reporting on officers in the General Classification)

....Branch.

....19

(Christian Names in full)　　　　　　　(Surname in capital letters)

Date Joined Branch	Present Duties	M. or S.	Date of Birth	Date Joined Service	Salary

ADVICE TO REPORTING OFFICERS.

1. Rate all the officers, upon whom you are reporting, upon one quality at a time. This helps you to keep the quality distinct in your mind and to keep your standard constant.

2. Make sure you have a clear idea of the quality. Don't consider the name only—the defining statement should be carefully considered.

3. Put a cross in the bracket against the descriptive phrase which best fits the officer in respect of that quality.

4. Consider the officer in relation to others with a similar length of service in the Bank.

5. Try not to let the officer's strength or weakness in one quality cloud your judgment of his standing in another.

6. Don't hesitate to give both very high and very low ratings. In a typical group of about twenty general classification officers it is likely that for each quality there is someone who deserves a top rating and not unlikely that there is someone who deserves a bottom rating.

7. If you find yourself giving a great proportion of high ratings or low ratings, pause to consider whether this results from—

   (a) Your having an unusually good or unusually poor group of officers compared with those in the service generally, or

   (b) Your tendency to be lenient or harsh in your judgment of them.

   If you find yourself giving scarcely any ratings outside two or three grades, pause to consider whether this results from—

   (a) Your having a group in which there is much less variation than is usual amongst those in the service generally or

   (b) Your reluctance to make reasonably marked distinctions in your judgment of your officers.

   When your answer is (a) in either case, then a covering note giving a brief justification is required; when it is (b) you should try to revise your standards of judgment.

8. Use the space for comments to qualify a rating which doesn't quite fit, to draw attention to some unusual circumstances affecting the officer, to add to the descriptive phrase when it does the officer too little or too much justice, to give brief evidence in support of an unusual rating, etc.

9. An answer or comment is to be given for each of the questions under the heading "Special Comments."

Fig. 1—A Standardised Reporting Form.

ACCURACY

To what extent is he able to work without errors?

Seldom makes errors ( )
Tends to make more errors than most officers ( )
Makes many errors ( )
Exceedingly accurate ( )
Reliable and reasonably accurate ( )

Comments

SPEED

What is his effective output? Is he slow in performing tasks allotted to him, or does he complete his work with the utmost expedition?

Very fast worker, consistently produces a considerable volume of work ( )
Consistently slow to complete his duties, tends to hold up the work of the office ( )
Normal output of work; able to keep up with a normal flow of work ( )
Quick worker, output is greater than the usual run of officers ( )
Not a fast worker but usually manages to complete his work in a reasonable time ( )

Comments

APPLICATION

Consider energy and attention given to work day in and day out. Is he consistently enthusiastic or does he work in fits and starts or does he put little effort into his work?

Industrious, keen and energetic; a very willing worker ( )
Applies himself steadily and attentively to his work ( )
Half-hearted and indifferent; does no more than he has to ( )
Not always diligent and attentive; does not display much enthusiasm ( )
Unusually energetic; a consistently diligent and enthusiastic worker ( )

Comments

PERSONALITY, APPEARANCE AND ADDRESS

Consider the impression he makes on others by his manner, speech, appearance and general mode of address. Does he inspire confidence and make a good impression? Or does he tend to antagonise or leave people dissatisfied or unimpressed? A bad impression may be created by both the over-aggressive, over-confident and by the neutral, shy and colourless personality. Poor appearance may detract from the general impression made, although other qualities such as a confident, tactful and helpful approach may compensate.

Unimpressive; carries little weight with others; tends to be unfavourably received ( )
Most impressive, inspires confidence with all with whom he comes in contact ( )
Tends not to make a good impression; others tend not to respond favourably to him ( )
Normally well received, but does not make an outstanding impression ( )
Rather impressive; favourably received by others. ( )

Comments

TEMPERAMENT

Consider his balance and steadiness in dealing with a situation. Does he go to pieces under pressure; does he rush into a situation impetuously? Or does he remain unruffled in an emergency; does he act with discretion? It is important not to confuse the quality defined with mere stolidness.

Unusually well-balanced; can always be relied upon even under pressure to act with sense and discretion ( )
Quite steady and balanced in most situations; not inclined to act rashly ( )
Calm and effective even under pressure. Difficult to ruffle; rarely acts hastily ( )
Not steady and balanced; becomes ruffled or acts impetuously ( )
Although normally steady, sometimes acts impetuously or becomes ruffled in an unusual situation ( )

Comments

MENTAL ALERTNESS

Does he readily grasp the essential points in a problem? Does he profit by experience? or is he slow to grasp the point or to learn? Consider intelligence and readiness of understanding and not glibness of tongue and brightness of manner.

Quick in understanding; readily picks up the threads of a new task ( )
Slow to learn a new task or see the point even with fuller explanation than most officers would require ( )
Very quick in grasping the essential points and in learning a new task, with a minimum of explanation ( )
Fairly apt in grasping a new idea or in learning a new task ( )
Usually requires longer time to learn a new task; may not grasp a new idea at first but can do so with fuller explanation ( )

Comments

KNOWLEDGE

Consider his all-round knowledge of the Bank's work, bearing in mind his length of service. Consider his understanding as only of his present duties but also of those related or immediately ahead of him.

Has just sufficient knowledge to cope with general requirements, but not with anything at all unusual.. ( )
Well informed; has a good knowledge of all matters he is likely to encounter .. .. ( )
Needs to refer too frequently for information; not well informed even upon general requirements .. ( )
Fair knowledge of the Bank's work; knows how to deal with most matters he is likely to encounter in his work .. .. ( )
Very well informed; has an unusually sound knowledge for an officer of his length of service .. .. ( )

Comments

INITIATIVE

Consider his ability to go ahead with work without being guided in every detail. Does he anticipate requirements or does he wait to be told what needs to be done? It is important to distinguish this quality from both application and mental alertness.

Able to work without close supervision after general direction; shows some capacity for anticipation and some resourcefulness .. .. ( )
Very resourceful and self-reliant; shows distinct evidence of foresight and constructiveness in his work ( )
Performs more straightforward work with general guidance, but tends to show little resourcefulness and foresight .. .. ( )
Needs sustained guidance in his work; little resourcefulness; not able to work independently .. .. ( )
Resourceful in meeting difficulties; usually anticipates what needs to be done .. . .. . ( )

Comments

SPECIAL COMMENTS

Does the officer lack a reasonable standard of punctuality, regularity of attendance, co-operation, trustworthiness, neatness of work?

Is the officer's efficiency impaired by outside interests, domestic or financial difficulties, or indifferent health?

Has the officer's attention been drawn to shortcomings with a view to improvement? If so, in what way and with what result?

In the case of all officers over twenty years of age, give a brief statement, commenting upon

(a) His present usefulness

(b) His promise of development

Is promotion or transfer specially recommended? If so, state suggestions and reasons

Does the officer desire transfer? If so, forward (for purpose of record and for consideration at the Bank's convenience) a signed application giving full particulars, if this has not already been done.

OTHER REMARKS.

Manager, or at Capital Branches Officer making Report.

For use at Capital Branches.

Manager's Comments (if any):

Manager.

The institution of a regular standardised staff reporting scheme, although it enables the administration to discriminate between officers in terms of their overall efficiency and the individual factors contributing to it, must not be regarded as productive only of good effects. Like most of the techniques introduced by the personnel administrator, it may have a significant bearing on human relationships, particularly those between the supervisor and the person reported on. There will always be some persons who will be rated in the lower half of the distribution and, despite their efforts, will be unable to improve materially on their level of performance. Others, too, will not be pleased with their identification with the norm of the group. Thus a regular reporting scheme that continually reveals and emphasises the relationship of these people to their fellows must have a depressing effect on their morale, and make it even more difficult for them to achieve a high standard of adjustment and performance. The importance of such effects has not received the attention of the research worker to the extent that it really deserves, and is an aspect of staff reporting that is avoided more frequently than it is dealt with. It offers a fruitful field of research to the psychologist and sociologist.

Whatever the advantages or disadvantages of a regular reporting system, it is unquestionable that, where critical decisions are made concerning such actions as placement, termination, promotion, etc., reports must be made; and the "Yes-or-No" report, or the prose report, the content of which is left entirely to the discretion of the reporting officer, is not good enough, in these circumstances, the standardised reporting form of the type illustrated in Fig. I, or a prose report which requires the reporting officer to comment on certain specific qualities, is highly desirable ; and the only question to be decided in each case is the extent and nature of the detail to be provided.[11]

OBTAINING AND USING INFORMATION ABOUT POSITIONS

The origination of effective techniques and practices depends to a great extent on the availability of precise information about positions. A knowledge of the actual duties of the positions is fundamental to efficient personnel administration, and a knowledge of the persons who are employed in these positions, or who may be applicants for them, become meaningful only against a background of such information. A careful study of the job is necessary to ensure effective selection and placement, equitable determination of salaries, efficient training schemes and well-balanced organisation and method.

Job Study

The technique used in job study depends on the purpose for which the study is to be used and, to a lesser extent, the type of position being examined.

In the carrying out of job studies, or job analyses, as they are often called, observation by a trained person is the principal method used. Such aids as a movie camera, stop-watch, thermometer and aptitude tests may be used to provide the necessary details and to increase precision. In the examination of simple repetitive positions such as those which abound in large-scale

---

[11] The arguments for and against systematic reports are contained in Isabel E. P. Menzies and E. Anstey, *Staff Reporting*, 1951.

industrial enterprises, a camera may be used to record the physical move-ments involved in the performance of a task. By running the film through slowly it is possible to isolate unproductive movements, failure to make the fullest use of physical capacity, delays caused by unco-ordinated hand movements and poor plant, material and man relationships and, following this examination, to determine the simplest and most efficient way of carry-ing out the task.

In the development of piece rates for workers employed in similar situations, the rate setter, after first breaking up the job into the most conveniently timed elements, times a number of runs—usually consecutive ones—with a split-second stop-watch. Following a close examination of the times taken for the individual elements and an assessment of the degree of skill and energy applied by the operator, a rate is set that then becomes the basis of the normal rate of working of the operator. The aim of the application of such a scheme is to credit the operator for any production achieved in excess of the normal rate.

In an attempt to determine more precisely the minimum and maximum abilities necessary for the effective performance of a particular type of position, psychological tests are administered to persons already employed in such positions. Critical scores can thus be obtained which may then be used to determine whether applicants for the positions are likely to be successful.

However, most of the information sought about positions by the Per-sonnel Administrator must be obtained through simple observation and inquiry. Not only is detailed information about positions vital in selection, placement([12]) and promotion, salary determination, the design of training courses and the improvement of work methods; problems of morale may be more effectively dealt with if the Personnel Administrator is aware of the satisfactions and frustrations that are likely to be experienced by employees through the very nature of the duties they perform.

Job Information

A system designed to provide this information would involve the following steps:—

    (1) The determination of the precise information required about a position if the various problems of the Personnel Administrator are to be solved.

    (2) The design of the method by which the information is to be obtained.

    (3) The classification and indexing of the material.

If a close examination is made of the information required for the purpose of selection, training, position evaluation, and so on, it will be found that the same critical data are required in each case. Once this information has been obtained, it will be necessary only to supplement it with greater detail as required by the particular purpose.

([12]) The "Index of Army Duties" prepared by the Australian Military Forces (1943) and the "Worker Descriptions" prepared oy the Commonwealth Em-ployment Service provide two examples of job specifications used for selection and placement purposes.

These critical factors are as follows:—

(1) *The subject matter with which the work is concerned.*—This factor is important in selection to meet the preferences or prejudices of applicants and, for obvious reasons, in training. It also simplifies the task of job classification.

(2) *The qualification requirements of the position.*—While this factor is basic to selection it also provides a convenient starting point in examining a position for evaluation purposes.

(3) *The difficulty and complexity of the duties involved.*—This factor finds its greatest importance in position evaluation and in determining what predictive tests and selection standards are to be used.

(4) *The responsibility assumed by the holder of the position.*—The greatest value of this factor, also, is found in evaluation, as it may be the final determinant of the level at which the position is placed within an organisation.

The investigator should seek information concerning the duties and responsibilities of the position in such a way as to highlight each one of these factors. This can be done by observation and inquiry by an investigator who prepares the basic record of the duties, or by the occupant himself. Experience has shown, however, that the best method of approach is to require the occupant of the position to prepare his own statement of duties in accordance with provided instructions. This statement is then tested by the investigator by further examination of the occupant of the position, his supervisor, and his branch head.([18])

The importance of sound instructions resulting in the uniform presentation of the specifications of a position (in terms of layout, detail and example) is quite clear—particularly where the duties are recorded by the occupant of the position. There is little doubt that personnel administration, and administration generally, have been much the poorer for the absence of statements of duties which have been carefully prepared in accordance with well-designed instructions. If the purpose of seeking job information is well understood—for example, that it is to be used for selection and training as well as for job evaluation—then special attention can be given to the manner in which the information is presented. A description of the position must, of course, be comprehensible, but it must also be comprehensive enough to meet the demands of the various purposes for which it will be used.

The information required in considering both factors (1) and (2) will be apparent from the tested statement of duties.

In considering the third factor, difficulty and complexity, the investigator will determine first what happens to the work *before* the employee gets it, then *what* the employee does with the work and, finally, what is done to the work *after* the employee has done his part. Is his contribution to the work he handles a major one? What are the limits of the action which he takes? Having established these limits, the investigator then proceeds to further questions. What is the degree of originality entailed in the officer's

---

([18]) See Appendix VI for the instructions for preparation of statements of duties issued by the N.S.W. Public Service Board.

work? Is he required to use judgment, knowledge or experience, or can he solve the problems likely to be encountered by referring to a few office rules, regulations or, say, a printed handbook? Does he make his decisions independently or under supervision? For example, a stenographer who is in a position to seek the advice of the officer in charge of the typing pool, and perhaps has her letters checked, is not doing as difficult a job as one who prepares the letters independently for signature.

In considering the degree of complexity of a particular position it is important to determine the number of different functions, or aspects of one function, which are performed. For example, an officer who is required to deal with submissions on *different* matters from four clerks of the same grade is doing more complex work than if his subordinates were all dealing with the same subject-matter. Finally, in considering this factor, the investigator must determine the extent of the organisation required in order to carry out the work programme for the job and the frequency with which this organisation must be modified to meet changing demands.

The fourth factor—responsibility—must be clearly distinguished from the third. It is a commonplace that the most difficult job is not always the most important or the highest paid. To what extent are an officer's decisions subject to review? How far can he take independent action? Does he make policy decisions, or merely conform? Do his determinations affect the safety of others? Funds and revenue? Public and personnel relations? And to what extent, compared with others in the organisation? These are the critical questions to be asked about responsibility.

It is now necessary to classify and index the information obtained so that it will be possible to readily locate, say, a position which is similar to or identical with a position which is to be created and graded, or one which, although of higher or lower degree of difficulty, may involve working in a similar situation or enable its occupants to satisfy similar interests. Similarly, the information should be arranged so that it will be relatively simple to locate positions requiring good verbal ability, legal training, work requiring contact with the public, and so on.

A classification in terms of salary grades will be inevitable in any well-planned system. This classification is the most difficult one to make because of the necessity of equating the various factors. A position evaluation scheme involves the assigning of a number of points to each factor so that a final assessment can be made as to the total demands of the position on the person occupying it. In coming to this assessment, and when comparing positions, it is necessary to equate the various factors in their various forms. It is necessary to decide whether more or less points should be assigned to this particular administrative responsibility as opposed to this degree of supervisory responsibility, or whether the same number of points should be assigned, say, to a four-year part-time University degree course as to a three-year full-time course.

Such problems are not capable of solution by the application of any simple formula ; consequently, the making of the decisions places a considerable strain on the objectivity and capacity of the person or persons doing the evaluating.

HUMAN RELATIONS

Research has shown that while an organisation's selection methods may be good, its wage structure sound, and information concerning the strength and weaknesses of its employees ample and readily available, it may still operate at a poor level of efficiency because its members do not possess those attitudes towards their place of employment, their fellow employees, their duties and their employer which enable them to be happiest and most productive. When these attitudes exist in a high degree, morale is regarded as high. When they are present in small measure, morale is regarded as poor.

The attitudes which determine the morale of a group are generated by a number of interdependent items, which can be broadly classified into those which find their origin in the individual and his personal circumstances and those which find their origin in the administration.

Those items more closely associated with the employee are personality, physical health, home circumstances, recent and remote experiences, and the restrictions of behaviour and attitudes imposed on their members by informal organisations of employees. These informal organisations, or cliques, may, e.g., be groups of employees suffering from common frustrations; the imposition of unofficial "dargs" and the holding of regulation strikes are typical of their effects.

Items more closely associated with the administration are rates of pay, security, sickness and pension benefits, physical working conditions and the expression of the employer's attitude, first in the written personnel policy, and second, in the behaviour of each person with a supervisory function.

It would seem that the employer can control or influence only those items with which he is directly concerned, for undoubtedly the attitudes of workers are often shaped by circumstances not even remotely connected with the work situation. But it is possible for him to exert a considerable influence even on these factors. For instance, the provision of a counselling service may enable material assistance to be given to an employee at a time when there is a serious illness in his home, thus enabling him to divert his attention from his personal problems to his job; or it may assist him in sorting out worries which originated in the conflicts and frustrations of every-day life.

If the administrator is to deal effectively with these problems of human relations, he must determine not only the wants and needs of his particular group of employees, but their relative significance and the most effective methods of satisfying them.

Attitude Survey

Information concerning the wants and needs of employees may be obtained by the use of an attitude survey.[14] Such a survey may be carried out either by requiring employees to complete one or more questionnaires, or through a series of standard interviews designed to elicit the desired information.

Hull and Kolstad carried out a study in a group of companies and found

[14] A questionnaire used in a survey of certain groups of N.S.W. Public Service officers is illustrated in Fig. II.

PERSONNEL SURVEY

First, indicate in numerical order those characteristics that would provide you with the greatest possible satisfaction in your job. Then, if you consider there are any other important items not listed, write them in what you regard as their correct position.

Do not place your name on the questionnaire

Section 1.

An opportunity to discuss grievances without fear of discrimination. ☐

An opportunity to contribute towards alterations in the work procedures with which you are concerned. ☐

An opportunity to engage in social and recreational activities provided by the Department. ☐

A high salary. ☐

Liberal recreation leave conditions. ☐

A pleasant physical work environment. ☐

Working for a supervisor who seeks your advice concerning ways of improving your work procedures and those of the branch in which you are employed, and who only rejects those ideas that he can prove to you are unsuitable. ☐

Congenial working companions. ☐

An opportunity to do the work for which you consider you are best fitted. ☐

Security of employment. ☐

An opportunity to be of service to the public. ☐

Promotion by seniority. ☐

Promotion strictly in accordance with the principle of "the best man for the job" regardless of service with the Department. ☐

Work offering plenty of variety of duties. ☐

Liberal sick leave. ☐

Availability of training schemes paid for by the Department or carried out in departmental time. ☐

The existence of a scheme that enables you to take part in the formulation of *all* departmental policy. ☐

Close proximity of your work place to your home. ☐

Section 2.

Indicate—

I am completely satisfied with my Department and derive the greatest possible degree of satisfaction from my job. ☐

I am well satisfied with my Department but action by the administration would make me more so. ☐

I am satisfied but cannot display any great enthusiasm. ☐

Dissatisfied. ☐

Extremely dissatisfied. ☐

Hereunder give the reasons for your endorsement.

Fig. II—An Attitude Survey.

that the average morale score for different companies showed significant variations, and that employers could influence the score to an important degree. The following items, listed in their order of importance to employees, were found to be determinant of morale—([15])

(1) A fair hearing and square deal on grievances.

(2) The prospects of a satisfactory future.

(3) The company's knowledge of the employee's qualifications and progress.

(4) Recognition of, and credit for constructive suggestions offered.

(5) Friendly and helpful criticism of work or correction of errors.

(6) Pay increases when deserved.

(7) Recognition and praise for unusually good work.

(8) Selection of best qualified employee for promotion when a vacancy arises.

(9) Amount of work required not unreasonable.

(10) Pay at least as high as the going rate for the same type of work elsewhere.

(11) Freedom to seek help when difficult problems arise in work.

(12) Freedom from unjust reprimand.

(13) Satisfactory daily working hours.

(14) The company's vacation policy.

This survey and others appeared to indicate the relative unimportance of such items as pay and the company's vacation policy, and the importance of items which concerned the personal relationships of the employees with the management. In another study by James C. Worthy, who analysed 12,000 responses to an attitude survey in the Sears Roebuck Company,([16]) it was shown that "pay in comparison with other jobs in the same unit" ranked in eighth place among the elements related to high morale. Rates of pay as such ranked in fourteenth place, and the low influence of hours of work was revealed by the fact that it was located in twenty-first place. However, there is no consistency of response to such attitude surveys; and pay can clearly become a significant factor under certain circumstances.

The general conclusions reached after an examination of numerous morale studies are:—

(1) Many of the factors commonly considered to be of primary importance, such as pay, bonuses, leave conditions, etc., in many instances play only minor roles.

(2) High morale does not result simply from being "nice" to people and plying them with favours.

(3) The importance of serious shortcomings on the part of an employer in such matters as pay and physical working conditions is likely to be magnified so that they become significant factors in morale.

([15]) Norman R. F. Maier, *Psychology in Industry*, pp. 83-84.

([16]) James C. Worthy, "Factors Influencing Employee Morale" *Harvard Business Review*, XXVIII, June, 1950.

On the other hand, attractively furnished and painted offices, washrooms and cafeterias and other amenities cannot in themselves develop high morale.

(4) It is often necessary to look below surface conduct in assessing group attitudes and individual motives.

(5) The supervisor is the most potent force in the building of morale —provided he is not the victim of poor handling by his own superior. Training programmes aimed at improving the social skills of supervisors are likely to lose their effect unless corresponding attention is given to executives.

The Role of the Supervisor

The importance of the supervisor was well revealed in the Hawthorne experiment, when it was shown that the quality of the relationship between the employee and management was more important to the productivity and happiness of the worker than any other factor. This finding has been corroborated by other investigators. In two departments in the same plant in which the work was identical, only 29 per cent. of the employees in the department with the better physical conditions of work had favourable attitudes towards the management, whereas in the other department 71 per cent. of the workers had favourable attitudes. The difference in attitudes of the two groups was shown to be bound up in differences in the quality of supervision.

Once the importance of the supervisor in administration has been realised, the question is naturally asked, "What can be done to improve the quality of supervision?"

Before attempting to answer this let us look at the basic functions of the supervisor.

He must—

"(1) Understand the duties and responsibilities of his position.

(2) Plan how best to accomplish the mission of his unit and determine what is needed to accomplish it.

(3) Evaluate and improve work methods, processes and procedures.

(4) Improve his own knowledge, techniques and skills, both as a technical expert and as a leader.

(5) Introduce new people in the best way, determine areas in which subordinates need training, and provide it both for new and old personnel.

(6) Evaluate employee performance in relation to production.

(7) Assist employees to adjust their problems and develop good discipline. Correct mistakes.

(8) Keep the subordinates informed about the policies, regulations and procedures of the organisation and about changes to be effected.

(9) Collaborate with colleagues and seek advice and assistance when he needs it.

(10) Deal with complaints and dissatisfaction and with suggestions."(¹⁷)

The range and nature of these duties are so complex that those employed on them should be as carefully selected and trained as those employed in any other complex field of activity.

Selection and Training of Supervisors

It appears, then, that sound supervision depends largely on the sound selection and training of supervisors.

Selection must not be made solely, or even perhaps to a major degree, on the basis of the capacity of an employee to deal efficiently with the mechanics of his day-to-day job. He must have the ability and personality to cope with all the personnel and technical problems that may arise. He must be sufficiently secure and stable to be objective ; ready to assume the role of the democratic leader, and have enough imagination and initiative to maintain leadership in action and ideas. He must be able to give just as much regard to the capacities, the personalities and the individual and group needs of his staff as he gives to the cost, capacities and maintenance needs of his machines or the "life" of his records. Training must be such that it creates an awareness of the latent power that can be released by a group of persons in the interests of efficiency through skilful handling and the application of effective principles and practices.

As pointed out in Chapter 16, training in the main will consist of confronting the trainee in advance with the situations with which he is most likely to have to deal and providing some guidance in their solutions, so as to minimise failures and damage which would result from the indiscriminate use of trial and error methods.

Ideally, supervisors should be selected and then placed on probation to confirm the predictions of the selection procedure. Of course, where selection has already taken place the need for training is even greater. It is possible to combine selection and training by instituting a system of selective training. People chosen for such a course would be those who not only carry out their present duties efficiently, but also show a predisposition to those characteristics which it is hoped to develop in training. Again, the method that would be used would require the group to be presented with actual cases, involving a range of human problems akin to those which will arise in the course of supervisory duties, for the purpose of discussion.(¹⁸) Observers would then appraise the reactions of each member of the group, looking for those critical personal factors, such as degree of tolerance, objectivity, sensitivity to the feelings of others, and capacity to display imagination and leadership in ideas and action. From the evidence so obtained, the selection of supervisors could be made.

(¹⁷) Hartvig Nisson, "Some Human Aspects of Administration", *International Institute of Administrative Science*, 1951.

(¹⁸) This method of training is generally described as "role-playing" and has found increasing use in training in human relations, e.g., in social case work, interviewing, as well as supervision. *A Human Relations Casebook for Executives and Supervisors*, by F. S. Drake and Charles A. Drake, 1947, provides excellent examples of the types of case history that might be used in training.

Counselling.

A few more words should be said about those factors affecting employees which are not originally related to the work situation, and so do not come under the ostensible influence of the employer. Such factors may influence the motivation of individual wokers and so have their effects on the morale of the group. Domestic discord, lack of money, or illness may prevent an employee from making his proper contribution to the group effort, and his poor motivation and conflicts may find expression in complaints about the quality of supervision or the attitude of management, or perhaps the lack of amenities or poor physical working conditions.

In one such case, a female worker cited specific and apparently genuine instances of poor supervision. It turned out, however, that the supervisor reminded her of her stepfather, whose conduct had made her home circumstances very difficult. The identification of the two men, only partly realised by her, was causing her domestic life to have a very decided impact on the work situation.([19])

In such cases it is not the relationship between worker and supervisor which must be revised, but the adjustment of the employee's personal problems. A wise administrator will appreciate the effect on attitudes of these external pressures. Some organisations provide counselling services with the object of bettering morale by improving the adjustment of individual employees. Such manifestations of maladjustment as chronic unpunctuality, outbursts of emotion, unreasonable complaints and frequent absences, are regarded by the counsellor as symptoms of more serious underlying causes, and the cases of employees who display them are sympathetically but thoroughly investigated. The cause, once located, may often be removed by counselling([20]) or, where material assistance or advice is required, by reference to some social agency—perhaps, in a large public service, to one of its own departments. The New South Wales Public Service Board has for some years employed a professional counsellor part-time in an attempt to improve the adjustment of its Service officers. It is interesting to note that some responsibility for arranging counselling services is to be placed on the full-time Training Officer whose appointment was decided on by the South Australian Commission just before the publication of this volume.

The Place of the Personnel Administrator

The personnel administrator is not concerned with completely new activities, but rather with the improvement, regulation and co-ordination of certain activities which have always been an essential part of administration.

In the past, selection, training, job evaluation and staff reporting have all been components of general administration; but their importance has not been sufficiently realised to justify their being placed under the control of a trained specialist. The personnel administrator assumes some of the functions that have been vested in the departmental secretary, senior clerk, or other senior administrative official who has been concerned with the selection of new clerical staff and is the arbiter of inter-personnel squabbles; the legal

---

([19]) Roethlisberger and Dickson, *Management and the Worker*, pp. 307-310.
([20]) *Ibid.*, pp. 590-604.

officer, who has been concerned with employment conditions and job evaluation; and the various other officers who have dealt, often in a haphazard way, with the training and motivation of staff. It is not suggested that these people will no longer be concerned with these items; but the appointment of a suitably trained officer allows the formulation and expression of a personnel policy, the application of specialised personnel techniques, and the provision of guidance in their use to all members of the staff.

Why have such qualified people been absent from administration in the past; First, there is no doubt, sweeping as the statement may seem, that many people in the top administrative strata, although aware of the existence of human problems, seem completely to overlook their importance in administration. This can be ascribed only to faulty training which emphasises things rather than people, and results in a pre-occupation with statutes, regulations and procedures, so that the question whether the human element could possibly require the same degree of attention as these items has not even been considered. Second, there are those who tend to discredit the personnel administrator by comparing him with the physical scientist, with his precise prediction of performance and events. Only too often he is expected to make predictions with the mathematical accuracy with which an astronomer forecasts the time of passage of a meteor, or the occurrence of an eclipse. The personnel administrator does not suggest that he can do this; but he does claim that the over-all results of his efforts can have a significant and beneficial effect on the efficiency of the organisation. To suit the accountants, it might be put another way—the value of the contribution of the trained personnel administrator far outweighs the cost involved in his appointment.

An improvement in the effectiveness of personnel administration appears to depend on three items—the realisation by top administration of the value of the contribution of the personnel administrator, an increase in the scope of administrative training so that it will include studies in Personnel Management Practices and Techniques, and increased attention to research.

Of the Australian Public Services, the Commonwealth and the New South Wales Service alone appear to be making a systematic attempt to provide skilled personnel administrators in departments. However, like them, South Australia has now embarked on a vigorous scheme for the training of supervisors and senior administrators which will ensure a fuller appreciation and application of personnel policy.

An examination of courses in Australia suggests the need for more emphasis on techniques and practices such as are outlined in this chapter. Present courses appear to define problems of management, but do little towards the prescription of precise techniques for their solution.

Research is sadly disregarded so far as general personnel problems are field is the Personnel Practices Branch of the Industrial Services Division concerned; the only organisation in Australia carrying out research in this of the Department of Labour and National Service. Practically nothing is being done by employing organisations themselves to contribute through developmental research to the refining of their day-to-day problems—in some cases, where there are tens of thousands employed, not even one or two are engaged in research. It is not difficult to demonstrate that concentrated attention on apparently pedestrian items, such as the revision of an application form, the setting out of standard instructions for the preparation of statements of duties, and the development of standards for job evaluation would produce immediate and important results.

APPENDICES

APPENDIX I
THE PLACE OF GOVERNMENT IN THE ECONOMY[1]

In 1957 Commonwealth, State and Local Governments employed about 23 per cent. of the work force, and undertook about one-third of capital works expenditure.

Development and utility services

Many of these are discussed in Chapters 3 to 6 of this book.   Here government plays a major role.

Natural resources : Government forests comprise 80 per cent. of the total forest area; these forests are controlled and improved by government, but are usually exploited under licence by private enterprise.   Government controls water resources, constructs dams and irrigation works and provides soil conservation services.   Of the minerals, government has interests in uranium, tin and coal mining.

Communications : Government has a monopoly or near monopoly of posts, telegraphs, telephones, telecommunications, railways, tramways, roads and bridges and port development and administration.   It shares with private enterprise the provision of airline, shipping, ferry, road motor, broadcasting and television services.

Other utilities : Government provides all public water supply and sewerage services, and substantially all electricity and about two-thirds of gas for public consumption.

Finance and Industry

Government plays an important role in banking; about 15 per cent. of trading bank business is done through government owned banks; at present about 90 per cent. of total saving banks deposits are at Government savings banks; central banking, including note issue and the minting of currency, is a government prerogative.   Government financial institutions contribute to private rural and industrial development through loans.

Government plays a minor role in insurance; government insurance offices were established for the purpose of providing insurance for government property and also to provide compulsory workers' compensation and third party motor accident insurance in competition with private companies.   Of recent years, these offices in two States have transacted all classes of insurance; government also operates superannuation schemes for its employees.

Government administers several trust funds—funds that it has itself set up, and, as Public Trustee, private funds placed in its care.

Government in competition with private concerns, conducts lotteries and provides betting facilities at race courses.

Government has only minor direct interest in industrial undertakings; those it owns are of a service nature or else are considered important to defence or development; examples are sawmills, brickworks, grain elevators and abattoirs, and aluminium production.   Government has also many regulatory functions in this field, see Chapter 3.

Social Services

See Chapter 5.   Seventy-five per cent. of school enrolments are at government schools.   Most technical education and all university education is provided by publicly owned or subsidised institutions.   Government takes a major part in scientific and industrial research.   Government, by loans and through its own housing programmes, is responsible for about one-third of houses being built.   About one-fifth of the houses are actually erected by Government.   Most hospitals are publicly owned or subsidised.

---

(1) The references to natural resources, communications, utilities, finance and industry, and social services are cited from *Public Corporations in Australia*, 1958, a paper prepared in the Department of National Development for E.C.A.F.E.; and the references to the Tariff Board from the *Tariff Board Index*, 1958.

Marketing of Primary Products

Marketing Boards for various primary products exist in every State and also at the Federal level. The views of primary producers' organisations have greatly influenced the degree of government intervention, and primary producers are strongly represented on the boards. However, in spite of their " producer " character, they are generally regarded as part of the machinery of government, and so merit a mention.

The Federal Boards are mainly concerned with the regulation of exports; any concern with internal marketing involves Commonwealth government agreement with the States, who have most of the constitutional powers in this field. Schemes vary considerably; some commodities, *e.g.*, wool, are marketed freely, though an Australian Wool Bureau acts in an advertising and advisory capacity. Others, *e.g.*, wheat, butter, cheese, are more closely controlled. (In these three cases there are also government price guarantees, met partly by fixing home consumption prices in co-operation with the States and sometimes partly by subsidy.)

The most important Commonwealth Boards are the :

    Dried Fruits Control Board (1924)
    Australian Dairy Produce Board (1924)
    Australian Meat Board (1935)
    Australian Wheat Board (1939)

but there are also boards for wine, apples and pears, etc. Usually they consist of a Government representative as chairman, and elected representatives of different sections of the industry. They work mainly by regulating private exporters (*e.g.*, by quotas), though in some cases they can handle the produce themselves. The Wheat Board, for instance, handles all overseas and domestic marketing.

The State Boards act mostly as marketing pools within the State. Four States (Queensland, N.S.W., Victoria, Tasmania) have general legislation providing for the creation of a board for any primary product at the request of producers. The Boards include government nominees, but the majority of members are elected by the producers. They usually themselves either handle the product, or the distributors act as their agents; producers are paid from the pooled proceeds. Dairy products, eggs, milk and dried fruits are controlled by most States, and a variety of other products in particular States, *e.g.*, sugar in Queensland. Some of these boards are set up under the general legislation; others have been created by separate acts, *e.g.*, the Dried Fruits Board and the Milk Board in New South Wales, and Sugar Board in Queensland.

A few boards depart radically from the usual pattern; for example, the Milk Board in New South Wales, which controls all milk sales in the Sydney and Newcastle areas, with the distributors acting as its agents, and which can also regulate conditions of production generally in the State. In this case the members are government nominees, including a producers' and a consumers' representative, and the Board is subject to Ministerial direction.

Overseas Trade

The two main instruments for government regulation of imports are (i) tariffs (ii) import licences. The machinery for controlling the latter, and for stimulating exports, is well-described in J. G. Crawford, " The Organization of the Department of Trade ", *Pub. Admin.* (*Sydney*), Vol. XVI, Dec., 1957 : see also Chapter 3 above.

In fixing tariffs, the Government is advised by the Tariff Board (1921). The Board is an independent body the members of which are appointed for fixed terms and can only be removed from office by action in the Parliament. Appointments are made so as to reflect the diverse interests of the community. Its functions are purely advisory and, whilst it has considerable powers of investigation, it has no executive authority. Although the Board is authorized to conduct inquiries into certain subjects on its own initiative, the subject matters of its inquiries are normally those referred to it by the Minister for Trade.

The Tariff Board consists of the Chairman and six other members who are appointed by the Governor-General for periods of from one to five years and who are eligible for re-appointment. The Act provides that at least two (but not more than three) members must be, at the time of their first appointments, officers of the

Department of Trade.   The remaining members are men with wide experience in such fields as commerce, industry, banking and primary production.

The majority of the Board's hearings take the form of public inquiries with evidence being taken on oath.   All interested parties are entitled to appear before the Board, including manufacturers, traders, importers and consumers.   The rights of United Kingdom producers to appear or be represented at Tariff Board inquiries are specially stated in Article 9 of the United Kingdom-Australia Trade Agreement. Although not guaranteed by treaty, representatives of producers or other interested persons or organizations in any other country are also accorded full rights of appearance at Board inquiries.   Some evidence of a confidential kind is taken in private.

After hearing the evidence presented at the public hearings and obtaining all other relevant information which may be available, the Board prepares a report for the Minister.   All reports containing recommendations for assistance to industry whether by means of duty or bounty are submitted by the Minister to Cabinet for consideration.   They are then examined by Cabinet in the light of overall Government policy.   In the great majority of cases they are adopted.

APPENDIX II

New South Wales State and Local Government Finance

I. *Receipts of State Consolidated Revenue Fund*, 1956–57 (£m)

Source : Auditor-General's Report and Public Accounts.

Payments to State by Commonwealth ([1]) :

Income Tax Reimbursement	58.35
Special Financial Assistance	6.93
Towards interest on Public Debt	2.92
Hospital Benefits	2.20
Tuberculosis	1.62
Pharmaceutical Benefits	0.45
Milk to school children	1.09
Other	1.01
	74.57

Taxation ([2]) :—

Stamp Duties	10.10
Probate and Death Duties	10.89
Racing Revenue	2.70
Licenses	3.25
Land Tax	3.35
	30.30

Other Receipts :—

State Lotteries	4.63
Land Revenue (sales, leases, mining, etc.)	4.62
Fees, fines, etc.	4.01
Harbour and tonnage rates, etc.	2.20
Forestry	1.31
Other	6.35
	23.12

Total Receipts	127.99

I. *Present basis of grants to States*

(a) *Tax reimbursement grants.* The total grant is determined first. The basic grant to the States of £45m., paid in 1947–8, is adjusted by (i) the increase in the population of the Commonwealth since July 1947, and (ii) the increase in the average annual wage since 1945–6. (N.B. this formula is not related to what the Commonwealth gets from income tax, nor does it make any allowance for increase in incomes other than wages, *e.g.*, farm incomes.)

Note—The formula was changed at the 1959 Premiers' Conference. A new "per capita" grant (*i. e.* grant *per head of population*) fixed for each State in the base year will change in future according to the percentage change in average wages for Australia as a whole. Instead of using the actual increase in wages, a figure 10% higher than this will be used–this is the so-called "betterment factor". So the total grant will vary with (1) population (2) average wages (3) the "betterment factor".

The base "per capita" grant for New South Wales (1959-60) is £22. 2. 9. For the other states, it is: Victoria £21. 12. 10, Queensland £25. 2. 3, South Australia £30. 4. 2, Tasmania £31. 16. 11, Western Australia £35. 6. 7.

([1]) The Commonwealth also contributes to other expenditure, *e.g.*, £8.43m. to roads from petrol duties.

([2]) State receipts from motor taxation are excluded, as these are paid into special road funds. This applies also to one or two other minor taxes, *e.g.* ,on poker machines, paid to Hospital Fund.

(b) *Special Financial Assistance.* In addition to the grant determined by the formula, the Commonwealth gives special financial assistance to the states. In 1951–52 this amounted to £33.6m., in 1953–54 £21.9m. These special grants are at the discretion of the Commonwealth, and the outcome of bargaining. NOTE— These "supplementary grants" have now been discontinued.

(c) *Special Grants to Claimant States.* The special needs of the "claimant States" (Western Australia, South Australia and Tasmania) have, since 1933, been looked after by an independent body, the Commonwealth Grants Commission (see main text). Students should read some of its reports, *e.g.*, the 3rd, 6th, 16th and latest reports. The basic aim of the Commission is to redress the inequalities (found in all federations) in the resources of different States, and, by means of special grants to the claimant States, help them to place their social and other services on a "normal" Australian level. The grants are made under Section 96. NOTE—These grants have since 1959 been considerably reduced.

(d) *Other Grants-in-aid.* The Commonwealth also pays a number of grants towards specified services. The most important grants are for *roads*, universities and *hospital benefits*. The others are a very mixed assortment indeed. They may contain a proviso that for every £1 granted by the Commonwealth the States must raise so-and-so much. This, for example, applies to part of the Commonwealth grants for *universities*. Roads grants to all States were £31.3m in 1956–57, public hospital benefits £5.9m. The N.S.W. figures are given in Table I. There were also grants for tuberculosis benefits, school milk, pharmaceutical benefits, various payments to States for primary industry, etc.

III. *Payments from New South Wales Consolidated Revenue Fund,* 1956–57 (£m)

Departments :

Minister for Education	35.98
Minister for Health	23.42
Colonial Treasurer	14.57
Premier (¹)	7.58
Secretary for Public Works	4.36
Attorney-General (and Justice)	4.02
Minister for Agriculture	3.38
Minister for Conservation	1.88
Minister for Child, Social Welfare	1.77
Secretary for Lands	1.50
Other	9.98
	108.44
Loan liability to Commonwealth	19.01
	127.45

(¹) Includes Police (£6.95m), Public Service Board, etc.

IV. *New South Wales State and Local Enterprises* :

Revenues of State business undertakings and State enterprises (1956–57) were about £160m., including :—

Railways ([1])	..	..	..	..	£80.5m (deficit £5.8m.)
Trams and Buses ([1])	..	..	..	£14.4m (deficit £1.2m.)
Electricity	..	..	..	..	£39.1m (surplus £0.1m.)

Revenues ([2]) of local authority trading undertakings (1955) were over £50m., including :—

Electricity	..	..	..	..	£44.5m (surplus £1.9m.)
Water and sewerage	..	..	..	£3.2m (surplus £0.8m.)
Abattoirs	..	..	..	..	£2.6m (surplus £0.1m.)
Gas	..	..	..	..	£1.0m. (surplus £0.1m.)

V. *State and local authority loan expenditure* (£m)

Source : Auditor-General's Report and Commonwealth Statistician.

State (1956–57) :

Railways, tramways, etc.	..	..	..	..	..	13.5
Electricity	..	..	..	..	..	10.5
Schools, universities	..	..	..	..	..	7.3
Water conservation, soils, forests	..	..	..	..	6.9
Hospitals	..	..	..	..	..	4.6
Land settlement	..	..	..	..	..	3.8
Water, sewerage, drainage	..	..	..	..	2.8
Harbours and rivers	..	..	..	..	..	1.9
Housing	..	..	..	..	..	0.1 ([3])
Roads and bridges	..	..	..	..	..	0.6
Other	..	..	..	..	..	2.3

£54.3m

Local (1955) :—

Electricity	..	..	..	..	..	6.8
Roads and bridges	..	..	..	..	..	2.5
Water and sewerage	..	..	..	..	..	2.5
Other	..	..	..	..	..	3.9

£15.7m

([1]) Transport revenues include certain transfers from general State revenues, mainly borne on the Treasury vote e.g. contributions to losses on developmental lines, to superannuation funds, and to meet the cost of travel concessions, track removal and road restoration.

([2]) Including government grants, water and sewerage rates.

([3]) Excluding expenditure under Commonwealth-State Housing Agreement.

VI. *Municipalities and Shires, Ordinary Services, Details of Revenue, 1955.*

	Sydney Metropolitan		Total		
	City of Sydney	Suburbs	Municipalities	Shires	Total
REVENUE	£	£	£	£	£
General Rates	3,142,950	8,310,147	14,055,371	7,137,206	21,192,577
Loan, Local, Special Rates	...	806,122	1,158,999	1,542,396	2,701,395
Extra Charges, Overdue Rates	6,337	48,460	79,265	55,192	134,457
Total Rates and Extra Charges ...	3,149,287	9,164,729	15,293,635	8,734,794	24,028,429
Payments in Lieu of Rates	61,484	26,195	116,566	9,920	126,486
Miscellaneous Licence Fees, Charges for Gas, Electric Mains, etc.	56,514	172,281	265,614	100,227	365,841
Sales and Charges—					
Contributions to Works	147,712	534,628	941,050	439,319	1,380,369
Sanitary and Garbage	142,680	1,238,572	1,688,737	1,134,757	2,823,494
Parks, Baths, Beaches	41,685	272,219	444,444	140,676	585,120
Public Markets	329,926	5,953	422,745	26,277	449,022
Libraries	4,066	7,713	45,659	3,812	49,471
Council Property	314,957	190,361	815,019	489,087	1,304,106
Housing—Instalments ...	790	84,216	116,041	18,478	134,519
Sale of Assets	3,584	220,373	419,925	200,740	620,665
Other	226,738	281,773	664,622	316,333	980,955
Total Sales and Charges	1,212,138	2,835,808	5,558,242	2,769,479	8,327,721
Total Raised by Councils	4,479,423	12,199,013	21,234,057	11,614,420	32,848,477
Government Grants—					
Endowment	...	5,665	3,660	219,345	223,005
Works (Roads, Streets, Bridges)—					
Main Roads Department	28,491	504,563	647,889	4,065,832	4,713,721
Other	40,729	229,434	434,176	1,774,122	2,208,298
Flood Damage Repair	...	738	161,554	392,270	553,824
Libraries	14,486	63,080	121,356	31,670	153,026
Baby Health Centres	...	26,537	28,433	17,255	45,688
Subsidy for Interest on Loans ...	...	912	1,719	3,732	5,451
Parks, Gardens, Baths, Beaches ...	...	2,970	33,372	60,343	93,715
Other	...	1,816	20,255	102,002	122,257
Total Government Grants	83,706	835,715	1,452,414	6,666,571	8,118,985
Total Revenue on Account of Ordinary Services	4,563,129	13,034,728	22,686,471	18,280,991	40,967,462

VII. *Municipalities and Shires, Ordinary Services, Details of Expenditure from Revenue, 1955.*

EXPENDITURE	£	£	£	£	£
Works and Services—					
Administration	392,526	885,389	1,633,507	1,083,434	2,716,941
Works—Roads, Bridges, etc.—					
Contributions to Main Roads Dept.	40,848	689,051	661,814	93,074	754,888
Other	1,370,135	4,796,374	8,040,578	12,058,905	20,099,483
Street Lighting	104,926	497,265	750,931	201,738	952,669
Sanitary and Garbage	298,377	1,735,895	2,389,043	1,116,864	3,505,907
Parks, Baths, Beaches	457,403	1,086,619	2,053,867	443,688	2,497,555
Baby Health Centres	1,278	52,791	68,986	21,292	90,278
Health Services	139,910	262,193	502,986	174,506	677,492
Public Markets	229,081	4,161	292,825	20,800	313,625
Libraries	73,352	204,987	456,742	97,303	554,045
Noxious Animals and Weeds ...	...	12,578	29,718	122,964	152,682
Fire Prevention	41,123	146,926	212,002	170,283	382,285
Cattle Straying	1,214	18,272	37,383	38,723	76,106
Donations	54,976	48,583	127,120	29,089	156,209
Housing (Construction and Advances) ...	...	...	2,697	9,834	12,531
Council Property	402,697	562,898	1,354,805	443,682	1,798,487
Town Planning*	70,875	242,415	292,703	74,193	366,896
Other	390,539	372,634	1,011,871	475,961	1,487,832
Total Works and Services ...	4,069,260	11,619,031	19,919,578	16,676,333	36,595,911
Debt Charges—					
Interest on Loans, etc.	372,030	459,391	980,555	321,551	1,302,106
Repayment of Loans, incl. Contrib. to Sinking Funds	287,685	988,743	1,751,002	1,128,358	2,879,360
Total Debt Charges	659,715	1,448,134	2,731,557	1,449,909	4,181,466
Total Expenditure from Revenue ...	4,728,975	13,067,165	22,651,135	18,126,242	40,777,377

*Includes contributions to County Councils.

APPENDIX III.
New South Wales Estimates : A Typical Page.
Source: Estimates 1957–58 p. 145.

MINISTER FOR EDUCATION

Sub-heads under which this Expenditure will be Accounted for	1957–58 Estimate	1956–57	
		Appro-priation	Expenditure
PRIMARY EDUCATION	£	£	£
Salaries and Payments in the Nature of Salary			
A1. Salaries and Wages, as per Schedule, page 158	14,734,212	14,491,261	14,429,359
A3. Allowances	208,603	214,263	214,263
A4. Payments for Leave on Retirement, Resignation, etc.	150,000	125,000	110,039
A5. Overtime	100	200	26
	15,092,915	14,830,724	14,753,687
Maintenance and Working Expenses			
B2. Expenses in connection with Buildings—			
Rent	12,000	15,500	12,178
Maintenance, Alterations, Additions and Renewals	1,710,000	1,640,000	1,556,159
Cleaning	70,000	73,000	66,454
B3. Subsistence and Transport Expenses—			
Travelling, Removal and Subsistence Expenses	77,000	77,000	71,116
Freight, Cartage and Packing	22,000	21,000	20,926
B4. General Expenses—			
Postal Expenses	25,000	22,000	23,856
Fees for Services Rendered	2,700	825	1,158
Stores, Provisions, Furniture, Equipment, Minor Plant, etc. (including Maintenance and Repairs)	532,000	485,000	514,238
Other Insurance...	2,600	1,400	1,420
Minor Expenses not elsewhere included	25	25	5
£	2,453,325	2,335,750	2,267,510
Other Services			
C1. Nursery Classes and Nursery Schools— Wages and Materials in connection with preparation of meals for very young children	11,000	9,500	10,855
C2. Payments for Conveyance of Children to School	687,000	670,000	686,773
C3. Hospital Schools—Expenses	3,000	3,000	2,980
C4. Survey of Sites	50	50	......
C5. Reimbursement of Telephone Rentals in Staffed Schools	5,250	4,250	5,047
C6. Subsidies towards cost of purchase of Pianos for School use	5,000	2,000	2,699
C7. Subsidies towards cost of purchase of Receiving Sets for Broadcasting in Schools	750	750	725
C9. Grants to Parents and Citizens Associations for Minor Repairs to Schools ...	20,000	8,000	9,717
... Non-recurring Service	....	....	287
£	732,050	697,550	719,083
Total—Primary Education ... £	18,278,290	17,864,024	17,740,280

APPENDIX IV

WHAT THE COMMONWEALTH THIRD DIVISION DOES

Estimated Distribution of Permanent Third Division Officers According to Major Function of their Position at 31st July, 1956.

Source : Sample Survey, July 1956, Commonwealth Public Service Board.

Functional Group	Number of Officers	Percentage of Officers in each group	Explanatory Notes
Accounting..	4,000	14	Includes office accounts, pay, etc.
Audit	700	3	Includes internal audit.
Assessing and Finance ..	2,500	9	Includes tax investigations.
General clerical ..	3,600	12	Includes some senior officers in general administration.
Statistics	600	2	All levels of statistical work.
Personnel	1,700	6	Staff and industrial, methods, recruitment, etc.
Office Services	1,100	4	Registry, library, etc.
Stores and Transport ..	1,600	6	Includes office stores. Excludes marine and air transport.
Engineering	2,200	8	All types excluding pure research.
Architecture and Drafting	1,000	3	Includes engineering drafting.
Non-Tech. professional ..	1,100	4	Legal, foreign affairs, economics, psychology, etc.
Other professional ..	1,200	4	Medicine, physics, chemistry, geology, survey, etc.
Technical	1,100	4	Weather service, property and buildings inspection, pharmacy and other technical work.
Customs	1,100	4	Functions peculiar to Customs Department.
Miscellaneous	1,800	6	Includes marine, patents, electoral, immigration, employment service and some postal work.
Postal positions not surveyed.	3,200	11	
Total Third Division ..	28,500	100	

APPENDIX V

LOCAL GOVERNMENT FUNCTIONS IN NEW SOUTH WALES

Source : Department of Local Government.

Local Government in New South Wales is mainly regulated under the Local Government Act, 1919, although certain local government powers and duties are exercised or performed under other legislation, *e.g.*, the Public Health Act, 1902–1944, Noxious Trades Act, 1902, Cattle Slaughtering and Diseased Animals and Meat Act, 1902, Dairies Supervision Act, 1901, and so on. All these Acts are public Acts and, as and when the powers of Councils as the local governing bodies are increased, the necessary authority is given under public Acts. Councils are not required to approach Parliament by way of private Bills for enlargement of their powers.

The Local Government Act, 1919, is an Act to make better provision for the government of areas; to extend the powers and functions of local governing bodies; and to establish bodies to take common action on behalf of areas.

(a) Public Health

In its role as protector of the health of the community a council may do all things necessary from time to time for the preservation of public health, safety and convenience. In addition to the normal functions of providing proper *garbage* and *sanitary* services a council may control and regulate the use or premises for the *sale of food* and the *preparation of serving of food* in *restaurants, hotels, cafes,* and the like. It licenses *butchers' shops, smallgoods shops, barbers' shops, boarding houses* and *houses let in lodgings.* It may control the keeping of *dogs* and *cats* on premises, so as to avoid insanitary conditions, and the keeping of *animals* and *poultry* at distances from habitable rooms. It may distribute and sell *milk* or regulate the sale and distribution of milk in areas not controlled by the Milk Board under the Milk Act and may conduct *abattoirs, preserving or freezing works* and sell *animals* and *foodstuffs.*

Other services which may be extended to their areas by councils are *diphtheria* or other *infections* or *contagious disease immunization,* the provision of *medical and nursing attendance* for sparsely settled country districts, and the subsidising of *life saving clubs, civil ambulance brigades, hospitals, pre-natal* and *baby health clinics, kindergarten and day nurseries,* settlements for aged persons, and organizations in respect of the *transport of children to and from school.* The Government is encouraging councils to provide *women's rest centres* at selected sites and is offering a subsidy up to 50 per cent. of the cost of constructing and equipping such centres.

(b) Public Recreation

In this important field of operation a council may provide facilities for the physical as well as the cultural and educational welfare of the community. It may provide and care for *public recreation reserves, children's playgrounds, gardens, golf courses, tennis courts;* provide *public baths,* regulate *beach bathing;* provide and control *community centres, public libraries, gymnasia, schools of art, museums, art galleries* and *public bandmusic* or other forms of *musical* or *public entertainment.* It may regulate *skating rinks* and appliances, such as *merry-go-rounds* and *shooting galleries,* used for public amusement and games. It may control *structures on wheels, caravans, tents,* and set aside *camping areas.* A council may acquire and preserve places of *historical interest* or of *scenic attraction,* and may *advertise* the *advantages of the area* and conduct a *tourist* bureau or act as *agent* for any Government tourist bureau or for other persons conducting tourist businesses.

(c) Building—Housing

A council has a direct responsibility to protect the interests of the home builder. Not only does this extend to the *type of building* to be erected, but also to the *quality of the materials* used in construction. It may enforce the repair or demolition of *ruinous buildings* and may require the provision for proper *cooking, bathroom* and *laundry* facilities and of an adequate *water supply* and the renewal or repair of *roofs, guttering* and *downpiping* or *gas* and *electricity* installations in premises. It may *finance home builders* and undertake *housing schemes.*

(d) Public Roads

In addition to providing *public roads*, their construction, improvement, protection maintenance, cleaning and lighting, a council may repair, drain or otherwise improve land used as a private thoroughfare at the expense of the owners of land adjoining such thoroughfare, license *street photographers*, control structures, e.g. *petrol bowsers* on roads, provide *parking areas* near or on roads, control *dogs* and the menace of *broken bottles* on roads and provide *bicycle tracks* in roads.

(e) Public Utilities—Trading

Councils may establish trading undertakings for the supply of *electricity* and *gas* and for *public transport*, *ferry services*, *carrying*, *quarrying*, *supply of ice*, *abattoirs*, *community hotels*, *public markets* for the sale of cattle or of food, the supply of *building materials*, and the operation of a *coal mine* and the supply and distribution of *coal*. Councils can also provide *water supply*, *sewerage* and *drainage* services other than in areas controlled by the Metropolitan and Hunter District Water Boards.

(f) Town and Country Planning

A council may, by resolution, decide to prepare a *town and country planning scheme* with respect to land within its area and may join with other councils in preparing joint schemes. The Minister may direct a council, or councils jointly, to prepare a scheme if it is apparent that a council is holding up the planning of contiguous areas or is clearly letting its residents down.

(g) Acquisition and sale of land

Councils are empowered to acquire land within or outside the area by lease, purchase, appropriation or resumption. The Governor's approval must first be obtained before a council may proceed to resume any land. Councils may also sell, exchange or lease any land or building or other real or personal property vested in or belonging to the Council.

(h) Miscellaneous

Other facilities and services which may be provided by councils include *public wharves*, *pounds*, *cemeteries* and *crematories*, *drinking fountains*, *weighbridges*, *clocks*, *buildings for public purposes*, *commons*, *aerodromes*, *telephone services* for out-lying districts, *light lines of railway and tramway*, *employment registries*, *sheep dips*, *community forests*, and *wireless broadcasting services* for prescribed purposes. Councils may regulate *burials and cremations*, compel the destruction of *noxious weeds*, regulate and license *public vehicles* and *drivers of public vehicles* in areas not subject to the Metropolitan and Motor Traffic Acts, provide, establish and manage *bush fire brigades*, carry out dredging, regulate *advertisement hoardings* and *advertisements*, write off or reduce *rates* owing by *old-age* and *invalid pensioners* towards which the Government will grant a subsidy of 50 per cent. of the amount written off, supply firewood and acquire land for the purpose of providing *small holdings*.

APPENDIX VI

THE STATEMENT OF DUTIES [1]

It is not uncommon for a statement of duties to be regarded simply as a guide for the new occupant of a position. When he takes over his new duties he is shown the statement, which tells him what his range of duties will be and acts as a reference point while he is learning the job.

Even for this single purpose, the statement of duties must obviously present a clear and detailed picture. There are, however, other purposes for which it is used.

The statement of duties :

(1) is important in *selection and placement* because, by showing the full extent of the duties to be performed by its occupant, it indicates the demands it will make on him and thus assists a selecting officer or committee to choose the person best suited in physique, abilities, temperament, education and experience to fill it;

(2) contains the basic data from which information is drawn to enable the *evaluation* of the position—that is, the determination of its grading, the occupant's place in the organisation and the salary he will receive;

(3) provides the most vital items of information required for the design of *training* courses;

(4) simplifies *salary-fixing* procedures by facilitating the grouping of positions which require similar qualities and involve similar duties and for which similar rates of pay are, therefore, justified;

(5) by defining the duties of officers, shows their *precise relationship* to one another;

(6) provides a datum point for the departmental or Public Service Board inspector conducting an *organisation and methods* survey.

To satisfy all these purposes the statement of duties must be as accurate, concise and informative as possible. The attached directions aim at assisting officers to achieve these ends.

Instructions to officers completing Statements of Duties and to Examining Officers.

In writing a Statement of Duties, the officer should present as true and as complete a picture of his job as is possible within the space available.

In order to achieve this end, the following rules should be adhered to :—

(A) *Introduce the Statement of Duties* with a brief summary of the job to assist in its ready identification.

(B) *Classify your duties under a number of headings but name your basic function first.* Every person has a basic function and this is usually identified in the title of the position; for example, a position with the title " Salaries Clerk " would be principally concerned with the maintenance of pay records and the payment of salaries, even though, say, in a small Department, the Salaries Clerk may be allotted several other functions. Other functions should then be described in the order of the demand they make upon the officer's time; thus the duties of a Salaries Clerk in a small Department might be classified under the following headings :—

SALARIES CLERK

(1) *Payment of salaries, overtime, general and travelling expenses.*

(2) *Maintenance of Office Leave Records.*

(3) *Salaries inquiries.*

(4) *Estimates.*

---

[1] Based on N.S.W. Public Service Board Circular of 27th February, 1952.

(C) *Show not only " what " is done but " how " it is done.*

Indicate the processes which contribute to carrying out the basic function. Where space permits, indicate the processes involved with the other functions. Obviously the amount of detail that can be contained in the descriptions of the processes is determined by the amount of space allowed to write the description—one page.

The process of dividing each function into its contributing components can be carried to a ridiculous point; *e.g.* the opening and closing of a filing drawer are tasks which contribute to the objective of filing a paper but, apart from indicating a physical motion which could be accomplished by practically any person, they are not sufficiently important to matter in a statement of duties.

The processes contributing to two of the functions of a Salaries Clerk would be presented as follows :—

SALARIES CLERK

(1) Payment of salaries, overtime, general and travelling expenses—

    (*a*) Maintains salary cards for 78 officers from files, vouchers or verbal advice.

    (*b*) Calculates salaries, commissions, tax, superannuation and miscellaneous deductions and general and travelling expenses payments.

(2) Maintenance of office leave records—

    Calculates and certifies leave due and records leave approved on leave cards.

(D) *Be economical in the use of words.* This can be best achieved by commencing the description of each process with a " doing " word : for example, " opens mail and stamps with date stamp "; by the careful selection of words and the deletion of the personal pronoun and definite article. The statement of duties is not expected to be a literary effort, but to be descriptive and have the greatest possible meaning.

(E) *Be definite.* Select the most appropriate descriptive terms. It would not be sufficient for a shorthandwriter to say—" I take dictation and transcribe my notes ". What kind of dictation—letters, reports, conferences, deputations, formal meetings ? What subject matter—administrative, medical, engineering, legal ? What is the official position of the people who dictate to you ? Do you have occasion to compose your own letters ? How often ? In what kinds of cases ? Do you do any other clerical work? If so what are these other clerical tasks ? How much of your working time do they take up ? Describe them in as much detail as your stenographic duties. If your position requires you to have unusual speed and accuracy as a stenographer, say so and why. Again, it is useless to use such a loose and indefinite expression as : " I handle correspondence " without going into more detail. An executive, a stenographer, a messenger, a mailing clerk, a file clerk, may all handle correspondence, each in his own way. In the case of an employee who dictates or writes rough drafts for, or in any way originates, correspondence, it is essential to show what class of correspondence it is, what the employee does in order to get the information required to answer the letter, what sort of review or approval the letter requires, and other facts that will indicate the degree of independence with which the letter is composed and the subsequent check to which it is subjected.

(F) *Give examples of your work.* Sometimes the best way to make the statement clear is to use typical tasks as illustrations. Avoid the unusual or exceptional task that occurs once in a lifetime as it cannot serve as a basis for classification. The tasks used as illustrations should be such as are typical of the duties occurring time and time again.

(G) *Quote figures.* If you are employed in a supervisory capacity, indicate not only the grades of the people who are *directly* responsible to you, but also their numbers and the total number employed in the branch or section. If you are Salaries Clerk, indicate the number and classification of persons employed and the total fortnightly or annual salary. Where possible, figures should be quoted on an annual basis.

(H) *Name the tools with which you carry out your work.* For example, name the Acts, Regulations, Instructions or any handbook you use as a basis for providing of information by phone or correspondence.

Indicate the machines you use, and *where appropriate* the make, type and model.

(I) *Indicate the relationship of your job to the work of your superiors and your subordinates.*

(J) *A special note for the senior officer.* Although all officers should check their jobs against the following questions, they apply in particular to senior officers.

If you are an administrative officer, the description of your work will naturally be broader than otherwise. In such cases a satisfactory answer can be prepared by considering replies to such questions as the following :—

(1) What functions do you direct, supervise, and control ?

(2) What part do you play in the formulation and development of operating plans, programmes, methods and policies ?

(3) Upon what types of problems do you make decisions that do not require higher approval and that generally are unrevised ?

(4) Upon what matters do you generally have only recommending authority ?

(5) Over what geographical territory do you have administrative jurisdiction ?

(6) Give some indication of the size of your establishment by showing such facts as the number of your assistants and subordinates, the annual amount of receipts, expenditure, collections, or other figure or figures that will serve as an index.

(7) With what other administrators, public or private, do you make contact in carrying out your work ? For what purposes ?

A specimen :—

SALARIES CLERK

Summary—

Responsible to the senior clerk for the drawing up and payment of salaries, overtime, general and travelling expense vouchers, maintenance of office leave records, and answering salary inquiries, compilation of information for estimates.

Duties.

1. *Payment of salaries, overtime, general and travelling expenses.*

   (a) Maintains salary cards for 78 officers from files, vouchers, or verbal advice.

   (b) Calculates salaries, commissions, tax, superannuation and miscellaneous deductions and general and travelling expenses payments.

   (c) Prepares vouchers, cash sheets and dissections for payment of salaries and overtime (£62,000 p.a.), examination fees, laundry charges, etc. (£5,000 p.a.).

   (d) Maintains appropriation ledger from salary cards and vouchers.

   (e) Writes cheques and covering letters merely identifying purpose for which the cheque is paid.

   (f) Cashes cheques and pays officers.

2. *Maintenance of Office Leave Records.*

   Calculates and certifies leave due and records leave approved on leave cards.

3. *Salaries Inquiries.*

   (a) Answers verbal inquiries *re* salaries payable under awards and agreements.
   (b) Answers individual officers' inquiries *re* salary payments, deductions, etc.

4. *Estimates.*

   Compiles staff details and salaries for Estimates.

BOOK LISTS

General reference material

The *Commonwealth Year Book* and the various State Year Books are full of useful information on administrative developments.

Public Administration (Sydney, 1937 onwards), the journal of the Australian Regional Groups of the Royal Institute of Public Administration, contains many valuable articles, some of which are cited in the text and below. A consolidated *Index* to the end of 1956 was published in 1957. There is a journal of the same name published by the Institute in the United Kingdom.

F. A. BLAND : *Government in Australia*, (2nd ed., Government Printing Office, Sydney, 1944) consists of extracts from government reports, with a commentary.

Current Commonwealth and State official publications are listed in the *Annual Catalogue of Australian Publications*, Commonwealth National Library.

Three other useful sources of reference for material on Australian public administration are :

J. CRAIG (ed.) : *Bibliography of Public Administration in Australia, 1850–1947*, University of Sydney, 1955.

D. H. BORCHARDT: *Check List of Royal Commissions, Select Committees and Boards of Inquiry*, Stone Copying Company, Cremorne, N.S.W., 1958.

Consolidated Index to (Commonwealth) Parliamentary Papers, 1901–49, Government Printer, Canberra, 1955.

On the United Kingdom :—

W. J. M. Mackenzie and J. W. Grove : *Central Administration in Britain*, Longmans, 1957, has useful book-lists.

Chapter One

E. BARKER : *The Development of Public Services in Modern Europe*, Cambridge U.P., 1944.

W. J. M. MACKENZIE and J. W. GROVE : *Central Administration in Britain*, Longmans, 1957.

Sir E. BRIDGES and OTHERS : *The Making of the Administrator*, Manchester U.P., 1956.

H. A. SIMON : *Administrative Behavior*, 2nd ed., Macmillan, N.Y., 1957.

J. D. MILLETT : *Management in the Public Service*, McGraw-Hill, N.Y., 1954.

P. M. BLAU : *Bureaucracy in Modern Society*, Random House, N.Y., 1956

F. DUNNILL : *The Civil Service—Some Human Aspects*, Allen and Unwin, 1956.

See also articles and books referred to in the text.

Chapter Two

K. C. WHEARE : *Federal Government*, 3rd ed., Oxford U.P., 1953.

G. SAWER and OTHERS : *Federalism in Australia*, Cheshire, 1949.

G. SAWER (ed.): *Federalism, an Australian Jubilee Study*, Cheshire, 1952.

Chapter Two—continued

The best general history of Australian government is :

G. GREENWOOD (ed.): *Australia : A Social and Political History*, Angus and Robertson, 1955. Some of the constitutional cases referred to may be read in :

G. SAWER (ed.) : *Cases on the Constitution of the Commonwealth of Australia*, 2nd ed., Law Book Co. of Australasia, 1957.

Chapter Three

G. SAWER : *Australian Government Today*, 5th ed., Melbourne U.P., 1957,

J. D. B. MILLER : *Australian Government and Politics*, Duckworth, 1954.

L. F. CRISP : *Parliamentary Government of the Commonwealth of Australia*, 2nd ed., Longmans, 1954, esp. chapters VII & IX.

S. R. DAVIS (ed.) : *Governments of the Australian States*, Longmans (forthcoming).

The Government of Victoria : Dept. of Political Science, Melbourne, Melb-U.P., 1958.

F. C. GREEN, " Changing Relations between Parliament and the Executive ", *Pub. Admin. (Sydney)*, XIII, June 1954.

S. ENCEL, "Cabinet Machinery in Australia ", *Pub. Admin. (Sydney)*, XV, June 1956.

J. G. CRAWFORD, " The Role of the Permanent Head ", *Pub. Admin. (Sydney)*, XIII, Sept. 1954.

" Commonwealth Policy Co-ordination ", (Report of Canberra Research Group), *Pub. Admin. (Sydney)*, XIV, Dec. 1955.

The *Federal Guide* lists Commonwealth departments, functions, chief officials. See also e.g. *State Departmental Guide* (New South Wales) and *Annual Reports* of Commonwealth and State agencies.

Chapter Four

A. H. HANSON (ed.) : *Public Enterprise*, International Institute of Administrative Sciences, Brussels, 1955.

W. FRIEDMANN (ed.) : *The Public Corporation : a comparative study*, Carswell, Toronto, 1954.

(both books contain chapters on Australian public corporations.)

" Public Enterprise in Australia ", Special Issue, *Pub. Admin. (Sydney)*, XVI, March 1957.

W. J. CAMPBELL : *Australian State Public Finance*, Law Book Co. of Australasia, 1954.

F. W. EGGLESTON : *State Socialism in Victoria*, King, 1932.

F. A. BLAND, " The Government as Entrepreneur ", in : *Planning the Modern State*, 2nd ed., Angus and Robertson, 1945.

L. C. WEBB, " Freedom and the Public Corporation ", *Pub. Admin. (Sydney)*, XIII, June 1954.

On individual corporations, see also their *Annual Reports* and e.g.

L. F. GIBLIN : *The Growth of a Central Bank*, Melbourne U.P., 1951.

The Railways of New South Wales, 1855–1955, N.S.W. Dept. of Railways.

Chapter Four—continued

Australian Aluminium Production Commission, 21st and 22nd Reports of the (Commonwealth) Joint Parliamentary Committee on Public Accounts, 1955.

I. K. MACKAY : *Broadcasting in Australia*, Melbourne U.P., 1957.

JOAN RYDON, " The Australian Broadcasting Commission, 1932–48 ", *Pub. Admin. (Sydney)*, XI, March and Dec., 1952.

On United Kingdom experience, see :

W. A. ROBSON (ed.) : *Problems of Nationalized Industry*, Allen and Unwin, 1952.

Chapter Five

R. MENDELSOHN : *Social Security in the British Commonwealth*, Athlone Press, 1954.

M. P. HALL : *Social Services of Modern England*, 2nd ed., Routledge and Kegan Paul, 1953.

E. M. BURNS : *Social Security and Public Policy*, McGraw-Hill, 1956.

T. H. KEWLEY, " The Development of the Social Services ", in C. H. Grattan (ed.) : *Australia*, University of California Press, 1947.

T. H. KEWLEY, " Social Services ", in G. W. Paton (ed.) : *The Commonwealth of Australia*, Stevens, London, 1952.

R. I. DOWNING : *Raising Age Pensions*, Melbourne U.P., 1957

P. D. ABBOTT and L. O. GOLDSMITH, " History and Functions of the Commonwealth Health Department, 1921–52 ", *Pub. Admin. (Sydney)*, XI, Sept. 1952.

J. H. L. CUMPSTON, " Public Health Administration ", *Pub. Admin. (Sydney)* XII, March 1953.

T. H. KEWLEY, " Child Endowment in Australia ", *Pub. Admin. (Sydney)*, XVII, Sept. 1958.

See also *Health* (Commonwealth Department of Health, quarterly) and *Education News* (Commonwealth Office of Education, bi-monthly), and the *Annual Reports* of Commonwealth and State departments and agencies. The New South Wales Council of Social Service publishes a *Directory of Social Service Agencies* (latest ed. 1957) and *Social Service* (bi-monthly).

Chapter Six

F. A. BLAND : *Government in Australia*, 2nd ed., Government Printing Office, Sydney, 1944, ch. XVII and XVIII.

F. A. BLAND : " Is There a Future for Local Government ? " *Pub. Admin. (Sydney)*, VI, Dec. 1946.

A. R. BLUETT: *The Local Government Handbook*, 5th ed., Law Book Co. of Australasia, 1954.

F. A. LARCOMBE : *History of Local Government in New South Wales*, Local Government and Shires Associations, Sydney, 1955.

A. F. DAVIES : *Local Government in Victoria*, Melbourne U.P., 1951.

J. R. H. JOHNS, " Development of Local Government in Western Australia ", *Pub. Admin. (Sydney)*, VIII, Dec., 1949.

L. BLAIR, " Local Government in South Australia ", in R. J. Best (ed.): *Introducing South Australia*, A.N.Z.A.A.S., 1958.

Pub. Admin. (Sydney), V, March, 1945 contains articles on the local government systems of all States except New South Wales.

Chapter Six—continued

On metropolitan and town-planning problems, see also :—

J. D. B. MILLER, " Greater Sydney, 1892–1952 ", *Pub. Admin. (Sydney)*, XIII, June and Sept. 1954.

A. F. DAVIES, " Local Government in Melbourne ", *Pub. Admin. (Sydney)*, XIV, June 1955.

F. A. BLAND, " Sydney ", in W. A. Robson (ed.) : *Great Cities of the World*, Allen and Unwin, 1956.

J. R. H. JOHNS : *Metropolitan Government in Western Australia*, University of W.A., 1950.

Royal Commission on Local Government Areas (County of Cumberland), *Report*, 1946.

D. WINSTON : *Sydney's Great Experiment* : *The Progress of the Cumberland County Plan*, Angus & Robertson, 1957.

G. F. ANDERSON : *Fifty Years of Electricity Supply*, Sydney County Council, 1955.

On decentralization and New States see :—

Decentralization, Australian Institute of Political Science, Angus & Robertson, 1948.

New States for Australia, Australian Institute of Political Science, 1955.

The Local Government and Shires Associations of New South Wales publish periodical conference reports and papers e.g. R. S. PARKER, " Highlights of New South Wales Local Government Legislation over the Last Fifty Years " (1956).

Local government periodicals and bulletins include the *Shire and Municipal Record*, monthly and *Local Government Service*, bi-monthly (N.S.W.), the *Australian Municipal Journal*, monthly (covering Victoria, South Australia and Tasmania), *Local Government*, monthly (Queensland), and *Local Government Administration*, the Federal organ of the Institute of Municipal Administration.

Chapter Seven

G. F. SHIRRAS : *Federal Finance in Peace and War*, Macmillan, 1944.

W. PREST : *The Economics of Federal-State Finance*, Joseph Fisher Lecture, University of Adelaide, 1955.

L. F. GIBLIN, " Financial Aspects of the Constitution ", in G. Sawer and others : *Federalism in Australia*, Cheshire, 1949.

F. A. BLAND : *Budget Control* (on N.S.W.), Angus & Robertson, 1945.

W. J. CAMPBELL : *Australian State Public Finance*, Law Book Co. of Australasia, 1954.

R. C. CHAMBERS : *Accounting and Action*, Law Book Co. of Australasia, 1957, ch. 12, " Governments ".

R. I. DOWNING : *National Income and Social Accounts*, Melbourne U.P., 1957.

(U.K.) Committee on the Form of Government Accounts, *Report*, Cmd. 7976, 1950.

The (annual) White Paper on *National Income and Expenditure* now presents the " social accounts ". See also the *Treasury Information Bulletin* (quarterly), *Finance* (the annual bulletin of the Commonwealth Statistician), the *Annual Reports* of Commonwealth and State Auditors-General, and of the Commonwealth Grants Commission. The (Commonwealth) Joint Parliamentary Committee on Public Accounts has published a number of reports on Commonwealth financial practices, e.g. 2nd, 3rd, 8th, 16th, 17th, 18th (The Form and Content of Financial Documents presented to Parliament), 29th, 31st (Supplementary Estimates), 34th (Trust Funds).

Chapter Eight

R. ANDERSON, " The States and Relations with the Commonwealth ", in R. Else-Mitchell (ed.) : *Essays on the Australian Constitution*, Law Book Co. of Australasia, 1952.

G. GREENWOOD : *The Future of Australian Federalism*, Melbourne U.P., 1946.

S. R. DAVIS, " Co-operative Federalism in Retrospect ", *Historical Studies*, Nov. 1952.

F. O. GROGAN, " The Australian Agricultural Council ", *Pub. Admin. (Sydney)*, XVII, March 1958.

C. G. HEADFORD, " The Australian Loan Council ", *Pub. Admin. (Sydney)*, XIII, March 1954.

See also Royal Commission on the Constitution, *Report*, 1929, and articles referred to in the text.

Chapter Nine

C. T. CARR : *Delegated Legislation*, Oxford U.P., 1921.

W. A. ROBSON, " Administrative Law in England, 1919–1948 ", in G. Campion (ed.) : *British Government since* 1918, Allen & Unwin, 1950.

W. FRIEDMANN : *Principles of Australian Administrative Law*, Melbourne U.P., 1950.

D. G. BENJAFIELD, " Statutory Discretions ", *Sydney Law Review*, Vol. 2 Jan. 1956.

H. STREET : *Governmental Liability*, Cambridge U.P., 1953.

A summary of judicial decisions affecting Australian public administration is given by G. SAWER in periodical articles in *Public Administration (Sydney)*. See also books and articles referred to in the text.

Chapters Ten and Eleven

H. R. G. GREAVES : *The Civil Service in the Changing State*, Harrap, 1947, chs. I, II, VI.

W. A. ROBSON (ed.) : *The Civil Service in Britain and France*, Hogarth Press, 1956, esp. T. Padmore, " Civil Service Establishments and the Treasury ".

F. A. BLAND : *Shadows and Realities of Government*, W. E. A., Sydney, 1923.

F. A. BLAND (ed.) : *Government in Australia*, 2nd ed., Government Printing Office, Sydney, 1944, Introd. and chs. I—IV.

R. S. PARKER : *Public Service Recruitment in Australia*, Melbourne U.P., 1942.

H. A. SCARROW : *The Higher Public Service of the Commonwealth of Australia*, Duke U.P., 1957.

C. J. HAYES, " The Commonwealth Public Service ", and " The Administration of State Public Services ", *Pub. Admin. (Sydney)*, XV, March and June 1956.

S. ENCEL, " The Recruitment of University Graduates to the Commonwealth Public Service " and " The Commonwealth Public Service and Outside Recruitment ", *Pub. Admin. (Sydney)*, XII, Dec. 1953, and XIV, March 1955.

See also *Annual Reports* of Commonwealth and State Public Service Boards and Commissions and *Reports* of Royal Commissions and other inquiries referred to in text.

Chapters Twelve to Fourteen

L. BLAIR, " Employer-employee Relationships in the Federal Public Service of Australia ", *Public Administration*, London, XXXV, Spring 1957.

E. E. CRICHTON, " The Development of Public Service Arbitration ", three articles in *Pub. Admin. (Sydney)*, XV, June, Sept., Dec. 1956.

J. D. B. MILLER, " Public Service Staff Associations and Politics ", *Pub. Admin. (Sydney)*, VI, Sept. 1947.

V. SUBRAMANIAM, " Evaluating Personnel Efficiency in the Commonwealth Public Service ", *Pub. Admin. (Sydney)*, XVI, Sept. 1957.

G. WEIR, " Promotion in the Public Service ", *Pub. Admin. (Sydney)*, XIII, Dec. 1954.

See also *Annual Reports* of Commonwealth and State Public Service Boards and Commissions and: Committee on Systems of Promotion and Temporary Transfers, *Report*, 1945.

Chapter Fifteen

H. O. DOVEY : *Handbook oj Organisation and Methods Techniques*, International Institute of Administrative Sciences, Brussels, 1951.

T. D. KINGDOM : *Improvement of Organisation and Management in Public Administration*, International Institute of Administrative Sciences, 1951.

D. G. ANDERSON, " A Departmental Approach to O. & M.", *Pub. Admin. (Sydney)*, XII, Sept. 1953.

R. M. OSBORNE, " O. & M. in the Australian Post Office ", *Pub. Admin. (Sydney)*, XIII, June 1954.

Other articles by Mr. GRAINGER will be found in *Pub. Admin. (Sydney)*, XIII, June 1954 and XVII, Sept. 1958.

See also the *O. & M. Bulletin* (U.K. Treasury, monthly) and *Annual Reports* of Commonwealth and State Public Service Boards and Commissions.

Chapters Sixteen to Eighteen

E. ANSTEY and E. O. MERCER: *Interviewing*, Allen and Unwin for R.I.P.A., 1956.

F. BRAY and others: *Training Managers in the Public Services*, Allen and Unwin for R.I.P.A., 1955.

J. A. C. BROWN: *The Social Psychology of Industry*, Penguin Books, 1956.

D. H. FRYER and others: *Developing People in Industry*, Harper, N.Y., 1956.

H. W. KARN and B. V. H. GILLMER: *Readings in Industrial and Business Psychology*, McGraw-Hill, 1952.

I. E. P. MENZIES and E. ANSTEY: *Staff Reporting*, Allen and Unwin for R.I.P.A., 1951.

J. D. MILLETT: *Management in the Public Service*, McGraw-Hill, 1954.

J. A. PATTON and C. L. LITTLEFIELD: *Job Evaluation*, R. D. Unwin, 1957.

O. G. STAHL: *Public Personnel Administration*, 4th ed., Harper, N.Y., 1956.

F. J. TICKNER: *Modern Staff Training*, U. of London Press, 1952.

Commonwealth Public Service Board: *Better Teaching*, Training Handbook No. 5.

(U.K.) Committee on the Training of Civil Servants, *Report*, Cmd. 6525, 1944.

H. J. WRIGHT, " Recent Developments in Administrative Training in the Commonwealth Public Service ", *Pub. Admin. (Sydney)*, XIII, Sept., 1954.

Other articles on training in the Australian public services will be found in *Pub. Admin. (Sydney)*, VI, Sept., 1946, March, 1947; VIII, June and Sept., 1949; XI, June, 1952. See also articles and books referred to in the text.

INDEX

INDEX OF NAMES

INDEX OF SUBJECTS